West Elevation.

IMPERIAL GOTHIC

G. A. BREMNER

IMPERIAL GOTHIC

RELIGIOUS ARCHITECTURE AND HIGH ANGLICAN CULTURE IN THE BRITISH EMPIRE

c. 1840–1870

PUBLISHED FOR THE PAUL MELLON CENTRE FOR STUDIES IN BRITISH ART BY
YALE UNIVERSITY PRESS ◆ NEW HAVEN AND LONDON

Designed by Emily Lees
Printed in China

Library of Congress Cataloging-in-Publication Data

Bremner, G. A., 1974–
Imperial gothic : religious architecture and high Anglican culture in the British empire, *c.*1840–70 /
G.A. Bremner.
pages cm
Includes bibliographical references and index.
ISBN 978–0–300–18703–8 (cl : alk. paper)
1. Church architecture – Great Britain – Colonies – History – 19th century. 2. Architecture, British colonial – History – 19th century. 3. Anglican church buildings – Great Britain – Colonies – History – 19th century. 4. Architecture and society – Great Britain – Colonies – History – 19th century. 5. Nationalism and architecture – Great Britain. I. Title.
NA4829.A6.B74 2013
726.509171'241 – dc23
2012028576

A catalogue record for this book is available from the British Library

Image on p. i Mosaic floor decoration at Christ Church cathedral, Christchurch, New Zealand, *c.*1880 (fig. 182).
Frontispiece: Christ Church cathedral, Dublin, restored (1871–8) to designs by G. E. Street (fig. 355).
Image on p. vi: The octagonal turret on the west tower of St Paul's church, Chippendale, Sydney (1848–75), by Edmund Blacket (fig. 248).

TO EMMA, WHO TOOK THE JOURNEY WITH ME.

IN MEMORIAM D. VICTOR ('VIC') SPENCER
1926–2005

CONTENTS

ACKNOWLEDGEMENTS

A project such as this accumulates innumerable debts. Many people have contributed both their time and knowledge towards its realisation. To these people – unfortunately too numerous to mention all by name – I am greatly indebted.

There are those, however, to whom I owe a particular debt of gratitude. These include Simon Bradley, Peter Coffman, Michael Hall, Deborah Howard, Ian Lochhead, Peter Mandler, Andrew Saint and Frank Salmon, all of whom continually supported and encouraged my work, either by reading and commenting on sections of the original manuscript, or by assisting with grant applications, or both. Without their kind assistance and generosity, this project would not have been possible.

Many colleagues offered advice or assistance along the way, especially during my long periods abroad conducting field research. Among these were Margaret Alington, Brian Allen, Brian Andrews, Barry Bergdoll, Michael Berning, James Bettley, Geoff Brandwood, Judith Bright, Mark Crinson, Colin Cunningham, Lynne DiStefano, Amol Divkar, Mark Dorrian, Leonie Duncan, Ian Dungavell, Chris Eve, Federico Freschi, James Grant (former Anglican Bishop of Melbourne), Manolo Guerci, Peter Hoffenberg, Colin Holden, Gill Hunter, Gordon Johnson, Katharine Jones, Paul Kotze, Tom Kvan, Howard Le Couteur, Ho Yin Lee, Miles Lewis, Sarah Longair, David Lung, Nancy Mallett, Jonathan Mane-Wheoki, Henry Mbaya, Chris Miele, Amlan Mondal, Paul Murray, Harriet Partridge, Alistair Pask, Leela Pienaar, Derek Pratt, Hannah le Roux, Gavin Stamp, Jane Teal, Malcolm Thurlby, Rachel Travers, Louise Trott, Geoffrey Tyack, Rachel Underwood, Catherine Wakeling, Susan Walton, Chris Webster, William Whyte, Jane Wild, Camilla Wright Premachandra, and the Master and Fellows of Queen's College, University of Melbourne.

I also wish to acknowledge the generous support of those agencies and foundations that assisted in funding the project, including the British Academy, the Arts and Humanities Research Council (Early Career Fellowship), the Graham Foundation for Advanced Studies in the Fine Arts (Chicago), the British Institute in Eastern Africa, the Carnegie Trust for Scottish Universities, the J. R. Smallwood Foundation for Newfoundland and Labrador Studies, the Society of Architectural Historians of Great Britain, the Macgeorge Fellowship (University of Melbourne), the University of Edinburgh, the visiting fellowship scheme at St John's College (University of Oxford), the Friends of the Alexander Turnbull Library (National Library of New Zealand) and especially the Paul Mellon Centre for Studies in British Art (Yale University), which initially awarded me a Postdoctoral Fellowship to commence this project and continued to fund it generously thereafter.

The staff at numerous libraries, museums and archives have been very helpful in enabling me to locate, view and reproduce relevant material for this book. These institutions include the Anglican Diocesan Archives in Sydney, Melbourne, Kolkata, Adelaide, Christchurch, Victoria (BC), Eastern Newfoundland and Labrador (St John's), Montreal and Newcastle (NSW); the Alexander Turnbull Library, Wellington; the Archives of Ontario, Toronto; Bishop's College Archive, Cape Town; Bishop's College Library and Archive, Kolkata, India; the Brotherhood of the Ascended Christ Library, Delhi; Canterbury Museum, Christchurch; Centre for Newfoundland Studies (Memorial University Libraries), St John's, Newfoundland; the Cory Library, Rhodes University, Grahamstown; Drawings and Archives Collections, RIBA Library; Elphinstone College Library and Archive, Mumbai; the Huntington Library, San Marino; John Kinder Theological Library, St John's College, Auckland; the Mitchell Library, State Library of New South Wales, Sydney; National Archives of Singapore; National Library of Scotland; the Provincial Archives of New Brunswick, Fredericton; Rare Books and Manuscripts, Cambridge University Library; Rare Books and Special Collections, University of Cape Town Libraries; Rare Books and Special Collections, McGill University Library; Rare Books and Special Collections, University of Sydney; Selwyn College Library Archive, University of Cambridge; State Library of South Australia, Adelaide; the State Library of Victoria, Melbourne; the Tasmanian Museum and Art Gallery, Hobart; the Tasmanian State Library and Archives, Hobart; The Rooms Provincial Archives, St John's, Newfoundland; Trinity College Library, University of Melbourne; University of Newcastle Archive (Auchmuty Library); William Cullen Library, University of the Witwatersrand; Zanzibar National Archives; as well as the numerous church and cathedral vestry archives consulted. A special mention must be made of Lucy McCann and Tony Hill at the Bodleian Library of Commonwealth and African Studies, Oxford, for their unending patience in assisting with material from the archive of the United Society for the Propagation of the Gospel (formerly the Society for the Propagation of the Gospel in Foreign Parts). This archive was fundamental to the study.

The editorial team at Yale University Press has been both extremely professional and efficient in their handling of the material for the production of this book. In this regard I would especially like to thank Gillian Malpass, Emily Lees, Sarah Faulks, Charlotte Grievson and Rosemary Roberts. Without their ever friendly patience and guidance this book would not have been able to take the form that it has.

Friends and family have helped out in various ways during the preparation of this book. In this respect, I wish to thank first and foremost all those members of my family who offered assistance, especially my parents, Anne and George, who have been unerring in their support and encouragement from the beginning. I also wish to acknowledge the support of Claudia Bolgia, Tim Brittain-Catlin, Jonathan Conlin, Louise Curran, Marla Ferreira Gomes, Giovanna Guidicini, Kathryn Ferry, Kate and Vesa Kangaslahti, Jonathan Lamb, the Rev. Jack McDonald, James McGregor, Bridget Orr, Judith Trimble, and last, but by no means least, Emma Frow, to whom this book is dedicated.

PREFACE

It is just over half a century since the publication of Basil Clarke's *Anglican Cathedrals Outside the British Isles* (1958). By no means a scholarly work, Clarke's book (by his own admission) is more a country-by-country, building-by-building compendium of nearly every extant Anglican cathedral built outside Britain between the late seventeenth and early twentieth centuries. In the foreword John Betjeman observed that Clarke's book would come as both a 'shock and [an] encouragement' to those who supposed that Anglican dioceses abroad were nothing more than places where 'a few old colonels keep the flag flying and where the bishop is a glorified vicar'.[1] Although it is debatable whether colonial dioceses were perceived in such naïve terms after about 1840, the point was taken: by the late 1950s Britain had all but lost its former colonial empire, and the idea that it – let alone its Anglican dioceses – ever amounted to anything much was on the wane. Clarke's book was therefore a product of its time, a kind of annotated photo album that served as a reminder of the fact that there was indeed an Anglican Church outside the British Isles and that it had actually achieved quite a lot.

But as Alan Gowans pointed out in his review of Clarke's book in 1959, this was a rich and diverse subject that deserved far greater attention than Clarke had given it.[2] To be sure, Gowans's review was perhaps something that only a scholar gazing from across the Atlantic at the demise of Britain's empire could have written. The subject was surely too sensitive, or even embarrassing, for a British scholar to have expounded at length. Nevertheless, Gowans's criticism remains valid, that the material covered in Clarke's book warrants closer and more serious examination.

In the fifty-odd years that have elapsed since the publication of Clarke's book, the intellectual climate in Britain has changed considerably. Gone is the cringe that once accompanied the study of empire. The last two decades in particular have witnessed a sea change in the way Britain's imperial past is perceived, and the scholarly genre of 'new imperial history' has played a significant role in providing a more complex (and complete) understanding of Britain's economic, political and social development during the modern era.

More recently an interest in the way religion, especially Protestantism, helped shape Britain's imperial experience has emerged, with the publication of a number of specialist studies dealing with aspects of this phenomenon in detail.[3] However, the history of Anglicanism (especially Tractarianism) vis-à-vis empire remains seriously under studied, particularly in comparison to Nonconformism and other strands of evangelical Christianity during the Victorian period.[4] The role that High Anglican churchmanship played in the development and characterisation of Britain's empire during the mid- to late nineteenth century is still unclear. As Pamela Welch and others have argued, our understanding of Anglicanism in all its forms would benefit greatly by being set in a much wider social, cultural and geographical context.[5] Rowan Strong's *Anglicanism and the British Empire, c.1700–1850* (2007) has taken major steps towards addressing this problem. But, again, the majority of Strong's analysis resides in the Georgian and Regency periods and deals predominantly with church organisation and the influence of Evangelicals.[6]

Given that the formal expression of divine worship was so important to High Church Anglicans, one of the most advantageous ways of measuring their contribution to empire (spatially and culturally) is through a study of architecture. Indeed, as Andrew Saint has recently observed, churches were the most important buildings the Victorians built.[7] They were at the very heart of Tractarian activity in the colonies, and a great deal of care was taken over their design and construction. Buildings of this kind not only provide clues as to the theological inclination of those who created them but also tell us where and to what extent High Anglicans were active in the empire and how they used architecture to achieve their goals, both politically and spiritually.[8] Thus, in the spirit of Gowans's appeal, and in light of the work that remains to be done on the global reach of Anglican culture during the Victorian age, now seems an opportune moment to revisit the history of Anglican architecture and its reverberations worldwide.

As the writing of this book took me to a great many locations that were part of Britain's vast and sprawling territorial empire during the nineteenth century, it called to mind the sheer ambition (and at times cupidity) of Britain's imperial enterprise. At its height Britain's empire extended over some 13 million square miles and included nearly a quarter of the world's population. By 1860 it had already reached two-thirds this size, and had penetrated every corner of the known world, including Europe, North America and the Caribbean, Africa, India and south-east Asia, Australia, New Zealand and the Pacific Islands.[9] Indeed, as Lord Salisbury grumbled in 1861, Britain's empire really was one upon which the sun never set.

In the same way that Salisbury's carp was intended to highlight the unwieldy nature of Britain's empire, my experience of gathering research material for this book forced me to reflect upon the limitations imposed by distance. Despite this 'tyranny', as Geoffrey Blainey once described it,[10] I never lost sight of the unique opportunity that this project represented: the possibility of considering as a whole, and for the first time, the influence and impact of Anglican ecclesiology throughout the British world – a broad analytical and comparative sweep from Britain to Barbados, Newfoundland to New Delhi. Although something is undoubtedly lost in working at this scale, particularly with respect to the number of buildings included and the degree to which they can be discussed, much is also gained. This is especially true in the uncovering of those wider associations and trends that both drove and informed the export of Anglican ecclesiology abroad. It is these broader aspects, and what they reveal about architectural theory and practice in the nineteenth-century British imperial world, that might otherwise escape the attention of more localised studies. Undertaking the research for this book certainly reinforced the reality that the spread of Anglicanism was a global enterprise, and that the mid-Victorians understood it as such.[11]

In considering the architectural achievement of the Anglican Church across so wide a geographical area, and over a time period of some thirty years, I found that such a study raised numerous problems concerning both methodology and terminology. These involved not only the issue of 'centre' versus 'periphery' but also the particular preoccupations of architectural history versus the much broader and more fundamental perspectives demanded by political, cultural and religious historiography.

One of the most immediate and pressing problems was the complex and, as yet, unresolved relationship between the historiography of 'British' architecture on the one hand, and that of 'British colonial' architecture on the other. Typically, these two subjects have been treated separately, both geographically and historically. But are they separate subjects, or can they be seen as integrated or even indivisible? Although there is no easy or absolute answer to this question, it was clear to me that the majority of Anglican churches I investigated for this book could not simply be labelled 'colonial'. Not even the term 'British colonial' was entirely satisfactory, for that term in itself has come to indicate something much greater (culturally, politically, geographically) than what historians have generally taken it to mean.

This initial observation forced me to ask what it actually meant to speak of 'British' and/or 'British colonial' architecture. Did the term 'British' in reference to architecture merely pertain to an account of those buildings and monuments that existed within the political boundaries of what is today referred to as the United Kingdom of Great Britain and Northern Ireland? Or, did it include those buildings that were designed and erected by British soldiers, merchants, architects, government administrators and settlers throughout Britain's former colonial empire?[12] To put it another way, and in the context of this particular study: are the Anglican churches designed by George Gilbert Scott in Newfoundland, India, South Africa and Australia, for example, any less 'British' than those by him in Edinburgh, Yorkshire, Cambridge, or on the Channel island of Alderney?

Although it could be argued that there is no such thing as 'British architecture' or, indeed, 'British architectural history', it would seem that the way most historians have conceptualised the subject – at least since the second World War, and particularly in the wake of the dismantling of British power structures abroad, including territorial empire – suggests that British architecture and its history have been confined largely to the British Isles. This of course raises further questions about the distinctions and correlations between the architectural traditions of England, Ireland, Scotland and Wales. Despite this, there has never been any serious or systematic attempt to include British colonial architecture within a study of the history of British architecture narrowly defined.[13] Take the topic of 'Victorian architecture', for example. Very few, if any, books on that subject make mention of architecture in the wider British empire during the Victorian age – the one obvious exception, perhaps, being Asa Briggs's *Victorian Cities* (1963), which includes a chapter on Melbourne.[14] If there has been a tendency to look abroad in an effort to understand the history of British architecture in some wider geographical context, it has almost always been with reference to continental Europe or the United States.[15]

This same narrowness of scope also applies to the history of architecture in Britain's former colonies. Histories of Australian, Canadian and New Zealand architecture, for instance, have tended to partition off the architectural heritage of their respective regions and reconstitute it within the collective history of the post-colonial nation state.[16] Although this has a great deal to do with the constraints of geography and the shaping of a subject for the purposes of publication, the apparently coherent narrative that these histories present gives the impression (but does not necessarily intend) that even buildings from the earliest colonial period may be considered 'Australian', 'Canadian' or from 'New Zealand'. Buildings and movements from Britain and elsewhere are necessarily mentioned in such histories but usually only as points of comparison or with respect to stylistic influence, never as the basis for a historiographical argument concerning a shared or common architectural heritage.[17] The problem with such an approach, however, is that many of the formal, spatial, technical and ideological characteristics that connect architecture in Britain to that of its colonies are lost in this partitioning – taken for granted, down-played, or completely ignored.[18]

As the bibliographic essay at the end of this book examines further (pp. 436–41), these connections suggested to me that there could be no clear or simple division of buildings into categories such as 'British' or 'colonial'. Such a division can apply – indeed, make sense – only if one maintains a strict (even arbitrary) geographical distinction between Britain and its overseas empire. Moreover, this division can be misleading, not only in its disintegration of those connections and associations that made the internal dynamic of empire possible but also, and more generally, for the way it presupposes a necessary antagonism between coloniser and colonised.[19] One of the ambitions of this study is to take the discussion of British colonial architecture beyond the binary categories of 'self'/'other', European/non-European, and coloniser/colonised to present a more nuanced, complex and even fractured picture of colonial agency and its architectural manifestations. European imperial powers were, of course, far from culturally homogenous or socially unified entities.[20] Indeed, as this study demonstrates, they were sometimes confused, oftentimes ideologically diffuse, and nearly always internally competitive and politically discordant – differing in each place at each time. This does not mean, however, that particular organisational structures or forms of agency within the broader imperial project, such as Christian churches, did not have a degree of coherence according to their individually specified missions. Clearly they did, which is in large part the story of this book. But they also fought among themselves, sometimes viciously, and were frequently at loggerheads with colonial officialdom.

With this in mind, Anglican architecture, if it is to be understood properly, should not be viewed as merely an

English invention that found its way to foreign shores from time to time but instead as something that had become a fundamentally global phenomenon by 1850. It may have been closely associated with home-grown movements such as Tractarianism, but Anglican architecture was also extended (and developed) beyond the British Isles through the global expansion of the English Church. This was a process that informed architectural debate as much at 'home' as it did in the colonies, particularly in the pages of *The Ecclesiologist*, and especially during the thirty-year period between about 1840 and 1870 at which time the new age of English Church expansion coincided precisely with the rise of ecclesiologically 'correct' forms of Gothic Revival architecture. Therefore, by tracing and recovering the sinews of nineteenth-century Anglicanism worldwide, the aim of this book is to take the study of Victorian architecture in new and exciting directions, opening up a novel methodological approach to understanding the *expanded* nature of British architecture.

At a more personal level, the writing of this book forced me to reflect upon my own experience of growing up in rural Australia. To me, the fact that Australia was once part of a worldwide empire – a 'British' empire – is given, but the process of investigation nonetheless allowed me to understand that experience in a different and more nuanced way. Many Australians today see the present and future of that country as lying firmly in the Asia–Pacific region, but only a generation or two ago Australians (such as my grandfather) could still be heard talking about the 'mother country'. Indeed, the residue of empire still persists most conspicuously in the form of Queen Elizabeth II, who remains the head of state of a number of Commonwealth countries, including Australia. Nor could I escape awareness of the fact that being a person of Anglo-Celtic descent I was quite obviously an intruder in a land previously occupied by an indigenous people, who had arrived some 40,000 years earlier. Now based in Scotland, from where my forebears originally came, I have had what seems like a strange homecoming, having gone full circle 160 years later. Again, all of this merely served to remind me of the vast and interconnected nature of the 'British world' during the nineteenth century.

I was also reminded, while conducting my research, of the rather fragile, even artificial, nature of colonial culture. The tension between the natural world (that is, 'wilderness' or 'outback') and 'civilisation' in a place like Australia was, and to a certain extent still is, one of the defining characteristics of that country's landscape. This tension or 'edge condition' played itself out in many aspects of Australian life, from domestic politics, settlement patterns and sport through to literature, the arts and architecture. The way buildings are situated in the landscape in many parts of Australia, even today, gives one a heightened sense of *architecture* as an act of intervention. This is particularly evident, for instance, in the paintings and drawings of early colonial artists such as John Glover and Conrad Martens, where buildings are depicted in uneasy juxtaposition to the densely forested wilderness beyond. As far as church architecture is concerned, this condition – in all its earnestness and, at times, misplaced optimism – has been captured most vividly in more recent times by Peter Carey in his novel *Oscar and Lucinda* (1988). Carey's trope of the glass church in the environmental context of Australia points up the over-burdensome promise of permanence and stability that was to be realised not only through religion but through architecture as well (in a material, spiritual and social sense). As I shall demonstrate throughout this study, the ever present tension between faith and folly was, in reality, close to the mark for many Anglican clergymen and their circumstances.

It is the experience of architecture as such, not just in Australia but throughout the former British colonial world, that revealed to me both architecture's essential character and its central task in the process of British imperial expansion. In this sense, as Mark Crinson has observed, architecture echoed, inflected and was integral to many of the other practices and relationships that empire required for its furtherance.[21] As we shall see, Anglicanism and its architecture were very much bound up in this process.

ALEX BREMNER
Edinburgh, July 2012

ABBREVIATIONS

ADAENL	Anglican Diocesan Archives of Eastern Newfoundland and Labrador, St John's, Newfoundland
ATL	Alexander Turnbull Library, National Library of New Zealand, Wellington
BC	British Columbia (Canada)
Bodl.	Bodleian Library, University of Oxford
Bodl. CAS	Bodleian Library of Commonwealth and African Studies, Oxford
BPML	Bishop W. G. Broughton Papers at the Mitchell Library, State Library of New South Wales, Sydney
CBF	Colonial Bishoprics' Fund
CCS	Cambridge Camden Society
CMS	Church Missionary Society
CNLS	Centre for Newfoundland Studies, Memorial University Libraries, St John's, Newfoundland
CPSA	Church of the Province of South Africa
Eccl.	*The Ecclesiologist*
ICBS	Incorporated Church Building Society
JCCHS	*Journal of the Canadian Church Historical Society*
JSAH	*Journal of the Society of Architectural Historians*
JSSAC	*Journal of the Society for the Study of Architecture in Canada*
NSW	New South Wales (Australia)
OAS	Oxford Architectural Society
RIBA	Royal Institute of British Architects, London
Rules and Proceedings	*The Rules and Proceedings of the Oxford Society for Promoting the Study of Gothic Architecture*
SA	Selwyn College Library Archive, Selwyn College, University of Cambridge
SPCK	Society for Promoting Christian Knowledge
SPG	Society for the Propagation of the Gospel in Foreign Parts
UMCA	Universities' Mission to Central Africa
UP	University Press
USPG	United Society for the Propagation of the Gospel

ALASKA
DOMINION
OF CANADA
(from 1867)
Vancouver
Winnipeg
Montreal
Toronto
Halifax
St John's
London
UNITED STATES
OF AMERICA
ATLANTIC
OCEAN
Honolulu
Hawaiian Islands
BRITISH
HONDURAS
Jamaica
(British)
MOSQUITO
COAST
GAMBIA
SIERRA LEONE
GOLD COAST
Georgetown
BRITISH
GUIANA
PACIFIC
OCEAN
St Helena
(British)
Tristan da Cunha
(British)
Falklands
(British)
British Empire, c. 1850

Constantinople
(Istanbul)
EGYPT
Aden
Lahore
Delhi
Kanpur
Allahabad
INDIA
Calcutta
Bombay
Madras
Ceylon
Colombo
Hong Kong
PACIFIC
OCEAN
SARAWAK
from 1860's
Singapore
Zanzibar
INDIAN
OCEAN
Magomero
Morambala
Darwin
AUSTRALIA
Brisbane
Perth
Adelaide
Sydney
Melbourne
Hobart
Auckland
Wellington
Christchurch
NEW ZEALAND
Cape Town
see inset below
Vaal
Indian
Ocean
ORANGE
FREE
STATE
NATAL
Orange
Pietermaritzburg
Port Natal (Durban)
Umlazi
Atlantic
Ocean
CAPE COLONY
(SOUTH AFRICA)
BASUTOLAND
Protectorate, 1843
Grahamstown
Great Kei River
Uitenhage
KAFFRARIA
to Cape Colony, 1866
Swellendam
Caledon
George
Port Elizabeth
Cape Town
Belvidere
Knysna

ALASKA
GREENLAND
Baffin Island
NORTH WESTERN TERRITORY
Hudson Bay
NEW CALEDONIA
Vancouver
Victoria
Hope
New Westminster
Stanley Mission
RUPERT'S LAND
LABRADOR
St Francis Harbour
Battle Harbour
Forteau
NEWFOUNDLAND
St John's
Oderin
Mapleton
Winnipeg
QUEBEC
OREGON TERRITORY
Newcastle (Miramichi)
PRINCE EDWARD I.
NEW BRUNSWICK
Charlottetown
Quebec
MINNESOTA TERRITORY
Montreal
Fredericton
NOVA SCOTIA
Halifax
ONTARIO
Ottawa
CALIFORNIA
UTAH TERRITORY
Hamilton
Toronto
New York
Philadelphia
NEW MEXICO TERRITORY
Williamsburg
UNITED STATES OF AMERICA
Bermuda (British)
Hamilton
TEXAS
ATLANTIC OCEAN
Bahamas (British)
MEXICO
Gulf of Mexico
Cuba
Hispaniola
Antigua (British)
Jamaica
Kingston
St Kitts (British)
BRITISH HONDURAS
Caribbean Sea
Barbados (British)
MOSQUITO COAST
PACIFIC OCEAN
Georgetown
VENEZUELA
BRITISH GUIANA
COLOMBIA
BRAZIL
British Empire, c. 1850
Original Thirteen Colonies, c. 1775

British Empire, c. 1850
CHINA
INDIA
Kanpur
Allahabad
Calcutta
Baruipur
Magrahat
Bombay
Arabian Sea
Bay of Bengal
BURMA
ARAKAN
TENASSERIM
SIAM
ANNAM
CAMBODIA
Hong Kong
Formosa
Hainan
South China Sea
Philippine Islands
PACIFIC OCEAN
Madras
Colombo
Nuwara Eliya
Galle
Ceylon
BRUNEI
SARAWAK from 1860s
Kuching
Borneo
MALAY STATES
Singapore
Sumatra
Celebes
DUTCH EAST INDIES
New Guinea
Java
Solomon Islands
INDIAN OCEAN
Darwin
NORTHERN TERRITORY from 1911
QUEENSLAND
AUSTRALIA
WESTERN AUSTRALIA
SOUTH AUSTRALIA
NEW SOUTH WALES
Fiji
New Caladonia
Norfolk Island
Lutwyche
Brisbane
Armidale
Merriwa
Muswellbrook
Allynbrook
Newcastle
Bathurst
Sydney
Yass
Goulburn
Canberra
Cooma
Perth
Busselton
Poonindie
Adelaide
VICTORIA
Daylesford
Ballarat
Geelong
Melbourne
Tasman Sea
Hagley
Buckland
Hobart
TASMANIA (Van Diemen's Land)
SOUTHERN OCEAN
Te Waimate
Auckland
New Plymouth
Mt Taranaki (Egmont)
NEW ZEALAND
Wellington
Christchurch
Lyttelton
Dunedin

1 *A Colonial and Missionary Church Map of the World*, 1843, produced on behalf of the Society for the Propagation of the Gospel in Foreign Parts (private collection).

INTRODUCTION

Anglicanism and the British Colonial World

TRANSPLANTING THE FAITH

But no! a different history of His Church was traced by the finger of God at Calvary. As is the Head, such must the members be. It is not by the easy unsacrificing multiplication of copies of the written word, but by self-sacrificing labour; it is not by the written word only, but through the Word of God, living in and quickening His chosen temples, sanctifying them, and testifying His own presence by the holy awe of the habitation wherein He dwells, that so great a work must be accomplished.

E. B. Pusey, *The Church the Converter of the Heathen* (1838)

The Church of England was late into the mission field. Moreover, it was lax in extending its privileges – a constitutional right, according to some – to those who arrived to live and work in the far-flung corners of Britain's colonial empire. To make matters worse, European Protestant churches and Nonconformist sects had been operating with vigour throughout Britain's overseas territories since the mid-eighteenth century. This only made the established Church look more negligent with regard to its responsibilities. It was even said that Roman Catholics had done more.

At first glance this seems odd, given that the Church of England had not one but three affiliate missionary organisations by 1800. These were the Society for Promoting Christian Knowledge (SPCK, 1699), the Society for the Propagation of the Gospel in Foreign Parts (SPG, 1701) and the Church Missionary Society (CMS, 1799). These organisations, although founded with the best of intentions, were not particularly dynamic in executing their directives; nor were they especially discriminatory in their neglect, forsaking Europeans and non-Europeans alike.[1] To be sure, this had much to do with the frustrations met by the SPG in its attempts to establish proper ecclesiastical governance abroad during the eighteenth century.[2] But even when this had been rectified to a degree, the SPG continued to focus what energy and resources it had on servicing the souls of expatriate settler communities. This was despite the fact that its mandate included from the beginning the 'conversion of natives'.[3] The SPCK, on the other hand, considered itself more a facilitator of missionary activity, focusing its attention on education, funding and publicity. It too had made modest attempts at launching missions to the heathen, especially in India (Tirunelveli), but devolved this responsibility to the SPG during the course of the eighteenth century.

Although much later on the scene, the CMS had arguably done more than the SPCK and SPG put together by 1840. This was partly owing to its Evangelical composition and partly to its ecumenical attitude towards recruiting missionaries (it was willing to accept German Lutherans, for example). Not hindered by an insistence on episcopal oversight, the CMS was able to go direct into the mission field. Its missionaries were sent to the farthest reaches of the British empire (and beyond), bringing the gospel to indigenous peoples, learning their languages and translating the scriptures. But the largely voluntary organisational structure of the CMS during the early nineteenth century led to disciplinary problems with local Anglican bishops.[4] Thus, although it was more enthusiastic and active than its SPG counterpart, the success of the CMS up to the time of Henry Venn (Secretary, 1841–72) was both patchy and controversial.[5]

Going Global: Founding the Colonial Bishoprics' Fund

If the 1830s were a difficult time for the Church of England generally, then the year 1840 offered new promise. This marked the moment at which the hierarchy of the Church suddenly awoke from its 'fat slumbers', as Gibbon once put it, regarding its imperial responsibilities. This perceived duty was something that had been smouldering in the background but was now suddenly enflamed. The initiative was headed by Charles Blomfield (1786–1857), bishop of London, in an open letter to the archbishop of Canterbury, William Howley (1766–1848). In this letter Blomfield highlighted what was generally considered to be the half-hearted attempt by Britain to make 'provision for the spiritual wants of its colonies', which 'at no time [had] been completely and effectually carried out'.[6] To Blomfield, who, as bishop of London, had nominal jurisdiction over Anglican clergy in the colonies, such provision was considered the 'sacred duty' of a Christian country. He argued this point not on spiritual grounds alone, as if that were not enough, but on temporal premises too; that the English Church was the established Church and therefore an inextricable component of the nation's constitutional settlement. Although the SPG had laboured against indifference to supply this provision to the best of its ability, Blomfield observed, it had done so inadequately. The time had now arrived to force the issue and make amends.

Up to this moment, episcopal provision in Britain's colonies was rather informal. Until the appointment of the first Anglican bishops in Nova Scotia (1787) and Quebec (1793) in the late eighteenth century, clerical oversight in the colonies came under the remit of the bishop of London. Indeed, until the death of the Rev. Edmund Gibson in 1748, the bishop of London had letters patent authorising him to appoint commissaries in his absence to scrutinise and discipline colonial clergy.[7] However, distanced from the locus of activity by several thousand miles, this system of 'remote control' proved to be less than adequate.[8] But few options were available. As English overseas expansion in the late sixteenth and seventeenth centuries was unforeseen at the time of the Reformation, no legal machinery had been devised to enable the extension of the diocesan pattern of the English Church. Successive attempts on the part of the SPG to raise bills in parliament for the erection of new dioceses and the appointment of colonial bishops in North America met with failure. Although the English Church was established by law in several American colonies, principally Virginia and Maryland, there was simply not the political appetite to appoint bishops. As Boyd Stanley Schlenther has observed, introducing Anglican bishops might have aided the colonial Church of England but it would unnecessarily have incensed the overwhelmingly non-Anglican population.[9] In Virginia, especially, the Church of England was associated almost exclusively with the interests of the planter élite. Even among the clergy there existed a degree of anticlericalism associated with long-held fears about the extension of imperial power through episcopal tyranny.[10] The colonial authorities in London were aware of this and consequently avoided anything that might agitate the situation and potentially tear at the sinews of the imperial commercial system.[11]

Thus, despite the erection of bishoprics in British North America, the Caribbean, and India following the American Revolution, the government did little to advance the national Church beyond Britain.[12] Even in the context of the French Revolutionary and Napoleonic Wars, when Church–State relations were reinvigorated for political and ideological reasons,[13] systematic reform and legal extension remained slow, if not elusive. By the second decade of the nineteenth century, however, it was clear to Howley (then bishop of London) that the *status quo* was largely ineffective with regard to episcopal jurisdiction – nothing more than 'a usage of ancient standing'.[14] As Britain's empire continued to expand, especially eastward into Asia (and beyond), the urgency of the need to rectify the situation intensified.

The implication of Blomfield's appeal, therefore, was that transplanting the State *in toto* to the scattered communities of the British empire would have additional benefits beyond the merely spiritual (as important as that was). Essentially, his proposal was to institute proper spiritual ministration through the provision of organised worship, pastoral care and the basic rites of passage (baptism, marriage and death) according to the authority and ordinances of the English Church.[15] But if the Church was too slow in pursuing this task, or faltered in its delivery, he warned, then 'kindred episcopal Churches' (that is, the Roman Catholic Church) would take its place, fraying the loyalty of British subjects and potentially fragmenting the empire.

Although contrived to agitate political opinion, such rhetoric was sincere. Indeed, the association between religion, culture and politics – those aspects 'vitally interwoven', according to the bishop of Montreal – is something that dawned on many within the Church following the American Revolution.[16] By fostering closer ties between colonial institutions and their English counterparts, as well as emphasising the idea of a pan-global 'Christian Commonwealth' through the auspices of the established Church, it was believed that the loyalty of settlers throughout Britain's empire could be secured.[17]

To be sure, appeals of this nature had been heard before.[18] As mentioned earlier, numerous among Blomfield's predecessors had pleaded with government in years past for what they considered to be the inalienable 'rights' of the English Church vis-à-vis Britain's colonial empire. To them the situation was straightforward. 'The proper and only remedy hath long since been pointed out', observed Robert Lowth (bishop of London) of the American colonies in 1771: 'the appointment of one or more resident Bishops . . . for the administering of the solemn and edifying rite of Confirmation; for ordaining Ministers, and superintending their conduct; – offices to which the members of the Church of England have an undeniable claim, and from which they cannot be precluded without injustice and oppression'.[19] The implementation of these ordinances was of course fundamental to an episcopal Church worthy of the name, but, for Archbishop Thomas Secker (1693–1768), there were wider benefits still, particularly with respect to evangelisation. Speaking on missionaries and the Seven Years' War in 1758, he observed: 'we ought to have more upon the frontiers . . . For Missionaries there might counteract the artifices of the French Papists; and do considerable services, religious and political at once, amongst the neighbouring Indians; both which points the Society [SPG] hath been heavily charged, on occasion of the present war, with having neglected.'[20] The colonial theorist and administrator William Knox (1732–1810) had also recognised this in the aftermath of the American Revolution. For him 'the Prevalence of the Church of England in those Colonies is the best Security that Great Britain can have for their Fidelity and attachment to her Constitution and Interests'.[21] The problem was, however, that to date very little had been done.

By the 1830s the situation in some areas had become critical. Hope of proper establishment was all but lost, especially with the ascendancy of the Whig reformers in parliament.[22] Just as 'Atheism and Impiety' had sprung up in the American Colonies, wrote Bishop William Broughton (previously archdeacon) of Sydney in 1834, 'there is reason to apprehend that the absence of religious ordinances will be still more certainly attend [*sic*] with the same lamentable consequences in the Australian Colonies'.[23] Three years later he reminded his friends and colleagues at home that: 'it is not enough that the Church of England be secured *in* England, but that its principles must be carried out to the most distant quarters of the English empire. Wherever our language is, there our Church *should* be. Would to God that our rulers took any such view of their duty, and felt that the security of the *nation* would be most effectively supported by *such* a discharge of the national obligations.'[24] The feeling was that colonial clergymen were swimming against a growing tide of secularism and indifference, and might be overwhelmed unless more systematic efforts were made.

The eventual outcome of these appeals by both Blomfield and his predecessors was the formation of the Colonial Bishoprics' Fund (CBF) in 1841. The object of this fund was to provide the means necessary to increase the provision of proper episcopal governance in Britain's empire, according to the doctrine and discipline of the Church of England. The fund was inaugurated with donations totalling some £80,000, with the SPCK and the SPG giving £10,000 and £5,000 respectively. However, owing to its High Church sympathies, the fund was effectively administered by the SPG, with the approval of government, and comprised a committee including W. E. Gladstone (honorary treasurer), Sir John Taylor Coleridge, Archdeacon William Hale and the Rev. Ernest Hawkins (honorary secretary). Over the next thirty-one years the CBF would provide for the erection and endowment of some thirty new sees, making a substantial difference to the presence and impact of the Anglican Church abroad.[25]

Like Blomfield's appeal leading up to the CBF's foundation, the meeting held in Willis's Rooms, London, in April 1841 to resolve the fund's mandate was also concerned with the wider social and political implications of establishing a colonial episcopate. The spiritual needs of the empire were, of course, at the top of the agenda, but a number of those who spoke were keen to press further the temporal advantages that a full and consistent application of 'true Religion' would bring to the security of the British empire. Again, this is one of the most important defining characteristics of the CBF: that it was driven by political as well as spiritual imperatives. In this sense, the spiritual welfare of both colonists and converts was considered coterminous with their mental and moral wellbeing. If they were inculcated with the tenets of the true faith then their inclination would be to sympathise with the national character of that faith, in effect contributing to the creation of a pan-global Anglican polity. This is precisely what Broughton had envisaged in 1837 as the 'one body' of world Anglicanism.[26]

After proceedings were opened by the archbishop of Canterbury, it fell to Blomfield to make the first speech. Quoting from a letter he had received from New Zealand, he noted how the presence of bishops of the established Church in that colony would, if nothing else, make for a basic social improvement. Their addition, he insisted, would allow such a colony to 'increase its respectability, and . . . to attract to it persons from a very valuable class, who would not else be likely to join it'.[27] The insinuation here was that the mere presence of such a 'class' would raise the moral and fiduciary tone of the place, thus ensuring its political stability. This was something that Evangelicals and High Churchmen alike could appreciate. Following Blomfield, the Earl of Chichester, a well-known Evangelical and president of the CMS, ruminated over what these deeper ties might be. He considered how the establishment of the Anglican Church in all its ministerial integrity would engender among colonials a natural bond with their homeland. It had occurred to 'those who care not for religion on its own account', he opined, 'that the absence of it has led to a state of things most adverse to the mere Civil prosperity of the Colonies, and to the stability of their connexion with this country'. 'They are beginning to see', he added,

> that as with the child and its parent, so with the colony and its mother country, there must be some bond more binding than that of a mere mercantile partnership. . . . We have found that a common language will not do this; – we have found that an assimilation of the laws and civil institutions of the new country to those of the old will not do it. But we believe that one thing will do it, and that is the preservation of our common faith.[28]

These sentiments were reiterated by the bishop of Winchester, who pointed to the fact that the 'Romanists' had done more than his own Church in establishing bishoprics in the empire, having erected twenty three compared to the Church of England's ten. But it was John Labouchere, a noted London banker and merchant, who drove the point home most forcefully in his castigation of government lethargy. Like Secker and Knox before him, Labouchere could see clearly the broader political benefits that would accrue if the English Church was extended systematically throughout the empire. Although crediting the government for attempting to secure the temporal welfare of the colonies (through trade and civil institutions, etc.), he regretted that he could not give them 'equal credit for their anxious desire to promote the spiritual welfare of those Colonies, or to uphold the interests of a Church which is so eminently calculated to promote the moral and religious welfare of all who are brought under the shadow of her wings'. He continued: 'In this respect I conceive the Government of this country to have been very remiss, and unmindful, moreover, of this important consideration – that, in neglecting their duty in this respect, they have . . . neglected to make use of one of the most efficient means of ensuring the allegiance and attachment of the inhabitants of those Colonies.'[29] As the fund's honorary treasurer, W. E. Gladstone, put it, the object of colonisation was the 'reproduction of the image and likeness of England'.[30] If so, the Church of England was crucial.

The underlying tenor of the speeches delivered that day was clear: that failure to preserve and extend the doctrines, traditions, rites and ceremonies of the English Church abroad was, in effect, bad economy. That, although the initial pecuniary outlay might be considerable, it would cost Britain and its empire far more in the long run – as the American colonies had shown – if the cohesion of the empire were jeopardised for want of implementing so basic and natural an institution. This may have been considered special pleading by some, but, as history had already demonstrated, it was felt that the prospects for Britain (indeed civilisation) were bleak unless decisive action was taken.[31]

The global extent of this challenge was captured compellingly in a map published by the SPG shortly after the inauguration of the CBF (fig. 1). This map, entitled *A Colonial and Missionary Church Map of the World*, is not only a bald statement concerning the global *imperium* of the British State, but also a striking representation of the Church's boundless ambition in a single image.[32] 'Two objects arrest the observer's eye, when he opens the "Colonial Church Atlas," and turns to the map of the world', it was observed in the *Quarterly Review* of 1844: '[t]he first is a dark shadow, overspreading the larger part of the earth's area: the second is a red line encircling a considerable portion of her coasts'.[33] More arresting still was the accompanying table giving the vital statistics of these features. These were no ordinary statistics concerning the British empire. Overall area and population were given, but these were presented in a way that emphasised the colossal (and worthy) task that lay ahead. The land mass of the entire globe and the British empire were compared to that of England, showing them to be a thousand and 160 times greater than England respectively. Then the total population of the world was shown in relation to 'British subjects', revealing that Britain's empire contained approximately one-seventh of the world's population. The English-speaking portion was included alongside this, showing, again, that the vast majority of the Queen's subjects were essentially non-European. This all led to the final and, as far as the authors of the map were concerned, most relevant statistic: that the world was composed mostly of 'idolaters'. This last statistic was represented in a visually dramatic way by the 'dark shadow' of ignorance that literally veiled three-quarters of the earth's surface. Only Christ, it was believed, could penetrate these satanic kingdoms and lift this diabolical fog. The one question remaining was could the Church of England make a difference?

A Special Responsibility? Anglicanism and the Providence of Empire

The association made between religion, identity and national responsibility at the inaugural meeting of the CBF is critical to understanding the relationship between Anglicanism and empire during the mid-nineteenth century. It was clear that religion had become a central plank in Britain's wider imperial 'mission' by the 1840s. This mission was not concerned merely with developing the world commercially, as had once been the case, but with 'improving' it through the inculcation of key civilisational institutions such as Christianity.[34] To the Victorian frame of mind, anything less was unconscionable.

Complicating this idea, however, was the fact that Anglicanism was really only the 'national' religion of England, Wales and Ireland at the time. Scotland had its own religion, Presbyterianism, organised under the general banner of the Church of Scotland.[35] If the empire was 'British', then it ought necessarily to include Scotland and Scottish interests. Indeed, the complaint was often heard in the colonies that the Church of England was just that, the Church of 'England', and therefore should not have privileged status in a 'British' empire (see p. 240). But although complications such as this whetted the appetite for disestablishment and religious plurality in the colonies, they did not stop the Church of England (or more precisely, Anglicanism) perceiving itself as the only 'true', superior, and therefore 'national' religion. This arrogance, so to speak, was aggravated by the fact that the Church of Scotland was never properly 'established' in the same way as the Church of England, thus allowing the English Church to reckon itself as the Church of empire *de facto*, if not *de jure*. Much of the rhetoric and enthusiasm surrounding English Church extension abroad during this period reflected this general assumption, even in the face of reform and calls for disestablishment.

Nevertheless, it was the Church of England's awakening to its perceived obligations during these years that induced and normalised the establishment of a colonial episcopate as one of its principal aims. Indeed, as emotive and impellent as the language at the inaugural meeting of the CBF may seem today, it was by no means unusual for the time. This was the beginnings of the 'great age' of empire, and discussion and debate over Britain's status as an imperial nation was both assertive and impassioned. For some time churchmen of an Evangelical persuasion had appreciated Britain's role and responsibilities in proselytising the non-Christian world. To the Evangelical mind, the Christian duty of spreading the gospel was not merely an individual one but a national one, too. Nations were like individuals in that each was subject to God's sovereignty and, ultimately, his judgment. Unlike individuals, however, nations would have no existence in a future world; their punishment and reward would be meted out in this one. This idea led to the theory – referred to as 'providential nationalism' – that God would protect those nations that championed his cause in promoting the message of Christ.[36] Extending the gospel into heathen lands was understood to be an especially important aspect of this commitment.[37]

The idea was not limited to Evangelicals. As we have seen, when such notions began rubbing off on those in the higher echelons of the Church of England, pressure mounted for it to act. Although, as Rowan Strong has recently shown, this claim to an alliance between God and the British nation had its antecedents in the pronouncements of the bishops about the evangelisation of India following the French Revolutionary and Napoleonic Wars, it had begun to influence those of the highest of High Church persuasion.[38] Long before Blomfield had brought the shame and inconsistency of the Church to public attention in 1840, Edward Bouverie Pusey (1800–1882), a leading Tractarian and supporter of the missionary cause, had censured the Church for its neglect of those 'special responsibilities' that God had bestowed upon it. In a series of sermons delivered on behalf of the SPG in 1838, Pusey sought to remind those present that the duty of the English Church was in fact that of the nation. In a similar way to those who had spoken out on India, Pusey couched this idea in terms of collective debt and obligation. 'To this petty island,' he exclaimed,

> once a nation of savages, separated from the whole world, and esteemed the extremity of the world, . . . He has given might and dominion and power and strength and glory, far beyond what once seemed the Empire of the World, the heathen Rome, whom we once served . . . . He has given us possessions in every quarter of the globe, in America, Africa, Asia, as well as Europe . . . . It seems not in vain, that to us, to whom He has given this power and influence, He has given a pure Church . . . [a] nd surely thereby He points out to us a high destiny, that wherever His good Providence has, (not for our righteousness, for we have therein often dealt very wickedly,) but wherever He in His mercy has prospered us, there we should plant branches of that Catholic Church.[39]

Such impassioned rhetoric illustrates the fact that providential theology – often considered the preserve of Low Churchmen – was not beyond even Tractarians. High Churchmen, too, could see that nations, like individuals, were responsible before the eyes of God.

This wider, nationally incurred dimension of the Church of England's imperial mission gained further impetus in the years that followed. Influential statesmen and clerics such as the Prince Consort, the Rev. Anthony Grant, W. E. Gladstone, Lord Salisbury, Herman Merivale, the Rev. Charles Wordsworth, Lord John Manners, among others, took it upon themselves to underscore the honour and righteousness of this cause.[40] The call came echoing back from those who were already labouring in the mission field and could see plainly the results of such neglect. 'Here is a country open to evangelization', pleaded the bishop of Montreal in 1845, 'to what power does it belong? To what Church does it address the call, *Come over, and help us*? . . . it is an appendage to Britain, to Christian Britain, to the first empire on earth with a Christian Government . . . with responsibilities before God who rules over [those] kingdoms . . . which are here enumerated.'[41]

At subsequent meetings of the CBF this responsibility and its attendant associations were explicitly reiterated. In 1847, for instance, resolutions were passed stating that it was 'the duty of this Church and nation to provide the means of grace for the Colonies and Dependencies of the British Crown', and that 'with a view to the more effectual discharge of this duty it is most important to plant the Church in the full integrity of its government and order in these countries'.[42] Such events also provided the opportunity to take stock of the fund's activities to date. At the second Public Meeting of the CBF in 1853, called to raise money for the division of the dioceses of Cape Town, South Australia and Toronto, it was vaunted how in the twelve years since the fund's creation fifteen new bishoprics had been erected and a further 146 clergymen installed. In some cases this represented a five- and six-fold increase in the number of clergymen in the colonies before the creation of the new sees.

Many of those who spoke at this meeting were keen to reinforce the connection between the civil functions of the Church and the political ambitions of the State. Again, somewhat alarmist comparisons were made, in particular the perceived calamity respecting the loss of the North American colonies. Blomfield, picking up where he had left off in 1841, declared that the advantage the Church had gained since that time should not be wasted. 'I do not hesitate to express my conviction', he stressed, 'that if efforts made in this respect during the last twelve years, had been made in the middle of the last century, those vast territories [North America] might have remained connected with this country.' Unless the Church of England continued 'in the course now marked out for us,' he warned, 'similar disastrous consequences will follow in respect to other Colonies now belonging to the British Empire'.[43] In emphasising this point Blomfield was insinuating that if the government had been ready to abdicate its responsibilities in this regard, then the Church was not.

Henry Pelham-Clinton (5th Duke of Newcastle), then Secretary of State for the Colonies, moved to reassure the bishop. Taking the stand, he made a point of advocating the extension of the episcopate. As a 'humanizing and harmonizing and religious influence,' he affirmed, 'the advantage of the Colonies would be greatly promoted by placing over the heads of the Clergy, Bishops to superintend their functions'. Moreover, it was the 'superior character' of Anglican clergymen that was most telling. This was considered especially important with respect to missionary work among the heathen. As Britain had recently emerged from a long and costly war with Xhosa tribesmen in South Africa (the so-called Kafir Wars), and with the bishop of Cape Town, Robert Gray, present at the meeting, the culturally specific nature of Anglicanism and the effect this could have on the indigenous peoples of the British empire was obvious. Attempting to underscore notions of cooperation and common cause between State and Church, the duke observed that it was 'a holy and sacred function of these Bishops to encourage and promote loyalty among those natives where it existed, to soften asperities, and to bring back to their allegiance those, wherever they might be, who from accidental circumstances departed from it'.[44] In facilitating this function, as it were, the British State could be perceived as living up to its moral obligation.

But, as the bishop of Cape Town noted, if the government had shown adequate foresight it might have realised that the cost of extending the episcopate would have been a great deal less than the £3 million it had spent prosecuting the recent wars, especially given that the result was a victory only on paper. Indeed, such an amount of money would have been 'sufficient to support a body of 2000 Missionary Clergymen for ten years'! If the Church of England could be 'planted among them it would be the most effectual instrument of preventing any future outbreak'.[45]

Missionary activity, particularly in peripheral areas where 'primitive' aboriginal populations existed, was therefore understood by colonial theorists, administrators and clergymen alike as easing the way for more subtle and complex systems of colonial authority to follow.[46] Missionaries were often considered the shock troops of empire whether they realized it or not. The basic perception was that in educating and converting indigenous peoples to Christianity, missionaries were essentially 'civilizing' them, manipulating and adjusting their consciousness in ways that made them more conducive and susceptible to European political and cultural domination.[47] This tactic was considered both morally prudent and politically expedient for it was seen to prevent the isolation, exploitation and ultimate destruction of indigenous populations at the hands of unruly settlers and frontiersmen.

Evidence of the apparent efficacy of this policy can be found elsewhere in British society at the time, including the arts. Works such as the Albert Memorial (1863–74) and Thomas Jones Barker's painting *The Secret of England's Greatness (Queen Victoria Presenting a Bible in the Audience Chamber at Windsor)* (*c.*1863) communicate clearly the importance that Christianity was understood to have as a civilising force in Victorian Britain. In Barker's extraordinary image none other than the Queen herself, head of State and Church, presents an authorised version of the Christian Bible to a figure who, although evidently African, is intended to signify the indigenous peoples of the non-European world (fig. 2). Watching attentively is Prince Albert, long-time supporter of the British missionary cause; while in the background lurks Lord Palmerston, then Prime Minister, and Lord John Russell, Foreign Secretary.[48] Similarly, at the rear of the large group titled *Africa* on the Albert Memorial are two figures representing a related theme: one, a female identified as Europe, with book in hand, instructing another, an African youth (fig. 3). 'Surprised in his warlike costume,' noted the artist, William Theed, 'the Heathen Kaffir is listening to the dictates of Truth and learns the precepts of a religion whose motto enjoins, "Peace on earth – good will towards men," [a]nd whose adoption is the basis of civilization, the "Herald of Progress".'[49]

The bishop of Oxford, Samuel Wilberforce (1805–73), son of the anti-slavery campaigner William Wilberforce and indefatigable champion of the SPG, was one clergyman who fully appreciated the overlapping concerns of indigenous conversion and British national interest. In a speech

at the Mansion House in 1840 (then as archdeacon of Surrey), only days before the publication of Blomfield's letter to Howley, he sought to remind those in attendance that it was an obligation incumbent on both Church and State that the holy sacraments be administered in *all* Britain's territories. Importantly, this should not be seen as the preserve of colonial settlers but a right of the aboriginal

Top 2 Thomas Jones Barker, *The Secret of England's Greatness (Queen Victoria Presenting a Bible in the Audience Chamber at Windsor)*, *c.*1863, oil on canvas (National Portrait Gallery, London).

Bottom 3 Europe instructing Africa from William Theed's *Africa*, 1864–9, part of the Albert Memorial, 1863–75, Hyde Park, London.

inhabitants among whom those settlers dwelt. As 'Christian Englishmen' had been active in destroying indigenous people and their communities, they should not stand idly by as the remainder of these people sank into vice and moral decay. In highlighting this predicament, Wilberforce was in fact drawing attention to the long-standing friction within the colonial Church of England and SPG between the so-called 'suffragan Church' and 'missions to the heathen' – that is, the distinction between establishing a Church for foreign emigrants and extending the gospel to indigenes.[50] Both were clearly important, it was only that the emphasis had been skewed in favour of the former. This was one of the recognised failings of the SPG during its first two centuries of operation, especially in North America and the Caribbean.[51]

Thus, characterised by a distinct air of providential nationalism, Wilberforce's speech was, in effect, an appeal to the nation's conscience. The task that he had laid before the English Church was presented as a form of repentance and a means of reparation for the evils that Englishmen had committed against indigenes through the process of colonisation. After all, he thundered, this project was a 'glory which God seems to have designed for England when he made England what it is'.[52]

There were also immediate and serious political consequences with respect to this task. For example, failure to act in a place such as South Africa, noted Wilberforce, might jeopardise the integrity of the empire as a whole. In a speech of 1858 on the evangelisation of the indigenous peoples of southern Africa, he pondered the reasons surrounding Britain's presence at the Cape of Good Hope. 'No doubt its value consists in this,' he observed, 'that it is the half-way house to India, and that the maintaining it in our strength is essential to our maintaining, unshaken, the Indian Empire which God has given to us; and, therefore, we must look at the question [of extending British religious and cultural influence among the indigenous inhabitants of southern Africa] as mixed up with the great question before us.'[53]

Similarly, Daniel Wilson, Evangelical bishop of Calcutta (1832–58), had cautioned that unless Britain took seriously its imperial responsibilities 'the same hand which has raised us to such a summit, can in one moment sink us to the lowest depth'.[54] Some years earlier Pusey, too, had realised that the Church's effort needed to be directed at the heathen as much as 'our own people'; that *all* should be 'gathered into the garners of the Lord' if the extension of the true faith throughout Britain's empire was to be successful and not lead to 'unnatural contest' and ultimate separation between Britain and its colonies.[55] This relied, of course, not just on good will and determination but on the systematic implementation of the ordinances of the English Church.

It must be said that the initiative of the CBF, and the anxiety that accompanied it, was largely a reaction to the spectre of Church reform and its legacy during the 1820s and 1830s. The repeal of the Test and Corporation Acts in 1828, followed by Catholic Emancipation in 1829, had significantly eroded the Church of England's privileged position vis-à-vis the constitution. If the writing was not already on the wall for the Church in the wake of these fateful amendments, then it appeared with unmistakable clarity after the Third Reform Bill gained royal assent in June 1832. In such stirring times, observed Richard Church in 1891, 'it was felt by men who looked forward, that to hold their own they must have something more to show than custom'.[56] So it was with the Church of England. Considered by many to have lost sight of its key spiritual mission, and grown fat and torpid on excessive and unwarranted endowments, the established Church had been exposed as an obvious target for root and branch reform.

Reform would anyway have been a bitter, if necessary, pill for the Church to swallow, but it was the Grey ministry's amalgamation of the Irish bishoprics under the Irish Church Temporalities Act (1833) that really raised the hackles of self-respecting churchmen, leading to John Keble's somewhat alarmist cry of 'national apostasy'.[57] In such an atmosphere, the time had come for the Church of England to assert its independence. In so doing, it released considerable energies that made it a formidable competitor for the allegiance and sympathy of wider British society.[58] It was in this spirit that Blomfield and Howley took matters into their own hands regarding the CBF, in the certain knowledge that in a climate of religious pluralism and retrenchment government grants for the endowment of colonial bishoprics would not be forthcoming. Thus, as Hans Cnattingius argued in 1952, it was this drive for self-sufficiency, not only in Britain but, importantly, across the entire British empire, that transformed the Anglican Church from what was essentially a parochial Church concerned with local matters into a 'World Church'.[59]

The Church Manifest: Tractarian Idealism and Ecclesiastical Architecture

These changes had an architectural dimension. With the idea of the colonial episcopate now elevated in the official mind of the Church, the consecration of colonial bishops became a public affair. These ceremonies graduated from the rather secluded environs of Lambeth Palace chapel to the splendid surroundings of Westminster Abbey.[60] Suddenly the idea of the colonial episcopate was invested with all the grandeur and significance that a setting such as the abbey could afford. The abbey was not only the home of royal coronations and state funerals but also an 'outward symbol', as R. E. Prothero would later observe, of national imagining, with its monuments and memorials to the great and the good of British history.[61] The first consecration of colonial bishops took place at the abbey in 1842 involving the bishops of Barbados, Guiana, Antigua, Gibraltar and Van Diemen's Land (Tasmania; fig. 4).[62] But it was the consecration of the bishops of Melbourne, Adelaide, Newcastle and Cape Town in 1847, attended by some 1,600 persons, including 760 communicants and numerous bishops from around Britain and the empire, that most spectacularly showcased the idea of colonial episcopacy. 'Surely,' remarked the *Colonial Church Chronicle* upon witnessing the event, 'there has not been such a Communion seen in this our day, nor, as we believe, for ages in the Church here in England.'[63] If the expansion of the colonial episcopate was considered a national responsibility, then there was no more fitting or appropriate setting than Westminster Abbey, in its 'union of the regal, legal [and] lay element of the nation with its religious, clerical ecclesiastical tendencies'.[64]

4 Engraving of the consecration of the bishops of Barbados, Guiana, Antigua, Gibraltar, and Van Diemen's Land (Tasmania) in Westminster Abbey, 1842 (private collection).

This increase in the ceremonial majesty of the colonial episcopate was not unrelated to the swell in High Church sentiment that had come to characterise the SPG and its activities by the 1840s. Although by no means Tractarians, Blomfield and Howley both welcomed and appreciated the general tenor of Anglican renewal and its call for a return to the core spiritual values of the Church. But these tendencies within the society caused much controversy in the early days of the CBF. Claim and counterclaim rocked the SPG as the Evangelical party crossed swords with their High Church adversaries. When Ernest Hawkins, a man of moderate Tractarian inclination, accepted the secretariat of the society in 1843, protests poured in condemning his appointment.[65] Many had misgivings about Wilberforce, too. Although a High Churchman of the old school, he was far from unmoved by the ideas of Newman, Keble and others, and his continued involvement in the society worked to raise suspicion and to steer it further from Evangelical concerns.[66] Over time, as the CMS refused to cooperate with certain colonial bishops and, as a consequence, became further estranged from the operations of the CBF, the SPG came to rely upon the support and influence of High

Churchmen. Thus, by the 1850s the SPG was moderately Tractarian in constitution.

These tensions were bound to arise given the factional nature of the Church of England during the early to mid-nineteenth century. Much of this tension had to do with debate over the sacramental nature of Anglican theology and doctrine, as well as the reform of English liturgy and worship. It concerned the use and interpretation of the Book of Common Prayer (a kind of manual for the order and character of the English Church service), and the observance of particular forms of liturgy considered fundamental (or not) to Anglican worship and ceremonial. Followers of the Oxford reformers, such as the Cambridge Camden Society, felt that the spiritual character of worship in the English Church had sunk into a state of decay by the early nineteenth century, to a point of near indignity (fig. 5).[67] In many churches, Holy Communion was almost never celebrated, and the chancels of churches were either shut off or put to purposes for which they were never intended (or so the story went). It was even reported, at one point, that an ancient stone altar had been removed from a church in Northamptonshire and employed as a horse trough.[68]

The Evangelical or 'Low' end of the Anglican spectrum, however, cared little for liturgical formalities, tending to focus instead on the 'Word' rather than 'mystery' in Anglican worship. The 'feeling' of faith was important to Evangelicals, and, although this was considered rather too 'enthusiastic' for some, Anglican Evangelicalism should not be confused by association with latitudinarianism, antinomianism, or moral laxity. Many Evangelicals also believed in emphasising the reformed, 'Protestant' (that is, Calvinist) nature of the Church of England as an institution established by law – what Tractarians would come to deride as 'Erastianism' (the theory of State primacy over Church

5 Thomas Rowlandson (attrib.), *A Church Service*, *c.*1800 (private collection). The scene depicts the disorder into which parish church services had descended by the turn of the century. Of particular concern to reformers were rented 'box' pews (*lower left*), which segregated the congregation according to material means. Other 'abominations' included the blocking up of chancels and the introduction of galleries (*far right*), from where unruly parishioners sometimes caused general disruption or hurled abuse at the priest.

affairs). This view they shared with so-called 'high and dry' or 'old High' clergy, who were essentially a product of the late Hanoverian period. However, in placing emphasis on the rational basis of faith, men of this stamp tended to promote a more austere if orderly (that is, 'dry') form of worship, in contradistinction to the 'excitement' desired by their Evangelical cousins. In propagating this rather narrow, orthodox and legalistic interpretation of the English Church, 'high and dry' men were often criticised for taking too secular a view of religion, and for utilising the Church as an instrument of social and political preferment rather than one of spiritual observance and devotion.

Those at the Tractarian, or 'High', end of the spectrum, on the other hand, were very much concerned with the full and proper observance of liturgical practices vis-à-vis divine worship, including what were referred to at the time as 'externals' – such as ceremonial, vestments, décor and architecture. As will be discussed below, the Camdenians were at the forefront of this movement. They shared a concern for spirituality with their Evangelical counterparts, but, unlike Evangelicals, focused more on those aspects of Christian worship and liturgy that had come down to, and were preserved within, the English Church (via the Book of Common Prayer and the Thirty-Nine Articles) from pre-Reformation times. In other words, they were intent on extracting as much out of the so-called *via media* ('middle way') as ecclesiastical law would allow. In so doing they preferred to see themselves as 'catholic' – meaning that they sought the revival of, and emphasis on, the 'purity' of early Church custom before the onset of the perceived 'corruption' of Rome. The anti-Erastian stance of Tractarians also meant that they preferred a clear divide between spiritual and secular power in the affairs of Church and State, although few wished to see the Church wholly disestablished.

Thus, through this understanding of themselves, Tractarians viewed their reform 'movement' as a getting back to what was considered basic and 'real' within the Church of Christ, including notions of apostolicity, baptismal regeneration and other sacramental rites, such as Holy Communion – a movement to which J. A. Froude would later refer, somewhat wryly, as 'the Oxford Counter-Reformation'.[69] For all this, Tractarians were frequently criticised for dragging the English Church back to Rome and thereby betraying its reformed and Protestant principles. The one apparent irony in this is that several among the leading lights of the Oxford Movement seemed to have cared less about externals, in some cases cautioning against them. But this is only part of the picture. To be sure, men like Pusey, Newman and Keble were wary of hollow 'aesthetick' gesturing, or men 'playing at Popery', as Newman described them (proponents of his so-called 'gilt-gingerbread school'),[70] but this does not necessarily imply that they neither desired nor appreciated solemn, well-ordered and/or 'correct' forms of worship.

Nor were their attitudes towards architecture antithetical. Their main concern was that externals not be fetishised, which they felt was beginning to happen under the rise of Ritualism (they were not alone in this view, even among High Churchmen). After all, Newman was involved with the Oxford Architectural Society from the beginning,[71] and his church at Littlemore testifies to his broad sympathy for revived medieval architecture.[72] Pusey, too, appreciated the fundamental role that externals played in the veneration of God (as the epigraph to this introduction indicates). Some of the suspicions surrounding Tractarianism were well founded, as Newman's 'going over' would eventually prove, but, as we shall see throughout this study, much of the debate and tension surrounding ideas of 'High' and 'Low' within the Church of England had to do with how it *was*, and indeed *wished* to be, identified as both a cultural and a religious institution.

This struggle, as it were, affected significantly the way the idea of Church extension was perceived and presented, both at home and abroad. In his sermons on behalf of the SPG, for instance, Pusey warned against sending missionaries abroad without proper authoritative leadership (that is, a bishop). To Pusey, as to Tractarians in general, there was no 'Church' outside the organised, apostolic tradition sanctioned by Christ himself. '*The* Missionary Society set forth in the Prophets', he insisted, 'by our Lord and His Apostles, is, the Church'.[73] Indeed, to labour under the lack of such a principle would do more harm than good. This was the problem with the CMS, believed Pusey – its indifference towards ordinance and liturgy.[74]

For Pusey, the SPG was different, and so it should remain. If it were to be dragged down the 'popular' route of missionary work, then all hope of planting the 'true Church' among the heathen would be lost.[75] This clash of cultures (theological and liturgical) would rage in the mission field. It was felt not only among Anglicans of High and Low Church persuasion but also between Anglicans, dissenters and Roman Catholics, becoming, as we shall see, a characteristic feature of the religious scene in Britain's empire throughout the mid- to late nineteenth century.

The absorption of Tractarian principles by the SPG meant that it not only condoned notions of apostolic succession and ecclesiastical discipline but also the new spiritual sensibilities that accompanied them. It was hoped that, in sending out an educated, pious and disciplined clerisy to the colonies, the underlying ideals of British and, in particular, Anglican culture would be duly transmitted.[76] Thus, the majority of bishops and clergymen who served under the auspices of the SPG during the thirty-year period covered by this book were usually earnest, Oxbridge-educated men of moderate to high Tractarian persuasion. From time to time Evangelical bishops were appointed, such as Charles Perry (Melbourne, 1847) or Henry Cotterill (Grahamstown, 1856), but these were the exception rather than the rule. Most serving members reflected the values of the society. As Brad Faught has observed, this is in part because the Oxford Movement's own sense of mission – those same ideals that infiltrated the SPG and influenced thinking on the CBF – accorded precisely with an age given over to the imperatives of exploration, redemption and improvement.[77] But, as mentioned above, and as Edward Pusey himself observed, this mission could not be realised without a solid foundation and a true, tried and tested organisational structure.

The High Church conformation of the SPG had significant consequences for the way Anglicanism was made manifest in the colonies and throughout the empire. The Tractarian attitude towards architecture is one such consequence, and it is particularly important to an assessment of the impact of High Church Anglican culture in the British empire. This is because the neat and, in many cases, spectacular churches built by Anglicans in different parts of the empire were not only the most conspicuous form of Anglican activity but also a form that embodied and represented the spiritually reinvigorated nature of Anglican worship. The presence of cathedrals, too, marked the organised and hierarchical structure of the English Church, imparting a sense of authority that reflected and reinforced Church governance at home.

This period witnessed the high or mature phase of the Gothic Revival movement in architecture. By the 1840s, led by luminaries such as A. W. N. Pugin (1812–1852), Anglicans, in particular, held that medieval forms of architecture – notably English Gothic – were the only legitimate source for ecclesiastical buildings. Although the range of sources for ecclesiastical design in Britain would broaden considerably during the 1850s to include models from continental Europe, especially French and Italian, the middle ages remained very much the *belle époque* in the minds of High Churchmen and their architects.[78] This penchant for the romance and authority of the middle ages was coupled to ideas concerning identity and nationhood in architecture, especially as the wider debate over the choice and appropriateness of architectural style in Britain reached its climax during the late 1850s and 1860s.[79] In the remote corners of Britain's empire, thousands of miles from 'home', the expression of cultural identity mattered. For example, the Rev. Henry Master White, brother of the English architect William White, captured this sensibility perfectly when he observed that English medieval architecture, although not perfect, was 'best adapted to the English national character in its noblest features, and so the best to be perpetuated in English colonies'.[80] As we shall see during the course of this study, the role that such ideas played in the spread of Anglican culture and its architectural manifestations across the world from 1840 was significant.

This emphasis on 'externals' transformed the liturgical, ceremonial and material aspects of the Church of England fundamentally during the 1840s and 1850s. As far as architecture was concerned, the transformation came in the form of an insistence on the 'correct' liturgical arrangement of space, in a style of architecture that was deemed to reflect true Christian values. This agenda was pursued at the University of Cambridge, where a number of devout and idealistic undergraduates focused their energies on reforming church design in Britain. These young men achieved considerable notoriety throughout the middle decades of the nineteenth century for their broad application of Tractarian ideals in ecclesiastical design. The key protagonists were John Mason Neale, Edward J. Boyce, Benjamin Webb and Harvey Goodwin, all of whom would become Church of England clergymen.[81] Indeed, it was Neale who observed that the 'Tract writers [had] missed one great principle, . . . Aestheticks'.[82] Thus, in 1839, the hugely influential Cambridge Camden Society (later renamed the Ecclesiological Society) was formed, one of the aims of which was to promote (oftentimes to the point of intimidation) 'real' ecclesiastical architecture.[83]

The Camden Society's principal organ, *The Ecclesiologist* (1841–68), quickly became a popular and important periodical among High Church architects and clerics, affecting the work of some of Britain's foremost up-and-coming designers, including William Burges, R. C. Carpenter, G. E. Street, George Gilbert Scott, G. F. Bodley and William Butterfield. The society was accompanied – indeed preceded – in its endeavours by the Oxford Society for Promoting the Study of Gothic Architecture (hereafter Oxford Architectural Society), formed two months before the Cambridge Camden Society, in February 1839. Although not as doctrinaire as the Camdenians, the Oxford society was also heavily influenced by Tractarian theology. This influence shaped its understanding of ancient church architecture and the endorsement of it as the only proper basis for a true and worthy Christian architecture.[84]

The Camden Society's initial adherence to the perceived conventions of English medieval church architecture led to the development of an approach known as 'ecclesiology'. It was according to the dictates of this new 'science' that the society's ideas pertaining to correctness in Anglican church architecture were initially formulated. Through publications such as the *Transactions of the Cambridge Camden Society*, *The Ecclesiologist* and *Instrumenta Ecclesiastica*, the views of the Camden Society were widely disseminated. The Oxford Architectural Society's principal organ, the *Rules and Proceedings*, also found favour among architects and the clerical élite. Indeed, many of the clergymen who would eventually go on to work in the colonies and become colonial bishops were affiliates of one or both these societies.

Importantly, both the Cambridge Camden and the Oxford Architectural societies had always perceived their mandate as extending beyond the British Isles. The very first report that appeared in *The Ecclesiologist* was, in fact, for the design of parish churches in New Zealand, while the Oxford Architectural Society made it their business throughout much of the early 1840s to supply designs for the Afghan Memorial church in Bombay (Mumbai) and wooden churches in Newfoundland.[85] In 1845 it was even stated, in the preface to the new series of *The Ecclesiologist* (when the Camden Society changed its name), that one of its principal aims was to support church building 'in the colonies'. As these places were perceived to be frontier environments – zones of emigration, opportunity, social experimentation and confrontation – the need to encourage correct and proper church design in them was considered paramount.

The Ecclesiological Society's sympathy for the cause of the Church of England abroad was maintained throughout the lifetime of *The Ecclesiologist*. Between 1841 and 1868 it carried more than two hundred and fifty articles and reports on aspects of ecclesiastical design in Britain's overseas territories. Indeed, just when the society was at its lowest ebb, having been mauled publicly for its apparent 'Romanist' leanings, it seemed to find solace in the appeals for assistance that came flooding in from across the empire. Responding to a letter from the Rev. Frederick Cox of Tasmania, the society recorded its 'pride and pleasure' in providing assistance to such a worthy cause, adding that 'the more we are repudiated at home, the more prized by us are our colonial relations'.[86] By 1848 the society could boast that Britain's colonies were now 'some of its best friends, and may see the most gratifying results of its exertions'.[87]

It was not just the regular correspondence kept up between the society and colonial clergymen that led to these results. The publication of *Instrumenta Ecclesiastica* from 1844 proved a useful aid in promoting correct church design in the colonies. As will be discussed in detail below, this series of publications – in effect, pattern books for the design of churches and church furnishings, based on medieval precedent – were produced primarily to 'improve' the quality of ecclesiastical design in such places.[88] In addition to *Instrumenta*, the Ecclesiological and Oxford Architectural societies both published series of model church designs. These included plans, elevations and details of known exemplars of English medieval church architecture that could either be reproduced *in toto* or be adapted for colonial purposes.[89] Indeed, so far did the influence of the Ecclesiological Society extend, some historians have suggested that almost no Anglican church in the world was left untouched by its reforming zeal.[90]

Before this watershed moment for both the English Church and its architecture, the situation was very different. Much as in Britain, the Church of England in the colonies had either sunk into a state of spiritual turpitude or was dominated by Low-Church tendencies. This had architectural consequences. Anglican churches right across the empire were still being erected, whether in timber or masonry, in a broadly classical or Anglo-Palladian style well into the nineteenth century. The Gothic Revival had begun making small inroads, however haphazardly, but classicism remained the dominant mode. This is clear wherever one cares to look: in India, Australia, South Africa, Canada or the Caribbean. We shall come across some of these buildings later, but it is worth making a few comments at the

6 St John's church, Calcutta (1784–7), by James Agg.

outset about conventional usage in the preceding Georgian era, as some of these usages persisted in the colonies long after their light had faded in Britain. This will help to set the changes that occurred in context.

Much of the easy rapport between Anglicanism and classical architecture during the eighteenth century had to do with the rise and circulation of pattern books. The principal culprit in this regard was James Gibbs's *A Book of Architecture* (1728), which carried several plans for churches and steeples, the most notable of which was that for St Martin-in-the-Fields.[91] These designs, and derivatives thereof, were replicated in many parts of the empire, especially India. The major Anglican churches in both Calcutta and Madras, for example, were heavily reliant on such patterns, as were the Presbyterian kirks. If one considers St John's, Calcutta (1784–7), or St George's cathedral, Madras (1816), then this is evident not only in the overall massing and plan of these buildings but most obviously in their steeples (fig. 6). Other churches in this vein included St George's, Agra (1826), and St Mary's, Benares (*c.*1810).[92] Aggravating this pattern-book phenomenon was the fact that these churches were designed not by architects but by military engineers, who tended to rely more on ready-made, formulaic solutions. This was common practice in eighteenth- and early nineteenth-century India.

The situation was similar in both Australia and the Cape Colony. In New South Wales the convict architect Francis Greenway produced designs for two Anglican churches during the early nineteenth century – the smaller being St Matthew's, Windsor (1817–20), and the larger St James's, Sydney (1820–4) (fig. 7). Styled in a restrained Anglo-Palladianism, these churches were less pattern-book copies than conventional prescriptions.[93] The architectural historian J. M. Freeland has described them as 'clean uncomplicated buildings, lightly but firmly designed to meet the needs of uncompromisingly Protestant congregations'.[94] Initially, the scene in Tasmania and Victoria was little different. In Melbourne there was the church of St James (old cathedral) – the so-called 'pepper pot of Collins Street' – opened for service in 1842 (fig. 9),[95] while in Hobart the scene was dominated by St David's, built between 1817 and 1823 (see also fig. 111). Around the same time as these efforts in Australia, on the other side of the Indian Ocean rose the church of St George (later cathedral), Cape Town

7 St James's church, Sydney (1820–4), by Francis Greenway.

(1834) (see fig. 246), which was based on John and Henry Inwood's design for St Pancras church, Euston Road, London (1818).[96] As we shall see, although a neat specimen of its kind, St George's was roundly condemned by the Rev. Robert Gray, first bishop of Cape Town, for what he considered to be its un-churchlike appearance and garbled internal arrangement. Condemnations such as Gray's marked the beginning of the end of classicism's reign in the colonial Church of England.

In America the classicising tendency and its legacy can be traced much further back in time. From the very beginning, Anglican church architecture in the North American colonies, the Caribbean, and what would later become Canada (British North America) was based in one form or other on English classical prototypes. In Virginia, for example, where the parish system had been established from earliest times, this pattern was especially clear. As Virginia was the largest, wealthiest and most populous of the American colonies during the eighteenth century, it exhibited a marked loyalty to the English Church, establishing it by law in 1632.[97] Here churches, whether large or small, adhered for the most part to a simple variation of Anglo-Palladian classicism in brick, adopting the 'auditory room' form common to the City churches of Sir Christopher Wren.[98] They were in no way direct copies of Wren's churches but represented, instead, the calibration of known eighteenth-century principles (formal and liturgical) to localised contexts. Although there were some rare examples of what might be termed 'Gothic Survival', dating from the seventeenth century, such as St Luke's, Newport, Isle of Wight County (1682), most American colonial churches bore the mark of this English classicising influence. Among the more prominent examples of this 'colonial style' in the Chesapeake Bay region are Bruton parish church (fig. 10), Williamsburg (1711), Ware church, Gloucester County (1715), and Christ Church, Lancaster County (1732). Even in Jamaica, where episcopal oversight from London had been all but disabled, Anglican church architecture still assumed a broadly metropolitan character. This is evident, for example, in St James's church, Montego Bay (1774), where a possible source for the building's neat Palladian detailing was Batty Langley's *The City and Country Builder's and Workman's Treasury* (1740).[99]

Further north, in the populous urban centres of Pennsylvania, New York and Massachusetts, there evolved a much larger and more pretentious form of this classical church style. Buildings such as Christ Church, Philadelphia (1727), St Paul's chapel, New York City (1764) (fig. 8), and Christ Church ('Old North'), Boston (1723) were all con-

8 St Paul's Chapel, New York City (1764), attributed to Andrew Gautier and James Crommelin Lawrence.

9 St James's church (the old cathedral), Melbourne (1839–47), by Robert Russell.

10 Bruton parish church, Williamsburg, Virginia (1711), by Alexander Spotswood.

11 Etching, 1759, of St Paul's church, Halifax, Nova Scotia (1750), adapted from designs by James Gibbs (Nova Scotia Museum, Halifax).

scious emulations of the Wren or Gibbs urban type, standing out as they did within the surrounding urban fabric. Less elaborate versions of the same type subsequently rose in Cambridge (Christ Church, 1759), Swedesboro (Trinity Church, 1784), and Portsmouth (St John's, 1807).

This vision of Anglican church architecture followed the Loyalist clergy – into what is modern-day Canada – when they left the newly constituted United States in droves after the Revolution. To be sure, the broader Anglo-Palladian tradition had already found its way there, namely in the form of St Paul's church, Halifax (1750), which was a relatively modest structure modelled on Gibbs's design for Marylebone chapel (St Peter's, Vere Street), London (fig. 11).[100] But several major churches were to rise in early nineteenth-century Quebec and Ontario that deliberately perpetuated this trend. In this mode we find Holy Trinity, Quebec City (1807), St James's church, Toronto (1833), St George's, Kingston (1825–7), and Christ Church, Hamilton (1837–42), all of which were broadly based on Wren–Gibbsian models (fig. 12).[101] So connected was this image of church architecture with the sober, Low-Church practices and traditions of Anglicanism in Canada that after the second iteration of St James's was severely damaged by fire in 1839 it was rebuilt along similar lines.[102] It was Bishop Strachan who would eventually sever the tie between classicism and the Anglican faith at St James's, insisting on a Gothic Revival structure after the church was gutted by fire again in 1849 (see Chapter 2).

Thus, as we can see, the Wren–Gibbs idiom held out in pockets of the empire right down to the 1840s. The Gothic Revival had begun to push its way through, but only in that tepid, picturesque fashion later condemned by Pugin. Indeed, as in Britain at the time, early examples of this type display a rather superficial approach to the use of Gothic detailing (what the ecclesiologists would later call 'Commissioners' Gothic'), evidenced in buildings such as St John's, St John, New Brunswick (1824), and St Thomas's, Port Macquarie, New South Wales (1828) (fig. 13).

12 Holy Trinity church, Quebec City (1807), by Captain William Hall and Major William Robe.

13 St Thomas's church, Port Macquarie, New South Wales (1828), by Lieutenant T. Owen.

Crucial, therefore, to the eventual triumph of the Ecclesiological and Oxford Architectural societies in raising the standard and consistency of Anglican church architecture in the colonies was a wholesale change in mentality. As I shall argue, this endeavour was reliant on the complicity of Church of England clergymen. Because many of the bishops, priests and deacons who ventured out into Britain's empire during the mid-nineteenth century were Oxbridge educated, they were able to stimulate change by means of their considerable social and religious authority. Moreover, while at university, or soon after graduating, these men were brought directly within the ambit of the Oxford and Cambridge societies. Their Tractarian sympathies also assisted them in developing a concern for the spectacle of Christian worship. This is important because, outside the design of large and complex structures such as cathedrals, a high proportion of the Anglican churches erected in Britain's colonies during the period under consideration were designed not by architects but by clergymen. In most locations, particularly early on, and beyond the confines of major settlements, professional architectural expertise was sorely lacking. This left the design and construction of churches either in the hands of insensitive builders at extortionate rates or in the care of the local clergyman. Having acquired knowledge of ecclesiology while studying at university, and helped by the response to appeals home for good and inexpensive church plans and models, many clergymen were able to perform the function of architect with relative ease. And 'Why not?' asked *The Ecclesiologist*; after all 'William of Sens, and Alan of Walsingham, and William of Wykeham were priests'.[103] Indeed, so crucial was a knowledge of architecture and the mechanical arts considered to be in some quarters, that it was encouraged as part of the formal training of colonial clergymen.[104]

This degree of non-expert participation in the design and construction of churches and chapels by Church of England clergymen is one of the most remarkable aspects of the spread and consolidation of Anglican culture throughout the British empire during the Victorian period. Like the Franciscan missionaries of New Mexico two centuries before them, who designed and built their own churches, the presence and influence of these architect–clerics cannot be overstated, for without them the colonial scene would have been very different indeed, perhaps unrecognisable. As we shall see presently, the early pioneering days of the colonial episcopate were dependent on the dedication and piety of the new colonial bishops and their determination to organise religion upon reformed catholic and apostolic principles, including architecture.

I

In Principio

THE FOUNDATIONS AND EARLY DEVELOPMENT OF COLONIAL ECCLESIOLOGY

Our English word *To Build* is the Anglo-Saxon Bẏlðan, To confirm, To establish,
To make firm and sure and fast, To consolidate, To strengthen . . . .

John Horne Tooke, *The Diversions of Purley* (1829)

A mountain is not climbed by leaps and bounds, but step by step.

Advice from Gregory the Great to Augustine of Canterbury (*c.*600)

Do they think of us in our English homes,
Who fondly remember yet
How they were two
Of our joyous crew
In the 'Ladye Margarette'?

'The Ladye Margarette in the Days of Old' (Ode to bishops Selwyn and Tyrrell)[1]

If Anglican clergymen indeed promoted the precepts of ecclesiology throughout the British empire during the mid-nineteenth century, then we must ask how this was done. A large proportion of the bishops first appointed under the Colonial Bishoprics' Fund scheme were Oxbridge-educated men of High Church persuasion, many of whom were naturally sympathetic to the formal expression of Anglican spirituality and worship. To them, as Robert Gray, bishop of Cape Town, would later observe, architecture was one of the chief 'appliances' at their disposal.[2] But who were these bishops (and their attendant clergy) and how exactly did they extend church architecture? Why did they consider architecture important when so many other immediate concerns demanded their attention? What were the key ideas and difficulties, and how did they implement and overcome these? It might be supposed that local circumstances affected their architectural response in each case, but precisely how did these circumstances impinge? These are important questions if we are to explain the spread of High Church Anglicanism and its architectural manifestations worldwide.

Back to Basics:
Bishop Selwyn and the Origins of Colonial Ecclesiology

The best place to start such an investigation is at the beginning – the beginning for the purposes of this study being the establishment of a global Anglican episcopate through the CBF. The first diocese erected under this scheme was that of New Zealand (1841), which had become a formal colony of Britain in 1840. This was followed shortly afterwards by the dioceses of Antigua, Guiana, Tasmania and Gibraltar, all erected in 1842. Then came Colombo (Sri Lanka) and Fredericton (New Brunswick) in 1845, followed two years later by Cape Town, Newcastle (NSW), Melbourne and Adelaide. An analysis of the foundational years of some of these dioceses will form the basis of the current chapter. A number of Anglican dioceses were extant before 1841, including those created under the Colonial Episcopates Act (1786) in British North America and the Caribbean: Nova Scotia (1787), Quebec (1793), Jamaica (1824), Barbados (1824) and the one Asian diocese of Calcutta (1814). The British North American dioceses were further divided in 1839 to form Toronto and Newfoundland, while Calcutta was reformed to include Madras (1835), Sydney (1836) and Bombay (1837). Aspects of some of these earlier dioceses will also be considered.

It is during the earliest phase in the establishment of these new colonial dioceses that we see many of the problems first appear that would test the expansion of the English Church abroad. These included access to resources, availability of materials, climate, religious competition and local politics. All of these, in some form or other, plagued Anglican clergy in their attempts to establish a foothold and gain influence in their respective regions. These problems were bound to affect architecture more than other activities associated with the colonial Church because the consumption of resources was so great with respect to building. In places where communication channels and professional expertise were either severely limited or non-existent, the problem was even greater. But, as we shall see, this led to the development of rather innovative compensatory measures that enabled an architecture to evolve that was practical and durable while remaining appropriate and dignified.

Many of the early attempts at erecting church buildings in Britain's post-1841 colonial dioceses were concerned with the imitation of correct ecclesiastical models. The term 'correct' – much used at the time – was taken to mean a church that both exhibited and exemplified proper liturgical arrangements according to the ordinances of the English Church, in a style of architecture that was considered 'Christian'. If the Church of England was to recreate its organisational structures abroad, then it was entirely reasonable to assume that the physical manifestation of its liturgical practices would follow. By the time the diocese of New Zealand was created in 1841, the winds of change had swept through the English Church, transforming it almost entirely. Ecclesiastical reform, in conjunction with the rise of Tractarianism, had made for a leaner, more serious and spiritually rejuvenated institution. This mood infused the new architectural societies in Oxford and Cambridge, leading in turn to an equally serious approach to the study and understanding of medieval architecture. Thus, when the Rev. George Augustus Selwyn (1809–1878), first bishop of New Zealand, requested assistance in the form of 'good' designs of English churches to take with him to his new diocese, his call was met with enthusiasm. Indeed, it had always been the aim of the Cambridge Camden Society to supply advice on matters of 'taste or architectural propriety' with respect to church design.[3] The Oxford Architectural Society, too, was keen to assist. The installation of an Anglican bishop in a new British colony was seen as a tremendous opportunity, architecturally speaking, to start afresh on a true and proper footing.

In many respects Selwyn was an Anglican clergyman typical of the age (fig. 14). Like those of the preceding generation, he was a man of learning and calm decision in the gentlemanly parson mould. Unlike his predecessors he displayed that air of seriousness and piety that would become the hallmark of Tractarian-inspired clergy of the mid-Victorian period. It would be wrong to describe Selwyn as Anglo-Catholic, for he was no enthusiast for ritualism, but he was influenced appreciably by the guiding principles of the Oxford Movement. His connections with the élite of English society (clerical and political) were extensive. For example, while a pupil at Eton he established a close and lifelong friendship with the High Church protagonist and future Prime Minister, W. E. Gladstone (1809–1898).[4] In 1827 Selwyn proceeded to St John's College, Cambridge, where he excelled not only as a scholar, coming second in the classical tripos, but also as an athlete, obtaining a blue for rowing in 1829. As we shall see, this not unseemly blend of piety and physical prowess would serve him well in his endeavours at establishing and organising his new diocese, which covered some 95,000 square miles (the equivalent land mass of Great Britain).

Selwyn's earnest spirituality and scholarly aptitude drew him naturally towards the finer points of ecclesiastical architecture. On being elevated as bishop in 1841 he was made a patron member of the Cambridge Camden Society, an association that would prove useful to him in his early days in New Zealand. Before leaving for his new diocese in December that year, Selwyn asked the Camden Society to furnish him with 'designs and models' for a cathedral and several parish churches. It was noted that one model of a good parish church would be sufficient at first, for the churches he intended to erect would be some two hundred miles apart.[5] It was also observed that the architectural style of choice was the rather simple yet solid Norman. This style was considered appropriate for a number of reasons. First, it was understood as a faster and cheaper method of building than fully developed Gothic. This was essential as the cost of building in New Zealand at the time was higher than in Britain. Second, building in such a 'primitive' style drew a parallel with the endeavours of the early Church fathers, such as Augustine of Canterbury in the 6th century.[6] It must be remembered that New Zealand was perceived by many as an antipodean equivalent of the British Isles, and Selwyn as a nineteenth-century incarnation of Augustine.[7] This would partly explain why the Camden Society was willing to deviate from its usual insistence on Decorated Gothic – or what they termed 'Middle Pointed' – for the design of ecclesiastical buildings in New Zealand. And, finally, because it would be both wise and natural 'to teach them [the native Māori] first that style which first prevailed in our own country; while its rudeness and massiveness, and the grotesque character of its sculpture, will probably render it easier to be understood and appreciated by them'.[8]

14 Engraving by Samuel Cousins after George Richmond of George Augustus Selwyn (1809–1878), first bishop of New Zealand, *c.*1842 (Staffordshire County Buildings Picture Collection). Selwyn was appointed under the Colonial Bishoprics' Fund in 1841.

It is important to note here that this insistence on the Norman style of architecture for New Zealand was not, as one might expect, based on a naïve assumption that Māori were necessarily less intelligent or less capable than Europeans. On the contrary, Selwyn often noted in his diary and letters, as had Samuel Marsden before him, how the Māori were just as intelligent and sensitive as their European counterparts, if not more so.[9] Rather, this appeal to Norman architecture had more to do with Whiggish notions of history as a temporal unfolding of civilisation through progress, and the idea that *history* could, in a sense, be replayed in Britain's colonies where European settlers came into contact with pre-existing indigenous cultures.[10] This 'civilisational' perspective, as Peter Mandler has described it, naturally set alien and primitive cultures against a backcloth of European progress and development. Thus, as a peculiarly modern form of anthropological evaluation, this historical standpoint contained within it both a *secularisation* and a *naturalisation* of time that enabled the construction of a comparative framework through which to observe, contrast and 'objectively' assess relative states of

15 Māori *whare*, lithograph illustrating indigenous wood-carving practices, from George French Angas's *The New Zealanders Illustrated* (1847).

civilisation among different peoples.[11] This framework, of course, tended to present civilisation as a kind of social-evolutionary slope or ladder. On this scale Europeans and 'modern primitives' were seen to be at different stages – or on different rungs, to extend the analogy – in their ascent towards cultural and technological attainment.[12] In this respect, as John Lubbock and other natural scientists would later observe, certain indigenous cultures, such as the Māori, were perceived as akin to 'living fossils'. The Māori may not have been at the same point on this scale as Europeans, but it was possible to bring them into a higher state of being through the right kind of intervention and tutelage. In this scenario, of course, reformed Christianity would join forces with the fundamental tenets of Enlightenment rationality, including commerce. After all, this was one of the basic objectives of missionary Anglicanism: not just to convert but to civilise.[13] For Selwyn and the Camdenians, architecture was seen as an agent in this civilisational process, a medium through which to inculcate not only the precepts of Christianity but also a set of technical and craft-based practices that would place the Māori on the right step on the ladder of social progress in order that they might learn and develop as had the Anglo-Saxons.[14]

In addition to this early Victorian view concerning the social progress of humankind, there was a growing interest in publications relating to Britain's colonies and their native inhabitants. Before Selwyn's departure to New Zealand numerous reports of Māori culture had reached Britain from, among others, agents of the Church Missionary Society.[15] There was also a handful of general publications outlining the conditions and prospects of New Zealand for would-be immigrants, including accounts of its indigenous

16 Plan, elevation and details of Than church, Normandy, from A. C. Pugin's *Architectural Specimens of Normandy* (1828).

population. Some of these publications carried illustrations of Maori craftsmanship, indicating how their skill might be turned to architectural ends.[16] One of the most elaborate of such publications, although produced some years after Selwyn's departure, was George French Angas's *The New Zealanders Illustrated* (1847). This publication included an astonishing array of highly detailed and informative lithographs, illustrating everything from Māori domestic architecture and weaponry through to handcrafted artefacts and social customs (fig. 15).[17] To European eyes the highly stylised and apparently 'rude' figures represented in Māori carving seemed to resemble earlier and less refined periods in the history of European sculpture, such as that found on the Norman church at Kilpeck, Herefordshire (1140).[18] As spurious as it might seem to us today, it was precisely for this reason that the Cambridge Camden Society believed the massive and 'grotesque character' of Norman architecture to be a suitable starting point for engaging with the Māori and encouraging them to participate in Christianity and, ultimately, European civilisation.

To aid Selwyn in his endeavours, the Cambridge Camden Society was to supply him with a plan for a simple parish church in the Norman style based on that of Than near Caen in Normandy.[19] The church at Than was a reasonably well-known ecclesiastical antiquity, having appeared in a number of notable publications on continental church architecture since 1820, including John Sell Cotman's *Architectural Antiquities of Normandy* (1822), A. C. Pugin's *Architectural Specimens of Normandy* (1828) and J. L. Petit's *Remarks on Church Architecture* (1841) (fig. 16). It was considered an ideal exemplar of ecclesiastical architecture because it was, as Cotman had noted, an 'unaltered' specimen in the 'true

17 St Mary's church, Iffley (near Oxford), from John Britton's *Architectural Antiquities of Great Britain* (1826).

Norman style' – a style that, appropriately enough, had been brought to the shores of Cotman's own country by 'Teutonic colonists' 750 years earlier.[20] The other exemplar that was considered suitable for New Zealand was the parish church of St Mary, Iffley, near Oxford (fig. 17). Like Than, Iffley was a well-known Norman relic. Indeed, it had captured the attention of antiquaries and architectural enthusiasts from Oxford owing to its reputation as one of the most complete and impressive Norman churches in England.[21] It was the well-preserved details of Iffley, rather than those at Than, that would serve as working models for Selwyn's Norman cathedral, plans for which were to be supplied by Anthony Salvin.[22] The Camden Society was assisted in this through its sister society in Oxford. At the bishop's behest, casts of the important details of Iffley, including the nave capitals and mouldings from around the door and window arches, were to be made.[23] It is not known if these particular casts were ever taken, or, if they were, whether they reached Selwyn. Casts answering to this description did, however, end up in the possession of the Oxford Architectural Society.[24] Given the circumstances surrounding Selwyn's request, it is possible that some or all of these casts were intended at some point for New Zealand.

Despite these lofty and noble ambitions for colonial ecclesiology, the reality on the ground was less promising. When Selwyn arrived in New Zealand from Sydney aboard the *Bristolian*, disembarking at Auckland on 29 May 1842, he quickly saw that his vision for a land scattered with Norman-style churches would be years in the making, if it could be realised at all. A much more immediate solution for church accommodation was required. Indeed, the problem of architecture had begun weighing on Selwyn's mind the moment he set sail. While *en route* he was concerned that provision be made for dignified Anglican worship. In order to realise this, he was allowed by the captain of the *Tomatin*, upon which he sailed to Australia, to transform the deck from time to time into a makeshift church. True to his High Church principles, Selwyn left nothing to chance. Although without walls and a roof, the furnishings of this 'ship church' – or 'Tomatin Cathedral', as his wife called it – were arranged in as correct a manner as possible (fig. 18).[25] Writing home to his mother in January 1842, Selwyn noted of one act of worship:

> You would be much pleased with our Church. I and my Chaplain sit at the part of the Ship which is used for our Communion table, which is covered with a red flag. The Capstan covered with another flag is our Pulpit and Desk, and the seats are arranged round, and covered with all the Ships signals. . . . Our communion table was spread with Mr. Mackerness's Altar Service Books, Mr. Few's Communion Plate, with a Cloth given by one of my Windsor Parishioners.[26]

The ship's passengers were certainly impressed. One noted how the whole scene was as close an 'imitation' of a real church as circumstances would permit.[27] This instance may not strike one initially as having much to do with the ecclesiology of New Zealand, but the 'Tomatin Cathedral' was, in a sense, the first Selwyn church. It was not only a carefully considered example of spatial programmatics, but also revealed Selwyn to have been highly sensitive to issues of ordinance and discipline in Anglican worship, regardless of context.

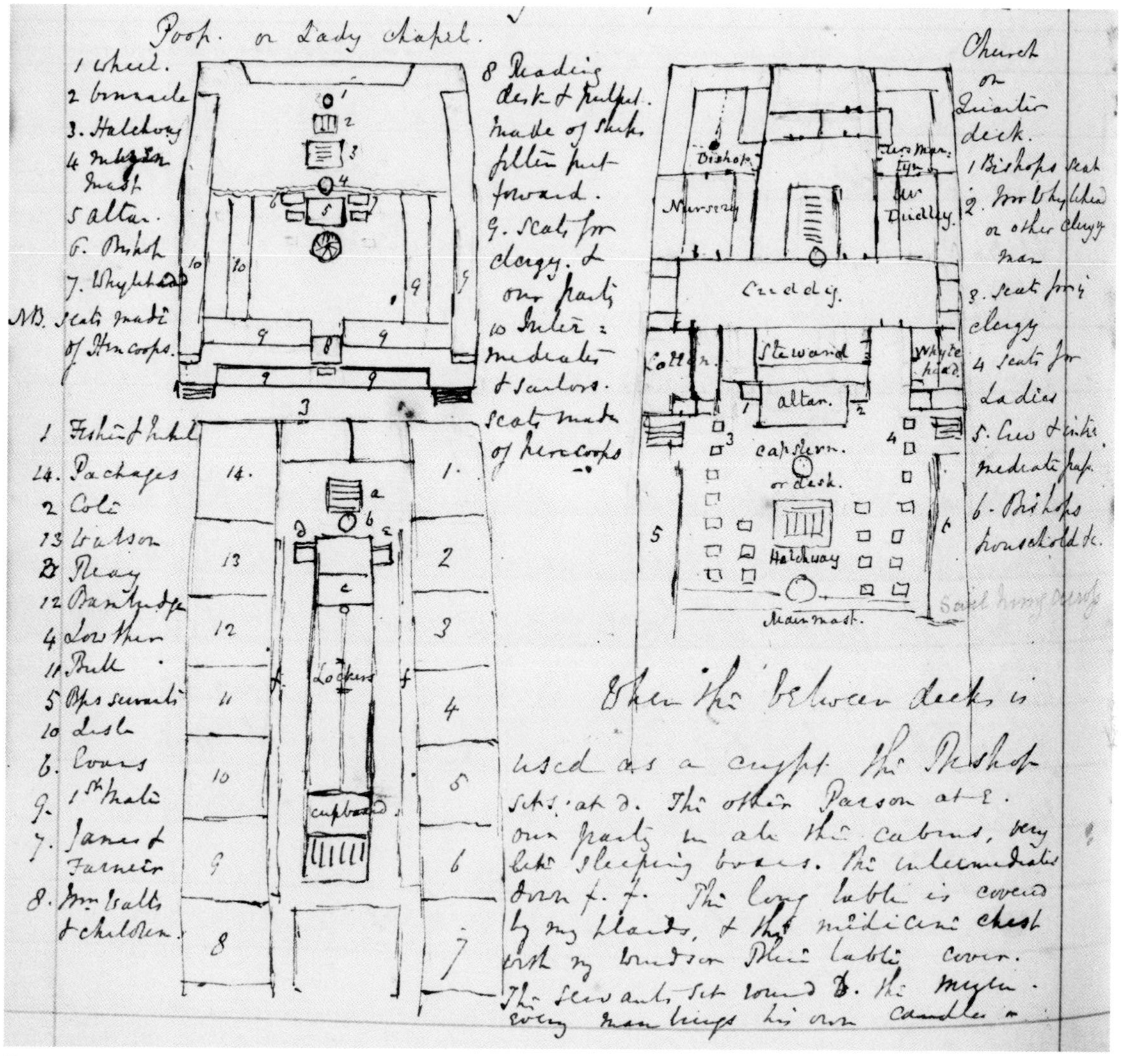

18 William Cotton's sketches of the 'Tomatin Cathedral' from his journal for 1842 (State Library of New South Wales, Sydney).

Selwyn was supported in his ecclesiological ambitions by two clerical understudies who accompanied him to New Zealand: the Rev. William Charles Cotton (1813–1879) (fig. 19) and the Rev. Thomas Whytehead (1815–1843). More than Selwyn himself, Cotton was a clergyman of clear and decided Tractarian sympathies.[28] Having studied first at Eton and then Christ Church, Oxford (where he took a first in classics, 1836), he was influenced considerably by the teachings of the Oxford reformers. Cotton's High Church leanings, combined with his keen interest in ecclesiastical architecture, had drawn him within the ambit of the Cambridge Camden and Oxford Architectural societies.[29] His father, William Cotton (1786–1866), was also a leading figure in the Incorporated Church Building Society (see Chapter 7).[30] The 26-year-old Whytehead, a former Bell Scholar at St John's College, Cambridge, was also a High Churchman and keen ecclesiologist. As a member of the Cambridge Camden Society, he was quickly co-opted as New Zealand correspondent for *The Ecclesiologist*.[31]

As church accommodation was lacking in New Zealand, Selwyn's mission party started out using a tent, which had been donated by Cotton's father. This apparatus, known variously as the 'Church Tent' or 'canvas Cathedral', was fitted out with all the appurtenances of divine service that one would have expected to find in a proper parish church.[32] So complete was it when erected that one

19 Margaret Carpenter, portrait of William Charles Cotton (1813–1879), on the occasion of his leaving Eton College, 1832 (Eton College). Cotton later became chaplain to Bishop Selwyn in New Zealand.

observer described it as 'a very seemly substitute for a more substantial building'. Selwyn himself considered it 'a most complete cathedral, with pulpit, reading-desk, communion table, rails, kneeling-boards, &c.'[33] As a structure it was quite large, measuring some 60 feet by 30 feet – large enough to contain 200–300 people (fig. 20).[34]

Architecturally speaking, the significance of this 'Church Tent' was twofold. First, it was a portable structure, enabling Selwyn and his aides to conduct appropriately ordered divine service while on the move. This was particularly useful in the early years of Selwyn's episcopacy, when he was on visitation journeys through his vast diocese, having to be away for weeks at a time.[35] Whether he was preaching to colonial settlers in newly established towns (such as Nelson and Wellington) or proselytising Māori in their native tongue, the tent brought a degree of dignity and character to Anglican worship that would otherwise have been lacking. Indeed, the very tension that existed between the impermanence of the tent itself and the authority of its interior fittings reflected the fragile if determined nature of the particular brand of Anglicanism that Selwyn hoped to institute in New Zealand. What better device could there have been in the struggle to extend 'true' religion than a 'church' that was potentially everywhere and nowhere at once?

Second, the use of a tent in substitution for a more substantial structure had significant symbolic value for Christians. It was representative of the very first church, the so-called Tabernacle ('tent of meeting' or 'holy of holies') which was a portable shrine constructed under the direc-

20 Watercolour sketch by an unknown artist of the Purewa campsite (near Auckland) showing Cotton's 'Church Tent', *c.*1845 (Alexander Turnbull Library, Wellington).

tion of Moses during the wandering of the Israelites in the wilderness.[36] The parallels with Selwyn's own situation are striking. He was, as it were, a Church father in the 'wilderness' – New Zealand being considered an uncultivated place in the 1840s, both physically and spiritually. Selwyn appreciated fully the biblical and historic synergies.[37] He believed that in taking up episcopal authority in such a place – one in which very little if any ecclesiastical governance existed prior to his arrival – he had been granted more than any other English bishop in history 'a power to mould the institutions of the Church from the beginning'.[38] In this sense, the tent or 'tabernacle' was a true beginning, ecclesiologically at least. Even the proportional relationship of its dimensions mirrored those described in Exodus: a length to width ratio of 2:1. So authentic and magisterial an idea had the tent become in the mind of Cotton, with all its sacred and precious accoutrements, that he recalled one occasion when the bishop was forced to conduct divine service 'in the "Mechanics Institute"', which was 'by no means so Episcopal a building as the Tent'.[39] As the illustrations here reveal, the idea of the 'tent' could take different forms depending on the context. In the scene at Orona, Lake Taupo (1843), later published in *The Ecclesiologist*, Selwyn and Cotton are shown officiating from their camping tents, as though standing in Gothic niches, while the remains of an old canoe forms a makeshift altar (fig. 21).[40] Selwyn's attitude towards such a spectacle is summed up in his parting sermon, delivered in Exeter cathedral on 12 December 1841:

> 'How shall we sing the Lord's song in a strange land?' . . . we have to leave these glorious temples of our native Church, to find in the wild woods our school of architecture, and to worship God under the open canopy of heaven, or under the shade of overarching trees, or in the tabernacle, which must be the forerunner of the temple. . . . God's promise is sure to those who build in faith upon the foundation of Christ.[41]

Although Selwyn's expectations were naturally lowered upon arriving in New Zealand, he did not desist from imagining the architectural possibilities. As early as the voyage out, he began sketching his vision for a 'Collegiate

21 Sketches showing Selwyn and Cotton officiating from their tents during Māori services at Orona, Lake Taupo, and Wakapapa River, 1843 (Alexander Turnbull Library, Wellington).

Institution' – an initial rendition of what would eventually become St John's College, Bishop's Auckland (see p. 52). Again, heeding the advice of the Cambridge Camden Society, these sketches show a series of buildings in a distinct Norman/Romanesque idiom.[42] They are carefully considered sketches that demonstrate not only a facility for design but also a sound understanding of ecclesiological principles. Their particular character also indicates a likely source. It is known that upon leaving England Selwyn was gifted a small library of books by his friends from Eton.[43] Among these books were works on architecture, including John Louis Petit's *Remarks on Church Architecture* (1841). Petit's book was full of quaint if rather crude sketches of many of the notable Romanesque churches of France and Germany. Aspects of Selwyn's sketches closely resemble Petit's, suggesting that he had this book to hand.[44]

In the event, Selwyn's and the Cambridge Camden Society's vision for a reconstituted early medieval architecture for New Zealand was never realised. Nevertheless, their imagining of the situation as one akin to that of the early Church fathers – out in the 'wilderness' laying down the foundations of the apostolic tradition – not only set the tone for the future direction of ecclesiastical architecture in New Zealand but also presented a model for bishops and clergymen to follow elsewhere in the colonial world. Selwyn's growing acclaim as a heroic pioneering cleric, along with the accounts in *The Ecclesiologist* of his early endeavours, ensured that his example would not go unnoticed.

A Matter of Mere Economy? Early Developments in Australia

New Zealand was not the only place that became a testing ground for a revived Norman- or Romanesque-style architecture. Across the Tasman Sea the Rev. William Grant Broughton (1788–1853), bishop of Australia, had been making busy for quite some time with plans to extend and entrench the influence of the established Church, including its architecture.

Broughton, who had been archdeacon of Australia from 1829, was made bishop of Australia when the diocese of Calcutta was divided in 1836 (see fig. 223). He was primarily a churchman of the 'high and dry' school, with a marked dislike of Roman Catholicism. Later he would come under the spell of the Oxford Movement, inspired mainly by ideas of spiritual dignity and ecclesiastical independence. Most importantly he was a man of considerable talent in both learning and administration, and soon developed a reputation for clear-sightedness and tenacity.[45]

Despite his abilities, however, Broughton quickly found himself having to defend the existence of the English Church in New South Wales. The suspension and eventual repeal of the Church and Schools Corporation (which granted one-seventh of land in Australia to the established Church) in 1833, followed by the institution of religious pluralism through the Church Act of 1836, left Broughton in little doubt of what lay in store: disestablishment and open competition for resources with other Christian denominations.[46] Selwyn faced a similar predicament in New Zealand (see pp. 237–8). In such an environment, filled as it was with the winds of reform blown from the motherland, Broughton realised that the Church of England in Australia would have to stand on its own two feet, and it was under these conditions that the ideas of the Oxford reformers began exerting their influence.

Like Selwyn, Broughton was very much concerned with the role that architecture might play in this new and uncertain world of religious pluralism. To be sure, it would bring much needed order and discipline to the public ceremonial of Anglican worship, but he could see how it might also be used to enhance the physical presence of the Church, thus asserting both its dignity and identity.[47] In this sense, architecture was a part of Broughton's wider policy that the English Church must present a respectable and strong intellectual face to the colonists of Australia if it was to counter indifference, encourage loyalty and combat the growing tide of Roman Catholicism.[48] It had been a definite concern of Broughton's almost since his arrival in Australia that there were no buildings for the 'decent celebration of the Worship of God'.[49] Indeed, as his predecessor, the Rev. Thomas Hobbes Scott, had observed, Anglican church services in Australia were 'administered much more after the manner of a Methodist Chapel than of a Church'.[50] As one of the prime movers behind the establishment of the CBF, Broughton understood perhaps better than anyone in Australia the benefits that organised religion and its architecture could bring to the development of civil society in a fledgling colony.[51]

To this end Broughton worked tirelessly to promote the cause of church building in Australia. Although his greatest achievement was St Andrew's cathedral, Sydney (1837–74), he encouraged the erection of correct, 'churchlike' buildings when and wherever he could. Again, like Selwyn, Broughton displayed a personal interest in architecture, oftentimes getting involved in the design and building of churches himself.[52] This was mainly owing to a dearth of capable architects and builders in Australia during the 1830s and 1840s.[53] Few were cognisant of the recent developments that had taken place in ecclesiastical architecture in Britain, and even fewer would have understood or appreciated the particular needs of a High Church cleric like Broughton. Fortuitously, a capable pair of hands did arrive in Sydney in November 1842 – a knowledgeable young man from Yorkshire by the name of Edmund Thomas Blacket (1817–1883). Blacket became acquainted with Broughton soon after his arrival, as he came carrying letters of introduction to him, including one from the archbishop of Canterbury; Broughton put him to work almost immediately designing churches of a proper ecclesiastical character.[54]

One such was the tiny parish church of All Saints', Bathurst (about a hundred and fifty miles west of Sydney) (fig. 22). As with the proposals for New Zealand, this building was erected in brick to a Norman design. The exact provenance of the design remains uncertain, but the plans were prepared by Blacket in 1844. It has been suggested by Joan Kerr that Blacket based his drawings on Than, assuming that Selwyn either left or copied the design given him by the Cambridge Camden Society during his visit to Sydney in 1842.[55] While All Saints' bears a passing resemblance to Than, it was certainly not beyond Blacket to have designed the church himself. After all, he claimed to know something about Norman architecture, having lectured on the topic in 1843.[56]

The reasons for adopting Norman architecture in this case, however, are not clear. It might reasonably be assumed that, if not for the sake of the local indigenous population (it was not a mission church), it was chosen for reasons of economy, being a style that, if done properly, was at once churchlike and cheap. Evidence for this reasoning can be found elsewhere. In South Africa, for instance, the Rev. John Fry had hoped that the Society for the Propagation of the Gospel might send him 'a plan and elevation of a

22 Sketch by an unknown artist (probably Blacket) of All Saints' church, Bathurst, New South Wales (1844), by Edmund Blacket (State Library of New South Wales, Sydney).

23 The Norman-style church of St Mary, Busselton, Western Australia (*c.*1845), by J. R. Wollaston.

Norman Church, that being the style easiest erected here [that is, cheap]', while the bishop of Cape Town had advised the parishioners of St Helena to adopt the Norman style of architecture because it was 'the least expensive'.[57] Closer to home there was the example of St Mary's, Busselton, a hundred miles south of Perth (fig. 23).[58] This charming rustic structure in the Norman style was designed by the Rev. J. R. Wollaston (later archdeacon of Western Australia) and built cheaply using locally sourced materials. Although located several thousand miles from Bathurst, it is possible that Broughton knew of plans to erect this church. Norman-style architecture may have been cheap, but this did not mean it was undignified. In 1848 St Mary's was described by a clergyman visiting from Adelaide as one of the neatest specimens of colonial church architecture he had seen, while the bishop of Adelaide noted that it was 'no bad specimen of the earliest style of Church Architecture'.[59]

Indeed, churches like All Saints', Bathurst, and St Mary's, Busselton, were not initially disapproved of by the Cambridge Camden Society. In the early years of the society's existence Romanesque architecture, especially Anglo-Norman, was considered acceptable under certain circumstances, even encouraged. This was not only the case in the colonies, but also in Britain.[60] For example, the Norman-style church of St Nicholas, East Grafton (Wiltshire), by Benjamin Ferrey was 'cordially approved' by the society in 1842.[61] The timing of this particular design (probably executed late 1841) suggests that it might well have been under consideration by the society as a 'model' church for the colonies.[62] There is no evidence linking the two designs, but All Saints' does bear some resemblance to Ferrey's design for St Nicholas's, although on a much reduced scale.

As the diocese of Australia was too large for a single bishop, the diocese of Tasmania was formed in 1842. The Rev. Francis Nixon of Sandgate, Kent, was consecrated bishop in Westminster Abbey on 24 August that year, and reached Hobart in July 1843. A further subdivision took place in 1847, in which the see of 'Australia' was dissolved and re-formed as the separate dioceses of Melbourne, Sydney, Newcastle and Adelaide. In this restructuring Broughton, restyled bishop of Sydney, became metropolitan of both Australia and New Zealand – acting in a fashion as 'archbishop' of the region. With the exception of Charles Perry (bishop of Melbourne), the new Australian bishops were of decided Tractarian disposition. Of these, Nixon, and the Rev. Augustus Short (1802–1883), bishop of Adelaide, were particularly High Church.[63]

After deliberating for some time over whether to take the bishopric of Cape Town or Adelaide, Short finally arrived off the coast of South Australia in December 1847 (fig. 24). What he discovered upon arrival, however, was a

24 Engraving by J. Hogarth after George Richmond of Augustus Short (1802–1883), bishop of Adelaide, 1849 (private collection).

25 S. T. Gill, contemporary sketch of Trinity Church, North Terrace, Adelaide, 1838 (State Library of South Australia).

religious scene that, unlike New South Wales, had been all but pluralist since the beginning.[64] Created in 1836, the colony of South Australia was founded in an atmosphere of radicalism and reform – a so-called 'paradise of dissent'. This condition dictated equality among all denominations, leading in short order to the withdrawal of state funding and a reliance on 'voluntaryism'.[65] In this respect South Australia was similar to New Zealand in the government's attitude towards disestablishment. Thus, although Short was lucky in that his bishopric had been endowed to the tune of £20,000 by the heiress to the Coutts banking fortune, Angela Burdett-Coutts (1814–1906), and in that the governor, Lieutenant-Colonel F. H. Robe, somewhat favoured the English Church, he did find himself in a situation that demanded no small amount of self-reliance and resolve.[66] Added to his woes was the fact that the Church of England in South Australia had been of a very Low kind, certainly up until the time that the SPG sent reinforcements in 1846. The problem was so great in rural areas that fraternisation with Nonconformists had already occurred – a condition referred to by the colonists as 'common Christianity'.[67] Where no clergyman was resident, and no Prayer Book services available, it was lamented, '[Anglican] settlers . . . are ready to unite with the first congregation that presents itself conveniently to them'.[68]

One of the means by which Short tackled this low state of affairs was to reassert the identity and traditions of Anglicanism through architecture.[69] He had commented on the flimsiness of many of the existing churches that he encountered upon arriving in the colony, describing Trinity Church, North Terrace (1838), for example, as 'too low' and St George's, Magill (1847–8), as 'rough' (fig. 25).[70] Among his first initiatives was to reinvigorate the numerous proposals to erect churches that had lapsed owing to vagueness or lack of funds. Principal among these was Christ Church, North Adelaide (1848–9) (fig. 26). The location of North Adelaide, situated across the river Torrens, away from the main settlement, was chosen for its commanding views and sedate environs. The decision had been taken in 1847 to 'abandon' the central part of the town to 'Dissenters'.[71] This was considered unwise by some but nonetheless gave the Church of England the opportunity to reassert its presence (and independence) in what was becoming an increasingly crowded, and perhaps all too cosy, denominational milieu. It was here, on the gently rising slope of Montefiore to the north-west of the city, that Short laid the foundation stone of his new church in June 1848. His hope was that, when complete, it would be 'a large and handsome structure . . . seen in every direction'.[72]

The only way that Short could ensure a suitably 'handsome' edifice, however, was to design it himself. Like Selwyn and Broughton before him, Short realised upon arriving in Adelaide that dependable labour was scarce and expertise in modern ecclesiastical design virtually non-existent. Thus, we find him noting in his diary for the morning of 28 January 1848: 'Drew plans for N. Adelaide Church.'[73] It has long been assumed that Henry Stuckey, one of Adelaide's foremost architects of the period, was responsible for designing Christ Church.[74] But Short's diary entry suggests an alternative scenario: that it was in fact the bishop who designed the church, passing his sketches on to Stuckey, who then took and used them to prepare the necessary working drawings.[75] As we have seen, it was by no means unusual for Anglican clergymen to assist in the design and construction of churches in Britain's colonies at this time, especially those who were naturally interested in architecture and who had links with the Cambridge Camden and Oxford Architectural societies.

Short, like many High Church clerics of his time, was well versed in the finer points of ecclesiastical architecture. He was someone who appreciated what Pusey had called the 'visible part of devotion', and was determined to raise the decency and order of Anglican worship in the colony of South Australia.[76] He even considered himself informed

26 Sketch by an unknown artist of Christ Church, North Adelaide (1848–9), shortly after its completion (State Library of South Australia). The church was designed by Bishop Short.

enough to give public lectures on the topic.[77] But, as with Broughton in New South Wales, it soon dawned on Short that funds for church building in South Australia were extremely limited. Not wanting to compromise the ecclesiastical dignity of his new church, he opted for the simple yet solemn Norman style. His reasoning for this was straightforward: the Norman style was 'most suited to the materials brick and stone and the finances at our command'.[78]

Looking at the building, there appears to be more to Short's decision than mere economy. First, the church as built comes nearer to the original Norman design supplied to Selwyn by the Cambridge Camden Society than anything ever erected in New Zealand. This suggests that if Short had not seen Salvin's drawings he might at least have read or heard about them, and been inspired to produce something similar.[79] Although mere speculation, this is certainly not impossible. Appreciating the fact that he was in a land the civil society of which was in a state of infancy, he may have felt it prudent to heed the advice given to Selwyn. Second, the window architraves at the east end of the building are carved with pilasters topped by Norman capitals (fig. 27). This was no inane attempt at giving the building a semblance of dignity or correctness, nor was it a gesture towards ecclesiastical pretension. Short's intentions were more considered than this. What he wanted was not a Norman church *per se* but, more specifically, an 'Anglo-Norman' one.[80] Whether the outcome was an identifiably English variant of the Norman style is rather debatable, but this nevertheless seems to have been a conscious decision on Short's part, wholly calculated to signal the newfound integrity of the English Church in South Australia and to pronounce clearly its national origins and affiliation.[81]

Christ Church, North Adelaide, was not the only church built in this so-called Anglo-Norman style during the early years of Short's episcopacy. All Saints', Hindmarsh (1849–50), was another (fig. 28). This church has also been attributed to Stuckey. However, given the timing and circumstances surrounding the design of Christ Church, it is likely that Short was involved here too. The same

27 East end of Christ Church, North Adelaide (1848–9), showing Norman detailing.

materials are used (brick and stone), and many of the principal features have been replicated. The main difference is the addition of a corbel table in red brick, giving the building a pronounced Norman appearance, in spite of the fact that the roof pitch is rather too high to make for a convincing Norman-style church.

Although most of the other early churches in Adelaide would be built in some form or other of Gothic, this Norman style appeared again several years later in the mission church of St Matthew, Poonindie (1855), sixteen miles north of Port Lincoln (fig. 29). Selwyn may never have realised his ambition to implement a church-building programme in the Norman style for the Māori of New Zealand, but there is evidence to suggest that a like scheme was attempted with Australian aboriginals at Poonindie. Here, under the watchful eye of the Rev. Mathew Hale, archdeacon of Adelaide, the indigenous converts of the station were taught bricklaying and other mechanical skills for erecting and maintaining the station's buildings, including the church.[82] It cannot be known whether the Norman style was chosen in this specific instance for social evolutionary reasons. But teaching indigenous converts technical

28 All Saints' church, Hindmarsh, Adelaide (1849–50), by Augustus Short and Henry Stuckey.

29 St Matthew's mission church, Poonindie, South Australia (1855).

skills, and utilising those skills to erect the house of God, was considered by Anglican missionaries as part of the broader civilising process. Again, as with All Saints', Hindmarsh, St Matthew's appears rather more like a small Early English parish church with round-headed windows than a distinctive Norman-style chapel. To be sure, it is not a building that would have attracted praise from ecclesiologists, but it was one that would nonetheless have been considered appropriate under the circumstances.

It should be stressed that the point of such buildings was not to imitate authentic Anglo-Norman architecture with archaeological precision, for Short and his colleagues had neither the means nor inclination to achieve this. Rather, it was an initiative designed to give the churches of the colony an appropriate, if modest, air of ecclesiastical grace befitting the history and traditions of the English Church. Indeed, the view that architecture had an innate capacity to embody essential ideas about religion and identity put Short in broad sympathy with his fellow labourers Broughton and Selwyn. Together they represented an entirely new attitude towards ecclesiastical architecture in Britain's antipodean colonies, demanding new levels of beauty and integrity consistent with the rubrics of the English Prayer Book, especially those concerning ceremonial and the order of Holy Communion.

Gothic Resurgent: Manly Middle-Pointed and the Ecclesiology of Endurance

Although simplicity was the leitmotif that governed the development of much early colonial ecclesiology, Norman was not the only style of architecture considered either socially appropriate or economically viable. The hardening attitude of organisations such as the Cambridge Camden Society towards pointed styles of architecture, in particular the Decorated or 'Middle-Pointed' variety of English Gothic, meant that Norman architecture was widely perceived as too basic or even 'primitive'. Moreover, pointed architecture need not be expensive.[83] Many of the underlying liturgical principles were the same as those found in Norman churches, while the construction of pointed arches was not necessarily more difficult than that of round-headed ones. Indeed, the implementation of simple yet correct Gothic forms would lead to a wholly more refined and 'churchlike' appearance. After all, as crude and ill-conceived as many of the earliest Gothic Revival churches may have been in Britain's colonies, they at least proved that pointed-arch construction was feasible. There were those who would continue to champion the Romanesque cause on grounds of symbolic value, such as E. A. Freeman of the Oxford Architectural Society, but it would never find favour among serious ecclesiologists again. Most were now of the opinion, as Pugin had stated so emphatically in *Contrasts* in 1836, that the only *true* Christian architecture was pointed.

As this idea pervaded the architectural societies in England during the early 1840s, it found its way to the colonies with the new breed of Oxbridge-educated clergymen, who had been taking up positions with increasing frequency since the establishment of the CBF.[84] Apart from Selwyn and his colleagues in New Zealand, the Rev. W. H. Walsh (1812–1882) of Sydney was among the first to translate these ideas into a colonial context. Being a member of the Cambridge Camden Society, Walsh was keenly aware of what constituted proper church architecture. In 1843, in the teeth of considerable indignation from Evangelicals, he successfully transformed the internal arrangement and fittings of Christ Church, St Laurence (1840–5), one of the first Anglican churches built in Sydney after Broughton's elevation as bishop (see pp. 246–7).

But perhaps the two most ardent advocates of this new tradition were to be found over six hundred miles south, in the colony of Tasmania, originally a convict dumping ground off the southern coast of Australia known as Van Diemen's Land. Naturally, one of these proponents was the Rev. Francis Nixon, bishop of Tasmania, the other, an enthusiastic young priest by the name of Frederick Holdship Cox (1821–1906) (see fig. 239). These men would change the face of Anglican church architecture in Tasmania almost overnight. Both were staunch Tractarians, and both members of the Cambridge Camden Society.[85] Nixon, in particular, being a vain and ambitious man, was keen to be seen conducting himself in a proper, High Anglican fashion. 'He was a remarkable man,' observed a diarist in 1847, 'tenacious in his rights, extremely anxious to be correct with regard to costume and all other points of etiquette, devoted to the fine arts and a beautiful draftsman.'[86] It was this aesthetic sensibility, no doubt honed while Nixon was one of the 'Six Preachers' at Canterbury in the early 1840s, that would drive his determination to introduce 'correct' church architecture in Tasmania.

30 Lithograph by an unknown artist, *c.*1850, of the church of St John the Baptist, Prosser Plains (1847–8), showing the original timber porch (private collection). The design was based extensively on R. C. Carpenter's St John the Baptist, Cookham Dean (1844).

Upon reaching Hobart in 1843, Nixon wasted little time in denigrating the ecclesiastical architecture he found there. He described the cathedral, a plain neo-classical edifice after the manner of Gibbs, as 'secundum artem' and 'totally devoid of all architectural character'.[87] St David's, as this building was known, was in many respects typical of late Georgian church architecture, not just in the colonies but in Britain as well (see fig. 111). It represented what *The Ecclesiologist* was wont to describe as 'Government Grecian', and signified everything that was considered wrong in ecclesiastical architecture. 'Pass but a few years,' declared Nixon, 'and I hope we may see our way towards something better.'[88] For him, the state of ecclesiology in Tasmania was somewhat akin to its people: 'unnatural' and 'hideous'.[89] As it turned out, the feeling was mutual (see Chapter 5).

In order to rectify the situation as he saw it, Nixon busied himself traversing his diocese and planning the erection of new churches. By October he had identified, along with the Rev. R. R. Davies, ten locations for churches and laid the foundation stones of several. His motto was dignity through simplicity. Describing this plan, Nixon's wife, Anna Maria, observed: 'I believe they will be very small and very humble, but still they will be set apart for God's service, "tabernacles" where holy worship may be performed.'[90]

One of these was the little church of St John the Baptist, Prosser Plains (now Buckland), about thirty miles north east of Hobart (figs 30 and 31). This is where Cox enters the picture. A former Bell Scholar at Pembroke College, Cambridge, Cox was a relatively spirited High Churchman and keen ecclesiologist. He was appointed curate at Prosser Plains by Nixon almost immediately upon his arrival, where he assumed responsibility for the erection of the church. In a letter to the Ecclesiological Society in 1847, Cox noted how he found himself having to act 'not only [as] secretary and treasurer, and actually *master* of nearly all the men employed, but [also] architect and clerk of the works'. This, he hastened to add, was because 'architects here are anything but ecclesiastical'.[91] The design adopted was that for St John the Baptist, Cookham Dean (1844), by Richard Cromwell Carpenter (1812–1855), one of the

31 St John the Baptist, Prosser Plains (Buckland) (1847–8).

young hopefuls of the Ecclesiological Society. A model and plans of Carpenter's design (along with those of two other churches) had been sent to Nixon by the society a few years earlier.[92] The timber porch, added later (now rebuilt in stone), was adapted from that of St Edburgha's, Yardley (Worcestershire), as illustrated in Plate 49 of *Instrumenta Ecclesiastica* (1847), copies of which had also reached Australia.[93]

The church at Cookham Dean was considered an appropriate model by the Camdenians because it met all the requirements felt necessary for a parish church in the colonies: unpretending, 'decent' and, most importantly of all, in the 'Middle-Pointed' style. Moreover, costing only £900, it proved the point that churches in the Gothic style could be built relatively cheaply. Upon its completion Cox observed that the building was 'by far the most church-like church in the island', while the *Hobart Town Courier* was sure that in its simplicity and beauty it would usher in 'a new era in the ecclesiastical architecture of the colony'.[94] In fact, when opened for service on Trinity Sunday 1848, this small, unassuming edifice was arguably the most substantial, ecclesiologically correct Anglican church in the southern hemisphere.

One of the most telling features of the little church of St John the Baptist, Prosser Plains, was the massiveness and solidity of its appearance. Such characteristics were important to both the idea and practice of colonial ecclesiology. The vast distances and adverse environmental conditions of many of the new colonial dioceses meant that church building in some areas, particularly remote areas, was especially trying. Lack of funds, inadequate building materials, little or no architectural expertise, and extreme weather conditions all militated against the realisation of proper church architecture. In such places it might have seemed easier simply to build quickly, cheaply and temporarily, with a view to erecting something more worthy later when, if ever, adequate funds became available.[95] Indeed, as the Rev. William Tyrrell (1807–1879), bishop of Newcastle (NSW), would later observe, it was often difficult to know where to plant the foundations for permanent churches, given that the population in some areas was at best unstable and oftentimes itinerant.[96] This was especially a problem on the Victorian goldfields, where the mining population was highly mobile. Mission clergymen often followed diggers from place to place, preaching out of tents or in the open air. On a visit to the diggings in 1852, Bishop Perry was forced to use a tree stump for a pulpit.[97]

But the erection of temporary churches was not only bad economy, many believed, but also an unsustainable footing upon which to build the colonial Church both physically and spiritually. Given that resources were particularly scarce in such places (money, materials and manpower), it dawned upon certain clergymen, such as Broughton, that when a church was to be built it should be built carefully and substantially from the first. This led to what might be described as an anxiety regarding solidity and endurance in the Anglican mind. These qualities suddenly rose up as paramount among Anglican clergy as they found themselves battling continuously against circumstance. Added to their woes was competition from Roman Catholics and Nonconformists, and often indifference and resistance from within their own ranks. When they arrived in their new dioceses for the first time, it did not take these clergymen long to realise that they really were in the realm of the Church militant, and their letters and diaries are littered with tales of hardship, frustration and despair.

In many respects, High Church Anglicans were able to turn this predicament to their advantage by making a virtue out of necessity. Having a keen sense for patristics and Church history in general, they saw themselves as not only labouring in the spirit of the early fathers but also, as in the case of Nixon, establishing entirely new branches of the catholic and apostolic Church. By definition, these new branches had to start out as 'primitive'.[98] As the Rev. John Strachan (1778–1867), future bishop of Toronto, observed as early as 1825, 'the churches are indeed thinly scattered over this vast country [Upper Canada], and bear a striking resemblance to the small congregations of primitive Christians in the days of the Apostles'.[99] The heroic virtue implied in re-enacting the stages of the Church in its earliest and purest phase was perceived by many High Church Anglicans as not only a privilege but also a means of participating in the idea of the divine.[100] Allied to this was the increasingly esteemed status accorded practices of asceticism and self-sacrifice among High Church clerics, particularly those in broad sympathy with the Oxford reformers, many of whom were now making their way to the colonies.[101] As the Rev. Richard Chenevix Trench so poignantly observed on the occasion of the first anniversary of the Universities' Mission to Central Africa: 'Africa, rich in martyrs already, shall be richer still.'[102]

But all this came at a price. Isolation, physical and psychological stress, as well as potential death, threatened constantly. A flavour of the exertion to which colonial clergy were exposed can be found in an account by bishop Tyrrell: 'I have visited every part of my extensive diocese, journied [*sic*] and preached where no minister of the Gospel *has ever* been heard or seen before: and my visitation rides on horseback have been very frequently 200, 300, & 500 miles; once 1,000, at another time 1,200; and last year one ride to the extent of 1,500 miles with the same horses.'[103] Likewise, Strachan, having just returned from a visitation of 2,300 miles in 1843, spoke of 'the fatigue of these journeys'. But having to contend with 'the deep mud-holes, the fallen trees to be cut out of the path, the jolting on the log cause ways, exposure for months to a summer Canadian sun, and the autumn rains, &c. &c' was all part of the job, he insisted (fig. 32).[104] For the weak, however, this kind of exertion led to exhaustion and death, as in the case of the Rev. John Armstrong (1813–1856), bishop of Grahamstown, in 1856, or the Rev. Thomas Whytehead, Selwyn's chaplain, in 1843.[105]

The particularly arduous nature of colonial ministration led to a particular type of clergyman being sought – what Selwyn described as 'men of the right stamp'.[106] For too long colonial clergy had been characterised as men of inferior power and attainment, particularly those associated with Low Church organisations such as the CMS.[107] Part

32 Illustration from the *Mission Field* (1867), showing a missionary clergyman dressed and equipped for the harsh conditions of the Canadian winter.

of the problem was money. With low stipends on offer and little prospect of promotion in the colonies, it is a wonder that any but the most devout and dedicated went abroad. Some had no choice but to make for distant lands, such as the numerous Irish-born and -educated clergymen whose opportunities in Ireland had diminished significantly owing to Church reform, poverty and the effects of the 'tithe war' (1830–6). Others were simply not good enough to obtain preferment in England, trying their luck in the colonies instead.[108] At least in part because of these factors, it had become all but unofficial SPG policy by the 1840s to source young men of an especial temperament and character.[109]

Those sought had to be, quite literally, a breed apart – men capable of taking 'a more enlarged view of the question', as Broughton perceived it.[110] Thus, letters started coming in from all corners of the empire stressing the particular qualities needed in a colonial clergyman. Words and phrases such as 'physical power', 'moral courage', 'earnestness', 'simplicity', 'endued with energy', 'sound in body', 'strength of character', 'self-denying' and 'manly' were used to describe the necessary attributes. The bishop of Melbourne summarised this sentiment when, in a letter to Ernest Hawkins, he observed:

> . . . with respect to the men who come out, I must repeat, what I have continually said before, that they must be fitted for their work. . . . They must be devoted to their masters work; not seeking 'their own, but the things which are Jesus Christ's'. They must be naturally energetic, and of cheerful disposition; not easily discouraged. They must be frank and manly, and yet prudent and judicious. They must also be strong in body, and capable of enduring fatigue and hardness.[111]

It was precisely this capacity to endure, Broughton had noted some years earlier, that 'a Clergyman stationed in charge of a parish in England cannot easily conceive'.[112] One wonders what the genteel clerics of Barsetshire would have made of Nathaniel Merriman, future bishop of Grahamstown, preferring to travel on foot rather than by horse, sometimes forty miles a day.[113]

Indeed, it is extraordinary the extent to which the reputations of this new breed of colonial clergy were built on their physical prowess and ability to withstand privation. Piety was one thing, but the aptitude to realise it in a foreign land with discipline, moral courage and fortitude was another. Such men, as the Rev. Samuel Wilberforce observed, had to be ready to give up home 'with its securities and its comforts'.[114] This was sometimes imposed *in situ*, as colonial bishops began establishing local training colleges to meet their needs. At Queen's College, St John's (Newfoundland), for example, Bishop Edward Feild was keen to promote ideals of physical health and plain living, insisting that his students forgo such luxuries as milk for the Spartan joys of hard bread and fish. Through a near monastic regime of constant prayer, study (including architecture) and practical application, Feild made sure that his clergy were 'spiritually fit' to serve in colonial parishes.[115] Although this concern for 'fitness' had a great deal to do with the cult of the clerical hero in mid-Victorian culture and the need to raise funds for the colonial Church, it was based in fact.[116] A remarkable number of such clergy were known to have been athletic and to have excelled at sport, in particular cricket and rowing. Such sports were, of course, encouraged at the time in both the public schools and universities of England for their character-building

33 Portrait by an unknown artist of William Tyrrell (1807–1879), bishop of Newcastle, New South Wales (private collection).

capacities.[117] The ancient Greek ideal of 'healthy body, healthy mind' was experiencing a renaissance, mixed up as it was with the equally pervasive and evolving notion of 'muscular Christianity'.

Bishops Selwyn and Tyrrell are typical in this regard. Both were members of Lady Margaret Boat Club (St John's College, Cambridge), and both rowed in the same headship crews of 1828, 1829 and 1830. Selwyn went on to gain his blue for Cambridge in the first university boat race in 1829. It was said of Tyrrell that he had a 'strong and active frame', which he kept 'well under control' through 'prudent and regular habits' (fig. 33).[118] Selwyn prized Tyrrell for his 'physical strength', wishing that he had made the journey with him to New Zealand. Selwyn was no slouch either. He too had acquired a reputation for his physical and spiritual prowess. On occasions he spent days, weeks, even months at a time rowing, riding and sailing around his extensive diocese.[119] Others of this ilk included Cotton, Short, Bishop Patteson of Melanesia, Bishop Mountain of Quebec, Bishop McDougall of Labuan (Sarawak), and the ill-fated Bishop Mackenzie of Central Africa.[120] It was recorded of Mackenzie, who had rowed in the 1st VIII for Caius Boat Club (Gonville and Caius College, Cambridge), that he was a rare combination of 'manly strength' and simplicity, an 'active missionary, vigorously employed in breaking up virgin soil – coming to his desk with hands blistered and cramped'.[121] Thus, the legend of the tough, selfless and manly missionary hero in the Carlylean mould was born – a notion devised as part psychological crutch and part professional compensation for the sacrifices these men were making in the eyes of their contemporaries back home. This image of the missionary as a 'good soldier of Christ' was further extolled and made popular through the writings of Anglican establishment figures such as Charlotte Yonge (*The Daisy Chain* and *The Trial*), herself an acquaintance of Selwyn and beloved cousin of the Rev. J. C. 'Coley' Patteson, Bishop of Melanesia.[122]

The distribution and promotion of this human resource owed a great deal to specific agencies in Britain. Some of these have been discussed already, such as the CBF, the SPG and the CMS, as well as individuals including Blomfield and Wilberforce (see Introduction). Broughton, for instance, had the Rev. George Gilbert of Grantham assisting him, while Bishop Feild of Newfoundland had the Rev. William Scott of Hoxton.[123]

But perhaps the single most effective, if forgotten, agent for the identification and supply of manpower and money to the colonial episcopate was the Rev. Edward Coleridge (1800–1887) – nephew of the famous poet, housemaster at Eton, personal friend of colonial bishops and clergymen (see fig. 200). It is difficult to say exactly how much Coleridge assisted the SPG and its cause, but his efforts were considerable.[124] After all, he had reason enough to assist the colonial Church. His cousin was the bishop of Barbados, his nephew the bishop of Melanesia (Patteson), and he had counted Selwyn since their time together at Eton as the 'most dear of all dear friends'.[125] In fact, he was the fulcrum around which much of the effort in England on behalf of the colonial Church revolved, acting not only as prime mover in the establishment of the Missionary College of St Augustine, Canterbury (1848), but also securing, among many other benefactions, £35,000 from Angela Burdett-Coutts for the endowment of the bishoprics of Adelaide and Cape Town.[126] His was a name, declared Nixon, 'that all in this hemisphere [that is, southern] must

34 Watercolour by J. A. C. Willis showing the newly completed church of St Mary the Virgin, Allynbrook, New South Wales, designed by Bishop Broughton, 1843 (State Library of New South Wales, Sydney).

love to honour',[127] and it was he to whom many a colonial bishop entrusted the recommendation of new and able-bodied young clergy for colonial service.[128]

This is not to suggest that colonial clergymen were rampant, muscle-bound 'thickheads' who believed the mission field to be an extension of the rugby pitch or cricket oval. On the contrary: as we have seen, all were highly learned and pious men, many of whom would have risen high within the ranks of the English Church had they remained at home. Their response to colonial conditions was in many respects practical: a survival tactic that necessitated a certain degree of strategic thinking, even if cloaked in a little romance. There is no doubt that the conditions experienced by these men, and the mentality that they fostered, affected their attitudes towards architecture. The anxieties concerning permanence and stability they felt were allayed, it may be argued, in the presence and security of built form. After all, as John Ruskin would later recommend in *The Seven Lamps of Architecture* (1849), 'it is always more honourable, and it has a tendency to render the style of architecture both more masculine and more scientific, to employ stone and mortar simply as such, and to do as much as possible with the weight of one and the strength of the other'.[129]

Bishop Broughton was one clergyman who perceived church architecture in precisely these terms. To Broughton, the parish system and its 'manifestation' through architecture was the most important means by which the presence of the English Church in Australia could be extended and fortified. It was essential, he believed, particularly in the outlying pastoral districts of the colony, that 'depositories' of 'visible religion' in the form of church buildings be established – buildings 'set apart for the decent and orderly administration' of the Anglican faith.[130]

In assessing Broughton's efforts, *The Ecclesiologist* noted how a colonial bishop must be a church builder. As a result, a conviction of the 'importance of externals' would necessarily grow upon him, it was claimed. In his capacity as bishop, Broughton did indeed design churches. One can point to numerous examples of this. We find him, for instance, 'maturing plans and calculations' for a timber 'slab church' with a local magistrate at Lake George, or jotting down designs on the back of an envelope for a church in Geelong (near Melbourne), or sending detailed diagrams to his son-in-law at Allynbrook.[131] In fact, St Mary the Virgin, Allynbrook (1843) (fig. 34), was among his earliest efforts in this regard, a building that was, to his great satisfaction,

35 Christ Church, Cooma, New South Wales (1845–50), designed by Bishop Broughton.

both 'strong' and 'secure' in foundation and 'so church-like that it cannot be mistaken for anything else'.[132] Typical of Broughton's approach was Christ Church, Cooma (1845–50) (fig. 35). After having arrived in the area (near Canberra) during his diocesan visitation tour of 1845, he 'drew out a rough sketch of a small church, in the Early English style of architecture, which, although a mere plagiarism and compilation from other examples, would have sufficient character about it to form a striking and respectable object in the wild and little-frequented neighbourhood where its erection was undertaken'.[133]

Plagiarised or not, this little church is indicative of early colonial ecclesiology in three ways. First, it reiterates, as highlighted by *The Ecclesiologist*, the importance of Anglican clergy in church design and construction. Second, as in the case of St John the Baptist, Prosser Plains, it illustrates the desire and expectation that Anglican architecture in the colonies should be a true 'Christian' art in its deployment of the pointed style, while remaining cheap; this included the 'prescribed forms of adoration', as Broughton called them, by means of correct liturgical arrangement. And, third, through its 'goodly', compact form and massive construction (built of local granite), it symbolised the struggle of the English Church in the colonies, standing as a monument to the perseverance of the faith in what was understood as a 'wild' and God-forsaken land.[134] As the Rev. W. H. Walsh would observe some years later, the contrast struck between the strangeness of the uncultivated environs in which such structures stood and the familiarity of their churchlike appearance established a productive tension that both excited and encouraged feelings of reverence among the scattered inhabitants.[135] This is what Broughton referred to as the 'spiritual efficacy and impressiveness' of proper church architecture.[136] In this sense, Christ Church was not only an 'externalisation' of Anglican faith and doctrine, as the ecclesiologists would have it, but an expression also of the psychology of endurance that characterised the mindset of High Church clergy in the colonies.

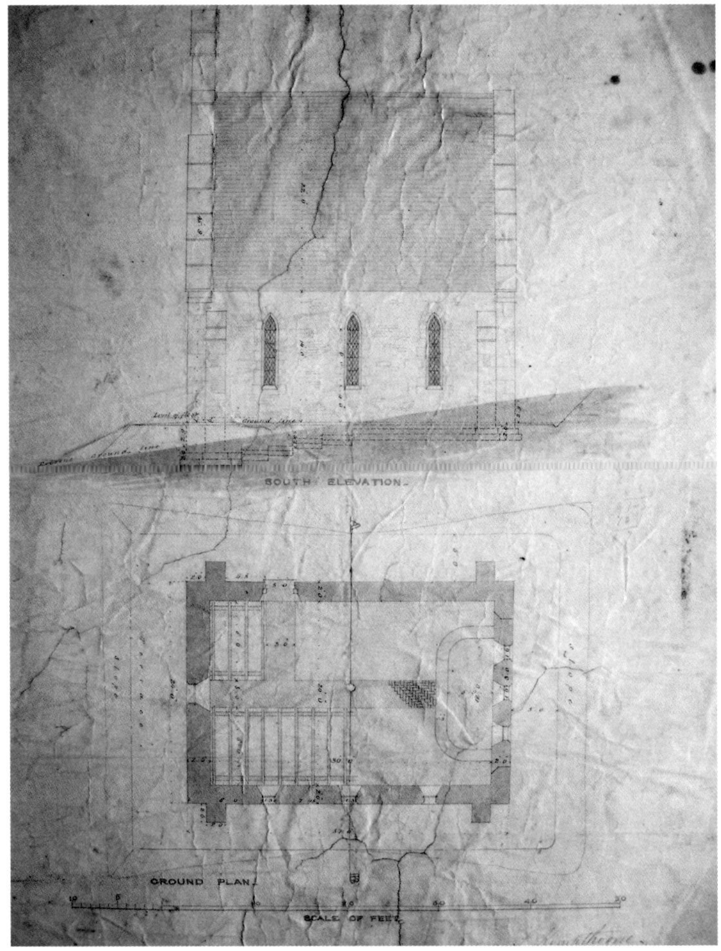

36 Ground plan and elevation drawings for St Stephen's chapel, Judges Bay, New Zealand (1844), by Sampson Kempthorne (John Kinder Theological Library, St John's College, Auckland).

Volcanoes in the Vineyard: Confronting the Challenges of Wilderness

The place where these concerns achieved their most consistent mode of expression was not Australia but New Zealand. The early years of Selwyn's episcopacy were pioneering in every respect, leading to the development of an architecture that was an embodiment of the Church of England's resolve to establish itself in the antipodes and to defy nature's every impediment. As with his colleagues in Australia, Selwyn's vision for architecture necessitated the employment of substantial materials. But where materials such as stone were either too difficult to obtain or unreliable, Selwyn and his colleagues developed a tradition of ecclesiastical architecture in timber. This is important because it demonstrated that ideas associated with solidity, impressiveness and endurance in colonial church architecture need not have been dependent on masonry alone, but that timber buildings were able to embody and communicate these same ideas, only in a different way.

As with Broughton, the concern to establish a permanent form of ecclesiastical architecture weighed heavily on Selwyn's mind. We have already seen how it was his intention to erect stone churches in the Norman style, and that whatever was built would 'be built solidly'.[137] Although his image of grand Norman minsters dotting the New Zealand landscape fell by the wayside, Selwyn never lost sight of the fundamental principle of solid stone construction. He had some success. Early buildings such as St Stephen's chapel, Judges Bay (1844), St Thomas's, Tamaki (1843–7), and St Mary the Virgin, New Plymouth (1844–6) were all built in stone.

This success was limited, however. Both St Thomas's and St Stephen's were condemned and abandoned shortly after completion. They were designed by the English architect Sampson Kempthorne (1809–1873), in consultation with Selwyn. Before immigrating to New Zealand in 1841, Kempthorne had achieved some notoriety as an architect of model workhouses for the Poor Law Commissioners in England.[138] He had also been responsible for a number of small churches and chapels. Thus, knowing that Kempthorne was professionally trained, Selwyn was keen to secure his services. As only minimal funds were available, both St Thomas's and St Stephen's were envisioned in the first instance as the chancels of what would eventually become much larger churches. This piecemeal approach to church construction was not only practised in medieval times but had also been sanctioned by the Cambridge Camden Society.[139] Consequently, both buildings were very small.

St Stephen's was intended as Selwyn's private chapel, and a place where he could preach the gospel to Māori who had resorted to the area around Auckland (fig. 36). Kempthorne's plan shows a single-cell building with seating for around forty people. Although minute, St Stephen's was distinguished by its correct formal and spatial arrangement. It was built in a plain yet identifiable Early English style, using locally sourced stone (scoria), with a raised platform at its east end. It was undoubtedly an extremely modest beginning for the science of ecclesiology in New Zealand, but as a work of architecture it embodied that mantra of 'plain solid work' which Selwyn had insisted on introducing.[140] Most importantly, St Stephen's conjured images of the familiar. On the day of its consecration the wife of Chief Justice William Martin, the chapel's warden, described it as a 'goodly stone building with high gabled roof. . . . We can see it from all our windows, and it has hallowed and made homelike our still sweet Bay.'[141] Selwyn's wife, Sarah, also observed how the rough, grey appearance of its stonework conveyed an air of massiveness and antiquity, qualities that were seen to possess a certain charm in 'this land of newness'.[142] Unfortunately for them, the chapel collapsed in 1847.[143]

St Thomas's fared little better (fig. 37). Although built of solid stone and described as a 'venerable looking building', it too was condemned and later collapsed – this time owing to inadequate foundations.[144] Like St Stephen's, it

37 St Thomas's church, Tamaki, near Auckland (1843–7), by Sampson Kempthorne.

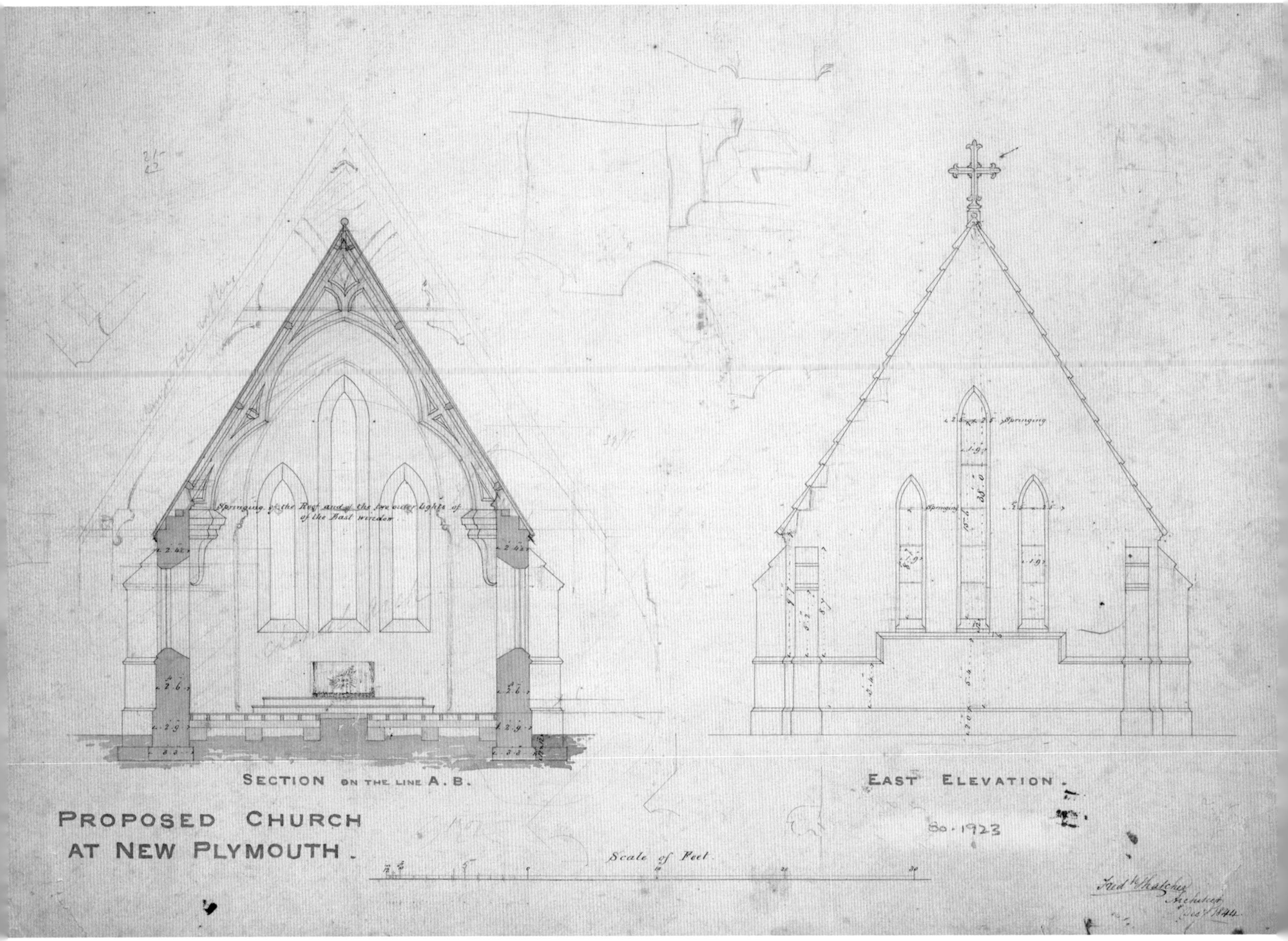

38 Cross-section and elevation drawings for St Mary the Virgin, New Plymouth, New Zealand (1844–6), by Frederick Thatcher, 1844 (Alexander Turnbull Library, Wellington).

was built of the greyish-blue scoria rock quarried at Mt Wellington, rough hewn, with local sandstone dressing for the windows and doors. Evidence that the building was intended as the chancel of a larger church is clear on the west wall where a blind arch was inserted, providing the link to a future nave.[145] In 1849, however, St Thomas's had to be abandoned. Large cracks had appeared in the walls and the soft dressing stone around the windows and doors had eroded.

But not all was lost. Perhaps the most successful early stone building by Selwyn was the church of St Mary the Virgin (1844–6), in the coastal settlement of New Plymouth, a hundred and fifty miles south of Auckland (figs 38 and 39). St Mary's, like St Stephen's and St Thomas's, was a very modest structure in the Early English style. As Margaret Alington has pointed out, although the émigré architect Frederick Thatcher was responsible for preparing the plans, there is strong evidence to suggest that Selwyn played

39 Watercolour sketch of the church of St Mary the Virgin, New Plymouth (1844–6), shortly after completion (Vestry Archive, St Mary's church, New Plymouth).

a leading hand in devising the building's overall form and appearance.[146] In a number of letters to the local vicar, the Rev. William Bolland, Selwyn described in detail how he wanted the church to look. 'I wish the main part of the wall to be uncut rough stone,' he advised, 'and the windows, doorcases, and stringcourses as being hewn thus.'[147] He included a small sketch illustrating the different textures of stonework required for the plinth, the string course, quoinning and openings. Other letters describe how he wished aspects of the church to be modelled on those of St Stephen's.[148] Its walls were built using a form of local granite (Egmont andesite), and its roof was composed of a native timber known as rimu (red pine). When completed in 1846, St Mary's was undoubtedly the most churchlike and 'correct' work of Anglican architecture in the colony, serving as an example of what could be achieved if the right combination of materials and expertise were applied.

To be sure, none of these early attempts at stone construction in New Zealand were impressive by English standards, but this had never been Selwyn's ambition. Owing to the dearth of materials, expertise and manpower in the colony, simplicity and solidity were his initial aims.[149] In the High Anglican mind, plainness was in no measure cognate with meagreness.[150] Like his original vision for Norman architecture, these buildings were seen as representing the very beginnings of a process of architectural development that mirrored the development of the Church itself – the foundations of a tradition that sought primitive beginnings but which would, in time, blossom into a much more elaborate and sophisticated entity. As Russell Walden has correctly observed, these initial attempts at Anglican ecclesiology in New Zealand were about instituting permanency.[151] They were simple, bold statements in stone comprising high-pitched roofs, prominent buttresses and deeply recessed lancet windows – built deliberately, as Selwyn had promised, in the manner of 'our ancestors'.

This concern for boldness and mass in the early Anglican architecture of New Zealand was entwined with the wider environmental context in which Selwyn and his colleagues found themselves. While travelling through New Zealand on visitation, both Selwyn and Cotton commented regularly on the surrounding landscape as it unfolded before their eyes. What impressed them most of all were the spectacular geological formations, features such as soaring mountains, active volcanoes, sheer cliffs and serrated escarpments. The New Zealand landscape, of course, was much younger, geologically speaking, than that of Britain. Neither Selwyn nor Cotton would have experienced anything like the intensity and drama of these South Pacific islands, unless they had visited the Swiss Alps or the Scottish highlands. In his diary of 1843 Selwyn described this dynamic and sublime landscape as 'bristling' with 'bold' and 'beautiful' forms (fig. 40).[152] Cotton, too, was dazzled, evoking notions of primeval energy in his recollections of volcanic eruptions, hot springs and gas vents.[153] This landscape was exciting and revelatory, with its seismic and volcanic activity demonstrating the forces of creation at work. Although this

40 Pencil sketch of mountain ranges on New Zealand's North Island, from Bishop Selwyn's diary, *c.*1843 (Selwyn College Archive, Cambridge).

was clearly God's plan, it was also interpreted – going back to our earlier discussion – as a specific understanding of the unfolding of time. Unlike the 'civilisational' perspective applied to the relative states of human progress, this reading of time necessitated a certain theological exegesis. Here we find Cotton recording his particular interest in exposed geological strata[154] – evidence, perhaps, of his seeking out the 'proofs' of 'an Infinite and Eternal Being', as Lyell had put it, in the awe-inspiring expanse of geophysical time.[155]

The reaction of Selwyn and Cotton to the New Zealand landscape is important because it prefigures the significance that concepts of geology would come to have in British architecture during late 1840s and 1850s (see pp. 112–13). The rising influence of natural theology in the curricula at Oxford and Cambridge would leave its mark on leading theorists such as John Ruskin and James Parker, who, in searching for deeper meaning and relevance in modern architecture, turned to the developmental theses of scientists such as Charles Lyell, William Buckland and Robert Chambers.[156] To Selwyn and Cotton, the rugged environs of New Zealand represented a beginning not just spiritually but geologically too. Both were particularly learned men and would no doubt have appreciated the theological implications of what they saw.[157] Although their ultimate aim was an increasingly sophisticated Middle-Pointed Gothic, a primitive and unrefined form of architecture would have seemed – for the time being at least – especially suited to such a land. After all, they had begun their mission with the most primitive and basic of all forms of ecclesiastical architecture, the tent.

Indeed, one of the problems that Selwyn faced was the landscape itself. It was prone to earthquakes, which could severely damage or even destroy solid stone buildings. The collapse of St Stephen's and St Thomas's was a premonition of what might happen to more substantial stone structures if exposed to considerable seismic activity. There was a solution, however: timber. Timber construction will be discussed at length in Chapter 3. Suffice it to say here that, on the whole, timber was cheaper and faster to erect than stone. It was already in use as a material for church building in Canada (see pp. 144–52), and was thought by both the Oxford Architectural and Cambridge Camden societies to be a worthy material where good stone was unobtainable.[158] In New Zealand CMS missionaries had also developed a hybrid ecclesiastical architecture in timber, incorporating traditional Māori building and craft techniques (see pp. 169–70).[159] But, more importantly, timber construction was better able to withstand earthquakes. Selwyn was aware of this, and realised that if he was to get up his mission headquarters, then the majority of its buildings would have to be erected in timber. This was not a problem, for New Zealand had a plentiful supply of suitable timbers for construction. Woods such as kauri, rimu, puriri (equivalent to English oak) and rata were all abundant and each was known for its particular characteristics.[160] Although it had never been Selwyn's vision to erect timber buildings in his new diocese, he soon got used to the idea. Timber construction was the norm in early colonial New Zealand, especially in rural areas, as Selwyn realised after arriving at his first outpost, the existing CMS station at Te Waimate, near the Bay of Islands (Northland). The buildings there, including the church, were constructed in timber and clad in weatherboards (horizontal planks) (see fig. 235).[161] The church, perhaps the most striking work of architecture on the station, was 'not a very handsome building,' Selwyn recalled, 'but in New Zealand it is a great point to have a church at all'.[162] Although it was clearly not to his liking, Selwyn did manage to fit the church up in a manner that was 'sufficiently Ecclesiastical', including removing the ceiling boards to expose the roof beams.

Selwyn and his mission party's stay at Te Waimate was short-lived, however. It was only ever intended as a temporary abode, but no sooner had they settled than a misunderstanding with the CMS hierarchy in London forced them to vacate in November 1844. They removed themselves some hundred miles south, to Tamaki, on the outskirts of Auckland, near to where St Thomas's would eventually rise (and fall). Here Selwyn began in earnest to establish his 'collegiate institution', St John's College, on a virgin site of 378 acres especially chosen for the purpose. The party initially set up camp at a place called Purewa, on the side of a hill overlooking the site. Here Cotton's 'Church Tent' took pride of place (see fig. 20).

Based on Selwyn's beloved Eton, with aspects of Cambridge thrown in for good measure, St John's College was envisaged as the 'acorn' from which the mighty oak of New Zealand Anglicanism would grow.[163] Selwyn's hope was that substantial buildings in stone might be erected immediately, but, once again, he soon realised that this would not be possible. The outbreak of war between the Māori and British government forces in 1845 (the so-called Northern War) caused the cost of building to escalate,[164] leaving

41 St John's College chapel, Bishop's Auckland (1847), designed by Bishop Selwyn in conjunction with Frederick Thatcher.

Selwyn with no alternative but to resort to timber, save for the kitchen and the bishop's 'palace' which had already been built. Luckily, he was able to secure the services of Frederick Thatcher (1814–1890) (see fig. 329), who had come to Auckland in 1845 to act as superintendent of public works under Governor FitzRoy. As Cotton had noted, Thatcher was 'in every way superior' as an architect to Kempthorne, who had initially been retained by Selwyn to start the college buildings.[165] Thatcher, who would himself train for holy orders at St John's, seemed particularly well suited to the task. He was not only in sympathy with the ideas of the Cambridge Camden Society but also had experience in designing timber buildings. Moreover, Selwyn felt he could trust Thatcher as he had already liaised with him over the successful completion of St Mary's, New Plymouth.

The most important and interesting building that Thatcher was involved with at the college was the chapel (fig. 41). Designed and built in 1847, in a nominal Gothic

42 Sketches by Bishop Selwyn of proposed buildings for St John's College, Bishop's Auckland, *c.*1842–4 (State Library of New South Wales, Sydney, and Selwyn College Archive, Cambridge).

style, it remains an extraordinary work of ecclesiastical architecture. It is a building that exemplified in many ways those anxieties over strength and endurance that preoccupied the minds of leading Anglican clergy. Knowing that he could not build in stone, Selwyn sought a form of timber construction that would at once embody and express solidity. As timber was widely regarded to be a temporary building material, the aim was to make the chapel structurally sturdy, employing 'honest' construction techniques, while giving a distinct impression of stability. This was important to Selwyn because, in striving to establish his collegiate institution, and in his efforts to inculcate the discipline and ordinances of the English Church, he believed that the authority and independence of his episcopal office rested on its perceived strength. Weakness in this regard was fatal, both physically and morally. Seen against this backcloth of ecclesiastical independence and self-determination, the chapel had particular significance. If the Anglican Church was to be taken seriously in New Zealand, then it was crucial that it be *seen* to be strong, useful and real. Thus, although Thatcher was essentially responsible for the chapel's design, the process was collaborative, with Selwyn advising closely on what was required, in much the same way he had at New Plymouth.[166]

Evidence for this can be found in the chapel's unusual massing. The cruciform plan, with its dual apsidal composition, is a radically different concept from that of Thatcher's other known church designs of the period and more sophisticated. In her 'Reminiscences', Selwyn's wife, Sarah, recalled how it was built 'on a peculiar plan, in wood suitable to building, a plan much favoured by the Bishop, partly his own and partly gathered from drawings by Mr Petit of Lichfield'.[167] Sarah was referring to J. L. Petit's *Remarks on Church Architecture*, a copy of which, as mentioned, Selwyn possessed (see p. 25). By the time of his move to Tamaki in 1844, Selwyn had become somewhat obsessed with the idea of St John's College. As Cotton's journals and Mrs Selwyn's diary reveal, he was often found sketching designs for the college, sometimes late into the night.[168] 'For two days after the Gov. had left us,' recorded Cotton in September 1844, 'he worked at the plans as steadily as tho' he had been an architect and nothing else' (fig. 42).[169] This confirms Selwyn's insistence on controlling the architectural character of his diocese, particularly in the early years. Thus, although the chapel as built is not based directly on any of the churches illustrated in Petit's book, one can see how Selwyn might easily have culled and combined various aspects of these illustrations in his design, advising Thatcher accordingly (fig. 43).

The chapel's impression of strength comes from the particular manner in which it was built. The main structure is composed of kauri, a good medium-to-high strength native timber, with some totara. But the distinguishing feature is the way the principal bracing elements are exposed externally. This is something that Thatcher probably brought to the design, having used a similar technique on the CMS chapel he had designed at Maraetai (Port Waikato) two years earlier.[170] This external bracing certainly gave the chapel added strength. But there was an aesthetic purpose, too. Today the whole of the exterior is painted white, but when first completed, the bracing elements were deliberately picked out in a darker colour so as to give a 'substantial look'.[171] This effect would also have given a pleasing 'English' appearance to the building, recalling ancient half-timbered structures from home. The external cladding was composed of vertically orientated tongued-and-grooved kauri planks with 'oxlip' joints, making for a 'much more sightly' building than the church at Te Waimate.[172] The overall effect is one of compactness and vigour.

The interior of the chapel is equally spectacular (fig. 44). Composed entirely of timber, and stained deep auburn, it is an intense yet contemplative space. Contributing to the effect are the small windows which admit only a limited amount of light, evoking feelings of devotion and capturing that sense of 'dim religious light' so prized in the medieval churches of England. Upon his arrival in Auckland in 1855, the future bishop of Melanesia, the Rev. J. C. Patteson, observed with some surprise that the interior was like that of a 'really good ecclesiastical building in England . . . Here my eye and mind rested contentedly and peacefully . . . [it] is already dear to me.'[173] Indeed, it is only when inside the chapel that one can make sense of its dual apsidal composition – one apse at the east end for the chancel, the other at the west for the font.

This mode of construction – referred to as 'Selwyn Gothic' – was rolled out in other parts of Selwyn's diocese during the late 1840s, especially in the vicinity of Auckland.[174] Near replicas of the chapel at St John's College were to be found at Remuera (St Mark's) and Parnell (St Barnabas's), both designed by Thatcher, and both with his trademark external bracing (figs 45 and 46). St Barnabas's was intended initially for Māori converts, replacing St Stephen's after its collapse in 1847. There were a number of other, larger timber churches erected in the area, including St Peter's, Onehunga (1848), and All Saints', Howick (1847), both of which were prefabricated in the carpentry workshop at St John's College (see figs 149 and 150). All Saints',

43 Sketch by J. L. Petit of St Albin's church, near Dijon, from his *Remarks on Church Architecture* (1841). Selwyn took cues as to the formal arrangement of his chapel from the many sketches that appeared in Petit's book.

44 Interior of St John's College chapel, Bishop's Auckland, New Zealand (1847), constructed using local timbers.

45 J. Kinder, watercolour, 1857, of St Mark's church, Remuera, New Zealand (1847), by Frederick Thatcher (Auckland Art Gallery).

46 Sketch by J. Kinder, 1858, of St Barnabas's church, Parnell, near Auckland, (1848), by Frederick Thatcher (Hocken Collections, University of Otago).

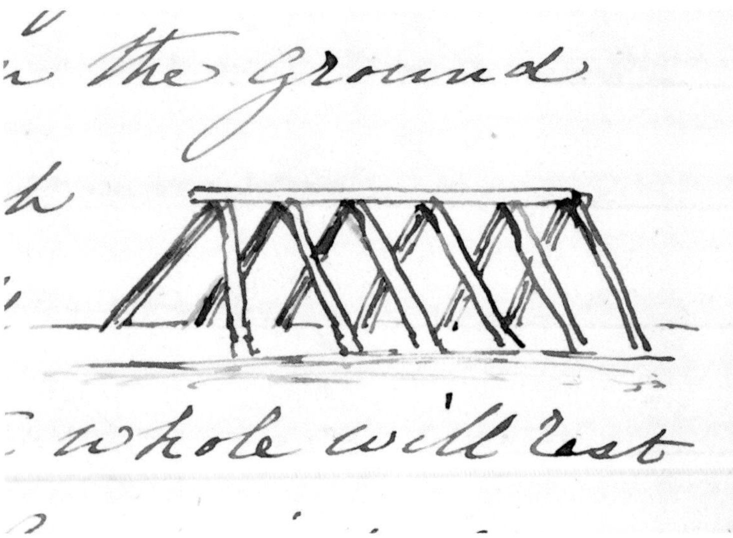

47 Sketch by Bishop Selwyn of a structural 'truss' system for church design in New Zealand, 1845 (Alexander Turnbull Library, Wellington).

like the chapel at St John's, also employed external bracing, although in this case with diagonal timbers.

It was not just the threat of earthquakes that necessitated a 'reinforced' architecture in New Zealand, but also the exceedingly high winds. Selwyn was very much aware of this and began devising a comprehensive structural system that he hoped would solve the problem. In a letter to his brother William, he observed of this system that: 'the main timbers of the roof are to rest on the ground and to be concealed in the walls of the Porch and transepts, so that the side walls will have little or no weight to support; and the whole will rest upon a base nearly twice as wide as the Church itself'.[175] What Selwyn described in his letter was effectively a rigid structure in the form of a triangular truss (fig. 47). Such a structure would not only resist the huge pressure exerted by gale-force winds but also float like a raft across moving ground during earthquakes, all the while remaining intact. This system did, it must be said, have certain affinities with traditional Māori architecture, in particular communal meeting houses (*whare hui*). Although, according to his wife, Selwyn had begun thinking about his new structural system for New Zealand before leaving England, he might well have been confirmed in his suspicions as to its appropriateness once having encountered Māori architecture first hand.[176] Whether this was the case or not, Selwyn's invention was ingenious. It demonstrated both his comprehension of physics and his desire, as a clergyman, to involve himself deeply in matters architectural.

Selwyn's rigid-frame system was eventually incorporated into a number of timber churches, including the CMS chapel at Maraetai and St Stephen's, Judges Bay (rebuilt 1856).[177] But the one that came closest in both form and appearance to his original idea was the small church of St Bartholomew's, Kaiapoi, near Christchurch (fig. 48). Like the chapel at St John's College, this too is an extraordinary piece of colonial ecclesiology. It was designed in 1854 by Benjamin Woolfield Mountfort (1825–1898), an émigré architect trained in the office of R. C. Carpenter. Not surprisingly, Mountfort was both associated with the Ecclesiological Society (although never a member) and a devout Anglo-Catholic. As Ian Lochhead has observed, he also seems to have been aware of Selwyn's concept.[178] One can see clearly how the triangular, A-frame technique devised by Selwyn has been adopted in full at St Bartholomew's, making for an impressively compact and rigid structure.[179] In a land where good building stone was difficult to procure, there was perhaps no better example of a correct, robust and ecclesiologically appealing church than this, embodying everything that early colonial ecclesiology stood for in the High Anglican mind.

Models and Modality: The Transmission of Forms and Ideas Abroad

One of the most important factors in the rise of ecclesiology throughout Britain's colonial empire during the mid-nineteenth century was the idea of the model. In places where very little knowledge of ecclesiastical architecture existed, let alone centuries of historical precedent, the transmission of ideas in the form of working models was crucial.[180] We have heard already about Selwyn's vision for Norman-style churches in New Zealand, a vision that was dependent on access to good, working models (see pp. 23–6). At the time the term 'model' was taken to mean more than just a miniature, three-dimensional representation of a building in wood, plaster or cardboard – what is commonly understood by the term 'architectural model' or 'maquette' today; included within it was the attributive notion of an ideal – that is, a 'model' or exemplar in the Platonic sense. Thus, 'models' could be and were transmitted

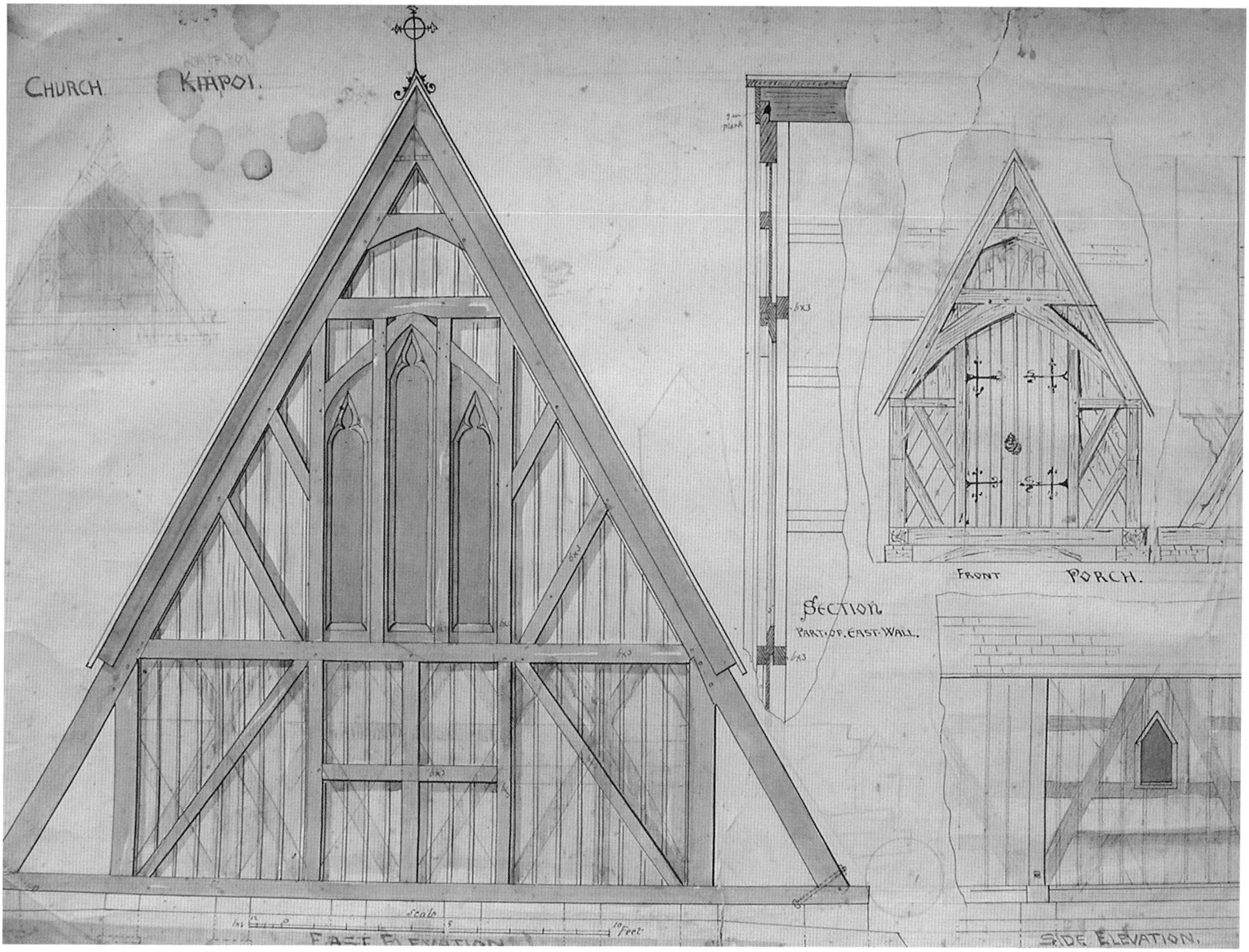

48 Elevation and section drawings for St Bartholomew's church, Kaiapoi, near Christchurch, by B. W. Mountfort, 1854 (Christchurch Anglican Diocesan Archive).

in three-dimensional form, on paper (drawn), or even as a written or verbal description: their mode of transmission was not critical as long as the *idea* was communicated effectively. This wider, slightly more abstract understanding of the term is what Selwyn meant when he noted that 'one model of a parish-church' would be sufficient for his needs (see p. 23). Exactly what *form* this model would take was up to those supplying it, in this case the Cambridge Camden Society.

The Camden Society was keen on models. In this respect it viewed both Britain and its colonies as a single field of operation and influence. It was felt that following 'good' ecclesiastical models was essential to proper and dignified worship in the Anglican faith, wherever the Church might be. This, of course, was an agenda that the Camden Society pursued in conjunction with its sister society in Oxford. Discussions of what constituted good working models for new parish churches littered the pages of *The Ecclesiologist* and the *Rules and Proceedings*. Only when 'real ancient designs' were selected for exact imitation, it was claimed, would a 'new and happy era in the history of modern church-building' commence.[181]

49 Perspective drawing of St Mary's church, Littlemore, near Oxford, by Henry Underwood, published by the Oxford Architectural Society, 1843.

This modality of thought and practice had its roots some years before the advent of the university architectural societies. The general gusto for a revived medieval architecture owes much, of course, to the polemics of A. W. N. Pugin. Despite Pugin's overt Roman Catholicism, his *Contrasts* (1836) and *True Principles* (1841) resonated in High Anglican circles.[182] But it was within the wider context of Anglican renewal, and that of the Oxford Movement in particular, that the most serious and far-reaching transformations in Anglican architecture were enabled to take place.

As early as 1837, the *Christian Remembrancer*, in a review of William Bardwell's *Temples, Ancient and Modern* (1837), noted how the subject of church architecture was 'beginning to excite an interest in some degree proportionate to its real value and importance'. The hope was that a wholly new 'scientific' approach to the design of ecclesiastical buildings would develop, taking as its cue the 'true principles' of Gothic art. Two years later this appeal was echoed by the Rev. Thomas Mozley (1806–1893), who penned a series of articles on architecture for the High Church organ the *British Critic*. Mozley, John Henry Newman's brother-in-law, and one of the *enfants terribles* of the Oxford Movement, observed that in light of the increased amount of church-building activity in England 'we may safely begin to ask that it . . . be well done'. Again, the implication of Mozley's article was that a true Christian architecture had once existed in England and that it ought to be revived. With this in mind, he pointed his readers in the direction of simple but correct parish churches as models for new designs. He singled out publications such as George Hamilton's *Designs for Rural Churches* (1836) as a starting point (although he could not recommend its designs), and called attention to several recently completed buildings, including a Kempthorne chapel at Buckhold, Berkshire, and the newly consecrated church at Littlemore near Oxford.[183]

The latter edifice is of particular significance as it was the initiative of Newman. Designed in 1835 by the Bristolian architect Henry Underwood (1804–1852), Littlemore church was, in many respects, the model small church of its day (fig. 49).[184] Although it had faults, claimed *The Eccle-*

siologist, it was nonetheless 'the first unqualified step to better things that England had long witnessed . . ., not so much a sermon-house, as a temple of the MOST HIGH.'[185] Moreover, it embodied the correct sentiment. For *The Ecclesiologist*, it was clearly the work of 'priestly architects' – those who were not only '"Religious"' but also committed to the principles of the emerging 'science' of ecclesiology. As Peter Howell has since noted, the church was considered exemplary because it combined economy with strength: unpretentious, set upon deep foundations, and built using solid materials.[186] This combination of attributes is precisely what was required in new parish churches. As Littlemore's reputation grew, it naturally acquired imitators.

Although Littlemore was an exemplar sought and used by colonial bishops, by the early 1840s the charge for 'good ancient models' was being led on a wider front by the university architectural societies.[187] The problem with modern church design, as far as the Cambridge Camden Society could see, was unwarranted and ill-conceived invention. The 'mannerisms' associated with modern Gothic were a gross distortion of the true principles of ecclesiology, 'which nothing but a close adherence to ancient models is likely to remedy'.[188] Why opt for 'original conceptions', it was asked, when one could 'be content to copy acknowledged perfection'.[189] Again, as if responding to Bardwell, or even Pugin, these 'models' were doubly worthy because they were English Gothic – a style at once 'truly religious and truly national'.[190] By August 1844 the Camdenians could boast that they had several complete sets of working drawings of ancient parish churches under way, including St Mary's, Arnold; All Saints', Hawton; St Andrew's, Heckington; and All Saints', Teversham (near Cambridge) – all examples in the Decorated or 'Middle-Pointed' style of the early fourteenth century.[191] For their part, the Oxford Architectural Society had produced drawings of St Giles's, Oxford; St Michael's, Stanton Harcourt; the exquisite St John the Baptist, Shottesbrooke; and, of course, Littlemore.[192]

The Camden Society went further in selecting buildings which it felt would be particularly useful in the colonies. These were, for the most part, modest structures. Perhaps the most notable among them was the small village church of St Michael's, Longstanton, about five miles north of Cambridge (see fig. 245).[193] This church – a stone structure dating from the mid-thirteenth century – was valued for its low, broad nave with aisles, high-pitched roof and manifest chancel. It was distinguished not only by its simplicity of detail and massiveness of form, but also by a signature feature of two substantial buttresses running down its west front either side of a small curvilinear window. Although not copied directly, derivatives of this basic format could soon be found throughout the empire, particularly in Canada and Australia.[194] St Anne's chapel, Fredericton (1846–7), for instance, bore more than a passing resemblance to it, as did later churches in the city of Toronto, such as St Stephen-in-the-Fields, College Street (1858) (see fig. 299), and St Peter's, Carleton Street (1865).[195] St John the Baptist, Prosser Plains, was also part of this genre (Carpenter's church at Cookham Dean was itself based on that of Longstanton),[196] as were a number of Blacket's schemes for rural churches in New South Wales, including his unbuilt design for Holy Innocents, Cabramatta (now Rossmore; fig. 50).[197]

But the most concerted and systematic effort to produce working models came in the form of *Instrumenta Ecclesiastica*, the first numbers of which were published by the Cambridge Camden Society in 1844. This publication was the closest the Camden (later Ecclesiological) Society came to producing a pattern book for church design. The first full volume (a consolidation of the individual numbers so far published) appeared in 1847 and, although intended for

50 Perspective sketch for Holy Innocents, Cabramatta, New South Wales (*c.*1847), by Edmund Blacket (State Library of New South Wales, Sydney). Blacket probably adapted an English design supplied to Bishop Broughton.

use wherever professional expertise was found wanting, including England, it was 'chiefly undertaken for the sake of the colonies'.[198] The remarkable thing about *Instrumenta* is its seriousness and attention to detail. These were no desultory sketches run off in an effort to feign concern for the plight of colonial clergymen, but a set of carefully considered, fine-line, working drawings, produced by professional designers such as William Butterfield and R. C. Carpenter. The first volume contained some seventy printed plates of all aspects of ecclesiastical design, from plans for churches and schools, pulpits, stalls, sedilia, litany desks and font covers through to church plate, door handles and hinges. Even headstones and coffin lids were featured. *Instrumenta* was produced primarily in response to the large number of requests that the Camden Society had received from 'our possessions'.[199] The aim, therefore, was to supply in a 'cheap and convenient form' an aid that might work to 'improve' church architecture both in Britain and its colonial empire.

When the seventh part in the series appeared in 1845, it was announced that copies of the whole would be sent to Anglican bishops residing in the colonies. There is evidence that copies of *Instrumenta* were indeed sent, received and utilised abroad. For instance, it was reported in the January 1846 number of *The Ecclesiologist* that the society had received testimonials regarding the 'practical value' of the publication from New South Wales and Canada.[200] In South Africa the Rev. Henry Master White (1820–1892) recorded how he had modelled a lectern for his church at Woodlands, near Cape Town, on Plate 2 (St Andrew's, Norfolk);[201] while the Rev. W. H. Walsh of Sydney had followed Plate 47 (Great St Mary's, Cambridge) for open seating designs at Christ Church, St Laurence.[202] As mentioned, the Rev. Frederick Cox in Tasmania had also made use of *Instrumenta*, adapting Plate 49 of a porch for his rural church of St John the Baptist, Prosser Plains. Later, in the 1850s, there was the example of Benjamin Mountfort, whose church of St John the Evangelist (1857–9), Heathcote, New Zealand, was modelled on Carpenter's design for a 'Chapel-School' which appeared as Plates 43–7 in the second series of *Instrumenta Ecclesiastica* (1856) (see figs 351 and 352).[203] The publication also proved useful in the United States. At New Brighton, Pennsylvania, for example, where the church was designed largely by the incumbent, *Instrumenta* was used extensively as the source for furnishings and other liturgical accoutrements.[204]

Not everyone was satisfied, however. Some did complain about the complex and relatively expensive nature of many of the patterns contained in *Instrumenta*. Among those voicing dissatisfaction was the bishop of Toronto, John Strachan. In a letter to Ernest Hawkins of the SPG he lamented that, although 'very beautiful in themselves, yet they are merely drawings of Church ornaments which are of little or no use to us'. Clearly something more basic was required. What Strachan really wanted were 'plain drawings of Churches from which to take a pattern'.[205]

Many such drawings were sent to clergymen in the colonies, some of which have been discussed already. Both the Oxford Architectural and the Cambridge Camden societies were active in supplying plans.[206] There were other sources as well from which clergymen and their architects could glean information about church architecture. Bishop John Medley of Fredericton, for instance, recommended that his clergy consult M. H. Bloxam's *Principles of Gothic Architecture* (1836) as well as Raphael Brandon's *Parish Churches* (1846–7) and *Open Timber Roofs of the Middle Ages* (1849), and himself used the latter to design the roof at Fredericton cathedral.[207] In New Zealand similar sources existed. Bishop H. J. C. Harper of Christchurch had in his possession several publications by the Camden Society, including *A Few Words to Church Wardens* (1841) and *Church Enlargement and Church Arrangement* (1843). Selwyn's library at St John's College contained Camden Society publications too, notably *A Hand-Book of English Ecclesiology* (1847). It also stocked J. H. Parker's *A Glossary of Terms Used in Grecian, Roman, Italian, and Gothic Architecture* (1840), J. L. Petit's *Remarks on the Principles of Gothic Architecture* (1846) and the Oxford Architectural Society's *A Guide to the Architectural Antiquities in the Neighbourhood of Oxford* (1840).[208] Selwyn did in fact use these books when planning the buildings for St John's College. William Cotton records how Selwyn, when working one night at his designs, declared that he was 'going to send down Pugin's works, and other books of architecture, together with his plans, that the architects may get correct details'.[209]

Blacket had also transported a small library of architectural books to Australia. This collection included, among other publications, well-known architectural pattern books and treatises such as the Pugins' *Examples of Gothic Architecture* (1838–40), Pugin and the Le Keux's *Architectural Antiquities of Normandy* (1841), James Barr's *Anglican Church Architecture* (1841) and, later, Edmund Sharpe's *Treatise on the Rise and*

Progress of Decorated Window Tracery in England (1849).[210] Blacket's first church, Holy Trinity, Berrima (1846–9), for example, was based on a series of illustrations of Biddestone church, Wiltshire, found in *Examples* (vol. 3, Plates 72–6) (figs 51 and 52).

Others, however, found circumstances more trying. Even with such models and patterns to hand, there was no assurance that they could be used. As H. M. White lamented in a letter to his brother William, 'architectural books generally have all the fine things wh. are out of ones power here: nor is it easy to turn a perspective sketch into working drawings'.[211]

Despite White's pessimism, South Africa is one place where model plans were used extensively during the late 1840s and early 1850s. Most of the early church-building activity that took place in that province was orchestrated by the first bishop of Cape Town, the Rev. Robert Gray (1809–1872) (see fig. 202). Gray's most important collaborator in this regard was his wife, Sophia (*née* Wharton Myddleton). Sophy, as she was known, made it her business to sketch designs, produce working drawings and participate in the building of churches and chapels throughout South Africa. Indeed, so prolific was she that Gray described her as 'architect to the diocese'.[212] However, although Sophy was an accomplished amateur architect in her own right, she was no innovator. Many of the church plans she produced for her husband's diocese were adapted directly from designs she had carried with her from England. It is not known exactly how many designs the Grays brought with them, but they did have plans by architects such as G. G. Scott, Henry Woodyer and William Butterfield.[213] They also had in their possession designs by Henry Underwood, in particular his plan for Littlemore, as well as his series of chapel schemes for burial grounds (1849).[214] Significantly, Gray noted how many of the new churches in his diocese would be 'small but . . . built upon correct Ecclesiastical principles, either from designs published by the Architectural Societies in England, or from plans kindly furnished to me by Architects in England'.[215] For instance, St Mark's, George (1849), was essentially a facsimile of Littlemore (see fig. 203).[216] Indeed, this prototype served as the model for a number of Sophy's rural church designs of the 1850s, including St James's, Graff-Reinet (1850) and St Peter's, Pietermaritzburg (1851–7).

Like Selwyn, the Grays were deeply interested in architecture, and it is known that they had read *inter alia* J. H. Parker's *Glossary* (1836), Thomas Rickman's *Essay on Gothic Architecture* (1825), Pugin's *True Principles* (1841) and Bloxam's *Principles* (1836).[217] Such knowledge proved particularly useful in their new environs, where the science of ecclesiology was entirely unknown.

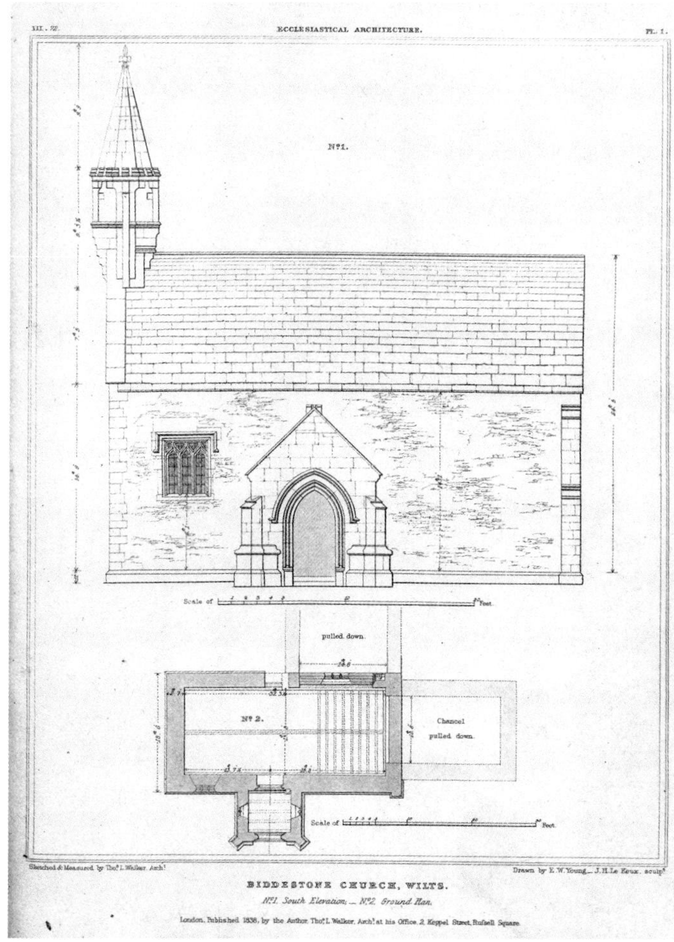

51 Elevation and ground plan drawings for Biddestone church, Wiltshire, from A. C. Pugin and A. W. N. Pugin's *Examples of Gothic Architecture* (1838–40), used by Blacket as the basis for his design for Holy Trinity, Berrima, New South Wales (1846–9).

Sketchbooks were also a useful aid in places where professional expertise or printed sources on architecture were lacking. Such books often came in the form of compendia of select architectural details. For example, Edmund Blacket took a number of pre-prepared sketchbooks with him to Australia. These contained dozens of drawings of medieval church details (and some plans) taken *in situ* and from printed sources such as the *Gentleman's Magazine* and *The Builder*,[218] including windows, doors, arcade capitals, mould-

52 Holy Trinity church, Berrima, New South Wales (1846–9), by Edmund Blacket.

ings, gargoyles and fonts in styles ranging from Anglo-Norman through to Perpendicular (fig. 53).[219] A number of these details appear in Blacket's church designs for Sydney and elsewhere. Sophy Gray also took a sketchbook with her to South Africa. Hers was an extraordinary creation, containing hundreds of carefully ordered, fine-line drawings of architectural details from medieval churches and castles, which she had made while on tour around Yorkshire and her home county of Durham (fig. 54).[220] Although she did not rely on this book to any great extent in her design work, it comprised exemplar specimens of medieval church architecture and would have provided all the models necessary had she required them.

Selwyn pleaded regularly for good working models, even though the Cambridge Camden Society had already gone out of its way to assist him. In a letter to Edward Coleridge, who had become a member of the Oxford Architectural Society in 1842, he implored: 'I greatly want some working drawings of existing Parish Churches, merely representing the Church as it was intended to be; the plainer and simpler the better, provided the outline be good. Small sizes, or if large, with good chancels, such as could be built first in the form of chapels.'[221] If such plans were forthcoming, he had earlier observed, 'I will use no other, propitiating the Colonial Architects by the usual per centage [*sic*] for the superintendence alone'.[222] His prayers were answered, it seems,

when a box containing 'Plans of Wooden Churches, Books, & c.' arrived at Auckland in 1845.[223] Exactly what plans this box contained, and by whom, is not known, but as they were plans for timber churches, they may well have been influential in changing Selwyn's attitude towards church architecture in New Zealand.

It is likely that Selwyn had Kempthorne base his designs for St Stephen's and St Thomas's on model plans. In many respects, Kempthorne's New Zealand churches resemble his designs for small churches in England, in particular his chapel at Buckhold, which itself was modelled on that of Littlemore. Indeed, St Stephen's does appear much like a compressed version of the Buckhold design (see fig. 36).

Top 53 Drawings of Gothic architectural details from Edmund Blacket's sketchbook, *c.*1842 (Rare Books and Special Collections, University of Sydney).

Bottom 54 Drawings of English medieval church fonts from Sophy Gray's sketchbook, 1836–1847 (William Cullen Library, University of the Witwatersrand, Johannesburg).

55 Wooden model of a prototype church, *c.*1850, produced on the recommendation of Bishop John Medley of Fredericton, New Brunswick, now in Christ Church, Maugerville, New Brunswick.

It might also have been based on a measured drawing that Selwyn received from the Camden Society prior to his departure. This was probably a plan of the chancel of St Mary the Virgin, Cobham, Kent, a drawing of which later appeared in the first series of *Instrumenta Ecclesiastica* (Plate 6), where it was noted in the accompanying text that: 'The want of such a Plan of a Church, with Ecclesiastical Buildings attached, has been felt in the Colonies.'[224]

Physical models, or maquettes, were also carried and utilised by colonial clergy. Medley, for one, advised his clergy that when planning to erect a new church, 'let a wooden model be always made'.[225] We see this in the wooden model kept at Christ Church, Maugerville (New Brunswick; 1857), which appears to have been used as a generic prototype by Medley (fig. 55). There are many examples of this phenomenon that one could point to, including the large alabaster model of Calcutta cathedral produced in the early 1840s.[226] But perhaps the most striking instance is that of Bishop Nixon of Tasmania. An extraordinary photograph of Nixon survives in the Tasmanian State Archives showing him seated, in full clerical attire appropriate to his rank (cut-away coat and episcopal apron), before a large church model (fig. 56). The model, intended as the design for a cathedral, is most likely one of the 'three models' produced by R. C. Carpenter and sent to Tasmania by the Cambridge Camden Society in 1844 (see p. 314).

The photograph is revealing in the sense that it is a formal portrait. It suggests that Nixon saw himself as a church builder in more ways than one. Here was a colonial bishop, who imagined himself as an early Church father, presented in a way that was reminiscent of medieval representations of clergymen holding votive models. Nixon's image of himself as a cleric, confident in his ability to transform his diocese both spiritually and architecturally, could not have been less ambiguous. Although no church matching the model's description was ever erected in Tasmania – the cost would have been prohibitive – St Mary's church, Hagley (1861–2), fifteen miles west of Launceston, comes closest (see Chapter 6).

Models were useful in other ways. As Medley had complained, 'it is always difficult to make people understand mere plans on paper; but, if they had a model, they could walk around it, and examine it, and see what it was made of and how it was made.'[227] He found models particularly useful in persuading the Anglican community in New Brunswick to adopt change. The lip surrounding the wooden plinth upon which Nixon's model sat hints at another purpose to which architectural models were put: fundraising.[228] It is likely that the model had a lid of some kind that would have joined to the plinth forming a container. The model could then be transported without being damaged, and revealed for display when required at church fetes, village gatherings or inside the entrance to public buildings. A similar model box survives for a church designed by G. F. Bodley at St Peter Port, Guernsey.[229]

Larger detail models were also used regularly during the mid-nineteenth century in both architectural education and as the basis for new designs. This type of model was

56 Bishop Francis Nixon of Tasmania, with a church model produced by R. C. Carpenter, *c.*1844, and presented by the Cambridge Camden Society.

57 Cardboard model of St Mary's church, Iffley, produced in 1840, probably for the Oxford Architectural Society.

life-size and often came in the form of a plaster cast – what the ancient Greeks referred to as a *paradeigma*.[230] As mentioned, there had been a proposal to send casts of various details of St Mary's church, Iffley, to Selwyn in New Zealand, but, again, it is not known whether these were ever sent (see p. 26). There was, however, a small scale model of Iffley church produced in 1840 which may have been intended for Selwyn at one point (fig. 57).[231] It is likely that this model was originally commissioned by the Oxford Architectural Society for its own use, but when it became known that Selwyn was looking for a good working model of a Norman church the idea may have occurred to send it, especially as Iffley had already been identified as the appropriate exemplar. Evidently the model was never sent, but its connection with the Oxford Architectural Society at the time of Selwyn's request is both intriguing and suggestive.

One of the largest and most detailed models associated with colonial ecclesiology is that of St Andrew's cathedral, Sydney (fig. 58). This model, produced in cardboard by J. C. White, and presented to Bishop Broughton in 1849, was a precise scale maquette of Blacket's final design.[232] At its most basic, this model was intended to indicate the composition and appearance of the building as it would be.[233] However, it was clearly more than this. Given that St Andrew's took nearly forty years to build, going through several design and redesign stages, the model came to stand in for the building itself. It was the only complete representation of the cathedral that Broughton had – indeed, would ever have, as he did not live to see the building's

58 Cardboard model (to scale) of St Andrew's cathedral, Sydney, produced by J. C. White and presented to Bishop Broughton, 1849 (St Andrew's Cathedral, Sydney).

completion. In this sense, White's model played an important role as a conduit through which Broughton could imagine and communicate ideas not only about architecture but also about the divine and transcendent power of the Almighty and his Church militant on earth.

This wider, figural dimension of the maquette is central to a nuanced understanding of the nature and uses of architectural models in colonial contexts. It must be remembered that Broughton struggled tirelessly, for years, to raise the necessary funds to realise his vision of a cathedral and 'Mother Church' for the Anglican faith in Australia. As someone who put great stock in the 'edifying' capacities of architecture, he saw the model as signifying the coming of a New Jerusalem in the southern hemisphere,[234] a 'landmark of holiness', it was said, that, in its magnitude, would stand as a 'symbol of "the breadth, and length, and depth, and height" of that "love of Christ which passeth knowledge"'. Equally important for Broughton, the model represented a fabric that would rise as a monument to the vigour and determination of the Church of England in Australia, a 'fortress', to use his terminology, against those evils of secularism, infidelity, parsimony, Nonconformism and Roman Catholicism that were perceived to characterise the Australian colonial scene.[235] In this sense, the model may be understood to have played the role of a *multum in parvo*-type object, one that was heavily invested not just with promise but also with mission – a microcosm, one might say (a 'model' in the widest sense of the term), of the Anglican world view and its global ambition. It was this expression of magnitude (material, moral, missionary) through miniaturisation that gave the model of St Andrew's cathedral its relic-like power, a power that it retains, as an historical artefact, to this very day.

Far from being an insignificant or incidental concern of Anglican clergy in the colonies, architecture was, from the beginning, central to their spiritual and material vision of extending the English Church abroad. They may not have had the same access to resources as clergymen in Britain, but they were careful to utilise what they did have effectively. Where professional expertise was lacking, they designed and built churches themselves. This is significant for, without the enthusiasm and involvement of Anglican clergy in church building, the architectural legacy in Britain's former colonies would be very different. Given their educational background and theological sympathies, this was a task that came naturally to these men.

It is clear that in such environs alternative principles were adopted in justifying and expressing the 'externals' of Anglican worship. Values associated with chasteness, simplicity, solidity, mass and permanence were given precedence, reflecting those qualities of modesty, discipline, self-sacrifice and strength sought in the recruitment of colonial clergy. The meshing of these values and qualities through architecture highlights a synergy between the material and spiritual dimensions of the Church in early colonial Anglicanism – a synergy that was celebrated through the activities of the key protagonists discussed here. To be sure, colonial clergy did rely on assistance from home, but they also drew upon and adapted to their own surroundings. This led to an architecture that was deliberate in representing the condition of the Church itself: the landscape, the architecture and the clergy in each place co-evolved to form unique variations or 'species' of English ecclesiology. In this respect it is misleading to view the ecclesiological creations of these clerics and their architects as unsophisticated or bastardised versions of what could be found in England. It is important to remember that given the circumstances under which these men laboured – lack of resources and antipathy to their initiatives – it is remarkable that they were able to achieve anything. Naturally they drew confidence from their cause, but help from home agencies such as the university architectural societies was crucial. By this means they were connected to a dynamic and ever-growing network that saw its remit and influence as extending well beyond the British Isles, bestriding 'the narrow world like a Colossus', as Benjamin Webb had said.[236] Architects and clergymen, wherever they might be, therefore adhered to the same basic principles of church design and arrangement, forming what was, in effect, a continuous field of Anglican agency and activity that stretched around the globe.

In the final analysis, Anglican clergymen were all attempting to follow the one 'great model' set down by kings Solomon and David at the Temple in Jerusalem. This was a well-worn trope with respect to church building in Anglican circles.[237] Colonial bishops, too, realised that, as the Lord became flesh, he did not suppress those emotions that the grandeur and sublimity of outward symbols worked to arouse. For, as Broughton was keenly aware, architecture functioned not only to accommodate 'the assemblage of the greatest numbers to hear His word', but also 'to awaken in them, by the help of outward impressions, a readier disposition to receive with seriousness the tidings of great joy which He came to preach'.[238] What were the ultimate effects and purpose of this realisation in the colonies? Here the Rev. W. H. Walsh shall have the final say:

> None but those who have been in new colonies can tell of what vast importance Her aesthetical work is to the due Christianization of the people of what infinite power over the heart the externals of religion, care in the form, and structure, and arrangement of the church, and decency, and order, and solemnity of ritual, have with those who have cast themselves into the wilderness in a strange land, where their occupations, and habits, and associations all tend to produce forgetfulness of God.[239]

2

The Colonial Cathedral

MONUMENTALISING THE APOSTOLIC TRADITION

Let all things be done decently and in order.

1 Corinthians, xiv. 40

[W]hen some future historian is recapitulating the material triumphs of English enterprise between 1800 and 1900, when he has told of the railroads and the docks, the Menai Bridge and the Britannia Bridge, the Palace of Westminster, the Exhibition Building, the stalks of gigantic mills, and those huge town-halls which our growing manufacturing towns are rearing, he may be able to add, this century likewise witnessed the foundation of the new cathedrals in this place and that.

A. J. B. Beresford Hope, *The English Cathedral of the Nineteenth Century* (1861)

The early years of Church extension abroad witnessed a modest but concerted effort to realise an ecclesiastical architecture worthy of the name. As small and as basic as some of these churches may have been, they were nonetheless manifestations of a common and influential set of principles that were transmitted around the globe. These modest beginnings, however, did not preclude thinking on a grander scale. Architectural ambition was not in short supply where ecclesiology was concerned, either among the new cohort of 'university-bred' colonial bishops, or the architectural societies at home. This much we have seen in Selwyn's initial aim of establishing a reconstituted Norman-style architecture for New Zealand, and in Broughton's efforts to raise a 'mother church' in Sydney. This ambition was partly fuelled by recognition that the colonial Church represented an opportunity not seen since antiquity to build the institutions of the Church from scratch, realising many of the reforms that had proved difficult or impossible in Britain. Again, this is what Selwyn meant when he observed that he had been granted more power in New Zealand to mould the institutions of the Church from the beginning than any English bishop in history (see p. 29).

Among the key institutions of the ancient Church was of course the *ecclesia cathedralis*, or cathedral church. Despite the abuses to which this institution had been subjected in England since the Reformation, the idea of the cathedral still held great importance in the minds of High Church Anglicans. It was, they were wont to claim, the basic institutional unit from which the discipline and ordinance of the Church issued forth. More than this, it was, in most cases, an architectural ornament the symbolic function of which was the glory of the English Church and the maintenance of its apostolic tradition.[1]

Colonial bishops, too, were keenly aware of this idea, and understood fully the cathedral's institutional and architectural significance. To be sure, recognition of this duality was in part a chasing after romantic ideals, especially those surrounding the early Church, but it was also rooted in practical politics and the logistics of reality. It was the pressures of reality that enabled romance to grow up and flourish with renewed relevance and meaning in the minds of colonial clergy. This is why we see, even from earliest days, colonial bishops concerning themselves intently with issues of Church independence, ecclesiastical governance, apostolic succession, and the role of cathedrals. Thus, as colonial bishops and their attendant clergy the world over struggled to build the Church both physically and spiritually, they never lost sight of the importance of the cathedral institution. As Broughton's unerring endeavour in this regard demonstrated, many were adamant that cathedral institutions were not only desirable but necessary. Indeed, as A. J. B. Beresford Hope later observed, it was the English Church in the colonies that was in the vanguard in this respect. What had been achieved overseas, particularly in the so-called 'white settler dominions', represented a working model of what might be accomplished at home, where the parochial system tottered under the immense strain of population growth and the expansion of the nation's chief industrial cities.[2]

In this chapter we shall trace the significance of the cathedral idea. We shall consider its importance to the High Anglican frame of mind, its application in the colonies, and how a number of Britain's foremost architects of the mid-Victorian period were responsible for realising this idea in its full architectural glory. The tensions between principle, propriety and pecuniary resources led to some novel if irregular results.

The Cathedral Idea in the Colonies

Whether at home or abroad, the notion that episcopacy required cathedrals was understood by most Anglicans. It had been thus in ages past, and so it would be in the new era of the colonial Church – or so the argument went. Again, this was no banal appeal to convention for convention's sake, but, rather, an idea that was deeply ingrained in Tractarian ideology and the emphasis it placed on apostolic succession. This idea may be summed up in the words of the High Church grandee and sometime chairman of the Ecclesiological Society, A. J. B. Beresford Hope. Writing for *The Times* in 1857, Beresford Hope noted simply that:

> The Church of England is episcopal, and it is established. The former attribute concentrates the staff who regulate, and that main body for whose welfare the staff itself exists, into certain groups called dioceses, under a head called bishop . . . . Thus the episcopal aspect of the church is that of aggregation. In the early days of Christianity, . . . each town had its bishop or overseer, with his staff of presbyters under him. Each bishop had at least one place of worship in that town, containing his chair or 'cathedra', and therefore called his cathedral church.[3]

Four years later, in his plea for cathedral extension in England, *The English Cathedral of the Nineteenth Century* (1861), he added: 'A Cathedral is, as every one knows who has thought ever so little upon the matter, both a building and an institution. As a building it is supposed to fulfil certain architectural and artistic conditions, and as an institution to carry out certain religious and charitable objects.'[4] Thus, the cathedral was, as it always had been, a 'mother church' that was the administrative and spiritual centre of the diocesan system. More often than not it was also a work of art befitting its status as such.

But this rather innocuous view of cathedrals was by no means universally accepted, even within the Church of England. Thirty years earlier, at the height of the Church reform movement, many took a dim view of cathedrals and their supposed function. Leading statesmen and clerics of the day, such as Lord Henley and Thomas Arnold, had come out against cathedral institutions.[5] Like much to do with the Hanoverian Church, cathedrals were considered to have lapsed into a moribund, ineffectual and thereby superfluous state. They were criticised as places where corrupt and indifferent clergymen holed up with sinecures, pluralities and other non-resident privileges, while poverty-stricken priests and deacons did all the work in the parishes. This, of course, was a caricature, but many had reason to believe it. Thus, moves were made under the Ecclesiastical Commission (established in 1835) to reduce cathedral institutions and redistribute their wealth. Progress was slow, but change did occur, even if not on the scale or at the speed that the reformers had originally intended.[6]

To be sure, cathedral reforms in England were, as Owen Chadwick put it, a 'half-turn' towards the place reached by the Swiss, Dutch and Scots two and a half centuries earlier. But the debate is important to the translation and implementation of the cathedral idea overseas, where such institutions had to be built, quite literally, from the ground up. To what extent would government interference be tolerated? Critics of the English reforms saw a clear danger in the Church and its institutions being run by government commission – nothing appeared more Erastian.[7] One of the most articulate critics of cathedral reform was the Rev. E. B. Pusey, who, in his *Remarks on the Prospective and Past Benefits of Cathedral Institutions* (1833), argued that the cathedral system ought to remain largely intact for the key role it played in the education and training of English clergy.[8] Pusey's trenchant defence of cathedrals was augmented by others, including one G. A. Selwyn, future bishop of New Zealand. In a pamphlet titled *Are Cathedral Institutions Useless? A Practical Answer to the Question* (1838), Selwyn argued that the problem with cathedrals in the modern age was not that their role as institutions was redundant, but that they were simply not being put to the uses for which they were intended. Citing the charter and statutes of Ely, Selwyn observed how, if administered properly, cathedral institutions were in fact central to the efficient and orderly operation of the parochial system – the diocese was seen as the fundamental unit of Church governance, not the parish. The dean and canons, their school and its scholars, the duties with regard to public preaching, hospitality, daily service and the exercise of patronage through the chapter and its resources were all presented as not only beneficial but also a bulwark against tyranny and corruption.

Selwyn's defence would have been no more than special pleading had it not been for his underlying point that the cathedrals of England were originally instituted to function in such a way; that one need not go so far as to abolish them but merely needed to empower the Church to reinstate what was already instituted by definition. Importantly, this idea followed Selwyn to New Zealand, where he envisioned from the outset a grand cathedral overlooking the Thames firth in Auckland – in the manner of Durham, Christchurch (Oxford) or even Romsey – acting as a beacon of diocesan organisation.[9] Indeed, it was to such efforts, Beresford Hope insisted, that England ought to look in contemplating cathedral extension in its own rapidly expanding industrial cities. He challenged his detractors to look for proof of the feasibility of his proposal not at home but to 'that great England beyond the seas, the British Colonies, where the Church has had to constitute itself in every particular, without the material advantage of being "established"'. It was in these places, he added, that 'the cathedral system has been, within the last quarter of a century, evolved out of nothing as the foundation of a great creative work'.[10]

Like Selwyn, Broughton too had considered the merits of cathedral institutions. However, despite Beresford Hope's optimism, the situation was not so easy for Broughton. As we have seen, he had toiled for many years in Sydney against indifference, Low Church sentiment, and disestablishmentarianism. In a place where profanity and 'mammonism' reigned supreme, gaining the support necessary to build a cathedral church was a considerable challenge.[11] The common retort to Broughton's ambition was lack of funding. Why should such a large portion of the community's hard-won resources be wasted on a single building, it was asked, when they might be distributed more evenly on a number of smaller, more humble edifices? In a sermon titled *Cathedral Churches, Useful and Necessary* (1849), Broughton reassured his congregation that the allocation of scarce resources was not a question of economic rationality or expediency, but one of religious principle. A cathedral church was both a visible sign and an institutional manifestation of Christian ordinance and discipline. 'Therein the bishop sat in his *cathedra*, or episcopal chair, surrounded by the presbyters . . . , his advisors and counsellors in the superintendence of the faithful', Broughton observed. This was entirely right and proper, he suggested, for it was 'an arrangement obviously borrowed from that institution or ordinance of Christ, – "Ye shall sit upon twelve thrones, judging the twelve tribes of Israel."'[12]

This was in part an attempt to dissuade the Anglican community in Sydney from their suspicions concerning episcopal tyranny and corruption. It was also a plea that they should consider what was fundamental to the organisational structure of Christianity and to the long-term interests of the English Church in Australia. Much like Selwyn ten years earlier, Broughton was keen to emphasise that 'it is with a view to promote the growth of piety and holiness, order and devotion, and faith and truth, and hope and charity, among ourselves, that we are building; and all these ought to find – and may find – encouragement in Cathedral institutions, if they be founded in the proper spirit, and carried out in the spirit in which they were founded'. Indeed, far from bad economy, the erection of a cathedral church would bring in its wake innumerable benefits and efficiencies. 'I must say', he boomed, in a partially veiled rebuke to his critics:

> the Cathedral is appropriately termed the Mother Church, inasmuch as wherever it lifts its majestic form, there it is invariably found surrounded by a numerous progeny of the ordinary class of churches. . . . where do we find the parish-churches numerous beyond the general proportion, and supplying ample room for the rich and poor to meet together, inclusive even of the vast augmentation of numbers that have risen up in the advance of society? It is in the Cathedral city.[13]

It was from such institutions, he would later claim, that, 'as if from a common centre, the stream of pure doctrine should proceed to fertilize all the land'.[14]

Selwyn had outlined a similar mandate for cathedral churches in the colonies only days before his departure for New Zealand. In a sermon titled *'How shall we sing the Lord's song in a strange land?'*, delivered in the appropriately episcopal surrounds of Exeter cathedral, Selwyn pointed to the actions of the early Church fathers, and to those of St Augustine of Canterbury in particular. Drawing an analogy between pagan Britain and New Zealand, he asked the Psalmist's question: "How shall we sing the Lord's song in a strange land?"

> The question leads us to think of the past as well as of the present. For, there was a time when they who planted the Church of Christ in this country, then a wilderness and a strange land, coming from countries where God was worshipped with customary reverence and stated service. . . . looked upon the wide forests, and the rude inhabitants of Britain, as we now look upon the woods and the people of New Zealand, as a noble field of Christian enterprise. . . . They who first planted in England a new branch of the vine of Christ, took care to fence it round, that the wild boar of the forest might not trample it down. Our cathedral precincts were the fenced and guarded vineyards of the Lord, the stationary camp of the soldiers of the Cross . . . . Within the cathedral precincts the bishop held council of his presbyters, as a central organ, to act as the moral heart of man, . . . in circulating the life's blood throughout the extremities. This was the system upon which the whole system hung . . . . May we have both the spirit to preach the Gospel, and the strength to arise and build the temple of the Lord! May we also have our cathedral church, in which we may sing the Lord's song with a voice of melody![15]

Although Selwyn would not realise this vision initially, he never lost sight of its value and importance.

Most significant of all, however, whether in Australasia or elsewhere, was the way in which cathedral churches – both as buildings and as institutions – symbolised the idea of apostolic succession. This was not just a matter of scriptural authority but also an acknowledged aspect of the post-Reformation English Church. As Peter Nockles has shown, High Churchmen, both before and after the Oxford Movement, believed in and adhered to the doctrine of apostolicity.[16] To such men, the episcopal system of Church government and the lineal succession of the episcopate were the veritable *esse* of the Church. All of the colonial bishops, especially those appointed under the Colonial Bishoprics' Fund, were of this ilk and thus firm believers in apostolicity. This not only included well-known Tractarians such as John Medley (Fredericton), but also those of a more traditional evangelical stamp, such as Daniel Wilson (Calcutta) and Charles Perry (Melbourne).[17]

This unwavering devotion to apostolic succession and all that it signified had been forged in the cauldron of Church reform and Anglican renewal during the 1830s. One of the principal aims of the *Tracts for the Times* had been to reiterate the centrality of episcopacy. The fundamental view of Tractarians regarding the Reformation was that no 'new Church' had been founded in England, but that the 'rights and the true doctrines of the Ancient existing Church' were simply reasserted and established against the error of Rome.[18] Thus, from the outset, in Tract 1 ('Thoughts on the Ministerial Commission'), we find Newman declaring: 'I fear we have neglected the real ground on which our authority is built, – OUR APOSTOLICAL DESCENT. . . . It is plain then that he [a bishop] but *transmits*; and that the Christian Ministry is a *succession*. And if we trace back the power of ordination from hand to hand, of course we shall come to the Apostles at last'.[19] After all, this was one of the 'four marks' of the Christian Church contained within the

Nicene Creed: belief in 'the one holy catholic and apostolic church'. The titles of many of the *Tracts* capture the centrality and importance of this doctrine.[20] To be sure, as Nockles points out, the Tractarians somewhat overstated the level to which ideas on apostolicity had sunk during the eighteenth and early nineteenth centuries. But in the context of the Church Temporalities (Ireland) Act (1833) and, later, the Dean and Chapter Act (1840), one can see why many were alarmed and therefore felt the need to defend vigorously the *sine qua non* of episcopacy, even if their claims of recovery were exaggerated.

In the religious context of the colonies, it is clear how such ideas gained in power and relevance. Given the effective separation of Church and State in much of the British empire, the notion of episcopacy and its ancient associations of deliberative cooperation had a rawness and immediacy that the Church at home could only wonder at. As we have seen with clerics like Francis Nixon, the idea of apostolicity was no hollow custom, to be transported wherever the Church went for its own sake, but a vital instrument of Church extension, alive with renewed purpose (see p. 41). It was in such places, and at such times of pending separation, Selwyn observed, that 'the privileges of our apostolic Church seem to grow upon our hearts, and to increase in value as the time of losing them draws nigh'.[21] For Bishop Strachan of Toronto, apostolicity thus became the fountainhead of truth and unity in the English Church as it faced division, dissent and disestablishment in the new world.[22] This thinking naturally informed the attitude of colonial bishops to the purpose and meaning of cathedral churches.

The question of size was also a factor. Many critics viewed cathedrals as symbolising excess and luxury; an unnecessary 'ornament', as it were, of Church organisation and governance. But, again, for advocates of the system, scale and magnificence were not fundamental: it was the *idea* that was important. Beresford Hope had made this point in *The English Cathedral*, observing that 'a cathedral is simply and merely a church, however small, in which the bishop's "cathedra" or throne is fixed'.[23] Despite the efforts of some colonial bishops to make their cathedrals as large and as architecturally impressive as possible, this was not essential. Indeed, as we shall see, nearly all Anglican cathedrals built in Britain's colonies during the mid- to late nineteenth century were rather modest in scale compared to their ancient European counterparts, in some cases no larger that parish churches. St John's, Winnipeg (Manitoba), and St Peter's, Pietermaritzburg (KwaZulu-Natal), for instance, were when they were first erected no bigger than Littlemore (see p. 307). This was somewhat appropriate given that many had to double as parish churches. In a passage that recalled Selwyn's 'cathedral' tent, Beresford Hope advised that the cathedral idea was in essence nothing more than the 'embodiment of the machinery of the Christian Church in the fulness [*sic*] of its divine constitution. . . . [T]he one church or chapel which they may raise or adopt, be it but a hut or a tent, is the rudimentary Cathedral'.[24] Thus, by definition, a cathedral 'ought to exist as an institution from the very first, and as a building from the earliest moment in which any building at all can be provided; or in other words, the first missionaries ought to be a rudimentary Cathedral'.[25] As we shall see, this is how colonial bishops understood and appreciated the cathedral idea.

Early Efforts: Calcutta, Sydney, and Toronto

One of the first Anglican bishops in Britain's overseas empire to implement the cathedral idea was the Rev. Daniel Wilson (1778–1858) of Calcutta (see fig. 332).[26] But Wilson was no Tractarian. In fact, he was implacably opposed to the Oxford reformers, describing their ideas as fatuous and 'wrong'.[27] He was, rather, an Evangelical's evangelical, having attended St Edmund Hall, Oxford (later tutor and vice-principal), before becoming a member of St John's chapel, Bedford Row.[28] However, this did not mean that Wilson was a Low Churchman. On more than one occasion, owing to his orthodox opinions and imperious demeanour, he was mistaken for a High Churchman.[29] This is hardly surprising for his views on apostolicity, ironically enough, were broadly in line with those of his Tractarian rivals. 'That the Apostles had a full authority over all the Ministers and teachers of the primitive Church has never been disputed', he wrote in 1833, 'nor can it be doubted whether this order of ecclesiastical government was designed, in its general features, to continue as the Apostles left it'.[30] To Wilson, 'order', above all, was necessary in Church governance, especially in a see the size of Calcutta.[31]

Such a strict view of apostolicity naturally affected Wilson's thinking on cathedral institutions.[32] He was keen to see the Church of England have a conspicuous presence

59 St Paul's cathedral, Calcutta (1839–47), designed by W. N. Forbes.

in India, not just through the erection of parish churches and chapels, for which he was a tireless campaigner, but also through the raising of an impressive 'mother church'. Writing about this idea in 1839, he mused: 'I seemed to myself like Moses surveying from Mount Pisgah the promised land. I figured to myself my beautiful spire, rising up two hundred and twenty feet, – the fine, deeply buttressed Gothic nave, chancel, and transepts, marking the massive grandeur of the Christian religion.'[33] Again, this vision was not so much a romantic yearning to replicate the greens of Salisbury plain as it was a desire to make manifest the institutional order and discipline of the English Church. Such a building would lend authority to that 'apostolic commission' prized by Wilson, giving 'a local habitation and name to Christianity, . . . [to] incorporate and fix it in the soil as part of the permanent institutions of the country'. 'All this is as directly applicable to India now', he claimed, 'as it was to Asia Minor, Africa, and Europe, in primitive ages.'[34]

By September 1839, Wilson had secured the plans for his cathedral. It was to be named after the great apostle St Paul and built on the open spaces of the Maidan, a mile or so south-east of Fort William. The designer was a military engineer (as was the case with so many churches in British India) by the name of Major W. N. Forbes. There is evidence to suggest that Forbes, in designing St Paul's, resurrected a similar plan for a cathedral he had presented to the Marquess of Hastings, former governor-general of India, in 1819.[35] This helps explain the 'Commissioners' Gothic' character of the design, rendered in a rather whimsical late Gothic or Perpendicular style (fig. 59). The foundation stone was laid to great fanfare on 9 October 1839, and the building opened and consecrated eight years later on 8 October 1847, having cost over £50,000 to complete.[36]

Despite giving the appearance of stone, the main structure of St Paul's was solid brick, coated in a particularly hardwearing, lime-based render known as *chunam*. This was a construction technique adopted widely in British building throughout the tropics during the late eighteenth and early nineteenth centuries (discussed further in Chapter 3). The original tower and spire were over 200 feet high and loosely based on those at Norwich, while the building's east end contained stained glass by Benjamin West (fig. 60).[37] Naturally, the Ecclesiological Society was unimpressed. Although it could not commend Wilson's cathedral on architectural grounds, *The Ecclesiologist* did acknowledge, however, that the bishop ought to be congratulated for initiating so important a first step in improving the state of church architecture in India.[38] 'The fact . . . of a Christian Bishop in a great metropolis considering a cathedral as indispensable', the magazine reassured its readers, 'is a great and cheering spectacle, and one which we trust is the prelude to better days.'[39]

60 Etching of the interior of St Paul's cathedral, Calcutta (1839–57), showing the original east end window by Benjamin West, from A. J. B. Beresford Hope's *The English Cathedral of the Nineteenth Century* (1861).

34. Interior of Calcutta Cathedral.

Just over two years before St Paul's was begun, the foundation stone of St Andrew's cathedral, Sydney, was laid (May 1837) (see fig. 228).[40] Broughton, who orchestrated the event, was known to Wilson, having been archdeacon of New South Wales within the diocese of Calcutta before his elevation to the bishopric of Australia in 1836. As they were both ardent proponents of ecclesiastical discipline, Broughton's and Wilson's views on the value of cathedral institutions naturally coincided, setting a new agenda for dignifying the episcopal office through architecture.

Broughton's promotion of the cathedral project at Sydney demonstrated once again the use of models and the involvement of clergymen as amateur architects. During his visit to England in 1834, Broughton was exposed to the changes that were beginning to transform ecclesiastical architecture there. It was clear to him that ancient models, along with a certain degree of archaeological accuracy, were fast becoming the order of the day in ecclesiastical design.[41] On his return to Australia in 1836, Broughton suddenly realised what was required for Sydney. For the time being, however, he was saddled with a local architect, James Hume (1798–1868), whom he had once sardonically described as 'a Presbyterian quite ignorant of architecture'. Hume was incapable of realising such a grand vision, so Broughton was forced once again to rely on his own wit and initiative. Some time in 1837 he composed a design for the cathedral based on an amalgam of St Mary's church, Oxford, and Magdalen College tower.

Although he had already designed a number of churches in Australia, Broughton never claimed to be an architect, and was therefore satisfied with this pattern-book approach. He had requested detailed drawings of the tower at Magdalen from the college authorities, which duly arrived,[42] and appears to have modelled the remainder of the building on the sections of St Mary's contained in A. C. Pugin and E. J. Willson's *Specimens of Gothic Architecture* (vol. 2, 1821) (fig. 61).[43] Writing some years later to his friend and agent

61 Lithograph by Conrad Martens, 1840, of Broughton's design for St Andrew's cathedral, Sydney (State Library of New South Wales, Sydney). The image was produced and distributed for fundraising purposes.

in England, the Rev. George Gilbert, Broughton was gracious enough to admit: 'I formed the design in 1837, when those societies did not exist [Camden and Oxford Architectural societies], and no person here has the slightest ability to give me a hint or to suggest a correction. At that time I was more proud of my production than I have been since, or am now, subsequent study of church architecture having revealed to me many mistakes and anachronisms.'[44]

Like St Paul's cathedral in Calcutta, Broughton's design for St Andrew's was largely in the Perpendicular or 'Third-Pointed' style, something for which it would later be criticised by the Ecclesiological Society. Nevertheless, as Joan Kerr has observed, it is remarkable for being the first attempt at a church design in Australia that was consciously medieval rather than merely 'Picturesque', incorporating scaled-down replica components of genuine Gothic buildings.[45] In this sense, Broughton was moving unwittingly in the direction of what would later become the 'science' of ecclesiology.

With the foundation stone laid, work progressed rapidly until severe drought followed by economic depression brought proceedings to a halt, first in 1839, with subscriptions all but drying up, and again in 1842, when operations were finally suspended.[46] The site remained abandoned until April 1846, when, with depression lifting and £4,000 having been raised, the building committee was re-formed and work resumed. It was at this time that Edmund Blacket was appointed in place of Hume as superintending architect.[47] Unlike the Presbyterian Hume, Blacket, a pious Anglican, seemed a singularly appropriate choice for such

62 Drawing by J. W. Jones of Edmund Blacket's revised design for St Andrew's cathedral, Sydney, showing the twin-towered west front and crossing tower, *c.*1846.

an endeavour, entering upon it, William Cotton observed, as though 'upon a holy work'.[48] Blacket took his new responsibilities so seriously that upon accepting the commission he immediately began redesigning the cathedral, extending the nave by three bays, adding a crossing tower (supposedly based on that at Bath), and substituting double towers for Broughton's single west tower (fig. 62).[49] He also embellished the whole with a profusion of correct Perpendicular detailing, the end result being a much more convincing, cathedral-like structure.

Blacket's inspiration for the twin-towered west front came from York Minster, drawings of which had been sent to him by his father.[50] This was a significant alteration to Broughton's original design, for it was generally conceded that a cathedral with a single tower at its west end was unknown in England and therefore anathema. Selwyn, who happened to be in Sydney at the time Broughton was deliberating over the twin-tower proposal, concurred with Blacket, noting that a double-towered front was the norm for an English cathedral.[51] This was symbolically important, for Sydney was soon to become a metropolitical cathedral, when Broughton was made metropolitan of Australasia in 1847. The two ancient metropolitical cathedrals of York and Canterbury both had twin towers. As with Calcutta, *The Ecclesiologist* was naturally disappointed with the choice of style, but was nevertheless pleased with Blacket's attempts at avoiding 'the effect of a mere parish-church' by adding a 'front of the recognised type'.[52]

As will be discussed further in Chapter 5, the backdrop to Broughton's anxiety and exertions over St Andrew's went further than his attempts merely to secure the position of the Church of England in Australia. They were partly inspired by his all-consuming fixation with the presence and agitation (as he saw it) of the Roman Catholic Church.

Indeed, St Andrew's was a cynosure of that anxiety, every stone on the way to its completion representing a victory in the struggle for ecclesiastical privilege and authority that characterised the religious scene in Sydney during the middle decades of the nineteenth century. Many now recognised that the completion of St Andrew's was a matter of national importance, particularly as the Roman Catholics had erected their own cathedral in 1839.[53]

The years during which St Andrew's lay dormant rankled and shamed Broughton. It must have been especially humiliating when a female vagabond was reported as having said that she was 'about to remove to the neighbourhood of that old cathedral which they are repairing'.[54] That St Andrew's would be a building to compare with, even surpass, the Roman Catholic cathedral of St Mary's on a point of 'architectural pretension' became a minor obsession for Broughton. Writing to Edward Coleridge in 1837 he lamented how 'without such a stronghold of the faith we cannot keep our position'.[55]

We have heard something already of Broughton's thoughts concerning the importance of cathedral institutions, but in the 'egalitarian' context of Sydney he was equally keen to reiterate the peculiar confessional nature of St Andrew's, constantly reminding his congregation that their cathedral was not only a centre of discipline and worship but also, and perhaps more importantly, a bastion of that 'Reformed and Protestant Church'.[56] He did not live to see the project completed, however. St Andrew's was consecrated on 30 November 1868, but the building was not finished until 1874. It took nearly forty years to build at a cost of some £60,000.

The situation experienced in Calcutta and Sydney was similar to that in Toronto. Like Wilson and Broughton, the bishop of Toronto, the Rev. John Strachan (fig. 63), was a High Churchman of the old school. Unlike Wilson and Broughton, however, he was a Scot and born a Presbyterian, educated initially at King's College, Aberdeen, and then the University of St Andrews. At first Strachan did not take holy orders, obtaining employment as a teacher instead. It was on the promise of a professorship at a new academy in British North America that he emigrated to Upper Canada (Ontario) in 1799, only later seeking ordination as an Anglican priest (1804). Despite his somewhat opportunistic origins as a cleric, Strachan proved to be a proud and loyal servant of the British crown, and someone who saw it as his duty to uphold and defend the status and privileges of the English Church. In this respect he was very much a product of the geopolitical context in which he first found himself as a clergyman, having moved to the parish of York in 1812 (archdeacon from 1827) when tensions between Britain and the newly formed United States of America were at breaking point.[57]

Again, as with his episcopal brethren in India and Australia, Strachan maintained a forthright and uncompromising stance on apostolicity and Church discipline. In a land increasingly infiltrated by dissent (which he associated with republicanism), Strachan believed that the tradition of order within the Church was what made it not only 'true' but also unified – a factor that would result in either its success or its failure in the colonies.[58] Facing political pressures similar to those that beset Broughton and the Church of

63 John Strachan (1778–1867), first bishop of Toronto. Strachan was formerly a Presbyterian who converted to Anglicanism; he was appointed bishop in 1839.

64 Lithograph by Thomas Young, *c.*1835, showing St James's church, Toronto, as intended in its second incarnation, though the spire was not built (private collection).

England in Australasia, Strachan found solace in the Oxford Movement and its position on Church governance.[59] Although he had expounded the sanctity of apostolic succession as early as the 1820s,[60] while in England in 1839 he felt compelled to write to Newman, thanking the authors of the *Tracts* for their 'able defence of the true Church' and 'elegant and profound elucidation of the foundation on which she ought to rest'.[61]

Strachan was consecrated bishop of Toronto at Lambeth Palace on 4 August 1839. Earlier that year, St James's church in the city of Toronto was severely damaged by fire, having been rebuilt only six years earlier.[62] Like many town churches in British North America at the time, St James's was a rather simple 'auditory church' in the late Georgian style, with box pews and gallery (fig. 64). Strachan immediately set about rebuilding the church for a second time. Now that Toronto had a bishop, he felt that St James's ought to assume the presence of a cathedral. Despite the fact that the Gothic Revival was well under way in Britain, the Church authorities opted for a neo-classical design with steeple, after Gibbs's St Martin-in-the-Fields. Plans were prepared by a local émigré architect, Thomas Young, and the building was restored by Christmas 1839.[63] However, it did not meet Strachan's increasingly sophisticated view of what constituted a 'cathedral' church.[64]

Disaster struck again in 1849. On the morning of 7 April, with a large area of the city of Toronto ablaze, St James's caught fire and was burned to the ground. For Strachan, this was a blessing in disguise. It restored his ambition to erect a building befitting his status as a bishop of the English Church. In his letters to England he insisted that the new church be of a 'Cathedral Character', and in 'a style much more splendid than before'.[65] As with Broughton and the building of St Andrew's, Strachan faced opposition from the Low Church element within his congregation, who saw no occasion to spend money indulging the exter-

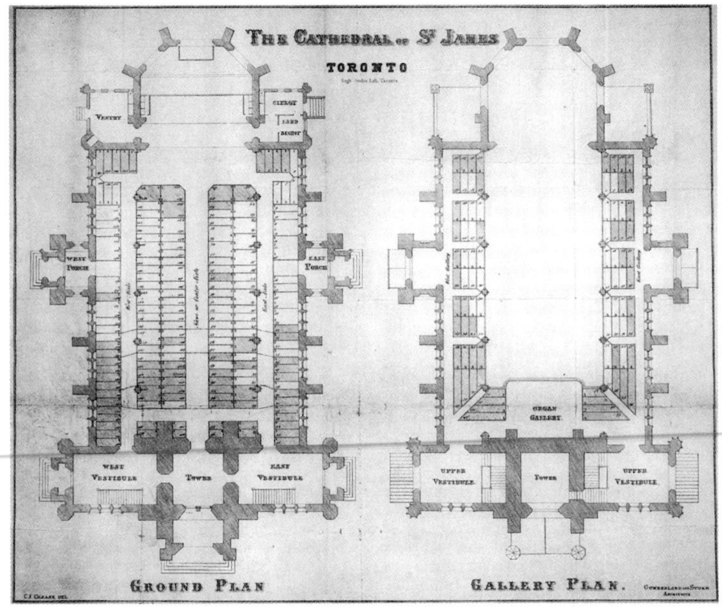

65 Ground floor and gallery plans, 1849, for St James's cathedral, Toronto (1850–3), by Frederic Cumberland of Cumberland and Storm architects (Archive, Cathedral of St James, Toronto).

nals of worship. But Strachan did not give up easily.[66] He took every opportunity to make the case for a building worthy not just of the Anglican community in Upper Canada but also of the episcopal office and its institutional character. In an open letter to his parishioners, he pointed to the original exemplar of Solomon's Temple, observing how it was built rich and magnificent at the express command of God. Thus, he added, 'Christians having this all-prevailing authority before them, have frequently in their churches and cathedrals surpassed the Temple itself as far in size, beauty, and costliness. . . . In regard to the restoration of the Church of St James, it will not do to make it of less dimensions, . . . nor ought it to be so plain and destitute of architectural beauty as the one we have lost.'[67] This proved convincing, for it was duly resolved by the vestry committee on 23 March 1850 that 'a handsome Parish Church in the Gothic Style . . . , denominated the Cathedral Church of St James', was to be erected in place of the ruined building.[68] The dimensions of the principal cathedrals of England were immediately sought, including Ely, Wells, Durham, Exeter, Peterborough, Winchester, Canterbury, Salisbury and many others.[69] Aspirations were clearly high, perhaps too high, but the idea that St James's graduate from being a glorified parish church to a proper cathedral finally stuck, focused, perhaps, by the completion of the Roman Catholic cathedral of St Michael in 1848.

Initially the building committee considered sending to England for plans, but in May 1849 opted for a local competition instead. The winner was the little-known Frederic William Cumberland, an English-born architect who had come to Toronto in 1847. Cumberland was very much aware of the developments that had taken place in ecclesiastical architecture in England over the preceding decade, and turned out a competent Early English design with the choice of a double- or single-towered front (fig. 65). In the event, pecuniary resources were not sufficient to erect the more traditional cathedral front, so the single-tower option was adopted. The foundation stone was laid on 20 November 1850, and the whole built of 'white' Toronto brick. As will be discussed further in Chapter 5, what makes St James's interesting as an early experiment in cathedral design in the colonies is the compromise it represented between the old-guard, Evangelical element within the Canadian Church and the more progressive High Church spirit drifting across from England. As a result, the building was not as grand as Strachan had been hoping for, nor was the increasingly repugnant system of pew rents done away with (it was considered necessary to help fund the project). When it was finished in June 1853 (except for the tower), at a cost of nearly £19,000, the new cathedral did not receive much attention from *The Ecclesiologist* (fig. 66). In an article on Christ Church, Montreal, it was observed in passing that, 'although the new [cathedral] at Toronto would, if completed, be larger, it is as yet unfinished, and on (we believe) a much inferior and less correct plan'.[70]

John Medley and Frank Wills: An Epoch in Transatlantic Ecclesiology

One of the most celebrated of colonial bishops is John Medley (1804–1892) of Fredericton, New Brunswick (Canada) (fig. 67). Medley has attracted a considerable degree of scholarly attention, not only for his vigorous and able superintendence as a bishop but also for his marked Tractarianism and interest in architecture.[71] The stand-alone monument and crowning glory of his long-serving episcopacy is without doubt Christ Church cathedral, Fredericton

66 St James's cathedral, Toronto (1850–3), as it stood *c.*1860, shortly after completion. The tower and spire were not finished until 1874.

(1845–53): a building that received plaudits both in England and in North America for its strict adherence to ecclesiological principles (fig. 68).

Medley's interests and inclinations necessarily make him one of the central figures in the story of colonial ecclesiology. He was among the first of the Anglican bishops in Britain's empire to have made a serious study of architecture, and, next to G. A. Selwyn, the one who arguably made the greatest contribution to it.[72] Medley was also a well-connected cleric, associated with celebrated figures across Britain and the British empire and known for his activities in ecclesiastical circles. For instance, he was acquainted with Bishop Selwyn, and, like Selwyn, was a friend of the great Victorian statesman W. E. Gladstone.[73] Moreover, he was a patron member of both the Oxford Architectural and Cambridge Camden societies, which regularly carried articles in their publications on his church-building exploits. He was also an active member, along with the Rev. John Armstrong, of the Exeter Diocesan Architectural Society (founded 1841).[71] Armstrong would later go on to become bishop of Grahamstown, South Africa, where, like Medley, he would raise the banner of ecclesiology (see pp. 98–100, 220–5).

Although Medley did not witness the Oxford Movement first hand (Wadham, BA, 1826), he soon became involved in its cause. He was a friend of both John Keble and E. B. Pusey,[75] and Thomas Mozley identified him in his *Reminiscences* (1882) as among those who stood out in 1820s Oxford for their 'high qualities and considerable promise'.[76] After ordination in 1828, Medley went to Truro as curate of Southleigh. His move to St Thomas's, Exeter, in 1838, however, placed him firmly within the High Church milieu of the Rev. Henry Phillpotts (1778–1869), bishop of Exeter. Here he mingled with the likes of the Coleridge family of Ottery St Mary and the Tractarian acolyte George James

67 John Bridges, portrait of John Medley (1804–1892), bishop of Fredericton, New Brunswick, 1848, showing Christ Church cathedral in the background (Christ Church Cathedral, Fredericton).

Cornish, a contributor to Keble's *The Christian Year.* True to his developing Tractarian sensibilities, Medley came out strongly in defence of apostolicity in 1835 with a pamphlet titled *The Episcopal Form of Church Government: Its Antiquity, Its Expediency, and Its Conformity to the Word of God.* This opus brought him to the attention of Keble, who had initially planned to include it as one of the Oxford *Tracts.* Later Medley would assist in translating the *Homilies of St. John Chrysostom* (1838) for that other great Tractarian enterprise, the Library of Fathers (1838–85).

Like Pusey, Medley was something of a providential nationalist when it came to the extension of the English Church abroad. If Britain failed to live up to its obligations respecting religious extension, he exclaimed, then 'what will our great Judge say to us?' 'These are critical times,' he stressed in a sermon on behalf of the Society for the Propagation of the Gospel in 1843, 'when every man is sifted and tried, when our empire is tried. We cannot go back: we must support Christianity [in the empire] or we fall.'[77] This sermon was preached shortly after the inauguration of the CBF, of which Selwyn was the first affiliate. Medley was present at Selwyn's final sermon in the cathedral at Exeter in December 1841. As W. O. Raymond has observed, Medley would no doubt have been inspired by Selwyn's

68 Christ Church cathedral, Fredericton, New Brunswick (1845–53), by Frank Wills and William Butterfield.

affirmation of the apostolic commission and his insistence on the necessity for cathedral institutions.[78] Following Selwyn's example, Medley later gave his own lecture on cathedrals and cathedral institutions before the New York Ecclesiological Society in 1851.[79]

All of this demonstrated how absolutely central apostolicity and its institutionalisation were to Medley. At the heart of his approach, Eugene Fairweather has noted, was a conception that the Church was a supernatural society, independent of the State, acting by the authority of Christ alone.[80] This put Medley very much in the same camp as Selwyn, Nixon and Short (born within seven years of one another), all of whom come from that generation of high-minded, university-educated clerics who saw such tenets as the *sine qua non* of the reformed Catholic Church.

Upon his elevation as bishop of Fredericton in May 1845, the first thing Medley did was to begin planning a cathedral. To this end he had designs prepared by the young architect Frank Wills (1822–1856), pupil of William Butterfield. On 12 May 1845, at a public meeting held in Exeter, Medley was presented with a parting gift of over £1,500 for his cathedral project. At this meeting his old friend, the Rev. William Hart Coleridge (1789–1849), who himself had been a champion of church architecture while

69 The medieval church of St Mary, Snettisham, Norfolk, used as the 'model' for Christ Church cathedral, Fredericton.

bishop of Barbados and the Leeward Islands (1824–42), rose to praise him for going beyond that 'wholesome doctrine' to supply 'before the eyes of your people . . . the scriptural ritual of that church, in all the fullness and impressiveness of a faithful outward observance'. 'For this end,' Coleridge continued, 'you have judged rightly, my Lord, in proposing to erect, with as little delay as possible, . . . an adequate and becoming edifice for the public worship of God – worthy – I might hesitate so to speak, even of the costliest achievements of architectural science – yet worthy, in some sense – . . . of that Being, who, though he dwelleth not in temples made with hands, ever deserveth the best from us.'[81]

There was, however, one telling passage above all in Coleridge's speech – namely, his reference to the proposed cathedral as being '[b]uilt, as you are desirous it should be, after an ancient model, of singular beauty, and cathedral appropriateness'. This 'ancient model', it turns out, was the

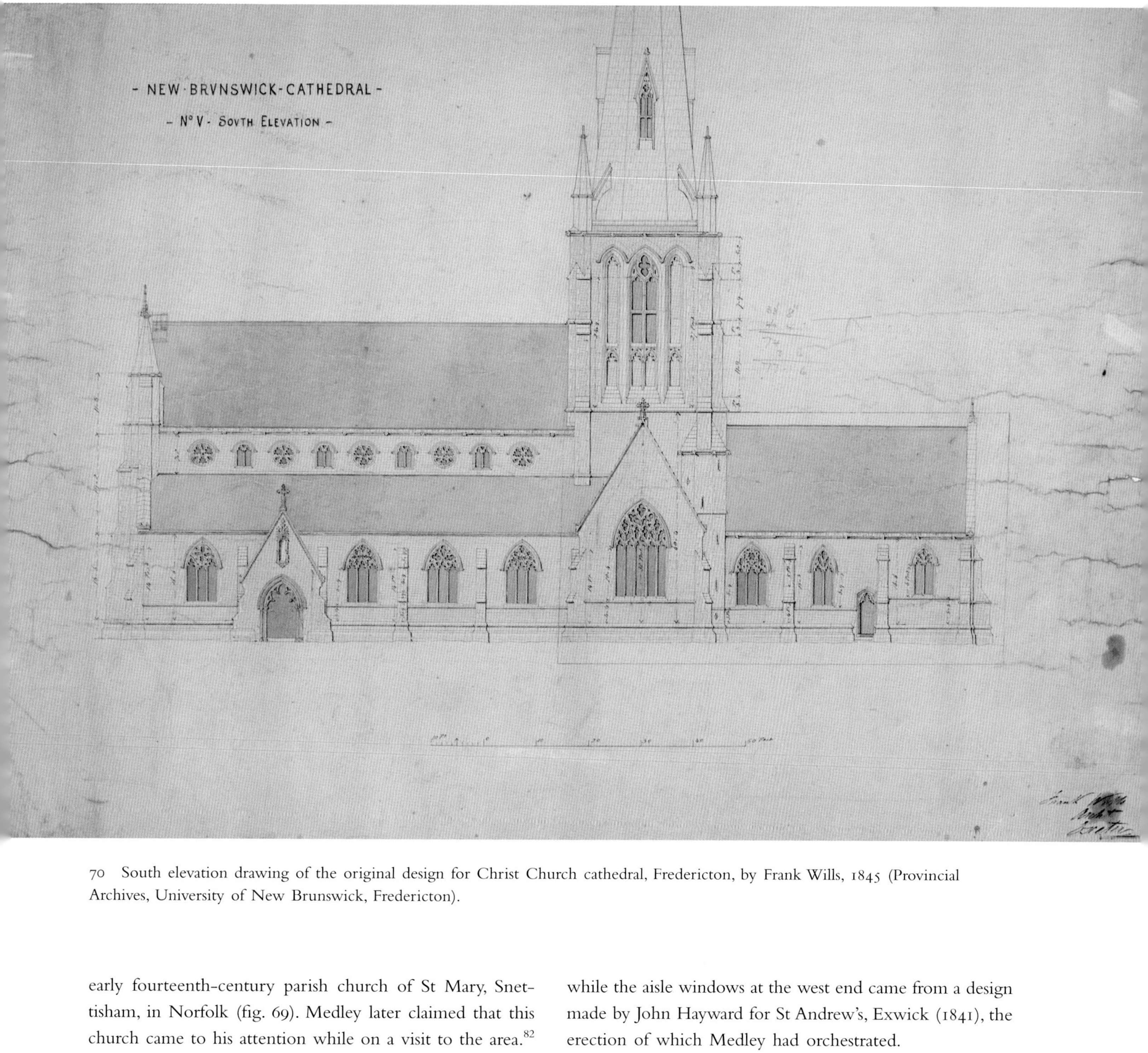

70 South elevation drawing of the original design for Christ Church cathedral, Fredericton, by Frank Wills, 1845 (Provincial Archives, University of New Brunswick, Fredericton).

early fourteenth-century parish church of St Mary, Snettisham, in Norfolk (fig. 69). Medley later claimed that this church came to his attention while on a visit to the area.[82] Stimulated by the efforts of his friends, Medley sent Wills, 'then a young draughtsman in an Architect's office in Exeter, to take the measurements'.[83] St Mary's was a partial ruin at the time, but Wills's plans show a building with the chancel and transepts St Mary's originally had (fig. 70). The design for the east window was taken from that of Selby Abbey, while the aisle windows at the west end came from a design made by John Hayward for St Andrew's, Exwick (1841), the erection of which Medley had orchestrated.

Ecclesiologically speaking, the selection of Snettisham as a working model was significant. It was, in many ways, everything that the Cambridge Camden Society had encouraged in modern church design. More important still (unlike the cathedrals at Calcutta, Sydney and Toronto), it was a specimen in the 'Middle-Pointed' style. This all boded

71 Bishop Medley's alternative design for Christ Church cathedral, Fredericton, from the *Illustrated London News* (1848), showing the transept towers.

72 F. Nash, engraving of the medieval church of Ottery St Mary, Devon, 1822. This was one of the inspirations for Medley's 'alternative' proposal of 1848 for Christ Church cathedral, Fredericton.

well indeed, as far as *The Ecclesiologist* was concerned. But there was a problem. '[T]hough magnificent as a parish church', St Mary's was 'essentially such, rather than a cathedral'. It was to be regretted that, in so 'holy an undertaking', Medley had failed to aspire to the 'characteristic features of an English cathedral'.[84]

Unperturbed, Medley set sail for New Brunswick within three weeks of his consecration, arriving in his new diocese in June 1845. He wasted little time, laying the foundation stone for the cathedral at Fredericton on 15 October.[85] Wills arrived shortly afterwards and work progressed steadily on the building until the early months of 1848. However, funds dried up when only the nave and aisles were complete. At this point, with Wills having left for greener pastures in the United States, Medley returned to England to raise more money. While there, he was invited to speak on the progress of ecclesiology in New Brunswick at the anniversary meeting of the Ecclesiological Society (9 May). No doubt sensible of the society's criticisms, he outlined an alternative solution, suggesting twin transept towers in the manner of the parish church at Ottery St Mary or Exeter Cathedral (figs 71 and 72).[86] In the end, he accepted a design by William Butterfield comprising a simplified crossing tower with splayed-foot spire and choir at nave height – a scheme of which *The Ecclesiologist* 'entirely approved' (fig. 73).[87] The foundation stone of the new tower was laid by the bishop's children in May 1849 and work recommenced. Further alterations were made to the design, with Medley partially reinstating the tower arrangement from Snettisham and adding two small transepts. The whole was completed and consecrated on 31 August 1853 at a cost of some £16,000. It was constructed using a locally sourced, hard-grained sandstone, with weatherings of stone from Grindstone Island. The dressings were of Caen stone shipped from England.[88]

Although Christ Church cathedral was a triumph for Medley and colonial ecclesiology, it did not come easily. Like Strachan before him, Medley had come to a realm dominated by Low Church tendencies. Consequently, the church that preceded Medley's new cathedral was typical of what he found upon arrival in New Brunswick. Also known as Christ Church, this building (erected in 1794) was nothing more than a 'rude and simple' Georgian box, based on Portland chapel in London.[89] Thus, Medley had to fight hard and consistently to raise standards, both architecturally and liturgically.[90] Despite suspicions sur-

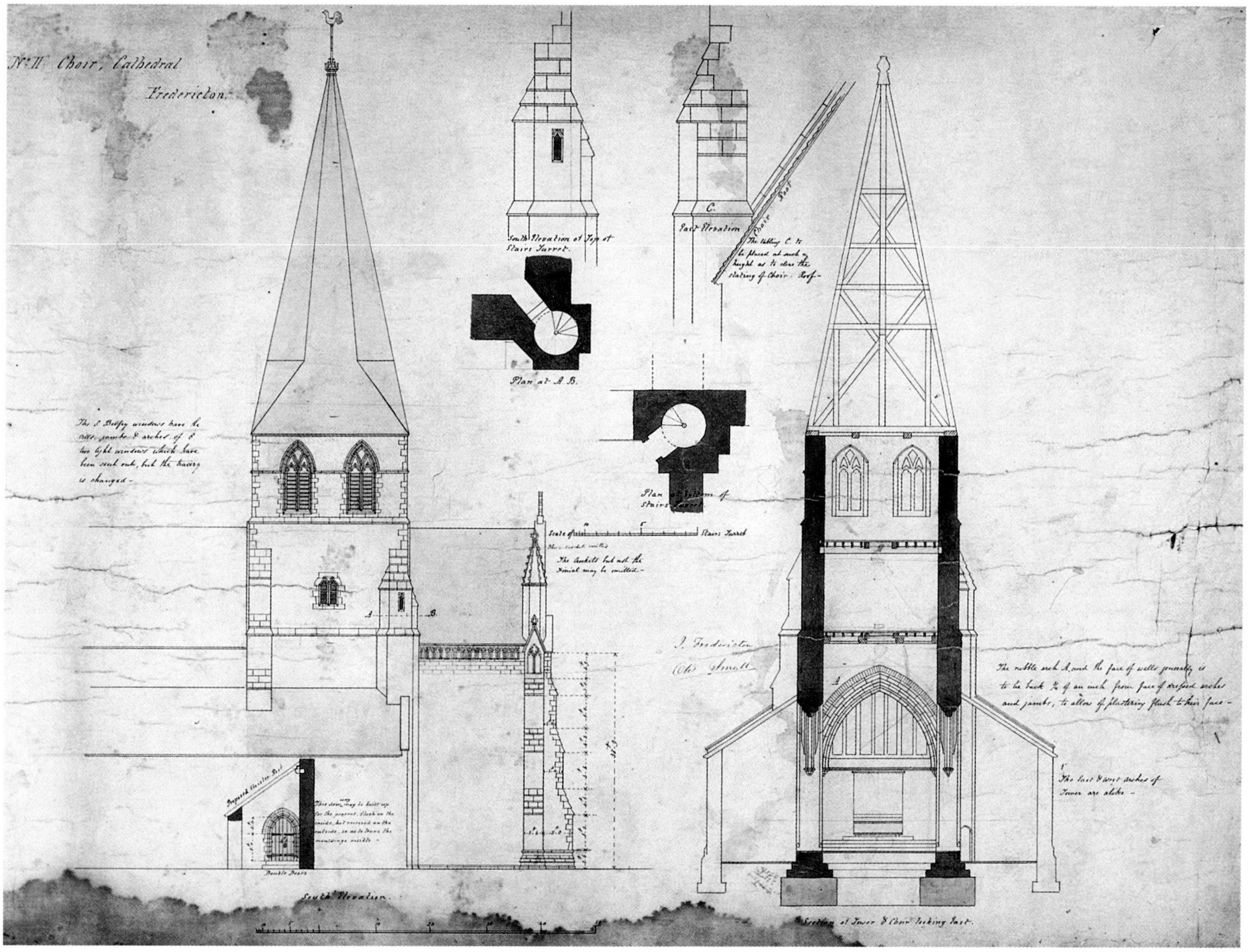

73 William Butterfield's revised scheme for the crossing tower and choir of Christ Church cathedral, Fredericton, 1848 (Provincial Archives, University of New Brunswick, Fredericton).

rounding his churchmanship, Medley continued to challenge his congregation's preconceptions concerning architecture. In a similar manner to Broughton, he spoke repeatedly in his sermons and charges of the scriptural truth and Christian duty of beautifying the house of God. Holiness may not be 'ensured by the observance of external rites,' he exclaimed, 'but is it ensured by their neglect?' '[L]et us be well assured', he insisted, 'that God is not the more spiritually worshipped, when our meanness refuses to offer him the best of what we have.'[91]

Wishing to avoid accusations of mere 'formalism', Medley drew on the moral authority of John Ruskin in addressing his clergy: 'Have not men in all ages considered the Temple of God to be a proper subject of honour, dignity, and beauty? Does Paganism rear its Pantheon to idol deities, and shall we do less honour to the God of Heaven? . . . I trust you will agree with me that we ought to do our best to make the outward form and internal arrangements of God's House, reverent and decorous.'[92] To Medley, churches were not 'square rooms, mean barns, Spectatoria, and Auditoria, but Houses of Prayer; long, rather than square, lofty, rather than low, with means of kneeling all together in humble adoration'. The cathedral church represented the pinnacle of this idea, architecturally and institutionally: it was, in short, 'Domus mansionalis omnipotentis Dei'.[93] In a sermon titled *The Staff of Beauty and the Staff of Bands* (1847), Medley was able to summarise this idea – the relationship between church architecture and episcopal ordi-

74 Christ Church cathedral, Montreal (1857–*c.*1860), by Frank Wills.

nance, between outward form and inner spirituality – by simply asking the Anglicans of Fredericton to consider their cathedral as that place in which 'outward and inward holiness are promoted by an union of Christians in a rightly constituted and well-ordered form of government and worship'.[94] When completed, Christ Church cathedral was the largest and most correct Gothic Revival church on the North American continent.[95]

It did not remain so for long. In 1857 Wills was engaged to design a new cathedral for the recently erected diocese of Montreal, divided from Quebec in 1850 (fig. 74). As at Toronto, a new building was required when the existing cathedral – an edifice of 'the old-fashioned Establishment type' – was consumed by fire on the morning of 10 December 1856. The old building, designed by William Berczy in 1805, was somewhat similar to the Gibbs-style one that still stands in Quebec City (Holy Trinity) (see fig. 12).[96] After some delay over the acquisition of an appropriate site (the old site was no longer considered serviceable), noted architects, including William Hay (see below), were invited to submit sketch proposals. In the event, Frank Wills was awarded the commission, having not only convinced the building committee of his undoubted talent as an ecclesiastical architect but also having brought with him testimonials from eminent clergymen, architects and builders from both Canada and the United States, including Medley.[97] It must be remembered that by this time Wills had become a successful ecclesiastical architect in the United States. He was a leading member of the New York Ecclesiological Society and had designed some fifty churches including St Peter's, Milford, Connecticut (1850–1) and St George's, Flushing, New York (1853–4).[98] If any further evidence were required as to his competence in this arena, he had produced in 1850, shortly after leaving Medley's employ, an impressive treatise on medieval church architecture – a publication the essence of which was concerned with elevating the standard of ecclesiastical architecture on the North American continent.[99] All of this placed Wills in the vanguard of those who were considered serious church architects in North America at the time.

Wills probably thought he was onto a winner with the bishop of Montreal, the Rev. Francis Fulford (1803–1868). Like his colleague further east, Fulford was a cleric of discernible Tractarian inclination.[100] As bishop, however, he was keen to exercise discretion on 'party' matters and was noted for his generosity and openness on all sides.[101] But when it came to church architecture he appears to have been firm in his convictions, fully cognisant of the effect that an impressive and liturgically correct church could have. As first editor of the *Colonial Church Chronicle*, he had read numerous accounts of the authority that good architecture commanded on the colonial frontier. Most important of all, Fulford, like Medley, was alert to the enlarged moral and spiritual capacities of architecture. Whenever he commented on the cathedral's design he was mindful to stress the significance of architecture as a means of celebrating God's glory. To quote the words of Solomon, as he often did: '[t]he house I build is great, for great is our God above all Gods' (2 Chronicles, ii. 5).[102]

The design Wills produced for Montreal was a slightly larger and more elaborate version of the Snettisham prototype used at Fredericton (figs 75 and 76). On the whole, *The Ecclesiologist* approved. 'Montreal cathedral will, when completed, mark an epoch in transatlantic ecclesiology,' the journal rejoiced. 'It will be the largest completed cathedral in America of our communion . . . [and] the only cathedral which approaches the normal dimensions of such a building, for Fredericton cathedral is in size only a moderate parish church, and of that of Newfoundland the nave only has been erected.'[103] It is clear that Wills had developed confidence and flare as an architect while in the States, becoming a master of the Middle-Pointed idiom. But this was both his strength and weakness as a designer. By the late 1850s such Middle-Pointed perfection as he showcased at Montreal was considered unprogressive if not obsolete among serious ecclesiastical architects, especially in Britain. To be sure, such a building in such a place was undoubtedly a great boon for the Anglican Church, but, as Phoebe Stanton has observed, Wills and his buildings were essentially unoriginal, rooted firmly in the practice and theory of the 1840s.[104]

There were other problems, too. Not only did Wills die within months of his appointment, but the architect commissioned to realise his design, T. S. Scott, proved less than competent. Insufficient foundations, combined with shoddy workmanship and unsuitable stone for the superstructure, led to subsidence and the eventual demolition of the tower in 1927.[105] The imported Caen stone used for the windows and exterior trimmings of the building proved unsuitable for the harsh Quebec winters, eroding rapidly and requiring complete replacement with Indiana limestone in 1920.[106] When opened, the cathedral also retained the old

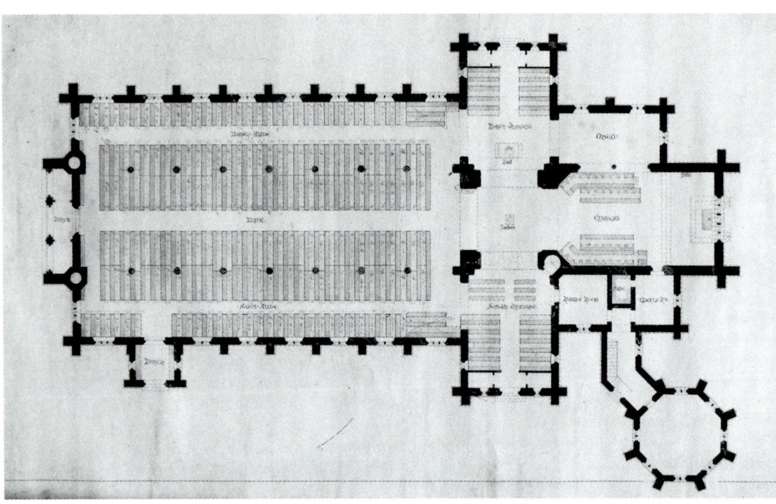

Top 75 West elevation drawing for Christ Church cathedral, Montreal (1857–*c.*1860), by Frank Wills, 1857 (Archive, Christ Church Cathedral, Montreal).

Bottom 76 Floor plan of Christ Church cathedral, Montreal, by Frank Wills, 1857 (Archive, Christ Church Cathedral, Montreal).

pew rental system, a practice that ran contrary to advanced Anglican discipline. The first official service was held in the cathedral on 27 November 1859. However, owing to outstanding debts, the building was not consecrated until 1867. Despite these failings, Christ Church cathedral, Montreal, was the 'neatest' and most impressive work of Anglican church architecture in North America at the time, representing a high if essentially imitative point in the development of ecclesiology on the other side of the Atlantic.

Beyond Imitation: G. G. Scott in the Colonies

As far as British architecture in the nineteenth century is concerned, few stand taller than George Gilbert Scott (1811–1878) (see fig. 199). He was among the first and greatest architects to champion the more mature phase of the Gothic Revival in Britain, beginning with A. W. N. Pugin and the university architectural societies. Indeed, by his own admission, he was inspired by Pugin, noting later in his memoirs that it was the 'thunder' of Pugin's writings that awoke him from his 'slumbers'.[107] He was also involved from an early date with the Cambridge Camden and Oxford Architectural societies, becoming a member of the former in 1842 and the latter in 1843. As is well known (and was at the time), Scott was something of an ideologue with respect to the value and meaning of medieval architecture. Although claiming he was no 'medievalist', he wrote on the subject throughout his career, and, as his numerous buildings demonstrate, commanded a deep and sympathetic understanding of the art and architecture of the Middle Ages.[108]

Although known primarily for his work in Britain, Scott also made designs for a number of buildings overseas, including several churches in Britain's colonial empire.[109] Among these were three of the largest and most impressive Anglican cathedrals erected outside the British Isles – St John the Baptist, St John's, Newfoundland (first phase 1846–50); St Michael and St George, Grahamstown, South Africa (1861–1912); and Christ Church cathedral, Christchurch, New Zealand (1862–1904). For this reason alone, Scott's colonial cathedrals warrant separate treatment. What makes them particularly interesting in the context of this study – beyond their obvious architectural merit – is the extent to which Scott engaged with them as projects. This is perhaps not surprising, considering Scott's family background. His grandfather, the Rev. Thomas Scott (1747–1821), was heavily involved with the Church Missionary Society, while his mother, Euphemia Lynch, was of Antiguan planting stock. Therefore, Scott's familiarity with, and empathy for, colonial causes was more developed than most.[110]

He entered fully and enthusiastically into the cathedral idea, in the case of Grahamstown offering his services 'pro Deo' (that is, for no fee).[111] Thus, as a pious Anglican, and with his prior knowledge of colonial conditions, Scott was well placed to consider how cathedral architecture might be articulated to embody a specific ecclesiastical purpose, at the same time celebrating (within the means available) the beauty and integrity of medieval design. His cathedral in Newfoundland heralded the dawn of a new era in colonial church architecture, in which original design, based on sound ecclesiological principles, took precedence over the adaptation or imitation of pre-existing models.[112]

The foundation stone for St John the Baptist had, in fact, been laid some years before Scott's involvement, on 21 August 1843. It was initiated by the first bishop of Newfoundland, the Rev. Aubrey Spencer (1795–1872), who felt a necessity to 'revive and extend' the institutions of the English Church in the face of what he perceived as papal aggression in Newfoundland.[113] As the existing church was considered both 'frail' and dilapidated, he appointed an Irish stonemason-cum-architect, James Purcell, to prepare plans. The Oxford Architectural Society had sent drawings to Newfoundland at the request of the Rev. Thomas Bridge in 1842,[114] but Purcell thought he knew better.[115] However, by June 1845 the scheme had fallen flat, the bishop reporting that 'the subject is never raised, even in talk'.[116]

Comparatively speaking, the diocese of Newfoundland was extremely poor. Funding for substantial churches was therefore difficult to obtain. Thus, the project stalled until the arrival of the new bishop, the Rev. Edward Feild (1801–1876) (see fig. 242), in early July 1844. At first Feild was exasperated by the predicament in which he found the project, describing it as a 'pretty colonial mess'. 'Nothing can be more deplorable,' he complained. 'The cut stone has arrived from Ireland, so that we are committed to the proposed plan in its details which are hideous.'[117] An incredible £3,797 had already been spent on materials and services by October 1844 without a single stone having been laid, other than the foundation.[118]

Feild was a paternalistic High Church Tory in the Phillpotts mould. Like Selwyn, he possessed marked but not

77 James Purcell's original design for the cathedral of St John the Baptist, St John's, Newfoundland, 1843 (The Rooms, St John's, Newfoundland).

excessive Tractarian tendencies, making it the principal objective of his long episcopacy to put the Church of England in Newfoundland on a secure and independent footing.[119] Unlike his neighbour Medley, however, Feild was no ecclesiologist. He was more a stickler for liturgical discipline than a 'priestly architect'. He nevertheless knew what made for a decent and well-ordered church.[120] Having decided that Purcell's plans would not do, he was initially unsure whom to approach in order to develop the project (fig. 77). What he required was something solid and simple, but not without 'ecclesiastical character'. Confirmed in his suspicions of Purcell, whose plans were pronounced by the Ecclesiological Society as 'abominable', he left the matter in the hands of Ernest Hawkins of the SPG and his trusted friend and agent in England, the Rev. William Scott.

It was around this time that G. G. Scott (no relation of the clergyman) entered the scene. A devastating fire in June 1846 destroyed great swathes of the city of St John's, including the Anglican church. This necessarily invested the cathedral project with renewed impetus. In response to the bishop's appeal, Hawkins began approaching architects in England, including Edward Blore, William Butterfield and Charles Gabriel (pupil of Benjamin Ferrey).[121] He also suggested that Feild seek advice from Medley and Wills. In the event, Scott responded most readily to Hawkins's solicitations, and in the summer of 1846 sent two sketch proposals to Hawkins, which were forwarded to Feild.[122] These sketches were for alternative arrangements: one, a parish-style church with nave, chancel, and western tower; the other, a cruciform plan with transepts, choir and crossing tower (figs 78 and 79).[123] Both designs were rendered rather minimally in the Early English style, in response to the bishop's request for something 'simple and severe'.[124] Although 'brother Fredericton's Cathedral looks nice on paper, it will not be built,' Feild advised Hawkins (wrongly, as it turned out). What was needed in the rugged and unforgiving climes of British North America was something more substantial. He had earlier mentioned to his friend William Scott the twelfth-century cathedral of St Magnus, Kirkwall, on the island of Orkney, as a potential model, later pointing to Pugin's design for St Wilfrid's, Manchester (1839–42) (figs 80 and 81).

By March 1847, it was decided that a version of the cruciform plan submitted by G. G. Scott would be adopted.[125] Scott seems to have favoured the cruciform arrangement from the beginning, observing in a memorandum to Hawkins:

> The cross form has always been considered to rank the highest among the forms adopted for a church – it has not only been adopted for probably nearly all cathedrals but for a majority of churches which were expected to take any degree of precedence among the churches of their neighbourhood. . . . This argument applies to the present instance . . . , it [St John's] must rank high as the Mother Church, and that belonging for a time at least more peculiarly than others to the Bishop.[126]

He cautioned, however:

> The ideas attached to the word *Cathedral* are often unduly affected by the magnificent scale of those to which we are accustomed – a scale to which they have grown by slow degrees and which however glorious

78 One of two formal perspective drawings for the cathedral of St John the Baptist, St John's, Newfoundland, by G. G. Scott, 1846 (Bodleian Library, Oxford). It shows a standard parish church arrangement of west-end tower, nave, aisles, south porch and chancel.

79 Second of two formal perspective drawings for the cathedral of St John the Baptist, St John's, by G. G. Scott, 1846 (RIBA Drawings Collection, Victoria and Albert Museum, London). This design shows an alternative 'cathedral' layout with nave, aisles, transepts with crossing tower, and choir.

> rather operates against their utility .. . . [A] cathedral built for our worship would probably be better on a far less scale – and a Colonial Cathedral as it appears to me ought to be no more than a Parish Church of a superior dignity to others . . . by its outline and more impressive form. . . . The only essentials then to constitute a cathedral are a somewhat larger size, a more dignified outline, and a larger proportion of Chancel . . . .[127]

In an attempt to head off 'needless alarm' over the cathedral, Scott went on to note that many of the cathedrals in England, as presently used, 'differ widely from their original intention', and that Newfoundland offered an opportunity to avoid 'error and perplexity' by getting back to basics.[128] In this memorandum, Scott, revealing himself to be every bit a 'religious architect', demonstrated his understanding of and investment in the cathedral idea. It is clear that he worked through the meaning and implications of St John's 'as a cathedral' from first principles. His thinking on the matter also reveals his appreciation of the debate surrounding cathedral institutions and their uses in England. Moreover, his conclusions chimed with what Beresford Hope would later say about cathedral churches – that sheer magnitude was no prerequisite.[129]

This was just as well, for Feild was most anxious to get a suitable but cost-effective building. A sum of nearly £15,000 had been raised in England for the purpose, but he feared that this was not nearly enough. Exacerbating the problem was Feild's highly principled position on what he considered necessary with respect to Church organisation and governance. Like Selwyn, whom he described as 'my gifted brother', Feild was known for his asceticism and 'primitive simplicity'.[130] In the highly vexed religious and political context that was 1840s St John's (often likened to Belfast), Feild was keen to demonstrate propriety and eschew excess. In a communication with his parishioners over the building of the cathedral in 1848, he argued that to waste a huge and disproportionate sum of money on a single building, when the diocese was in desperate need of clergymen and churches, was unconscionable. In this respect he took the opposite line to Broughton (see p. 71), suggesting that the 'Mother Church' should lead by example through its chasteness and dignified humility. As a result, Feild reassured his flock that there would be no tower or transepts to begin with, only a nave. If funds permitted and the need arose, then the remainder of the church could be erected at a later date.[131]

These limitations were appreciated by Scott.[132] By the middle of 1847 he had developed the cruciform design,

following, it would appear, the suggested precedents of Kirkwall and St Wilfrid's (figs 82 and 83). The windows were to be single lancets, the larger ones towards the east containing plate tracery with geometric patterning. As a form, St John's thoroughly embodied Feild's arcane notion of rugged asceticism, rising vigorously from its sloping site like some great ecclesiastical fortress.[133] For Scott it was a masterly if overly stern essay in the essentials of what he later called the 'perfect' English or 'lancet' style.[134] Ironically, despite being 'scrupulously correct', the design was considered by Benjamin Webb (writing for *The Ecclesiologist*) to have been so compromised that it tended towards lacking invention

Top 80 J. Kidd, watercolour, 1808, of St Magnus cathedral, Kirkwall, Orkney (National Gallery of Scotland, Edinburgh).

Bottom 81 A. W. N. Pugin's design for St Wilfrid's church, Manchester, 1839.

and originality.[135] Be this as it may, Scott might well have felt vindicated after the fact by Ruskin's notion that Gothic art was born of the cold and 'rude' landscapes of northern Europe, thus making it particularly suited to the wilderness environs of a place such as Atlantic Canada.[136] Of more immediate concern to Feild was the fact that Scott's design could be built in separate sections: the nave first, with the remainder to follow when further funds became available.

The Scottish architect William Hay (1818–1888) was appointed clerk of works, and set sail for St John's in April

Top 82 Perspective drawing of G. G. Scott's final design for the cathedral of St John the Baptist, St John's, Newfoundland, from the *Illustrated London News* (1849).

Bottom 83 Plan of the cathedral of St John the Baptist, St John's, from *Building News* (1885). The walls in black indicate the extent of construction up to the building's consecration in 1850, when the east end wall comprised a temporary timber structure; a north doorway with a porch was later added. The eastern part of the building was completed by G. G. Scott Jr between 1880 and 1885.

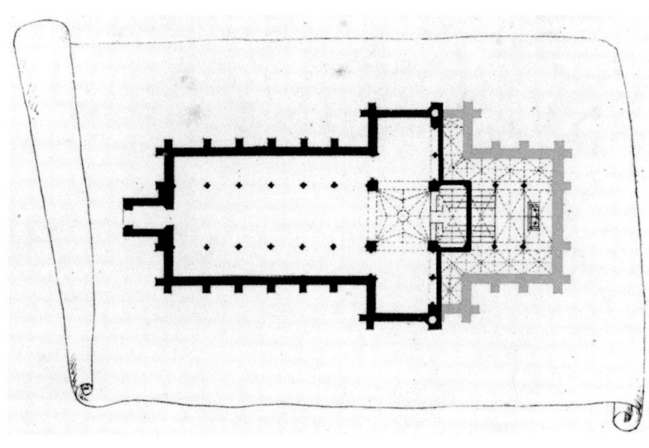

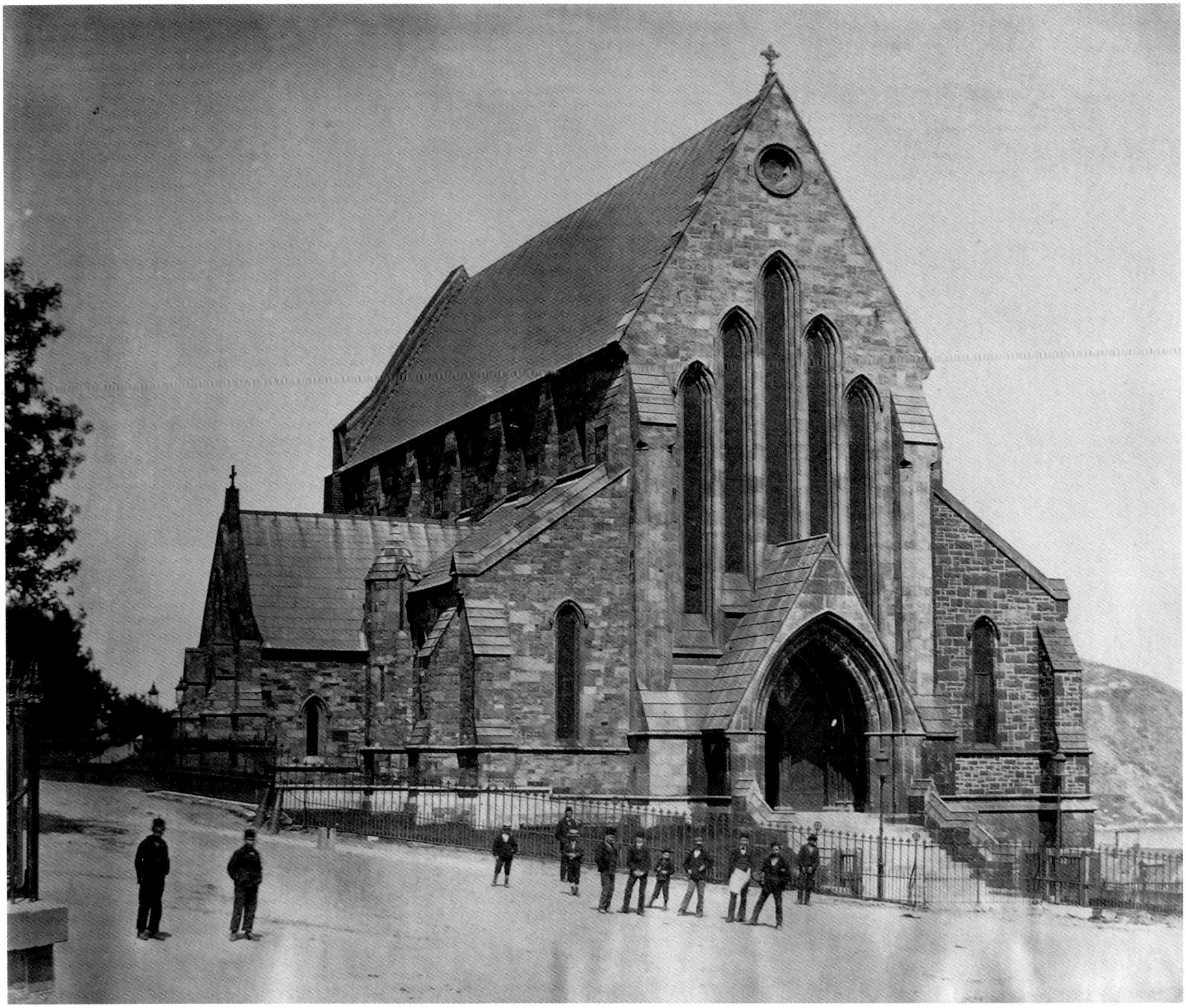

84 The cathedral of St John the Baptist, St John's, as it appeared before work began on completing the east end, under the direction of G. G. Scott Jr, in the 1880s.

1847.[137] Hay worked steadily on the cathedral until the nave was completed, oftentimes in the face of considerable difficulty.[138] This part of the building was constructed using a greyish sandstone from nearby Kelly's Island, with ready-worked dressings of Giffnook stone, sent from Britain.[139] The completed nave was consecrated and opened for divine service on 21 September 1850 (figs 84 and 85). Although the building was plain, *The Ecclesiologist* was willing to acknowledge that, on 'an island the most inhospitable upon which the Caucasian race has permanently settled' – St John's – 'by its durability and solid size, as well as by its unmistakable English and authenticated character, [it] will . . . fully and very credibly represent our Church in one of the most cheerless of its seats'.[140] The choice of the term 'cheerless' turned out to be rather inauspicious. The transepts and choir were

85 The north nave arcade of the cathedral of St John the Baptist, St John's (1847–1905), as it appears today.

completed between 1880 and 1885 under the direction of G. G. Scott Jr, but less than seven years later, in July 1892, fire swept through St John's once again, leaving the cathedral severely damaged. It was not fully restored and completed until 1905.

Ten years would elapse before Scott was given the opportunity to design another colonial cathedral, at which point two commissions came almost simultaneously. The first of these was the cathedral of St Michael and St George in Grahamstown, South Africa (fig. 86). Like St John's, Newfoundland, the commencement of this building predated Scott's involvement. The initial idea was to make the existing church of St George more 'cathedral like' by simply adding a new and more imposing tower. The design for this was prepared in late July 1860 by a local architect, Joseph Flashman. The cornerstone of what was known as

86 West front tower and spire (the Alfred Tower) of the cathedral of St Michael and St George, Grahamstown, South Africa (1861–1912), designed by G. G. Scott and J. O. Scott.

the Alfred Tower was laid the following month (9 August) by Prince Alfred himself, while on tour in South Africa. It was some time after this, in July 1861, that Scott was approached by the bishop of Grahamstown, Henry Cotterill (1812–1886), to 'remodel' the entire building, incorporating Flashman's tower.[141] Scott seems to have accepted the commission 'pro Deo', sending plans to Grahamstown at some time after August 1861 (figs 87 and 88).[142]

The existing church of St George had raised the hackles of Anglican clergy ever since the diocese of Grahamstown was erected in 1853. For the newly arrived bishop, John Armstrong (1813–1856) (fig. 89), St George's was an abomination. As mentioned, Armstrong was a close colleague of Medley's in Exeter. He was also an accomplished ecclesiologist and, like Medley, keen to apply his knowledge. He criticised St George's for being 'plain and uninteresting in the extreme' and, although many more immediate and pressing concerns claimed his attention, hoped that he might one day raise 'a better and more worthy structure' (fig. 91).[143] His chaplain, Nathaniel Merriman (1809–1892) (see fig. 205), another enthusiastic ecclesiologist, had done his best to make the interior of St George's churchlike and 'as comely as possible'.[144]

Although the rebuilding campaign was not formally initiated until 1860, there is evidence to suggest that Armstrong had been considering such an endeavour as early as 1855. A sketch exists in one of his journals labelled 'Vision for a Cathedral' showing a single-cell, Perpendicular-style structure, close in form and scale to a college chapel (fig. 90).[145] It is difficult to know whether or not this sketch actually represented Armstrong's idea of a cathedral for Grahamstown, as there is no indication that it was developed any further. It is possible that it signified nothing more than the type of building he might have expected under the circumstances. Given that magnitude was no prerequisite for a cathedral church, Armstrong may have been considering a similar approach to Selwyn's by erecting first the chancel end of what would eventually become a much larger and more commodious structure.[146]

Owing to difficulties with the site, building work on the cathedral did not commence until 1876.[147] In the meantime Armstrong had died (1856). Merriman, now bishop, was nevertheless determined to raise a new and more substantial structure, worthy of Armstrong's original vision for a building proclaiming itself 'the heart and centre' of the diocese.[148] As very little documentary evidence concerning the project survives, it is difficult to ascertain the precise course of events. What is clear, however, is that Scott did not incorporate Flashman's tower into his own design. Instead, he prepared an entirely new set of drawings. The formal characteristics of this new design also betray Scott's thinking on colonial cathedrals, namely that a simple but no less dignified rendition of the Early English style was most applicable. As we have seen, he pursued this line of

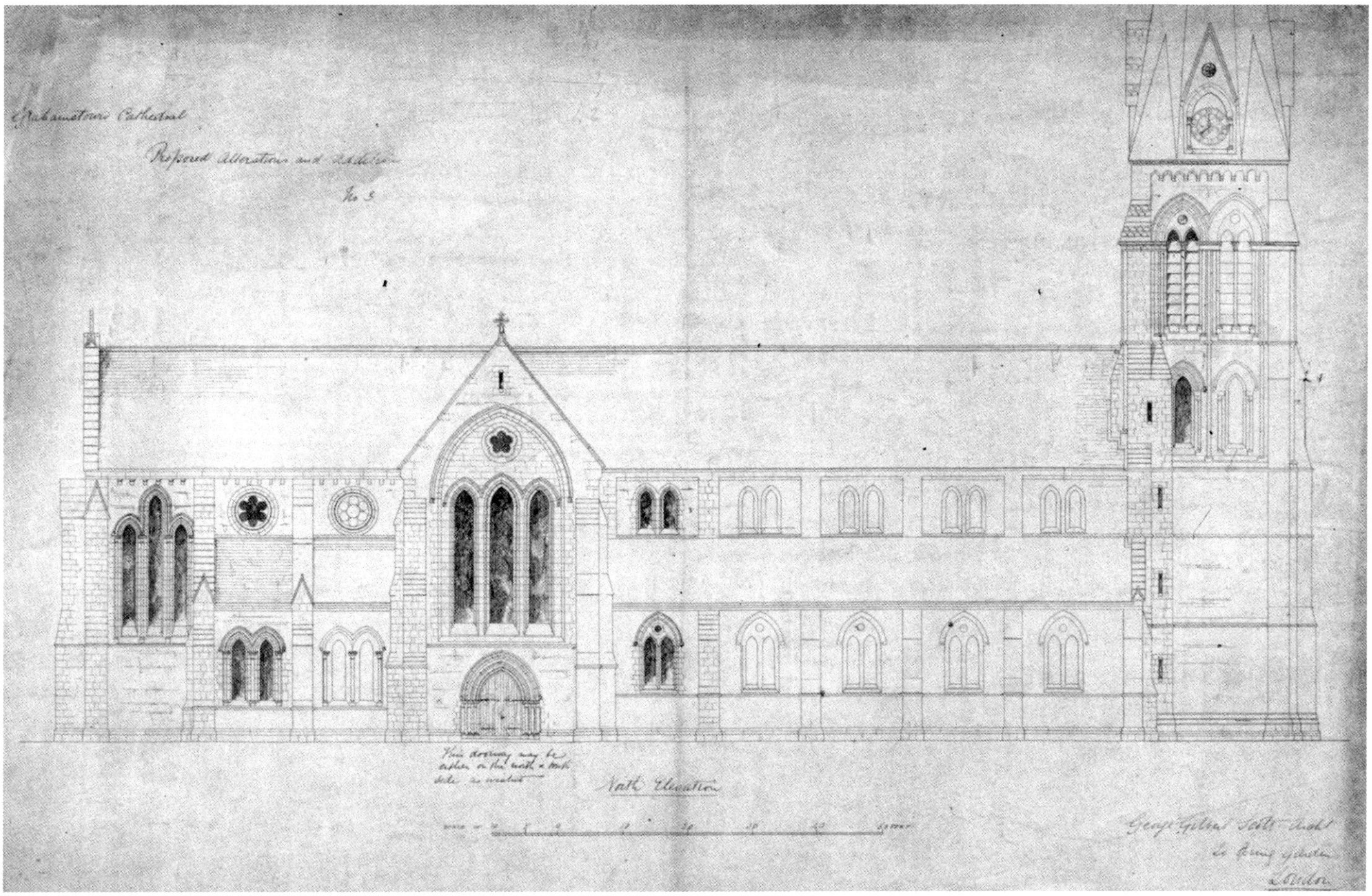

87 G. G. Scott's original north elevation drawing for the cathedral of St Michael and St George, Grahamstown, *c.*1861 (RIBA Drawings Collection, Victoria and Albert Museum, London).

88 G. G. Scott's original plan for the cathedral of St Michael and St George, Grahamstown, *c.*1861 (RIBA Drawings Collection, Victoria and Albert Museum, London).

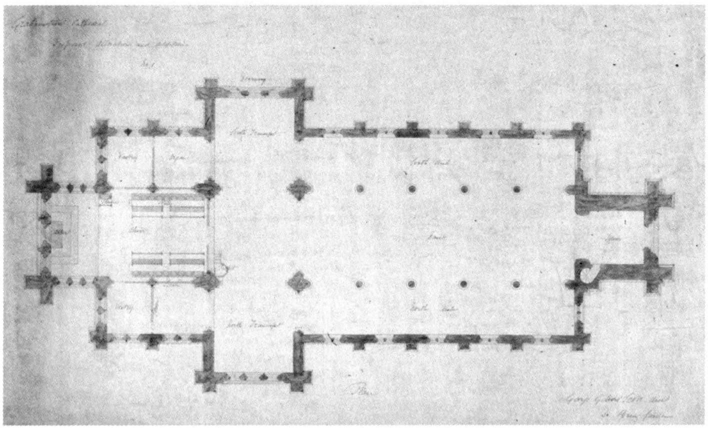

reasoning at Newfoundland. He had also claimed some years earlier that the Early English was not only a 'pure' style but one that was readily adaptable to 'the varied circumstances of the British colonies'.[149] Thus, a simple, cost-effective, yet recognisably 'English' style was evidently perceived as ideal for a rugged frontier environment such as the Eastern Cape.

Looking at the design, one can see that Scott was keen to emphasise the building's 'cathedral character'. The bold, uncomplicated lines impart a sense of grandeur that belies the building's comparatively modest scale. Although *The Ecclesiologist* would not have appreciated the single west-end tower, the plan is straightforward, compact, and cathedral-like in its arrangement, incorporating the 'cross-plan' identified by Scott as the *sine qua non* of English cathedrals. In many ways, Grahamstown cathedral is the embodiment of Scott's notion that a colonial cathedral ought to be no more than a parish church of superior dignity. Indeed, it is instructive to compare this design with one of his initial

89 Portrait of John Armstrong (1813–1856), first bishop of Grahamstown, from T. T. Carter, *A Memoir of John Armstrong* (1857).

sketches for St John's, Newfoundland, fifteen years earlier. Was Grahamstown the fulfilment of this original vision for a cathedral in the colonies (fig. 92)?

In the event, the cathedral was not built exactly to Scott's original plan. An 'improved' design based on a duplicate set of Scott's original drawings was produced and sent to Grahamstown in July 1874.[150] At first only the tower was erected (completed 1879). As with St John's, the project was taken over by one of Scott's sons after his death in 1878, in this case John Oldrid Scott (1841–1913). Drawings for the nave and choir were sent in 1890 and 1906 respectively, and the cathedral opened for service in August 1912.[151]

Scott's third colonial cathedral, the commission for which came at around the same time as Grahamstown, was that at Christchurch, New Zealand (figs 93 and 94). Although Scott was approached to design a cathedral for the settlement of Canterbury as early as August 1858, he did not produce his first set of drawings until February 1862.[152] A bitter and protracted process concerning the appointment of a bishop, along with a degree of dithering on the part of the Church authorities over the sort of building required, caused significant delays. This is not surprising when one considers the problems that plagued the early development of Christchurch as a colony.

Ever since the Canterbury Settlement in New Zealand was established in 1850, it had failed to live up to expectations. According to its foundation document, the settlement's objective had been to 'send out a colony, to be composed entirely of members of our own Church, accompanied by an adequate supply of Clergy, with all the appliances requisite for carrying out her discipline and ordinances'.[153] The reasoning for this was simple enough. It was argued that English colonisation to date had been only a half-hearted affair. Without all the rights and privileges of English society transferred, Britain's colonies presented 'only a defaced and caricatured resemblance to . . . the parent state'.[154] These concerns, of course, echoed those stated at the inauguration of the CBF a decade earlier (see p. 4). How could men of 'station and character, of cultivation and refinement' be expected to migrate to such places, it was suggested, if the most basic provisions respecting the

90 Ink sketch by Bishop Armstrong, 'Vision for a Cathedral', 1855 (Bodleian Library, Oxford).

91 The 'old' church of St George, Grahamstown (1824–30), before its reconstruction.

92 One of G. G. Scott's early sketch designs for the cathedral of St John the Baptist, St John's, Newfoundland, 1847 (Bodleian Library, Oxford).

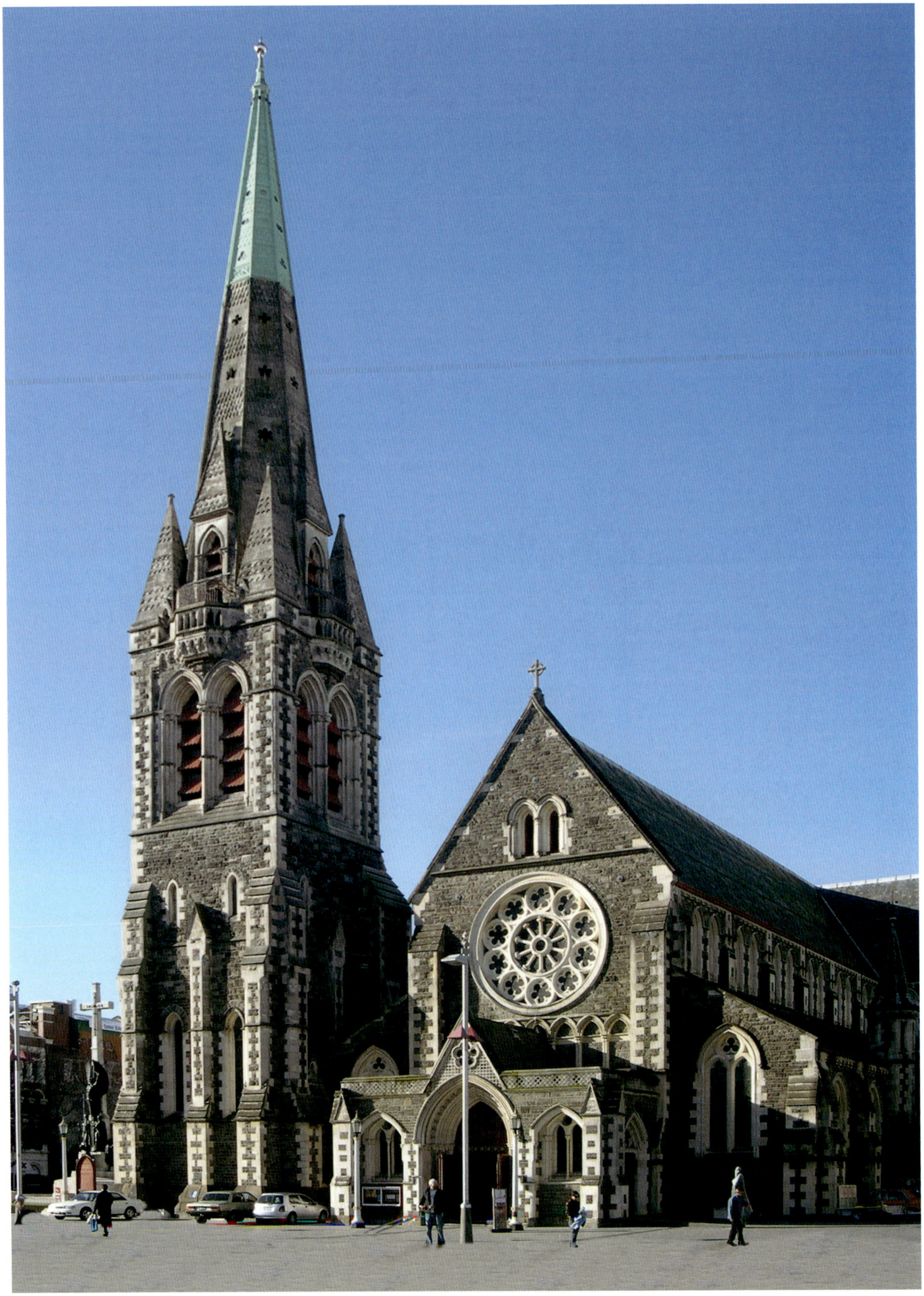

93 Christ Church cathedral, Christchurch, New Zealand (1862–1904), by G. G. Scott and B. W. Mountfort.

94 Interior of Christ Church cathedral (1862–1904), looking east down the nave (*c.*1890).

national Church were inadequate or non-existent? Many claimed that the time had now arrived in Britain's long history of colonisation to establish fully and systematically a purely Anglican colony. At the heart (quite literally, as Edward Jollie's original map shows) of this 'establishment' would necessarily reside a cathedral. Only the most accomplished of architects would do for such a visionary undertaking, and G. G. Scott was quickly fingered – he was, after all, as W. E. Gladstone affirmed to the settlement's superintendent, J. E. FitzGerald, 'the best ecclesiastical architect in Europe, and therefore the world'.[155]

Despite the initial flurry of support for an Anglican colony in New Zealand, development was slow; nor did the enterprise remain 'pure' as initially intended. The colony's Committee of Management had wished to restrict the sale of land to 'bona-fide' English churchmen, but the Colonial Office refused.[156] The settlement did remain predominantly Anglican, but by the mid-1850s other denominations had infiltrated, comprising approximately 30 per cent of its population. Thus, by the time Bishop Henry John Chitty Harper (1804–1893) arrived in 1856, he entered upon a scene that was anything but a bustling Anglican utopia in the South Seas. Rather, he encountered a rough and somewhat ramshackle pioneer village of a few thousand people.[157] With the principal church of the settlement considered by many as nothing more than a 'miserable

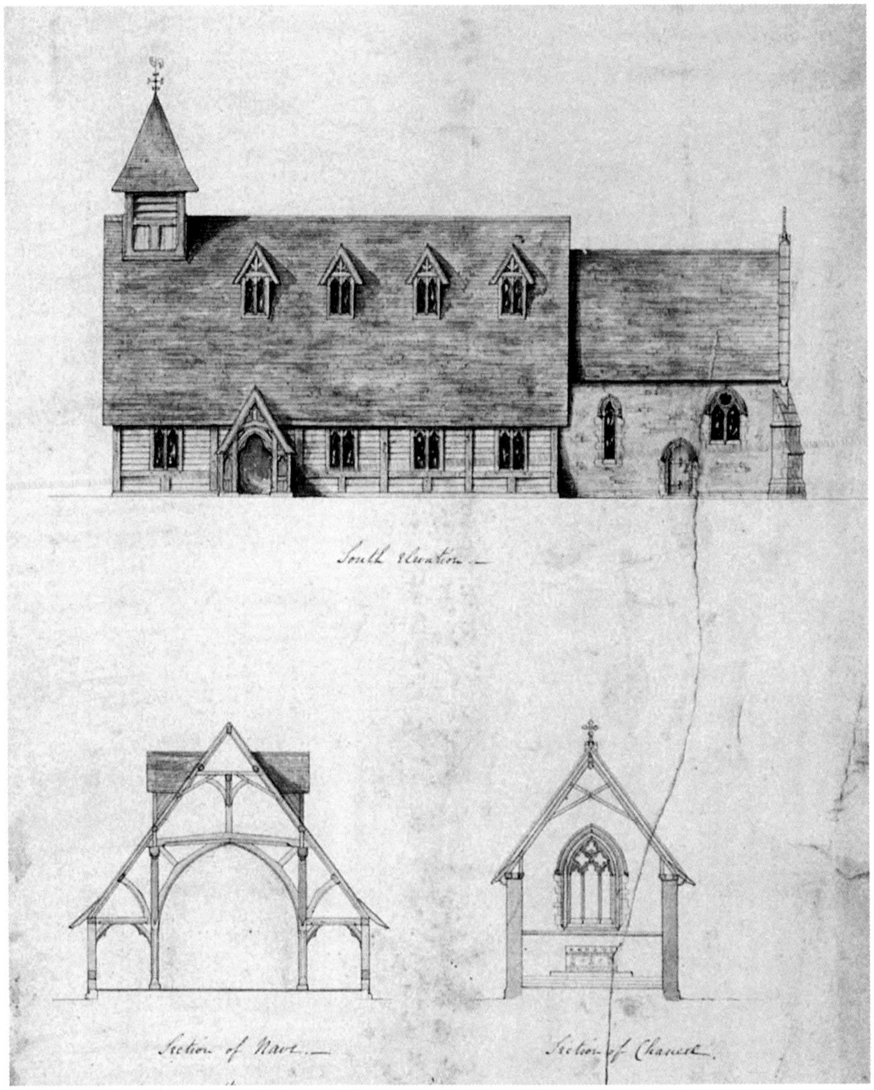

95 G. G. Scott's unexecuted design for a church with timber nave and stone chancel for Christchurch, New Zealand, *c.*1850 (Christchurch Anglican Diocesan Archive).

barrack', Harper made it his priority to erect a more fitting and worthy structure. A public meeting of members of the Church of England, held at Christchurch in October 1862, confirmed the need for such a building.[158] The Cathedral Commission, established shortly afterwards, reported that the 'purposes' of a cathedral in such a colony were manifold, not least being its role as the chief church of the diocese, 'where the Bishop's cathedra or chair is placed, and therefore representing a branch of the great Christian Society in its complete organisation'.[159] In this sense, the cathedral idea was elevated in the minds of the citizens of Christchurch to a status as nothing less than 'a perpetual and conspicuous witness' to Christian holiness and its peculiar English incarnation.

Scott was involved at the Canterbury Settlement before his work on the cathedral. He had designed a small timber church with stone chancel for Christchurch some time around 1850, the plans for which were never executed (fig. 95). He was therefore acquainted with the particular demands of the New Zealand context. But the cathedral was on an all together more imposing scale. His first scheme is notable for its integrated hybrid structure, combining an internal roof and arcade of timber with an external cladding of stone (figs 96 and 97). As Ian Lochhead has

96 Detail drawings of the elevation and longitudinal section of Scott's original design for Christ Church cathedral, illustrating the timber construction elements, 1862 (Christchurch Anglican Diocesan Archive).

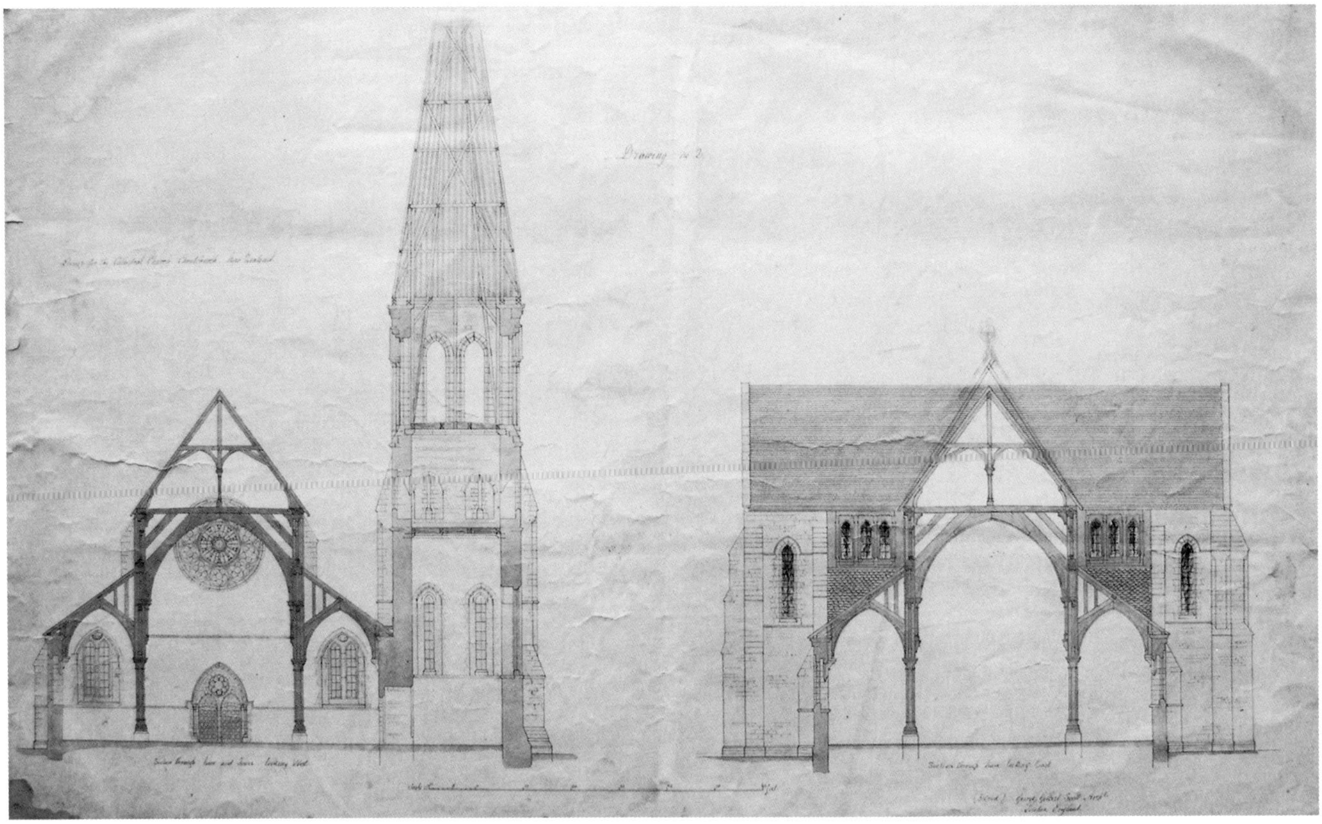

97 East and west cross-section drawings of G. G. Scott's original design for Christ Church cathedral, showing timber arcade, clerestory, and roof construction, 1862 (Christchurch Anglican Diocesan Archive).

observed, the novelty of Scott's solution was the way it imparted a necessary degree of permanence and dignity through its stone exterior, while taking advantage of the lightness and flexibility of timber.[160] FitzGerald, who had visited Scott's office to peruse the drawings during their development, immediately recognised the benefit of the scheme to New Zealand. Not only did it respond to local circumstances with respect to materials, but 'a large oak framing would . . . be so strong that in an earthquake it would stand if the walls were shaken'.[161] As we have seen, this was a concern that dates back to Selwyn's experiments in the mid-1840s (see pp. 46–56).

The hybrid concept was most probably inspired by a design produced by Henry Woodyer several years earlier for the Rev. Charles Abraham, a close friend of Selwyn's. *The Ecclesiologist* reported that Woodyer's design was 'ingeniously carried out', incorporating for its walls 'rubble stone, no dressed work at all being required[,] with internal arcades and the tracery to all the windows of wood'.[162] Other sources included the magnificent tithe barns in England that had survived from the middle ages, such as that at Harmondsworth, which Scott knew well. There is little doubt that the great oak frames that supported these barns provided a precedent for Scott.[163] These sources and concerns, it may be suggested, place Scott's scheme in a genealogy of ideas, the pedigree of which can be traced back to Selwyn's original vision for an ecclesiastical architecture in New Zealand. Indeed, in many respects, it may be seen as representing the ultimate expression of that vision.[164]

Unfortunately, the scheme was short-lived. Considerable discussion arose as to whether it would not be more prudent to begin with a less substantial, temporary structure. Moreover, if Scott's scheme was to be adopted, then it was suggested by some that it ought to be carried out entirely in stone. Those in favour of a stone structure included the bishop himself. Scott was therefore asked to prepare an alternative set of drawings (fig. 98). Although the idea of a permanent, full-scale cathedral built partly in

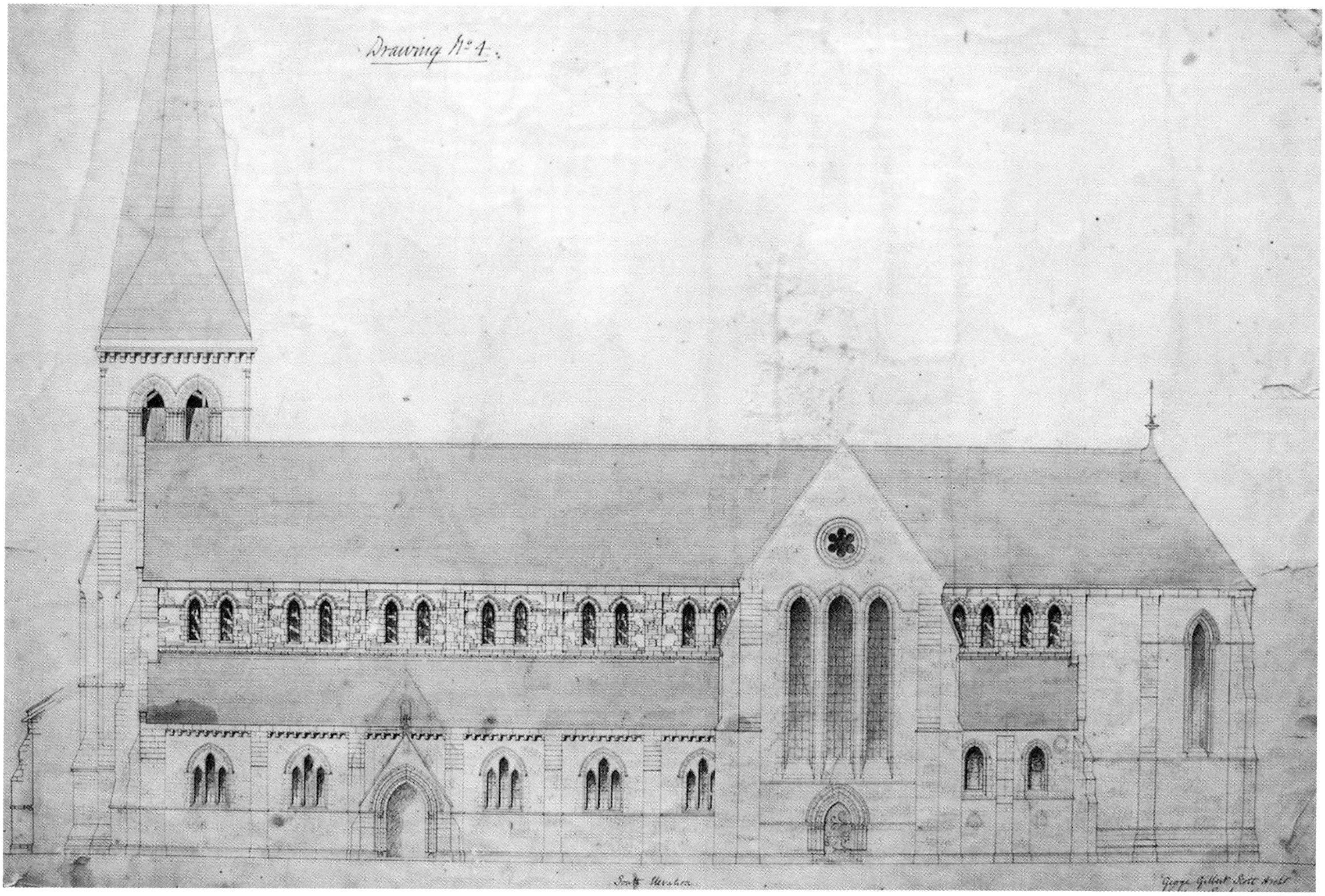

98 South elevation drawing of Scott's second design, in stone, for Christ Church cathedral, 1863 (Christchurch Anglican Diocesan Archive).

timber was no doubt anathema to Harper and his associates, the reason given for abandoning the hybrid scheme was that a suitable supply of building stone had recently been discovered near Christchurch.[165] Moreover, the huge kauri logs required for the arcade columns would have to be shipped from Auckland at considerable expense, thus undermining the argument of economic expediency.

But these were not the only problems threatening the cathedral's realisation. Further delays were caused over the appointment of a superintending architect. Despite Scott's insisting that a 'gentleman on the spot', namely Benjamin Mountfort, would make the best clerk of works, the Cathedral Commission, motivated by no small amount of colonial prejudice, were determined to appoint a 'professional' from England.[166] The commission eventually got its way, and Robert Speechley, a former assistant to William Slater, arrived at Christchurch on 6 September 1864. Not wishing to let the matter rest, *The Press* newspaper (a supporter of Mountfort) observed that Speechley would no doubt be '*speechless* with surprise' to know that he had come to the other side of the world to 'advise on a matter on which the whole population are much better judges than him'.[167] The foundation stone for the cathedral was finally laid on 16 December 1864 – six years after the idea had first been mooted, and fourteen years after the arrival of the first Canterbury settlers.

Architecturally, Scott's design bears comparison with his earlier two efforts. As with Newfoundland and South

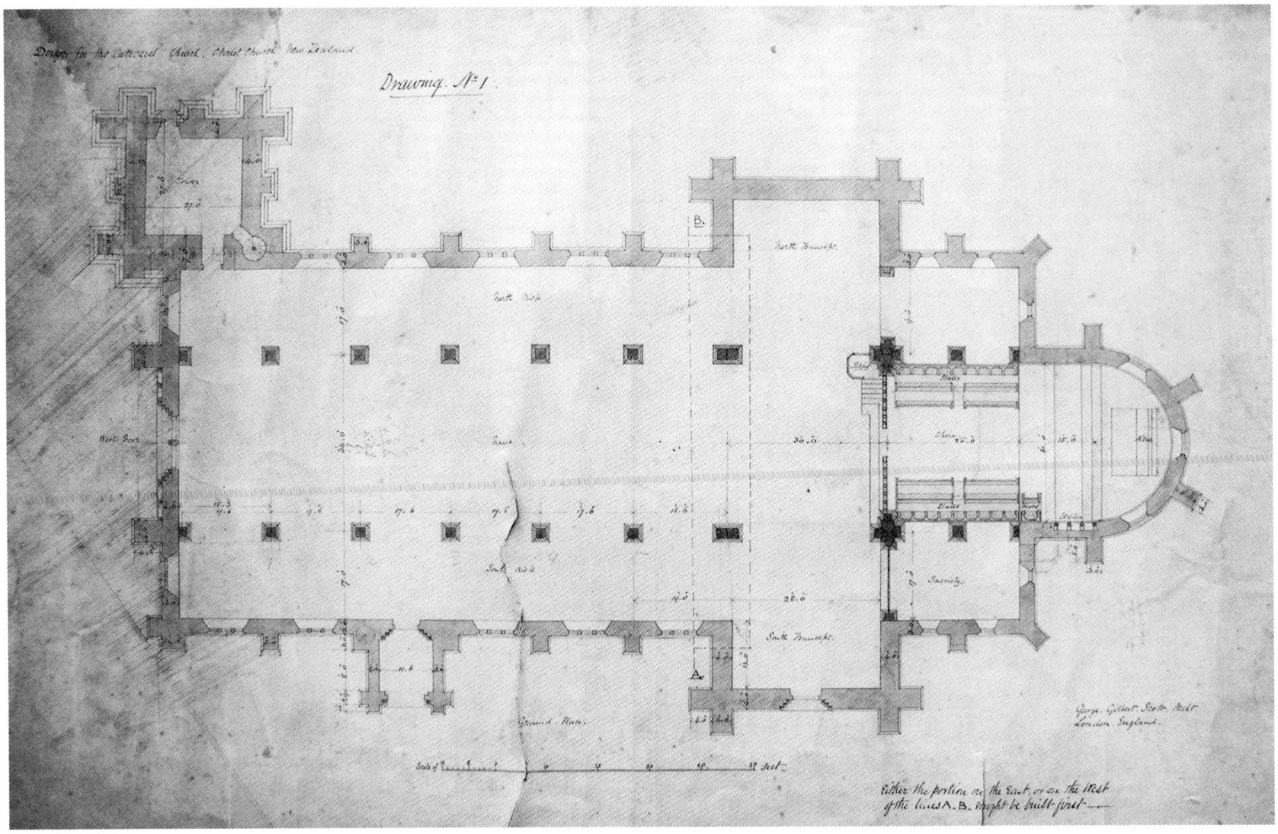

99 Plan of Scott's second design, in stone, for Christ Church cathedral, 1863 (Christchurch Anglican Diocesan Archive).

Africa, we see a rather simple and severe rendition of the Early English style. The plan is nearly identical with that at Grahamstown, save for the extra bay, apsidal choir and semi-detached west-end tower (fig. 99). It also incorporates the all important 'cross-plan'. The tower has an impressive splayed-foot spire which emerges from the roofline like a great crystalline shard, recalling Butterfield's attempts at Fredericton and, later, at All Saints', Margaret Street (1849–59). Although, externally, there is the same degree of quiet strength in the massing of forms, a small number of continental elements have crept into the design, such as the large west-end rose window and the apsidal arrangement of the choir (fig. 100). However, these are neatly constrained within an articulation of forms and spaces that remains recognisably 'English'.

Work on the cathedral progressed slowly. By the time Speechley left for Australia in 1868 (taking the plans with him and all but copying them for the newly proposed cathedral in Melbourne, 1869), only the foundations had been laid.[168] Building activity stalled until the commission handed the superintendence of the project to Mountfort, officially appointing him architect in August 1873. After a brief but failed attempt at reviving the hybrid scheme, work progressed steadily on a stone building.[169] Although Scott, looking back on his experience at Newfoundland, advised on erecting the east end first, efforts were concentrated on raising the nave.[170] By 1880 the whole was virtually complete (excepting the choir) and the cathedral was consecrated the following year on 1 November 1881. Mountfort introduced a number of minor alterations, in particular a remodelling of the spire, but the whole remained largely faithful to Scott's original design.[171]

Seen together, Scott's colonial cathedrals appear very much like variations on a theme. His Newfoundland experience taught him early on that conditions (pecuniary and environmental) in the colonies were such that only a limited range of formal options was available to an architect preparing plans for large-scale buildings, especially within the parameters of 'correct' ecclesiastical design. It would be wrong to suggest that Scott operated according to a formula,

100 Exterior of Christ Church cathedral (1862–1904) from the south-east, showing the apsidal arrangement of the east end.

but it does seem that by the late 1840s he had resolved in his own mind what a colonial cathedral ought to be. Because of this, his designs for colonial cathedrals have a certain confident deliberation about them: consistent and distinctive in their solemn yet massive dignity. Even at Holy Trinity, Shanghai (1868–70) – his only other cathedral outside the British Isles – we see the same basic format, only this time in a much more dramatic 'Ruskinian' style. Nevertheless, it is important to note that the basis of Scott's aesthetic was as much intellectual as it was practical, a process in which he clearly weighed up the various factors involved in each case. His writings on the subject – both public and private – demonstrate that he was indeed concerned with understanding what it actually meant to design a church in the colonies, rather than merely regurgitating his English work for a foreign context. Although Scott no doubt saw each of these buildings as an experiment in its own way, that did not prevent him from appreciating them as a species of what he called 'our architecture' abroad. In this respect he has made a significant contribution to our perception of cathedral architecture in the colonies.[172]

Progressing the Cathedral Idea: Development and Refinement in the 1860s

There are numerous other cathedrals in Britain's empire that one could point to in a study such as this.[173] The prevalence of cathedral churches – big and small – increased steadily from about the mid-1850s, as further dioceses were erected and as the colonial world became more populated, organised and wealthy. For example, a number of cathedrals were built in tropical and semi-tropical areas, including those by William Slater (Honolulu), R. C. Carpenter (Colombo), William Hay (Bermuda), William Emerson (Allahabad) and Frederick Thatcher (Wellington). These buildings are particularly interesting for their adaptation to climatic conditions, and will be discussed separately in Chapter 3. Of the remainder, several warrant closer attention. These are the ones that either represent the full flowering of a particular stylistic phase in the development of ecclesiology, or embody the significant aesthetic transformations that ecclesiastical architecture underwent during the High Victorian period.

Perhaps the greatest exponent of the latter 'High' phase of Victorian architecture is William Butterfield (1814–1900). As an architect, Butterfield was among the favoured few of the Cambridge Camden Society. His early churches, such as those at Coalpit Heath, near Bristol (1844–6), and Sessay, Yorkshire (1847–8), along with his efforts in preparing designs for *Instrumenta Ecclesiastica*, had ensured his reliability in the eyes of ecclesiologists. His second design for St Peter's cathedral, Adelaide (1868), would have been – if executed as planned – one of the most original and spectacular cathedrals built anywhere in the Anglican world during the nineteenth century. His involvement with the project dated back as far as 1847, when he prepared a set of plans for Bishop Short to take to Australia. These plans were exhibited at a meeting of the Ecclesiological Society, the following description of which appeared in *The Ecclesiologist* in December that year:

> It is of extremely plain design, and in dimensions not larger than a moderately sized parish church: but it has a very peculiar character. Although cruciform, the transepts do not extend beyond the outer walls of the aisles; the choir in its north wall exhibits two high three-light windows, with tracery of the simplest geometrical kind . . . . At the intersection of the cross is a square tower, very low and broad, with but one stage above the gables of the roofs . . . . The tower is surmounted by a low embattlement, within which is a pyramidal capping.

Considering the aesthetic appeal of the design, it was added: 'Nothing could be more severe than this design, and yet it has a character of its own which it is perhaps impossible to describe: it has just that individuality which we admire in our ancient churches. The building, although plain to excess and of a material so mean as brick, will be religious and imposing from its unusual height and marked outline.'[174]

As discussed in Chapter 1, colonial clergymen had long been requesting 'simple' church designs, and Butterfield did not disappoint in this regard. According to Beresford Hope, the severity of his design was calculated specifically to demonstrate at how cheap a rate the 'cathedral character' might be obtained in a colonial church.[175] The only real problem was the proposed use of brick, which was a material barely acceptable to serious ecclesiologists at the time. Unfortunately, these plans no longer survive. We get some idea of what the building may have looked like, however, by considering Butterfield's second design, which dates from 1868. In preparing the drawings for this design, Butterfield produced at least two versions of the same building, one less elaborate than the other. The plainer of these was probably a developed version of his 1847 design, with the addition of twin western towers and the substitution of an octagonal lantern for the original crossing tower (fig. 101). It was also more complex in plan, with the introduction of a second set of transepts *à la* Salisbury. It was over the crossing of these minor transepts that the lantern sat (fig. 102).

Although the source for the original 1847 design is not known, one cannot help but suppose the 1868 design to have been influenced by the twelfth-century minster at

Southwell in Nottinghamshire.[176] If one were looking in England for an appropriately robust model for a colonial cathedral, then this was it.[177] There were also Butterfield's own buildings, such as his earlier design for St Ninian's cathedral in Perth, Scotland (1847–50), and the parish church of St Cross, Clayton, near Manchester (1862–6) (fig. 103). Whatever the exact source for Adelaide, the result is

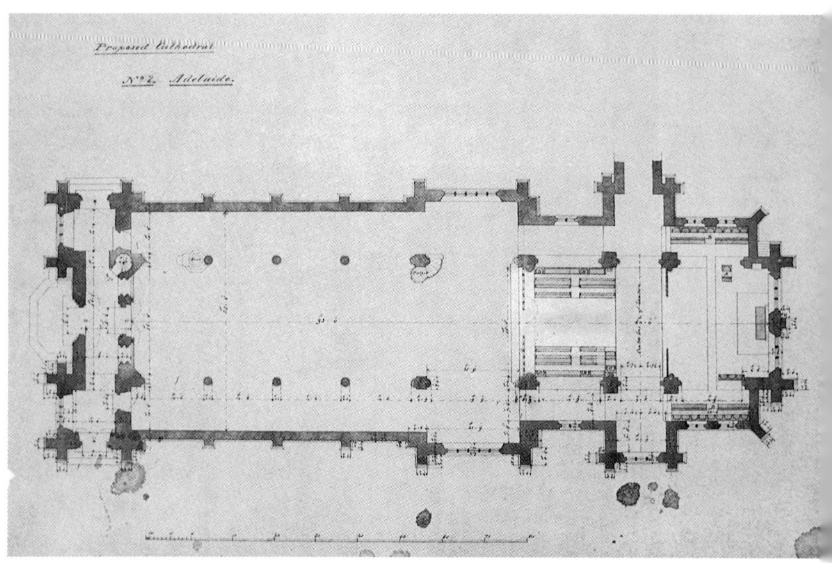

Top 101 Perspective drawing of the plainer of William Butterfield's two versions of his second design for St Peter's cathedral, Adelaide, 1868 (State Library of South Australia, Adelaide).

Bottom 102 Plan of Butterfield's second design for St Peter's cathedral, Adelaide, showing the double transept arrangement, 1868 (Archive, Woods Bagot Architects, Adelaide).

103 The church of St Cross, Clayton, near Manchester (1862–6), by William Butterfield.

a powerful and dynamic ensemble of forms, rising sheer like an ancient striated butte from some desert plateau. The lower sections of the building especially, composed of panels of windowless brickwork, are formidable in their fortress-like solidity. Indeed, the whole is overwhelmingly defensive in its appearance, no doubt calculated to combat the harsh conditions of the Australian climate. The other, more elaborate version of the design was very similar, except for the conventional Decorated window tracery (particularly in the clerestory), canopied buttresses and the substitution of gabled spires (fig. 104). This was an extreme building for extreme conditions, capturing the primitive simplicity of the early church through what J. Mordaunt Crook has called 'the sublime abstraction of reductive geometry'.[178]

The most obvious and spectacular deviation from the original 1847 design was the wholesale introduction of banded polychrome brickwork. In this respect, Butterfield's design for Adelaide cathedral is a superb example of the aesthetic transformations that characterised ecclesiastical architecture in Britain during the early 1850s, especially within High Church Anglican circles. Butterfield's very own All Saints', Margaret Street (1849–59), was the first site of this great experiment, setting the tone for years to come with its rich, varied and progressive architectural vocabulary. Moreover, the call of Benjamin Webb, John Ruskin and G. E. Street for British architects to lift their eyes to the spectacular but no less 'true' forms of continental Europe, in particular the medieval buildings of Spain, Belgium and Italy, suddenly made brick an acceptable, even desirable, material.[179] Indeed, commenting on Butterfield's work in 1852, Street was able to appreciate the full 'extent to which brick may be used, and the variety of colour of which it is susceptible', leading to a

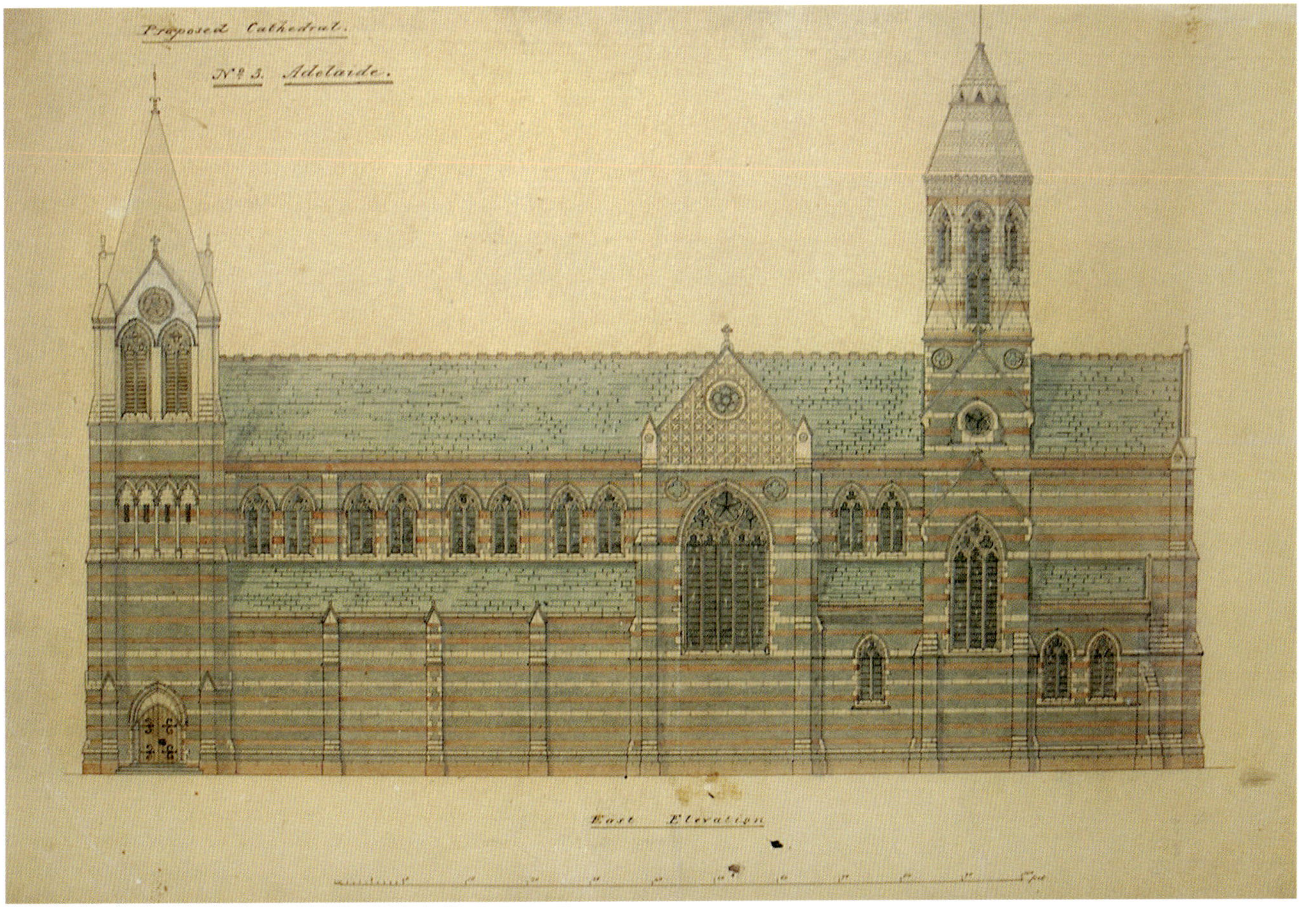

104 East elevation (liturgical south) of Butterfield's second design for St Peter's cathedral, Adelaide, showing an alternative scheme for spires and fenestration, 1868 (Archive, Woods Bagot Architects, Adelaide).

new kind of invention in English architecture.[180] This was the 'possibility of developement [*sic*]'.

The theory of 'developement' was central to the evolution of what is now referred to as High Victorian architecture, and has a rather complex history, incorporating aspects of theology, the arts, liberal Anglicanism and natural science, including geology and the theory of evolution. It was a notion that militated against superficial eclecticism in favour of a deeper, more synthetic, approach to architectural design. As an idea, it reached those interested in architecture via Anglican theology, in particular the ideas of W. G. Ward and J. H. Newman.[181] Among the first to be affected by its rumblings was E. A. Freeman (1823–1892), a student (then fellow) at Trinity College, Oxford, during the early 1840s. Freeman, who was also a leading light of the Oxford Architectural Society, had been influenced, while an undergraduate, by Newman's pronouncements on the subject of doctrinal development. He had also been inspired by notions of historical 'unity', which he had picked up from lectures given by the regius professor of history, the Rev. Thomas Arnold (1794–1842). Synthesising these different but related strands of thought, Freeman was able to devise a historical concept of architecture that presented formal change over time as a teleological process of evolution from lower to higher forms based on the civilisational attainment of any given society or culture – a theory which he later expounded in full in his first book *A History of Architecture* (1849).[182]

As Freeman's concept began to be publicised and debated in the pages of *The Ecclesiologist* and the *Rules and Proceedings*, it was picked up by Beresford Hope, who offered his own version of it, which he later called 'progression by eclecticism'.[183] Although the Camden Society formally rejected Freeman's theories, there is little doubt that they had an effect in shifting its hard-line stance on 'correct' ecclesiological design during the mid-1840s.[184] Picking up so many threads central to the Victorian world-view, the theory of 'developement' in architecture soon acquired other associations, especially those based on insights emanating from the rapidly advancing discipline of natural science.

As Michael Hall has shown, this associated interest in the natural world had a significant impact on the aesthetic transformation of religious (especially Anglican) architecture during this period. With the publication of Charles Lyell's *Principles of Geology* (1830–3), William Buckland's *Geology and Mineralogy Considered with Reference to Natural Theology* (1836), and Robert Chambers's *Vestiges of Creation* (1844), British architects began considering how architecture – especially religious architecture – might reflect this new understanding of the world.[185] In *The Stones of Venice* (1851–3) Ruskin, too, had recommended the study of geology to architects, evident in his concept of the 'wall-veil' with its reliance on geological metaphor. The 'introduction of horizontal bands of colour' was valuable, Ruskin claimed, because it suggested 'the natural courses of rocks and beds of the earth itself'.[186] Was this not indicative of the process by which God, the 'great Builder', worked?

Thus, theories concerning 'developed' architecture were more about the expression of ingrained or 'genetic' traits, so to speak, rather than the mere grafting of superficial elements onto a building according to need or context. This had obvious implications for colonial ecclesiology in the sense that colonial church architecture, in many instances, was compelled to adapt by mutation. This reality both affected and transformed thinking on ecclesiology in Britain, forcing the pace of debate and change. As we have already seen, and as will be discussed further below, architects, too, such as G. F. Bodley, William Burges, G. E. Street and William White, used their colonial commissions to experiment in this new developmental mode of design, thus making the evolution of High Victorian church architecture a truly global affair. Benjamin Webb was also a key player in this debate, pushing the limits (along with Beresford Hope) of what actually constituted Anglican ecclesiology. His contribution is discussed in the following chapter.

If there was one architect who understood and embraced these developments in Victorian architecture, it was William Butterfield.[187] However, it seemed that colonial society in Adelaide could not stomach such modern innovations. Although Bishop Short, like his colonial brethren elsewhere, understood the need to plant cathedral institutions as 'symbols' of Church authority,[188] it seems that not even he could tolerate a second-rate material such as brick for so important a building. Despite having visited All Saints', Margaret Street, in 1866 – no doubt the reason behind his recommissioning of Butterfield – he probably realised that so radical a design would fall flat in the antipodes.[189] Paul Thompson has rightly noted that the rejection of Butterfield's polychrome scheme was no doubt influenced by the potential difficulty it posed for raising funds.[190] But Short had his own doubts. Cognisant of the wider evolutionary concepts associated with horizontal banding in modern church architecture, he wryly remarked to Hawkins in 1870: 'I am sorry to say that Butterfield having introduced brick into the design for our Cathedral has occasioned much delay and embarrassment inasmuch as our *primitive* paleozoic country of S. Australia disdains those comparatively modern beds of brick clay in which England rejoices . . . . Happily we have very good stone.'[191]

This wit reveals that no cathedral was possible in Adelaide that did not conform to colonial taste. Short attempted to persuade Butterfield to redesign the building in stone to no avail. He was therefore left with no option but to purchase the plans from Butterfield and engage a local architect, E. J. Woods, to alter the design. The foundation stone for the first part of the cathedral was laid on 29 June 1869. This is the only part of the building that remains faithful to Butterfield's original 1868 scheme, minus the polychrome brickwork (fig. 105). When this section of the building was completed in 1878, work on the remainder was postponed until 1890. At that time the nave was added and the unsympathetic front and apsidal sanctuary tacked on.

Another cathedral design worth mentioning, although it was never built owing partly to a series of misunderstandings, is that by William Burges (1827–1881) for the semi-tropical city of Brisbane, Australia (1860) (figs 106 and 107).[192] This design is somewhat reminiscent of Scott's cathedrals in its stout, almost stunted conformation. However, Brisbane was influenced much more by continental precedent than anything we have discussed so far. In describing the plans, *The Ecclesiologist* observed that they were 'carried out in that solid and massive early French which is his [Burges's] style of predilection'.[193] Like Butterfield, Burges was one of those High Victorian architects

105 Choir and crossing of St Peter's cathedral, Adelaide, as completed in 1878. This was the only part of the cathedral erected largely in accordance with Butterfield's second design, including double transepts but excluding polychrome brickwork.

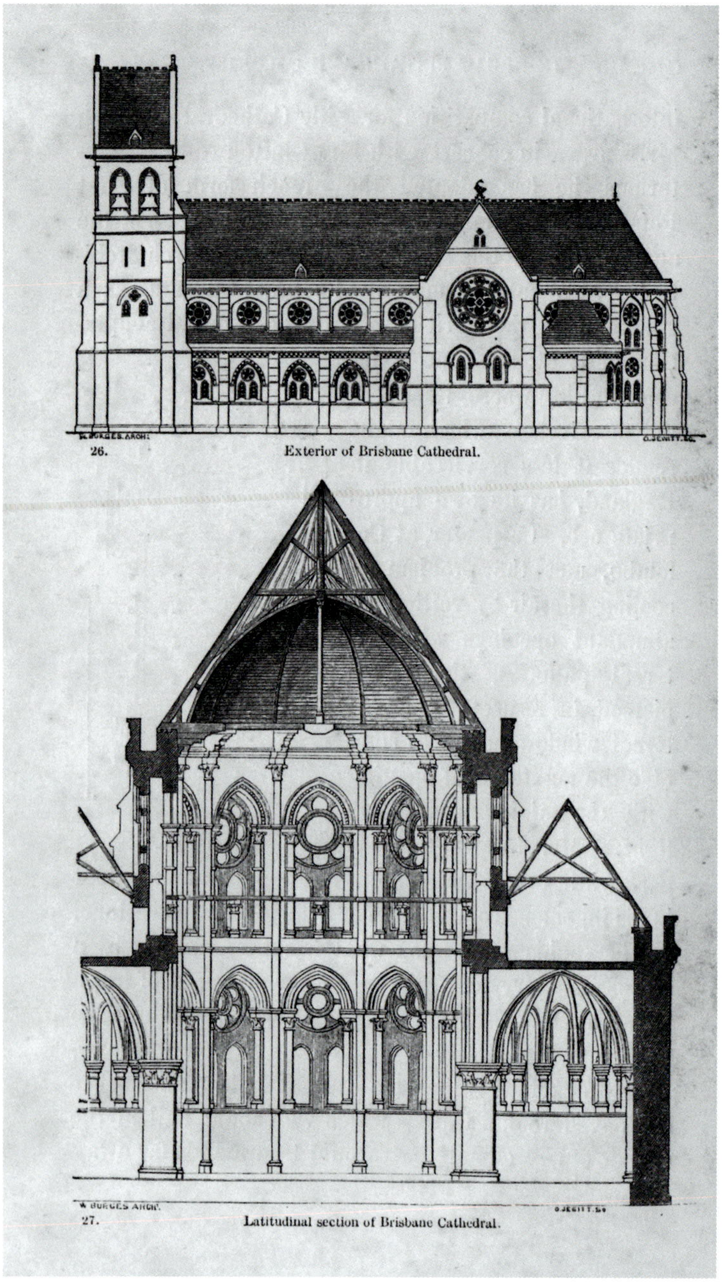

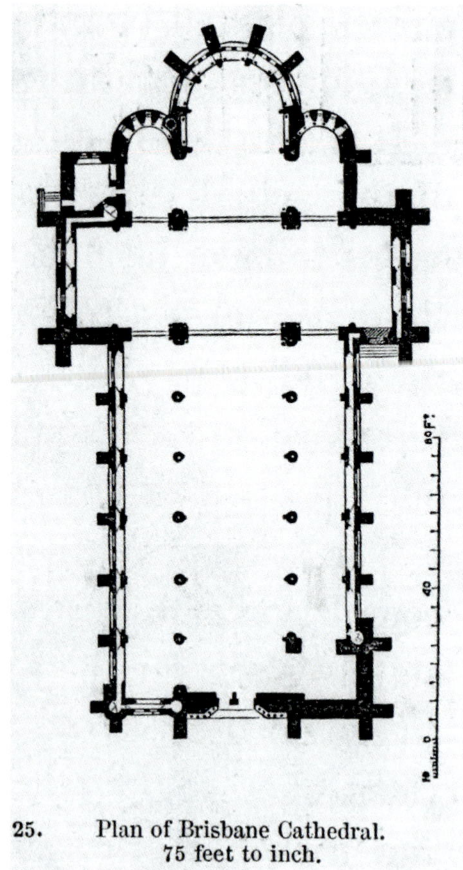

Left 106 Elevation and section drawings of William Burges's unexecuted design for Brisbane cathedral, 1860, from A. J. B. Beresford Hope's *The English Cathedral of the Nineteenth Century* (1861).

Right 107 Plan of William Burges's unexecuted design for Brisbane cathedral, 1860, from A. J. B. Beresford Hope's *The English Cathedral of the Nineteenth Century* (1861).

whose output was distinctive to the point of idiosyncrasy. One of the distinguishing features of his style was the energetic tension he achieved through the combination and compression of bold architectural elements. We see this coming out in his design for Brisbane, with its pronounced buttressing, heavy plate tracery and low saddle-back tower. Internally, too, there is a sense of depth and plasticity to the architecture, which imparts a spatial quality or 'thickness' to the fabric that is almost Michelangelesque in its intensity (fig. 108). In this respect, Brisbane represents that other branch of 'developement' which was concerned not with polychromy but with extending and manipulating the formal vocabulary of English architecture by looking directly across the Channel to France, especially Normandy. This was a movement that imbued English ecclesiology with a certain muscularity through an emphasis on unbroken planar surfaces and simple geometric volumes.[194]

108 Interior perspective of William Burges's design for Brisbane cathedral, looking towards the east end, from *Building News* (1860).

Burges's 'penchant' for early French Gothic, as Beresford Hope described it, achieved its earliest and most notable manifestation in his winning entry for the cathedral competition at Lille (1856; unbuilt), reaching its apogee at St Fin Barre, Cork, in Ireland, several years later (1865–78) (see fig. 361).[195] Brisbane was an exercise that lay – formally and chronologically – between his various unexecuted designs for the Crimean War Memorial church in Istanbul (1856, 1859 and 1861). These were experiments in adaptation (cultural and climatic), utilising the so-called 'speluncar' method of thick walls and small windows (see pp. 129–43). Brisbane is closest to the 1861 design for Istanbul. There is no polychrome banding, only the 'reality' and rawness of natural stone. Nothing detracts from the firmness of its overbearing form; nor is there anything delicate or whimsical – it is a truly 'muscular' edifice, which captures perfectly those notions of strength and endurance that were so relevant to the concerns of Anglican clergymen abroad. In its sheer

massiveness, Brisbane provided what Ruskin had alluded to in another context as not merely physical security but 'security to the imagination'.[196]

At Hobart we see many of the same concerns rehearsed and affirmed (fig. 109). The building was designed by the eminent English architect G. F. Bodley (1827–1907) in 1867, and erected in three stages: 1868–74, 1891–4 and 1929–36. The first of these stages, as in the case of a number of the buildings discussed so far, was the nave. The bishop at the time was the Rev. Charles Henry Bromby (1814–1907) (fig. 110), who arrived in 1865 after Nixon's retirement. Bromby

Top 109 St David's cathedral, Hobart (1868–1936), by G. F. Bodley. This photograph shows how the building appeared shortly after the first phase of construction had been completed in 1874.

Bottom 110 Charles Henry Bromby (1814–1907), second bishop of Tasmania.

was a man who knew his own mind. Educated first at Uppingham School, Rutland, and then St John's College, Cambridge (BA 1837, MA 1840), he was a cleric of decided but not excessive High Churchmanship. Aware that he was stepping into a political and theological maelstrom in Tasmania, he was keen to exercise tolerance and present himself as someone who might reconcile rather than exacerbate differences. While still in England, Bromby had set his sights firmly on the existing cathedral at Hobart.[197] He had no doubt heard reports of its poor condition as well as its unworthiness as a cathedral church. It was, as we have already seen, considered 'secundum artem' by Nixon (see pp. 39). Although Nixon had dreamed of rebuilding St David's, he had neither the funds nor the support to achieve this during his episcopacy (fig. 111).

111 The classically inspired lines of the original St David's cathedral (Old St David's), Hobart, alongside the recently completed nave and transepts of G. F. Bodley's new Gothic building, *c.*1875. The temporary timber chancel of the new cathedral can be seen on the right.

Thus, only days after arriving in Hobart, Bromby made it known publicly that foremost in his mind was the erection of a new cathedral.[198] The Tasmanian *Church News* agreed. Invoking the memory of past bishop–architects such as Poore, Walkelyn and Wykham, the paper was excited at the prospect of Bromby taking his rightful place among these 'great Church-builders of old time'. In the manner of Broughton and Medley, it felt cause to reprove secular interests for pouring huge amounts of money into government building projects while the English Church was left to languish in poorly designed and often inadequate accommodation. 'Surely', it lamented, 'those who occupy them [the government buildings] must think sometimes of the self-reproach of King David, as they look upon the poor old church which, happening to bear his name, still stands in the midst of them, – "Behold, we dwell in houses of cedar, but the ark of God dwelleth within curtains".'[199] Bromby had himself made similar remarks, adding that 'our houses of God should be places of beauty'.[200] What was required in Hobart was a structure that would stand as a 'material type' of the Church of England in Tasmania.

Like Scott and Beresford Hope before him, Bromby had thought carefully about what the idea of an Anglican cathedral actually meant in the modern age, especially for a place such as Tasmania. 'The English cathedrals . . . were expected to meet the demands of the medieval period,' he reminded his flock in a pastoral letter of 1866, ' . . . they have lost much of their architectural meaning since the Reformation. We need now rather a superior type of parish Church, less expensive by far, yet beautiful in form, and imposing in proportions.'[201] With this in mind, he was fortunate in having G. F. Bodley as his brother-in-law. As Bromby was disposed to nepotism, it is not surprising that Bodley got the job of designing the new cathedral. He had also employed Bodley before, on the design of the Normal College in Cheltenham (1852), of which he had been the principal.[202] Bromby therefore had firsthand knowledge of Bodley's ability.

An additional factor in Bodley's appointment would have been Bromby's eldest son, Henry Bodley Bromby (1840–1911). Henry was an undergraduate at Jesus College, Cambridge, in the early 1860s, where he excelled at sport (rowing, cricket, running, football). He was 'full of pride in his muscularity', recalled J. V. Walters some years later.[203] At the time, Jesus was a notorious hotbed of undergraduate Anglo-Catholic sentiment, with Henry in the thick of it. Importantly, it was during Henry's time at Jesus that his uncle, Bodley, was commissioned to design All Saints', Jesus Lane (1863–70). As the living was within the college gift, the fellows and students naturally exercised a degree of influence over the design.[204] Given Henry's fondness for art, and the fact that his uncle was the architect, it is reasonable to assume he took a special interest in the building's progress. Shortly after graduation Henry followed his father to Tasmania. There he was made curate at St David's, then incumbent at St John's, Hobart (see pp. 320–1), before becoming a canon of the cathedral. When the cathedral committee was formed some time in the early months of 1866 to oversee the cathedral's design and construction, prominent among its members were H. B. Bromby (secretary) and F. H. Cox (chairman).[205] Although Bodley was a renowned architect in his own right, there was clearly little transparency with respect to his appointment. This is a classic example of the Anglican clerical network pulling rank, and evidence of the advantages that a well-connected bishop could bring to a colonial diocese such as Tasmania.

Although many of the arguments made about the need for cathedrals were well worn by this time, the architecture in this case is different. Like his design for All Saints', Jesus Lane, Cambridge, Bodley's St David's cathedral is indicative of his move away from the overtly muscular, continental manner of his youth to what Michael Hall has described as a more 'refined' approach through a return to English precedent.[206] At Hobart we have a design that was simple yet thoroughly 'English', the west front of which was based, as at Fredericton, on that of St Mary's, Snettisham (fig. 112). Indeed, commenting on Bodley's drawings, *The Ecclesiologist* noted that 'the whole design is a marked reaction from the earlier type of Foreign Gothic which Mr. Bodley formerly affected'.[207]

Interestingly, Bodley's first design (about July 1865) – subsequently rejected by the cathedral committee – was rather different.[208] In the belief, perhaps, that such a context required something slightly more robust, he produced what appears to have been quite a compact and vigorous proposal. After all, this was typical of his approach to colonial design (see pp. 180–4, 222–3). The plans for this initial scheme no longer survive, but the written description suggests that it was very much in his 'former' style:

> The ground plan . . . is an almost unbroken rectangle, (the Nave-aisles being continued along the chancel,) . . . . The Chancel occupies almost exactly one-third of the whole length. There is a South Porch but no Transepts. . . . Turning to the Elevations, we find, as the most striking feature, that the Chancel is considerably higher than the Nave, an arrangement more usual on the continent of Europe than in England. The Architect has evidently sought to produce his main effect by loftiness rather than by elaborate detail. . . . the East window . . . is in fact three in one, two three-lights side by side, with a good rose or wheel in the apex . . . . A handsome canopied and niched buttress runs up the centre of the East wall half way up the window, and adds materially to the general effect of the Elevation. . . . In the side

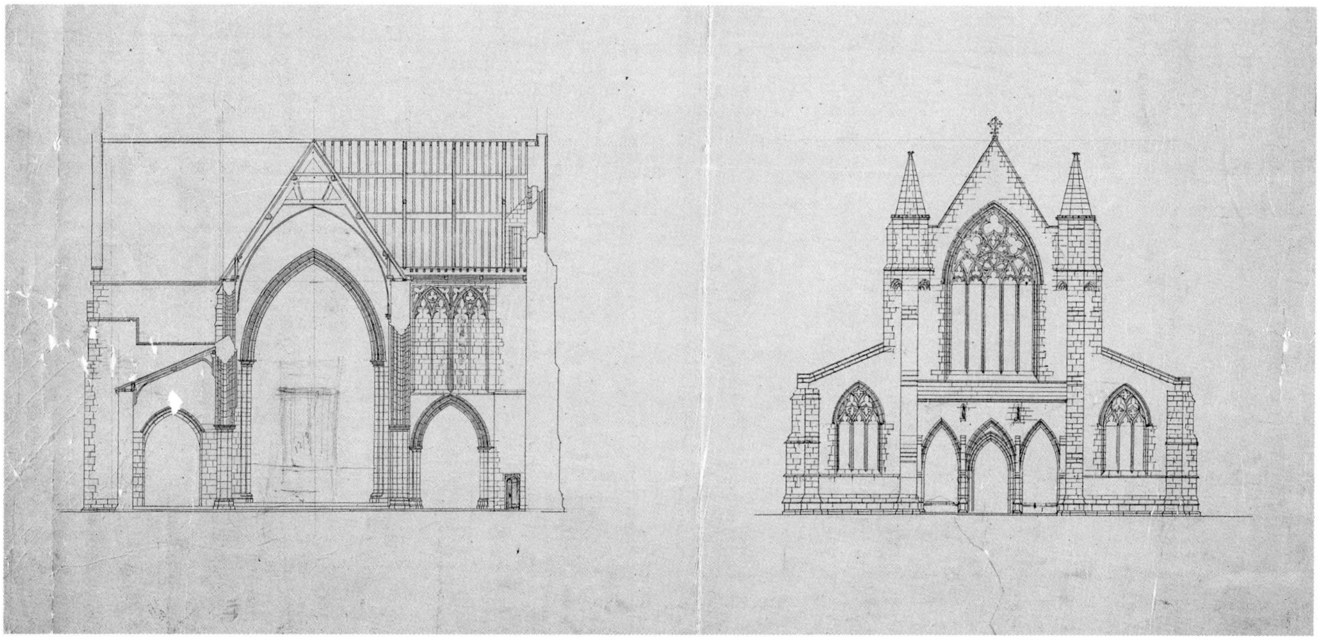

112 Front elevation and section drawings of G. F. Bodley's second design for St David's cathedral, Hobart, 1867 (Archive, Tasmanian Museum and Art Gallery, Hobart).

> Elevation, we miss the usual clerestory to the Nave . . . and it gives a very heavy effect to the great extent of roof, which is almost unbroken between the nave and aisles.[209]

It was later observed that the 'effect' of this design was 'not obtained by expensive and elaborate detail, but by commanding height and true proportions'.[210] This initial design bears some comparison with a number of Bodley's earlier church schemes in England. The raised chancel idea is one that had medieval precedent in the recently restored example of St Mary, Stone (Kent), and one that he had experimented with at St Stephen's, Guernsey (1861), a few years earlier (fig. 113).[211] Simple geometric volumes, planar surfaces, and 'wheel' windows are of course all associated with his early works such as All Saints', Selsley (1858), St Michael and All Angels, Brighton (1858), and St Martin's, Scarborough (1861).[212]

This design, however, did not last long. It was challenged on two fronts: first, the building, as was the case with many colonial cathedrals, was required to double as a parish church; and, second, certain of the proposed building's features raised the hackles of Evangelicals. Such a long choir was felt to impede the proper 'seeing' and 'hearing' of the service for a large town congregation, while the raised sanctuary was perceived as giving undue, and therefore alarming, prominence to 'exaggerated ritualism'.[213] Bromby was aware of and sensitive to these concerns. Just before coming to Tasmania, he had delivered a sermon in the church of his living at Cheltenham, in which he noted the danger of what he described as 'worshipping the imagination in religion'. He added: 'The young and well educated are principally exposed to this tendency, and I solemnly warn them. Ecclesiastic architecture and ecclesi-

113 St Stephen's church, Guernsey (1861), by G. F. Bodley.

astic music are examples of this tendency, dangerous if uncontrolled.'[214]

Whether Bromby actually believed this is not entirely clear, for his own son was principal among those 'young and well educated' who displayed such tendencies. Nevertheless, he was anxious to reassure his flock that the new cathedral at Hobart would indeed be a 'Cathedral Parish Church' for 'the entire Diocese', not just for one party.[215] It is likely that the concerns expressed over the initial design were communicated to Bodley either by Bromby or his son (probably Henry), with the suggestion that something less unconventional was required. It was clear that many among the existing Anglican community in Hobart were suspicious, even frightened, of 'foreign' and unfamiliar assemblages. In response Bodley produced his second, more conventional English design (about January 1867), which formed the basis of the building we see today. The foundation stone was laid on 8 January 1868 by Prince Alfred (who had earlier laid the foundation stone at Grahamstown), and the nave, with transepts, was consecrated on 3 February 1874. The chancel followed seventeen years later (1891–1909), with the tower not being completed until 1936. Local architect Henry Hunter (1832–1892) served as superintendent.

As a work of architecture, St David's cathedral has the grace and poise of an old English minster, somewhat like a distilled version of Glasgow cathedral without the crossing tower. Designed and built at the end of the period covered in this book, its air of refined Englishness reminds one of that 'model' cathedral designed and built twenty years earlier by bishop Medley at Fredericton, demonstrating that, in a way, stylistic development in ecclesiastical architecture had come full circle by 1870.

❁

It is clear that the cathedral idea had considerable symbolic value in the colonies. Cathedral churches were one of the principal means by which Anglican bishops both asserted their legal authority and made manifest the confessional identity of Anglicanism in the wider colonial landscape. It was an idea that also cut across party lines, allowing Tractarians, traditional High Churchmen and Evangelicals (often bickering with one another) to find common ground. This was partly because apostolicity demanded it, and partly because, in contexts where the Church was all but disestablished, cathedrals provided evidence of the unity and independence of the English Church in 'conspicuous guise'.[216] Opinions may have differed on the size and elaboration of cathedral churches, but most Anglicans were convinced of their merit and did what they could to erect them.

In terms of planning and arrangement, colonial cathedrals were eminently useful and 'reformed'. In other words, they were 'modern' in their shedding of many of those spatial and liturgical superfluities associated with medieval Romanism – those 'parasitical and indefensible accretions', as Beresford Hope called them – in favour of something 'natural and practical'.[217] This obviously referred to the eradication of certain ritualistic practices associated with pre-Reformation cathedral institutions. It also included the shedding of architectural redundancies associated with monasticism, such as cloisters, leaving modern cathedrals looking more like French rather than English prototypes. Although there had been some talk of resurrecting cloisters in some parts of the empire, such as in the tropics, this was mainly as a means of avoiding the sun, even though they might also have conjured up romantic associations.[218] These modernising tendencies had much to do with the expanding horizons of English ecclesiology as architects peered across the Channel, absorbing aspects of foreign traditions that were considered consistent with Anglican needs. They also had to do with strict budgets, site constraints and/or shorter construction times under modern contractual conditions. For instance, Truro cathedral (1881–1910) – the first on English soil since the rebuilding of St Paul's – was very modern in this respect, making it more like a colonial cathedral than an ancient English one.[219]

But there were deeper, cultural reasons for rationalising the architecture of cathedral institutions in the modern age. On this point Beresford Hope observed of post-Reformation architecture that 'the reformed Church of England was, in its externals, the reformation of the English Church'. The logic of this was clear:

> The retention of the reformational modifications of the medieval cathedral is the correlative of the historical progress of the English people, who now in the days of Victoria, as once in the days of Edward III., possess their House of Lords and House of Commons, their courts of common law and equity, and their espiscopal church –

> the same in their basis, yet altered, developed, improved, and reformed by the progressive wisdom of centuries.[220]

Thus, the 'false antiquarianism' of attaching a cloister to a modern cathedral merely because ancient cathedrals in England had them was illogical: if there should be a practical reason for them, insisted Beresford Hope, then adopt them; if not, do not. At any rate, he added, 'the current of general feeling and legislation will probably make [the cloister's] revival more and more impossible'.[221]

The personnel involved in cathedral extension abroad also reveals the extensive yet intimate network of knowledge, expertise and resources that was drawn upon from across the Anglican world, whether ecclesiological, professional, pecuniary or theological. In this respect, the cathedral idea and its institution abroad, as Beresford Hope observed, gave to the English Church 'order, system, power, and magnitude of operation'. It is this that best characterises the aims and ambitions of the global Church of England during the mid-nineteenth century.

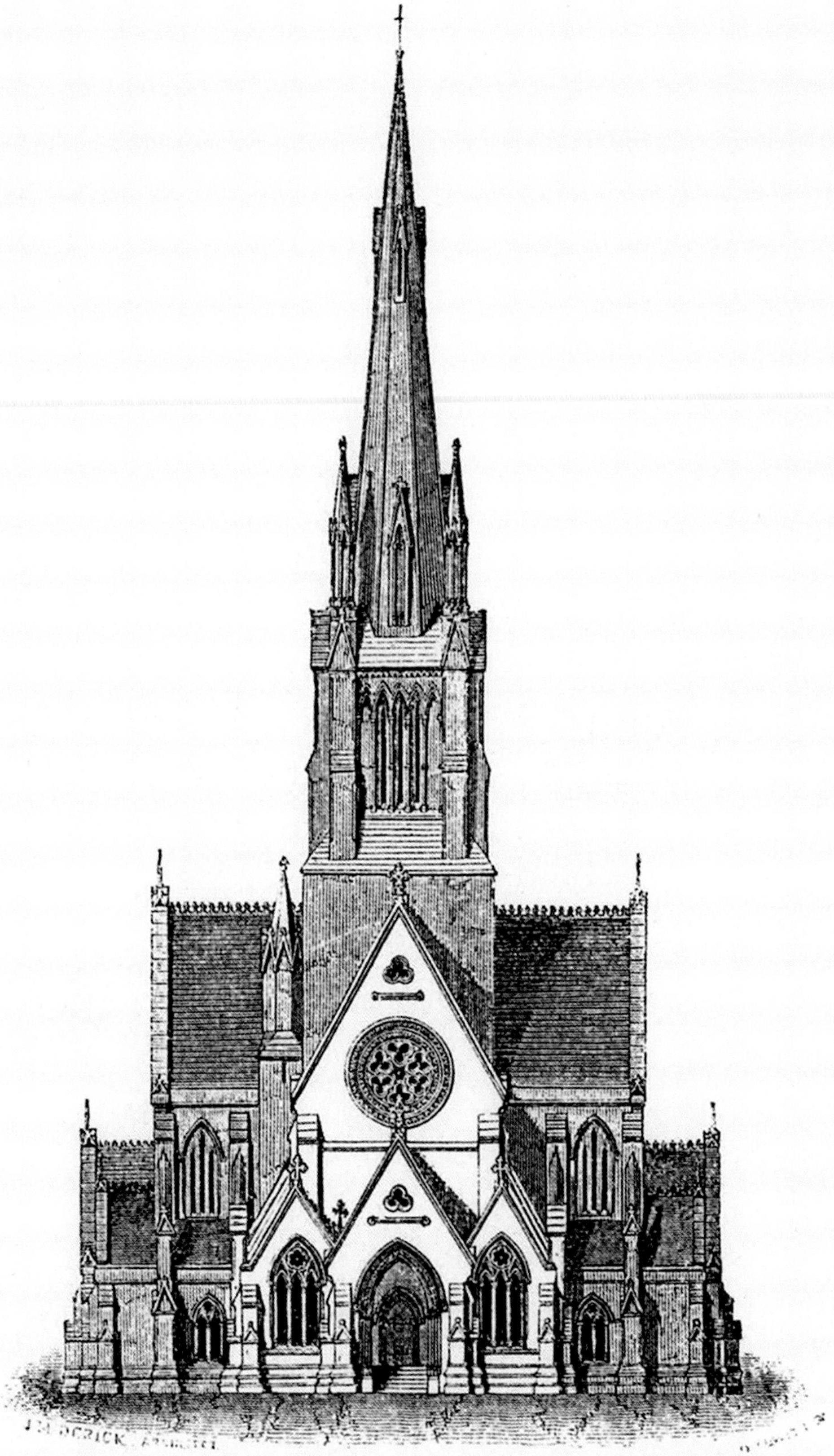

114 J. M. Derick's design for the Afghan Memorial church, Bombay, 1843, from *Rules and Proceedings* (1843).

3

Adaptation and Invention

THE THEORY AND PRACTICE OF ACCLIMATISATION

We should remember that Great Britain reigns over the torrid and the hyperborean zone.

A. J. B. Beresford Hope (1846)

What is wanted is that our Colonial fellow-Churchmen should learn Ecclesiology. Let them master this, and then they will be as competent to develope [*sic*] as we are, and will have every facility for doing so. . . . If the church be of mud, it may still be a church; properly arranged and suitable for Catholic worship. This is the first thing to be secured: afterwards the style and the sumptuousness of the building should be considered.

The Ecclesiologist (1847)

Both the Oxford Architectural and Cambridge Camden societies realised early on that their initiative would necessarily extend beyond the British Isles as the Anglican Church spread and consolidated its influence throughout the British empire. They lent much advice (and criticism), both practical and theoretical, to clergymen who were keen to promote correct church architecture abroad. The question of adaptation was at the forefront of their thinking on this matter, particularly as they began receiving letters from clergymen and architects overseas reporting their peculiar circumstances and enquiring as to how they might adjust architecturally. We have seen something of how these men attempted such an adjustment through the revival and transmutation of key religious and architectural ideas, as well as through the substitution and adaptation of materials. But one of the most pressing concerns of colonial clergymen was that of climate. Much of Britain's empire was located in parts of the world with radically different climates from northern Europe. These climates ranged from the frozen (or 'hyperborean') climes of Newfoundland and Labrador to the tropical (or 'torrid') zones of South Asia and the Caribbean; from the semi-alpine retreats of New Zealand and British Columbia to the arid outposts of Australia and southern Africa. The architectural societies approached this problem with some trepidation. 'We ourselves are only feeling our way to the successful revival of Pointed architecture in this country,' declared *The Ecclesiologist* in 1847. 'Its development in other climates must be a much harder task, and it is clear that we at home are the least fitted to attempt it. . . . [A]fter all, the Colonies alone can help themselves in this want. We in England can only theorize.'[1]

Nevertheless, it was apparent to all concerned that simply transposing English Middle-Pointed Gothic to these regions, unaltered in any way from its original context, would not work. It was recognised that English Gothic was itself an environmentally determined species of Christian architecture and that a similar process of adaptation was to be expected when it came to developing an appropriate ecclesiology for the colonies. The British, of course, had considerable experience of living in extreme climatic conditions, so the concept of architectural adaptation was far from unfamiliar to them. But ecclesiastical architecture had, by and large, evaded the demands of climate. Thus, the time was now right, declared Benjamin Webb in 1845, 'to call upon our members [in earnest] to assist in discovering some principles which may be laid down for church-building in all varieties of climate'.[2]

Developing a Strategy: General Approaches to Climate Control

Although adaptation seemed commonsensical, it keyed with wider debates over 'developement' in Anglican church architecture during the mid-nineteenth century. The Camden Society was itself undergoing a reformation at this time as it began lifting its horizons in a bid to reinvigorate its own agenda and head off accusations of 'copyism'. Webb had also pointed out that although an Englishman abroad might well prefer the architecture of his own country, and 'English Pointed' was certainly recognised as having a peculiar excellence, it could not be condoned as 'the model for every church in any climate'. To be sure, the 'essentials' of the Middle-Pointed style ought to remain as the basis of proper ecclesiastical architecture, but appropriate modification was now vital to its successful transmission abroad. This particular line of reasoning was pursued by Beresford Hope, who extended it beyond climate into the realm of culture. His notion of progressive eclecticism – or 'developement' by another name – encouraged a cross-fertilisation of styles and forms that would reflect the increasing reality of Britain's position in the world as the metropolis of a burgeoning global empire.[3] 'We must not for this discovery confine ourselves to England or to the Western Church,' he urged; 'we must penetrate to the East and her venerable heredity uses . . . we must be as familiar with San Clemente, Santa Sophia, and the church of the Holy Sepulchre, as with Heckington and York Minster.'[4]

Such thinking had wider implications with respect to what would become the 'Battle of the Styles' debate and the search among British architects for an original and 'modern' nineteenth-century mode of expression.[5] It also had a precedent in the architecture of Spanish, Portuguese and Dutch missionaries in the Americas and South Asia during the sixteenth, seventeenth and eighteenth centuries, of which ecclesiologists were cognisant even if they were somewhat reluctant to imitate it. English ecclesiologists and architects may have harboured an aversion to this kind of architecture on stylistic grounds, but key lessons were learnt. One such was the necessity of cultural adaptation – a process later referred to in Roman Catholic circles as 'inculturation'. As we shall see, this would be important in creating a church architecture that was both responsive and flexible to the challenges that Anglican missionaries faced in attempting to establish a foothold and make conversions in foreign lands. In such contexts only an architecture that met the demands of both climate and culture would succeed. Thus began a discussion about adaptation and invention within the Church of England and among the university architectural societies that would test the limits of ecclesiological theory in Britain and push the boundaries of what was considered to be 'correct' church architecture within the Anglican confession.

Among the first serious attempts at developing a strategy for climatic control in Anglican ecclesiology was Benjamin Webb's 'On the Adaptation of Pointed Architecture to Tropical Climates', published in the *Transactions of the Cambridge Camden Society* in 1845. Originally read as a paper before a meeting of the society in February that year, Webb's thinking was as straightforward as it was logical: to what extent was Pointed architecture capable of modification and, if it was, how might that be achieved under certain climatic conditions? His principal concern, of course, was that whatever modifications were recommended, the end result should remain both 'truthful' and 'churchlike'. On this point he criticised the Oxford Architectural Society's attempt at intervening in the design of the Afghan Memorial church at Colaba, Bombay (Mumbai), as well as his own society's efforts at procuring a plan for the Protestant church in Alexandria. Both designs fell at the first hurdle. Not only did they fail the 'reality' test, they also neglected the strict liturgical requirements fundamental to a proper Christian church. Rule number one in developing an 'Anglo-tropical' architecture, as far as Webb was concerned, was that 'the bones . . . be constructed before the flesh which covers them. Chancel and nave, altar and font, secured, any thing else may be boldly added.'[6]

With these fundamentals established, the architect was then free to investigate structure, form and materials. This process, however, was not concerned with external effect alone. Webb was aware of the need to develop an architecture of integrity; that is, an architecture that was systematic in its approach to the problem of climate while being rooted in a contextual understanding of architectural form. Referring to the way in which Christian architecture had been studied in Europe, he observed:

> [We] have traced carefully enough the first introduction of the arch springing from its piers; have theorized upon the origin of the pointed arch, and have classified mouldings: but we still want a comparison of the different ways in which different people and climates embodied their type of a church. . . . Had Church Architecture been so treated, our present subject would not have been built from the first ages in every kind of climate: whether the churches of Africa had peculiar features, and why: whether those in Abyssinia. We should know more of the churches of the Christians of S. Thomas in Malabar than we can now glean from meagre hints in the Researches of Buchanan.[7]

Webb's use of the term 'embodiment' here took his interest in ecclesiology beyond the narrow confines of antiquarianism – an approach that had, by and large, dominated the study of architecture in Britain until the late 1840s – into the realm of what today would be called anthropology. He was not so much concerned, in this case, at least, with *where* the pointed arch came from, or *how* it was brought and integrated into northern European architecture (as interesting as that may have been), but *why*. In other words, his interest focused upon the relationship between generic architectural features and their specific cultural expression. For Webb, these two things were inextricably linked. Environmental factors (culture, climate, materials) played as great a role in the evolution of architectural forms as raw technology. In this respect, as E. A. Freeman would later articulate, Webb viewed architecture as somewhat analogous to plant life: the underlying essentials of good plant growth were everywhere observable, only each species of plant differed in form from the others according to the prevailing context and conditions in which it was located.[8] Thus, it was important to appreciate the difference between 'essentials' and 'accidentals', argued Webb, if a genuine 'Tropical Pointed' was to be developed in Britain's colonies. 'If the result *be* unlike an English church,' he exclaimed, 'what will that matter, provided we have a building correct in plan and detail, and accurately suited to the particular climate?'[9]

In seeking solutions to this problem Webb turned initially to the churches erected by Spanish and Portuguese missionaries in India and the Americas during the sixteenth century. But it was the cathedral at Funchal in Madeira, along with the remains of late Gothic churches in the Canary Islands, that received particular attention. These were buildings that Webb's friend and colleague John Mason Neale knew from first-hand experience.[10] The lesson to be learnt from these examples, according to Webb, was the recurrence of certain characteristics such as increased area, greater height, solidity of walls, and the prevalence of 'internal gloom' (owing to few and small windows). The problem with proposing these buildings as models, however, was their style – a debased admixture of late Gothic and Renaissance classicism – which was totally unpalatable to the modern ecclesiologist.[11] But what about the architecture of southern Europe, especially Italy, Spain and Portugal, where the climate was much hotter than in Britain? In these climes all the features Webb had identified were predominant. 'Let us, then, picture to ourselves', he mused, 'a church with low roof and few small windows, disposed irregularly at a great height, and as much out of sight as may be; also with great breadth and with very lofty aisles'. The net effect of these features would not only be a cool, dark interior but also a massive, heavy fabric. Again, as long as the essential characteristics of a church were in place, such an architecture would be no less 'truly Gothic' than an English parish church.

Although he did not realise it at the time, Webb was edging towards a theory of ecclesiastical design that would later become known as *speluncar* ('cave-like'). This theory was based on the principle of thermal mass – that is, hugely thick walls acting as insulation against heat gain from the external environment. Small and few windows would also prevent direct sunlight from penetrating the building and raising the temperature of the interior. The 'speluncar' concept first gained currency in an article by the Rev.

William Scott that appeared in the February 1851 edition of *The Ecclesiologist*.[12] In this piece Scott was keen to disabuse his readers of the notion that 'cave architecture' was necessarily barbaric, and to convince them that, in fact, wherever it occurred in civilised societies, such as India, Ethiopia and Sicily, it was adopted first and foremost for practical reasons. 'To live, and therefore to assemble for worship, in a tropical climate,' observed Scott, 'man has to contend with his fierce enemies, sunlight and the burned midday air. For this purpose he buries himself; and where he cannot do this, the more his house, or church, is like a cave, and fulfils the speluncar idea.'[13] Thus, recalling the sentiments of John Ruskin from his influential *Seven Lamps of Architecture*, Scott concluded that 'unless you can beat mountain and precipice, forest and fell, tree and river, in their own chosen seat of majesty, do not wage an unprofitable contest with them'.[14] By considering aspects of built form that went beyond outward appearances, Scott was arguing for a 'developed' rather than eclectic approach to architectural adaptation.

Referring to the Spanish colonial cathedral of Santa Ana, Las Palmas, Gran Canaria (*c.*1500 onwards), Scott pointed out that: 'Without saying that Las Palmas cathedral has sufficiently thrown off the traditions of a more temperate climate, that it is a very cool church [situated within less than 5 degrees of the tropics] may safely be attributed to the thickness of its walls and the paucity of its windows.'[15] For such a theory to be fully appreciated, however, Scott reminded his readers that it was necessary for English architects and ecclesiologists to forgo their prejudices regarding matters of style, warning that: 'objectors, especially professional architects, must be told, that till they have seen the sunshine, or in other words, till they have visited the tropics, they have . . . little rational right to give opinions about what amount of light or ventilation is wanted in these regions'.

The Ecclesiological Society had an advantage in this respect as a number of its members were already located abroad and thus able to relay first-hand knowledge of local conditions. Many weighed into the debate, and numerous alternative precedents were invoked. The architecture of Byzantium and the Eastern Church might provide lessons, as could buildings closer to home, such as St Peter's Basilica in Rome.[16] Even the Crusader churches of Palestine ought to be considered, especially for arid climates.[17] In terms of basic practical requirements, various techniques were suggested, including deep-set windows and the use of sun hoods. Some believed more sophisticated techniques were necessary, such as cavity walls filled with insulation, or the incorporation of wide, semi-circular buttresses that might double as stack ventilators.[18] All of these, it was hoped, would meet with approval by not interfering with the symbolic intentions of church architecture.

Others, however, were wont to go further. J. E. Millard of the Oxford Architectural Society, for instance, believed that Christian architecture in colonial dioceses where the 'national style' (that is, the indigenous style) had progressed beyond 'huts, caves or tents' ought to assume local forms entirely. In justifying this strategy he observed that 'our own pointed style, though in its present form so admirably adapted to, and representative of Christianity, is after all traceable to a heathen style'. Was there not great similarity already in the features of European Gothic and those of 'Mohammedan' architecture, he asked.[19] However, this went too far for the Ecclesiological Society. It was felt at the time that if Western Christendom was to achieve ultimate 'victory' over the 'impostor' prophet and his 'false religion', then European Pointed architecture must reign supreme.[20] Anything less was 'incredible'.

Much anecdotal evidence had also begun to find its way back to Britain, suggesting that the speluncar method did not work in all cases, and that the open 'draught-admitting' approach, as Beresford Hope would later describe it, was more effective.[21] Part of the problem was that discussions on the adaptation of Gothic architecture which appeared in the pages of *The Ecclesiologist* were confusing. Little, if any, distinction was made between arid, desert-like regions and those of a more humid, tropical nature – all were lumped together as 'burning' or 'hot'. Initially, at least, this led to the speluncar method being advocated as a universal solution. But Anglican clergymen stationed in Ceylon (Sri Lanka), for example, felt that opening church buildings on all sides and shading them with loggias and verandahs were a better way of achieving a satisfactory result. Many also believed that flat roofs were inadmissible in such climates because they were unable to shed the heavy tropical rains fast enough, leading to extensive leaks. The Rev. Dr Norman Garstin of Point-de-Galle (Sri Lanka), for one, noted the importance of admitting as much air as possible into a building. This was a strategy based on the principle of cross-ventilation, a solution that was in many respects opposed to that of the speluncar.[22] 'The problem to be solved [here]', Garstin observed, 'is to find such a plan as will give abundance of air through doors and windows, and yet, by the help of judicious provisions, and perhaps well managed *planting*, afford shelter from the tropical glare and tropical rains.'[23] Among these 'judicious provisions' was the incorporation of cloisters, which could be wrapped around the building to serve as a kind of verandah. The arches of these cloisters could then be filled with unglazed tracery, or, in some cases, decorative iron-work. In addition, the building's roofline could be extended to create large, overhanging eaves, thereby draining rainwater away from the edge of the building and shielding against direct sunlight. Thus, by 1851 two opposing methods for adapting Christian (that is, Gothic) architecture to torrid climates had emerged: the 'speluncar' and the 'draught-admitting' (thermal mass versus cross-ventilation). It remained to be seen whether one or the other, or a combination of both, would succeed.

Counter-intuitively, perhaps, the speluncar method was also considered applicable in cold climates. The same principles applied: thick walls would stop the cold penetrating the internal spaces of the building, while small windows would minimise heat transfer between inside and out. It was precisely this thinking that lay behind the design of St John's cathedral, Newfoundland.[24] In exceedingly cold climates, however, masonry construction was prone to disintegrate during prolonged periods of frost. Under these conditions, timber was seen as a more robust material, despite the necessity for continual maintenance. Even iron was countenanced in certain circumstances. Indeed, identifying and sourcing the most appropriate materials for construction was central to the idea of adaptation, as ecclesiologists sought to strike a balance between cost, practicality and appropriateness.[25] We have seen this already in the case of New Zealand, where, initially at least, good building stone was unavailable (see pp. 46–56). In order to justify different materials and methods, other types of medieval church building were suggested as models, such as the timber churches of Scandinavia, or, in the case of brickwork, Albi cathedral in southern France.[26] There were many examples to which one could point; the only question remaining was how theories of adaptation should be applied in practice.

Torrid Gothic: Tackling Heat and Humidity

The two university architectural societies had tried their hand at designing churches for torrid climates as early as 1842. The first of these was the Protestant church at Alexandria (St Mark's), the design for which was orchestrated by the Cambridge Camden Society and produced by one of the society's 'approved' affiliates, Anthony Salvin (1799–1881).[27] This effort, however, turned out to be a false dawn for Tropical Pointed architecture. No serious attempt was made by Salvin (or the society) to adapt the design to the prevailing conditions, and the proposal was swiftly rejected.[28] Looking back at the episode some years later, *The Ecclesiologist*, by way of excuse, was able to claim that 'Tropical Architecture was, in those days, a thing which we had not studied, and of which we had no experience.' The commission passed to James Wild in 1845 who produced a far more responsive, if controversial, design (see below).

The other early, but no less notorious, attempt at erecting an ecclesiologically correct church in the tropics was the Afghan Memorial church in Bombay. Intended as a memorial to British soldiers who had fallen during the First Afghan War (1839–42), the church was to be located at the perimeter of the military cantonment at Colaba, two miles south of the old fort. From the very beginning the British authorities in Bombay sought assistance from England. The Rev. George Pigott, chaplain to the East India Company, wrote to the Oxford Architectural Society in February 1843 requesting designs. This request was in itself unusual. Normal practice in the military was to engage a Royal Engineer to draw architectural plans. Pigott, however, was determined that his building should avoid becoming just another nondescript, 'Gothick' garrison church. As a member of the Oxford Society, Pigott clearly desired something more authentic. From the outset he was very much aware of the climatic adaptations that such a building required, noting in his letter to the society that the aisle windows should be unglazed and filled with 'Venetians . . . to secure a perfect ventilation', and that a trefoil vent be placed high up, directly under the gable, for the same purpose.[29] These recommendations were reiterated by the bishop of Bombay, the Rev. Thomas Carr, who observed that, in addition to 'complete ventilation', all openings should be shielded from the direct glare of the sun, and a *porte-cochère* incorporated for women arriving by coach. In

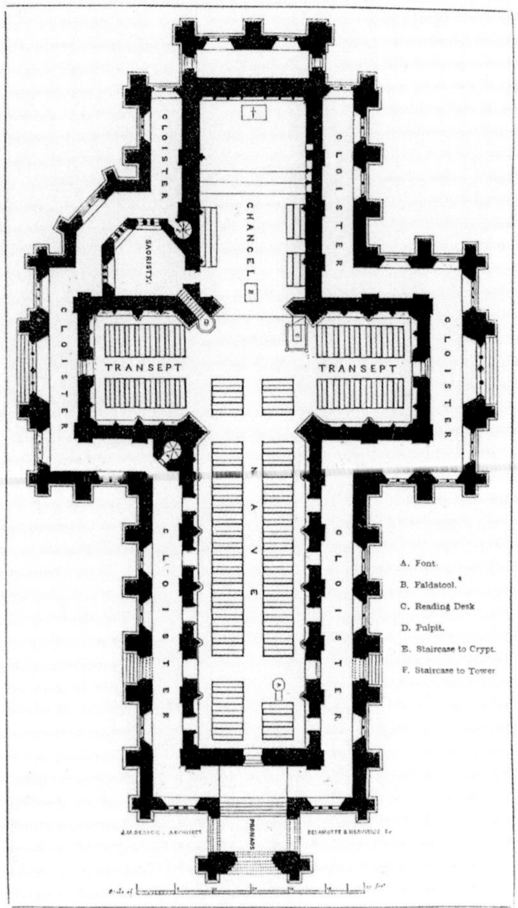

115 Plan of J. M. Derick's design for the Afghan Memorial church, Bombay, 1843, from *Rules and Proceedings* (1843).

case these recommendations were mistaken as mere suggestions, it was emphasised that such adaptations were 'of importance to us *in India*'.[30]

For their part, the Oxford Architectural Society engaged the 'approved' architect J. M. Derick to prepare plans. Before long the enterprise was being promoted under the 'joint sanction' of the two university societies, as there had been some confusion as to which had received Pigott's request first.[31] Derick's plans were submitted to the Oxford society for approval in November 1843, when it was noted with enthusiasm that 'great care had been used to adapt the design to the climate', and that 'Mr. Derick had shewn [*sic*] considerable skill by the manner in which he had carried out this object, without injuring the Church-like effect, or departing from the purity of Gothic Architecture' (fig. 114).[32] The printed plans show a compact cruciform structure with pronounced nave, chancel and transepts, rendered competently in a Middle-Pointed Gothic style. The most striking feature of the design, however, is the so-called cloister, approximately ten feet wide, shown enveloping the entire lower section of the building (fig. 115). In plan, this gives the distinct impression of a building within a building. The walls, as drawn, also appear at least four feet thick. These plans were accompanied with a commentary by the Oxford society, stating that the design was 'so contrived that the sun's rays can nowhere fall directly into the building, while there is a through current of air through every part of it, with the power of shutting out the hot wind at pleasure'.[33]

Although, on the face of it, this was a genuine attempt at adapting Gothic architecture to a tropical climate, it was considered a failure by some. As mentioned, for Webb, the result was entirely false. The cloister gave the impression of aisles, which the church did not have, while the clerestory was not a real clerestory. Consequently, 'this church, however satisfactory it may look on the outside, is most unchurchlike within'.[34] Moreover, as Webb had stressed in his essay, such a design process should not be treated as a simple case of transplanting an English parish church to a foreign land and applying 'sham appanages [*sic*]' for the sake of acclimatisation. The fundamental error that Derick had made was 'to read the problem thus. Given, an English church, to fit it for the tropics. Instead of, Given, the tropics, and such and such *principles* of architecture, to build by the latter a church to suit the former.'[35] In short, it was a lazy and un-thoughtful approach that led to an 'unreal' result. Perhaps Derick's biggest mistake was to fall foul of the Camdenians' changing attitude towards 'developed' ecclesiology – an ideological transformation he could hardly have foreseen in 1843.

Webb's criticisms also indicate his growing bias towards the speluncar idea and its apparent contextual associations. His ignorance of true tropical conditions – which, it must be said, he was willing to admit – led him to believe that the principles evident in the Christian architecture of southern Europe, and applied in the Canary Islands, were also applicable to the low-lying, sultry environs of Bombay and Calcutta. But the churches that were being erected by English clergy in such places were by and large too small to take advantage of the speluncar method. An alternative approach was required, namely the 'draught-admitting', which had been made known to the university architectural societies as early as 1839.[36]

In the event, Derick's design was not executed, condemned by the local authorities as not only too expensive but also 'not fit for the purpose'.[37] The church at Colaba was eventually built, but not through the direct assistance of the university architectural societies, nor with the 'special' climatic adaptations they might have hoped for (see pp. 295–7).[38]

Perhaps the most serious early attempt at devising a Tropical Pointed architecture for Britain's colonies was Colombo cathedral, Ceylon. This project was initiated by the bishop of Colombo, the Rev. James Chapman (1799–1879) (see fig. 221), former master at Eton and brother-in-law of Edward Coleridge.[39] In a letter to the Ecclesiological Society dated 16 December 1845, Chapman requested designs for a 'plain cruciform structure . . . of simple design, good and correct proportion'.[40] At the very least, it seems, Chapman was aware of and keen to implement the society's principles. Given the date of his letter, however, it is unlikely that Chapman knew of Webb's paper on tropical architecture, or the society's general endorsement of the speluncar method. Chapman's thinking on adaptation was informed by local considerations, in particular the churches already standing in Ceylon, such as those erected by the Dutch in the eighteenth century.[41] These buildings were generally large and often open on all sides to capture the prevailing sea breezes and to allow for adequate ventilation. They were also built massively of solid brick. Following this lead, Chapman suggested that the design of the new cathedral be Early English and include 'a cloister [all] round to serve as [a] verandah'. This would result in a church that was somewhere between a speluncar-style building, with thick walls, and a draught-admitting one, open on all sides. As Chapman's proposal was based on observation and the practicalities of context, his views were seen to carry considerable weight.

The Ecclesiological Society wasted little time in answering Chapman's call, advising that his hints on climatic adaptation be taken seriously. The task was entrusted to the society's young hopeful, R. C. Carpenter. A ground plan was ready for inspection by May 1846, with a full set of designs presented in October the following year (figs 116 and 117).[42] What Carpenter produced was an evolved version of the idea originally employed by Derick at Bombay. The core of the plan is that of a small cathedral, comprising aisled nave and transepts, raised choir with apsidal sanctuary, and an ambulatory formed by the continuation of the aisles past the choir and behind the sanctuary.[43] Added to this was an extra layer of spaces that served to encapsulate and thus insulate the core spaces of the building from the external environment. In plan, this additional space, or 'cloister' as it was called, formed what was, in effect, an extra aisle. Its purpose with respect to the function of the church is unclear, as it had doors and gates demarcating it from the main spaces of the building. In elevation and section we can see that these cloister spaces are articulated on the exterior of the building in much the same manner as a traditional single-aisled church, with a lean-to roof abutting the clerestory wall. What is

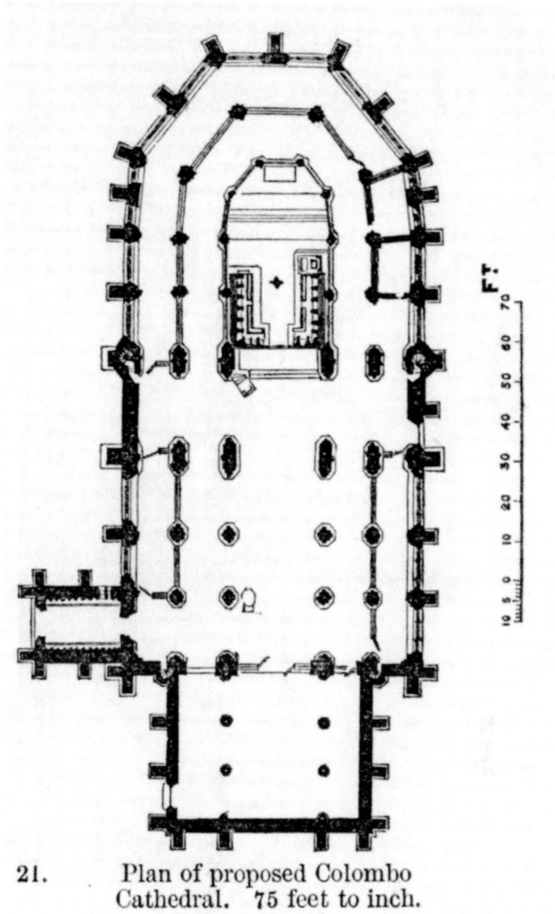

116 Plan of R. C. Carpenter's design for Christ Church cathedral, Colombo, Ceylon, 1846, from A. J. B. Beresford Hope's *The English Cathedral of the Nineteenth Century* (1861).

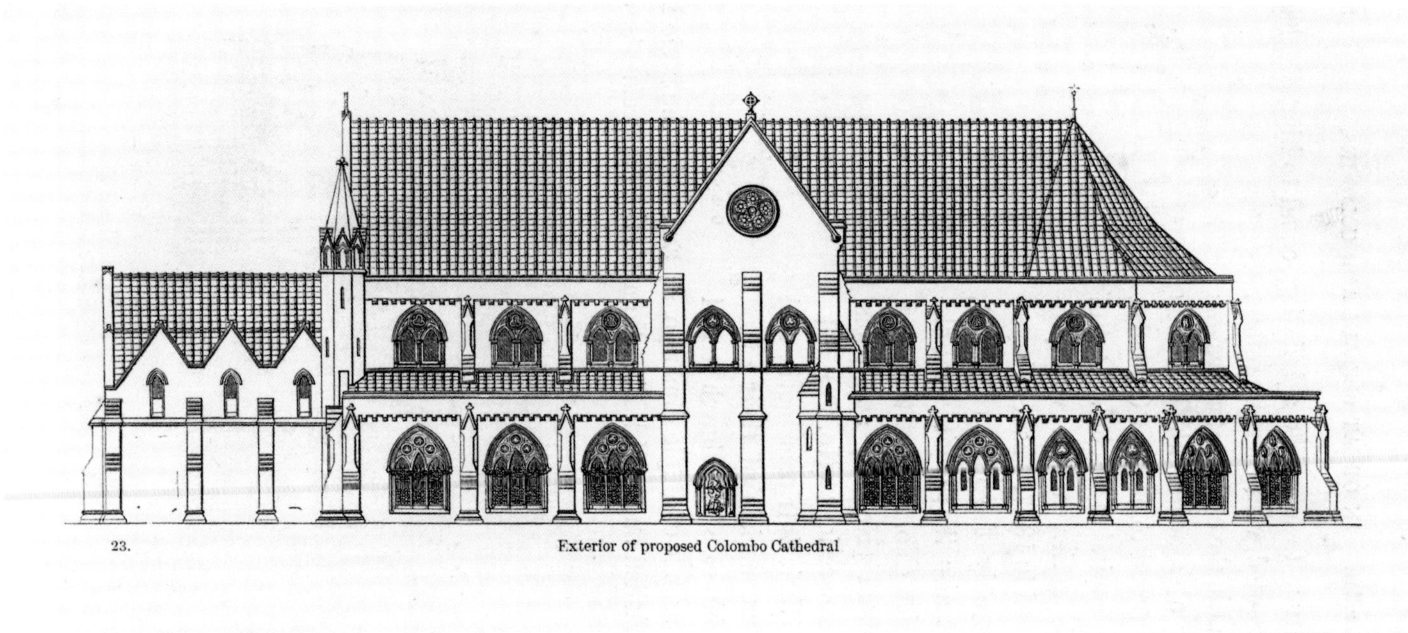

117 South elevation of R. C. Carpenter's design for Christ Church cathedral, Colombo (1847), from A. J. B. Beresford Hope's *The English Cathedral of the Nineteenth Century* (1861).

perhaps not immediately evident from either the plan or elevation, however, is that the clerestory of the church is in fact a double-height aisle in the manner of a German hall church, the key difference being that in this case the upper and lower levels of the aisle are distinct, with the upper level forming a kind of triforium gallery or passageway.[44] A sheltered clerestory of this kind without glass was considered 'indispensable' by the bishop of Colombo – 'we should be suffocated without it. . . . We *must* have air; and the more the better.'[45] Instead of glass it was envisaged that the window openings would be filled with jalousies (fixed but adjustable Venetian blinds for the moderation of air flow). The arched openings in the lower portions of the building were to be filled with ornamental cast-iron screens, as much for security as ventilation. Chapman also advised that the main roof of the church have an overhanging eave of approximately three feet to prevent the penetration of direct sunlight, but Carpenter, it seems, found this suggestion ecclesiologically unpalatable. Describing the design some years later, Beresford Hope summarised it as follows: 'The church it will be seen is of ample dimensions; and while the style is modelled on English First Pointed, the requirements of the oppressive climate are met by the open external aisle or loggia which encircles the entire building, in addition to the ordinary internal aisle, and by the clerestory galleries in the double thickness of the walls.'[46] Thus, the design for Colombo cathedral may be seen as a compromise, or hybrid, solution between the speluncar and draught-admitting approaches to Tropical Pointed architecture. What we end up with is an open, well-ventilated building, built in a simple yet massive style of architecture – a building that would allow a cooling breeze while preventing as much direct and radiated heat as possible.

Although simplicity was the 'one great requisite', as far as Chapman was concerned, Carpenter, perhaps mindful of the criticisms levelled at the memorial church in Bombay, was keen to demonstrate the 'reality' and correctness of his design. He would achieve this through a subtle yet clear articulation of architectural forms. The way the roofline is splayed at precisely the point where the outer clerestory gallery meets the inner clerestory wall, for example, is indicative. This is typical of Carpenter's sensitivity as an architect.[47] Adhering to the guiding principle of truth in ecclesiology, he reveals the internal organisation of the building to the exterior – there is no attempt here to cover up the fact that there is a double height aisle or 'clerestory gallery'.[48] As Webb had made clear, not even the dictates of an extreme climate should be allowed to negate the fundamentals of ecclesiastical architecture.

Other designs caught up in the debate over climatic adaptation included that for Point-de-Galle (Galle), also in Ceylon. As mentioned, the local incumbent, the Rev. Dr Norman Garstin, was a leading proponent of the draught-admitting approach to tropical church design. Like Chapman before him, Garstin's numerous letters to *The Ecclesiologist* stressed the need 'for *admitting* air, and . . . *excluding* the sun's direct rays'.[49] This was to be achieved not only through particular architectural adjustments but also through landscaping, including the planting of trees and shrubs for additional shelter. These additional measures were endorsed, on grounds of biblical precedent, in the *Colonial Church Chronicle*, where it was noted that Abraham not only 'builded an altar' but also 'planted a grove'.[50] Carpenter was again entrusted with the job of transforming these ideas into architectural reality. His design, now lost, was a smaller version of his plan for Colombo, except this time with the inclusion of overhanging eaves. Although the design was described in *The Ecclesiologist* as being 'quite correct', this feature alone would have distinguished the building from anything that could have been found in more temperate climes at the time, including England.

Despite Chapman and Garstin's interventions, the debate over climatic adaptation was far from settled. In the same number of *The Ecclesiologist* in which Garstin's letter appeared, William Scott's correspondence on the speluncar method was also published.[51] This was the same William Scott (of Hoxton) who had been involved in the design of St John's cathedral, Newfoundland. *The Ecclesiologist* was torn over which method it should endorse. 'On the one hand,' it observed, 'Mr Carpenter can scarcely be blamed for responding to the conditions laid down by persons long resident in Ceylon. . . . On the other hand, Mr Scott's views, though in our own opinion they almost carry conviction with them, have not yet been formally adopted by ecclesiologists.'[52] This was a dilemma for the Ecclesiological Society. Scott's reasoning in favour of the speluncar method may have been compelling, but it was limited, in the sense that it was based almost exclusively on his visit to the Canary Islands.[53] Moreover, despite their caution against 'theorizing' from home, it is clear that the society preferred the speluncar method for reasons other than those based on experience.

The society's saviour, so to speak, emerged in the form of the Rev. J. F. Bourne of Guiana. Having considered both arguments, and having lived in the tropics for some time, Bourne sided with Scott, observing:

> My own experience convinces me that a cave-like building would be best fitted for the Tropics. . . . [W]e generally enjoy such a strong sea breeze that we do not feel the mid-day heat. . . . At such times our churches are often tolerably cool, but at the cost of great inconvenience from the blowing about of our robes and the leaves of the books. At other times, when we lose the breeze, which is frequently the case in the rainy seasons and in some situations, it is not in the power of windows and doors or of openings to any extent to admit cool air, the whole atmosphere being sultry. I have on such occasions sometimes seen clergymen, the backs of whose surplices were thoroughly saturated with perspiration.[54]

It seems that certain types of adaptation were tolerable; clearly clerical vestments were not among them.

Bourne's conclusion would have suited Webb. Not only did it seem rational, it also appealed to his instinctual predilection for the speluncar type. This type took its cue from known ancient sources such as the medieval buildings of southern Europe and the Crusader churches of the Holy Land. Ecclesiologically speaking, it was safe. If any further arguments were required in favour of this approach, then there were always the ancient Hindu and Buddhist temples of India and Sri Lanka to which one could point. These, especially the rock-cut temples of Ajanta and Elephanta, were interpreted as pre-existing evidence of the speluncar method having been adopted in such climates.[55] As idolatrous as these religions were considered to be, their architecture hinted at what was seen as an appropriate precedent, even though the fact that they were not designed for congregations was conveniently ignored. The draught-admitting approach, on the other hand, was essentially new. It had no ready or obvious precedent in the world of ancient religious architecture (although plenty in domestic architecture) and was therefore considered potentially incoherent or, worse still, 'unreal'. The debates on climatic adaptation that graced the pages of *The Ecclesiologist* between 1846 and 1854 did, however, temper the society's attitude towards the draught-admitting approach, as the design for Colombo cathedral indicates.

In the event, neither of Carpenter's designs was executed as planned. Both were modified extensively. The cathedral at Colombo, completed in 1854, was much reduced in scale

118 Christ Church cathedral, Colombo (1854), as built by Royal Artillery engineers to extensively reworked designs by R. C. Carpenter.

119 Interior perspective and plan of Joseph Clarke's design for All Saints' church, Point-de-Galle (1861–2), from *The Ecclesiologist* (1861).

at the hands of military engineers, ending up as little more than a transplanted parish church (fig. 118).[56] This is precisely what the Ecclesiological Society had militated against. Although, as with the cathedral at Calcutta, *The Ecclesiologist* acknowledged the benefit of anything that approximated a proper church in Asia, they noted that 'no attempt has been made to give a *speluncar* character to the architecture. The building indeed appears, material and detail apart, to be simply a reproduction of an English country church.'[57] The church at Point-de-Galle (All Saints') fared better. Although Carpenter's plans were essentially discarded, the underlying concept was retained (figs 119 and 120). The task of reconfiguring the plans fell to the English architect Joseph Clarke (Carpenter was dead by this time).[58] Developed under the watchful eye of Garstin, the result naturally incorporated a number of draught-admitting principles, such as exterior cloisters. It also included a key speluncar feature in the form of double-thickness walls. In sympathy with these characteristics the architecture was given decidedly masculine overtones, being described at the time as 'very early Pointed, with plate tracery, and a strong infusion of early French'.[59]

This character likens Point-de-Galle to Burges's design for Brisbane. As mentioned in chapter 2, Burges's plan

120 All Saints' church, Point-de-Galle, Ceylon (1861–2), by Joseph Clarke. The original design for this church was supplied by R. C. Carpenter in 1850.

reflected the broader shift among British architects towards heavier continental styles, particularly the early Gothic of Normandy. In this case, at least, the Ecclesiological Society could take heart from the fact that an architect had finally paid attention to their call to follow speluncar principles. However, as Brisbane was in a semi-tropical location, *The Ecclesiologist* had to concede that Burges's design was only 'semi-speluncar'. Still, this was better than nothing. As at Point-de-Galle, the windows were numerous, but they incorporated heavy plate tracery, thus shielding the interior from direct sunlight.[60] This is similar to the approach Burges had adopted in his designs for the Crimean War

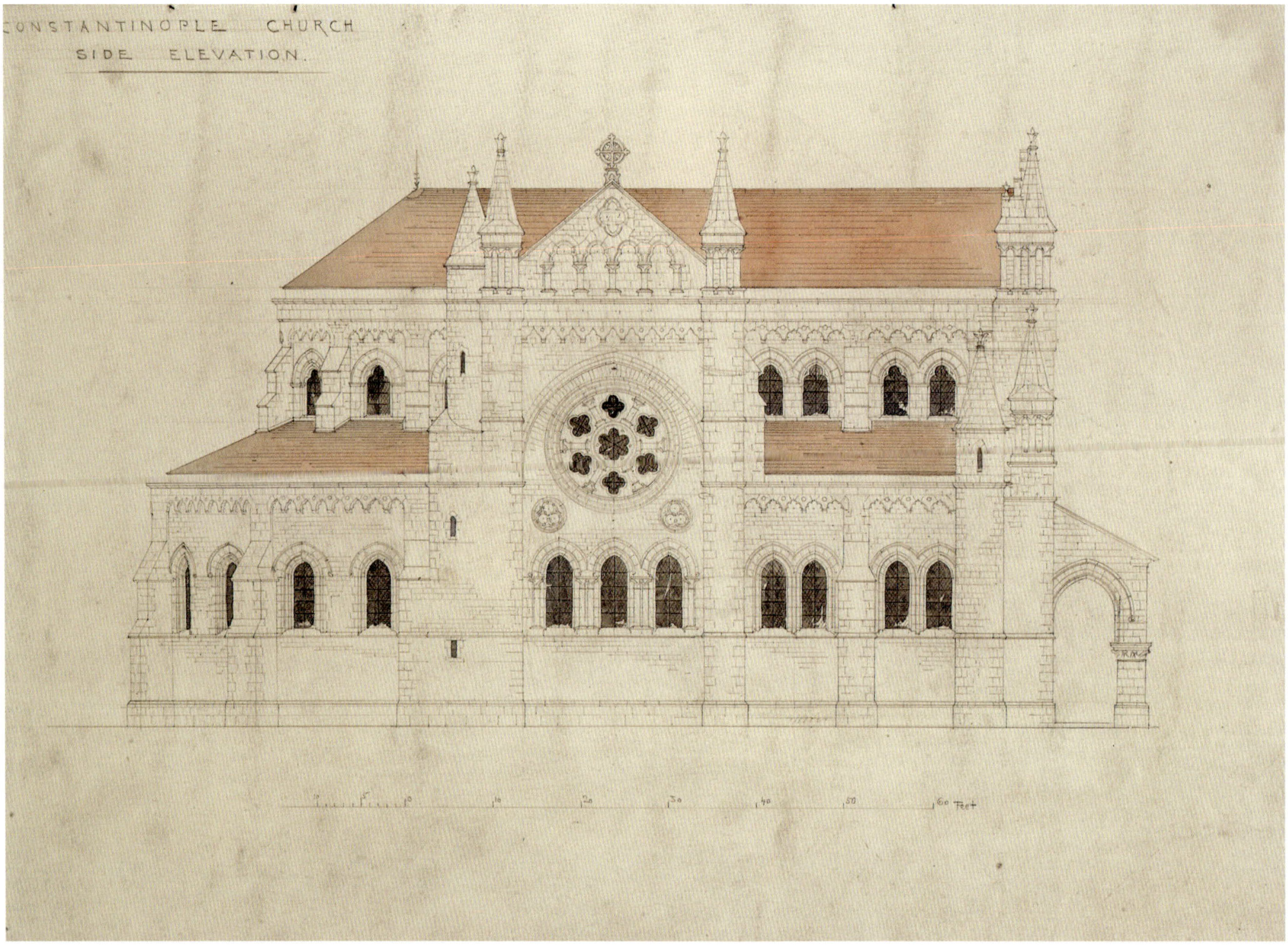

121 North elevation of William Burges's final design for the Crimean War Memorial church, Constantinople, 1861 (RIBA Drawings Collection, Victoria and Albert Museum, London).

Memorial church – a project that was still developing at the time he produced the plans for Brisbane (fig. 121). We not only see the same types of fenestration being used but also a clear concession to simplicity of form. G. E. Street's final design for the same church, the commission for which had fallen to him after Burges's withdrawal in 1863, was along similar lines (fig. 122). In both instances the architects have placed great emphasis on mass and solidity, allowing only small and narrow windows, all of which are set deep into the wall to guard against direct sunlight. As the original competition brief required a building to 'suit the climate', every effort was made to impart a speluncar effect.[61] In this respect, Street also incorporated large buttresses, small eaves, and deep relieving arches in an attempt to provide additional shading.[62]

It was hoped that the design for Brisbane would be carried out in full, for 'we have had enough', complained *The Ecclesiologist*, '. . . of the substitution of second-best for satisfactory cathedral churches'.[63] Unfortunately, as was the case with so many colonial churches, this was not to be. All was not lost, however. The commission was passed on to John Loughborough Pearson (1817–1897) in 1888, resulting in a building that, if somewhat more grandiose, was certainly no less 'cave-like' in its deference to southern European models.[64] It was the same story with G. F. Bodley's design for St Stephen's Mission church in Delhi (1861). Although praised by *The Ecclesiologist* as embodying the 'speluncar principle with great felicity' – and therefore 'the best design for a tropical church which has come under our notice' – it too was modified beyond recognition, only this time by a far inferior architect (see pp. 180–4). Piecemeal attempts were made elsewhere. For instance, in the small English church erected at Mauritius the windows were left unglazed. However, in this case no serious effort was made at systematic acclimatisation.[65] William Hay, on the other hand, tried harder. He had been called to Bermuda from Newfoundland to intervene in the construction of Holy Trinity, Hamilton (1842–68). He suggested inserting unglazed windows at clerestory level and allowing the beams of the roof to protrude through the external wall, thus creating a gap at ceiling height for ventilation.[66] This solution was intelligent but, again, *ad hoc.*

Despite the number of aborted and make-do attempts at climatic control in English church architecture abroad, some important churches were nevertheless completed in line with ecclesiological dictates on Tropical Pointed architecture. Two of the more notable examples were St George's, Basseterre (St Kitts), and All Saints' cathedral, Allahabad (India). Both of these buildings showed serious and systematic attempts at climatic adjustment. The first of them, St George's, Basseterre (1856–9), was under the direction of William Slater (1818/19–1872), former pupil and colleague of R. C. Carpenter. It was Slater's intention to design this church from first principles, incorporating all necessary adaptations as integral to the building's architecture. He was not particularly swayed either way by the speluncar or draught-admitting approaches. In fact he had initially received 'instructions' to adopt the latter.[67] However, as St Kitts was located in an earthquake- and hurricane-prone region, Slater thought it prudent to give the building a degree of sturdiness by adopting simple, low-lying forms and by making provision for ample internal bracing.[68] Adopting tactics similar to Selwyn's in New Zealand, he specified a roof (minus clerestory) with a pitch of 45 degrees for maximum strength.

There was precedent for this approach in the Caribbean. Whether Slater knew it or not, earlier generations of church builders had attempted to combat the particular seismic and climatic conditions of the region through strategies of mass and formal arrangement. In Jamaica, for example, many of the Anglican churches designed and built during the eighteenth century were compact, centrally planned structures, usually in the shape of a Greek cross. It was believed that this approach lent stability to a building in the event of high winds or moving earth.[69] This idea was revived briefly in 1850 with a suggestion (from the West Indies) that plans be prepared by the Oxford Architectural Society for an octagonal church in wood, specifically to resist the pressure and movement exerted by hurricane-force winds and earthquakes.[70] It was with these considerations in mind that a spire was not specified for Slater's church at Basseterre, as it was believed that it would simply be blown off in high winds (figs 123 and 124). When passing by the building in 1858, the bishop of Antigua noted that, although 'a good specimen of rather late Early English', the lack of a clere-

122 Perspective drawing and plan of G. E. Street's final design for the Crimean War Memorial church, Constantinople, from *Building News* (1868). Street was commissioned to design the church after William Burges withdrew in 1863.

123 St George's church, Basseterre, St Kitts (1856–9), by William Slater.

story made the roof appear too heavy.[71] He was evidently unaware of the reasons.

Commenting on this same heftiness, *The Ecclesiologist* came to the opposite conclusion to the bishop, rejoicing in the fact that the 'massive tower over the south porch' was 'boldly buttressed with sets-off at every stage'.[72] Despite the nave and tower being purposefully designed in a heavy and angular fashion, Slater opted for an apsidal instead of a square east end (fig. 125). In plan, this feature sits rather uncomfortably in relation to the rest of the building. The reasons for including it were probably stylistic, but it had been observed by the Rev. J. F. Bourne several years earlier that, 'like the bow of a ship, it [an apsidal east end] seems better adapted to resist the violent storm'.[73] As the church also incorporated several draught-admitting devices, such as large louvred windows, the design was somewhat reminiscent of Carpenter's 'hybrid' vision for Colombo. Given Slater's former association with Carpenter, the broad similarities in approach are not surprising. Nevertheless, *The Ecclesiologist* considered it a 'fresh contribution' towards the problem of Tropical Pointed architecture. Consecrated in March 1859, the church was destroyed by fire in 1867. It was later rebuilt.

At Allahabad we see what is, next to Street's final design for the Crimean War Memorial church, the most thoroughgoing and consistent attempt at Tropical Pointed architecture in an Anglican church anywhere during the mid-nineteenth century (figs 126 and 127). Designed in 1870 by William Emerson (1843–1924), All Saints' cathedral incorporates many of the principles and devices ecclesiologists had been insisting upon for over twenty years. Indeed, as a former pupil of Burges, Emerson designed a cathedral that can be seen as the full realisation of Burges's vision for Brisbane (fig. 128). Although inspired by the choir at Canterbury,[74] it is reminiscent of Burges's cathedral at Cork. The singular achievement of this church is that it manages to remain a distinctly Christian building in both form and appearance while incorporating several important and characteristic adaptive features. The most striking of these is its sheer size and mass. Like an Ely of the East, All Saints' rises from the flat plains of Uttar Pradesh like a great hulk. For this reason it is referred to locally as *pathar girja*, or the 'plateau church'.[75]

On closer inspection it is immediately noticeable that All Saints' is no ordinary church. It has been designed specifically for the context and adapted to suit the climate.

Left 124 Interior perspective of William Slater's design for St George's church, Basseterre, 1856, from A. J. B. Beresford Hope's *The English Cathedral of the Nineteenth Century* (1861).

Right 125 Plan of William Slater's design for St George's church, Basseterre, 1856, from A. J. B. Beresford Hope's *The English Cathedral of the Nineteenth Century* (1861).

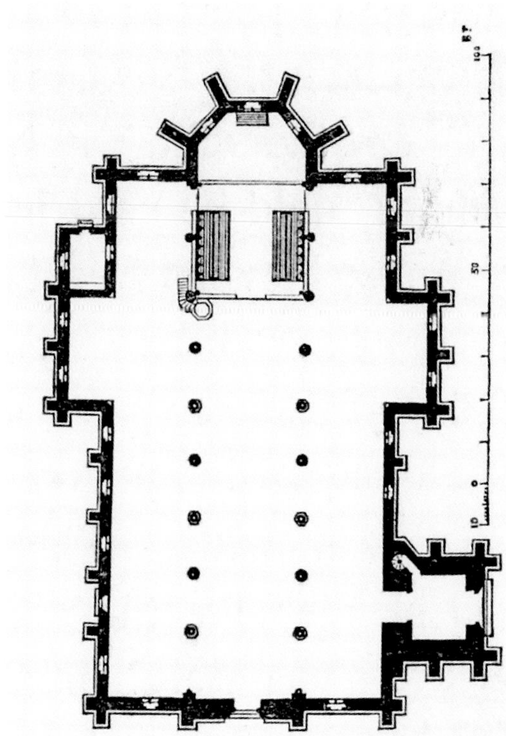

28. Plan of St. Kitt's Church.
75 feet to inch.

126 All Saints' cathedral, Allahabad (1870–87), by William Emerson.

Everywhere we see massively thick walls, a flat roof, sparing use of fenestration (in some cases windows are set several feet into the masonry), plate tracery, ventilation devices and, most striking of all, impressively deep eaves running around the entire building (excepting the transepts) at clerestory level. This last feature is fully integrated into the architecture through the incorporation of arches, resting on piers, which are then buttressed into the walls of the aisle beneath. The result is neat and visually coherent. Internally the church is not only correct but also spacious, dark and cool – precisely what ecclesiologists had been aiming at. Indeed, if *The Ecclesiologist* had still been in print at the time All Saints' was designed, one suspects that Emerson's efforts would have received hearty praise. Here was a genuine exemplar of Tropical Pointed. The foundation stone was laid in April 1871 and the building consecrated in 1887.

The only other cathedral design for India during this period that came close to All Saints' in terms of meeting adaptive criteria, both formal and spatial, was that for St

127 West front of All Saints' cathedral, Allahabad (1870–87).

128 Plan and longitudinal section of William Emerson's design of 1870 for All Saints' cathedral, Allahabad, from *Building News* (1877).

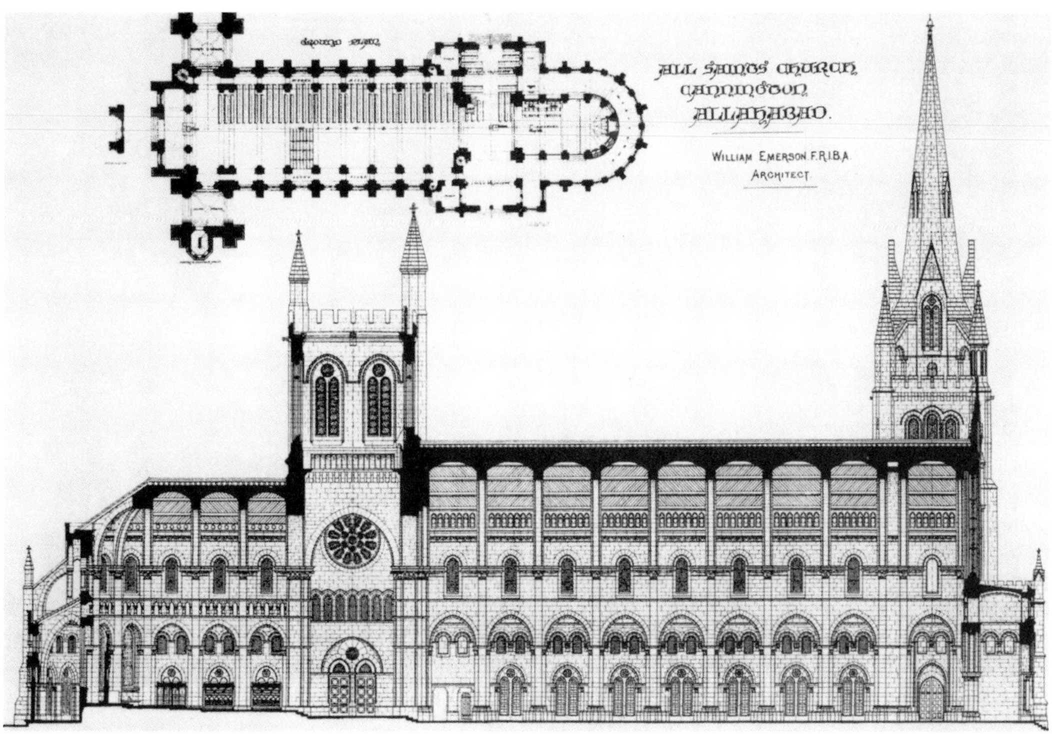

129 James Trubshawe's unrealised design for St Thomas's cathedral, Bombay, 1865 (Bodleian Library, Oxford).

Thomas's, Bombay (1865) (fig. 129).[76] This proposal was put forward at the behest of Archdeacon W. K. Fletcher by James Trubshawe (b. 1817), an English architect then working for the Bombay government. It was intended as a reconstruction of the existing cathedral, which had occupied the site since 1718.[77] Trubshawe's vision was extraordinary in its sheer scale and aesthetic bravado, betraying that sense of optimism which accompanied Bombay's cotton boom of the early 1860s. Much like Derick's design for Colaba, or Carpenter's for Colombo, Trubshawe surrounded his church with an open-air cloister, rising to two storeys at the west front. The rich exterior treatment was, of course, consistent with the architectural goings-on in Bombay at the time, later to be recalled in F. W. Stevens's magnificent Victoria Terminus building (1878–88). Nevertheless, it is very much a conscious work of ecclesiastical design in the High Victorian mode, with its exuberance of Mediterranean, Moorish and Arabic features, befitting its 'Oriental' location.

Unfortunately, the cotton boom had gone bust by the late 1860s and Trubshawe's vision all but came to nothing. The only part that was realised – and that in modified form – was the east end (see fig. 193). Although only a fraction of the original plan, it at least gives some idea of what this building would have looked like. If completed, it would have been one of the most stunning churches anywhere in the world, not only cementing Bombay's reputation as the *urbs prima in Indis* but also as the most spectacular city in the British empire.

It would not be until the early 1880s that the Indian subcontinent would see anything like these designs again. This time it was J. O. Scott's proposal for a magnificent brick cathedral at Lahore (1883–1914), in modern-day Pakistan, admirably adapted to the climate. But this building falls beyond the limits of the current study.

Hyperborean Gothic: Keeping Out the Cold

Strangely, and perhaps counter-intuitively, the speluncar method was considered equally applicable in cold climates. As with the heat, this had to do with the idea of thermal mass: thick walls and few openings that would obviate the worst effects of biting wind and frost. This was certainly how Scott and Bishop Feild viewed the problem at St John's, Newfoundland (see pp. 93–5). Its severe and simple early Gothic style, combined with massively thick walls, was implemented specifically to 'suit its hyperborean climate', as Beresford Hope later observed.[78] So interchangeable was the speluncar principle considered to be that some believed G. E. Street's original design for the Crimean War Memorial church 'would be admirably suited for the cathedral of some northern city where the winters are long and sharp', such as Ottawa or Montreal.[79]

There were others, too, who felt that church architecture in such climes ought to 'harmonise' with its surroundings, assuming a chaste and rugged character.[80] One such was the Rev. Thomas B. Fuller of Niagara. In describing the recently completed church of St Peter, Thorold (1845), Fuller was keen to present the building's architecture as an outgrowth in communion with the surrounding landscape. Located in the undulating terrain along the southern shore of Lake Ontario, perched high between the 'cultivated lands of the industrious farmers' and 'the noble trees of our primeval forest', it was imagined as a kind of other-worldly arbiter between civilisation and savagery. Straddling this boundary, the new church could not boast 'the marks of a thousand years on its walls', noted Fuller, 'but . . . look[ed] as if those marks might yet be there'.[81] In this respect St Peter's was the perfect country church, appearing as if it were somehow both natural and ancient.

The 'simple style' approach, which we have come across before and which was concerned with a certain practical and political economy, was also encouraged in cold climates because of the potential for heavy snowfall. As the Rev. Thomas Bridge of Newfoundland had indicated to the Oxford Architectural Society, 'it would be highly desirable [that] . . . the nave and aisles [of a church] should all be under a single roof; were there a separate roof for each the lodgement of snow in our snowy land between the roofs would be almost overwhelming to any structure'.[82] Building in stone also had its problems. Principal among these was the acquisition of good material at a reasonable price. This was a particularly pressing dilemma for fledgling dioceses in remote areas, where there were few resources and even fewer followers. A good stone church might be years in the making, during which time congregations would be left languishing in less than adequate (or appropriate) accommodation, if they had any at all. However, in the minds of some, there was an even more fundamental problem: stone was not necessarily as 'solid' and therefore suitable for cold climates as one might expect. Unless the right kind of stone was used and the correct mortar produced, buildings would literally 'shiver to pieces'.[83] As moisture seeped into the face of cut stone and between the joints, the stone tended to split or crack when it froze.[84] This made Bishop Feild quite anxious about his cathedral in Newfoundland, and it was a problem to which St Saviour's, Hermitage (1850–4), succumbed.[85] We have also seen how the Caen stone used at Montreal eroded under the severe conditions of that location (see p. 89). It was supposed by some that the worst effects of this kind of weather might be mitigated by employing dry-wall, 'cyclopean' masonry, composed of rough-cut boulders, but this was not practical in the case of cathedral-sized buildings.[86]

130 Lithograph by J. C. Dahl of a medieval timber stave church at Hitterdal, Norway, 1837.

Construction in stone was a tricky and therefore expensive business in sub-arctic regions.

The immediate solution to this problem was to look to another, cheaper, and more flexible material. This material was, of course, wood. The use of timber in Canada and New Zealand, for instance, made perfect sense. Both locations had it in abundance, and both had established forestry and sawmilling industries by the early nineteenth century. By the mid-1840s word had already come from Newfoundland and New Brunswick that good designs for wooden churches were required.[87] Ironically, despite being a 'rock' off the east coast of Canada with very few trees, Newfoundland was a location where it was still easier to obtain milled timber from the mainland than it was to procure a reliable supply of building stone. Thus, a concerted effort was made on the part of both university architectural societies to consider carefully the topic of wooden ecclesiology and to furnish the colonies with appropriate plans and models. The first serious utterances on the subject came from J. E. Millard of Magdalen College, Oxford, in 1845. In a paper on the design of colonial churches, read before the Oxford Architectural Society, Millard stressed that a wooden church could be just 'as Gothic in principle as a stone one, not by imitating in wood the features of ancient stone Churches, but by applying the same principles to a different material'.[88] This got ecclesiologists thinking: could there be a genuine and legitimate timber ecclesiology for the modern age? Perhaps; but this required Britons to look beyond their shores, even beyond the great centres of European medieval architecture. The idea probably first occurred to Millard when he saw the lithographs of medieval Norwegian stave churches presented to the society in 1843 by the Rev. J. L. Patterson of Trinity College (fig. 130). These lithographs, by the Norwegian artist J. C. Dahl (1788–1857), of ancient wooden churches in Hitterdal, Urnes and Borgund showed by no means perfect ecclesiastical specimens, but they at least encouraged new ways of thinking about how a genuine ecclesiastical architecture in timber might be formulated. There was, of course, a long-standing tradition of timber church construction on the North American continent, including, from the early nineteenth century onwards, a Gothic Revival style of sorts – so-called 'carpenter's Gothic'. This tradition had flourished in the United States and parts of modern-day Canada.[89] It was known to ecclesiologists in England, thanks mainly to the numerous letters the architectural societies had received from clergymen abroad, but was considered unworthy as a precedent, owing to the incorrect application of arrangement and style. With this in mind, Patterson would have hoped that his Norwegian models, despite their origins, 'might afford some useful hints for the erection of similar churches in countries where the same materials and no other were readily to be found, . . . more particularly Newfoundland and New Zealand'.[90]

The most substantial early contribution towards a more correct theory of timber ecclesiology came in 1848 from none other than the Rev. William Scott of Hoxton, Feild's friend and confidant. In a paper titled 'On Wooden Churches', Scott appealed to origins in making his case. The very first type of the 'Spiritual Church', he observed, was surely the ark made of 'gopher wood'. Thus, may we not 'detect in *wooden* churches a recurrence and witness to the first type of the Church itself'? Moreover, would it not therefore be 'thoughtless in ourselves to conclude that its material of WOOD were not invested with some peculiar claims upon Christian consideration'?[91] In making his argument in favour of wooden ecclesiology, Scott was able to invert the standard retort that stone was more real than timber by distinguishing between the 'accidents' of material and the fundamentals of form. 'I am not going to say that a stone church as such is not better than a wooden church,' he opined, 'but what I would suggest is, that if a stone church is developed from a wooden church, therefore the stone church implies and assumes the wooden idea.'[92] There-

131 Engraving of the ancient timber church of St Oswald, Lower Peover, Essex, *c.*1013, from *The Builder* (1849).

fore, in the timber church resided the 'archetypical plan'. More convincing still, perhaps, was the fact that several ancient timber churches remained in England in places such as Little Greensted (St Andrew's), Essex, Lower Peover (St Oswald's), and Marton (St James's and St Paul's), Cheshire (fig. 131). These were no less correct than stone churches and happily conformed to the prejudices of ecclesiologists. All of this was no doubt welcome news to the likes of Selwyn, Feild and all those other clergymen who had been struggling in the 'wilderness'. Indeed, as Scott reassuringly asserted, 'contemporaneously both with British and Saxon and Norman churches, arose in poor places, deficient in materials, quarries, and roads, wooden churches, just as they are required in Canadian forests, or at Newfoundland fishing-stations . . . or on the shores of Hong Kong'.[93]

With this idea established, and the case for wooden churches justified, the way was now open, in theory at least, for a modern ecclesiology in timber that would not necessarily be considered inferior to stone. Indeed, it was not long after Scott's appeal that the Ecclesiological Society produced its own design for a timber church, which appeared in the second series of *Instrumenta Ecclesiastica* (1856) (figs 132 and 133).[94] This was perhaps in response to Feild's call for 'one perfect pattern' in wood for the colonies.[95] But all was not right. There were potential problems with timber churches in freezing conditions. This was apparent in the plans of wooden churches sent to Feild by the Oxford Architectural Society in early 1845. These were possibly those drawn from ancient models by William Butterfield and G. G. Scott.[96] We first hear of them in a letter from Feild to William Scott dated May 1845, in which it was noted: 'I have received from the Architectural Society in Oxford nice drawings of wooden chs.' These drawings may have been 'nice', but they were far from ideal, it turns out. 'They are constructed after the model of the old wooden chs. in England,' complained Feild, 'with cross timbers and plaster, which would not suit here.'[97] Although churchlike and a decent alternative to stone (in principle), the problem was that 'outside plaster would not stand the weather'.[98] A simpler, more robust solution was demanded.

Enter the Rev. William Grey (1819–1872), Oxford graduate and keen ecclesiologist. Grey went to Newfoundland via Bermuda as chaplain to Bishop Feild in 1848. Born of 'high family connections', he was the second son of the Rev. Harry Grey of Knutsford (Cheshire), as well as brother-in-law of William White (architect) and father of the future 9th Earl of Stamford.[99] While at Magdalen College in the early 1840s, Grey was heavily involved in matters architectural, being a regular contributor to the events and publications of the Oxford Architectural Society.[100] He was, as Thomas Mozley later recalled, a 'thorough ecclesiologist',[101] and his impact on the development of church architecture in the hyperborean climes of Newfoundland and Labrador was profound. Indeed, owing to his extensive knowledge of ecclesiastical architecture, Grey had 'the office' of diocesan architect foisted upon him.[102] His arrival in Newfoundland was of course a great boon to Feild.[103] This was especially so given that Feild was able to appoint him, among other things, principal of Queen's (theological) College. In this capacity, Grey gave lectures on architecture to trainee clergymen twice a week. Like Broughton in Australia, it was his belief that clergymen in the colonies '*must* be architects'.[104]

According to Feild, Grey worked hard at devising a form of church architecture that would suit the particular conditions the Church faced in Newfoundland and Labrador. As with Selwyn and Fuller before him, this entailed careful consideration of the circumstances, including the availability of materials, local building expertise and the wider environmental context. This last consideration was especially important, it seems, as Grey wanted an ecclesiology that was appropriate to both the 'climate and scenery'.[105] After all, it was reported with grim remorse in the *Colonial Church Chronicle* that Newfoundland was a land 'without a

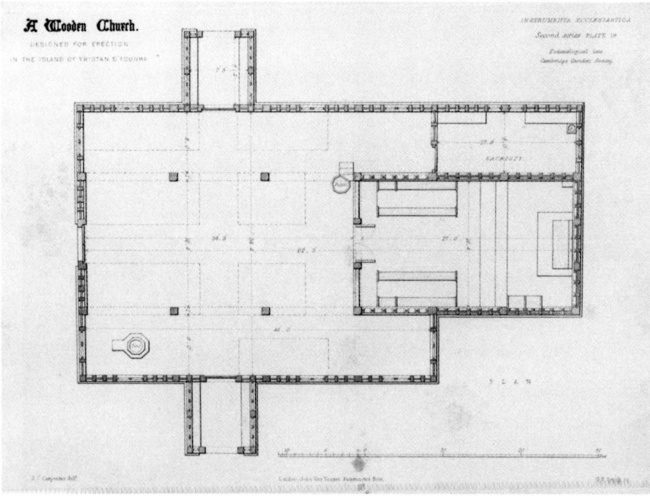

132 Plan of a 'model' timber church for Tristan da Cunha by R. C. Carpenter, 1850, from *Instrumenta Ecclesiastica*, 2nd ser. (1856).

133 Perspective drawing of R. C. Carpenter's design for a 'model' timber church for Tristan da Cunha, 1850, from *Instrumenta Ecclesiastica*, 2nd ser. (1856).

sheltering tree, or depth enough . . . earth to dig a grave', and where one could often expect nothing more than a 'crop of cold snow'.[106]

Given these harsh climatic conditions, and the problems with masonry construction, the outcome was a simple, even 'severe', ecclesiology in timber; what Feild referred to as Grey's 'particular style'.[107] We see evidence of this 'style' in the churches he designed for Forteau, Battle Harbour, Oderin and Portugal Cove (figs 134 and 135).[108] All of these places were coastal fishing villages, Forteau and Battle Harbour being particularly remote locations along the southern coast of Labrador. Again, like Selwyn and Cotton in New Zealand, Grey commented on and sketched regularly the impressively dramatic and rugged landscapes that he encountered on his travels around Newfoundland and Labrador; hence his desire to formulate an architecture that would harmonise with these environments (fig. 136).[109]

Unfortunately, most of Grey's buildings no longer survive, but we get some sense of just how simple and severe they were from original drawings and photographs. In each

134 William Grey's sketch of a design for his timber church at Battle Harbour, Labrador, *c.*1853 (Memorial University Libraries, St John's, Newfoundland). The church as built (1853–7) varies slightly from this design.

135 Sketch by William Grey of his mission church at Oderin, Newfoundland, *c.*1855 (Bodleian Library, Oxford).

instance we see an approach to ecclesiastical design that was broadly minimalist. Bold and simple forms, composed of solid stud framing in timber, exposed to the exterior, with infill panels of weatherboard.[110] In this respect, Grey's churches are somewhat reminiscent of Selwyn's in New Zealand, with a few small exceptions: there are generally very few if any external cross-bracing elements visible on the exterior, and the cladding is, on the whole, applied horizontally. This is somewhat peculiar given that Grey would have been familiar with the general demand among ecclesiologists for the 'churchlike' effect of vertical cladding. Although this was probably a concession to local building conventions, it was also related to ancient techniques known to Grey from England. It is evident in the way he introduces what are referred to as 'oblique' panels in the upper sections of the walls of his churches, usually arranged at opposing angles either side of the major structural elements. This technique may be seen at St Peter's, Forteau (*c.*1855) (fig. 137), and in Grey's sketch of St Peter's, Portugal Cove (1854). Apart from offering visual relief, this oblique form

136 Panoramic sketch by William Grey, of Petty Harbour, Newfoundland, 1857.

137 The timber church of St Peter, Forteau, Labrador (*c.*1855), by William Grey. The oblique timber sections can be seen in the upper part of the nave walls.

138 Timber mission church at St Francis' Harbour, Labrador (1850), by William Hay and William Grey, from the *Quarterly Paper of the SPG* (October 1850).

of cladding recalls the technique observable at Lower Peover, drawings of which were known to have been in Feild's possession.[111] Further evidence for this 'half-timbered' effect is found in Grey's suggestion that the framework elements of timber churches ought to be picked out in a darker colour than the weatherboarding.[112]

Grey was known to have employed a variety of techniques in the construction of his churches. For example, in his designs for Placentia Bay, Newfoundland (1852), and his collaboration with William Hay at St Francis' Harbour, Labrador (1850), we see the use of vertical instead of horizontal cladding (fig. 138).[113] This approach reflected better, perhaps, the perpendicular principle associated with true Christian architecture. Nor was Grey entirely against stone architecture. One of his most successful and representative designs was that for St Mary's (1869) in the city of St John's (fig. 139).[114] Peering across at Feild's cathedral from the

139 St Mary's church, St John's, Newfoundland (1869), by William Grey.

140 All Saints' church, McKeen's Corner, New Brunswick (1861), by Edward Medley.

other side of the harbour, St Mary's is a good example of hyperborean Gothic in stone. It followed speluncar principles to the letter, with its bold and simple forms in the Early Pointed style, thick walls, small (and few) windows, and uncomplicated, high-pitched roofs. On the whole, it presented a most severe and formidable outline; a veritable fortress against the fearsome Newfoundland winter.

The other place where we see the development of an ecclesiology responsive to cold conditions is New Brunswick. Bishop John Medley had initiated this cause through his engagement with the Ecclesiological Society in the 1840s. On more than one occasion he had solicited the society to consider seriously the topic of timber ecclesiology and to prepare model designs in wood for the colonies.[115] In fact, it was in response to the encouragement of clergymen like Medley and Feild that William Scott ventured to expound on the topic at length in 1848. But it was Medley's son Edward (1838–1910) who would do most in realising this cause. Trained initially as an architect under William Butterfield (with whom Medley had connections), Edward was later ordained an Anglican priest (1864) on his return to Canada.[116] In this role he was able to unite his expert knowledge of architecture with his vocation to produce some of the finest timber churches erected anywhere in the Anglican world. In this respect, Edward Medley was a 'priestly architect' in the Frederick Thatcher mould (see p. 51). A number of his churches recall the forms and techniques devised by Selwyn and Thatcher in New Zealand nearly twenty years earlier. All Saints', McKeen's Corner (1861), and St Mary the Virgin, New Maryland (1863–4) (fig. 140), for instance, are similar in their compact form, overhanging eaves, vertically aligned cladding, and exposure of structural elements to the exterior. As Douglas Richardson has observed, Medley was also influenced by 'board and batten' timber housing in North America and inclined to borrow directly from known published sources, such as the porch in Carpenter's design for Tristan da Cunha (see below).[117] These characteristics culminate in his most important and developed work, Christ Church, St Stephen (1863–4) (fig. 141). Internally, this is a spectacularly rich and sophisticated essay in carved native timbers, somewhat reminiscent of the framing techniques observable in

141 Christ Church, St Stephen, New Brunswick (1863–4), by Edward Medley.

142 Interior of Christ Church, St Stephen (1863–4), showing exposed timberwork construction.

the great tithe barn at Harmondsworth, recommended by G. G. Scott (see p. 106) (fig. 142).[118]

The innovations of William Grey and Edward Medley came closest to what *The Ecclesiologist* hoped would be 'a national style of wooden Christian architecture' in Canada.[119] With this in mind, it is mistaken to view their churches as necessarily inferior to those in Britain. They may have been basic in comparison, and were certainly not constructed of 'solid' materials, but they were no less sophisticated in their own way. After all, as we have seen, *The Ecclesiologist* had explicitly encouraged colonial architects and clergymen not to copy buildings from England but to formulate their own unique brand of church architecture and 'practically find what they are seeking'.[120] This is exactly what Grey and Medley did. Their churches represent a carefully considered form of ecclesiastical architecture, deliberately tailored to suit prevailing circumstances. Grey and Medley were no hacks in this respect. In fact, they were at the centre of the ecclesiological movement in Britain: Grey, an active and highly respected (even leading) member of the Oxford Architectural Society; and Medley, son of a noted Tractarian bishop and trainee of William Butterfield ('apostle' of the High Church school, as G. G. Scott described him).[121] Both men were fully cognisant of the 'science' of Anglican ecclesiology and applied it knowingly.

Materials and Materiality: Finding an Alternative Condition

As we saw in Chapter 1, materials and materiality were crucial to the development of Anglican ecclesiology abroad. Like climate, materials were considered a problem with regard to correctness and propriety in colonial church architecture. The default position of most ecclesiologists in Britain was that, under normal circumstances, churches ought to be built substantially and in stone. Brick eventually became acceptable, especially for urban churches, but less substantial materials such as timber were generally frowned upon. However, the circumstances faced by the Church in the colonies were far from normal. Alternatives had to be sought, and 'rules' relaxed, if proper ecclesiastical architecture was to flourish in Britain's empire. This much we have seen in relation to 'hyperborean Gothic' discussed above.

But there were more basic considerations. The availability of solid building material and the resources to procure it were major concerns for colonial clergy, especially those located in remote areas. There was a way round this predicament, however. One of the most important concepts in modern ecclesiology was that of propriety – that is, truth to materials and honesty in construction. This concept had gained credence among architects during the 1830s and 1840s, owing first to the agitations of Pugin, and then to the dictates of the university architectural societies, embody-

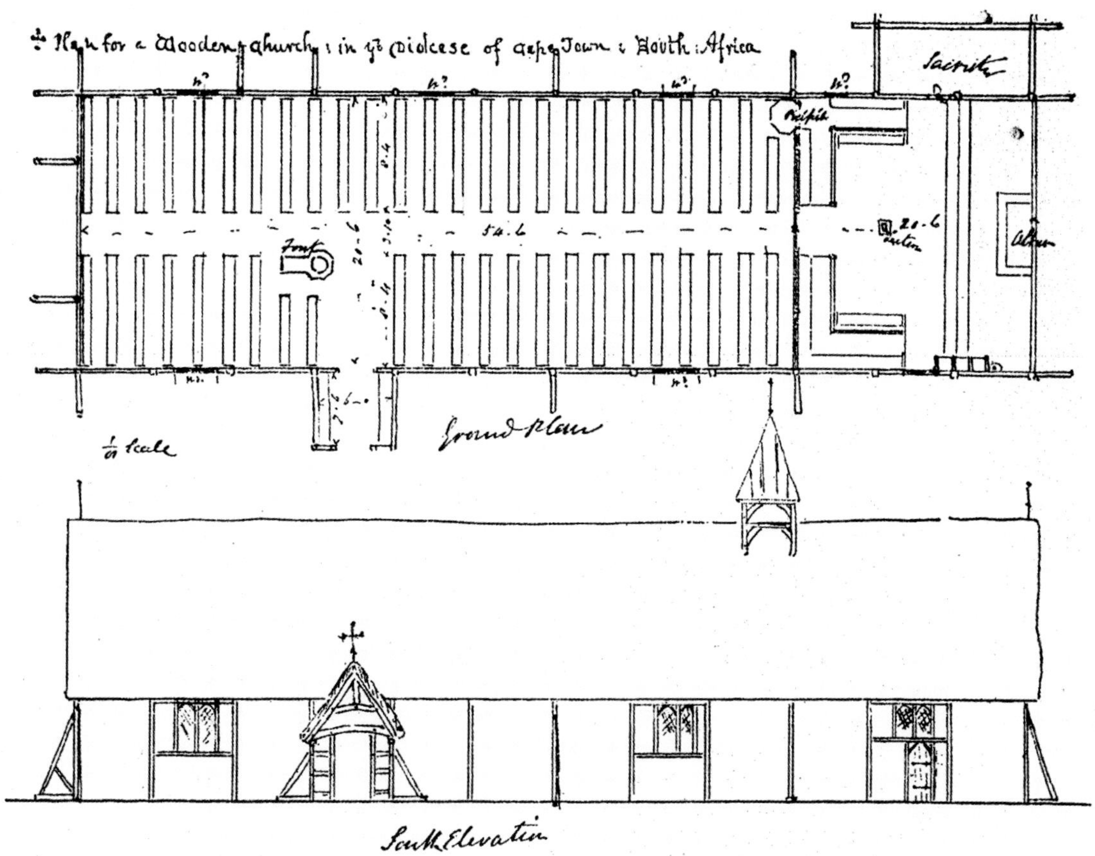

143 Plan and elevation drawings of William White's unexecuted design for a timber chapel at Woodlands, near Cape Town, *c.*1852.

ing that crucial swing away from notions of the picturesque in Gothic Revival architecture to those of archaeological accuracy and authenticity. Ruskin, too, had evoked the moral dimensions of this idea in his influential essay 'The Nature of Gothic' (1853), in which characteristics such as 'savageness' and 'changefulness' were presented as virtuous rather than defective.[122] All this led to a general shift in attitude among Anglican ecclesiologists on the point of appropriateness. Alternative materials were acceptable as long as the most basic and fundamental principles of Christian architecture were not violated.

We have seen perhaps the most extreme example of this in Selwyn's movable tabernacle, the so-called 'Church Tent or 'canvas Cathedral' (see pp. 27–9). Another, slightly less ephemeral, example was William White's unbuilt design for a small church in the diocese of Cape Town (*c.*1852) (fig. 143). In terms of spatial arrangement, White's church was neat and correct in every way. It had not only a distinct nave, chancel and side porch, but also open seating and an elevated altar (including sedilia with piscina). Despite this, the building was to be erected of the crudest, lightweight, ready-to-hand materials – in essence, nothing more than wattle and daub. Nevertheless, such buildings were considered 'suitable' under the circumstances.[123] Other examples of this kind include Holy Trinity chapel, Te Henui (New Zealand), Holy Trinity church, Merriwa (Australia), the Universities' Mission to Central Africa church at Chicamas, Morambala (Mozambique), and Holy Trinity church, New Westminster (British Columbia). The 'slab churches' of bishop Broughton in Australia (see pp. 4–5) also fall within this category of 'rustic ecclesiology'.

In every case the cheapest and most basic materials were used. At Te Henui (1845) rough-split slabs of rimu pine, with the bark still attached, were erected vertically to form

144 Holy Trinity chapel, Te Henui, New Zealand (1845), by Frederick Thatcher.

walls, while wild ferns were used for thatching (fig. 144).[124] Still, the outcome was perfectly churchlike, with its high-pitched roof, side porch, bellcote and gable cross – even the corner struts were an adequate substitute for buttresses. The churches at Merriwa and New Westminster were similar, and only slightly more refined. In the case of Merriwa (1850–5), the Rev. R. George Boodle (who designed it) made use of locally sourced timbers, including the infamously hard iron bark (fig. 146).[125] These timbers were split into slabs rather than sawn, giving the building a distinctly rugged, even coarse appearance.[126] Overhanging eaves and swinging shutters were also incorporated to protect against excessive sunlight. As Joan Kerr has observed, Boodle's church, much like those of Grey and Medley discussed above, was no 'untutored "vernacular" building erected by an ignorant amateur; it was a cheap rural church which knowingly combined English medieval associations with local materials, expertise and climate'.[127] The same applies to Holy Trinity, New Westminster (1860) (fig. 145). Although correct in every way, its nave arcade comprised 'massive pillars' of local fir 'with Gothic arches between'.[128] Perhaps the most extreme example of this type, however, was the UMCA church at Chicamas (1863) (fig. 147). Here indigenous building technologies and materials were adopted, including elephant grass and bamboo, to create a

145 Holy Trinity church, New Westminster, British Columbia (1860), by an unknown designer.

146 Holy Trinity church, Merriwa, New South Wales (1850–5), by George Boodle.

building that, like White's in Cape Town, was perfectly correct if radically unconventional in terms of its materiality and appearance.[129] When it was completed, the UMCA bishop, William Tozer (1829–1899), observed that the church may have appeared as nothing more than a 'poor cottager's hay stack', but in the highlands of Central Africa, where no 'architecture' was seen to exist, it was perceived as both novel and imposing.[130]

147 Edward Steere, sketches of a bamboo and thatch church (1863), erected by the missionaries of the Universities' Mission to Central Africa at Chicamas, Morambala (Mozambique) (Bodleian Library, Oxford).

These examples demonstrate what was both possible and tolerable at one end of the ecclesiological spectrum. In this sense they are something of a modern Anglican equivalent to the adobe churches erected by Franciscan missionaries in New Mexico during the seventeenth century.[131] Moreover, they are linked by the association made in the minds of their creators between materiality, missionary labour and the 'primitive church' ideal. Such buildings were understood as manifestations of a specific condition and location: that is, the Church in its most infantile state, in the process of becoming, in a particular place at a particular time. Although informed by a common set of design principles, they differ markedly with respect to the colour, density and texture of their materials. We get a sense of this in the account of Holy Trinity, New Westminster, at the time of its consecration: 'the internal fittings are of the handsomest description. The seats . . . are of fir, trimmed with the famous Californian redwood. The lectern or bible-desk . . . is of fir and the Columbian cottonwood; the poppy heads of redwood are admirably contrasted.'[132] Churches of this kind were at once universal and unique (that is, place specific). As discussed in Chapter 1, the building of such 'primitive' churches was imagined against the historical backcloth of the early Church and the hardship faced by the 'fathers'. More substantial buildings would no doubt have been preferred, but a certain sense of dignity and satisfaction was gained from extending the Church in this way through the employment of local materials and the application of technical ingenuity.

As we have seen, this attitude towards materials led to the development of whole new traditions in modern Anglican ecclesiology. In New Brunswick, for example, Bishop John Medley was certainly keen to make the most of wood as a cheap and abundant material. Triumphs in this regard included St Andrew's, Newcastle (now Miramichi; 1850) (fig. 148) and Christ Church, Maugerville (1857). These buildings were wooden versions, complete with imitation buttresses, of model parish churches, designs for which were sent from England.[133] This form of ecclesiology had also migrated to the United States via architects such as Frank Wills, whose 1850 book *Ancient English Ecclesiastical Architecture and Its Principles* contained his own design for Grace Church, Albany, New York (1849–52). Although this type of building attracted the general approbation of the Ecclesiological Society, there were problems. Essentially, it was already obsolete by the 1850s. Moreover, being literal transcriptions in wood of model parish churches, these buildings were seen to violate the fundamental ecclesiological tenet of reality.[134] In other words, they had not, as both Millard and Scott insisted they should, 'discarded rigorously and unceremoniously all that is essential to stone'.[135] Rather than imitate 'secondary forms' such as buttresses, ecclesiologists preferred the use of angled struts on timber churches. This was considered a more direct and therefore honest expression of load-bearing construction. As we have seen, things were different in Newfoundland, thanks mainly to Grey. In the United States, too, Richard Upjohn had developed a species of timber church architecture, evident in his design for St John Chrysostom, Delafield (1851–6), that addressed many of these concerns. But it was not until the return of Edward Medley from England in the 1860s that attitudes towards timber ecclesiology began to change in New Brunswick.

In New Zealand, on the other hand, timber was much more than an alternative building material. It formed the basis of an entirely distinct but no less correct species of Anglican church architecture. Even where good building stone could be found, timber was often preferred. Again, this was dictated largely by practical considerations, such as cost and the need to limit earthquake damage. Thus, in a peculiar inversion, like that experienced at Newfoundland, stone came to be seen as less permanent than timber.[136] Under such circumstances timber soon acquired an aesthetic economy of its own.

This is observable in the earliest efforts of Bishop Selwyn and the development of the so-called Selwyn style. From the beginning Selwyn was keen to make a connection between the education of a clergyman and the principle of labour. He recognised architecture as a means of encoding this connection. Following biblical precedent, and the example of St Paul in particular, he established a carpentry workshop at St John's College, Bishop's Auckland, in which the pupils were required to pursue practical skills, including the pre-fabrication of buildings, alongside their theoretical training. This was part of what Selwyn called his 'industrial system' – a necessary response to the missionary circumstances in which he found himself.[137] This system extended the 'embellishment of Churches with carved work of wood and stone'.[138] Apart from the college chapel, the first notable example of such a building was All Saints', Howick, built for a community of émigré pensioners in 1847 (fig. 149).[139] This church, designed and manufactured in the college

148 The timber church of St Andrew, Newcastle, New Brunswick (1850), erected under the auspices of Bishop John Medley.

workshop, and assembled on the banks of the Purewa Creek, was shipped to Howick using the college vessels *Undine* and *Marion*.[140] It is a plain but sturdy building, incorporating the exterior cross-bracing common to many Selwyn churches (see p. 53). On closer inspection one can see quite clearly the wrought nature of the individual components, revealing certain inconsistencies and imperfections. This gives the building a distinctive hand-crafted appearance. It has a peculiar 'roughness', as Ruskin would later describe it (or 'barbaric richness' as William Scott might have said), through which it is possible to appreciate the morality (that is, dignified labour) of the architecture and its means of production. In the end, as many as eight such churches were prefabricated in the workshop at St John's and erected in the vicinity of Auckland.[141] These included St Peter's, Onehunga (fig. 150); St Mark's, Remuera; and St Barnabas's, Parnell.

Thus, in the disciplined regime of St John's College, timber was associated with labour in a way that was both conspicuous and reverential. It became the medium through which the ideal of St Paul was expressed and given meaning. In such a context, timber was able to acquire a particular efficacy through its ready transformation from an essentially 'raw' (that is, wild) material into one of productive and spiritual value. Further significance was added as each prefabricated component accrued meaning through program-

149 All Saints' church, Howick, near Auckland (1847), prefabricated in the workshop at St John's College, Bishop's Auckland.

150 St Peter's church, Onehunga, New Zealand (1848), by Frederick Thatcher, prefabricated in the workshop at St John's College, Bishop's Auckland.

matic assemblage. Thus, surrounded by the signs of wilderness and 'savagery', Selwyn and his colleagues perceived architecture as a means of achieving salvation. This process was in a sense alchemical. The systematic prefabrication of timber churches was the material counterpart to the harvesting and conversion of souls – conversion, like building, involving the transformation of something from one state to another, from a base condition to an elevated and enhanced nature. Timber had become the missionary material par excellence, and its materiality a mark of the missionary condition. By analogy, Selwyn reminded his followers that 'we must have faith in the very nature of our work': 'A prophet's office is not in the courts of Kings, or in rich men's houses, where men wear soft clothing and fare sumptuously every day. John came neither eating bread nor drinking wine; yet Herod, from the midst of his palace, heard the fame of his preaching in the wilderness, and listened to his reproof, and respected his character. . . . Elijah the Tishbite, put not on his courtly garb to wait upon Ahab, but bound his hairy garment about his loins, with his leathern girdle, and went to meet him at Samaria, and preached to him the judgements of God.'[142] Thus, the humble and unpretentious timber church would do the work of God in the wilderness no less effectively than the sumptuous temple.

It was not long before the Ecclesiological Society began to appreciate the benefits of prefabrication. There had been some discussion in the pages of *The Ecclesiologist* on the export of ready-made churches, such as those by Peter Thompson of Limehouse, to different parts of the world, but there had been very little attempt on the part of the society itself to propose a more satisfactory solution (fig. 151). This changed with the publication of the second series of *Instrumenta Ecclesiastica* in 1856. Here there appeared two designs for prefabricated churches, one in wood, as mentioned, and the other in iron. The timber design, composed by R. C. Carpenter, was originally intended for the island of Tristan da Cunha, but was generally considered appropriate for temperate climates.[143] What is apparent in looking at this design is the way in which the material is celebrated. This is no mere carpenter's Gothic. There is no attempt to disguise wood as a substitute for stone. Rather, we see the development of a genuine ecclesiology in wood, in which the architect has identified and worked with the peculiar qualities and constraints of the material to produce a building that is both characteristic and 'real'. The way in which the individual components are brought together is calibrated specifically to the characteristics of the material at hand (fig. 152). The result is a form of joinery without nails – only a combination of lap boarding, tongue-and-groove boards and mortise-and-tenon joints with wooden pegs that recall medieval carpentry techniques. In this one design, propriety and precedent were accounted for in timber no less than they would have been in stone.

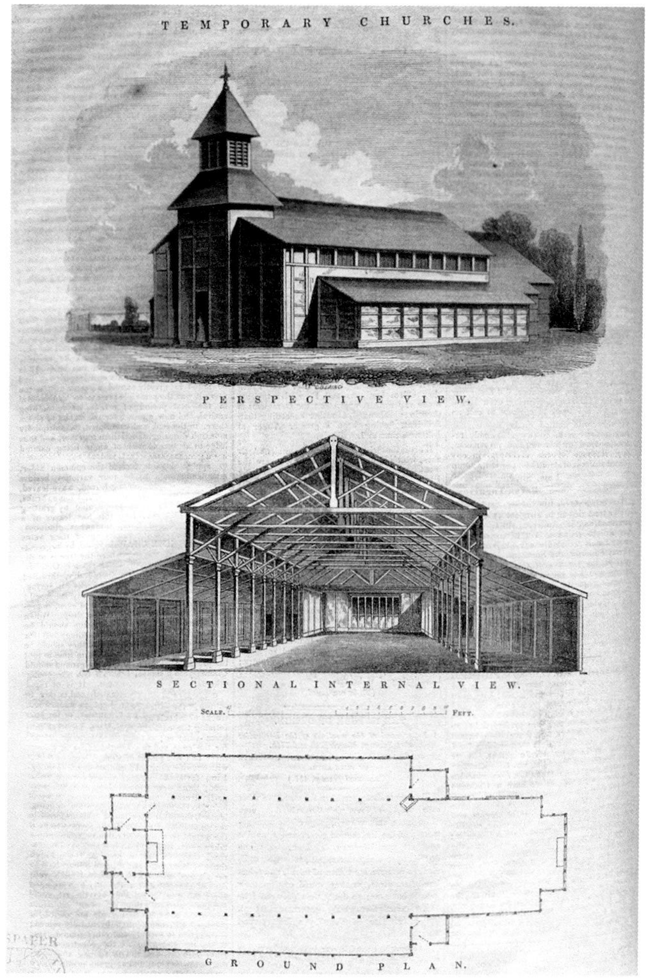

151 Design for a 'temporary' timber church by Peter Thompson of Limehouse, London, from *The Builder* (1844).

Although this particular design was never built, the principles it embodied were influential. We see this, again, in New Zealand where the tradition of timber ecclesiology reached its apogee in the work of architects such as Frederick Thatcher and Benjamin Mountfort. Thatcher's design for St Paul's cathedral, Wellington (1865–6), is a breathtaking example of the levels to which timber ecclesiology of this

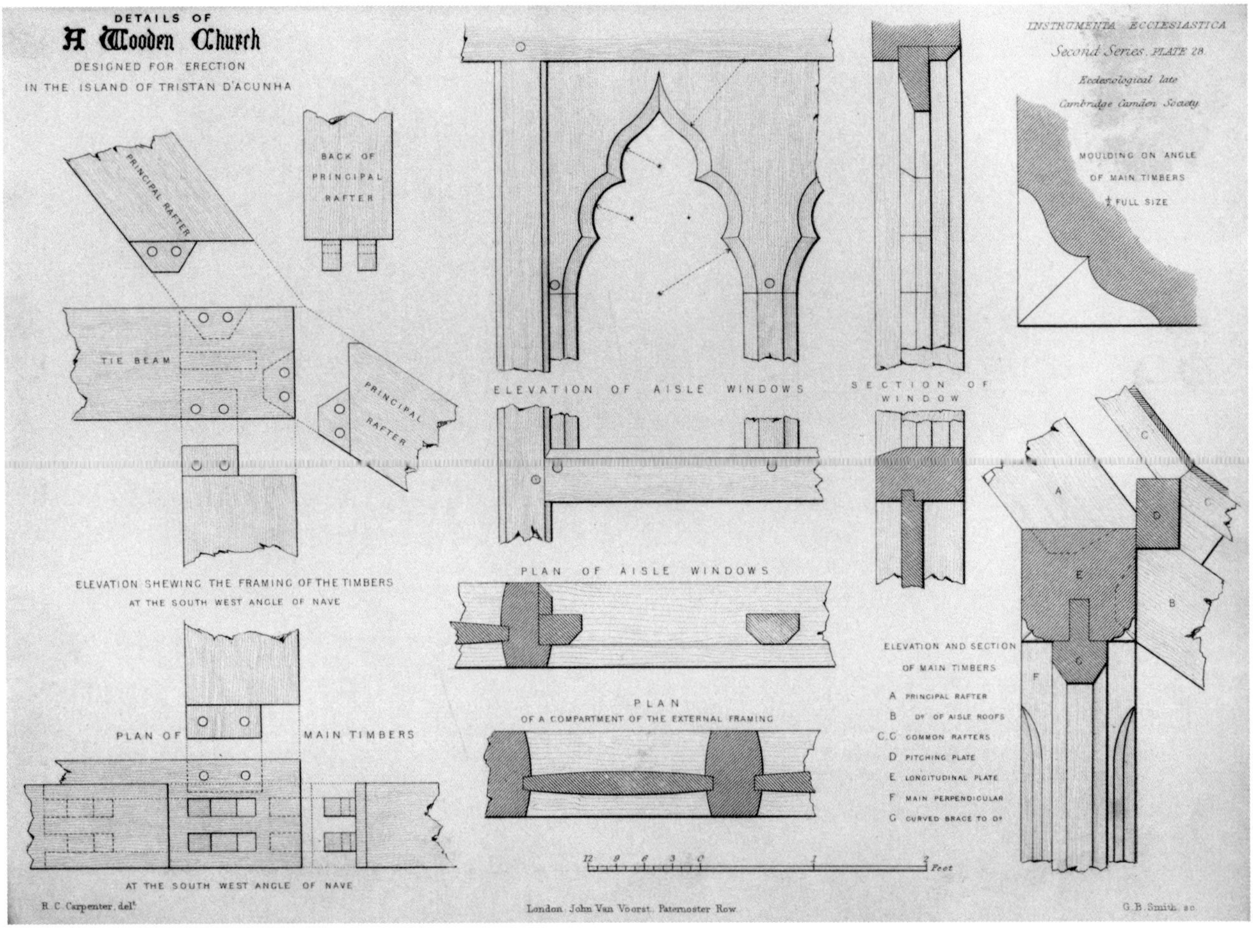

152 Details of timber jointing for R. C. Carpenter's church at Tristan da Cunha, from *Instrumenta Ecclesiastica*, 2nd ser. (1856).

kind was developed in the middle decades of the nineteenth century (fig. 153). Erected using an array of native timbers, including totara, rimu, kauri and matai, it is a building that announces and celebrates its material quality. The interior, especially, is a spectacular assemblage of wrought timber elements, carefully worked and stained to reveal their peculiar nature (fig. 154). One is struck immediately upon entering by the grains and textures of the different woods, as well as their specific scents. The exterior, too, pretends to be nothing other than what it is. In all, St Paul's offers a master-class in adapting timber to the formal requirements of the Gothic style. These qualities and influences are also evident in the work of Mountfort (see pp. 277–81). From the humble Hemingford Church (1851–3) to more grandiose and refined schemes, such as Holy Trinity, Lyttelton (1851–5), St Mary's, Halswell (1862), and even St. Augustine's, Waimate (1872) (see fig. 276), Mountfort rose to become New Zealand's premier ecclesiastical architect, demonstrating what was possible in the medium of wood.[144]

Timber was also used in tropical climates. Almost in spite of the debate raging over whether the speluncar or draught-admitting approach was more to be preferred in colonial church design, certain architects and clergymen forged ahead and built their churches in wood. In the case of the Rev. F. T. McDougall of Sarawak (on the island of Borneo, Malaysia), the factors to be considered were more practical than theoretical. His decision to build a church in wood at Kuching (St Thomas's) was, again, a solution associated with the exigencies of place (fig. 155). It was known to McDougall that houses in the region (Singapore and Malaysia) built of substantial materials such as brick did not last. 'Bricks I have found will not stand the climate – the best rot and crack and crumble away.'[145] Instead, McDougall turned to an indigenous timber known as balean or 'iron wood'. He

153 St Paul's cathedral, Wellington (1865–6), by Frederick Thatcher.

154 Interior of St Paul's cathedral, Wellington (1865–6), showing the magnificent exposed timberwork construction, using native New Zealand woods.

had heard it claimed by the Dyak peoples of Borneo that a house built of this material would last several hundred years.[146] The real benefit of balean was its relative indestructibility, its being resistant to rot and the rapacious white ant – two extremely important considerations for a church in this locale.[147] The downside, however, was that its use added to the cost of construction. It was so heavy that it could not be floated downstream ('it sinks like a stone'), and so dense that it quickly blunted the tools used to work it. Nevertheless, McDougall persisted. As with Selwyn, Broughton, Cox and others before him, he found himself acting as architect, clerk of works and even carpenter for a time. The foundation 'sleeper' of the church was laid in August 1849, and the building consecrated by bishop Daniel Wilson of Calcutta in January 1851 (fig. 156).[148] Again, what we see in St Thomas's is a building that embodies its adapted condition, not only through certain climate-control measures, such as open walls, overhanging eaves and verandahs, but also in its contingent materiality, all contained within a neat and correct Gothic design.

In the humid climes of Queensland, Australia, similar buildings could be found. The work of the English émigré architect R. G. Suter is a case in point. Educated at Trinity College, Cambridge, in the late 1840s, Suter would undoubtedly have been familiar with the activities of the Ecclesiological Society.[149] Moreover, his brother (the Rev. A. B. Suter) was an Anglican priest who later became bishop of Nelson in New Zealand (1866). This connection, along

155 The cathedral of St Thomas, Kuching, Sarawak (1849–51), by F. T. McDougall. It was built using native balean timber.

with his family's long-standing association with Sampson Kempthorne, who, as we have seen, emigrated to New Zealand in 1841 (see pp. 46–7), meant that the timber churches of Selwyn were known to Suter. In his designs for St Andrew's, Lutwyche (near Brisbane, 1867) and St Augustine's, Leyburn (1871), we see the adoption of a very similar exposed framing, or 'outside studding', technique (fig. 158). Although timber in this case was employed primarily for its cheapness as a building material, it is clear that Suter was keen to give his churches an air of ecclesiastical dignity, based on precedent. The half-timbered effect achieved was understood to approximate the traditional half-timbered buildings of his native England; in the Australian context, the dark brown hue of the iron-bark studding contrasted naturally with the yellowish/cream colour of the Moreten Bay pine cladding.[150] Climatic adaptations were also incorporated, such as extensive eaves and the elevation of the building off the ground to facilitate air circulation.

Timber was not the only alternative building material to stone or brick. Iron was another. To be sure, many clergymen perceived timber as too ephemeral, requiring constant maintenance and eventually deteriorating.[151] Most viewed timber as a temporary solution at best. Iron at least had greater potential for longevity. Increased industrial production and the development of pre-fabrication techniques in Britain during the nineteenth century made iron a viable alternative. Its use led not only to daring and novel archi-

156 Drawing by an unknown artist of the interior of St Thomas's, Kuching (1849–51), showing the clam-shell baptismal font, *c.*1855 (Bodleian Library, Oxford).

tectural experiments, such as the Crystal Palace (1851) and the courtyard atrium of the Oxford Natural History Museum (1854–60), but also to the production of portable buildings for shipment abroad.[152] In the minds of true ecclesiologists, however, the same concerns applied: could a genuine iron ecclesiology be developed on 'metallic principles'? The Ecclesiological Society certainly thought so, publishing a design for an 'Iron Church' by William Slater in the second series of *Instrumenta Ecclesiastica* (1856) (fig. 157).[153] This design is well known, as is the fact that it was never built.[154] The perceived advantage of such a design, in theory at least, was that it could be entirely pre-fabricated off site, flat-packed, and shipped anywhere in the world, thus making it ideal for colonial dioceses. Some commentators were less sanguine, however. Ruskin, for one, was at best ambivalent over the use of iron (especially cast iron), eventually coming to the conclusion that it should not be used for purposes of visible construction in Gothic buildings.[155] Scott, too, shied away from employing it openly in his churches, as did most other High Victorian architects. But for some the experiment was at least worth trying, especially where few other options remained.

Among the earliest examples of iron churches in the colonies were those sent to Victoria (Australia) in the 1850s. The first bishop of Melbourne, Charles Perry, received a grant in aid of £1,300 from the SPCK in 1853 to begin the importation of iron churches. Pre-fabricated buildings of this kind were considered necessary at the time because the Victorian gold rush had resulted in soaring and unsustainable labour costs in the colony. They had also been used in Britain (where they were called 'tin tabernacles'), espe-

157 West elevation of William Slater's design for a prefabricated iron church, from *Instrumenta Ecclesiastica*, 2nd ser. (1856), showing corrugated sheet-iron exterior cladding.

158 St Andrew's church, Lutwyche, near Brisbane (1867), by R. G. Suter.

cially for mission work among the urban poor in the country's rapidly expanding cities (for more on this see Chapter 7).[156] Produced by Samuel Hemming of Bristol, the first 'iron pot' church sent to Australia was that for Williamstown (Melbourne), which arrived in 1854.[157] Known as Holy Trinity, this building, not entirely unlike that illustrated in *Instrumenta Ecclesiastica*, consisted of a cast-iron and timber frame, sheets of corrugated iron (fixed vertically) for cladding, a felt ceiling, and a painted canvas interior (fig. 159).[158] Perry's hope was that he would receive ten such churches, but after the fourth one had arrived for the rural town of Bacchus Marsh in 1855, the rising cost of iron, along with the diminishing cost of wages in the colony, made importation uneconomical. Moreover, as such buildings were designated 'temporary edifices', they did not attract funding from the government.[159]

Perhaps the largest and most ambitious iron church sent to the colonies at this time was that for St John's, Victoria (Vancouver Island, British Columbia), erected in 1860 (fig. 160). Also produced by Samuel Hemming, this building was somewhat more pretentious than his earlier efforts in Australia. With its corner tower and spire, it certainly achieved a more pleasing churchlike aspect. In this case, however, the entire underlying structure and internal lining of the building was in timber, only the cladding was of iron.[160]

The main problem with iron churches was their impracticality. They may have promised expediency in the rapidly expanding parishes of cash-strapped colonial dioceses but they were ill suited to their context. The insulating properties of iron as a material were extremely poor, both acoustically and thermally. Initial plans to insulate these buildings artificially do not appear to have been carried out.[161] Thus, heavy rain or wind made it almost impossible to hear anything uttered inside these buildings, while the heat of the midday sun in locations such as Australia turned them into ovens – hence the term 'iron pot'.[162] Many ecclesiological

purists also felt they were fundamentally 'unreal' as church buildings.[163] The Ecclesiological Society had complained of the type sent to Australia and Canada as being 'merely wooden', not iron. 'Their framework is of wood, covered externally with corrugated iron. . . . What is such a building but a wooden structure encased in metallic plates?'[164] Their own attempt fared little better. It was criticised by some for violating ecclesiological principles in being nothing more than a metal incarnation of a brick or stone church.[165] But the society had always upheld the idea of truth to materials, and insisted that 'the framework of this design is of iron. The columns, instead of being cast imitations of stone forms, are composed of four detached rods, bound together by a spiral band' (fig. 161).[166]

Top 159 The prefabricated iron church of Holy Trinity, Williamstown, Melbourne (1854), by Samuel Hemming of Bristol.

Bottom 160 The prefabricated iron cathedral of St John, Victoria, British Columbia (1860), designed and produced by Samuel Hemming.

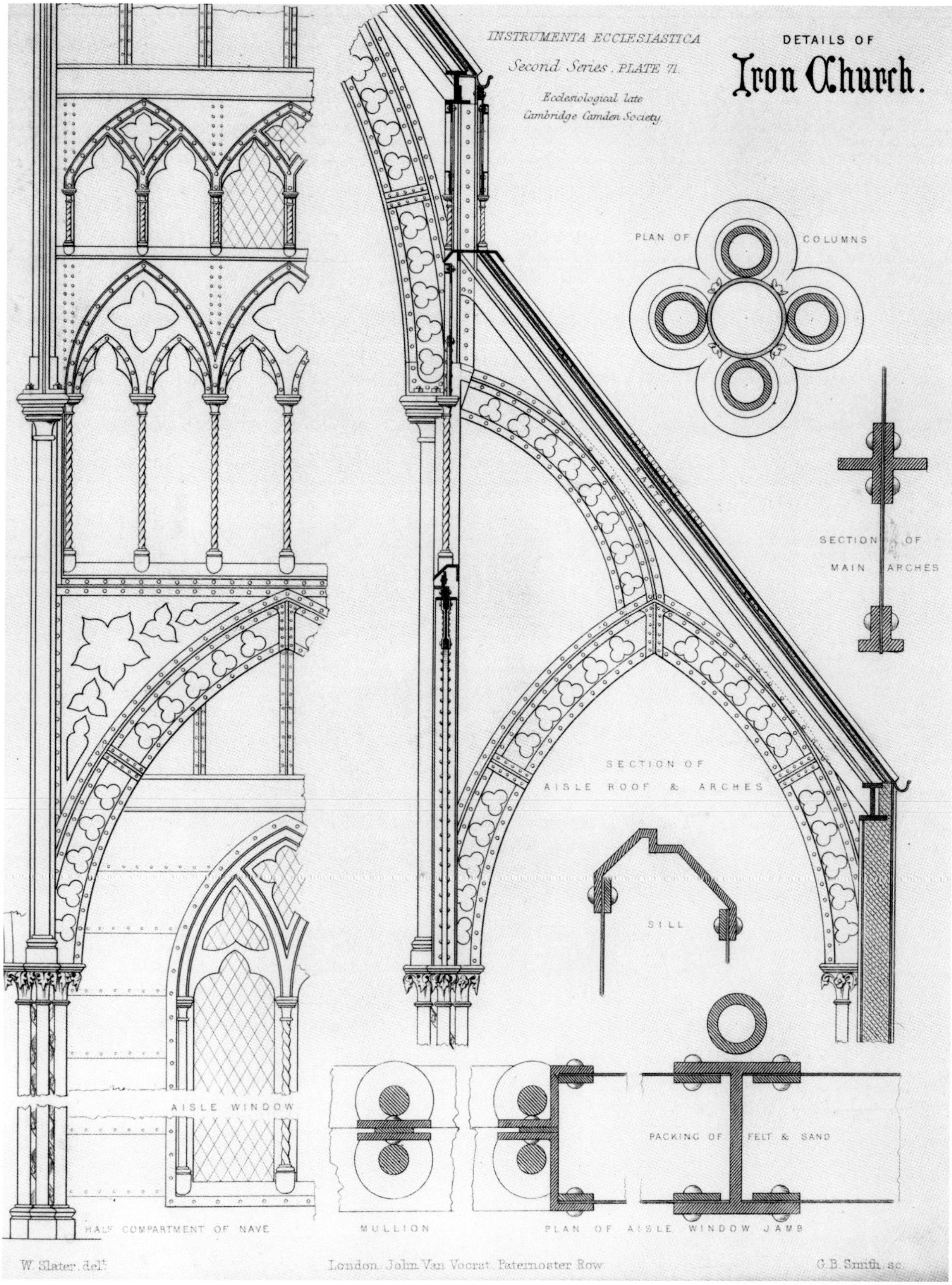

161 Details of connections for a prefabricated iron church by William Slater, from *Instrumenta Ecclesiastica*, 2nd ser. (1856).

If clergymen in the tropics were brave enough to opt for a more substantial material such as brick, then there were means of protecting it against the corrosive effects of the weather. At St Andrew's cathedral in Singapore (1854–62) (fig. 162), for instance, we see the application of an external rendering treatment known as Madras *chunam* – a cement-like composition, comprising shell lime (without sand), beaten with egg whites and coarse sugar or 'jaggery' to form a paste. Water (in which coconut husks had been soaked) was added to this mixture which was then plastered on the walls and columns of the church.[167] This produced a finish that was so hard that it was almost 'impossible to drive a nail into it'.[168] Where no conventional building materials were available, substitutes had to be found. In the case of Christ Church cathedral, Stone Town, Zanzibar (1873–80), this meant resorting to local and time-honoured construction techniques. Here walls several feet thick were built, using chunks of reef coral set in a heavily gritted mortar and finished with a lime-based render similar to *chunam*.[169]

162 St Andrew's cathedral, Singapore (1854–62), designed by Colonel Ronald MacPherson and consecrated by bishop Daniel Wilson of Calcutta in 1856. The cement-like substance known as *chunam*, applied to protect the masonry from tropical weather, may be seen in a deteriorated state on the walls of the building.

But stone had always been the most desirable of church-building materials. It was a material that had long associations with ecclesiastical architecture, and one that was recommended in preference to all other materials where it could be obtained in quantity and at the right quality. This was a tenet of ecclesiology that even Selwyn understood. Indeed, such was the aura of permanence and solidity that surrounded stone as a building material that, even where it could not be obtained, we find examples of stone churches entirely pre-fabricated in England being sent to the colonies.[170] The use and significance of stone in this regard is something that has been touched upon already. We have considered, for example, the material's psychological dimensions vis-à-vis church building on the colonial frontier. We have also discussed how the idea of heaviness or thickness in masonry was perceived as a defensive strategy against the penetration of heat and cold. Nevertheless, despite stone's perceived durability, experience showed that it had certain shortcomings with respect to extreme weather conditions. As mentioned, cut stone was prone to crack and crumble in severe frost. Likewise, in tropical conditions it was subject to erosion caused by heavy rain and wind. It had been suggested by the bishop of Bombay as early as 1843 that mouldings on church buildings in places such as India ought to be kept to a minimum or abandoned altogether as they 'soon fall down'.[171]

Fewer mouldings also meant less cost. As with timber construction, this principle of economy soon acquired its own aesthetic currency based on the idea of dignity through frugality, particularly with respect to mission churches. In some cases, such as Christ Church, Colombo, or William Slater's design for the cathedral in Honolulu (1862), simplicity was born of necessity, either because stonemasons of sufficient skill were unobtainable or the local stone was unsuited to carving.[172] Moreover, as discussed in Chapter 2, a more robust and chaste form of architecture was considered appropriate for colonial society. This principle, of course, mapped neatly onto the aestheticisation of clerical anxieties regarding privation and endurance. But the reasons for resorting to a severe brand of ecclesiology in colonial contexts, especially those in the tropics, were more elemental still for the Rev. William Scott. For Scott, basic 'atmospheric differences' were a critical factor in adopting such a strategy:

> Perhaps the first, and a very perplexing effect of tropical scenery, is its flatness. The most yawning chasms, and the deepest torrent gulfs, are absolutely lost in the sun-lighted aspect of tropical scenery. The sharpest lines of even volcanic mountain ridges, seem flat. . . . [W]hen every thing is forced into one plane by the immoderate force of light, they [church builders] would only waste time and labour in channelling and relieving, what after all, would never secure shadow. . . . In a word, it may be proposed, from this *rationale*, that a tropical architect should seek external effect chiefly by outline and mass, not by external variety and contrast of planes.[173]

Stone may have been the church-building material par excellence, but even its time-honoured traditions were forced to bend in response to colonial conditions.

Cultural Adaptation: Accommodating and Reconciling Difference

The adaptation to 'climate' also implied adjustment to different and often challenging cultural environments. This was especially the case where Anglican missionaries came into contact with pre-existing and long-established indigenous cultures. Regions such as South Asia, Africa and the Pacific Islands proved particularly trying for missionaries in cultural terms. As we shall see, the challenges faced by Anglican clergymen in these parts of the world had a direct effect on the development of church architecture.

The most immediate and pressing challenge facing Christian missionaries of all denominations in every part of the world was not architectural but, in fact, spiritual – what might be termed the pre-contact indigenous state of being. To many missionaries, non-European indigenes were, by European standards, at best uncivilised and at worst totally 'savage'. This is, of course, well known and was part of the general European attitude towards the non-European world during much of the early to late modern period.[174] But this fact need not incline us to essentialise all Christian missionaries as having the same views or adopting the same practices. It is important that we make distinctions, for there were as many different approaches to missionary work as there were missionary organisations, and, as we shall see in Chapter 5, these approaches (and organisations) sometimes came into direct conflict with one another. Anglicans, too, were no less divided among themselves as to how best to organise and implement a missionary enterprise. This was itself dependent upon whether those involved were of Low or High Church persuasion, as was the case with the Church Missionary Society and the Society for the Propagation of the Gospel respectively.

But there was a tendency among all Anglicans, of whatever persuasion, to study closely the culture and habits of their would-be converts. Although there were concerted efforts among Anglicans, particularly early on, to 'civilise' indigenous people, attempts were also made to incorporate aspects of existing indigenous belief for the purpose of facilitating conversion. This was a stated policy of both the CMS and the SPG during the period covered in this study.[175] Indeed, as Sara Sohmer has demonstrated in relation to Bishop J. C. Patteson's mission to Melanesia in the 1860s, this policy extended to viewing indigenous belief systems not as false but as so far 'incomplete', or partial, revelations of the true faith – an approach that was seen in much the same light as St Paul's treatment of the Athenians.[176] This enabled some Anglican missions, such as the UMCA and the Cambridge Mission to Delhi, to move beyond the civilisational creed that informed the tactics of so many Protestant missionaries during the nineteenth century.

Architecturally speaking, we see these tactics of incorporation first occurring in the mission churches of the CMS in New Zealand in the 1840s. Although the CMS was dominated by Low Church inclination, it is worth noting that its early experiments in missionary architecture highlight some of the concerns and practices it shared (at times) with the SPG. Perhaps the most striking example of this is the church at Rangiātea, erected near the CMS station at Ōtaki between 1848 and 1854. This project was overseen by the Revs Octavius Hadfield and Samuel Williams and given sanction, or *mana* (prestige), by the Ngāti Toa warrior chief, Te Rauparaha (*c.*1768–1849). As a centre of Christian worship, it was intended for both Māori and Pākehā (Europeans).[177] Externally the building was a rather conventional looking parish church (excluding chancel) in timber, complete with mock wooden buttresses. Internally, however, it was anything but conventional (fig. 163). The roof covering the main space rested upon a huge, single-wrought, ridge beam of totara (signifying the one true Christian God) which was in turn supported by three massive tree trunks

163 Lithograph by Charles Decimus Barraud, 1852, of the interior of Rangiātea Church, Ōtaki, New Zealand (1848–54) (private collection).

of the same timber (signifying the Holy Trinity). The rafters were decorated with a sacred motif known as the *mangōpare* (hammerhead shark pattern), while the walls were hung with woven *tukutuku* panels signifying the Milky Way (the heavens).[178] A number of such native chapels were built in the north island of New Zealand in the 1840s and 1850s, the largest and most magnificent being that referred to as Manutūkē IIB (1849–63), measuring some 45 feet by 90 feet. Although orchestrated by CMS clergymen, these chapels were fabricated almost entirely by Christianised Māori craftsmen. Thus, when compared with traditional Māori architecture, it is clear that many of the construction techniques employed in these buildings were indigenous in origin, resulting in a unique form known as *whare karakia* (house of prayer).[179]

Nevertheless, Rangiātea cannot really be described as a genuine amalgam or 'hybrid'. Instead, it had the strange effect of two buildings in one – a kind of architectural schizophrenia of interior and exterior. This disjunction is perhaps representative of the efforts made by CMS missionaries to reconcile the cultural and religious differences within colonial society without allowing the Church to lose its identifiable Christian character. In this respect Rangiātea may be seen as an attempt to give shape to Henry Venn's vision of a 'native Church' in New Zealand – a church that ought not merely 'transplant' established modes and practices into the new world but one that looked to what would later be called 'fraternal association', thus taking advantage of 'such national customs, notions, and tendencies' as were considered useful and appropriate.[180]

Selwyn is unlikely to have had much sympathy for this idea. His policy was one of assimilation and conformity with regard to Church organisation, leading to a vision of ecclesiastical architecture that was based on strict ecclesiological principles. As *The Ecclesiologist* would later observe of a CMS-style church erected near Otago, the idea of employing the 'wild but elaborate carving of the native New Zealanders' was venerable, 'but it should have been developed so as to Christianize and improve the native taste and skill, not merely to admit its savage grotesque power, just as it is'.[181] Nevertheless, both Selwyn and Cotton were keen observers of Māori architecture, including the CMS churches.[182] As mentioned in Chapter 1, it is owing to this interest in classic Māori architecture that Selwyn may have been influenced in his efforts to adapt Christian buildings to the seismic conditions of New Zealand (see p. 56).

Other attempts at adapting church buildings to prevailing cultural circumstances include the Protestant church at Alexandria and the Crimean War Memorial church in Constantinople (Istanbul). As Mark Crinson has shown, both these buildings sought to accommodate the exigencies of place with respect to religion and politics. The attempts made at Alexandria, however, did not find favour among hard-line ecclesiologists. Although James Wild was responding to diplomatic pressures, *The Ecclesiologist* thought that his 'Saracenic' design was nothing short of a betrayal (fig.

164).[183] In a place such as Egypt, the journal thundered, where the Christian Church was 'in a state of servitude and depression', surely the resurgent confidence and superiority of Christianity ought to be marked by the deployment of true Christian forms. It was ignominious to cower before or, worse still, honour the 'great scourge of Christianity [Islam]' by assuming its style. Here again we see the push for a 'developed' architecture as opposed to one content with superficial eclecticism. This was especially the case when appropriate models were seen to exist for such a building, in particular the Crusader churches of Syria and Palestine, or the basilica at Emmaus.[184] In the end *The Ecclesiologist* took a more phlegmatic tone, observing that: 'We trust that the Christian Church in Egypt will in her good time spoil the enemy; but the time has not yet come.'

Similar concerns were at the core of the competition for the Crimean War Memorial church. One of the key criteria of this competition was that the building be designed to 'suit the climate'.[185] Attracting entries from the younger, more experimental generation of British architects, including William Burges, G. E. Street, William Slater, G. F. Bodley and William White, this competition became one of the most publicised test cases in the history of Victorian architecture for the adaptation of Gothic forms to a foreign climate. Again, the term 'foreign' in this case referred to more than just the weather; it implied differences in local religion and culture.[186] Being part of the Ottoman empire, Turkey's population was, of course, predominantly Muslim. However, Islamic and Byzantine styles were expressly forbidden under the terms of the brief. Therefore, several of the competitors looked instead to the medieval architecture of Italy.[187] This deference to 'southern' types was undoubtedly influenced by John Ruskin's recently published *The Stones of Venice* (1851–3). The use of polychromy by many of the competitors, along with the incorporation of features more readily associated with architecture from the Mediterranean, is evidence of this (fig. 165).[188] For Beresford Hope,

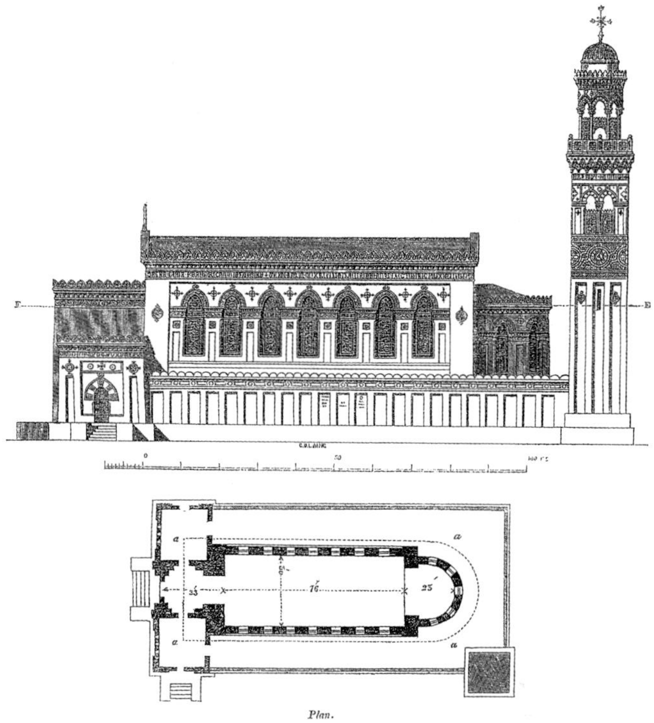

Top 164 Design by James Wild for the Protestant church at Alexandria, from *The Builder* (1846).

Bottom 165 Perspective illustration of William Burges's first design for the Crimean War Memorial church, Constantinople, from *The Builder* (1857). Banded stonework and small windows were considered particularly Mediterranean characteristics, the latter being an adaptation to warm climates.

it was just as well, as 'a single church in the middle of Constantinople built in Northern Gothic would have been in partial, if not offensive, contrast to every other building in that city, and would accordingly have proved an architectural failure, and not improbably the cause of much social heartburning'.[189] Likewise, no attempt was made to integrate local religious motifs, including representations of human or animal forms.[190] But the fact that the general context was acknowledged with a degree of sensitivity demonstrates how flexible the principles of Anglican ecclesiology had become by the mid-1850s.

A more radical approach to the incorporation of indigenous beliefs and customs is observable in the activities of the Universities' Mission to Central Africa. Formed in 1858 following David Livingstone's address to students at Cambridge in 1857, the UMCA was a rather quixotic High Church organisation, the aim of which was to abolish the east African slave trade and establish an autonomous 'negro church' in Africa.[191] The mission's early years (1861–4) were spent at stations in the Shiré Highlands and along the Zambezi river valley. Importantly, unlike most other Protestant missions at the time (both Anglican and Nonconformist), the UMCA eschewed ideas of civilisation. As their first bishop, the Rev. Charles Mackenzie, realised, it was they who would have to adapt to Africa, not the other way around. Indeed, Mackenzie's successor, the Rev. G. W. Tozer, argued that 'to Anglicize the people in all . . . respects would be a very doubtful gain. . . . [I]t is wonderful how much wisdom after a time you will discover in the use of customs which at first sight seem barbarous.'[192] Similarly, the Rev. Henry Rowley recognized early on that both the Mang'anja (Nyasa) and Achawa (Yao) peoples had a reasonably developed concept of a higher being akin to 'God'. He reckoned that 'seeking a groundwork in their common customs . . . [was] a surer way of making them Christians than by totally ignoring all they [knew] as useless'.[193] For Tozer and his successor, the Rev. Edward Steere, the physical appearance of indigenous peoples was of little significance. Forcing them to adopt European-style clothing and customs was unnecessary and potentially dangerous. Let Africans be African, was their philosophy, as long as their souls were attended to and a holy church built among them.[194]

This attitude dramatically affected the UMCA's approach to architecture. Its missionaries had not only a much more relaxed outlook on the adoption of indigenous building techniques and materials, as we have seen, but also a more liberal and, at times, politically savvy stance on the incorporation of other non-Christian motifs. This is not to suggest that the UMCA was any less strict when it came to correctness in church architecture, merely that the outward appearance of church buildings was secondary to their essential function and arrangement. In this respect UMCA clergymen were far more progressive than most of their colleagues in other parts of the world.

The most monumental expression of the UMCA's attitude towards missionary architecture can be found in the design of the so-called Slave Market church (Christ Church cathedral), Stone Town, Zanzibar (1873–80) (figs 166 and 167). Built over the old slave market, this building is a complex amalgam of stylistic elements and motifs, including Christian, Islamic and vernacular.[195] As a Christian mission, the UMCA obviously occupied a tenuous position in the Muslim-dominated environs of Stone Town. Both Tozer and Steere were acutely conscious of this and therefore unwilling to test the patience of their Arab hosts by erecting a building that did not harmonise with the local environment.[196] It is clear from the tenor of their letters that the 'Arabic' overtones of Christ Church cathedral were concerned with the self-conscious vulnerability of a small Christian community situated in the midst of a large Muslim one. The sultan had allowed them to build the cathedral – even gifting them a clock for goodwill – but only so long as its spire did not overtop the highest point on his palace. It is not surprising therefore that the cathedral's spire was built to look more like a minaret than the tower of a traditional Christian church.[197]

The other important cultural adaptation in this building was the addition of a narthex (figs 168 and 169).[198] This device was a necessary spatial concession to the Muslim inhabitants of Stone Town who wished to enter the church and observe divine service. As these 'inquirers' were non-communicants, a designated space was needed that would allow them to enter without trespassing upon and thereby defiling the sacred spaces of the building.[199] A narthex was a space of indeterminate size used in primitive Christian and medieval architecture that literally, as the name suggests, came before the nave in a church. Its use varied, but its primary function was to contain catechumens and to segregate miscreants, including penitents, energumens and inquirers.[200] The incorporation of such a space at Christ Church cathedral accorded precisely with the strict disciplinary practices of the UMCA. Indeed, narthex-type

166 The Slave Market church (Christ Church cathedral), Stone Town, Zanzibar (1873–80), by Edward Steere and C. F. Hayward.

spaces of this kind had already been used on the mainland during the mission's first phase of operation. In the 'grass church' at Morambala, for instance, the nave was divided in two by an ornate wooden screen, the 'western place being for the heathen boys', observed Tozer, 'and the eastern arranged as a choir for ourselves' (see fig. 147).[201] This division effectively split the church into a *naos* and *pronaos* – the *pronaos* acting in every respect as a true narthex.[202] As the UMCA clergymen perceived themselves to be labouring amid circumstances akin to those of the early Church fathers, they considered the rehabilitation of an equally early or 'primitive' spatial model appropriate for the purpose of discipline.[203]

This is not the first recorded example of such a spatial division in Anglican church architecture on the African continent. A slightly earlier version was implemented by the Rev. R. Robertson at the Umlazi mission station in the diocese of Natal in 1857. As at Morambala, this church, equally ephemeral in its fabrication, was divided in half, with separate spaces for 'Christians' and 'Heathen' (fig.

167 Interior of Christ Church cathedral, Stone Town (1873–80), looking west down the nave.

170).[204] There is a possible connection between this building and the one at Morambala. Before becoming bishop of the UMCA, Mackenzie had been a missionary in the diocese of Natal (1855–9). During this time, he and his sister, Anne, had established a friendship with the Robertsons. Much correspondence passed between the two parties, and Robertson may well have communicated his thoughts on the building of his church.[205] Indeed, it is likely that Mackenzie saw the building at some point. Once bishop, Mackenzie faced his own challenges concerning liturgical discipline and probably implemented a similar division at St Paul's, Magomero (Malawi).[206] It is likely that this tactic was then passed down to Tozer through other missionaries, ending up as the basis for the spatial arrangement in the church at Morambala.

Generally speaking, it was the Ecclesiological Society that played a key role in legitimating the use of narthex-type spaces in Anglican church architecture during the mid-nineteenth century. It was increasingly clear that foreign and colonial contexts presented particular chal-

lenges with respect to maintaining the solemnity of Anglican worship. As reports began to arrive back in England describing the difficulties experienced by clergymen in attempting to control crowds of onlookers, the Ecclesiological Society decided to assist. At a meeting of the society in May 1848, John Mason Neale raised the issue in a paper on the uses of the narthex in early Christian architecture, later developed in his *History of the Holy Eastern Church* (1850). One of the main points of this paper was to encourage the reintroduction of the narthex in missionary contexts.[207] This was reiterated some years later by Beresford Hope in his book *The English Cathedral of the Nineteenth Century* (1861), where he observed that 'a spacious narthex, or western vestibule, is suitable, accord-

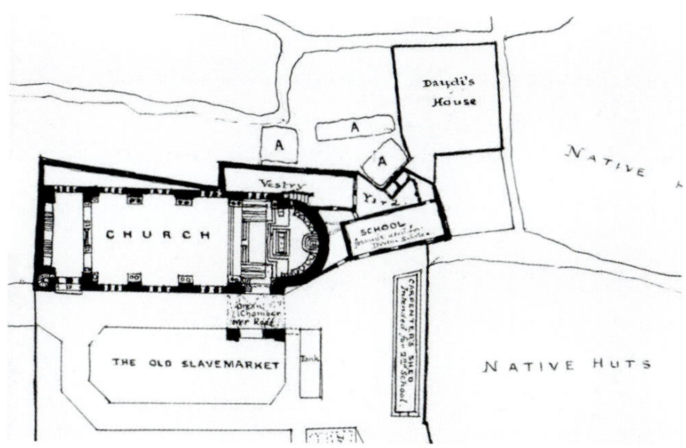

Top 168 Narthex and baptistery, Christ Church cathedral, Stone Town (1873–80).

Bottom 169 Site sketch of Christ Church cathedral, Stone Town, with a plan of the cathedral, showing the various delineated spaces – narthex, nave, choir, and sanctuary – designed by Edward Steere and C. F. Hayward, *c.*1873 (Bodleian Library, Oxford).

ing to ancient precedent, to a church planted in the midst of a vast heathen population, for practical no less than ecclesiastical reasons'.[208]

Anglicans were, of course, not the first missionaries to tackle the problem of adapting the spatial requirements of Christian liturgy to foreign contexts. Again, Spanish missionaries in central America had experienced similar difficulties with respect to discipline and conversion during the sixteenth century. In order to cater to huge crowds of converts in the New World – a problem largely unknown and therefore unaccounted for in the development of Christian architecture in Europe – these missionaries found themselves having to extend the communal precinct of their churches well beyond the confines of the church proper into large open areas in front, known as *patios* or *atrios*.[209] These spaces – so-called 'open-air churches' – were capable of holding tens of thousands of people at once for the purposes of mass preaching. They were augmented with additional spaces such as open chapels and *posas* (small, enclosed oratories) to aid the liturgical and ceremonial dimensions of Catholic worship.

As we have seen, ecclesiologists were aware of Spanish colonial precedent, but it is uncertain whether they knew very much, if anything, about these particular auxiliary spaces and their application. There is certainly no recorded example of an Anglican missionary church being arranged in this way during the mid-nineteenth century. Nevertheless, Anglican missionaries were inclined towards open-air preaching when necessary. We have already discussed the example of Selwyn in New Zealand (see p. 29), and Robertson did the same in Natal. The illustration here (fig. 171) shows Robertson (or possibly the Rev. H. Waters) preaching to a gathering of indigenous people in front of what appears to be a makeshift structure. The exact purpose of this building is unclear, but it appears to be a *posa*-like construct, designed to mark out and distinguish a sacred portion of ground, however crudely. Although no doubt doubling as a shelter from the elements for Robertson himself, it would also have answered his call for 'aesthetic teaching' through having some kind of 'house' set aside 'especially for the service of God'.[210]

Thus, in the face of difficulties of this kind everywhere, the narthex began to appear with increasing frequency in designs for Anglican missionary churches from the 1840s onwards. Among the first was Carpenter's design for Christ Church cathedral, Colombo (see figs 116 and 117).[211] Bishop Chapman had similar problems to those that confronted the UMCA in Africa. Surrounded by a predominantly Buddhist and Roman Catholic population, he felt the need to impose order, and realised that liturgical discipline was 'really necessary' if he was to wean the Singhalese from what he considered to be their mistaken habits of 'superstition'.[212] Although not built, Carpenter's incorporation of a narthex into his design for Colombo embodied (in theory, at least) the reinvigorated missionary agenda of the Anglican Church abroad, creating both a form and space that may be seen to have monumentalised the state of 'militancy' in which the Church found itself.

170 Sketch plan of the church at Umlazi mission station, Natal (1857), designed by the Rev. R. Robertson (Bodleian Library, Oxford). 'D' indicates the space for the 'Heathen', who were to be segregated from the Christians ('C').

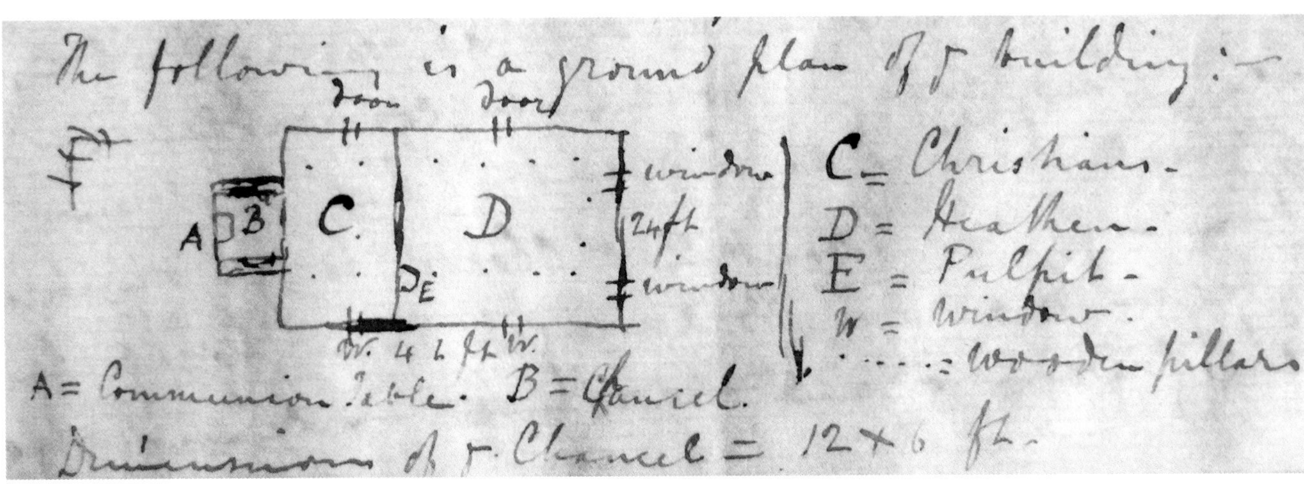

171 Watercolour sketch by an unknown artist, showing a cleric, probably the Rev. R. Robertson, preaching before converts from a makeshift shelter near Umlazi mission station, Natal, *c.*1857 (Bodleian Library, Oxford).

The idea emerged again shortly afterwards in the competition entries for the Crimean War Memorial church. Burges's winning design – based in part on the thirteenth-century church of Sant'Andrea in Vercelli (Piedmont) – included three deeply recessed portals at its west end with a low-pitched, overhanging roof.[213] This made for a semi-enclosed space at the front of the building approximately 20 feet deep (figs 172 and 173, and see fig. 165).[214] Apart from protecting the entrance to the building from the intense Mediterranean sun, this space may have been intended to serve as a *proaulion*, or porch for inquirers, in accordance with the disciplinary dictates of the early Christian Church, especially in the East.[215] This function is suggested in the changes Burges made to the design in 1861. It was reported in *The Ecclesiologist* that an 'open narthex, similar to that of S. Germain l'Auxerrois', had been substituted for the western-most bay of the nave. This alteration, it was noted, would still allow room 'for any probable congregation, and the accommodation of ample external shade will be given to the native attendants who may be as requisite for the service of the worshippers as they would be undesirable loungers inside the building'.[216] Burges was not alone in adapting his design in this way. G. F. Bodley's entry was also distinguished by what was described as a long and pronounced narthex. Again, the exact reason for this space is unclear, but one can only presume that it was intended to serve the same function as that in Burges's design. William Slater, too, who had received the 'extra' or fourth prize in the competition, had incorporated a narthex. Indeed, Slater would go on to include one in his design

172 Longitudinal section of William Burges's initial design of 1857 for the Crimean War Memorial church, Constantinople (RIBA Drawings Collection, Victoria and Albert Museum, London).

173 Plan of Burges's initial design for the Crimean War Memorial church, from *The Builder* (1857).

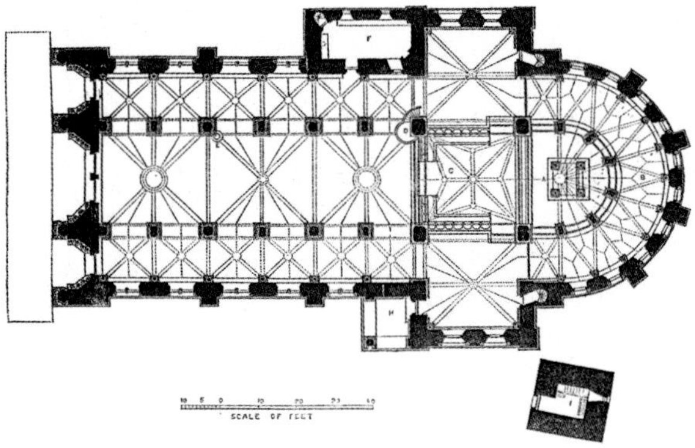

for the Anglican cathedral in Honolulu (fig. 174). In that design, the narthex was raised on four steps so as to contain a full-immersion font for adult baptism.[217] Although somewhat peculiar, this was a feature that not only had the authority of ancient precedent on its side but also betrayed the clear missionary intent of the building.

In India we see several of the very earliest examples of this type of spatial division found anywhere in the British empire. Among the first was St Paul's cathedral, Calcutta (1839–47) (fig. 175). Here it was intended that 'the Lantern, Transepts, Vestibule, and Verandah . . . receive a large number of Catechetical classes, Normal Schools, Sacramental catechumens, Audiences of Lecturers on the Evidences, &c.'.[218] It is difficult to say where Wilson got this idea from, but he was impressed by the ancient Syrian churches he encountered on his primary visitation in 1835–6. These churches, some of which dated back to the ninth century, all had nartheces (fig. 176).[219] Beyond Calcutta there were

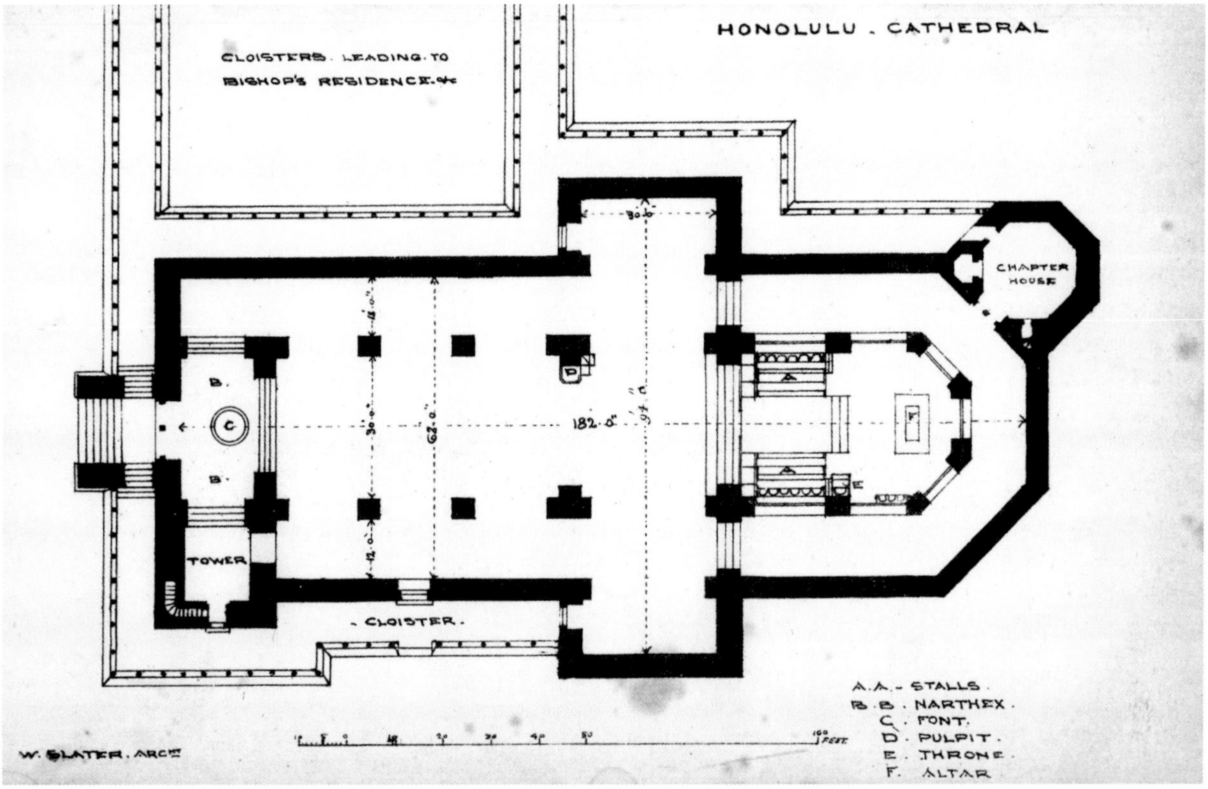

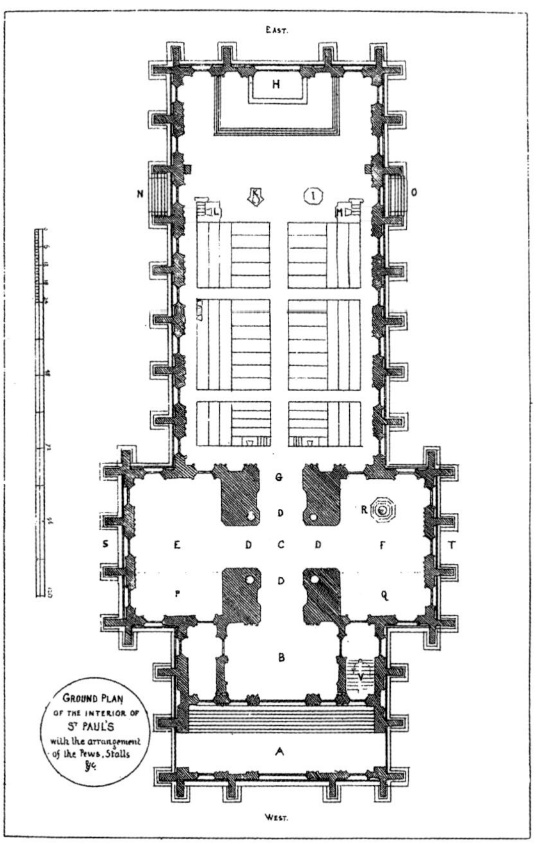

Top 174 Plan of William Slater's initial design for Honolulu cathedral, from *The Ecclesiologist* (1862).

Bottom left 175 Plan of St Paul's cathedral, Calcutta (1839–47), designed by W. N. Forbes. The spaces in and around the crossing were intended for catechumens.

Bottom right 176 Engraving of the Syrian church at Cottayam, India, from Josiah Bateman's, *The Life of the Right Rev. Daniel Wilson* (1860).

177 Engraving of St Peter's church, Barripûr, India, *c.*1847, from the *Quarterly Paper of the SPG* (April 1846).

a further three churches built in the early 1840s in which the segregation of catechumens from communicants was strictly enforced. These churches, overseen by the Rev. John Driberg (then a Catechist and a man of apparent Tractarian inclination), were erected in the villages of Barripûr (or Baruipur, now Kalyanpur), Mogra Hât (Magra Hat) and Jhanjera (fig. 177).[220] The spaces at ground level beneath the western towers in the churches at Barripûr (St Peter's) and Mogra Hât (St Andrew's) were designed as 'porches' that would 'add to the accommodation allowed to the Catechumens'. Although not labelled nartheces as such, it is clear that these spaces were intended to serve that purpose.[221]

Further afield we find the Rev. W. T. Humphrey proposing a church in the diocese of Madras with a screened choir for 'the faithful' beyond which (in the nave and transepts) were to be located catechumens and 'penitents'. 'It surely was not intended that unbaptised pagans should enter Christ's temple with as little ceremony as if walking into a toddy shop,' declared Humphrey, but cautioned against banning some members of the congregation from the building altogether, lest 'we unwittingly bar men's hearts against [the] reception [of religious truth] by too lavish dispersion . . . among those who are not yet prepared by previous discipline to appreciate it'.[222] Emerson had also provided for such a space at Allahabad. Looking at the cathedral's plan it is clear that the main spaces have been carefully delineated (see fig. 128). There is a narthex proper immediately following the *porte-corchère* (not built), and a vestibule-type space directly preceding the nave, which is a species of esonarthex into which the 'curious' could be corralled as they entered the building (fig. 178).

But perhaps the most striking example of a narthex in India was at the mission church of St Stephen the Martyr, Delhi (1865–7) (fig. 179). The idea for this building dated back to 1861, when G. F. Bodley was engaged to prepare a design for the Cambridge Mission to Delhi.[223] In the event, the design was altered radically by a local engineer. Nev-

178 The 'esonarthex' in All Saints' cathedral, Allahabad, India (1870–87), by William Emerson.

ertheless, the finished building included Bodley's suggestion of an external cloister and narthex, though, in this case, not extending to the clerestory (fig. 180). At the opening of the church in October 1867, Bishop Milman of Calcutta preached, observing that one of the primary functions of the new church was to afford 'an opportunity [for the heathen] of becoming acquainted with the ritual of the Christian Church and of hearing God's word read and preached'.[224] This 'acquaintance' was achieved by means of the narthex, where 'the heathen [might] be allowed to stand, except during the celebration of the Holy Communion, and from which they [could] watch the Christians

179 The mission church of St Stephen the Martyr, Delhi (1865–7) as built, to a radically reworked version of an original design by G. F. Bodley.

at prayer'.[225] Again, as at Zanzibar and elsewhere, the narthex at St Stephen's was intended to act as both a reception space and a zone of exclusion – restricting non-communicants to a particular area of the church while allowing them to witness and partake in certain aspects of the service. Here, according to ancient church precedent, the narthex was also considered the most appropriate place to locate a baptismal font – in the case of St Stephen's, two baptismal fonts: a normal one for infant baptism, and, as with Slater's design for Honolulu, a larger, full-immersion one for adults in the shape of a coffin (fig. 181).[226]

Coming back to Zanzibar we see Bishop Steere going even further in his attempt to adapt Christ Church cathedral to prevailing cultural circumstances. The narthex at the entrance to the building can be interpreted as an extension of the *baraza* tradition in Zanzibari architecture, in which stone benches were placed abutting the exterior of shops and houses, creating an interstitial space for public and

180 Interior of the mission church of St Stephen the Martyr, Delhi (1865–7), looking west down the nave to the narthex.

semi-public intercourse.[227] Steere had originally incorporated this idea in the 'mud house' he built on the slave market site before he erected the cathedral. Under the eaves at the front of this house he fashioned a mud bench so that he might 'sit there and talk to all comers'.[228] He upheld this tradition in the new church, coming down the nave to converse with those who had gathered in the narthex. Not satisfied, Steere continued to make alterations to the cathedral. Directly above the narthex he found it necessary to build what was described in the Holy Eastern Church as a *gynæconitis* or women's gallery, 'since in the present state of feeling', he observed, 'it would be impossible for ladies holding any position to throw themselves on the floor of the Church where the men worship'.[229] This was in itself a concession to the strict division between the sexes in Muslim society. But Steere's innovation was more than merely a sop to social convention, for such an apparatus was also found in the Shi'a mosques of Stone Town, where

181 Baptismal font in the shape of a coffin for full-immersion baptisms, located at the west end of the nave, immediately in front of the narthex, in the mission church of St Stephen the Martyr, Delhi (1865–7).

women were allowed to take part in religious ceremonies from behind screened partitions, either on the floor of the mosque itself or at the level above. With this in mind, Steere's introduction of a 'women's gallery' into the Slave Market Church was an ingenious ploy to create a point of intersection between two religious traditions through a shared architectural device. Thus, finding himself in a difficult situation, Steere was able to negotiate a *via media*, as it were, between the cultural reality of Zanzibar and his desire to maintain primitive Church custom.[230]

What we have seen in this chapter are the lengths to which both architects and Anglican clergymen went in adapting basic formal and liturgical principles to foreign contexts (climatic and cultural). The strategies that they developed in order to cope with these circumstances were clearly crucial to the efforts of the Church of England to spread out and exert its influence beyond what may be considered its traditional comfort zone – the familiar forms and environments of England and the urban centres of the white settler colonies. In this respect, the missionary and/or 'frontier' dimensions of the Church's activity came to prominence. Although this had been recognized as a challenge in Church of England circles before the advent of ecclesiology and the wider missionary movement, it was suddenly taken up with altogether more zeal and a greater degree of urgency and seriousness following the inauguration of the Colonial Bishoprics' Fund and the subsequent penetration of the Church into ever more extreme climatic locations during the mid-nineteenth century. Ultimately, as Bishop Mackenzie had realised with regard to central Africa, it was the Church that would have to adapt to such contexts if it was to survive, not the other way around.

The considerations were both material and spatial. Through the circulation of ideas via *The Ecclesiologist*, *Instrumenta Ecclesiastica* and other Church of England periodicals, such as the *Colonial Church Chronicle* and the *Mission Field*, as well as the personal correspondence and experiences of individual clergymen, clear and consistent patterns began to emerge as how best to cope with the problems faced. No dilemma seemed too complex, minor or distant to be tackled under the all-embracing aegis of ecclesiology as it evolved to acquire a collective sense of responsibility and influence on a planetary scale. To be sure, no one single solution to any given problem was ever enforced, but the constant process of reporting, debating and disseminating ideas and techniques between the centre and the periphery of empire fundamentally changed Church of England architecture and provided it not only with a distinct set of forms but also a coherent discourse through which to challenge and direct that change. In other words, the nexus established and extended throughout the 1840s and 1850s between architects, clergymen and the university societies in both Britain and the colonies created a 'system', as it were, through which the transmission and inculcation of a specific set of strategies worked to shape and expand the limits of Anglican ecclesiology, thereby transforming church buildings in ways that were at once liturgically generic yet formally specific.

4

Symbolism and Identity

FAITH, NATIONAL FORM AND THE POLITICS OF EMPIRE

[T]he proper material of ornament will be whatever God has created; and its proper treatment, that which seems in accordance with or symbolical of His laws.

John Ruskin, *The Stones of Venice*, vol. 1 (1851)

Coelum non animum mutant qui trans mare currunt.
['Those who go across the sea change their sky but not their soul.']

Colonial Church Chronicle

The wilderness and the solitary place shall be glad for them; and the desert shall rejoice, and blossom as the rose.

Isaiah, xxxv. 1

Adapting to foreign contexts involved more than finding practical solutions to the exigencies of culture and climate. It also concerned symbolism. An appreciation of the role of symbolism in Anglican church architecture had grown significantly by the mid-nineteenth century and was considered central to the agenda of organisations such as the Cambridge Camden and Oxford Architectural societies. A renewed concern for liturgy, in particular, raised the symbolic intentions of ecclesiastical architecture to levels not seen since the middle ages. Publications such as *The Ecclesiologist* and the *Rules and Proceedings* regularly carried articles on the meaning and importance of symbolism in church building. In addition, the Camden Society published specialist tracts on church arrangement and maintenance, including *A Few Words to Church Builders* (1841) and *A Few Words to Church Wardens* (1841), both of which sold in large numbers.[1] The discussion in these publications ranged from specific subjects such as western triplets, lychnoscopes and the proper locations of baptismal fonts to more general and abstract topics such as proportion and geometry in church design. After all, it had been among the explicit aims of the Ecclesiological Society to promote 'the connexion of architecture with Ritualism, the science of Symbolism, [and] the principles of church arrangement'.[2]

Through these publications the significance of symbolism was inculcated into a whole generation of Anglican clergymen and architects. It was part and parcel of what was now considered to be 'correct' church architecture. This concern reached its rather fastidious apogee, literarily speaking, in the translation by John Mason Neale and Benjamin Webb of the thirteenth-century treatise on church symbolism by William Durandus, the *Rationale divinorum officiorum*.[3] Prefaced by a 121-page 'Introductory Essay' by Neale and Webb, the translation was intended to prove the necessity of symbolism in church architecture. It was suggested that 'if architecture [be] anything more than a mere trade; if it is indeed a liberal, intellectual art, a true branch of poesy', then 'Sacramentality' was crucial. 'By this word', it was explained, 'we mean to convey the idea that, by the outward and visible form, is signified something inward and spiritual: that the material fabrick symbolizes, embodies, figures, represents, expresses, answers to, some abstract meaning.'[4] As the general sentiment of this 'philosophy' began percolating through the world of Anglican church building, it was not long before clergymen stationed in the colonies began pondering the implications of symbolism for themselves. How, for instance, would the principle of orientation be affected in the southern hemisphere? Or, what forms and motifs relating to church ornamentation were applicable in foreign and unfamiliar lands? Should architects and craftsmen turn to native flora and fauna instead of inanely replicating European species? These were all considered important questions in the context of 'appropriateness'. As mentioned in the previous chapter, some of these concerns overlapped with issues of materiality and hybridity. However, whatever one may have thought about symbolism – whether essential or 'Popish' – it was firmly back on the agenda, and it was global.

The concern for 'embodiment' and 'representation', reinvigorated by this interest in symbolism, also points to the broader but no less significant themes of identity and nationalism in Anglican church design. Symbolism was but another way of understanding built form abstractly and analogically. This necessarily had wider implications. One of the initial concerns of the Cambridge Camden Society was to settle upon a type of medieval architecture that not only represented perfection (formally and aesthetically) but one that was also identifiably English – a concern that Beresford Hope described as the 'Anglo-parochial age' of ecclesiology.[5] As John Mason Neale noted in *Hierologus, or, The Church Tourists* (1843), 'at a time when a taste for syncretism or eclecticism prevails among so many who ought to know better, . . . it seems important to recommend nationality of style'.[6] This had much to do with what Neale perceived to be the sources of beauty in ancient English churches; namely, 'situation, association, and legend'. All of these were calculated to gain our sympathy and inspire future works.

This geographical stricture was, of course, relaxed in the late 1840s and early 1850s as continental forms entered the repertoire of English ecclesiologists, but the desire to distinguish a specifically Anglican form of 'Catholick art' never diminished. The Anglican Church was the national Church. In the eyes of many it was therefore the 'truest' and best-fitted to preside over religious teaching in those lands under the sway of the British crown. Even Beresford Hope's call for a more progressive and wide-ranging form of eclecticism in British architecture relied on Gothic – preferably English Gothic – as its foundational style.[7] 'We need not be afraid', he later argued, 'of adopting it as the platform upon which we are to construct our own superior style.' But, he cautioned, this modern, 'superior' style 'should be emphatically northern and emphatically English, yet not narrowly northern nor narrowly English, any more than the most true-hearted Englishman, educated in the broad civilization of the day, is one whose patriotism is narrowed into prejudice and his home-pride soured into cynical self-idolatry'.[8] In this sense church architecture was considered coterminous with 'Englishness', if not formally then at least culturally. This idea, both architectural and confessional, would follow English churchmen wherever they went, playing a fundamental part in the way the colonial Church of England was made manifest in the landscape (spatially and culturally) and the role it was perceived to have in promoting and consolidating Britain's political interests worldwide. This chapter explores the symbolic and representational dimensions (and implications) of that role.

Laus Deo: The Challenge of Revealed Faith in the Colonies

The Ecclesiological Society was concerned with promoting sacramentalism as far and as wide as possible. As we have already seen, in its darkest hour, when under suspicion of Romanising tendencies, the society was quick to acknowledge the unwavering support of its 'relations' abroad (see p. 14). *Instrumenta Ecclesiastica* was proof of this desire to extend and entrench a particular symbolic regime with respect to church architecture the world over. In providing authoritative patterns for features such as chancels, gable crosses, sedilia, fonts, monograms, altar décor and so on, the hope was that Anglican church architecture would be elevated everywhere, not just in England. After all, Anglicanism was now a global phenomenon. In the society's annual address of 1851 it was observed with enthusiasm that, thanks to the efforts of its members, the colonies were now developing their own 'outward form'.[9]

We get some sense of this heightened awareness of symbolism and its colonial application in the writings of the Rev. William Scott. As one of the leading lights of the Oxford Architectural Society, and a controversial advocate of Church ritual, Scott was involved in advancing the cause of ecclesiastical symbolism at every level. Owing to his special interest in the colonial Church, he naturally wished to extend the benefits (and rites) of symbolism across the empire. In his 1848 essay on the value and legitimacy of timber ecclesiology, Scott was quick to point out that, despite the ultimate utility of stone, 'the symbolism of churches – the mystical import of the temple and its measurement – the significant decorations of the tabernacle and its furniture are but instances of a law which was for the first time promulgated on the building of the *wooden* ark'. Therefore, as mentioned in Chapter 3, timber churches, far from being symbolically or materially inferior to stone ones, were seen as embodying the 'archetypical plan' (see pp. 144–5). This was because of timber's original nautical associations. 'As long as the ship is the emblem of the Church,' Scott insisted,

> as long as one of every church's more familiar parts, the nave, is identical with the name of a ship, ναυς, – as long as we see in the inverted hull of a ship and its arched timbers the image of the church's wooden roofs, we shall in the reverse way not only detect in *wooden* churches a recurrence and witness to the first type of the Church itself – that great material prophecy, the wooden ark of Noah; but we shall at the same time find that a wooden church, with somewhat more vividness than even one of stone, suggests to us the great hold of Christian souls – the ship of the Christian Church.[10]

Thus, Scott's underlying message was that where an abundance of timber was found, and the skills existed to work it (both native and settler), the symbolism of wood vis-à-vis ecclesiastical architecture ought to be exploited. There was no necessary shame or deficiency in this. On the contrary: as Pugin had asserted in *True Principles* (1841), truth to materials in Christian architecture was itself symbolic. Again, resorting to locally available materials was not only an expression of the true and therefore 'honest' condition of the Church but also (and because of this) an embodiment of sacramentality. In this, architecture was understood as revealed morality. Moreover, the nautical associations of a material such as timber probably carried special meaning in the colonial world. Overseas colonisation represented not only a metaphorical but also a *literal* containment and passage of souls. To colonial immigrants, the timber church was at once a symbol of biblical origins and a poignant reminder of how they had reached their destination (fig. 182). Indeed, some colonial clergymen went so far as to turn actual ships into mobile churches. The most notable instance of this was probably Edward Feild's 'church ship' *Hawk*, which journeyed up and down the Newfoundland and Labrador coast, carrying and ministering the sacraments to isolated fishing villages (fig. 183).[11]

182 Mosaic floor decoration at Christ Church cathedral, Christchurch, New Zealand, *c.*1880, depicting one of the 'Canterbury Pilgrims' ships.

The relationship between church architecture and timber had further symbolic connotations. There was the age-old,

183 Engraving of the 'church ship' *Hawk*, in which Edward Feild sailed the coasts of Newfoundland and Labrador, ministering to remote communities, from the *Quarterly Paper of the SPG* (October 1844).

near clichéd, metaphor of the Gothic cathedral as forest – a notion that appears to have originated during the Renaissance and come down to contemporary thinkers through the picturesque tradition. This was an idea that Selwyn appealed to in his parting sermon, amid the veritable 'forest' of columns and vaulting ribs at Exeter cathedral, thanking the Lord that he was 'allowed to come here this day, to feast my eyes and to feed my mind with the sight of one cathedral more before I go far hence to seek for a place for the temple . . . , in the hope, like David, of finding it "in the wood"'.[12] Ruskin took this idea one step further in suggesting that the walls of Gothic buildings tended to dissolve into traceried windows, following 'a principle admitted by nature . . . in her woods and thickets'.[13] One wonders to what extent, if at all, this idea crossed G. G. Scott's mind while he was devising his first design for the cathedral at Christchurch, New Zealand (see pp. 100–10).

But there were more basic liturgical problems with respect to colonial ecclesiology. Where, for example, was the proper location for entrances into churches in the southern hemisphere? Traditionally, entrances to parish churches, especially for the laity, were located on the southern side of the nave or in the south aisle. As time went by, these developed into spaces of their own in the form of porches, which, in turn, were incorporated into the liturgical practices of the Church.[14] But did the location of porches have an innate symbolic value? Perhaps not, but the Cambridge Camden Society had insisted as early as 1841 that the 'position and arrangement [of doors and porches] are matters of extreme importance'.[15] It was certainly a question that exercised the Rev. Frederick H. Cox of Tasmania. Obviously conscious of the fact that he was in the antipodes, he wondered 'how far I am right in thinking that the entrance in this hemisphere should be as usually on the north side, as it is usually on the south in England'.[16] In the event, he put the porch to his church at Prosser Plains on the north side, as did many others in the southern hemisphere (see figs 30 and 31). This logic might have applied just as easily to the incremental orientation of chancels according to the dedication of churches, recommended by the Cambridge Camden Society in its publication *The Orientator* (1844) (fig. 184).[17] If a church was to be dedicated, say, to St Giles in Australia or South Africa, should its orientation be 13° 30´ north of east or south of east? No definitive solution was ever found for these problems, however.

More conventional forms of ecclesiological symbolism also weighed on the minds of colonial clergy, one example of whom – the Rev. John Frederick Bourne of Guiana – we met in the preceding chapter. Writing to the Ecclesiological Society in 1848 on the value of Spanish colonial churches, he observed of his own church that: 'I have endeavoured, as well as I am able, to attend to symbolism.'

> That of the three eastern lights, for instance, is well known; but I am not sure that I am right about my couplet. I believe that couplets are usually explained as symbolising the mission of the Apostles, as it is written 'He began to send then forth by two and two.' And where the lights are distinct and in rows, as in the north and south sides of the nave, this seems correct. I have inserted my southern couplet, however, with a different object, as symbolising another mysterious article of the Creed of S. Athanasius – 'Who although He be GOD and Man: yet He is not two but One CHRIST'; for this reason the lights splay into one internally. The single lights on each side of the sacristy are for each of the holy doctors, S. Paul and S. Augustine, the patrons of the parish and of the chapel; and the south-west single light is for the doctor and bishop of the diocese.[18]

High Anglican clergy in the colonies, if not fully compliant with the dictates of religious symbolism, were at least cognisant of its significance. They were apt to apply it when appropriate and where funds permitted. Even in the most humble of churches, basic provision was made. Commenting on the tiny mission church at St Francis' Harbour, Labrador, for instance, *The Ecclesiologist* was happy to report that 'the windows are rightly formed: adjacent plain lights, grouped in twos and threes, in the aisles, and trefoil-headed lights in the chancel. The east window is a triplet.'[19] Such symbolism could take numerous forms. Among the most immediate and impressive of these was stained glass. Unfortunately, an analysis of stained glass in colonial churches is beyond the scope of this study; suffice to say that all manner of Christian imagery could be (and, indeed, was) commu-

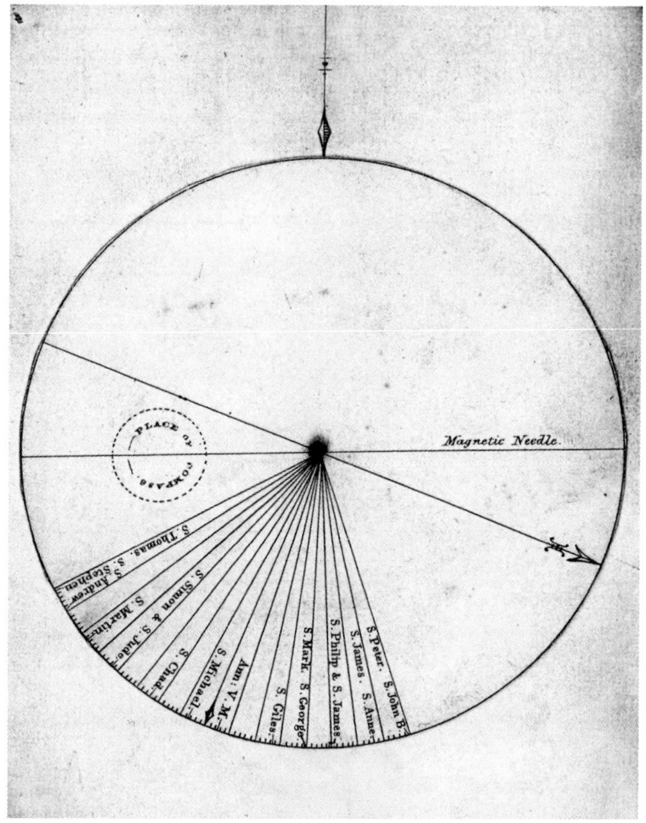

184 Church chancel orientation device from the Cambridge Camden Society's *The Orientator* (1844).

nicated through this medium. Moreover, all the key glass manufacturers loomed large on the colonial scene, including Clayton & Bell, Hardmans, Morris & Co., C. E. Kempe and others.[20] The same applies to other forms of interior decoration, in particular encaustic tiles.[21] Minton's, along with Maw & Co., were especially active in the colonial marketplace, supplying encaustic wall and floor finishes for hundreds of Anglican churches throughout the British empire during the mid- to late nineteenth century. Tiles of this kind can be found in nearly all the substantial churches discussed in this study, from those as small as St John the Baptist, Prosser Plains, and St Anne's chapel, Fredericton, all the way up to the largest of buildings, including St Andrew's cathedral, Sydney, Christchurch cathedral, New Zealand, and (later than these) St Paul's cathedral, Melbourne.

Forms of applied art such as painting, carving and stencilling were also prevalent, and numerous examples could be found in *Instrumenta Ecclesiastica* (fig. 185). At St George's church, Basseterre (St Kitts), for instance, the carved oak

185 Sample Gothic alphabet, designed by William Butterfield for use in stencilling or carving, from *Instrumenta Ecclesiastica*, 2nd ser. (1856).

pulpit was topically emblazoned with a central panel representing Christ's charge, 'Go ye into all the world'; while the marble pulpit at Christchurch cathedral, New Zealand, contains a series of interesting panels depicting the Christianisation of that country (fig. 186). Chancels, especially, were the focus of artistic attention, including the revival of altar décor such as embroidered frontals and church plate. Church plate was considered by many to be not only necessary for divine service but also indispensable in the process of conversion. Britain's key ecclesiastical designers were also involved with this, including William Butterfield, G. E. Street and William Slater (fig. 187). Some indigenous people, upon first seeing these implements, believed them to be imbued with mystical power. The so-called 'Windsor plate', given to bishop Selwyn of New Zealand, for example, had just such an effect on the Māori congregation at Te Waimate when they discovered that it came from England – clearly evoking their own concept of *tapu* (sacredness).[22]

It should be said that both Selwyn and the Rev. William Cotton were sensitive to Māori notions of *tapu*. Although they believed that Māori did not appreciate beauty in the same way as Europeans ('they have no word in their language to express it'),[23] they did acknowledge and even value certain modes of Māori cultural representation. For instance, like many Europeans, they were fascinated by Māori facial tattoos (*pukanohi*). What they recognised in this cultural practice were ideas of time, honour, status and identity (such notions as *iwi*, *whakapapa*, *mana*, *tapu*, etc.) – ideas that were at the basis of their own understanding of the English Church. Evidence of this can be found in Cotton's journal for 1843. Here we find an elaborate drawing or 'map' of a facial tattoo, carefully labelled with numbers and letters as a legend to its meaning and symbolism (fig. 188). Cotton perceived in this apparently 'barbaric' practice what he considered to be a strictly 'national' rather than 'heathen' custom, observing (unlike his Church Missionary Society colleagues) that 'it is a grave question whether all these national customs should not be carefully preserved'.[24] Such practices demonstrated, as far as Cotton was concerned, a sophisticated awareness by Māori of the

186 Carved limestone panel by John Roddis, depicting Bishop G. A. Selwyn proselytising the Māori of New Zealand, on the Selwyn memorial pulpit, 1883–8, by B. W. Mountfort, Christ Church cathedral, Christchurch.

187 Examples of church plate designs by William Butterfield, from *Instrumenta Ecclesiastica*, 2nd ser. (1856).

potential of art to express abstract and conceptual ideas. Did this make them peculiarly capable of perceiving and appreciating the symbolism and accoutrements associated with Anglican worship? Selwyn's wife, Sarah, certainly thought so. With such a deep and ingrained understanding of their own cultural and 'national' traditions, she indeed wondered 'what effect a handsome building – a real Church properly adorned – would have upon them'.[25]

The clergymen of the Universities' Mission to Central Africa were also aware of the symbolic value and power of proper church arrangement. Under the most trying of circumstances, deep in the African jungle, with death and disease lurking around every corner, they spared no effort in dignifying the chancels of their chapels and churches, the accoutrements of which were carried around in a specially made wooden box. On the occasion of the opening

188 William Cotton's sketch of a Māori face tattoo from his journal for 1843 (State Library of New South Wales, Sydney).

of the 'grass church' at Morambala (Mozambique) in 1863, Bishop Tozer noted in his diary how the east end was adorned in blue cloth, and the altar draped with a frontal donated by friends in England. A wooden corona, portable brass altar desk and set of crosses were used to enhance the effect (fig. 189).[26] After all, as the Rev. W. H. Walsh of Sydney had learned, nothing seemed to have a greater effect on the Christian spirit and character of a people than the externals and symbolism of correct, beautiful and proper ecclesiastical edifices.[27]

There was also considerable discussion about ornamentation in colonial churches. This included carved stonework for mouldings, finials, crockets, corbels, capitals and the like. In medieval architecture, ornament of this kind usually took the form of natural flora and fauna. For influential critics such as John Ruskin, the revival of architectural carving provided an unparalleled opportunity for the modern architect and craftsman to celebrate the infinite variety and beauty of God's creation, namely nature. The underlying moral lessons in nature were clear to Ruskin. The natural world was akin to a 'second book' of Revelation in which the power and imagination of the 'great Builder' was everywhere apparent. The associationist and allegorical character of Ruskin's conceptual schema on art gave his writings a force that immediately transformed the meaning and intent of ornamentation in ecclesiastical architecture, seizing it from the perceived clutches of Catholic mysticism.[28] In a typically Protestant reading of the natural world, we are told in *The Stones of Venice*, for example, that 'all noble ornament . . . is the expression of man's delight in God's work'.[29] Nature was important in this respect (in accordance with evangelical typology) because 'God has stamped those characters of beauty [in it] which He has made it man's nature to love.' Thus, good architecture drew its inspiration and subsequent power from the 'image it bears of the natural creation' (fig. 190).[30] According to this view,

189 Church built by the Universities' Mission to Central Africa at Newala, Tanzania (*c.*1882). This building, which used indigenous construction technology, was very similar to the one that the UMCA erected at Morambala.

church architecture could (indeed should) be a vehicle through which the ultimate truth of the world is made manifest – a literal 'sermon in stone'.

As early as 1872, Charles Eastlake, in his *History of the Gothic Revival*, recognised the immense impact that Ruskin and his ideas had had on the development of British architecture.[31] The 'praises' of his work, as G. G. Scott observed, 'were in every one's mouth'.[32] Indeed, in his own treatise in defence of Gothic architecture, *Remarks on Secular and Domestic Architecture, Present and Future* (1857), Scott put reference to nature high on his agenda.[33] Although somewhat critical of his obsession with Italy, and perturbed by his 'extreme' Protestantism, the Ecclesiological Society also viewed Ruskin's ideas favourably. Ruskin's principled line provoked the society to suppose that he had 'practically come to the same conclusions as ourselves'. Although they would later criticise Ruskin for his notions concerning ornamental typology, Neale and Webb had observed in their 'Introductory Essay' to the *Rationale divinorum officiorum* that 'Nature and the Church answer to each other as implicit and explicit revelations of God. Therefore, whatever system is seen to run through the one, in all probability runs through the other'.[34]

Thus, if it was indeed right and proper that nature take its place in church symbolism, whether ornamentally or analogically, then the only question remaining for colonial clergy was what forms and types should be included. Oak and ivy were commonly used in English medieval churches, but what about new churches being erected in Australia, Canada, Africa or the Caribbean? Again, the Rev. William Scott was clear on this point:

> [Do not] let the tropical architect forget how vast a variety of decoration in foliated capitals, and the like, and in carved work, both of wood and stone, is ready for his investigation and reverent study, in the unknown vegetable forms of southern lands. We have boldly pronounced the artistic excellence of Montaude, because, building in Las Palmas, he honestly seized on the indigenous truth of a palm-tree, and 'planted it in the house of the LORD, to flourish in the courts of the house of our GOD.' When another true artist has familiarised himself with the country of the aloe and the banana, – when he has imbued himself with the spirit of the ferns and euphorbias of the south, – when he has felt the delicacy and the majesty of the cocoa and the magnolia, he will not import into the rich bursting tropics the shrunken ball-flowers, or the timid ivy and oak-leaf of a temperate zone. The southern vegetation has yet to be consecrated to the service of religion; and in it we may reverently forecast a true development of Pointed art which the world yet demands. It seems a normal fact, that high art should always adapt the indigenous flora of the country in which it builds. . . . Why should Australia forget its acacias, – Brazil its parasitic orchideæ, – India its nelumbium, – Guiana its gigantic Victoria regia, – Ceylon its spice trees and pitcher plants, – Sicily its orange blossoms, – Africa its stapelias, – Mexico its cactus flowers? Is nothing to be learned from the characteristic forms of the dracæna and the bunyan? – nothing from the grotesque foliage of the pawpaw, or the majestic clusters of the strelitzia?[35]

In response to Scott, and in sympathy with Ruskin, Bourne noted that, for mouldings and other forms of decorative carving in foreign churches, 'there are fruits and flowers in immense variety, teaching us to render daily thanks and praise, and to adore the Creator of them'. 'Besides the gigantic Victoria Regia,' he observed of his own location: 'the passion flower is very abundant; and our forests abound in every direction in orchidious plants and other parasites. I think these last would be particularly appropriate for the capitals of columns. And they seem to

190 Detail sketch of carved stonework on a church exterior, showing weeds growing among the Gothic decoration, from John Ruskin's *Seven Lamps of Architecture* (1849).

me to be full of symbolism, depending entirely, as they do, on the moisture of the tree on which they grow for life, strength, flower, and fruit; reminding one of the words of Eternal Wisdom, "Blessed is the wood whereby righteousness cometh." '[36]

Looking to the local context in this way was considered to be an important ecclesiological principle. Indeed, one of the most basic recommendations in *A Few Words to Church Builders* was that 'style depends on locality'. In commenting on G. G. Scott's memorial column to Sir Charles Hotham (1806–1855), late governor of Victoria, *The Ecclesiologist* noted that Scott's 'genius' was about to teach 'the southern hemisphere that for this as well as all other needs Christian

191 Arcade column capital in Christ Church cathedral, Montreal (1857–9), depicting Canadian maple leaves.

art is all-sufficient'. The journal was referring here to native flora and fauna, which Scott was to use to decorate the memorial. 'We will not . . . suffer ourselves to regret that its *locale* is to be no city of Europe, but one of the new Australian world', it was happily conceded, 'recollecting as we do, that that land seems destined to be the seed-plot of urban nations – parents of art to half the globe.'[37]

Indeed, the symbolical and didactic capacities of architectural ornamentation in this sense were being played out at precisely this moment in the design of the Natural History Museum in Oxford. Here the embodiment of 'nature' and natural processes into the building's architecture and ornamentation allowed for a certain degree of theological mediation of the story of Creation. The scientific and theological questions that lay behind this kind of representation were what linked secular and sacred architecture theoretically in Britain during the 1850s.[38] Feeding into debates on ecclesiology, such concerns became part and parcel of the full and thorough-going adaptation of ecclesiastical forms to foreign contexts. This was the developmental ethos in ecclesiology at work.

Instances of this kind of ornamental adaptation are observable in colonial churches. They are not common, especially early on, as there was little money to embellish buildings in the way architects or clergymen might have wished. Notable examples, however, include the cathedrals at Montreal (fig. 191), Adelaide, Bombay (Mumbai) and Allahabad, where some of the arcade capitals, bosses and other decorative features depict different varieties of native flora and fauna.[39] At St Thomas's cathedral, Bombay, we see two instances of this; the first in the capitals of the pier shafts that surround the interior of James Trubshawe's polychrome east end, representing native flowers and foliage (figs 192 and 193); the second on the font, executed in England by James Forsyth under the direction of the Rev. Charles Boutell. This font was designed specifically to 'harmonise' with Trubshawe's original Lombardo-Romanesque proposal for the cathedral's choir and sanctuary (see p. 142). The base of the bowl is encircled by a carved filigree of lotus leaves, while the capitals of the stout columns contain lotus flowers intermingling with roses, signifying the union between England and India (fig. 194).[40]

But it is at Allahabad where the most astonishing array of contextually inspired ornamentation can be found. Here we see a veritable menagerie of beasts and plants that leave one in no doubt as to the building's location. Lotus buds, broad-leaf foliage, crocodiles, camels, buffalo and tigers abound (figs 195 and 196). This kind of thing also had its corollary in the metropolis, in secular buildings such as the India Office, where an appropriate decorative scheme, based around topical imagery, was considered integral to the building's symbolic function.[41] In the wonderfully 'Ruskinian' All Souls' Memorial church, Kanpur (1862–75) (fig. 197), we see more of the same (fig. 198).

This practice became much more common in the later nineteenth and early twentieth centuries, when extra money

192 Interior of the choir of St Thomas's cathedral, Bombay (*c.*1865), showing carved native flora on the shaft capitals.

was available and local architectural competencies had evolved. In Australia, for instance, native plants and animals became normal in church ornamentation. The narthex screen at William Butterfield's magnificent St Paul's cathedral, Melbourne, (1880–91), for example, has eucalyptus and marsupialoid motifs, while the pier capitals at Holy Trinity, Launceston, Tasmania (1902–39), are decorated with all manner of native shrubs, including banksia and wattle.[42]

193 The choir of St Thomas's cathedral, Bombay (*c.*1865). James Trubshawe produced new designs to reconstruct the existing cathedral, but the choir and sanctuary were the only parts of his scheme to be built.

194 James Forsyth's design for the font in St Thomas's cathedral, Bombay, from *The Builder* (1865).

195 Gargoyle in the form of a tiger emerging from the jungle on the crossing tower of All Saints' cathedral, Allahabad (1870–87).

196 Gargoyle in the form of a crocodile, with lotus leaves and blossoms, on the south transept at All Saints' cathedral, Allahabad (1870–87).

Other localised forms of décor also adorn internal fixtures such as fonts, as seen in the example of the giant native clam shell at St Thomas's, Kuching (see fig. 156). The incorporation of such motifs necessarily added to the place-specific character and appearance of colonial church buildings. Again, these 'accommodations' should not be interpreted as a secondary, inferior, or even debased form of ecclesiology. The idea that any pure or perfect type might have existed as far as Christian architecture was concerned had all but disappeared – if it ever really existed at all – by the late 1840s.[43] To informed ecclesiologists, correct colonial churches were as much a part of the extension and 'developement' of revived 'Catholick' art as St Paul's, Brighton, or All Saints', Margaret Street. As G. G. Scott observed in 1848, '[e]very ancient church, however simple and rustic, must . . . be viewed as a portion of the material of Christian art, – as one stone set apart for the foundation of its revival'.[44] This sentiment pervaded the project of ecclesiology as a whole, both at home and abroad.

Top 197 All Souls' Memorial church, Kanpur, India (1862–75), by Walter Granville.

Bottom 198 Arcade column capital, depicting native Indian flora, All Souls, Memorial Church, Kanpur.

A Greater Cause: Religion and Identity in the High Anglican Mind

The concern for symbolism in church architecture was explicitly associated with identity in the High Anglican mind. Symbolism was considered important precisely because it represented the liturgical practices of ancient (and therefore 'true') Christianity in a way that accorded with the authority and ordinances of the reformed English Church. In this sense, a correctly arranged Anglican church was a very particular cultural formation – a material and spatial manifestation of a peculiar and nationally ordained religious ideology. Whether it was located in England or elsewhere did not matter, as long as it was identifiable as such. Indeed, the ability of these forms to travel and adapt without losing their distinct essence was considered a mark of their cultural efficacy. Of course, the ideas of identity surrounding this formation were often measured and articulated against what they were not; that is, the 'perverted' doctrines of the Roman Catholic Church, the error of Nonconformism, or even the 'extremes' of Protestantism (more about this inter-denominational conflict will appear in Chapter 5). Although essentially a reformed and thereby 'Protestant' Church, the Church of England occupied a point on the spectrum between the perceived extremes of Rome and Geneva: hence, the all important notion of the *via media*. Anglican clergy were very much aware of the Church's position as the manifestation of this 'middle way', and consciously manipulated the vagaries associated with it, some staking their claim at the 'Low' end, others at the 'High'. Nevertheless, whether High or Low, the Anglican Church was identified by its distinct and national doctrines, practices and prejudices. Many of these took (or could take) architectural form.

The Gothic Revival itself had a long history in Britain of being pressed into the service of identity and nationhood.[45] In the early nineteenth century, in particular, antiquaries and architectural theorists were apt to suggest the English or wider Saxon origins of Gothic architecture.[46] Later, in the 1830s and 1840s, came greater concern for the specific value of English Gothic over Continental varieties, leading to a prejudice for 'national' forms. This is observable in the writings of well-known theorists and architects of the time such as A. W. N. Pugin, E. A. Freeman, G. G. Scott, G. E. Street and even John Ruskin, who, despite his clear love of Italian medieval architecture, considered English Gothic

199 Portrait of George Gilbert Scott (1811–1878), steel engraving after George Richmond, 1879.

of the 'earliest decorated' to be the 'safest choice' for a universally accredited, national style of architecture.[47] Ruskin was against the 'invention' *de novo* of such a style, but his thoughts on the issue nevertheless reflected the desire, then prevalent among the architecture fraternity in England, for a 'modern' and 'national' style. This desire, and the debates that attended it, were played out in an episode known as the 'Battle of the Styles' – an ideological tussle concerning the competing merits of Gothic versus classicism, which culminated in the design of the new Foreign and India Office buildings in Whitehall, London, between 1857 and 1861.[48] However, these concerns were evident in British architecture much earlier, especially in the design of the new Palace of Westminster (1836), in which associations of *genius loci* and English liberty were central.[49] The connection between architecture (with its capacity for didactic expression), identity and nationhood was one of the leitmotifs of mid- to late nineteenth-century British architecture.

An example of the far-reaching impact these ideologies had on architectural thought in Britain can be found in the writings of G. G. Scott (fig. 199). As architect of the controversial new Government Offices project in Whitehall, Scott was at the centre of the debate over style. He was also soon to become one of Britain's, if not (as Gladstone said) Europe's, most accomplished and influential architects. For instance, as early as 1848 we find him suggesting that the sympathies of an English architect lie most naturally with his own native country, 'with the very buildings to which he traces the earliest and most cherished of his architectural associations'.[50] Coming from this position, Scott believed that 'our' architecture 'should everywhere be both *English* and *Christian*'. It should not, however, be a lifeless imitation of past achievements; rather, and importantly for its extension beyond the British Isles, it was to 'have in it that intrinsic principle of life which would admit of its ready adaptation to the climate of the torrid or the frozen zone, to the scorched plantations of Jamaica or the icy rocks of Labrador'.[51] Scott therefore saw English Gothic as a form of architecture that was culturally identifiable yet pliable – a form that was suitable to the modern age (owing to its inherent adaptability) while remaining representative of a professed Christian nation. In this he was a disciple of Pugin. But he went further. In his *Remarks on Secular and Domestic Architecture*, we find Scott insisting that, in devising a modern style of architecture, the English architect might locate 'such a nucleus' for it 'in the native architecture of our own country, – the production of our own forefathers; men bearing our own names; whose lands still often remain in the same families; whose armorial bearings we are still proud to hold; to whom we owe our liberties, our constitution, and our national customs; and who, though living in simpler times, were the fathers of our modern civilization'.[52] Thus, he concludes, 'all that is really national and historical in the buildings around us must ever draw us towards the mediæval styles'.[53]

There is a subtext in this. Reminiscent of Goethe's appeal to nationalist myths of origin in architecture, it concerns the broader notion of 'civilisation'. Here we find Scott delving into racial theory – undoubtedly picked up from his friend E. A. Freeman[54] – in his defence of Gothic architecture as that style with the greatest claim to our attention and sympathy. In his Royal Academy lectures on medieval architecture (1857–73), for instance, he observed that the 'leading historical claims' of the Gothic style are that it is not only 'pre-eminently the architecture of our forefathers and of our own land', but also 'the architecture of the nations wholly or partially of Germanic origin, in whose hands the civilisation of the modern world has been vested'.[55] 'I am, however, only urging this as a claim which our old architecture has upon our own study', he added.

> If we investigate the architecture of Egypt, of Assyria, or of Persia, we find that it tells of races with whom we have no national or personal sympathy. If we go to the classic shores of Greece, though there we should be viewing the work of a race whose arts and literature are, more than those of any other people, the property of the world, we nevertheless fail to find anything to connect them in any special sense to ourselves . . . How different is the study of Gothic architecture! Its original exemplars are at our own doors; the very churches, perhaps, in which from our infancy we have worshipped; the monuments of our own forefathers . . . who spoke, in its pristine form, our own language; who sat in our own Parliaments . . . and laid the foundations of our liberties and of all those institutions which render the name of England illustrious among the nations of the earth.[56]

The revival of Gothic architecture was not the result of mere 'fashion', Scott retorted in response to its critics; no, it was 'a deep-seated, earnest, and energetic revolution in the human mind, and one which . . . pervades all the countries where Gothic architecture once flourished' – that is, 'our own family of nations'.[57] In other words, it had reached its apogee, as Freeman would have said, in the lands of the Teutonic races of northern Europe. Although, following Viollet-le-Duc, Scott ultimately argued for a commonsensical or 'rational' basis for Gothic architecture, he, along with many others, was clearly enamoured of the rich historical, cultural and, indeed, national associations that this style of architecture had accumulated over the intervening centuries. Such romantic sentiments were responsible in part for driving the Gothic Revival in Britain.

These kinds of association of course affected Anglican ecclesiology. In the early 1840s the Cambridge Camden Society was (in)famous for its forthright – even belligerent – advocacy of 'national' styles of medieval architecture, especially the so-called 'Middle-Pointed' or Decorated phase of English Gothic. It pulled no punches in this regard. The prevailing view among ecclesiologists at the time was that properly considered Christian architecture ought to 'suit the climate, scenery, manners, and national feelings' of those who produce it. 'What principle can be so reasonable as the adoption in each country of its own peculiar and

200 Portrait of the Rev. Edward Coleridge (1800–1887), engraving by J. H. Robinson after George Richardson, 1847 (King's School, Canterbury).

national variety of architecture?' it was asked.[58] English forms, it seems, were necessary for a purely English Church.[59] We have also seen how the idea of the cathedral – one of those institutional hangovers from pre-Reformation times – was considered not only an ancient and thereby sanctioned form of Church organisation but also one that was now a feature (nay 'ornament') of the English ecclesiastical system (see pp. 70–3). Moreover, if instituted properly, and in accordance with its original purpose, the cathedral system was perceived to be a form of governance that was liberal and representative in the best English tradition. There were many who thought otherwise. But the point was made: cathedrals and their architecture were among the greatest cultural achievements of the British people, and very much part of the constitutional settlement of the reformed English Church.

These wider connections between identity, form and purpose in the English Church, both at home and abroad, cannot be overstated. They were extensive and substantial. The obligatory basis of this connection, as far as the responsibilities of the Church were concerned, was established with the inauguration of the Colonial Bishoprics' Fund (1841), the reinvigoration of the Society for the Propagation of the Gospel, and the systematic establishment of Anglican dioceses abroad (see the Introduction). As Howard Le Couteur has observed, much of the nationalist sentiment that characterised the Church of England at this time derived from High Anglican notions of paternalism and the idea of a gentlemanly 'clerical caste', which were seen as exponents of English culture. This paternalist notion, in its modern sense at least, was grounded in an understanding, arrived at by Samuel Taylor Coleridge (the Rev. Edward Coleridge's uncle), of the established Church as a constitutional phenomenon, which served cultural as well as religious ends. Thus, the role of the Church of England was to transmit both national and Anglican culture wherever it went.[60] As we have seen, individual architects, including G. G. Scott, William Butterfield, G. F. Bodley and William Burges, among others, were instrumental in both Britain and its overseas territories in promoting the presence and authority of the Anglican cause through built form. There were also a number of clerics and statesmen who were vociferous in laying bare the greater purpose of the English Church vis-à-vis its national character and geo-political function – those who might be described as 'champions' of the cause, such as the Rev. Charles Blomfield, William Gladstone, the Rev. Edward Coleridge (fig. 200), A. J. B. Beresford Hope and the Rev. Samuel Wilberforce. Wilberforce, whom we met earlier, was perhaps the most enthusiastic (fig. 201). He was unwavering in his support for and promotion of the SPG. Indeed, he perceived the SPG as nothing less than the Church of England's 'missionary arm'.[61] As Bishop of Oxford, and a leading patron of the society, his views on the SPG as a quasi-political entity bear further scrutiny in light of their distinctly nationalist overtones and understanding of the wider responsibilities of the Church of England.

As mentioned earlier, Wilberforce, imbued with that Coleridgean sense of national paternalism, was aware of the role that orthodox religion played in the maintenance and stability of Britain's national interest. More than this, he pegged Britain's peace and prosperity at home squarely on the virtue of its activities and reputation abroad. As Britain, indeed England, was a Christian nation (a nation with its own divinely sanctioned and politically instituted Church), it followed that wherever Englishmen went they ought to take their Church with them, and that that Church, by definition, would become a moral and spiritual bulwark in the wider political 'game' being played out between Britain and its rivals across the globe. The scenario was simple: no Church (that is, no Anglican Church), no national prosperity (potentially). In the eyes of Wilberforce, this was a great sword of Damocles hanging over the head of the British nation. The idea is summed up in the following passage from one of his sermons:

201 Portrait of Samuel Wilberforce (1805–1873), bishop of Oxford, from R. G. Wilberforce, *Life of the Right Reverend Samuel Wilberforce*, vol. 2 (1881).

> Almighty God has given us that [prosperity], and, at the same time, in giving us an arm of strength, giving us ships which multiply our presence in every part of the earth, giving us colonies which enable us to reproduce our race and our Church wherever the sun rises and sets, He has intended, if we rise fully to the dignity of our birth-right, to make the English branch of His Church, spread now throughout America, spreading now throughout Australia, seated in New Zealand, carried out in South Africa, blended with the blood of Africa in the West Indies, entering from Sierra Leone into the northern part of Africa – that with this apparatus for spreading it, and this gift of God's truth to spread, His purpose for England is that she shall be the regenerator of our race and the maintainer of the purity of Christendom.[62]

This was in essence a zero–sum game, in which piety equated to profit.

For Wilberforce, the Great Sepoy Revolt or 'Indian Mutiny' of 1857 was a case in point, illustrating what happens when such grave responsibilities are eschewed. 'Will it be believed', he bewailed in a sermon on behalf of the SPG in 1857,

> that until the year 1783 a missionary was not allowed to reside in British India? . . . In 1783, when the charter was renewed, one, whose name it is my blessed privilege to bear, stood up for truth and right in England's senate, and proposed this resolution – 'That India must be held by the British nation for the moral and religious good of the natives thereof'. And what was done? The words were struck out of the bill and it was allowed to pass. In her highest hall of legislation, deliberately and avowedly, England – Christian England – rejected the bare general avowal that it was her duty to care for the moral and spiritual welfare of her Indian population. And what followed? . . . And therefore I desire every one of you, as Christians, and as Englishmen, to study this matter – to be ready to take a positive attitude of resistance, if God blesses our arms, to the resettlement of the Indian question upon anything but a Christian basis. . . . Our responsibility is great and if we neglect it we must expect to be smitten – to lose the gift of peace, to have the channels of grace diminished, to have less love, less faith, less holiness at home.[63]

What was worse, if Britain was unprepared to rise to the challenge in India, then 'some other people will be raised up to do the work of God there [that is, Russia], and we shall be put down because we refused to do it'.[64] Unfortunately for Wilberforce, the Queen's royal proclamation of 1858 did not institute Christianity as the basis of colonial government in India. On the contrary, it guaranteed freedom of religion.[65] But this did not stop Anglican clergymen and their supporters, both in Britain and abroad, lobbying government and promoting the interests of the Church vis-à-vis colonial society.[66] As we saw in the Introduction, Wilberforce was far from alone in his views on the matter.

If the likes of Wilberforce were fighting 'the good fight' at home, in the colonies there were clergymen doing their bit too. Bishop Medley of Fredericton, for instance, was keen to make his new cathedral as much a cultural and political statement as a spiritual one. For a time the old wooden church at Fredericton stood beside the newly completed stone one (this was a relatively common practice in the colonies during the rebuilding of churches). As Gregg Finley has pointed out, the contrast between the two buildings would have been striking. The one representing the now obsolete, classically inspired Georgian tradition with its Erastian associations; the other signifying the new, spiritually earnest and very Victorian worldview of revived medievalism and ancient Church custom. Here, in the space of a few yards, was captured the evolving condition of the British empire – not merely a temporal realm, as Finley contends, 'but an empire under God'; not an 'imperial presence once removed, but a direct, compelling sense of the Mother Country'.[67] In erecting the new cathedral, Medley made sure that none among his congregation missed the point: 'No express form of architecture is divinely given: Yet one can see no reason for going to pagan Greece and idolatrous Rome for our models, when we can find better in Christian England. . . . The parish church of our fatherland has been found convenient and suitable for the worship of millions of Churchmen for many centuries . . . why should it not be good enough for us?'[68] In this one building were bound up notions of architecture, religious nationalism and British imperial politics.

Similar notions concerning architecture and its relationship to identity prevailed in New Zealand – that 'Britain of the South'. Here, as Ian Lochhead has argued, the pangs of absence were felt as acutely as anywhere. In his poem *Patriotism*, for example, the Rev. Henry Jacobs reflected on the sentiment that if 'Greece is where the Greeks are', then ''tis England, where an English spirit dwells'. There is little doubt that the largely dashed expectations surrounding the early development of the Canterbury Settlement exacerbated such feelings. James FitzGerald, superintendent of the settlement, also mused over this predicament, suggesting that 'what Britain was in comparison with Rome, such to a considerable extent is New Zealand to England'. In Roman Britain, he continued – as if to assuage feelings of exile and despair – 'there were men who . . . endeavoured to propagate in the land of their adoption that beauty of form and colouring, with which they had been familiar in the country of their birth'.[69] Thus, it was indeed possible to recreate 'home' (or a semblance of it, at least) in a foreign land, and architecture was central to this endeavour. The desire to erect proper and, where possible, substantial Anglican churches was evidently part of the process – a process that involved reconstructing, as it were, old worlds from new. This was, of course, impossible, but the myth persisted nonetheless.

Across the Tasman Sea, in Australia, Bishop Broughton was also busy raising the banner of the English Church in its national and imperial capacities. In his speeches and sermons Broughton constantly reiterated the unique identity and national purpose of what he was wont to emphasise as the 'Reformed' English Church. As we shall see in the next chapter, this had much to do with his siege mentality, wedged, as he felt himself to be, between the creeping forces of Roman Catholicism on the one hand, and official indifference on the other. Nevertheless, there is little question that, much like Wilberforce, Broughton viewed the Anglican confession as having a divinely ordained mission to secure peace in the world and to promulgate the 'true' faith, especially through architecture (see Chapter 1).

Broughton was prepared to tackle the issue of religious politics head on. As mentioned in the Introduction, he wrote to Edward Coleridge in 1837 complaining of the predicament in which he saw the Church, making a connection between the duty of politicians and national security (see p. 3). Over the years Broughton's views on this matter hardened. In a sermon preached on Whitsunday 1849 at St James's church, Sydney, he explicitly connected the nature and spirit of the English Church with the achievements of the British empire. Unambiguously entitled 'The English Reformation, and the Empire of England', it was delivered in celebration of the tercentenary of the first use of the Book of Common Prayer during the reign of Edward VI – the English Prayer Book and the 'reformed' nature of the English Church being favourite topics for Broughton. 'This day', he boomed, '. . . memorably coincides with the three hundredth anniversary of the day on which the public offices of our religion were first solemnized by authority in a form of prayer, which, we may with admiration and gratitude contend, has done more than any other human composition whatever to cause the sound of the Gospel to go into all the earth.'[70] Critically, for Broughton, the Church in which *he* ministered the gospel was not merely Christian but English. This was important because to a cleric such as himself, who harboured a certain amount of Erastian sentiment, the Church of England was as much a political entity as it was a spiritual one. 'The existing circumstances of the British empire now render it no less manifest', he exclaimed, 'that it is set up to be a bulwark of that reformed and recovered Christianity which exhibits the genuine lineaments of heavenly truth'.[71] As he reminded his congregation:

> It is impossible to contemplate the position held by England at this moment, – as the central body of a vast system of colonization, the various members of which gravitate towards her, subject, like the planets and satellites in the heavenly regions, to a well-adjusted controlling influence which bends their courses into their several appointed orbits, maintaining the due relation of each to each, and the harmony of the entire system, – without being impressed with a conviction that things have been ordered thus by the fiat of an all-discerning Providence.[72]

Broughton's views concerning religion, empire and state are not at all surprising when we consider the fact that he spent seven years of his early life working at the treasury of the East India Company (1807–14).[73] His awareness of the extension of the British state and its limitations was more acute than most. Thus, like many of his clerical colleagues, he was inclined to view spiritual 'dominion' within the empire not as a fragmented, piecemeal phenomenon, but as a common and continuous force that was everywhere united in its purpose and objectives.

But the Church could not be lax or rest upon it laurels, it was felt, for danger and darkness lurked at every turn. This is where the visible externals of Anglican worship, such as architecture, played their part. 'Numerous bodies are already settled, and increasing numbers are daily establishing themselves,' warned Broughton,

> in regions where, if the soil be uncultivated, and consequently unfruitful in the products of nature, it exhibits but too accurate a picture, it supplies only too close an emblem of the total want of religious cultivation, and of the attendant danger which exists of an entire cessation of growth in grace. Hundreds of miles, – thousands, I might rather say, – of inhabited districts have I despondingly traversed, in which no holy fabric of the Church was visible, to put men in mind of heavenly things by its very external aspect; or to unfold its doors that they might enter in, and be taught the 'truth as it is in Jesus'.[74]

In this particular order of things – this Anglican worldview – more was at stake than either religion or architec-

202 Portrait of Robert Gray (1809–1872), first bishop of Cape Town, from Charles Gray, *The Life of Robert Gray* (1876).

ture alone. Both were pressed into the service of the nation's wider geo-political interests, becoming planks in Britain's self-appointed 'mission' to develop commercially, civilise and Christianise the non-European world.[75]

Pro Fide et Patria:
The Church and Architecture in South Africa

One place where we see the intersecting concerns of religion and secular politics played out on a grand scale is South Africa. Indeed, a recurring theme in Wilberforce's pronouncements on Christianity, empire and national prosperity was the strategic importance of the Cape of Good Hope. Before the opening of the Suez Canal in 1869, access to India by ship was via the Cape. It was therefore vital that Britain maintain a controlling stake in that part of the world in order to secure its empire in Asia. For politically minded clerics such as Wilberforce, brute force alone would not win the day. Gunboat diplomacy may have had its uses, but it was ultimately unsustainable. A more systematic and long-sighted campaign for the winning of hearts and minds was required – what clergymen at the time called the 'curing of souls'. It was obviously much more efficient in the long run to secure the loyalty of indigenes and settlers alike in Africa through the inculcation of national religion than by the coercive force of continuous and destructive warfare. This was the point that the Rev. Robert Gray, first bishop of Cape Town (fig. 202), made at the second public meeting of the CBF in 1853 (see p. 7). Wilberforce, too, was clear on the wisdom and righteousness of this strategy. As mentioned in the Introduction, he had made speeches to this effect before. One cause that was particularly close to his heart in this respect, and one for which he fought tirelessly, was missionary bishops. He was a leading proponent of the UMCA, for he understood the longer-term benefits that such a mission, operating outside official British territory, would have in promoting peace and prosperity in the region. In the wake of such a mission would come not only true religion but also political influence by way of English customs and commerce.[76] '[W]e are at this moment as a people so connected for good or for evil with that great continent of Africa', Wilberforce declared in a speech on behalf of the UMCA in 1860:

> The very fact that we possess the Cape of Good Hope is a wonderful call upon us. Remember, we could not maintain, humanly speaking, our great oriental possessions in India – upon the preservation of which we have spent so much, and upon the preservation of which so much of our wealth depends – if that half-way house, that natural citadel, jutting out upon the promontory, pointing into those stormy seas which roll ever round the Cape, were in the power of an adverse European nation. God has given us that as a safeguard for our Indian dominion; and I say, in giving us that, He has given us the basis of missionary operations in Africa.[77]

All this pointed to the need – apparent urgency, even – of planting the English Church fully in southern and central Africa. So much for the rhetoric; what about the practicalities?

Before the arrival of Bishop Robert Gray in the summer of 1848, Anglicanism in South Africa had only a small and select following. Its communicants came mainly from among the army and the governing élite, and it was not unusual for divine service to be conducted in secular buildings such as court houses or government offices. Although not uncommon in the British colonial world at the time, this rather makeshift approach to Anglican worship was purely pragmatic. Clearly, things were not as they should be. The English Church was considered by many to be indolent with respect to evangelisation in Africa. 'While English, French, and German societies, of various denominations, are sending out their Missionaries,' wrote one disgruntled Cape resident in 1846, 'our own Church does worse than nothing.'[78] It was therefore clear by all accounts that before the establishment of the new bishopric and the appointment of Gray, Anglicanism in South Africa, never robust, was in a moribund state, bordering on extinction.[79]

Historically, the propagation of Christianity at the Cape had been presided over almost exclusively by the Dutch Reformed Church. Although not particularly concerned with missionary work, the Dutch Church was nevertheless active in its own way. It was more widely followed and better funded than the Anglican Church, enabling it to have a strong visual presence in towns and cities through its numerous and well-appointed churches and chapels.[80] Evangelisation of indigenes had been left in the hands of independent missionary organisations such as the Moravians, who had been establishing missionary stations inland among the native peoples since the late eighteenth century.

From the 1820s onwards, however, the denominational demographic of the Cape began to change. As British emigrants started arriving in larger numbers, Nonconformist bodies such as the Wesleyan Methodists and the London Missionary Society (LMS) began playing an increasingly dominant role in religious affairs. When Gray took up residence in Cape Town at the beginning of 1848, it was clear to him that his Church was all but a new factor in a hitherto foreign and Nonconformist domain, and that he would have to rebuild it from the ground up, both literally and figuratively.[81]

Architecture was instrumental in Gray's campaign to reconfigure the religious landscape in southern Africa. But before we can examine his thoughts on architecture more closely, a word on his initial impressions of the Cape is necessary.

In his early writings on the subject we find Gray describing the apathy of the English Church in South Africa as a blot on the reputation of the British nation. Thus, even before he had left for his new diocese, Gray had been heaping guilt upon his fellow countrymen and their Church. 'The Presbyterians, Wesleyans, Independents, Moravians, Baptists, the Rhenish, Paris, and Berlin Societies, and the Americans, have all their Missions in active operation, *but the Church of England has none*,' he exclaimed in 1847; '[e]ven Mahometans appear to have been more zealous than we. . . . This is, indeed, a sad disgrace to us.'[82]

The nature of this charge is important. By raising the stakes in this way, Gray was attempting to prick the conscience of the established Church and its followers. His aim was to put a particular spin on the evangelical and missionary liabilities of the English Church. He believed, along with an increasing number of Anglicans at the time, that Britain had a duty to uphold with respect to its colonial territories, a duty that concerned not only the proper governance of its empire but also the rolling out of an 'empire of the spirit'. As long as the Cape of Good Hope was a British colony, he declared, the Church of England was responsible for the spiritual welfare of its inhabitants. By emphasising this sense of obligation, Gray was able to make the point that the Church of England's involvement in the wider mission field was as much a question of national accountability as it was of Christian duty.

With this in mind, Gray saw one of his initial and most important tasks in South Africa as making provision for church accommodation. While on the first visitation of his diocese in 1848, he commented frequently on the lack of buildings for proper and regular worship. In many areas no Anglican church existed at all. While on visitation between Cape Town and Uitenhage, a distance of some nine hundred miles, he reported having seen only one Anglican church.[83] Such was the extent of dereliction that before he had passed through a third of his new diocese Gray had arranged for the erection of ten new churches and pledged support for six additional clergymen.[84] In the 'battle' to cure souls and to prevent the defection of Anglicans to Roman Catholicism or Nonconformism, Gray knew that his efforts would be decisive. So important was this that he later identified the erection of churches and chapels as his 'chief concern'.[85]

Gray, however, was no Tractarian. He did, nevertheless, sympathise to a large extent with the Oxford reformers and their cause. In this respect he was similar to Selwyn. He accepted much of what had been espoused in the *Tracts of the Times*, even Tract 90, and believed that the Church of England ought to regain something of the humility and discipline of its catholic and apostolic roots.[86] These views naturally extended to his opinions on architecture. Although not a particularly intellectual man, Gray, like Walsh in Sydney, was percipient enough to recognise the potential that architecture had to inspire religious sentiment.[87] While passing through the north-western town of Springbok in 1866, for example, he recorded how 'a very nice and correct little Early English church has been erected'.[88] Comments of this kind appear frequently in Gray's letters and visitation diaries. Far from merely appreciative, they are symptomatic of his endeavours in deploying architecture to transform the visual and moral character of the African landscape. 'In order to carry on the work which lies before the Church in this land, which is the gathering of souls into the fold of Christ, and the preserving of those that are within, in the true faith, in holiness and righteousness of life that they may be saved through Christ forever,' he pleaded in 1850, 'means are needed; a machinery must be supplied.'[89] Architecture was a vital cog in this machinery. But not just any architecture would do. One that was identifiably English and Anglican was obviously necessary.

For Gray, church buildings were more than places of worship – they served a mnemonic function as well, both as markers of the recovery of Anglicanism in southern Africa and the extension of English cultural identity. Moreover, they were 'appliances' (to use his own language) in the struggle of the English Church over the 'strongholds of Satan' and therefore essential in the wider campaign to overcome his 'Romish' and Nonconformist rivals in the mission field.[90] 'It is delightful to see our old English churches repeated in this land,' he observed of St Mark's, while passing through the town of George in 1850: 'I am glad to find that it is generally admired and appreciated for it encourages me to persevere in my efforts to get correct churches built' (fig. 203).[91] Similarly, while at Beaufort in 1855, he recorded with satisfaction how the recently erected church 'put me very much in mind of some of the little churches in our Yorkshire dales'.[92]

Importantly, Gray was surrounded from the beginning by a band of younger, mostly Oxbridge-educated clergymen. Among these young hopefuls were the Revs James Green, Henry Master White (fig. 204), William A. Newman, Hopkins Badnall and Nathaniel James Merriman (fig. 205). Nearly all of these clerics immersed themselves in questions of architecture. White and Merriman, in particular, were staunch Tractarians.[93] Although not acquainted with one another before they embarked for South Africa, they arrived together at Cape Town aboard the *Gwalior* on 15 November 1848, having spent several weeks at sea getting to know one another and discussing future plans.[94]

White, a Wykehamist, was deeply ensconced in Tractarian circles. He was also soon to become the brother-in-law of the Rev. William Grey of Newfoundland (see Chapter 3), who married his youngest sister, Harriet, in 1849.[95] In White's final years at Winchester College, the High Church cleric George Moberly (1803–1885) was appointed headmaster. Moberly was known to have exerted great personal influence over his boys, and he no doubt played a significant role in shaping the theological outlook of the young

203 St Mark's church, George, South Africa (1849), by Henry Underwood and Sophy Gray.

White before he went up to Oxford in the spring of 1839. Although White matriculated at Balliol (Moberly's college), he moved shortly afterwards to New College (a Wykehamist bastion), where he was made fellow and mixed with other Tractarian stalwarts, such as James Edwards Sewell (fellow 1829, warden 1860–1903) and, through him, his brother the Rev. William Sewell, then dean of Exeter College.[96] Moberly was also good friends with John Keble (his neighbour at Winchester) and a close associate of Sewell's. William Sewell would later become president of the Oxford Architectural Society (1848–50), of which White was himself a life member.[97]

Merriman, over a decade White's senior, was also a Wykehamist, though too early to have been touched directly by the High Church idealism of Moberly. His innate moral sensibility and disciplined spirituality naturally inclined him towards Tractarianism and its concern for fundamental Church reform. He entered Brasenose College in 1829, and,

204 The Rev. Henry Master White (1820–1892), first principal of Bishops College, Rondebosch, and frequent contributor to the *South African Church Magazine*.

205 Portrait of Nathaniel James Merriman (1809–1882), archdeacon and then bishop of Grahamstown.

although the Oxford Movement was not yet fully under way when he came down in 1834, he witnessed its turbulent beginnings. This left a deep impression on the young Merriman's mind. After having been at his second curacy of Holy Trinity, Over Darwen (Lancashire), for less than a year, he was accused of being a 'Puseyite' and forced to resign.[98]

Thus, representing that new breed of colonial clergyman discussed in Chapter 1, it was only natural that these men carried with them to South Africa ideas on architecture they had picked up while at Oxford (or Cambridge). Indeed, not long after arriving at the Cape, Gray established a monthly publication entitled *The South African Church Magazine and Ecclesiastical Review*. Its editor, the indefatigable William A. Newman,[99] was a keen ecclesiologist, regularly including articles on church architecture. His own writing on the subject was rather turgid, expressing a deeply romantic, near saccharine adoration for the image of English medieval architecture.[100] His prose is shot through with poetic yearnings:

> [We are] deprived of the pleasing delight we once had in our college long vacations, of a kind of pilgrimage to our old English Churches, tracing, or pleased to think that we traced, the pure specimens, and first gradations of the Saxon, Norman, early English, Perpendicular. . . . We have seen these venerable piles in all lights and shades, – in the stillness of the moonlight, – and beneath the glare of a noon day-sun; – and in every hour, and in every light, they are alike the same, – solemn, grand, sublime. They are still daguerreotyped on our minds. We see them yet, – years and distance and other scenes cannot erase them; they are *palimpsests*; – other impressions may for a time usurp their place, – but Memory's alchymy [*sic*] can in a moment restore them.[101]

Such sentiments were no doubt exacerbated by the feelings of cultural and spiritual isolation Newman experienced upon his arrival in Africa. As with *The Ecclesiologist*, connections were regularly made in the *South African Church*

206 One of several sketches by John Armstrong of English country scenes, *c.*1852, which he took with him to South Africa (Cory Library, Rhodes University, Grahamstown).

Magazine between English medieval architecture and identity.[102] The suggestion here was that, although not perfect, English medieval forms were, to quote one of its authors, 'best adapted to the English national character in its noblest features, and so the best to be perpetuated in English colonies'.[103] Perhaps forewarned of the emotional distress he would experience in a place like Africa, the Rev. John Armstrong, bishop of Grahamstown (1853–6), came armed with a number of bucolic scenes containing churches that he had sketched before departing England. If not intended as the basis for future designs these scenes would have provided psychological comfort by way of 'Memory's alchymy' amid the harsh, sun-scorched and oftentimes barren environs of the Eastern Cape (fig. 206).

On the whole, the most consistent element in the writings of Newman and other contributors to the *South African Church Magazine* was their clear endorsement of the Tractarian view that architecture was the embodiment of belief. This sentiment was seen to carry particular weight in a land such as Africa, where Anglican clergy were reminded that the 'faithful study of the principles of the English Church will show that Churches, which are *like Churches*, are best calculated to promote devotion and holy life'.[104]

Typical of Gray's initiative in this regard was his intervention in the rebuilding of St Paul's church at Rondebosch (1848–72). When he learnt that the church was being built in 'the usual colonial fashion', he presented two sets of alternative plans to the vestry committee. These were ren-

207 Drawing by an unknown artist of St Paul's church, Rondebosch, Cape Town (1848–72), by William Butterfield and Sophy Gray (Vestry Archive, St Paul's church, Rondebosch).

dered in a simple, Middle-Pointed, Gothic style.[105] Knowing that he would face such difficulties in South Africa, Gray (and his wife) had solicited architectural plans and drawings from friends, architects and organisations such as the Oxford Architectural and Ecclesiological societies before their departure.[106] As a consequence, St Paul's was rescued from being yet another nondescript 'preaching box' and was transformed into one of South Africa's earliest correct Gothic Revival churches (fig. 207).

Not satisfied, Gray then focused his attention on erecting a 'collegiate institution' for the education of immigrants' children. This initiative was calculated as a means of inculcating orthodox English values in the settler community. In a similar fashion to St John's College, New Zealand, it was to replicate the English public school, consisting of a chapel, library, hall and dormitories, all built with 'due regard to ecclesiastical and architectural beauty'.[107] What Gray meant by this was that his new college ought to be built in a 'neat' and correct English Gothic style – a style concordant with the now established principles of Anglican ecclesiology. Gray appointed one of his young attendants, Henry Master White, as first principal. Rather fortuitously, White's brother was the English architect William White, whom we met earlier (see p. 153). In April 1849 White asked William to prepare designs for new college buildings, making the suggestion that he base them on the example of Radley College in Oxfordshire.[108] It was made clear from the beginning that the cost of building in South Africa was exorbitant and that only a very simple style of architecture could be afforded. Although the exact number of designs produced by White for the college is uncertain, it seems that he submitted at least two sets of drawings, both of which met with 'very favourable opinion' from the Ecclesiological Society.[109]

Owing to lack of funds, however, the 'cheap and simple' version was adopted. But this did not necessitate a less correct or complete building. In fact, as the project developed, White was forced to make complex alterations to his original plans not only to suit changing circumstances but also because the bishop demanded a 'grander and more dignified' style of building.[110] We can get some impression of what the original design may have looked like by considering White's plans for the small timber church at Woodlands, near Cape Town (see fig. 143). The first of the college buildings erected, however, were much more substantial than this, with stuccoed, solid brick walls and a roof of imported Welsh slate. Among these buildings, now part of Founder's House, Bishops College, are the dining hall (1862) and the range of rooms that form the eastern edge of the quadrangle (1852) (fig. 208).[111]

As mentioned in Chapter 1, one of Gray's most important collaborators in his architectural endeavour was his wife, Sophy (see p. 61). It is reckoned that Sophy was involved in the design of over a hundred buildings in South Africa between 1847 and 1872.[112] Her level of activity in this regard was truly impressive and can hardly be overstated. Indeed, most of the plans that Gray distributed among his numerous parishes were either drawn by Sophy or adapted from plans she brought from England.[113] Although Sophy was no originator, it nevertheless required considerable knowledge and skill on her part to adapt these plans to prevailing conditions. Many of the drawings she brought with her, including her own sketches, were applicable to England and English means. These buildings could not simply be copied in South Africa. They required extensive simplification, almost without exception. The working drawings she produced for St Peter's cathedral in Pietermaritzburg, for example, demonstrate her ability to reconfigure existing plans in this way. Importantly, Sophy, like her husband, was minded to perceive the Church as a vehicle for social and cultural change. She recognized the urgency and importance of erecting correct places of worship if the Church of England was to 'ma[k]e itself felt' in that land of 'floating' congregations.[114]

208 Founder's Quad, Bishops College, Rondebosch, Cape Town (*c.*1852), by William White.

Notable churches that relied on Sophy's involvement besides St Paul's, Rondebosch (1848–72) include St Saviour's, Claremont (1849–80), St Mark's, George (1849–50), Holy Trinity, Caledon (1850–5), and Holy Trinity, Belvidere (1851–3) (figs 209–11). The churches at Rondebosch and Claremont were probably adapted from William Butterfield's design for Coalpit Heath, Gloucestershire (1844–5), while that at George was based on Henry Underwood's design for Littlemore.[115] Holy Trinity, Belvidere, on the other hand, has a confused pedigree.[116] There is a likeness to one of Underwood's schemes for burial-ground chapels, although the date of this (1849) appears too late for the Grays to have carried the plans to South Africa (perhaps they were sent later). There is, however, an extraordinary, near identical, likeness to Harvey Eginton's design for Holy Trinity chapel, Trimpley (1844). As Butterfield was an assistant in Eginton's office between 1838 and 1840, it is quite possible, even likely, that the design for this building passed from Eginton to the Grays, through Butterfield.[117]

We get a sense of how this cultural agenda for the Church in South Africa was envisioned by examining one of Sophy's watercolour sketches of St George's church, Knysna, built between 1849 and 1855 (figs 212 and 213). Here we see a scene that might easily be of a parish in some remote, rural part of England. There is very little depicted in either the landscape or its flora that necessarily suggests a foreign context. The only thing that potentially gives the game away is the small cottage with a verandah perched on the knoll in the middle distance. It is clearly not the location that Sophy wished to emphasise in this

Top 209 Sketch by Sophy Gray, *c.*1850, of St Saviour's church, Claremont, Cape Town (1849–80), only partially complete (William Cullen Library, University of the Witwatersrand, Johannesburg). The church was based on a design supplied by William Butterfield and adapted by Sophy Gray.

Bottom 210 Holy Trinity church, Caledon, South Africa (1850–5), by Sophy Gray.

211 Holy Trinity church, Belvidere, South Africa (1851–3), by Harvey Eginton and Sophy Gray.

212 Panoramic sketch of Knysna and surrounding district by Sophy Gray, showing St George's church (1849–55), built to her design, *c.*1855 (William Cullen Library, University of the Witwatersrand, Johannesburg).

213 St George's church, Knysna, South Africa (1849–55), by Sophy Gray.

214 Watercolour sketch by Sophy Gray of the church of St Mary the Virgin, Woodstock, near Cape Town (1859–64), built to her design (William Cullen Library, University of the Witwatersrand, Johannesburg).

sketch but the cultivated nature of the scenario – that is, the bucolic idyll of the small country church and parsonage. However, there were other images by Sophy in which she deliberately contrasted Christian (that is, Anglican) civilisation and the rugged, untamed wilderness of the Cape. One such is her depiction of St Mary the Virgin, Woodstock (fig. 214). In this scene the distinct yet familiar form of the church is set firmly against the craggy terrain beyond, itself a cipher, perhaps, for the apparently uncultivated nature of the African continent as a whole. It is scenes such as these that the Grays and their followers (Newman and the others) wished to create in South Africa. Of course, there were limits to what could be achieved in this respect, but not for lack of trying. The idea obviously held great appeal. Indeed, Armstrong would later lament the trials of living in an environment destitute of 'antiquity', insisting that, 'no one knows what it is like to live in a country where there is nothing old 'til they have tried it'.[118] It was for this very reason, as we saw in Chapter 1, that Broughton and Walsh were so keen to get churches built that were not only neat but also distinctive – what was described as the 'spiritual efficacy and impressiveness' of proper ecclesiastical architecture (see p. 46). Gray and his colleagues could not have agreed more.

Faith in Action: St Philip's Mission Church, Grahamstown

The activities of Gray and his wife and the other clergy were all part of what Wilberforce considered necessary for 'securing' the Cape. Their attitude towards reforming and enhancing the influence of the Church of England in South Africa was part of Britain's wider imperial 'mission' to promote progress and inculcate civilisation (that is, English civilisation) into the local population. Like the great stone Ebenezer (1 Samuel, vii: 12), the buildings these men (and women) erected were understood as markers of God's will on earth, signposts pointing the way from 'barbarity' and 'ignorance' to the promise of a tempered life in the Anglican way. This concerned settlers and indigenes alike. The secular dimensions of this endeavour to ensure 'loyalty' among the populace were everywhere apparent. One small but nevertheless telling example of this was the Rev. William Greenstock's desire to keep the day of Queen Victoria's accession free for preaching 'the benefits of the extension and establishment of English rule in South Africa' (fig. 215).[119] In this respect, the Anglican missionary project in South Africa, represented by the serious and comprehensive nature of its church-building activities, was inextricably entwined in the broader aims and objectives of British imperial and colonial politics.

As we saw in the Introduction, missionary activity of this kind was seen by imperial administrators as creating a kind of civilisational bridgehead into the 'wilderness' landscape of indigenous communities, through which more formal systems of governance could later infiltrate (see p. 7). As Bishop Selwyn of New Zealand had observed in 1847, 'the Missionary must always expect that colonization will follow in his train'.[120] But the consequences of this tactic were double-edged. For although the indigenous populace was afforded a degree of protection under British colonial rule, it was simultaneously drawn into a network of political and economic relationships over which it had little control and which fundamentally dissolved its ancient beliefs and customs. This strategy was common to the missionary policies of Nonconformist, Roman Catholic and Anglican alike, as they assaulted the spiritual and mystical values underpinning the 'heathen' way of life.[121] The role of architecture was to structure and give spatial order to this offensive.

At the Umlazi Mission, south of Durban, for instance, the superintendent (Rev. W. Baugh) noted how the sight of the mission buildings appeared 'as a breach in the heart of heathenism'. 'Our settlement on such a spot will have doubtless a direct civilizing effect,' he added: 'The sight of a well-ordered European household and the cultivated ground with its vegetable productions will do their silent work of conveying new ideas and suggesting thoughts to the natives' minds'.[122] Mission stations therefore sought to effect a transformation in the mentality of indigenous peoples by reconfiguring their social practices around dis-

215 Sketch by William Greenstock, *c.*1856, of his church at St Luke's mission station, diocese of Grahamstown, South Africa, showing an English flag flying from the corner of the building (Bodleian Library, Oxford).

ciplines of time, orderliness, piety and labour.[123] Such discipline forced colonial indigenes to negotiate space in a manner that was not only alien to their culture but also explicitly designed to 'rationalise' their worldview, thus bringing them into the fold of European civilisation and making them participants in the colonial order of things.

Indeed, the effect that ecclesiastical architecture had on the indigenous population was discussed among Anglican clergy. As churches were considered sacred places, when Bishop Cotterill of Grahamstown (Armstrong's replacement) stipulated that mission chapels should double up as schoolrooms, some clergymen protested. Greenstock, for instance, who presided over St Luke's Mission station at Umhala's Country (Chief Mhala's territory, along the Kei river), cautioned that 'de-sanctifying' chapels in this way would lead to a loss in the clergy's ability to win over local chiefs and to convert the wider indigenous population. Writing to the SPG in 1857 he recorded, with unease:

> I have just read with sorrow and alarm the opinion expressed by our new Bishop, in a letter written from Brighton, that *school chapels* only are needed at first in our Kafir Missions. How shall we be able to teach the natives that reverence for the House of God which should be instilled from the very beginning? . . . The Kafir Chiefs, though unconverted, have a strong sense of the holiness of Churches. *Umhala* expressed this to me on a late occasion. I shall grieve much if this salutary feeling were weakened in any way.[124]

Similarly, at the laying of the foundation stone of St Peter's cathedral in Pietermaritzburg in 1852 it was noted how important the erection of a large and imposing structure would be in such a place, 'remembering that it is the first church in the district, in the capital town of that district, and in the centre of a large heathen population'.[125] As Henry Master White had reminded Anglican clergy in the *South African Church Magazine*: the Anglican Church in Africa was in a state of militancy and therefore must remain 'aggressive upon the world'. It was reckoned that if the 'Church faithfully uses her own powers' (that is, architecture), then many conversions might be hoped for, both Nonconformist and indigenous.[126] Similar concerns over the sanctity of churches were also expressed in New Zealand.[127]

In times of political strife, too, Anglican clergy more often than not sided with the government. In the case of the so-called Eighth Frontier (Kaffir) War of 1850–3, Gray noted that, although the 'white man' had failed broadly in his duty to the Xhosa, it was necessary to stamp out 'unlawful' practices such as cattle rustling, and that the colonial authorities were right in taking decisive action against it. Similarly, although the Hottentot peoples had been displaced from their land and relocated to 'one of the finest parts of the country', they had no excuse whatever, claimed Gray, for entering the war on the side of the Xhosa; only 'sobriety and industry [will] enable them to take their place among the landed proprietors of the country'.[128] Merriman agreed, reminding those Xhosa chiefs who came seeking his counsel that they must first act within the law before they could expect any sympathy.

However, as Mary Goedhals has pointed out, despite their hard line, Merriman and his colleagues were no imperial automata. It would be wrong to suggest that the Anglican Church in South Africa was merely an extra-gubernatorial arm of the colonial executive, for it was not, nor did it wish to be. After all, the underlying spirit of Tractarianism was one of ecclesiastical independence from the affairs of State. Anglican clergy were certainly aware of their perceived responsibilities in shaping the territory of South Africa and its inhabitants in a way that benefited the interests of British colonial politics, but they were also men of wider perception and compassion. The likes of Gray and Merriman may have seen empire and Christianity as going hand in hand, but they were determined that the empire and its officers be seen to be Christian also.[129]

In fact, Anglican clergymen were far from blind to the problems caused by European colonisation. Bishop John Armstrong of Grahamstown was well aware of how mutual suspicion and prejudice between black and white had led to an artificial sense of social segregation in the Eastern Cape, especially with respect to Christian worship, observing that 'the Church has to beat down boldly these walls of partition'.[130] Bishop Selwyn too was alert to such problems. In the New Zealand Wars of 1860–3 he was caught between the opposing Māori and colonial government forces. Selwyn had always concerned himself with the welfare of the native peoples of New Zealand, and was morally outraged by what he saw as the illegal purchase of land by the government in Taranaki and the subsequent declaration of martial law by Governor Browne. To Selwyn, such acts were in flagrant breach of the Treaty of Waitangi (1840). He was heavily criticised by the settler community

216 Cartoon of Bishop Selwyn, caught between a Māori warrior and a government soldier, from *Taranaki Punch* (1860).

for taking this stance, even being described by some as a traitor (fig. 216).[131] How could an English bishop act against the interests of the crown, came the protest. But for Selwyn the situation was clear: the law must be obeyed by native and settler alike, both God's law (moral) and the law of the land (legal). In taking this principled line, however, Selwyn was later to alienate himself from the Māori too. He therefore ended up in a position of distrust on both sides in his efforts to broker what he considered to be a fair and just resolution, a situation over which he deeply despaired.[132]

The intersecting and widely conflicting concerns inherent in the extension of British power were brought home from time to time by clergymen working in the field. For instance, Newman, on a return visit to England in 1855, was quick to point out that not everything in South Africa was as straightforward as it seemed. In his sermon preached in March that year before the parishioners of Tormohun church, in the diocese of Exeter, Newman couched the problem in terms of exploitation versus obligation (personal gain versus national responsibility), identifying the predicament of relations between coloniser and colonised as a conflict between freedom in Christ and the rise of a new and equally pernicious form of European slavery. 'Our nation's flag streams proudly in almost every port, our nation's name is revered amongst almost every scattered people, . . . our countrymen have colonized in every region of the earth, [and] they have mingled with every race,' he reminded those gathered. 'We have grown richer with the produce of every land, but, alas! we have not made the dwellers in those lands richer in Christian blessings. . . . We use their bodies, we profit by their labour, but, in the name of Christ, I ask you, what have we been doing for their souls? What endeavours, as a great Christian people, have we made that they may become Christ's freedmen?'[133] Although Newman's reproach was by then a familiar one in the context of the Anglican mission abroad, the point was made: much work still needed to be done. Being a clergyman who believed so earnestly in the promise of ecclesiology, there is little doubt that Newman would have understood architecture as being among the chief weapons in his armoury for the battle that lay ahead.

There are any number of Anglican churches in Britain's former colonial empire that one could point to as capturing the intersecting concerns of politics, religion and architecture in this way. But one of the most interesting and representative is St Philip's Mission church, Fingo, Grahamstown, South Africa (1863–7) (figs 217 and 218). Erected at the height of Anglican missionary fervour in the 1860s, St Philip's is at first sight a small, nondescript church, the likes of which could be found throughout South Africa – indeed, the entire empire – during the nineteenth century. On closer inspection, however, it reveals itself to be anything but ordinary. Both William White and the Rev. N. J. Merriman were heavily involved: White as architect and Merriman as fixer. The style of architecture adopted was also quite sophisticated for its time and place. Although a somewhat modest affair, St Philip's is full of vigour, embodying a clear sense of that reforming zeal, antiquarian ethos and overt 'muscular' energy that was the hallmark of mid-century Anglican ecclesiology.

The history of the building begins with the appointment of the Rev. John Armstrong (1813–1856) as bishop of Grahamstown in 1853. Like Gray, Armstrong was keen to institute change. He was a man of more than moderate Tractarian persuasion and would prove a useful ally to Gray, in promoting the cause of architecture. While priest-vicar of Exeter Cathedral in the early 1840s, Armstrong had developed an interest in the use of architecture as a devotional aid. He wrote and preached on the topic, and, along with John Medley, was instrumental in founding the Exeter Diocesan Architectural Society (1841).[134] Moreover, as one of the prime movers behind the Church Penitentiary movement in Britain, he had already made contact with

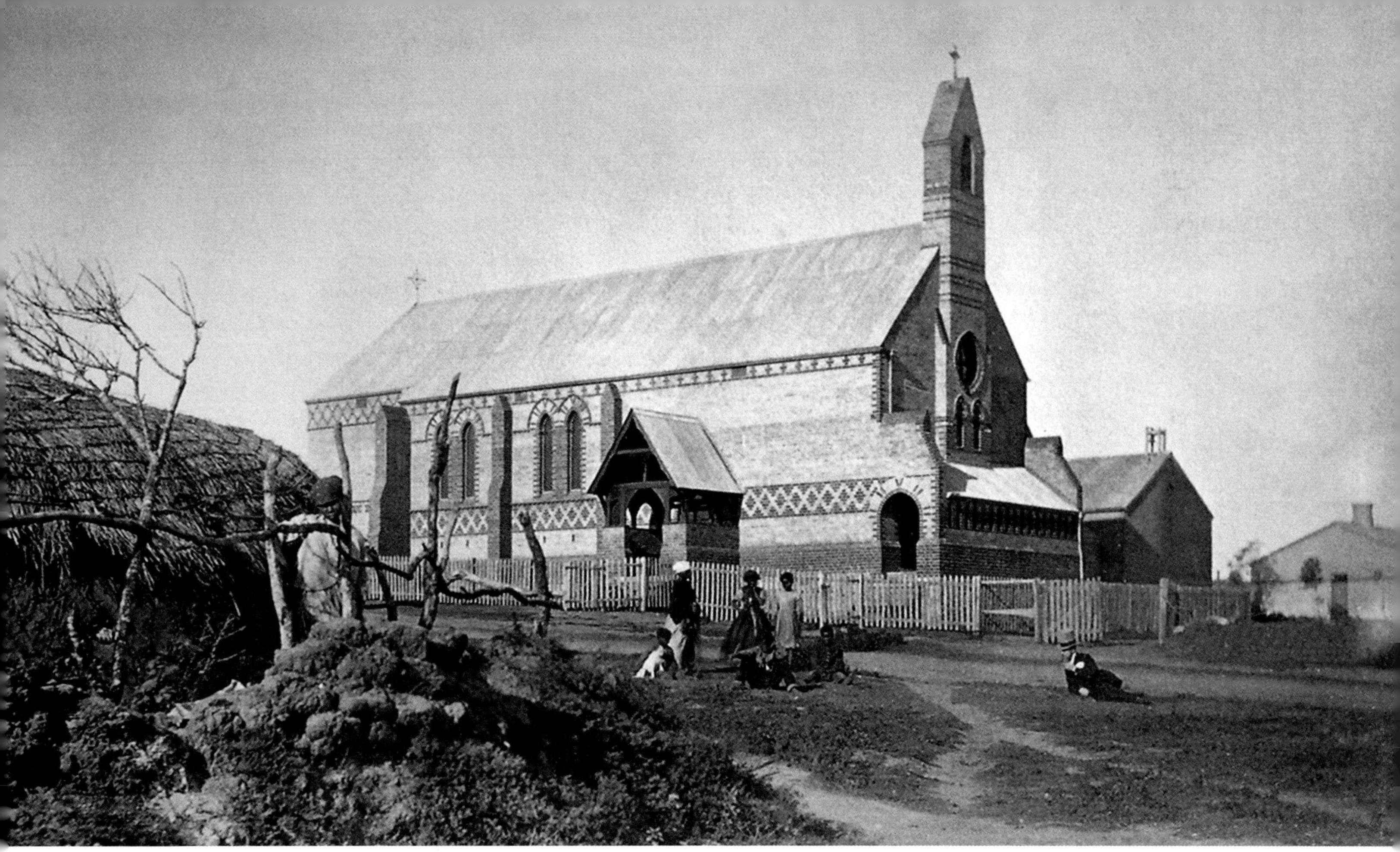

217 St Philip's mission church, Fingo, Grahamstown (1863–7), by William White.

218 Interior of St Philip's mission church, Fingo, Grahamstown (1863–7).

White before his departure for Africa.[135] It was during Armstrong's time as bishop that Merriman came across from Cape Town to take up the post of archdeacon of Grahamstown. Sharing Armstrong's keen enthusiasm for architecture, Merriman was instructed by the bishop to spearhead a building campaign for a new and more respectable parish church for the diocese.

It was at this point that William White first entered onto the scene at Grahamstown. The plans for Armstrong's new church – to be known as St Bartholomew's – were supplied by him (see Chapter 6). Although this church was for the English expatriate community of Grahamstown, Armstrong had not forgotten the local indigenous population.[136] After all, the express remit of the new colonial episcopates was to extend the gospel to 'the heathen'. This was, of course, the basis of Wilberforce's plea. To this end Armstrong established five mission stations in the Eastern Cape, one of which, St Philip's, was created for the largely refugee population – referred to as 'Fingoes' – that had been gathering on the outskirts of Grahamstown since the early nineteenth century.[137] St Philip's Mission was the result of a land grant from the colonial government in 1857.

This apparently innocuous beginning is important because it links St Philip's directly to the policies of the then British high commissioner to South Africa, Sir George Grey (1812–1898). Grey's vision was to assimilate, as he had attempted to do in New Zealand, the indigenous peoples of the Cape (especially the Xhosa), so that the province might be put on a more 'prosperous and tranquil' footing. It was apparent to Grey on his arrival in South Africa that maintaining 'frontier tracts' separating Europeans from indigenes would only exacerbate tensions and lead to further conflict.[138] Being a 'good Churchman', Grey's policies naturally included a scheme for Christianisation (here a euphemism for 'civilisation'). He was therefore willing to grant both land and money voted by the imperial parliament in London (some £45,000–£50,000) to those Church organisations willing to adopt 'industrial training' as a principal component of their missionary strategy. At first Anglican missionaries viewed Grey's proposal as an attempt to pollute their purely 'spiritual' endeavour, but soon came to the realisation that the incentives on offer were too good to refuse, especially if accepting them meant keeping pace with their Roman Catholic and Nonconformist rivals in the mission field.[139]

It was not until the early 1860s, however, that any decisive action was taken to erect a permanent structure at St Philip's Mission.[140] It was noted in the annual report of St Bartholomew's for 1862 that the native population 'who live amongst us' required further support, and that it had become 'necessary now to provide a separate Chapel for Divine Service'.[141] The following year plans arrived from England, along with pecuniary aid. Although the author of these plans was nowhere stated, it can reasonably be assumed they were by the hand of G. F. Bodley. In a note on new churches that appeared in the April 1860 number of *The Ecclesiologist*, it was reported that the society had received intelligence of a 'simple pointed design' for a church in Grahamstown by Bodley.[142] The plans certainly caught the journal's attention. What appealed was the design's simple yet bold character – perfect, it would seem, for a mission church. 'The internal arrangements are strictly correct. . . . The chancel proper stands below the tower, which is of massive and dignified proportions, and has a low square pyramidal capping. The aisles are very low, but the clerestory fully developed. The windows are plain, tall, chamfered lancets, but at the west end there are four arches rising from low cylindrical shafts. . . . Great character and a most excellent effect result from the good proportion of these simple details.'[143]

Whether the first design for St Philip's was by Bodley or not, the commission seems to have passed to White by 1862.[144] Having worked in the diocese of Exeter in the late 1840s and early 1850s, White had grown accustomed to designing small churches on limited budgets for what was effectively a missionary context.[145] This work also brought him within the ambit of the Incorporated Church Building Society, part of whose mandate it was to assist 'home missions' in places such as Cornwall and Devon. In fact, the character of White's corpus as a whole tended towards the unpretentious. Contemporary assessments of his work note how many of his buildings, although not without 'integrity and vigour', were 'simple, reserved, and eminently sincere'.[146] These were noble characteristics for any ecclesiastical building to have had at the time, especially one in the colonies. Some of White's designs for smaller churches in England have a great deal in common with the St Philip's commission. Christ Church, Smannell (Hampshire; 1856–7) (fig. 219), for example, exhibits the same continental influences and use of constructional polychromy. The general massing of Christ Church also tends to suggest a relationship with St Philip's that is more than coincidental.

219 Christ Church, Smannell, Hamphire (1856–7), by William White.

The apparent desire for dynamism in Anglican missionary architecture is also important in this context. As discussed in the preceding two chapters, it is true that much Anglican church architecture during this period was cast in a deliberately 'muscular' fashion – both at home and abroad.[147] White's friends Street and Bodley were deft exponents of this approach, as were other notable Victorian architects who contributed to the colonial scene, such as Butterfield and Burges. Although White does not seem to have been entirely comfortable working in this idiom, the idea of mass was nevertheless an important feature of his work. As Edward Kaufman has argued, such admiration for the 'power of mass' had thoroughly transformed thinking on ecclesiastical design in England by the 1850s, especially with respect to rural churches.[148]

It can be argued that such formal virility in ecclesiastical design had particular application in the harsh and unfamiliar environs of Britain's colonies. If the primitive allure of the early French Gothic had become a fitting antidote to the 'crying deficiencies of the age', as A. J. B. Beresford Hope insisted, then surely it was even more suited to the rugged and competitive domain that was the colonial mission field. After all, these were lands in which the dual iniquities of 'atheism and heathenism' held sway – Satan's own 'stronghold', as Bishop Gray had described them. As we have seen, this kind of thinking prevailed in the design of colonial cathedrals. But it was the metaphysics of Christian architecture that most forcefully pronounced its true 'missionary vocation'. In defending the use of continental forms in Anglican church architecture, Beresford Hope observed, with no small amount of moral probity: 'there now prevails a feeling in favour of the Early French, as pre-eminent for strength and dignity. . . . The grave, strong, Early French will be adduced as the preacher of righteousness, truth, and simplicity to a luxurious and crooked generation, and it will be urged that, in order to give cogency to the sermon, a somewhat dispendious use of material may in the end be true economy.'[149]

Much of the appeal associated with the muscular turn in ecclesiastical architecture sprang from notions concerning truth and sincerity. Concepts such as 'force' and 'power' that evolved out of these precepts were then taken to signify ideas of the Church militant. The notion that there was a relationship between mass, morality and 'militancy' in design had of course been championed by John Ruskin in the 1840s and 1850s, but it was a set of relations that had at least been prefigured (if not established) in the polemics of Pugin. As colonial dioceses were desperately poor compared to their English counterparts, concepts of truth and simplicity in architectural design were not optional. In most cases they were absolutely necessary. This was a rather happy coincidence, it turns out, for as we learnt in Chapter 1, strength, courage, self-denial and economy were qualities especially prized in colonial clergymen – qualities that found direct translation in missionary architecture. Indeed, the aesthetic stoicism and latent energy of a church like St Philip's would have appealed to a clergyman like Merriman, a man whose own reputation was built on demonstrable displays of resilience and frugality.[150] These associations were of course appreciated by White. Not only did he have a brother who was a colonial clergyman but he also knew that 'effect [in architecture] must be given by masses and breadth of surface and not by height of detail or manipulation of parts'.[151]

The foundation stone of St Philip's was laid on St Peter's Day 1863 and, according to the incumbent, the Rev. William H. Turpin, the church was completed in stages and consecrated in 1867.[152] Importantly, the construction of the church involved the mission's indigenous converts.[153] This was not a particularly common practice in the Anglican Church in South Africa at the time, and was restricted almost entirely to mission stations. To be sure, the necessity for such a practice was dictated in large part by limited resources, but it was also considered a responsible way of 'improving' the converts' lot in life, and preparing them for integration into modern society – Sir George Grey's policy of 'assimilation' at work.[154] Bishop Robert Gray was impressed with what he had seen at mission stations run by the Moravians, especially their belief that the dignity of labour was paramount, and the way in which all converts were taught a practical trade, including 'mechanical arts' such as bricklaying and carpentry.[155] This was a missionary ethos that, as we have seen, was already in operation in New Zealand, and one that would later animate both the Melanesian and UMCA missions in their desire to create self-sufficient religious communities among indigenous peoples.

It was an approach that also sat well with Armstrong and his views on church building. Ever since his days as incumbent at Tidenham, Gloucestershire, Armstrong had considered it a moral and spiritual duty of Christians to participate in the building of their own churches. In taking this view he was appealing to the 'pattern', as he called it, laid down by kings David and Solomon in the building of the first temple in Jerusalem, and insisted that parishioners ought to 'aspire to such noble and selfless acts', particularly in 'an Age which . . . seems especially called to be a Church-building [one]'.[156] The implication here was that churches should not be mere receptacles, erected to meet the need for larger accommodation, but should be understood as aids in the service of devotion, reflected in both their construction and use.[157] In this sense, the converts' participation in the building process at St Philip's would have been interpreted as fulfilling a dual function: their salvation and the means by which to attain it.

The employment of unqualified labour, however, did affect the quality of workmanship. For example, if one looks at the soffit of the arcade arch illustrated here, then a degree of inexperience is apparent (fig. 220). But blemishes of this kind were to be expected in a building that was erected piecemeal and in less than ideal circumstances. In fact, it might be argued that the problems experienced in the building of St Philip's were what ultimately secured its success. By being actively involved in the construction process, the converts were given a sense of belonging and ownership over the building. Again, this was part of the awareness of Anglican clergymen concerning the difference handsomely built churches could make in the mission field. As St Philip's neared completion one native parishioner noted that: 'in all the years that other Missionaries have been working amongst the Kafirs, there was not one Church like the English people's Churches . . . , but now . . . the Church of England was making a foundation for them, and . . . She taught . . . that God ought to be served in a good Church by them as well as by the English people.'[158] Thus, when considering the architectural quali-

220 Arcade arch soffit, St Philip's mission church, Fingo, Grahamstown (1863–7). The lack of skill of the builders is evident in the wavering lines of the moulding in the brickwork.

ties of a church like St Philip's, it is important to remember that part of the Anglican missionary strategy was to use architecture and its powers of persuasion in a very deliberate way.

A photograph taken only a few years after St Philip's was completed, illustrates clearly the visual impact the building had (and still has) in its original context (see fig. 217). Surrounded by indigenous forms of architecture, the church was understood as striking a contrast between the 'strongholds' of Satan and the hope of a New Jerusalem. The way the converts pose ingenuously beside the church, with the vestiges of their former life erased by the European-style clothing they wear, reflects the Church of England's broader aspiration to 'clothe' and 'domesticate' the colonial landscape. Again, this notion carried within it a distinct High Church agenda that appreciated the seriousness and solemnity of the Anglican missionary endeavour and the special role that 'externals' such as architecture were seen to play. As Turpin wrote shortly after the church's consecration in 1867: 'The time the Church was opened was about 6 years from when the first service was held in the open air [where] the missionary stood alone with the canopy of heaven as his church and school and wild heathens half naked, as his listeners, . . . now behold the contrast.'[159] It is in this contrast that resides not only the history of St Philip's but also that of much of the early Anglican Church in South Africa.

In the end, St Philip's can (indeed should) be interpreted as a clear and dignified statement of that 'missionary vocation' so prized by mid-century Anglicans like Beresford Hope and the Ecclesiologists. Rising up – almost as though it were a natural outgrowth of the reddish-hued earth upon which it sits – its dynamic, crystalline forms emerge like some sublime Ruskinian homily to the perceived righteousness of God's work among the 'heathen'. Its power seems to speak to an idea of redemption and wholesome rehabilitation in what was considered to be a harsh and God-forsaken land – again, an idea that very much reflected the vision and expectations of the colonial Church of England as a whole during the 1850s and 1860s.

The challenges presented by the pursuit of sacramentalism in the colonies gave new meaning and direction to symbolism in Anglican church architecture. What might otherwise have been considered less than ideal imperatives, such as the use of timber, suddenly became an opportunity to recast the range and intent of church design. This initiative covered all aspects of ecclesiology from overall form and materiality to ornamentation and arrangement. Recognising such challenges, ecclesiologists turned them into an opportunity to extend the ornamental repertoire of church architecture to include the representation of native flora and fauna. This was understood as a logical step in the development of true Christian architecture, lending a particular character and 'situatedness' to ecclesiology in the colonies. Such concerns may not have been on the minds of all Anglican clergyman abroad, but to those with refined architectural sensibilities, these were welcome and necessary advancements.

Similarly, considerations of identity – both national and confessional – were evidently a factor in the way the Church of England established and promoted itself overseas. Maintaining a strong and unambiguous presence in foreign lands was understood to be one of the principal means by which the Church could exert influence and instigate change. Equivocality and indecisiveness were potentially ruinous. The perceived role of the English Church in this regard – its desire, as Henry Master White had said, to remain 'aggressive upon the world' – gave it a natural, if somewhat self-imposed, duty to represent and protect the interests of the British state. In the context of nineteenth-century imperialism, Christianising and civilising people (and territories) was one thing, doing this in a manner that served English, and in particular Anglican, culture was another. As the case of South Africa demonstrates, to 'civilise' the landscape and its people was to erect churches. Such buildings became markers of English identity and culture, persuading (it was hoped) settlers and indigenes alike of the benefits of the orthodox, tempered and patriarchal brand of English civilisation represented by the Anglican faith.

This is not to say, however, that the Church of England was an unofficial arm of government. On the contrary, as many of the Tractarian-inspired bishops in this study indicate, there was a concerted effort to institute the Church on an independent footing. This occasionally brought Anglican clergymen into conflict with colonial officialdom. Nevertheless, the connections between the Church and the governing elite in British colonial society ran deep. Indeed, as we shall see in the next chapter, operating in the colonial mission field was a highly competitive and thus delicately balanced affair. Things were not as easy as many had initially thought, and any advantage that might be garnered was eagerly sought.[160] Once again, architecture would be crucial in maintaining this balance.

5

Conflict and Confrontation

ARCHITECTURE IN AN AGE OF SECTARIANISM

Here therefore I am; set in the front of the battle against the force of the Roman Catholics.

Rev. W. G. Broughton, Bishop of Australia (1836)

Call it by what name you please, the meeting at Sydney was, in fact and truth,
the first Council of the great Ecclesiastical province of Australasia.
The Bishops have met – have deliberated – have pronounced;
they parted . . . with extended plans and larger prospects of usefulness.
The Colonial Church is stirring with organic life: the thing is done.

The Guardian (May 1851)

Thus far we have considered the origins of colonial ecclesiology, its adaptation to foreign contexts (culturally and architecturally), its sense of identity and purpose, and some of its most elaborate manifestations in the form of the cathedral idea. All of this has provided us with an insight into the networks, practices and motivations that lay behind the global Church of England and its physical expression. But we are yet to discuss the sectarian tension that confronted and, in some cases, nearly crippled the Church in these contexts. This was a consequence of the liberal and reforming tendencies that swept through British society both at home and abroad during the early part of the nineteenth century, leading to the ambiguous legal status of the Church beyond the British Isles.[1]

As mentioned in earlier chapters, the Church of England was never properly established in the colonies during the nineteenth century. Where it was nominally 'established' for a time, as it was in British North America and New South Wales, it did not carry the same legal or constitutional status as the Church at home. By the 1840s the Church of England abroad was but one denomination among many – a 'mere sect', as Bishop Perry of Melbourne bemoaned – despite the soft advantage it maintained owing to its influence within the élite of British colonial society. The ambiguity surrounding the legal status of the Church in the colonies eventually forced synodical action and brought about effective regional independence, beginning with Australasia in the early 1850s, and sweeping through the major ecclesiastical polities of empire during the 1860s and 1870s.

This levelling of the religious playing field, so to speak, caused a great deal of conflict both within and outside the Anglican confession in the British empire. Unlike their brethren at home, Anglican bishops and clergymen in the colonies were faced with serious competition from Roman Catholics, Presbyterians and Nonconformists for the meagre resources on offer in the form of state aid, local voluntary support and largess from Britain. Some of the disputes born of this rivalry, as we shall see, were bitter and protracted, causing no end of personal and political nuisance. This tension, and the sectarian conflict that came in its wake, was a distinctive feature of the social and religious scene in Britain's colonial empire during the period.

Perversely, perhaps, this tension and conflict stimulated considerable building activity. Architecture quickly became one of the key battle grounds upon which the struggle for religious influence and ascendancy was fought. Much of the impetus for the church-building activity we have discussed so far was in fact generated by this rivalry. As the various denominations bedded down in the towns and cities, and in the wider mission field generally, throughout the British empire during the 1840s and 1850s, their ecclesiastical architecture began to take distinct forms according to the particular social, theological and environmental demands and constraints exerted upon it. In this respect, as we have seen already, Anglican architecture evolved in response to both internal and external pressures, which reflected not only shifting tastes in ecclesiastical design but also the views of individual bishops and clergymen as they sought to reform the Church and its image from within. Denominational sectarianism was one of these pressures.

Competition from Without: The Challenge of Roman Catholicism and Dissent

Denominational sectarianism was felt more keenly in some places than in others. In Ceylon (Sri Lanka), for example, Bishop Chapman was entering upon a field that had been occupied by Jesuit missionaries since the sixteenth century (fig. 221). For Chapman, architecture was crucial in his struggle against what he saw as the lingering effects of the Roman Church. But if this were not enough to contend with, added to his woes was the continued influence of the ancient religions of Buddhism and Hinduism, particularly Buddhism. The architectural pretension and magnificence of Jesuit mission churches, as well as Buddhist and Hindu temples, meant that it was important for Chapman to 'bring all spiritual appliances and aids to bear' in his missionary campaign.[2] The nominally Christian quarter of the Singhalese community may have been baptised under a 'faulty system', Chapman believed, but the Church of England was going to have to work very hard indeed if it was to convince the native population of the value of Anglicanism. Writing to the Society for the Propagation of the Gospel in 1850, Chapman communicated his anxieties: 'The Romish Church makes some pretensions to architectural style,' he observed with trepidation, '[while] our plain stone building close by its side, with its large square windows and doors, can only be mistaken for a bare conventicle or tasteless School. Anywhere else this might not matter *much*, but in this situation the *contrast* is far from pleasing.'[3] A church was required that would hold forth 'that light of God's truth . . . not faithfully alone, but visibly and prominently'.[4] It was with this concern in mind that Chapman had originally solicited plans for a cathedral of proper 'ecclesiastical character' from the Ecclesiological Society in 1847 – a building that was calculated to impress with its style, materials and 'associated influences'.[5]

Anti-Catholic sentiment was rife in British North America, too. Animosity towards Roman Catholics in Atlantic Canada had its roots in the initially small, but staunchly Protestant, communities of loyalist colonials who took refuge there following the American Revolution. These refugees, who were not all Anglicans, tended to associate Roman Catholicism with tyranny and political intrigue. Compounding these suspicions, of course, was the presence of the neighbouring francophone Acadian population of Quebec (Lower Canada), which was predominantly Roman Catholic. This dynamic gave the religious scene in Atlantic Canada distinct political overtones.[6] Thus, despite their clear Tractarian leanings, all the Canadian bishops were particularly alert to what they perceived as Roman incursions, especially as many among their adherents were imbued with innate prejudice in this regard. It was this concern that had spurred Strachan to redouble his efforts to complete the cathedral at Toronto, and this that had caused so much consternation and sectarian wrangling in St John's in the aftermath of the great fire of 1846.

Indeed, the reconstruction of St John's cathedral, Newfoundland, after 1846 is somewhat indicative of the tension that existed between Anglicans and Roman Catholics over

221 James Chapman (1799–1879), bishop of Ceylon (Sri Lanka).

access to resources, the role of resources in characterising the political landscape vis-à-vis religion and architecture, and the advantage they gave one denomination over the other. Generally speaking, this 'race' for resources made for a more extreme and vexed religious scene in the colonies than in Britain. For example, only weeks after the flames had receded in St John's, leaving much of the city in ruins, a petition was raised in London for what became known as the 'Queen's Letter' fund for the relief of victims. Although nominally intended as a general relief fund, the petition explicitly requested that monies be raised for the rebuilding of the 'Episcopal Church'.[7] The subsequent call for donations received some £29,000, all of which was forwarded by the Colonial Office to the government authorities in Newfoundland for distribution. However, this fund soon became a flashpoint of contention. The Roman Catholic bishop of Newfoundland, Fr M. A. Fleming (*c.*1792–1850), immediately contested the right of the Anglican community to its share of the money. In a letter to the Secretary of State for the Colonies, Earl Grey, Fleming complained that the Anglican cathedral was 'not intrinsically worth £200' before its destruction. This being the case, he insisted, why should Bishop Feild receive £15,000 for its rebuilding?[8]

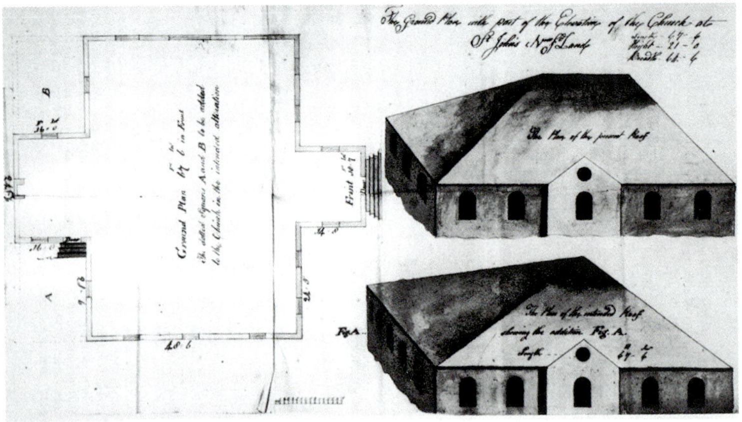

222 Plans, with dimensions, of the parish church of St John the Baptist, St John's, Newfoundland (designer unknown), before the great fire of 1846.

Fleming had a point. It is true that the pre-fire church was little more than a crude wooden shack, looking more like a badly designed house than anything approaching a church (fig. 222). How much it was worth is difficult, if not impossible, to say. Moreover, the population of St John's comprised a sizable number of Irish Catholics: why should Anglicans be disproportionately advantaged, wondered Fleming. However, despite the supposed value of the old church, what was certain was that plans were already well under way to replace it with a more comely structure before disaster struck. In response to accusations of misappropriation, Feild reassured Grey that not only had his fund-raising campaign for a new church been prematurely curtailed and therefore dashed because of the fire, but also such a claim on the funds was firmly 'in accordance with the expectations of the inhabitants generally of St. John's'.[9] 'To prove that there has been no misappropriation I need only refer to the printed Correspondence (printed by order of the House of Lords), and to the Petition of the London Committee appended thereto,' he later added. Wishing to retain the moral high ground, Feild observed of Fleming's remark about the value of the old church merely that it was 'far from being . . . correct', and concluded by saying that he would 'abstain from all imputations of unkind motives, or recriminating allusions'.[10]

It seems that the dispute arose over a misunderstanding as to how the monies raised by the Queen's Letter fund were to be distributed. Feild maintained that, according to the original petition, three-quarters of the fund was to be dedicated to the rebuilding of the Anglican cathedral, whereas Fleming believed that the money was intended as general relief.[11] In the event, Feild did receive the lion's share of the kitty.[12] Nevertheless, the sectarian tensions aroused in Newfoundland by the issue of the relief fund highlight the competitive, fundamentally insecure and potentially acrimonious environment in which the colonial churches operated, as each worked to advance its cause over rivals. As far as the Queen's Letter fund was concerned, these tensions resulted in one of the most original and correct works of Anglican ecclesiastical architecture to be found anywhere in Britain's empire at the time. Whether, without the grant, Feild could have raised the £15,000 necessary to complete the first phase of the project in the given time seems doubtful. This being so, it is plain that his response to Fleming's charge entailed no small amount of special pleading.

Perhaps the most anxious and vociferous of Anglican bishops in Britain's colonies during this period was the Rev. William Grant Broughton (1788–1853), bishop of Sydney and later metropolitan of Australia (fig. 223). As mentioned in earlier chapters, Broughton was predominantly a cleric of the 'high and dry' school, having been educated at Pembroke College, Cambridge, in the second decade of the nineteenth century (BA 1818, MA 1823). However, despite his deep attachment to the Hanoverian Church–State settlement, he came under the spell of the Oxford Movement during a return visit to England in 1834–5. The Tractarians' concern for reverence and spirituality certainly appealed to Broughton, but it was their stance on apostolicity and Church autonomy that had the greatest impact on his thinking and which he found most useful in his own predicament in Australia.

From his earliest days in Australia, Broughton had expressed concern for the colony's social and religious conformation. He abhorred not only the debased state of civil society in Sydney (a town which had begun life as a penal settlement) but also, and more importantly, its 'godless' character.[13] In this respect, Broughton certainly had his work cut out. Over the seventeen years of his episcopacy (and the preceding seven of his archdeaconry) he would combat not only irreligion, immorality and liberalism, but also dissension, the effects of papal aggression, and Low Church tendencies among his own adherents.[14] Australia in the 1830s and 1840s was certainly no place for a supine or fainthearted cleric.

223 W. Nicholas, portrait of William Grant Broughton (1788–1853), bishop of Sydney and later Metropolitan of Australia, 1843 (State Library of New South Wales, Sydney).

We know that Broughton, like Wilberforce, connected Britain's national prosperity with its obligation to extend 'true' religion throughout the empire.[15] But this was easier said than done. As mentioned, the main factor that Broughton had to contend with – and the one of which his 'mind was *full*' – was the sustained competition for resources and 'souls' he encountered from other Christian denominations.[16] Principal among these was the Church of Rome. To the staunchly loyal and Protestant sensibilities of a man like Broughton, Rome was the foremost enemy of true religion. Like the 'sons of Loyola' that he and his colleagues believed them to be, Roman Catholic priests, with their 'stealthy' and 'silent working means', were striving to 'roll their mighty machine over the length and breadth of the land' in a way that was scarcely conceivable to churchmen in England.[17] In 1843 Pope Gregory XVI erected Australasia into a Catholic archdiocese and elevated Dr J. B. Polding (1794–1877), then merely a titular bishop, to the official title of Archbishop of Sydney. These acts both alarmed and enraged Broughton, who viewed them as not only an arrogant and dangerous usurpation of the rights of the English Church in 'Her Majesty's realm' but also a demonstration of flagrant disregard for Episcopal authority 'in provinces where . . . [bishops] of the Church of England have already been instituted'.[18] Perceiving these measures as essentially 'schismatic', Broughton believed that the concurrent erection of a Catholic see under such circumstances, and any act of solemnisation therein, was 'utterly null and void'.[19] However, he was powerless to prevent its recognition by the colonial government. To rub salt into the wound, Polding was for a time given precedence over Broughton in the social hierarchy of New South Wales, an official ranking that was sanctioned by the Secretary of State for the Colonies, Lord Grey.

These events tested Broughton's patience in the extreme. Writing to Edward Coleridge in a tone of near desperation, he protested that the 'schemes' of Polding were 'bold, artful, and diversified beyond description or calculation'.[20] To Broughton, papal aggression of this kind in the colonies was not only without precedent but also portentous.[21] It was the first glimpse of 'that extended contest which all the signs of the times foreshow is about to arise in this Colony, and in this hemisphere, between our Church and that of Rome'.[22] Indeed, if left unchecked in New South Wales, it might provide succour to those with even grander designs. In a letter to the Archbishop of Canterbury in 1851, Broughton recalled with some satisfaction the warning he had issued eight years previously: 'every encroachment upon the spiritual rights and character of the Church of England which shall have been connived at, and so encouraged, if not legalized, within the Colonies, will sooner or later be transplanted from there to England itself'.[23] And so it was. In 1850 the Roman Catholic hierarchy was re-established in England and Wales after an absence of some three hundred years, and Cardinal Nicholas Wiseman (1802–1865) was elevated as Archbishop of Westminster.

Today the language employed by Broughton may be considered somewhat hyperbolic, even paranoid, but in the context of Catholic Emancipation, 'papal aggression' and the pluralist state of religion in many of Britain's colonies during the early to late nineteenth century, Broughton's anxieties were neither extreme nor abnormal. Similar protests at the time were to be heard not only in Britain but across the entire British colonial world – concern over Roman Catholic education in Ireland through an increase in the Maynooth Grant (1845) being one such controversy (see p. 351).[24] Both Nixon in Tasmania and Short in South Australia supported Broughton in his objections. They were fighting their own battles against what they perceived to be the 'illegal' usurpation of ecclesiastical authority in British territory by 'that diseased limb' of the holy Catholic Church.[25]

But despite the morally (and apparently legally) superior position many colonial Anglican bishops believed themselves to be in, thanks to Royal Supremacy, anxieties of this nature were felt more keenly abroad than at home.[26] The perception that colonial bishops and clergymen were struggling far from home with few resources and less honour, often against the opportunist and indifferent attitudes of British colonial officials, only worked to heighten feelings of isolation and betrayal.[27] As the realisation dawned that the Church abroad would never be 'established' in the same way as in England, ideals of Church autonomy and renewed spirituality began to take hold. Perversely, perhaps, this condition acted as a spur to action in a way that almost certainly would not have happened had the Church assumed all the same privileges it enjoyed at home.[28] For example, Broughton's growing status as the chief authority of an essentially independent Church gave him increasing liberty and power to act as he saw fit. Although he would never see full autonomy from either Whitehall or Canterbury in his own lifetime, he had embraced the new paradigm of imperial Anglicanism by 1850. Feeling 'bound hand and foot' by the doctrine of Royal Supremacy, he called a *de facto* Australasian synod (referred to as the 'Bishops' Conference') that year, following this up in 1853 with a trip to England in an attempt to place it on a proper legal footing.[29] Broughton's steady acknowledgement of the colonial condition during his time as bishop of Sydney had profound consequences for the way he and his episcopal brethren went about shaping the Church of England in Australia, indeed the world.[30]

Again, architecture was among the chief weapons in Broughton's armoury. If battle (or 'warfare', as he called it) was to be joined with determined opponents, then the most conspicuous and effective manner in which to pronounce the intentions of the English Church was through numerous, well-appointed and strategically placed churches. We have seen something of Broughton's strategy in this respect already (see pp. 31–3, 45–6), but his motivations were, on occasion, quite specific. For example, his anxieties over so-called 'papal aggression' were an important factor. In several of his many letters to the SPG in London we find Broughton complaining of the extensive resources at

224 Watercolour sketch by John Rae of Sydney, *c.*1842, showing St Mary's chapel (later cathedral), designed by Fr John Joseph Therry (State Library of New South Wales, Sydney). The temporary bell tower, designed by A. W. N. Pugin, can be seen at far left.

the disposal of the Roman Church.[31] These resources allowed Roman Catholics, he believed, to gain an advantage over the Church of England by making their presence felt through conspicuous building campaigns.

Lying close to the heart of this concern was Governor Bourke's Church Act of 1836, which pluralised the colony of New South Wales and made government subsidies available to all Christian denominations according to the distribution of their adherents. If Broughton had not already seen the writing on the wall with the repeal of the Church and Schools Corporation in 1833, then Bourke's act ended any lingering illusion he may have had respecting ecclesiastical establishment in Australia (see Chapter 1, p. 31).[32] The most immediate consequence of the Church Act was to put Anglicans in direct competition for grants with Roman Catholics, Methodists, Presbyterians and others. Aid came in the form of a pound-for-pound payment of up to £1,000, matched to the churches' own fundraising, and could be used for a wide variety of Church-related activities, including the erection of buildings. Broughton, of course, protested, as did Nixon in Tasmania. Despite this apparent affront to the assumed privileges of the English Church, it was one of the chief beneficiaries of the scheme. The scramble for funds during the late 1830s and early 1840s accompanied substantial growth in Christian culture in Australia.[33]

As early as 1836 Broughton informed Coleridge that his 'anxious desire' was to erect two additional churches for the Anglican community in Sydney. Rather ambitiously, these buildings – St Andrew's cathedral and Christ Church, St Laurence – were to make room for an extra 7,000 people (or 'Protestants', as he described them). His motives were clear. Although he claimed that providing a greater number of 'free sittings' was his prime objective, Broughton stressed that 'these Churches ought to have some such degree of architectural pretension [that is, neat Gothic Revival architecture] as may make them capable in some sort of bearing a comparison with the structure which the Roman Cath's are now completing'.[34] The 'structure' to which Broughton referred was St Mary's chapel (later cathedral), designed by Fr John Joseph Therry, rising to the east just a stone's throw from old St James's (fig. 224).

225 St Patrick's Roman Catholic church, Sydney (1842–4), by J. F. Hilly.

But this was not Broughton's only concern. A year earlier he notified Coleridge that 'every time I go to the Church [St Philip's, York Street] I observe the walls of a vast edifice to be called the Church of "St. Patrick" rising higher and higher [fig. 225]: and I ask myself where is the man to be found, who, in addition to contending with many other obstacles and discouragements . . . [can] keep together a congregation in opposition to the seductive earnestness and . . . sophistries which are at no very distant date to be addressed to them from the gorgeous altars of which I can already trace the foundations.'[35] Another notable Roman Catholic church rising in the city that would have caught Broughton's attention was St Benedict's, Broadway, produced from designs by none other than A. W. N. Pugin, the greatest Roman Catholic architect of them all. A very handsome and imposing edifice, it was completed in 1856, lending a degree of ecclesiological sophistication to Sydney's skyline (fig. 226). Pugin was also engaged to prepare designs for the projected monastery at St Mary's. However, only the bell tower was ever completed.[36]

To combat this 'great assault', warned Broughton, 'I must appeal to our Societies [SPG and SPCK] for means to make one decided effort towards completing our unfinished Churches; and the drain upon our resources to attain that and (a necessary and indispensable one) will endure for two or three years.'[37] There was good reason for Anglican bishops in Australia to fear the architectural capacity of the Roman Catholic Church, for, in the early days at least, Roman Catholicism was the only denomination that could compete with Anglicanism architecturally.

While Broughton was fussing over the appearance of a new, more pretentious brand of 'structure' in Sydney, Bishop Nixon in Tasmania had also been dealing with an artistic assault from Pugin. As Brian Andrews has shown, Pugin's reach extended down to Tasmania under the patronage of the first Roman Catholic bishop of that colony, Fr R. W. Willson (1794–1866). A friend of Pugin, Willson commissioned the architect to design not only churches (fig. 227) but all manner of ecclesiastical accoutrements, including church plate, altar crosses, candlesticks, vestments and even headstones.[38] The array of items produced by Pugin for Tasmania is truly extraordinary, and it put the Roman Catholic Church for a time at the vanguard of advanced ecclesiastical design in the antipodes. Roman Catholic churches were beginning to be erected in most towns and cities throughout Australia by the mid-nineteenth century; some of the more notable examples include St Patrick's cathedral, Ballarat (1857–63), Our Lady of Mount Carmel, Sunbury (1864), and the Pugin-designed churches of St Francis Xavier's (originally St Scholastica's), Berrima (1849–51), and St Stephen's, Brisbane (1849–50).

Broughton's answer to these challenges was to expand, and expand vigorously. He was not afraid to employ architecture to maximum advantage, having spent his entire SPG grant for 1837 on building churches.[39] As discussed in Chapter 2, it was with the power of architecture in mind that Broughton embarked on his greatest work, St Andrew's cathedral – that 'fortress', as he imagined it, of the reformed English Church in Australia (fig. 228).[40] Like a 'city set on a hill,' he declared only a few months after the laying of the foundation stone, '[it] shall not easily be hid. . . . It is easy to foresee both that without such a stronghold of the faith we cannot keep our position; and if it *be* finished . . . the influence which may thus be exercised upon the religious condition of this profane town must be immense.'[41]

Roman Catholics were only part (albeit the largest part) of the predicament facing Broughton. Dissent was another.

226 St Benedict's Roman Catholic church, Broadway, Sydney (1845–56), to plans by A. W. N. Pugin.

227 St Paul's Roman Catholic church, Oatlands, Tasmania (1850–1), by A. W. N. Pugin.

228 St Andrew's cathedral, Sydney (1837–74), by Edmund Blacket.

Although not as vigorous as the Roman Church, Nonconformist churches were active in New South Wales, as elsewhere.[42] Presbyterians, too, were on the scene. Indeed, at times Broughton felt himself to be the object of a pincer movement between Rome and Wesley. 'The Romanists on the one side and the Dissenters on the other allow me no rest,' he complained wearily in 1839.[43] His concerns in this respect were the opposite of those he feared from the Vatican. Writing to Edward Coleridge in 1838, Broughton couched his disquiet in political terms. The ultimate question at hand, he stressed in rather apocalyptic terms, 'was a very great one: no less than whether pure Christianity shall flourish or not over a sixth part of the habitable world; and in conjunction with true religion, civil liberty also will rise or fall'. Harbouring similar fears to Strachan in Toronto, Broughton believed that, rather than the 'spiritual and political despotism' that would follow in the train of Rome, it would be 'republicanism . . . triumphant in the same proportion' if Presbyterians and dissenters had their way.[44] Like the 'Romanists', came the warning, they (dissenters) 'eye the unguarded suburbs of our strong city with wistful cupidity'.

This concern was real in the sense that latitudinarianism was known to exist in parts of Australia. It was certainly a problem in South Australia, as Bishop Short discovered to his consternation in 1848. Again, although not as numerous or as well supported as Roman Catholic priests, Nonconformist preachers were to be feared, especially for their ability to tug at the loose and weakened ties of the nominal Anglican community in Australia, resulting in that sort of 'common Christianity' so abhorred by orthodox churchmen. The Rev. George King, then an SPG missionary in Western Australia, explained the problem in the following way:

> The Romish priests are travelling to and fro in the land, and evince much of the wisdom of the serpent in their intercourse with the people. . . . But from this quarter we have no apprehensions. The gulph which separates our Church from [theirs] . . . is easily recognized by the simplest of our people. It is the Dissenter chiefly whose plausible representations of our agreement on what is called the essentials of faith, are calculated to unsettle the minds of our people, whose erroneous teaching is to be guarded against. The Wesleyan preacher made a proposition to the patron of one of our Murray [river] Churches, couched in humble terms, and as it appeared to many, originating in pious motives – to assist the missionary's labours by an occasional visit to our Churches for the purpose of prayer and preaching. Mr. P – fearing that a refusal from him might perchance give offence, referred the matter to me: and I replied decisively; that I could not permit any individual to minister in Churches committed to my care, who had not received license from the Bishop to preach.[45]

Thus, it was precisely because he saw the vast expanses of the Australian continent as so many fronts on a battlefield, that Broughton wished to ensconce the 'proper systems' of Anglican polity – those orders of bishop, priest and deacon – throughout the land, and the parish church as its most visible and conspicuous emblem.

The situation was little better in New Zealand. There Nonconformism was particularly energetic. In reading the letters and diaries of Selwyn and his colleagues, it is clear that they were acutely sensitive to what they perceived to be the intrusion of Wesleyan missionaries on their patch.[46] Selwyn was clear in his belief that Wesleyans were 'schismatics' and could therefore expect no systematic cooperation from the Church of England.[47] The disdain of High Anglicans for Low Church sentiment (particularly Methodism) was sometimes articulated with reference to architecture. For example, one can find numerous comments on Wesleyan church buildings in the journals of the Rev. William Cotton. For instance, in describing the Wesleyan Institution at Auckland and a sketch Selwyn had made of it, Cotton recorded that:

> The Bishop was very funny about [it]. . . . He is rather sore at the Governor having given them 400 acres of land, while for us he has done nothing. . . . The Institution is near the Cemetery at Auckland. It presents a gable to the sea. In the front view the Bp. confesses to have drawn it too high and goodlooking, with a window in the most approved Ch warden gothic with wooden mullions. It looks like a chapel. But take a back view and there is a great kitchen chimney, with a queer shaped little window curiously fitted under the roof. The 'Transepts' are dormitories.[48]

The condescension did not stop there. While on visitation with the bishop in 1847, Cotton observed with alarm that 'as usual the Wesleyans have got up a chapel before ours is begun. They have two Wesleyans here and do their work by fraternizing with the other denominations, and use their chapels in common.' This was the same problem that Broughton and Short had experienced in Australia. But Cotton's most sardonic comments were reserved for Methodist architecture: 'On one side they [the Wesleyan chapels] have . . . architectural windows, on the other ordinary sashes. Dr. Arnold in his letters seems to have been wonderfully drawn to NZealand. . . . [the Wesleyans] anticipate his plan for Ch. reform, as far as relates to buildings being carried out here.'[49] Clearly, to the high-minded and sophisticated architectural tastes of Selwyn and his colleagues, this kind of building only reinforced their prejudice against the perceived 'error' of Nonconformism.[50]

Indeed, firmly inspired as he was by High Church notions of ecclesiastical autonomy, Selwyn opted out of the New Zealand government's Church Act (identical with Australia's), in which all denominations were eligible to compete for state subsidy. He felt that putting himself at the mercy of this scheme would only invite government interference.[51] Instead, he instituted his own 'principle of equivalency', in which he, as bishop (and therefore head of the Church of England in New Zealand), would match funds raised by parishioners. This initiative had direct architectural consequences. The regulations for the 'Church Fund', as it became known, stipulated that the plans of all buildings seeking aid were to be 'approved by the Bishop, or by some person appointed by him', thus enabling Selwyn to exert tight control over the type and quality of building erected in his diocese.[52] By acting in this way Selwyn was able to extricate himself from what he considered to be the undignified frenzy for government funding and the politics that necessarily accompanied it. It also freed him from 'any rights of lay patronage, jews [*sic*], or other incumbencies'.[53]

As mentioned in Chapter 4, bishops Gray and Armstrong in South Africa were confronted with a similar dilemma with respect to state aid. The advent of Sir George Grey's policy of 'frontier Christianisation' in 1855 suddenly plunged Anglicans there into a contest for resources with their denominational rivals, especially Methodists. As a considerable amount of government money was on offer (approximately £45,000–£50,000 per annum, voted by the imperial parliament in London), Gray and Armstrong were faced with a predicament not unlike Selwyn's in that they either accepted the money, thereby admitting government interference, or declined it, in which case they would maintain their independence but lose ground (and influence) to their competitors. This forced Gray's hand because he was already feeling considerable pressure from Wesleyan missionaries, who he believed were 'doing what they [could] to undermine us'.[54] After deliberating for a time, Gray and Armstrong made the opposite decision to Selwyn, accepting the money and using it to establish five mission stations in the Eastern Cape. In taking this money, Gray believed that he was putting the Church of England in an advantageous position, not just economically but politically, too.[55] The stations were to incorporate 'industrial education' (that is, carpentry, bricklaying, agriculture etc.) as the basis of a policy of indigenous assimilation – a 'system' that Grey believed would resolve the ongoing conflict between the 'barbarous races' and colonial frontiersmen in British Kaffraria once and for all.[56]

As discussed in relation to St Philip's (one of the five stations) in the preceding chapter, there were direct architectural consequences to this policy (see pp. 217–25).[57] St Philip's represented a deliberate use of architecture as a means to impress and convert indigenous peoples. After all, Pugin himself had observed that the Gothic Revival was 'most closely connected with the revival of the faith itself'. In this sense, as William Westfall has noted, Gothic was a missionary style of architecture that sought to inspire Christendom by impressing its meaning directly on the heart of the observer.[58] This is precisely the effect St Philip's and other mission churches were intended to have in South Africa.

By the 1850s Presbyterian and Nonconformist congregations had begun to absorb the lessons of the Gothic Revival as well. Until this point, architecture for Nonconformists, especially, had been a purely utilitarian affair. The otherworldly theology of orthodox Protestantism had not encouraged the pursuit of such lowly matters as architecture – almost any building, for example, could serve as a Methodist chapel. However, the publication of the Rev. Frederick Jobson's *Chapel and School Architecture* (1850) fundamentally changed this attitude. Jobson suggested that the Gothic style of architecture was not only economical but also preferable in northern climates. More importantly, as Christopher Wakeling has reminded us, Jobson declared in a manner redolent of Ruskin that 'Truth in Architecture is not necessarily connected with Error in Religion.'[59] Gothic was now safe for strict Protestant use.

In the colonies, Nonconformists wasted little time in adopting the new style. By the 1860s and 1870s nearly all the major Nonconformist sects were beginning to build, or had already built, churches in one or other medieval style. In some cases this occurred even earlier. We have already seen, for instance, Methodists adopting a churchlike, neo-Gothic aesthetic for their mission chapels in New Zealand. We also find evidence of this as early as 1845 in South Africa in Thornley Smith's design for the Commemoration Methodist chapel (1845–50), Grahamstown (fig. 229).[60] Although this was not a sophisticated use of the style (it would have horrified Pugin), it nevertheless demonstrates that Nonconformists were open to Gothic architecture. Why this occurred so early in some cases in the colonies is difficult to determine, but it perhaps (or even probably) had something to do with the perceived liberty to use medieval styles in a context where the Church of England was not established and where the taint of Roman Catholicism and its associations was largely absent.

229 The Commemoration Methodist chapel, Grahamstown, South Africa (1845–50), by Thornley Smith.

By the late 1860s designs for medieval-style churches for Independent and Presbyterian congregations were being erected in Melbourne. Two conspicuous examples, facing each other across Russell Street on the south-western edge of Eastern Hill, are St Michael's and the Scots' church. These buildings were complete by 1875, one in a richly polychromatic, neo-Lombardic style (St Michael's), the other in a rather heavy, nondescript, decorated Gothic (the Scots' church) (fig. 230). At the time, these buildings were comparable, if not superior, to the then Anglican cathedral of St Paul's on Flinders Street. It would be another decade before William Butterfield's much more impressive edifice began rising on the same spot. This pattern of denominational representation through church architecture was repeated in towns and cities across Australia in the latter part of the nineteenth century. Other, and even earlier, examples in and around the city of Melbourne include the Wesleyan churches on Lonsdale Street (1857) and the corner of Fitzroy and Princes streets, St Kilda (1857–8), and the Congregational church, Malvern Road, Prahran (1858) (fig. 231).[61]

In Canada, too, it is possible to trace the rise and challenge of Nonconformist architecture at this time. 'I confess', wrote an observer of architecture to the *Christian Guardian* in 1856, 'that I do not like to have a traveller ask, when passing the place where I worship, "is that a *mill*, or a *barn*, or a *factory*".' 'There should be something in the general appearance and

230 The Scots' Presbyterian church (*centre*, 1873–4), and St Michael's Independent (Congregationalist) church (*right*, 1867), on Collins Street, Melbourne, both by Reed and Barnes architects.

impression of the edifice which tells the passer-by, *it is a house of God*,' he insisted.[62] Perhaps the most spectacular realisation of this plea came in the form of Henry Langley's Metropolitan Methodist church in Toronto, designed and built between 1868 and 1872 (fig. 232). Envisaged on a huge scale, in a distinctive Decorated Gothic idiom, it was quite literally a 'cathedral of Methodism'. In terms of visual impact in the urban landscape, it certainly challenged if not surpassed the Anglican cathedral. Langley also helped to realise the aspirations of Baptist congregations in this regard through his designs for the New Baptist church, Port Hope (1867), and the Jarvis Street church, Toronto (1874).

Likewise, Presbyterians were forging ahead with distinctive and impressive designs of their own. In terms of religious equality in the colonies, adherents of the Church of Scotland had a point: after all, the empire was *British*, not exclusively *English*, and theirs was an established Church, too.[63] It was felt that their status as a Church should be precisely that of Anglicans. This was a point that had been made as early as 1835 by James Thomson in his *Remarks on*

231 Wesleyan Church, Lonsdale Street, Melbourne (1857), by Joseph Reed.

the Status of the Presbyterian Church in the British Colonies.[64] There had, of course, been a long tradition of classicism associated with Presbyterian churches in Britain's colonies, but Gothic was also being freely adapted by the mid-nineteenth century, often with distinctive results. The Scots' church, Melbourne, is one example of this, as is the intriguing design for St Andrew's, King Street, Toronto, with its Romanesque-cum-Scottish Baronial aesthetic (fig. 233). Elsewhere in Melbourne and surrounding areas Presbyterians produced several very fine specimens of Gothic and Romanesque revival architecture in local basalt ('bluestone'). These include St Andrew's, Sydney Road, Brunswick (1865), the Free Presbyterian church, Chapel Street, St Kilda (1864), and St Andrew's, Sturt Street, Ballarat (1862–4).[65]

Although coming after the Church of England's and, indeed, the Church of Rome's, systematic revival of Gothic forms, what these examples illustrate is that the Anglican Church slowly lost its monopoly on the use of medieval styles and their Christian associations in the Protestant arena. By 1870 Nonconformists and Presbyterians had

232 Metropolitan Methodist church, Toronto (1868–72), designed by Henry Langley.

233 West elevation drawing by William G. Storm of St Andrew's Presbyterian church, King Street, Toronto (opened 1876) (Archives of Ontario, Toronto).

essentially caught up, producing what can be regarded as some of the more advanced and experimental renditions of neo-Gothic architecture in Britain's empire.

Competition from Within: High Church versus Low Church

The vitriol of High Anglican clergy was not reserved exclusively for Nonconformists, Presbyterians and Roman Catholics. Low tendencies within their own Church received criticism in equal measure. In fact, it was in this domain that many of the newly appointed Anglican bishops experienced their fiercest opposition. Selwyn discovered things to be so bad upon arrival in New Zealand that in some parts of the country he found very little or no solemnity of worship at all. For example, in 1844 a young ordinand at St John's College recorded an incident in which he offered the communion cup to a parishioner during divine service, who responded, 'but I don't need a drink, sir'. Stunned, the ordinand (T. B. Hutton) replied, 'it's for the sake of our Lord,' at which point the parishioner snatched the cup from his hand and said, 'well, here's to the lord then,' and drank the entire contents.[66]

But the greatest challenge in the early years of Selwyn's episcopate came from the Church Missionary Society clergymen who were already stationed in New Zealand at the time of his arrival and over whom he was given nominal authority – or so he believed. In fact, as Hans Cnattingius, T. E. Yates and others have noted, the CMS and its missionaries reacted badly to Selwyn's authoritarian manner and much confusion reigned as to what exactly his powers were respecting the *in situ* organisation and placement of CMS clergymen.[67] The clash that occurred between Selwyn and the CMS was essentially one of two distinct cultures. Fundamentally, the CMS saw itself as an organisation that both existed and operated beyond episcopal control, concerning itself exclusively with native conversion. However, if Selwyn was to be 'bishop', and therefore head of the Church of England in New Zealand, then surely CMS clergymen (ordained Anglican priests) would come within the ambit of his authority.[68] This would include their ministering to European settlers as well as evangelising indigenes. Indeed, being an organisation that sprang from the Evangelical Revival of the late eighteenth century, the CMS was Low Church in both spirit and practice. Thus, the tendency of CMS missionaries was to view Selwyn in his disciplinarian manner as something of a 'Puseyite'.[69]

These divisions were evident in their differing attitudes towards architecture. Again, in the journals of William Cotton one can find illustrations and descriptions of CMS churches (fig. 234). Many of these were drawn by Hutton. As his comments upon entering St James's church, Sydney, make clear, Hutton's views on architecture were decidedly High. 'The arrangement of the Church', he observed while passing through in 1844, 'is the most singular that I have ever had the pleasure of seeing, or rather I should say the pain – for the annexed plan will show it is rather a painful thing to be in it. The Communion table (for it cannot be called an altar) is . . . surrounded with pews, and instead of having two candles on it, has one . . . lamp "*which gives off more light*".'[70] There is little doubt that the recording of the CMS churches by Hutton and Cotton was motivated by a certain amount of disdain for, and astonishment at, the levels to which 'church architecture' had apparently sunk in New Zealand. As mentioned in Chapter 1, Selwyn was

234 Sketch of 'New Zealand Church Architecture' from William Cotton's journal, 1842 (State Library of New South Wales, Sydney).

equally disappointed upon arriving at Te Waimate to discover that the church there was 'not a very handsome building' (see p. 50) (fig. 235). It was not all bad, however. Frederick Thatcher had designed quite a neat-looking church for the CMS at Maraetai. But, on the whole, what Selwyn and his colleagues found upon arriving in New Zealand only spurred their aspiration to elevate the standard of ecclesiastical architecture.

Low elements within the Church also tested Broughton. With their outlook shaped by a predominantly Georgian view of the English Church, the majority of Anglicans in Australia were either conservative or Evangelical or both.[71] Moreover, egalitarian and reformist sensibilities, combined with the influence of Arnoldian notions of ecumenism, meant that sections of the nominally Anglican community there would have appeared both archaic and potentially radical to Broughton.[72] If not out-gunned on this front, he was certainly outnumbered. Indeed, the peculiar, even extreme, Low Church character of colonial Anglicanism must have been all the more apparent to Broughton after his return visit to England in 1834–5, where he witnessed the tremendous transformation then overtaking the Church – a transformation that touched him personally. Although maintaining great respect for their bishop, Sydney Anglicans tended to view Broughton's firm position on the articles and liturgy of the English Church with suspicion, as though it were the imposition of an unnatural and illiberal form of clericy or, worse still, a brand of quasi-popish authoritarianism. Broughton's new-found Tractarian sympathies did not help the matter, and when the Revs Robert K. Sconce and T. C. Makinson (both Sydney clerics associated with Broughton) seceded to Rome in February 1848, full-blown controversy ensued.[73] The flames of these controversies were fanned by the liberal press. Just as Broughton was attempting to reassure his flock of the merits of erecting a cathedral, Robert Lowe of *The Atlas* described him as the 'Australian Pope, Patriarch and Pontiff', who was nothing more than a lover of stone altars and carved wood; while J. D. Lang (a Presbyterian) of *The Colonist* accused him of being a Puseyite and his cathedral as a 'Gothic superstructure of Episcopal power and influence', designed specifically to undermine hard-won colonial liberties.[74] His own clergymen – albeit Irish ones – attacked him from time to time for his 'despotic rule' and attempts to 'crush evangelical truth'.[75] There were even calls in some quarters to establish a 'Free Church of England' in the colony.[76]

235 Watercolour by an unknown artist of the timber church at the Church Missionary Society station, Te Waimate, New Zealand (*c.*1839) (John Kinder Theological Library, St John's College, Auckland).

Such suspicion put Broughton in a position of having constantly to justify measures which, to him, were scripturally sanctioned and merely authorised by the doctrines of the reformed English Church. Ultimately, episcopal discipline and colonial liberalism were unhappy bedfellows. We see Broughton asserting himself on this front in sermons concerning church architecture. Time and again he championed the necessity for solemnity and beauty in ecclesiastical architecture against what he considered to be wrongheaded policies of meagreness and economy. To be sure, he affirmed to his congregation, the 'correctness' of dignified architecture was connected with the extension of true Christian principles and with the 'defence and confirmation of the gospel'. This was good as opposed to bad economy, he insisted. Buildings of this kind were not to be viewed as popish accretions but as 'landmarks of holiness',

236 The Rev. William Horatio Walsh (1812–1882).

as bastions and bulwarks of the true faith. Thus, turning the fears and anxieties of his congregation to his advantage, Broughton implored them: 'Is, then, the aspect of the world, and of the things of the world, at the present moment, such that we may securely dispense with these appropriate means of protection? Is the Roman power enfeebled, or showing any symptoms of diminished hostility? Is sectarianism less positive, or dissent less acrimonious? Is infidelity less confident . . . ?' The answer was clearly no. They ought therefore to seek refuge in that 'fortress' which was their new cathedral, rejoicing among those 'pillars of the Catholic Faith in our Reformed and Protestant Church'.[77] Perversely, perhaps, it was suggested that the huge expense of the cathedral was in fact the most effective and economical way of both realising and defending their faith. However, despite his best efforts to elevate the tone of Anglicanism in Sydney, Broughton never managed to overcome the deep-rooted suspicion surrounding his episcopate. This led to the appointment as his successor in 1854 of the Rev. Frederic Barker (1808–1882), a staunch Evangelical who had come under the influence of the leading Evangelical churchman Charles Simeon during his time at Cambridge in the 1830s. The diocese of Sydney has remained Evangelical ever since.

The Rev. William Horatio Walsh experienced the debased state of Anglicanism in Sydney and its architectural consequences at first hand (fig. 236). After arriving in Sydney aboard the *Fairlie* in December 1838, in April of the following year he was offered the parish of St Laurence by Broughton. Initially there was no church. While making arrangements for a new building, Walsh

> found a good temporary place of worship in the wing of a large brewery generally lent from the first institution of the Parish in May 1839, by J. T. Hughes Esq. In this building a congregation of about 40 persons more or less used to assemble, together with a gang of Prisoners and the Sunday School. Altho' thro' the diligence and zeal of my predecessor there was a most kindly feeling and disposition amongst the Parishioners towards the Clergyman, still I found great difficulty in overcoming the prejudices that existed both among rich and poor against attending on Divine ordinances in an unconsecrated building. "The Brewhouse" was a sort of bye word and reproach; and especially in the case of Marriages it was no easy matter to reconcile the people to the legality of the ceremony when performed in this unassuming building.[78]

Given that Walsh would later become a member of the Cambridge Camden Society, and chief Australian correspondent for *The Ecclesiologist*, it is not surprising that he wished for something more worthy. At first Henry Robertson was given the job of preparing plans, and Broughton laid the foundation stone for what would eventually become Christ Church on 1 January 1840. Work stopped in 1842 with only the nave, chancel and tower base complete. In retrospect, Walsh described the building at this stage as distinguished only by 'features of poverty and incongruity'.[79] In 1843 Edmund Blacket took over as architect, rearranging the interior, designing the furniture, reconfiguring the windows and later adding a tower with

237 Christ Church, St Laurence, Sydney (1840–57), by Edmund Blacket.

spire (1857) (fig. 237).[80] However, as mentioned in Chapter 1, at the opening of the church in 1845, these adjustments caused great consternation and alarm among the evangelically minded parishioners of St Laurence.[81] Knowing the temperament of his parishioners, Walsh must have foreseen this reaction. He persisted nonetheless, and *The Ecclesiologist* was happy to report the following year that Walsh had 'succeeded in bringing about the completion of the church in a very satisfactory manner', making for 'a real improvement in church architecture and arrangement in Australia'.[82]

As Stuart Piggin and Colin Holden have shown, factionalism of this kind could erupt into acts of destruction and violence. For example, during the erection of the church at Jamberoo (NSW) in 1866, it was reported that 'every attempt at decoration is jealously watched by some who regard as the highest proof of piety to hate'. Such was this 'hate' among certain of the parishioners that it led to the pulling down and smashing to pieces of the building's gable crosses in the middle of the night.[83] A similar fate befell the gable cross on St Peter's, Eastern Hill, Melbourne, in

238 Watercolour by an unknown artist, *c.*1850, of St Peter's church, Eastern Hill, Melbourne (1846–8), by Charles Laing.

1846 (fig. 238). In this case the offending object was found nearby 'with a piece of rope around its neck'.[84]

The situation was also getting out of hand further south. Much like New South Wales, both South Australia and Victoria (a separate crown colony from 1851) suffered prolonged internal division. The high-minded Bishop Short of Adelaide struggled to assert episcopal control over Church affairs, in the end having to compromise with his Evangelical and liberal reforming rivals who feared 'prelatical dictation and encroachments' of the Tractarian variety. The trials Short faced were all the more difficult given that the grant-in-aid scheme established by the colonial government was withdrawn in 1851, leaving him high and dry. The need to gather funds from local members of the Church therefore left him in a vulnerable position, inevitably tempering his hard-line attitude towards Church discipline and giving the laity a much greater role in Church governance.[85]

But it was Tasmania, of all the Australian dioceses, that felt the effects of internal strife most severely. Bishop Nixon may have been a man who knew his own mind, especially when it came to questions of Church doctrine, but he was opposed by a considerable number of Evangelical laymen and clerics who banded against him (in the form of the Protestant Association) for what they considered to be his heavy-handed, near Roman authoritarianism. The fact that Nixon protested in no uncertain terms against the appointment of Bishop Willson, and, like Broughton, would eventually repudiate the notion of establishment in the colonies, did not prevent his Low Church rivals from attacking him at every turn. When news of the Gorham Judgment reached Tasmania in June 1850, stirring up egalitarian sentiment and reinforcing notions of 'ecclesiastical republicanism', the gap between High and Low only widened.[86]

Inflaming the conflict to the point of intractability were the rather extreme personalities of Nixon and his chief

239 The Rev. Frederick Holdship Cox (1821–1906).

antagonist, the Irish-born priest H. P. Fry (1807–1874). The struggle between Nixon and Fry was bitter and protracted. It lasted some six years (1851–7) and involved clerics we have already met, such as F. H. Cox (fig. 239). What worried Nixon most of all was the unruly and potentially schismatic position in which the Church in Tasmania found itself by the 1850s. Writing home of the turbulence in October 1855, he observed: 'You in your better ordered communities can but little understand the evil that *one* determined and unscrupulous clerical agitator can effect in a place where public opinion is a myth; where there is no aristocracy; and where each man is as good as his neighbour . . . no one wants support here, who lifts himself up against lawful authority, be it civil or ecclesiastical.'[87] Nixon's response was to deliver a firm charge condemning the Gorham Judgment and reinforcing episcopal authority.[88] In reply the Low Church faction published a *Solemn Declaration*, in which they stated five 'Principles of the Protestant Reformation', the most extreme being the denial of 'any Church or Minister to prescribe to individuals in matters of religion in opposition to their judgement'. Rather threatened by this 'declaration', Nixon wrote in dramatic terms to his ally, the Rev. R. R. Davies, presenting himself as a kind of new-age martyr: 'The laity of this Colony are as resolutely against the real principles of the Church of England as ever were the puritans . . . I should have Laud's fate to a certainty, – did the state of things permit it.'[89] It is not surprising that Nixon should liken himself to Laud, being an alumnus of St John's College, Oxford.

These divisions were felt architecturally, particularly with regard to internal arrangement and decoration. On his return from a trip home in 1851, Fry banished, in dramatic fashion, the Tractarian-style furnishings at St George's, Hobart. As Nixon had been busying himself since his arrival in the colony in elevating the liturgical tone of divine service, the tussle between the two men and their respective camps acquired distinct spatial overtones. Evangelical suspicion of High Church motives in Tasmania lingered long after Nixon's departure as bishop in 1865, as evinced in the protest against 'exaggerated ritualism' in Bodley's first design for St David's cathedral, Hobart (see p. 121).

In British North America architecture spoke directly of the Low and outmoded state in which the Church was seen to be languishing. Writing to the Ecclesiological Society in 1848, Bishop Medley of Fredericton observed how the 'ordinary type' of church to be found in North America before 1840 was of wood and 'borrowed from the buildings erected by the Puritans . . . , the Church having no form of its own, nor having apparently any reference to the ancient churches in the mother country'.[90] Flat roofs, low ceilings, poor and thin towers, and no chancels were just some of the architectural misdemeanours Medley had to contend with. However, one of his biggest bugbears was the continued use and sale of box pews. Medley viewed this practice as not only unchristian but also an ecclesiological anachronism, now widely condemned in England.[91] He considered it nothing short of 'class legislation', calculated to alienate the affections of innumerable worthy church-goers. What right did the wealthy have to build and divide churches among themselves, he asked; 'where would the blessed Apostles, who sold all that they had to follow Christ, find a seat in such Churches?'[92] Thus, on Medley's watch, pew rents were done away with at St Anne's chapel and Christ Church cathedral, allowing both churches to

240 St Anne's chapel, Fredericton, New Brunswick (1845–7), by Frank Wills.

become not only beacons of a new and more correct form of church architecture but also places where a modern and inclusive type of Christian worship could be instituted (figs 240 and 241).

Part of the problem was ignorance. It was therefore all the more important, Medley believed, that clergymen bound for the colonies should have some sort of architectural education. 'What are the best plans that can be devised in the hands of an ignorant Clergyman?' he asked. 'He falls helpless into the hands of some rude mechanic, whose superior practical knowledge makes him hopelessly conceited, and as the Clergyman can teach him nothing which he does not already know, he will listen to no advice, he ruins every plan, misunderstands every direction, and adopts just so much of the original design as to make the result more unsightly than it would have been if no attempt had been made to do better.'[93] Whether Medley's plea was exaggerated or not, he certainly considered architecture one of the principal means by which the tone of Christian worship could be elevated and transformed. Something so important could not be left in the hands of those who knew nothing of correct form or detail.

241 Interior of St Anne's chapel, Fredericton (1845–7).

242 Edward Feild (1801–1876), bishop of Newfoundland.

Bishop Feild was also hard at work ferreting out obsolete practices in Newfoundland (fig. 242). His able assistant, William Grey, described much of what he saw in the colony as long 'stale' in England. 'High pews and galleries are seen in several of the older churches,' he informed readers of *The Ecclesiologist* in 1853, 'though our good Bishop wages war against them.'[94] Like Nixon, Feild was a wilful cleric determined to assert Anglican rights and to create a strong, independent Church. Also like Nixon, he divided opinion with his uncompromising brand of High Churchmanship. Not wishing to make his Church beholden to secular authority, he rejected state aid and implemented a policy of self-support similar to that of Selwyn in New Zealand. All subscriptions were to be paid into a central fund rather than to individual churches, thus mitigating the worst effects of lay interference and coercion. This rankled with Evangelicals, including the colonial governor, Ker Baillie Hamilton (1852–5), who found it 'strange and alarming', believing it would marginalise the laity and empower the bishop.[95] But Feild was not one to pay much heed to popular opinion. 'If I were popular I would do much', he once remarked disparagingly, '– much to exalt myself, degrade the Church, and ruin souls.'[96] Nevertheless, despite his clear Tractarian leanings, Feild did not wish to be known as a party man. He was sensitive to the fragile condition of Church politics in the colony and oftentimes went out of his way to avoid accusations of partisanship, especially Puseyism. Writing to Ernest Hawkins before departing for Newfoundland in 1844, he declared: 'I cannot tell you how I was disturbed by the prospects for my Cathedral Church. Pews! Pewholders! Pew rents!!! What conventicle can be lower. All this between ourselves. Do not let any vague reports precede me of my being a Tractarian or Pestilential Fellow, or what not.'[97] Indeed, so concerned was he at his reputation being sullied in this respect – a particularly grave indictment in such an anti-Catholic community – he rejected his nomination as patron of the Cambridge Camden Society in 1845.[98] This was done for political reasons, for the society was then at the centre of a controversy concerning what many believed to be its increasingly 'perverted' inclinations.[99]

Thus, although not an ecclesiologist in the same vein as Medley, Feild nonetheless felt the need to remind his flock continually of the 'lessons' inherent in a well-designed and well-ordered church. He made his clearest statement on this point in 1870, in a sermon delivered at his winter retreat of Bermuda upon the completion of Holy Trinity church, Hamilton. Rather explicitly titled *The Means and Methods of a Christian Life, as Told and Taught by the Form and Arrangement of a Christian Church*, his words recalled those of Broughton in his attempt at convincing Sydney Anglicans of the scriptural merits of proper church architecture.[100] 'Does it [the Church] not speak, and preach as it were', Feild reminded those gathered, in a distinctly Ruskinian tone, 'to all who pass by – speak of higher and better things than gain and merchandise, of a greater Potentate than the kings and rulers of this world? . . . Such, dear brethren, are the means and appliances for our new birth and growth in grace, and for the work of prayer and praise, provided in every rightly constructed and properly furnished Christian Church.'[101]

Feild's experience was similar to that of Bishop Hibbert Binney (1819–1887) (fig. 243) of Nova Scotia, the oldest Anglican diocese in British North America (established 1787). Although born in the province, at the age of four

Binney went to England, where he was educated, finally taking a first-class honours degree in mathematics (second in Classics) from Worcester College, Oxford (1842). He did not return to Nova Scotia until he was appointed bishop in 1851 following the death of the Rev. John Inglis (1777–1850), who had been bishop there since 1825. Steeped in Tractarian ideals, Binney moved quickly to enforce episcopal authority in what was a largely latitudinarian and congregationalist domain.[102] This brought him into conflict with certain prominent clergy and laymen, who prized the puritan and Calvinist traditions of the Nova Scotian Church. Despite facing some of the most ardent resistance from lay members in the Church of any Canadian bishop, Binney was eventually able to institute a higher and 'better' form of worship at his new cathedral of St Luke's, Halifax (1864).[103]

Like many among his colonial brethren, Binney maintained a special interest in architecture. He could often be found giving advice on such matters, as in 1855 at Conqerall, where he instructed local parishioners on 'proper ecclesiastical proportions and architectural style' for their new church.[104] But perhaps Binney's greatest triumph in this regard was at Charlottetown, Prince Edward Island (fig. 244). In designating the proposed church of St Peter as an 'extra-parochial' chapel of ease in 1866, he was able to head off the fractious tension then developing among the parishioners of St Paul's (a traditionally Low Church congregation) over access and arrangement. These changes paved the way for the advent of a new and liturgically 'High' form of worship on the island, free from pew rents and proprietary statutes. This was a style of worship craved by many among the younger portion of the congregation at the time but denied them by the fiercely Protestant, Irish-born rector of St Paul's, the Rev. David Fitzgerald (1813–1894).[105] The new church of St Peter, which effectively divided the community, was officially opened in 1869 (it became a cathedral in 1873). It was a handsome edifice, composed of brick in a simple but distinct early Gothic idiom (the tower was added later), somewhat reminiscent of the now well-worn model of Longstanton, near Cambridge (fig. 245).

Clear examples of the way that architecture was often perceived by clergymen as representing – or, indeed, standing in for – differences between old and new, Low and High, within the Anglican confession can be found throughout Britain's empire at this time. The reaction of ecclesiologists in Britain to what was sardonically referred to as

243 Hibbert Binney (1819–1887), bishop of Nova Scotia.

244 Interior of St Peter's church (now cathedral), Charlottetown, Prince Edward Island (1867–9), attributed to David Stirling.

245 The ancient parish church of St Michael's, Longstanton, near Cambridge, identified as a 'model' church for use in the colonies by the Cambridge Camden Society.

'Government Grecian' is well known. As Pugin had so forcefully argued, classical architecture was considered by most to be incompatible with 'true Christian principles', and therefore quickly became associated with an obsolete and moribund order of things in the wake of Anglican renewal. We have already seen evidence of this attitude in the reaction of bishops Strachan and Nixon to the churches they encountered in their dioceses of Toronto and Tasmania. In Grahamstown and Adelaide, too, we have seen how even nominally Gothic structures came in for criticism. But at Cape Town we see what is perhaps the most patent remark regarding this kind of architecture. Here Gray and his newly arrived colleagues were keen to reform the image and practices of what they considered to be an essentially hollow and all but useless institution.

When the high-minded Nathaniel Merriman arrived in Cape Town on 15 November 1848, he was quick to pass judgment on what he saw: 'St George's is the principal English church in the town and in the colony. . . . the building goes at present by the popular name of 'The Cathedral;' but as it is nothing but a proprietary Chapel in the hands of trustees and shareholders, and as the interior of the building (to say nothing of its Grecian exterior) is fitted up in anything but cathedral fashion, being filled with large high pews, and with no chancel-like arrangements, it is to be hoped that ere long a real Cathedral will rise in the place of it.'[106] The building to which Merriman referred – the cathedral of St George the Martyr (1834) – was typical of most British colonial churches erected during the first half of the nineteenth century (fig. 246).

It was a neo-classical edifice based on the model of an existing building in England – in this case, the parish church of St Pancras in London. A prototype 'ordinance' church, St George's was built by the colonial government in conjunction with the sale of shares, the interest on which was taken out of pew rents.[107] This effectively made the church a private 'joint stock company', as Gray described it, with the proprietors being 'Jews and Atheists'.[108] Merriman's reaction to this building was in many ways typical of Tractarian clergy, who not only preferred the authenticity and spiritual purity of English Gothic but also advocated the abolition of 'pews' in favour of free sittings. A church such as St George's also whiffed of Erastian interference, a situation repudiated by clergymen of Gray and Merriman's ilk, who believed in episcopal autonomy. Gray disapproved so strongly of this building and what it stood for that only a few months after arriving at the Cape he had already made plans to 'throw [it] overboard'.[109] It was eventually replaced by a much grander, late Gothic Revival edifice (1901–36) designed by Herbert Baker, unfortunately far too late for Gray to have appreciated the change.

246 Pencil sketch by an unknown artist, of St George's cathedral, Cape Town (1834). The design for the cathedral was based on that of the church of St Pancras, London.

The Church of England was in many respects unsuited to the political climate of Britain's colonies. Neville Meaney has rightly observed that, as an institution, it was never really intended for export.[110] The ambiguity surrounding its exact legal status, which reared its head in most colonial settings – from concerns over Royal Supremacy in Australia and episcopal authority in New Zealand, to the Colenso affair in South Africa and the issue of Clergy Reserves in Canada – handicapped both its organisation and its reputation.[111] As we have seen, this confusion led to challenges concerning its perceived privilege from within and outside its own ranks. It was not until 1855–6 that any kind of clarity was achieved respecting its rights and privileges. In the colonies of South Australia and Victoria at this time independent Church constitutions were drawn up, with Bishop Perry of Melbourne receiving royal assent for his on 25 February 1856. This push for independent, constitutionally ratified government came in the wake of the 1850 Australasian 'Bishops' Conference' and the failed attempts in 1852 and 1853 by W. E. Gladstone and Archbishop Sumner to secure a constitution in the imperial parliament for the whole of the colonial Church. It was informed also by recognition on the part of most bishops that each colony (indeed, each ecclesiastical province) had its own particular needs, and thus required its own peculiar form of 'consensual compact' – this much we have seen in the way different bishops in different locations either accepted or declined state aid.[112] It was felt by many that the constitutional structure of the Episcopal Church in the United States might provide an appropriate model.[113]

Initially, synodical action in the colonies was viewed with caution by Canterbury and resisted (for a time, at least) by colonial laity, both of which had reason to believe they were losing influence and control. These reactions were perhaps coloured by rumblings at home over the renewal of Convocation (suppressed since 1717) and attempts in some quarters at instituting local diocesan synods (namely Exeter).[114] Bishop Gray of Cape Town had also noted the spreading tendency among churchmen to look towards synodical action for the proper organisation and governance of their dioceses.[115] Moreover, with many colonies having gained degrees of self-government by this time, Westminster felt it prudent to err on the side of caution, throwing the issue over to each and every crown colony legislature to decide for itself the legal status of the Church. In this sense Perry's and Short's breakthrough set a crucial precedent, and other colonial sees followed their lead in the ensuing years, including New Zealand in 1857, parts of British North America from 1857 (including the institution of the General Synod in 1861), and South Africa in 1870.[116] As *The Guardian* had warned, following the 1850 Australasian Bishops' Conference, 'the Colonial Church is stirring with organic life: the thing is done'.

Despite the confusion, and no small amount of frustration, attending the colonial scene, it is clear that the circumstances in which the newly invigorated Church of England found itself throughout much of Britain's empire during the mid-nineteenth century both stimulated its aspiration and hardened its resolve. Indeed, the often volatile political and economic context of the colonies encouraged rather than diminished notions of Church autonomy. As we have seen, the problems that faced colonial clergymen over issues of competition and Church governance were more or less the same. Recognition of this – communicated personally and through official bodies and organs such as the SPG and the *Colonial Church Chronicle* – encouraged sympathy, cooperation and collective action, both at home and abroad. In Australasia it drew the community together, leading to synodical action and legally binding constitutions. At home it prompted serious attempts at gaining a proper legal footing for the Church abroad, invigorated through personal connections such as that between Gladstone and Selwyn. Inspiration was felt in South Africa and British North America. Bishop Gray, for instance, observed of the Australasian conference that it was 'almost the only cheering church matter that has occurred for some time', resulting in his calling his own synodical gathering in 1851.[117]

This high-minded drive for independence and proper constitutional government may have brought with it internal strife, but it also focused attention on the different ways in which architecture could function in aid of religion generally and the Church of England more specifically. As the settler colonies of the empire became wealthier and more established throughout the course of the 1850s and 1860s, drawing extensively on resources both locally and at home, so too did church architecture become richer and more elaborate to meet the increased expectations of clergy and parishioners alike.

6

'A church [almost] as it should be'

THE HIGH NOON OF COLONIAL ECCLESIOLOGY[1]

Thither the children of England are thronging,
There for true riches securely to search;
Not for thy gold, California, longing,
But for sweet home, with enough, and a Church!

Martin F. Tupper, *New Zealand* (1850)

And they went forth, and preached every where, the Lord working with [them],
and confirming the word with signs following.

Mark, xvi. 20

The period between about 1850 and 1875 saw the colonies 'catching up' with ecclesiological developments in England as best they could as their populations grew, their economies expanded, and the identities of those who inhabited them began to transform. As the diocesan system was consolidated and parishes established, the Church, as we have seen, increasingly regarded itself as independent of (although in communion with) Canterbury. The reasons for this were as much legal as they were practical. Indeed, it might be more correct to speak of 'Churches' after about 1870 rather than a single, monolithic Church, if there ever really was such a thing, legally or functionally. The Anglican Church that we see today in those places that were once British colonies is a product of this slow and, in many cases, tortured process.

Nor were things always as they should be with regard to church architecture, which varied considerably across the empire as each colony – indeed, each diocese – fumbled its way to something better. As we discussed in the preceding chapter, this variation exposes the particular problems that the colonial Church of England faced in different places and at different stages of its development. Oftentimes this led to inconsistencies or anomalies in the implementation of Church practice, especially among those who professed High Church leanings. For example, in parts of Australia and Canada we find the retention of pew rents and galleries, which had not only been condemned in England but had all but disappeared by the 1870s. From this emerged the strange phenomenon of what were otherwise perfectly correct churches, administered by High

Church clergy, that maintained certain condemned practices, as at Christ Church cathedral, Montreal. But, as we shall see, owing to the political and financial circumstances that prevailed in some colonies, the arms of clergyman were occasionally bent against their better judgement.

In this chapter we shall consider some of the ways in which ecclesiology spread and was developed throughout Britain's empire. The 1850s and 1860s witnessed the full flowering of ecclesiology in many of Britain's colonies, including not only the realisation of correct Middle-Pointed designs but also the influence of High Victorian eclecticism, combined with aspects of local innovation. In locations such as South Africa, Canada and Australasia, especially, Anglican church design can be said to have entered a mature and distinct phase during this period. Here we can trace both those consistencies that united Anglican church architecture across the world and the differences that began to distinguish it in particular regions.

The Colony of New South Wales

In the case of Australia, this had a great deal to do with the increasing number of qualified architects, both émigrés and locally trained. To be sure, plans sent from England continued to be used, especially with respect to the design of large churches, but such plans became less important as the availability of specialist and professional literature increased and local networks of expertise grew. Nevertheless, the principles of correct church design remained the same, particularly at the High end of the Anglican spectrum.

In Sydney, these developments were led by the English immigrant Edmund Blacket. It is difficult to say how ecclesiastical architecture in the colony of New South Wales would have developed had it not been for the arrival of Blacket in 1842. As we have seen, much that passed for Gothic Revival church architecture in the colony before his appearance was designed either by clergymen, such as Broughton, or architects ignorant of the style's changing moral and scientific associations. It is safe to say that the sophistication in terms of correctness, accuracy and feeling that presided in England at the time with respect to the revival of Gothic architecture in the Church of England would have been retarded by another decade or so in Australia had Blacket not appeared when he did.

We have heard something of Blacket already (see pp. 32, 76–7), but the most important contribution he made to the Australian scene was to translate the true spirit of medieval architecture to colonial church design. Sensitivity to medieval ideas and aesthetics was by and large lacking in a place where no ancient architecture existed and where educated architects and their supporting institutions were for the most part absent.[2] Through his first-hand knowledge of medieval forms, as well as his familiarity with the writings of Pugin and other contemporary theorists, Blacket brought a working knowledge of the latest stylistic developments in Gothic Revival architecture to Australia, which made him the right man, in the right place, at the right time.

However, an irony that is often overlooked in light of Blacket's success as an architect in Australia is that he was not professionally trained at all, but actually began his career in the colony as an inspector of schools for Bishop Broughton. As Joan Kerr has observed, he had developed his skills as a designer through his interest in ancient churches, sketching them *in situ* and tracing them from publications, such as the *Gentleman's Magazine* and *The Builder*. He had also gained some practical experience as a surveyor while working for the Stockton and Darlington Railway Company in the late 1830s.[3] Writing to his brother shortly after arriving in Australia, he noted: 'I have however now fallen into such circumstances where I can indulge my Architectural propensities without one tinge of conscience, and hope to have a great hand in improving the taste of the discerning Public upon Ecclesiastical Architecture. I have already succeeded marvellously, and altho' I do not *officially* bear the title, yet I hear that I am pretty well known as the Church Architect. . . . The taste is reaching us here to study *decency* in churches as well as *economy*.'[4] Importantly, despite having been educated at a Congregationalist school, Blacket was a devout Anglican – 'a gentleman', it was recognised of him, 'thoroughly imbued with the spirit of church architecture'.[5] In this sense, much like G. G. Scott, he was one of those 'religious' architects that the Camdenians believed were so important to the cause of revived Christian architecture everywhere.

Thanks to Blacket's talent and tenacity, by the late 1840s and early 1850s Sydney and the surrounding areas could boast a number of moderately sized Anglican parish churches that bore comparison with some of the best economical designs produced in Britain. Reporting to the Ecclesiological Society in 1847, the Rev. William Walsh rejoiced in the fact that Blacket was 'beginning to design churches that are very church-like and proper and would certainly meet with the Society's approval'.[6] Apart from his work on St Andrew's cathedral, the three most important of Blacket's early ecclesiastical commissions in Sydney, and those that provide a good impression of his abilities as a church designer, were St Mark's, Darling Point (1848–70), St Paul's, Chippendale (Redfern; 1848–75), and St Philip's, Church Hill (1848–56).

Stylistically, these three churches move from late Early English, through Decorated, to Perpendicular. Indeed, as Blacket's sketchbooks and church designs reveal, he appears to have had a penchant for the latter phases of Gothic architecture, particularly complex window traceries, including reticulated and curvilinear. We see this coming through not only in his designs for the cathedral and buildings at the University of Sydney, but also in churches for other parts of New South Wales, such as Holy Trinity, Berrima (1847–9), Christ Church, Geelong (1844–7), St Mary's, West Maitland (1860–7), and, later, Goulburn cathedral (first design 1870).

Like many of Blacket's early designs, the church at Darling Point (fig. 247) was based on existing models, in this case Holy Trinity, Horncastle, Lincolnshire (1847), by Stephen Lewin, and pattern-book details.[7] Much of the nave and chancel are modelled closely on Lewin's original design, but Blacket added a leaner and more sophisticated west front with angle buttresses, and a pronounced south porch tower with stone broach spire (1853–70). The whole is rendered competently in a late 'First Pointed' or Early English idiom.

The church at Chippendale was along broadly similar lines, although in this case we have a square, west-end tower with projecting octagonal turret (figs 248 and 249). This configuration was based on Arthur Ashpitel's decidedly Decorated design for St Barnabas's, Homerton, near London, which Blacket found in a copy of *The Builder* (1847) (fig. 250).[8] The patterns for the building's window tracery, as Kerr has noted, came from Edmund Sharpe's *Treatise on the Rise and Progress of Decorated Window Tracery in England* (1849), of which Blacket possessed a copy (see pp. 60–1). This building also has some rather elaborate, even delicate, decorative carving, remarkable for an early Antipodean church, not only in its window tracery but also in the dripstone terminations, which take the form of portraits of English medieval kings and queens (fig. 251).

247 St Mark's church, Darling Point, Sydney (1848–70), by Edmund Blacket.

Blacket's most impressive and accomplished design of this period, however, was St Philip's, Church Hill (fig. 252). Rendered in a solid yet graceful Perpendicular style, it comprised a six-bay nave some 90 feet long, a fully formed west-end tower (modelled, like the original design for St Andrew's cathedral, on the tower at Magdalen College, Oxford), a distinct chancel with vestry, north and south porches with aisles, and a separate organ chamber. It replaced what was justly described at the time as 'the ugliest church in Christendom', illustrating just how far

248 The octagonal turret on the west tower of St Paul's church, Chippendale, Sydney (1848–75), by Edmund Blacket.

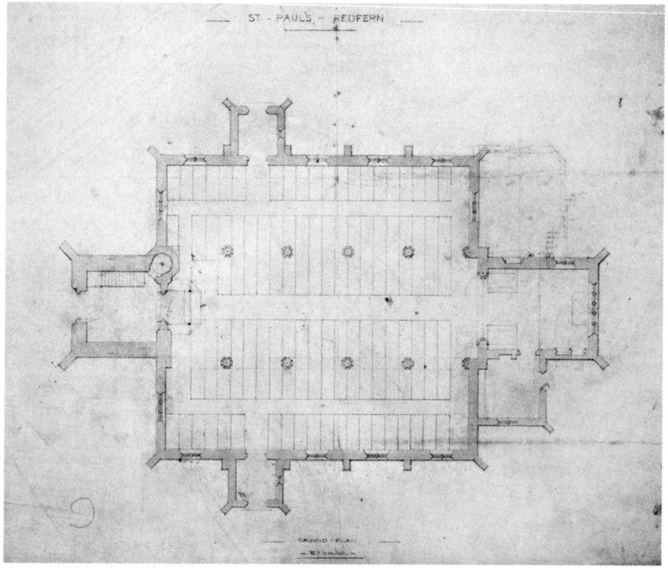

249 Plan of Edmund Blacket's design for St Paul's church, Chippendale, 1848.

250 Perspective drawing of Arthur Ashpitel's design for St Barnabas's church, Homerton, near London (1845–52), from *The Builder* (1847).

ecclesiastical art had come in Australia since the beginning of the nineteenth century.[9]

St Philip's was Bishop Broughton's reply to the challenge issued by the Roman Catholic church of St Patrick – that 'structure', as he called it – erected nearby only a few years earlier. Built using the wonderfully warm 'yellow block' Sydney sandstone, it must have presented a truly striking image when the tower, 102 feet high, was finally completed in 1858 – second only in terms of its grandeur to St Andrew's cathedral. Given Broughton's anxieties over what he perceived as papal aggression in the colony of New South Wales, Blacket was a godsend.[10] His loyalty to the Church and manifest devotion and dedication to ecclesiastical architecture thrilled both Broughton and Walsh no end, prompting them to appoint him diocesan architect in 1847.

Blacket had also been engaged to design churches outside Sydney, across the length and breadth of what was then the colony of New South Wales (which included modern-day Queensland and Victoria). These efforts to 'improve the taste' of the public in matters ecclesiastical began as early as 1844 with his design for Christ Church, Geelong. In January that year he recorded in his work diary: 'The Bishop gave orders to draw plans for Geelong Church upon a given plan.'[11] As mentioned in Chapter 1, Broughton had sketched his thoughts for this building on the back

251 Detail of a dripstone termination on the entrance doorway to St Paul's church, Chippendale (1848–75), showing the head of a medieval queen.

252 St Philip's church, Church Hill, Sydney (1848–58), by Edmund Blacket.

of an envelope the year before.[12] The end result was a small but correctly arranged edifice of four bays, with chancel, south porch and tower, built of sandstone mostly in the 'Third Pointed' or Perpendicular style (fig. 253).[13] Although Christ Church would not have garnered the approval of hard-line ecclesiologists in England, it was nevertheless among the first 'proper' Gothic Revival churches in Australia that could claim a pretence to architecture.

Numerous other small rural churches followed, including St Clement's, Yass (1847–50) (fig. 254), St Paul's, Carcoar (1845–9), St Mark's, Greendale (1848–9), and those at Berrima and Bathurst discussed earlier. By the 1860s, Blacket was, without doubt, Australia's most experienced ecclesiastical architect. He had established a recognisable style of his own, identifiable in his repeated use of motifs and pattern-book details such as the double-lancet and oculus window combination for the west fronts of his larger parish churches (as seen at Darling Point and St Stephen's, Newtown, 1871–9), his designs for reticulated and curvilinear window tracery, and the single-buttressed west front motif, topped with a bellcote, for his smaller rural churches and chapels.

His last and perhaps most accomplished work was St Saviour's cathedral, Goulburn (1874–1988) (figs 255 and 256). This work, described by Kerr as 'unmistakably a Blacket church', was orchestrated by the bishop of Goulburn, the Rev. Mesac Thomas (1816–1892). Although a man of Evangelical persuasion by the time he reached Australia, Thomas, it is worth pointing out, was among the founding members of the Cambridge Camden Society, having studied

at Trinity College in the late 1830s. He therefore had a special interest in, and knowledge of, church architecture. Although Thomas initially wanted a design from England, Blacket eventually received the commission, and in 1871 produced a set of drawings for what was, in effect, a large parish church in an elaborate Decorated style, with four bay nave, crossing, north and south transepts, two-bay choir, sanctuary and a large square tower rising from the south-east corner.[14]

Blacket's churches represent a competent, if essentially unimaginative, form of early to mid-Victorian ecclesiastical Gothic. They may not have been as sophisticated as what

Top 253 Engraving by Thomas Ham after R. Meredith of Edmund Blacket's design for Christ Church, Geelong, 1844 (Geelong City Library). A sketch plan for this church was produced by Bishop W. G. Broughton and handed on to Blacket for development.

Bottom 254 St Clement's church, Yass, New South Wales (1847–50), by Edmund Blacket.

255 St Saviour's cathedral, Goulburn, New South Wales (1874–1988), by Edmund Blacket.

could be found in Britain, but they nevertheless served an immediate purpose, raising the hopes of those among the Anglican clergy in Australia who had ambitions regarding architecture, especially Broughton and Walsh. It has been suggested that, through his access to architectural literature, Blacket was able to keep abreast of ecclesiastical fashion in Britain. But this is not entirely true. It is worth remembering that a church such as St Philip's, Church Hill, was broadly contemporary with Butterfield's All Saints', Margaret Street (1849–59). Although Blacket began experimenting with polychromy in the 1860s, his formal and aesthetic vocabulary lagged well behind developments in England.

To be sure, there are a number of possible reasons for this. Somewhat like G. G. Scott, Blacket was an ecclesiastical architect in the Puginian mould, inclined to work within medieval convention and precedent rather than strike out in bold colour and form.[15] The other factor that perhaps kept in check any attempt at experimentation, as Bishop Short had discovered in South Australia, was the conservative taste of Australian Anglicans. What the people wanted were churches that reminded them of the ancient landscapes of their homeland, and this is exactly what Blacket supplied them with – solid and respectable parish churches in a coherent and identifiable medieval idiom. If the rather

256 Interior of St Saviour's cathedral, Goulburn (1874–1988), looking east down the nave to the choir.

moderate liturgical 'innovations' introduced by High Church clergy were too much for most Australian Anglicans at the time, then a 'streaky bacon' or 'holy zebra' style of building, in the manner of Margaret Street or All Saints', Boyne Hill, would have been beyond the pale. It was not until the 1870s and 1880s that such architecture gained currency in Australia – hence, much of Blacket's oeuvre appeared stuck in the 1840s. He was not the only colonial architect to suffer this fate.

Perhaps the most daring and original architect operating in Australia in the latter part of the 1860s and early 1870s was John Horbury Hunt (1838–1904). Hunt was an immigrant from Canada via the United States, born into a staunchly Loyalist family from Nova Scotia. Because of his inculcated Loyalist sensibilities, Hunt always referred to himself as British North American as opposed to merely 'American': 'a Canadian – a Britisher – a Bluenose', as he was once quick to declare.[16] After arriving at Port Jackson aboard the *Tropic* in January 1863, aged just 25, he soon found employment in the office of Blacket. Hunt had trained with the Boston architect Edward C. Cabot, and therefore proved himself immediately useful to Blacket.

Indeed, he soon gained the full trust of his new master and was given responsibility for all manner of projects, including hospitals, churches and warehouses.

But it was Hunt's early involvement with Blacket's churches that gave him a feel for ecclesiastical requirements in New South Wales. This was an experience that would prove invaluable when he went out alone in 1869. However, where Blacket had been academic and conventional, Hunt was adventurous and expressive, pushing at the boundaries of what constituted ecclesiastical architecture in the colony at the time. As J. M. Freeland has noted, in order to understand the quality and character of Hunt's architectural output, one must first appreciate his personality.

By all accounts, Hunt was an intense, even restless man. Despite his socially conservative outlook, including ultra-Loyalist sympathies, he was fiercely individualistic to the point of being eccentric. This often brought him into conflict with those whom he believed to be lesser mortals, which happened to be most people involved in the Australian architectural scene during the late nineteenth century. He soon gained a reputation as something of an agitator, yet maintained tremendous respect as an architect. 'Such', observed Freeland, 'was the man who strutted onto the Sydney stage in 1863. A fiery, turbulent, bantam fighting-cock of a man, a perpetually tightly wound spring of energy, an egoist, an individualist and an excellent architect.'[17]

Shortly after leaving Blacket's employ, Hunt acquired the patronage of the Rev. William Edward White of Edenglassie in the Hunter Valley, north-west of Sydney. In fact, it was while superintending the construction of G. G. Scott's design for St Alban's, Muswellbrook (1864–9), that Hunt first met White, who was then the incumbent. White, although Australian born, had been educated at Oriel College, Oxford, matriculating in 1853 and graduating BA in 1858.[18] Not surprisingly, he was decidedly High Church. He also cultivated an interest in architecture, having been a member of the Oxford Architectural Society during his time in Oxford as a student.[19] This, along with his English experience, would have impressed Hunt.

The other association that proved fruitful for Hunt, both intellectually and architecturally, was with the recently appointed bishop of Armidale and Grafton, the Rev. James Francis Turner (1829–1893). Turner began his career as an architect in Cambridge, working first in the office of George Basevi, before moving to London under the tutelage of Philip Hardwick. However, a spiritual calling led him to matriculate at University College, Durham, in 1848; he took deacon's orders in 1851 and progressed to the priesthood in 1853. During his time in Durham, Turner busied himself with matters architectural. Not only was he honorary secretary of the Architectural and Archaeological Society of Durham and Northumberland, but he also designed the chapel at what is now Hatfield College, University of Durham. It was through these connections, in particular the influence and financial support of the White family, that Hunt was able to begin his solo career as an architect: they provided him with some of his most important commissions during the early to mid 1870s, including St Matthias's, Denman (1871–5), St Paul's, Murrurundi (1871–5), and St James's, Jerry's Plains (1875–9).

Unlike Blacket, Hunt was a self-consciously High Victorian architect. Freeland gives the misleading impression that he was somehow an alchemist when it came to designing churches, taking nominally Gothic forms and transforming them, almost *de novo*, into something powerful and unprecedented.[20] But it is obvious, especially when one considers the extensive library that he owned, and the professional magazines that were by this time readily available in Australia (such as *The Builder*), that Hunt was a keen student of the 'eclectic school' of architectural design, as Charles Eastlake described it.[21] His churches display all the classic features of this genre – the abstraction, the vigour, the continental influences and the experimental use of materials. These features characterised the churches of the movement's acknowledged masters from over a decade earlier, such as G. F. Bodley, G. E. Street, William Burges, William Butterfield and others. Given his Anglophilic tendencies, it is almost impossible to believe that Hunt was not aware of, and substantially influenced by, the works of these well-known architects.

Indeed, if one were to be critical, it could be suggested that Hunt, like Blacket, lagged considerably behind contemporary trends in England, not even having begun his career by the time G. F. Bodley was passing into his period of 'refinement'.[22] Moreover, just as Hunt's initial clutch of churches was being erected, the first book-length account of the movement appeared: Charles Eastlake's *A History of the Gothic Revival* (1872). Despite this lag, it is likely that Turner had been encouraging Hunt in the direction of contemporary developments.

We first see High Victorian tendencies in Hunt's architecture coming though in some of his earliest churches, in particular St Silas's, Waterloo (1867–8), and the Church of the Good Shepherd, Kangaroo Valley (1870–2). Both of these buildings demonstrate a return to Romanesque sources in the spirit of Ruskin. St Silas's, which was a project Hunt worked on in Blacket's office, is a small but assuredly High Victorian church, with bold, articulated features, compact form and studied use of structural polychromy (fig. 257). It also demonstrates the effect that Hunt's flair had on Blacket's practice in the 1860s.[23] The Church of the Good Shepherd, on the other hand, is often referred to as Hunt's first solo effort. This, too, is a building in brick, but there is little or no use of polychromy (fig. 258). Instead, Hunt picks out the various forms and features of the building through a basic interlocking of masses (chancel and nave in one, with north transept), and through different types of structural patterning in the brickwork, such as corbelling in the heads of the windows, the projecting string course at sill level and the double-ringed frame around the traceried bulls-eye in the west gable.

His Hunter Valley churches continue the trend towards muscular abstraction. Small churches became necessary as the settler population continued to expand in rural New South Wales during the middle decades of the nineteenth century. St Matthias's, Denman, is a classic example (fig. 259), demonstrating all the vitality and manly vigour that would come to distinguish Hunt's ecclesiastical work. Like Kangaroo Valley, it has a continuous ridgeline, encapsulating both nave and chancel, with a porch to the south and a vestry transept to the north. Here the porch protrudes from the extreme south-west corner, wrestling with the line of the west façade. The chancel is marked to the exterior by a single buttress on the south wall, followed by the staccato-like rhythm of five closely spaced slit windows. With its clean lines and planar surfaces, the whole appears as an emergent geological formation, its cavernous windows like slots punched into the face of a giant rock. But it is the

Top 257 Drawing of the west elevation of St Silas's church, Waterloo, Sydney, from the office of Edmund Blacket (probably from the hand of John Horbury Hunt), 1867 (State Library of New South Wales, Sydney).

Bottom 258 Church of the Good Shepherd, Kangaroo Valley, New South Wales (1870–2), by John Horbury Hunt, showing at the west end a slatted narthex designed to improve ventilation.

259 St Matthias's church, Denman, New South Wales (1871–5), by John Horbury Hunt.

west front that is most impressive. The attention to detail here is exquisite. A certain energy is perceptible in the way the bellcote, resting as it does on a row of dentilled corbels, pushes its way through the gable apex, while the windows beneath are grouped within a short but expansive blind arch with projecting sill, as though forming part of an exceptionally heavy plate-traceried window. Emerging further still are the bargeboards and bracing of the gable end, mirroring the arrangement of the roof timbers within. The resulting ensemble is unfussy yet sophisticated, imbuing the building with a sense of scale and proportion that belies its stature. It is a work of true High Victorian sensibility and imagination.

Similar features are evident at Jerry's Plains (fig. 260). Here a slightly more conventional arrangement is marked by a powerfully expressive sanctus bellcote with accompanying buttress. We also find the by now characteristic traceried bulls-eye window, in this case positioned in the north wall of the chancel. But Hunt's masterpiece is undoubtedly St Peter's cathedral, Armidale (1871–91) (figs 261 and 262). He began work on this building in 1870, producing a set of drawings that Turner felt comfortable

260 St James's church, Jerry's Plains, New South Wales (1875–9), by John Horbury Hunt.

taking to a meeting of the Church District Society the following year. Again, typically for the Australian scene, it was more a large parish church in scale than a cathedral. But as Beresford Hope had reminded those concerned with such matters nine years earlier, size was no prerequisite in a cathedral.[24] Turner defended the design, suggesting that there was 'nothing in it fairly chargable [*sic*] with extravagance'. Above all, he added, it was 'real, honest and true'.[25] Built entirely of locally sourced, 'Armidale Blue' bricks, it is an unparalleled *tour de force*. In the words of J. M. Freeland:

The Cathedral Church of St Peter Apostle and Martyr is a Gothic style building . . . like no other Gothic building that existed in Australia in the 1870s. . . . It was the first building in which bricks had been used from choice rather than economic necessity. . . . To elect brick because it was better was decidedly odd; only Hunt could be so odd. . . . He preferred brick for its constructional and its intrinsic qualities. . . . Using dozens, even hundreds, of different specially moulded bricks he created a blue-brown pile which probably has never been surpassed in Australia. Advancing series of

Left 261 St Peter's cathedral, Armidale, New South Wales (1871–91), by John Horbury Hunt.

Right 262 South transept of St Peter's cathedral, Armidale (1871–91).

> piers and buttresses, arched wall panels receding in three of four planes, course upon course of boldly dentilled arches, indented gables, bands of projecting diagonally laid bricks, and plain horizontal weather moulds are thrown into heightened relief by the bright New England sunlight.[26]

There may have been no church like it in Australia, but brick had of course become fashionable in Britain by the 1860s, as evinced in well-known and published exemplars such as St James the Less, Pimlico (1859–61), by G. E. Street, and St Peter's, Vauxhall (1863–4), by J. L. Pearson – buildings that were doubtless known to Hunt.

It turns out that the sun did much to inform Hunt's approach to ecclesiastical design in the antipodean context. The walls of his churches are invariably thick, and the windows small and deep set. His peculiar bulls-eye apertures are no mere affectation but, rather, a deliberate means of filtering light. Hunt was aware of the way in which intense light could adversely transform the solemn atmosphere of ecclesiastical space. Many of his churches also have pronounced, overhanging roofs, purposely intended to shed heavy rain and augment solar protection. His church at Kangaroo Valley, for instance, even has a narthex with horizontal slats for ventilation. In a word, Hunt's churches are cleverly and consciously adapted to their environment. In this respect, they may be considered a working realisation of the speluncar method of climatic adaptation first mooted by the ecclesiologists and later proposed by William Burges in his design for Brisbane cathedral. As Beresford Hope's *The English Cathedral of the Nineteenth Century* (1861), containing as it did both an outline of the speluncar theory and copies of Burges's design, was known to Hunt, it is not unreasonable to presume that Hunt was influenced by it. Indeed, distinguished by their singular strength and dignity, Hunt's churches were precisely those 'preachers' of 'righteousness, truth, and simplicity' that Beresford Hope had called for, and may be seen as the Australian equivalent of the small rural churches produced in England by the likes of Scott, Butterfield and Street in the 1850s and early 1860s, such as St Michael and All Angels, Leafield (Oxfordshire; 1859) (fig. 263), St Paul's, Hensall (Yorkshire; 1853–4), St John's, Howsham (Yorkshire; 1859), and All Saints', Denstone (Staffordshire; 1860–2).[27]

Outside New South Wales, in Tasmania, there was the rising star Henry Hunter (1832–1892), who had acted as superintending architect for Bodley's cathedral in Hobart. Having immigrated to Australia from Nottingham with his parents and three sisters in 1848, in the mid-1850s Hunter moved to Tasmania, where he was encouraged to practise architecture by the then Roman Catholic bishop of Hobart, Fr R. W. Willson – an association that would bring numerous commissions. Although not as adventurous as Horbury Hunt, Hunter nonetheless understood what made for a proper church, and was one of few architects in the region at that time who could claim to have an understanding of true ecclesiological principles. St John's Anglican church, Ross (1868), is a typical example of his approach – bold yet conservative (fig. 264). He was also responsible for adapting one of Carpenter's designs for St Mary's, Hagley, near Hobart (see pp. 314–15). Like Blacket, he was a disciple of Pugin. However, also like Blacket, Hunter's devotion to the Puginian ideal brought its own limitations, for, as Brian Andrews has pointed out, he was

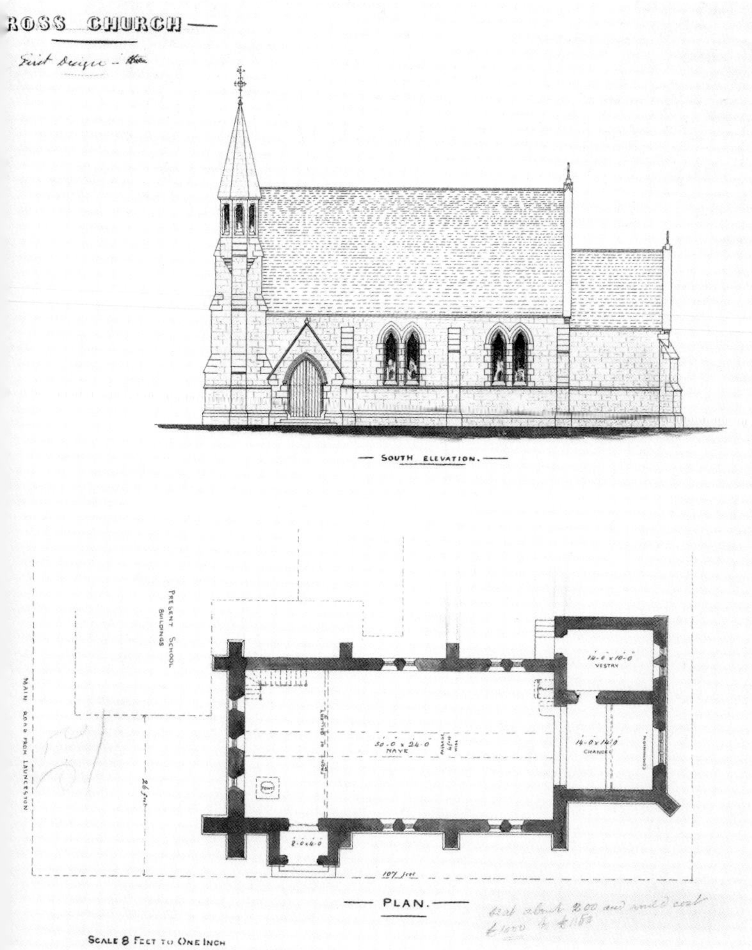

Top 263 St Michael and All Angels, Leafield, Oxfordshire (1859), by G. G. Scott.

Bottom 264 Plan and south elevation of Henry Hunter's design for St John's church, Ross, Tasmania, 1868 (Archive, Tasmanian Museum and Art Gallery, Hobart).

still producing archaeologically correct designs for parish churches long after such an approach had been abandoned by progressive architects in England.[28]

The Colony of Victoria

The rifts that developed between High and Low factions within the Church of England in Australia helped to focus thinking on architecture, enabling it to flourish in certain contexts as a manifestation of particular doctrinal positions and styles of worship. In the city of Melbourne, for instance, by 1860 there were already several parishes in which a moderate to High form of church liturgy was being performed, the most notorious of which were located at Eastern Hill and St Kilda. The advent of this liturgy, and its accompanying forms of ecclesiastical art, broadly coincided with the 'golden age' in the history of the colony of Victoria. The discovery of gold in the Ballarat and Bendigo areas in 1851 meant that the colony (formally separated from New South Wales that year) and its principal city accrued a considerable amount of wealth in the decades that followed. While the number of Anglican churches in Victoria languished at only five up to 1851, it had grown to some twenty-nine by around 1860, reaching nearly one hundred by 1865.[29] Initially, however, the Church was unable to take full advantage of the boon brought by gold.

The Anglican parishioners of Victoria, it turns out, were a proud and tight-fisted lot. Many were self-made men who jealously guarded what money they donated. Much to Bishop Perry's chagrin, these men were far less interested in giving to general funds – which needed support – than in dispensing their largess on things they could control and from which they benefited directly, such as their local parish church. This was a major problem for Perry who was desperate to extend the presence and influence of the Church of England right across Victoria, particularly in the goldfields where tens of thousands of new immigrants had arrived in the space of a few years.[30] Perry put this parsimony down to the apathy towards church finance that many Anglicans brought with them from England, 'accustomed as most of them have been', he bemoaned, 'to have provided for them free of all charge such ministrations'.[31] However, as discussed, the consequences of this neglect in the Australian context were potentially disastrous. Frustrated, Perry complained:

> Transplanted to this land the members of the Church of England have to learn the necessity of personal exertion which those of other denominations have been already taught. . . . , thousands upon thousands of intelligent and well meaning 'churchmen' among us, are possessed with the idea that the Church of England in this land is an institution upon which they have claims which it is its duty to recognize and discharge although they themselves withhold from it the smallest personal support.[32]

Thus, Perry found himself caught between, on the one hand, a niggardly unwillingness to support the activities of the Church by locals, and, on the other, a naïve belief in England that the Church in Victoria no longer required support owing to the discovery of gold. But, as he was quick to point out, it was precisely *because* of the discovery of gold that further support was required, especially as the cost of building and other supplies had escalated beyond all expectation.[33] For these reasons Perry remained a reluctant recipient of state aid.

The effects of this dilemma were not all bad. As the tendency of parishioners was to focus what money they gave on causes of self-interest, church building benefited. This was especially the case in areas that had well-to-do populations. In 1850s Melbourne, these areas included Toorak, South Yarra and St Kilda. In these places churches were eventually raised that were not only worthy of the name, befitting an increasingly sophisticated and prosperous new society, but also, and for the most part, moderate to High in their style of worship.

At St Peter's, Eastern Hill, the first church was erected between 1846 and 1848 to designs by Charles Laing, a Manchester-born architect. Laing became involved after an attempt to secure the services of Blacket fell through. But the building Laing designed, rendered in a rather nondescript Commissioners' Gothic, was quickly found to be too small (see fig. 238). In 1854 plans were submitted by Charles Vickers, a local architect, to extend the church by way of transepts and a new chancel. Later, around 1870, designs for a more elaborate apsidal east end, with choir, were prepared by Leonard Terry, who was not only among Victoria's most accomplished designers but also diocesan architect from 1860. Terry's addition (completed 1876) extended some 31 feet beyond the eastern wall of Vickers's transepts in order to accommodate a choir as part of the growing musical tradition at St Peter's (figs 265 and 266). Although by no

265 St Peter's church, Eastern Hill, Melbourne (1846–76), showing the reconstructed east end, with transepts by Charles Vickers (1854) and apsidal chancel by Leonard Terry (1876).

means impressive, these additions are notable for their simple but correct rendition of early Gothic forms in local basalt ('bluestone'). This stone – a dark grey-blue in colour – was extremely hard-wearing if difficult to dress, giving those buildings for which it was used an unusually heavy, even fortified appearance.

Here, in the one building, over a period of some twenty-five years, we see the slow move in Victoria from obsolete to modern ideas in ecclesiastical design. It was reported by a correspondent to the Oxford Architectural Society in 1852 that, although displaying a 'laudable desire to be Gothic', Laing's initial effort was essentially a dog's breakfast. 'Correct ideas on the subject [in the colony] are as yet in embryo,' it was observed regretfully.[34] This correspondent had not seen Christ Church, Geelong, however; nor did he comment on the nearly completed St Paul's, Swanston Street (1850–2). Although not exactly a prime specimen of

266 Drawing by an unknown artist of the interior of St Peter's, Eastern Hill (1846–76), showing the extensions by Charles Vickers and Leonard Terry (Anglican Diocesan Archive, Melbourne).

267 St Paul's church, Swanston Street, Melbourne (1850–2), by James and Charles Webb.

ecclesiastical Gothic, St Paul's, with its conspicuous bluestone tower, was the closest thing Melbourne had to a correct Anglican church (fig. 267).[35] Although condemning much of what he saw, the correspondent did admit that he had not been in the area long enough to make a proper assessment. By the time Terry took control at St Peter's in the 1870s, a new and more serious understanding of medieval architecture prevailed in Melbourne. But the real importance of the additions at St Peter's lay not in their fabric but in what took place within. Well before Terry's extension, St Peter's had become notorious for its increasingly High style of worship.

The church's fourth incumbent (installed 1854), the Rev. H. H. P. Handfield (1828–1900), was among Melbourne's leading High Churchmen. Although he did not have a university education, he came under the spell of the Oxford reformers during a visit to England in 1855. Upon his return, substantial changes in the style of preaching and worship at St Peter's became noticeable.[36] These were quite considerable changes for the Melbourne scene, as the staunchly Evangelical bishop had been vigilant in curtailing such practices. However, as the tastes and desires of Melbourne Anglicans became more sophisticated, and as Tractarian ideas began to exert their influence, Perry was bound to struggle in containing the slow creep of High Church liturgy.

Perry was described by Wilberforce as 'a Low Churchman of the narrow school', and, by his own admission, was neither a learned nor an intellectually inclined cleric.[37] This brought him into conflict with men of Handfield's persuasion. Although Melbourne was by no means a Tractarian stronghold, by 1865 Handfield had introduced a

268 All Saints' church, East St Kilda, Melbourne (1858–91), by Nathaniel Billing.

surpliced choir at St Peter's, despite Perry's protestations.[38] In the meantime, his parishioners (wealthy and educated Melburnians, keen to elevate the dignity and aesthetic spectacle of worship) had been busy donating all manner of finely made furnishings, including church plate and a new organ. All of these liturgical and ceremonial developments eventually inspired (indeed, required) Handfield to extend the church in a style that was more in keeping with this style of worship.

The other centre of High Churchmanship in Melbourne at this time was All Saints', East St Kilda (figs 268 and 269). Here, between 1858 and 1891, the Rev. J. H. Gregory oversaw the erection of a handsome five-bay church, with articulated aisles, transepts and chancel, to the designs of the immigrant architect Nathaniel Billing, former pupil of G. G. Scott.[39] In its correct arrangement, distinctive blue-

269 Interior of All Saints' church, East St Kilda (1858–91), looking east down the nave to the chancel.

stone fabric, with freestone dressings and Decorated detailing, All Saints' represented the height of mid-century Anglican Gothic in Melbourne. The first stage of the building was complete by 1861, and the church opened for regular service. Further work was carried out in 1868, before the transepts and chancel were added in 1875 to designs by Frederick Wyatt. These later additions were far more French in character than the earlier parts of the building, and were supposedly inspired by Gregory's return visit to Europe in the early 1870s, when he not only toured France but also (no doubt) witnessed ecclesiological developments that had taken place in England during the preceding two decades.

Through such architecture, Gregory recognised a means of achieving a deeper sense of devotion. The intention was clear: to erect a building worthy of the Church of England and to 'revive the hallowed and pleasing recollections of the parish Churches of our fathers, where our first impressions of public Christian worship were received'.[40] Like Handfield, Gregory did not have an Oxbridge education, but as a child he had attended Margaret chapel (the predecessor of All Saints', Margaret Street), London, where the Tractarian-style services of the Rev. Frederick Oakeley affected him deeply.[41] As at St Peter's, Eastern Hill, the parishioners of All Saints' played a prominent role in the affairs of the church, both financially and intellectually. Like many among their middle-class counterparts in England, they had developed, through wealth and education, not only an appreciation for order and beauty but also an interest in the spiritual and liturgical reforms of the Oxford Movement.[42] Although Gregory initially struggled to gather all the funds necessary to complete the building, he was quick to reassure those willing to part with their hard-earned cash that 'all the construction is real; and no attempt at . . . fading and temporary ornamentation has been made'.[43] A model of the final design was kept in the church to remind those arriving of their duty to assist in its realisation.

The building was dedicated in October 1868, with Bishop Perry presiding. It was reported in the *Melbourne Church News* that an altar was placed in the chancel and choristers were arranged on either side, 'according to the orthodox plan, very rarely followed in this colony'. As Stuart Soley has noted, this moment enabled Gregory to bring together both his teachings and ethos in an architectural setting that was conducive to a distinctly High Church style of worship, a full seven years ahead of Handfield's achievement at St Peter's.[44] Perry was no doubt mortified throughout the ceremony.

But these 'innovators' could not have it all their own way. One of the peculiar, even ironic, inconsistencies between local practice and their otherwise clear High position was the retention of pew rents. As mentioned earlier, charging for pews had been condemned as unchristian in much of the rest of the Anglican world by this time. However, the desire of the bishop to extend the Church in the face of growing competition, and the ambition of Handfield, Gregory and others to erect churches worthy of the name, meant that considerable amounts of money had to be borrowed.[45] With the Roman Catholic Church making ever bolder strides in infrastructural development, thanks mainly to the presence in Melbourne of the accomplished Gothic Revival architect and Catholic convert William Wilkinson Wardell (1823–1899), Perry, like Broughton, began to feel the heat. In this context, income generated through pew rents was deemed necessary to meet the repayment of loans tied up in substantial capital works projects and other basic expenses.[46] The adverse consequence of this predicament was the exclusion of poor communicants from church services and therefore the damaging perception that the Church of England in Melbourne was a largely plutocratic institution.

By the late 1850s and early 1860s more authentic and correct forms of Gothic Revival architecture were all but commonplace in the Anglican Church in Melbourne. Other notable examples – many of which are in bluestone – include Christ Church, South Yarra (1856–9, tower 1881–9); St John's, Toorak (1860–2); Christ Church, St Kilda (1854–81); St Mark's, Fitzroy (1853–76); and Holy Trinity, Coburg (1853–69) (figs 270 and 271). There were also a number of distinctive churches in outlying areas of the colony, such as Holy Trinity, Ceres (1855–7); St John's, Port Fairy (1854–5); St James's, Dandenong (1864–5); St Peter's, Ballarat (1864–7); Christ Church, Castlemaine (1854); St Paul's, Bendigo (1867–73); Christ Church, Daylesford (1862–3); and the tower of St Paul's, Geelong (1865) (figs 272–4). Many of these buildings involved the input of a new generation of professionally trained architects, including Leonard Terry, Percy Oakden, Nathaniel Billing, Joseph Reed and William Wardell. Through these men the age of ecclesiology had well and truly arrived in Victoria.

270 Christ Church, South Yarra, Melbourne (1856–9; tower and spire, 1881–9), by Charles Webb.

271 Church of St John the Evangelist, Toorak, Melbourne (1860–2), by William Wardell.

New Zealand and the Pacific Islands

Across the Tasman Sea, in New Zealand, considerable leaps forward were made in Anglican church architecture at this time. The centre of this activity was Canterbury, where the immigrant architect Benjamin Woolfield Mountfort was its foremost proponent (fig. 275). As mentioned in earlier chapters, Mountfort was an ecclesiologist of no mean credentials, having trained under R. C. Carpenter and been an associate of the Ecclesiological Society (though never a member). Thus, with his arrival at Christchurch aboard the *Charlotte Jane* in December 1850 came a thoroughly up-to-date and sophisticated brand of modern ecclesiastical Gothic. He was undoubtedly the most knowledgeable, inspired and professional revivalist architect New Zealand had yet seen, and his experiments in timber ecclesiology

Top 272 St John's church, Port Fairy, Victoria (1854–5), by Nathaniel Billing.

Bottom left 273 St Peter's church, Ballarat, Victoria (1864–7; tower added 1891), by C. D. Cuthbert.

Bottom right 274 Christ Church, Daylesford, Victoria (1862–3), by Leonard Terry

275 Benjamin Woolfield Mountfort (1825–98).

made him the inheritor of a tradition begun by Bishop Selwyn and Frederick Thatcher a decade earlier.

To be sure, Mountfort, as Ian Lochhead has shown, was more than a designer of churches. He was also responsible for many of the key health, educational and administrative buildings of the 1850s, 1860s and 1870s in Christchurch, including the Canterbury Provincial Council Buildings (1855–65), with its magnificent main chamber, the Canterbury Museum (1869–82), the town hall (1857), the hospital (1872–8) and aspects of Christ's College (1857–88), to name but a few.[47] He had also produced designs for a number of buildings before leaving England, including churches in the Black Country at Croft, Ogley Hay and Birmingham.[48] Indeed, it was in church design that one senses Mountfort's calling. A devout Anglican, his churches capture the spiritual essence of true ecclesiastical design, proving him to have been every bit the 'Godly architect' the Ecclesiological Society had hoped would come to dominate the profession.

We have discussed some of Mountfort's work already, namely St Bartholomew's, Kaiapoi (1854–62), and his involvement in the erection of Christchurch cathedral (see pp. 56, 107–8). His most remarkable early work, however, was Holy Trinity, Lyttelton (1851–5) (fig. 276). This building was intended as one of the first signs of Anglicanism that new settlers bound for Canterbury would see upon their arrival. Perched high on a hill overlooking the harbour, it was constructed using local timbers, arranged to form an elaborate cross-braced frame, between which were placed brick infill (or noggings). The noggings were then covered with a cement-based render, leaving, as the *Lyttelton Times* reported, 'the wood work appearing on the outside'.[49] The result was an extraordinary half-timbered effect.

Owing to a lack of funds, Mountfort's vision for Holy Trinity was only partly realised. In May 1852 the foundation stone was laid for what was intended as the first stage, which comprised the four westernmost bays of the nave (fig. 277). This part of the building was completed and opened for service in January the following year. However, despite the pride the new settlers had in this 'local work',

276 Perspective drawing of Benjamin Mountfort's design of 1851 for Holy Trinity church, Lyttelton, New Zealand (1851–5) (Canterbury Museum, Christchurch).

277 Watercolour sketch by J. E. FitzGerald, 1852, of the four completed bays of Holy Trinity, Lyttelton (Canterbury Museum, Christchurch).

they failed to take into account local conditions. An imprecise understanding of how the two native timbers used – totara and rimu – behaved meant that considerable shrinkage occurred, leaving parts of the structure unstable. In March 1854 a strong north-westerly wind – another local hazard – caused some of the brickwork to fall from the west gable. Under these conditions, with its high walls and steeply pitched roof, the church acted somewhat like a sail, catching the wind and transferring a huge load onto the structure. Thus, ironically, in his eagerness to implement the recommendations of the Ecclesiological Society, Mountfort ran into trouble. Following a failed attempt to remedy the situation with an alternative, scaled-down version in 1855, the structure was condemned and eventually demolished in 1857, never to be realised as originally intended.

However, as Ian Lochhead has pointed out, Mountfort's vision, although never realised, was nonetheless a reasonable attempt at adapting ecclesiological principles to local economic and material circumstances. In this respect Holy Trinity was a true form of colonial ecclesiology. Its sources were many and varied, including the well-known English precedents of Lower Peover and Greenstead, mentioned earlier, and Carpenter's plans for a timber church at Tristan da Cunha (1850), as well as G. G. Scott's 1850 design for a timber church with stone chancel, produced specifically for Canterbury. The other likely source was the design for a half-timbered church, illustrated in George Truefitt's *Designs for Country Churches* (1850), which was almost certainly known to Mountfort.[50] Ironically, the failure of Mountfort's and the Canterbury Association's ambition for Holy Trinity was ultimately symbolic of the dashed expectations of the colonists themselves and the less prominent role that Anglicanism would eventually come to play in the overall development of the settlement.[51]

278 St Mary's church, Halswell, New Zealand (1862), by Benjamin Mountfort.

But Mountfort was not deterred. He went on to design a number of churches not just in Canterbury but in other parts of New Zealand as well. Some of these have been mentioned already, such as Hemingford Church (1851–3), St John the Evangelist, Heathcote (1857–9), based on Carpenter's design for a 'chapel-school' in the second series of *Instrumenta Ecclesiastica* (1856), and St Augustine's, Waimate (1872). But there are others that date from the late 1850s and early 1860s worthy of mention as neat and progressive examples of ecclesiology in wood, including St Mary's, Halswell (1862) (fig. 278), the chapel at Barbadoes Street Cemetery, Christchurch (1856–63), and St Peter's, Riccarton (1857–8), the last of which Mountfort designed in partnership with Isaac Luck. All of these buildings demonstrate a clear, learned understanding of, and appreciation for, the ethos of medieval architecture and its flexible adaptation to new and challenging contexts.

Perhaps the most interesting structure produced by Mountfort during this period was the free-standing timber belfry (1861) for the existing church of St Michael and All Angels, Christchurch (fig. 279). This is a delightful confection, influenced by sources as wide-ranging as the bell tower at St Mary's, Sompting (Sussex), the timber belfries of the Essex countryside, and the designs based on Scandinavian models in *Instrumenta Ecclesiastica*.[52] Although not integrated as part of the original church, the belfry is nonetheless a solid and striking specimen of ecclesiastical timberwork. As Lochhead has observed, its harking back to Anglo-Saxon precedent was particularly appropriate in the context of Christchurch, where parallels between the primitive origins of English ecclesiastical architecture and the embryonic state of the Church in Canterbury resonated profoundly.[53]

Parallels such as this may have carried a particular romantic charm, but it was the apparent social inertia that accompanied them – this perpetuated infantile state, as it were – that rankled with Canterbury's Anglicans after a while. Much as elsewhere in the British colonial world at the time, at Canterbury the push to develop the Church visibly and spatially through architecture took place against a backdrop of increased competition among the various Christian denominations. As we saw in the Chapter 5, this had been a historic problem in New Zealand, but it carried an added sense of disappointment in Canterbury. It was no small humiliation to Anglicans that the settlement had not turned out the way its promoters had intended. To be sure, development was slow, but perhaps this was to be expected in such a place.[54] Much less acceptable was the fact that other denominations had not only got in on the act but had been far more vigorous in making their presence felt through the erection of churches. In the eyes of some, the lethargy of the Church of England on this score was disgraceful, especially as so many had been lured to the other side of the world on the promise of an Anglican paradise. Up until the mid-1860s, the half-hearted effort of St Michael and All Angels was all that Christchurch could show for this brave new world of Anglicanism.[55]

Patience wore thin. 'No such disgrace hangs over the Wesleyan or Presbyterian communities,' exclaimed *The Press* in 1862. 'A stranger driving through Christchurch could not fail to be struck with the churches erected by both these Christian bodies,' it declared, 'and would, no doubt, arrive at the conclusion that they constituted the most numerous, and most wealthy, and most influential sections of the community.' Adding insult to injury, the paper continued: 'He would, did he know nothing of Church history, imagine that it had been the dissenting bodies who had been the students and patrons of Church architecture, whilst the peculiarity of Episcopalians had been to promote simplicity, unsightliness and discomfort in their places of worship.'[56] It would not be until the mid- to late 1860s that Anglicans in Christchurch could begin to hold their heads

279 Belfry (*centre right*) of the church of St Michael and All Angels, Christchurch, New Zealand (1861), by Benjamin Mountfort.

high, with the initial stages of the cathedral approaching completion and the erection of additional stone churches such as St John the Baptist, Latimer Square (1864) (figs 280 and 281).[57]

❁

New Zealand was not the only field of endeavour that captured the Church's imagination in this part of the world. From his earliest days as bishop, Selwyn had shown a keen interest in extending his missionary work to neighbouring islands in the south-west Pacific. Indeed, he had always considered these islands – what constitute modern-day Norfolk Island, Vanuatu, Fiji, New Caledonia, the New Hebrides and the Solomon Islands – as part of his diocese, even though they were outside official British territory. This was owing to an error in his letters patent, which stipulated the northern boundary of his diocese to be 34° 30′ north instead of south. Just as did New Zealand, these islands represented a domain into which the Church of England might go in order to validate its new-found spiritual claims and demonstrate its credentials as the 'true branch' of the Christian faith by reviving the missionary model of antiquity.[58] But Selwyn's concern for these islands went beyond the spiritual. It also involved an appreciation of the wider geo-political context of competing European powers and

280 The church of St John the Baptist, Latimer Square, Christchurch, New Zealand (1864), by Maxwell Bury.

281 Plan and north elevation of Maxwell Bury's design for St John the Baptist, Latimer Square, Christchurch, 1864.

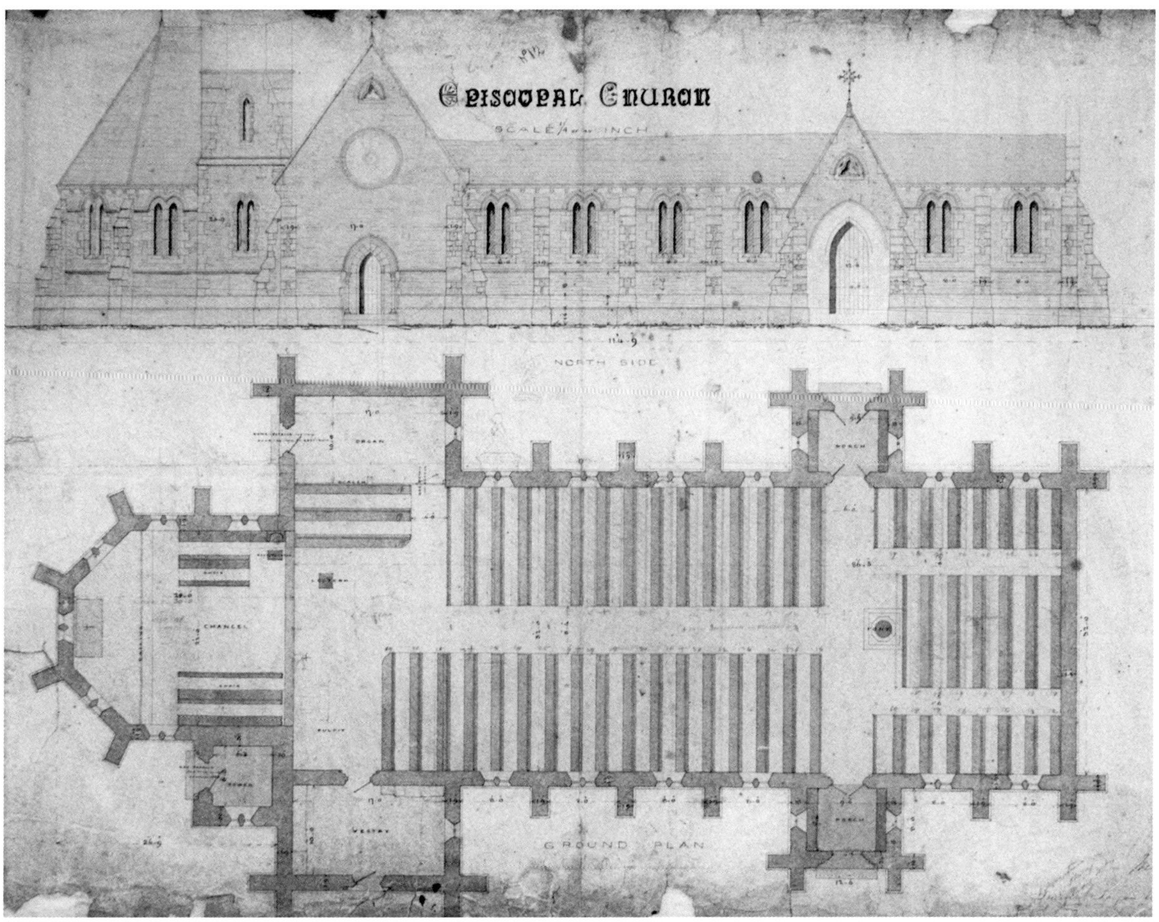

missionary organisations, including Roman Catholics. He was also concerned about the growing tide of violence between European sailors, labour traders and islanders, believing that an English mission might bring a degree of order and thereby ease tensions. In this sense, Selwyn's plans were expansionist. If Christianity was to be promulgated in that part of the world, then the Church of England, he believed, ought to be its authoritative agent. 'If it pleases God,' he wrote to his friend Gladstone in 1850, 'I hope in ten years to shake hands with the Bishop of Borneo.'[59]

With this in mind, Selwyn set about establishing what became known as the Melanesian Mission. Initially styled the 'Northern Mission', its headquarters were first located at St John's College, Bishop's Auckland (Tamaki), before moving down to the harbour below the college in 1859. This location, known as Kohimarama ('Focus of Light'), became the mission's first proper station, later taking the name St Andrew's College. The intention was to collect eligible boys from the surrounding islands using the college schooner, *Southern Cross*, bring them to the station for a period of time, educate them, and then send them back to the places they had come from. It was from this 'central reservoir', Selwyn envisaged (a kind of antipodean Iona or Lindisfarne), that true religion would emanate, resulting in a 'Native Ministry' of Melanesian clerics, who would Christianise their own communities from within.[60] In this respect, the Melanesian Mission was akin to the Universities' Mission to Central Africa, the objective of which was to create an independent 'negro church' before withdrawing from the field.[61]

The Melanesian Mission came into its own with the arrival of the Rev. John Coleridge Patteson (1827–1871) in 1855 (fig. 282). 'Coley', as he was affectionately known, was the nephew of the Rev. Edward Coleridge, Selwyn's close friend and agent in England (see pp. 43–5). Patteson had been sent to take charge of the enterprise, later becoming its first bishop (1861). Like Selwyn, he had been a pupil at Eton, before progressing to Balliol College, Oxford (BA 1848). Indeed, the Selwyn and Coleridge families had long been intimate. This aided Patteson in his dealings with Selwyn, who was known to be cantankerous and authoritarian at times, enabling a relatively trouble-free relationship, based on High Church principles. Patteson's arrival in New Zealand is an example of networking within the global Church of England at its most effective. Here was an Eton boy, with family connections, hand-

282 John Coleridge Patteson (1827–1871), first bishop of Melanesia.

picked by his uncle, who was himself an Eton man and friend of the bishop of New Zealand. At Patteson's episcopal consecration, Selwyn drew attention to these ties, observing that the ceremony involved 'three Eton bishops [Abraham, Hobhouse and Selwyn] . . . consecrating a fourth Eton man [;] . . . all trained in the same place of education; united in the same circle of friends,' and that, 'in boyhood, in youth, in manhood, we have shared the same sorrows, and joys, and hopes, and fears'.[62] Little did they know at the time that they would share further sorrow yet.

Architecturally, the mission began its independent life in modest timber accommodation, originally set aside for the crew of the *Southern Cross*. This was soon followed by the erection of additional buildings, including surplus structures brought down from St John's College. By December 1859 the site had been developed into three sides of a quadrangle, with a substantial stone building forming the western range

283 View from the west of the buildings forming the quadrangle of St Andrew's College, Kohimarama, near Auckland, as they appeared *c.*1865. Probably designed by Reader Wood, the college was the first independent headquarters of the Melanesian Mission.

(fig. 283). The timber structures were built in the so-called Selwyn style, under the superintendence of local architect Reader Wood. Construction of St Andrew's College was funded for the most part by proceeds generated from the sale of Charlotte Yonge's *The Daisy Chain* (1856).[63] Yonge was herself a member of the Coleridge clan and a key figure in popularising the Tractarian cause through fiction and children's literature. She was also Patteson's cousin. Writing to Yonge in 1859, Patteson was able to report:

> The buildings at present form three sides of a quadrangle, but the south side is only partly filled up. The large schoolroom, eighty feet long, with three sets of transepts, has been removed from the College [St John's], and put up again so as to form the east side of the quadrangle. This is of wood; so is the small wooden quadrangle which serves now for dormitories, and a part of which I occupy; my house consisting of three little rooms, together measuring seventeen feet by seven. These dormitories are the southern side of the quadrangle, but do not reach more than half way from the east to the west side, room being left for another set of dormitories of equal size, when we want them and can afford them. The west side consists of a very nice set of stone buildings, including a large kitchen, store room, and room for putting things in daily and immediate use; and the hall, which is the northern part of the side of the quadrangle, is a really handsome room, with simple open roof and windows of a familiar collegiate appearance. These buildings are of the dark grey scoria, almost imperishable I suppose, and look very well.[64]

Proposals for further development were put forward by the Oxford-based architect Charles Buckeridge in 1866, but these fell through when the college moved to Norfolk Island the following year.[65]

284 Interior of the chapel at St Andrew's College, Kohimarama, near Auckland, from *Mission Life* (1867).

Evidence of the care taken in erecting these buildings can be seen in the chapel. This was a small space, forming a wing of one of the larger buildings, composed in the style of the St John's College workshop, with its square-headed windows and exposed timberwork (fig. 284). The seating was arranged in a collegiate fashion, the altar raised and decorated, with a portable timber lectern positioned accordingly. A crude but effective attempt was also made at ornamentation.[66] But, as this was only a temporary arrangement, Patterson remained hopeful of better things.[67] As he wrote to his sister, Frances, in 1863:

> Sometimes I have a vision of a small but exceedingly beautiful Gothic chapel, rich inside with marbles and stained glass and carved stalls and encaustic tiles and brass screen work. I have a feeling that a certain use of really good ornaments may be desirable, and being on a very small scale it might be possible to make a very perfect thing. . . . It may come some day, and most probably long after I am dead and gone. . . . [A] really noble Church is a wonderful instrument of education, if we think only of the lower way of regarding it.[68]

It would come much sooner than he or anyone else could have imagined.

Tragically, Patteson was murdered in September 1871 while visiting the island of Nukapu, Santa Cruz. The attack was supposedly in revenge for the abduction of several native boys from the island by a European labour trader a few days earlier. Patteson instantly became a modern-day martyr, universally hailed as a missionary hero both in Britain and elsewhere. Shortly afterwards an appeal for funds was raised in England for a suitable memorial. This took the form of a building, the chapel of St Barnabas, Norfolk Island (1875–80) – the final, if untimely, realisation of that 'beautiful Gothic chapel' he had always wished for.

By this time, St Andrew's College had moved from Kohimarama to Norfolk Island (1867), the mission's new headquarters. Designed in 1874 by Thomas Graham Jackson (1835–1924), former pupil of G. G. Scott, the Patteson Memorial chapel is a small but beautifully composed structure (fig. 285). It was built using locally quarried, rough-cut reef stone, with interior finishes and fittings imported from New Zealand and England, including a marble pavement from Patteson's native Devonshire.[69] Externally, the massing is compact and unambiguous, exuding no small degree of missionary zeal. Indeed, the overall form of the chapel, with its clean-cut (to the point of abstract) delineation, has the appearance of being at once crude yet refined – undoubtedly a deliberate ploy on the part of the architect, given the building's location and context.[70] Internally, it presents a carefully arranged and decorated space (fig. 286). The layout is collegiate, with seating running parallel to the nave, while the apsidal east end is distinguished by a beautifully carved, dark walnut reredos, with banded stone walling. Placed immediately before the entrance to the nave is an extraordinarily powerful, octagonal-shaped font of black and salmon-pink Torquay and Devonshire marble. But perhaps the most significant element of the chapel's decorative programme is the stained glass, notably the five windows around the chancel. These are by Morris & Co., from the

285 St Barnabas's church (Patteson Memorial chapel), Norfolk Island, New Zealand (1875–80), by T. G. Jackson.

hand of Edward Burne-Jones (1833–1898), and depict the four evangelists and the Lord as 'Rex Omnipotens'. They are considered among the artist's finest work.[71]

There are, however, particular aspects of the chapel's formation that warrant further consideration and that communicate something of the mission's spiritual ethos. If we look at the fronts and ends of the stalls, for example, we find decorative carvings and inlaid shell-work, which point to a particular type of association (fig. 287). This work was carried out under the direction of the Rev. Robert H. Codrington (1830–1922), a friend of Jackson, and executed by Melanesian (Ulawa) boys resident at the college. Apart from traditional Christian scenes and symbols, the work contains a number of indigenous patterns and motifs. This carefully orchestrated cross-fertilisation of sacred and symbolic traditions, European and Melanesian, is representative of the theological approach that characterised the mission from its very beginning. Selwyn, Patteson and Codrington all believed that the missionary approach in Melanesia ought to be based around a thorough understanding and incorporation of indigenous beliefs and custom, where appropriate.

This missiology was designed to dispel the myths surrounding the notion of heathenism, in the process proving the universal efficacy of Christian truth, irrespective of outward appearances. Here developmental theology was an important factor in so far as 'truth' could not reveal itself but had to be 'interpreted' – this was the responsibility of an organised Church. Patteson and his colleagues were informed in this approach by the writings of Anglican divines such as Richard Hooker and Joseph Butler, as well as by the contemporary biblical scholarship of Joseph

286 Interior of St Barnabas's church, Norfolk Island (1875–80), looking east to the altar.

Lightfoot and Brooke Westcott.[72] As with their UMCA counterparts, the Melanesian missionaries, through their interpretative methodology, were able to set themselves apart from other Protestant (especially evangelical) missions that worked to erase rather than incorporate 'savage' or 'uncivilised' tendencies among their converts.

The incorporation of indigenous motifs in the decorative programme at the Patteson Memorial chapel can therefore be viewed as a formal manifestation of the mission's particular theological position, as opposed to merely a general aesthetization of the building's 'exotic' location. This is all the more plausible given that Codrington oversaw the entire process. Educated at Charterhouse, then Wadham College, Oxford (BA 1852), Codrington took control of the mission upon Patteson's death until the appointment of a new bishop in 1877. Like Patteson, he was a very sensitive man and a gifted linguist, who would later become a leading scholar of Melanesian culture.[73] Although he had certain misgivings about the plausibility of erecting such a building in the South Pacific, Codrington was on hand from the laying of the foundation stone in 1875 to the chapel's consecration and official opening in 1880. He was even involved in its construction, himself carving the capitals for the marble window shafts.[74] One of Codrington's key theological concepts was that of mediation, which he took from his reading of Butler. As Sara Sohmer has observed, mediation was a process of applying an understanding of the familiar to the unfamiliar. Codrington believed that the Gospel had to be presented in such a way that its relevance was apparent to general human conditions.[75] This would enable Melanesians to 'see that they themselves, without any teaching from us, know and recognize . . . some higher association than their own'.[76] In following this precept, Codrington was able to play on the indigenous concept of *mana*, a higher, supernatural force distinct from, but apparent in, the physical world, similar to the Christian notion of God almighty.[77]

Codrington's approach to mission also found resonance in the building's exterior. As a supreme example of High Victorian muscularity in ecclesiastical design, the Patteson Memorial chapel represented a particular type of church. Like St Philip's, Grahamstown, it was part of that genre in Victorian church architecture that was, as Henry White had so aptly observed, 'aggressive upon the world'.[78] It exuded all that 'abstract power and awfulness' that John Ruskin had come to identify with the true spirit of Gothic architecture, the 'savageness' that to his mind characterised its most impressive and enduring qualities. Thus, the uncompromising primitiveness of the chapel – its bold geometry and formal reduction – spoke of a forthrightness and manly vigour that captured precisely the mission's purpose and determination. As Codrington observed at the time, it had 'no rival in that hemisphere'.[79]

287 Stall end from St Barnabas's church, Norfolk Island (1875–80), containing inlaid shell-work, based on indigenous decorative motifs.

But, as the missionaries understood all too well, 'savageness' was a relative concept. As Patteson put it in 1859: 'It is strange to be living so peacefully among nations accounted savage & fighting each other, while you highly educated & civilized individuals [Europeans] act your barbarism on a more exalted scale & with a far greater refinement. It is very savage indeed to spear 3 or 4 men, but exceedingly valiant to leave about 3,000 dead in the field slain by the Enfield rifle . . . What scene in Melanesia ever exceeded the horrors of the sack of a town by British troops?'[80] In this respect, the memorial chapel was a truly a 'savage' construct – the ultimate, perhaps. In mediating, at the point of intersection, between two worlds, between two opposing but essentially equal states of savagery, it at once collapsed these perceived states of being and monumentalised their apparent relativity. Given the explicit and avowed theological position of the Melanesian Mission, the chapel's architecture can therefore be understood as a formalist lesson in interpretative missiology, 'preaching' to the world, as Beresford Hope would have it, the liberal and progressive credentials of a new religious civilisation. Its effect was profound. It not only proved a great attraction, thus aiding the mission in its cause, but was also replicated time and again, both in part and in full, throughout Melanesia.[81] It truly was, as Patteson had hoped, a 'very perfect thing'.

Meanwhile, some four thousand miles north-east of Norfolk Island, in the Kingdom of Hawai'i, preparations were under way to erect the cathedral designed by William Slater. Formerly referred to as the Sandwich Islands, Hawai'i was not official British territory. Rather, it was a one-time protectorate (1794–1843), over which Britain still maintained a degree of cultural and economic influence. The cathedral project was inspired by the appointment of the Rev. Thomas Nettleship Staley (1823–1898) as the Anglican bishop of Honolulu in 1861. Staley found himself in the Hawaiian Islands at the recommendation of Bishop Samuel Wilberforce, who had, through Queen Victoria,

288 Interior perspective of William Slater's initial design for Honolulu cathedral (detail), from *The Ecclesiologist* (1862).

received a personal request on behalf of King Kamehameha IV and his wife, Emma.[82] This request was made not only because the king had come to appreciate the ritualistic expression of Anglicanism more than any other form of Christian worship, but also because he wished to bolster the legitimacy of his own crown against the increasing political encroachment of the United States (which officially annexed Hawai'i in 1897).[83] Staley, it turned out, was precisely the man king Kamehameha was looking for – so much so that he joined battle almost immediately with the American Congregationalist missionaries ('Puritans', as he called them) who had dominated the religious scene in Hawai'i since the early nineteenth century. Like many of his colleagues elsewhere at the time, Staley was a steadfast Tractarian, having been a student, then fellow at Queens' College, Cambridge, during the 1840s. His doctrinal inclinations extended to architecture, leading him to become a member of the Cambridge Camden Society in 1844. He was, of course, a keen advocate of the cathedral project, being fully cognisant of architecture's role in both framing and emphasising the ritualistic dimensions of Anglican worship.

Slater's design went through at least two iterations. As discussed in earlier chapters, the initial design (1862) (see fig. 174), which Staley carried with him from England, was for an exceptionally plain, even abstract, structure in the

289 Interior perspective of the revised scheme for Honolulu cathedral by William Slater and R. H. Carpenter, from *The Ecclesiologist* (1866).

290 Exterior perspective drawing (with plan) of William Slater's and R. H. Carpenter's revised scheme for Honolulu cathedral, 1866, from *Building News* (1867).

'massive unchamfered Early Pointed of the middle and south of France'.[84] Its severity was broken only by the occasional flourish of carved woodwork and an elaborate programme of religious murals (fig. 288). The second and final set of plans (1866), designed in conjunction with R. H. Carpenter (Richard Cromwell's son), was a rehashing of Slater's competition entry for the Crimean War Memorial church, employing a slightly 'lighter' style of architecture to 'suit the Hawaiian temperament'.[85] This design was solicited directly by Queen Emma herself while on a fund-raising expedition to England in 1865, with the intention that it would double as a memorial to her late husband, who had died unexpectedly of an asthma attack in November 1863.[86] Internally, a resolute but decorative early French Gothic was considered appropriate, composed of Doulting, Ketton and Bath stone imported from England (fig. 289).[87] Oregon pine was specified for the ceiling, while the windows were to be fitted with timber Venetians to the interior. Externally, it was more of a mixture, with elements of transitional French and Italian Gothic, accompanied by a dash of Early English for good measure (fig. 290). All of this, of course, was a response to the climate, and represents one of the better and more interesting examples of Tropical Pointed ecclesiology during the mid-nineteenth century. In this respect, the church bears comparison with St George's, Basseterre (St Kitts), which Slater had designed a decade earlier (see pp. 137–8). The first phase of construction was completed in 1886, and the cathedral, known as St Andrew's, officially opened on Christmas Day that year. Subsequent phases were completed in 1888, 1908 and 1958.

South Asia

South Asia was a difficult field for Anglican missionaries. The pre-existing religions of Buddhism, Hinduism and Islam (and their variants) had been entrenched in local culture and custom for centuries. To convince the native population that Christianity was somehow better and 'truer' than what they already knew was an uphill struggle, particularly in a society where distinctions in social rank were ingrained and dependent upon established religious tradition. Moreover, up until 1858 the East India Company, which controlled British interests in the region, resisted what it perceived as the meddling and destabilising influence of Christian missionaries. Although missionaries received some concessions by government order in 1813, they were never welcomed with open arms. Nearly all missionary accounts of the mid-nineteenth century repeat the same basic complaint, that the successes were small and the reversals frequent. As resources were scarce and the distances to be covered vast, it is hardly surprising that clergy were difficult to recruit.[88] Thus, the combined forces of politics, native propriety and penury conspired against easy gains in the field.[89]

As elsewhere in the British empire, the confusion caused by the presence of other Christian denominations, especially Roman Catholics and German Lutherans, added to these difficulties. To be sure, Christians had been active in South Asia for nearly two millennia: the Syrian Church traced its origins back to the arrival of the apostle Thomas at Malankara in AD 52, and later Jesuit missionaries arrived, beginning with Francis Xavier in 1541. Protestants were, therefore, very much latecomers on the scene. In places 'where there is one Clergyman of the Reformed and Scriptural Church of England,' it was noted with regret by the archdeacon of Madras in 1848, 'there are often several ministers of that Church [Roman] which proclaims "another Gospel"'.[90] Alarm at this apparent lack of zeal on the part of the English Church reached fever pitch with the Indian Mutiny in 1857. This event was interpreted by many, both High and Low, as divine retribution for Britain's negligence with regard to evangelisation.[91] Thus, rather than curtail missionary activity on the basis of some misguided notion that Christianity had been the root cause of the rebellion (as some MPs and many EIC officials believed), the Church was called upon to redouble its efforts in accordance with the professed faith of the nation. Although the results failed to match the rhetoric, advances were made in the far south of the country in Tamil Nadu, especially around Tinnevelly (Tirunelveli).[92]

Despite the strong Evangelical character of Anglicanism in South Asia, the Church of England did make some progress architecturally. However, as mentioned earlier, much of this was rather generic and 'incorrect' in character, owing to the input of military engineers. Churches of this kind were built in garrisons and hill stations throughout India and modern-day Pakistan, such as St John's, Peshawar (1852–60) (fig. 291), Holy Trinity, Murree (*c.*1855), and Christ Church, Simla (1844–57).[93] But not all were struck in this mould. For instance, we have seen already how, under the leadership of Bishop Daniel Wilson, much was accomplished in terms of church building in the vicinity of Calcutta. In Uttar Pradesh there was not only the magnificent cathedral at Allahabad but also the striking All Souls' Memorial church, Kanpur (1862–75), designed by Walter Granville, with its richly coloured, Italianate Gothic exterior (see fig. 197).[94] The Bombay churches of William Emerson, too, were altogether different, if not unique, such as the wonderfully muscular Emmanuel Mission church, Girgaum (1867–9), built for the Church Missionary Society.[95]

There were also the efforts of Bishop Chapman in Colombo and Point-de-Galle in Ceylon. The 1850s and 1860s witnessed a spate of church-building activity in Ceylon as the Church of England began to expand its influence along the southern coast and into the coffee-planting districts of the central highlands. The churches at Nuwara Eliya (Holy Trinity, 1852), Hultsdorf (All Saints', 1865) and Tangalle (Christ Church, 1870) all represent efforts at aspiring to a more consistent and 'churchlike' form of Anglican ecclesiology (fig. 292). Chapman was particularly gratified by the completion of the church in Nuwara Eliya. Travelling there in February 1852, he observed with elation how it formed 'not only the brightest ecclesiastical ornament of the diocese, but an abiding witness, I trust, of Christian truth, and our Churches [*sic*] vitality in the centre and on the very summit of this heathen land'. Chapman perceived this building as extending a direct challenge to Buddhism on its own turf. Just as 'Buddhism has its shrine (a mere shed) on the summit of Adam's Peak, 7,800 feet above the sea level,' he relayed in a letter to Ernest Hawkins, 'Christianity has [now] built its nobler sanctuary on the elevated plains of Newara Eliya, direct

from which rises Pedro Tarasalla, the apex of Ceylon, to the height of above 8,200'.[96] Holy Trinity, Nurwara Eliya, had become Chapman's very own Temple Mount.

In Calcutta there was evidence of substantial church building during the 1860s. In 1861, for example, G. G. Scott produced a set of plans for a church that would later become known as St James the Great, Lower Circular Road (1862–4).[97] However, as had become common practice in South Asia, these plans were 'rejected' in favour of a design produced by a locally based architect, in this case C. G. Wray. Locally produced designs of this kind were often, in reality, nothing more than remodelled or diminished versions of original plans, bordering on plagiarism. Scott's original drawings for St James's no longer survive, and such a fate may have befallen them. A surviving watercolour perspective in the Asian Collections at the Victoria and Albert Museum shows Wray's alternative design for St James's, which was exhibited at the Royal Academy in 1864 (fig. 293).[98] Although there is no way of knowing what Scott's original design looked like, Wray's perspective is not

Top 291 St John's church, Peshawar, British India (1852–60).

Bottom 292 Engraving of Holy Trinity church, Nuwara Eliya, Ceylon (1852) (Bodleian Library, Oxford).

unlike something Scott would have produced for such a context. Indeed, it has many similarities to his almost contemporaneous design (1863) for Holy Trinity, Shanghai (fig. 294).[99] In both cases there is a characteristic use of corbelling between storeys and along the gable ends, which would appear to be more than coincidental. There is also a distinctly Lombardic spirit to both designs, including the use of wheel windows.

However, it seems unlikely (though not impossible) that Scott would have specified a rendered exterior for a brick building of this kind. As at Shanghai, the church in Calcutta provided the perfect opportunity to showcase the spectacular polychrome effects of Italianate Gothic. Moreover, the interior of the building, with its rather clumsy detailing, is not something that would have come from the hand of Scott. One possible scenario is that Wray, in 'redesigning' the church, retained much of Scott's impressive exterior while reducing the scale and splendour (and therefore the cost) of the interior.[100] The problem here is that the interior as built does not match the description given of Wray's design in *The Ecclesiologist*. A further complication is that Walter Granville's name was also associated with the church, possibly linking it to his design for All Souls', Kanpur.[101]

Top 293 Watercolour by C. G. Wray, 1864, of his design for the church of St James the Great, Lower Circular Road, Calcutta (1862–4) (Victoria and Albert Museum, London).

Bottom 294 Engraving of the Anglican cathedral of the Holy Trinity, Shanghai (1866–9), by G. G. Scott, from the *Illustrated London News* (1877).

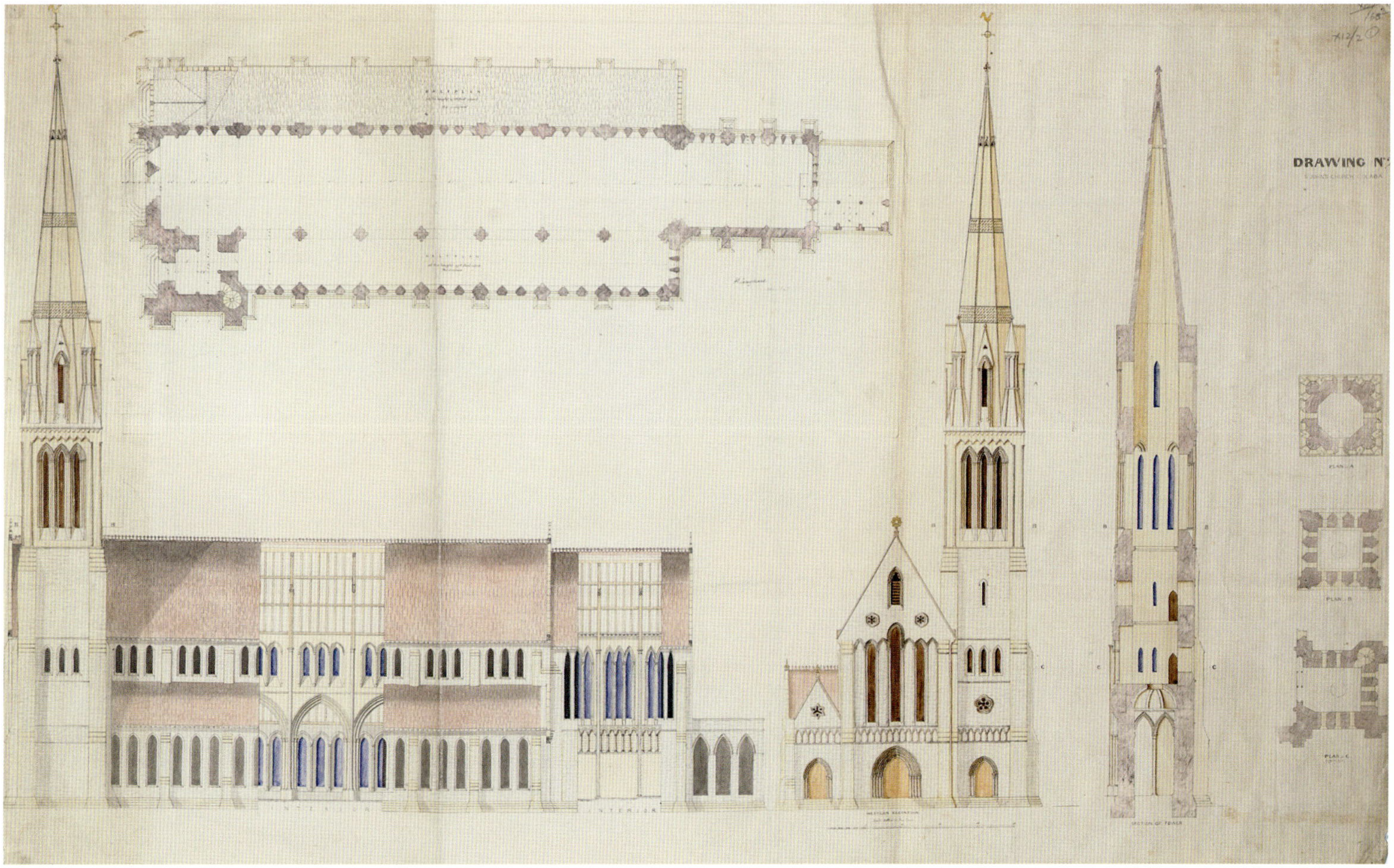

295 Design drawings by Henry Conybeare for St John's church (the Afghan Memorial church), Colaba, Bombay, *c.*1849 (RIBA Drawings Collection, Victoria and Albert Museum, London).

Whatever the case may have been, it would seem beyond the realms of fortuity that St James the Great and Holy Trinity, Shanghai, are so similar in their general form and detail if Scott had not had a hand in both. If this scenario is correct, then, when his Calcutta plans were rejected, Scott may have recycled aspects of his design for Shanghai. This would account for the similarities and timing.

Among the most concerted efforts at ecclesiological correctness in India during this period was St John the Evangelist, Colaba, Bombay (1847–65). As we saw in Chapter 3, this church was intended as a memorial to the Sind and Afghan campaigns of 1838–43, and was encouraged along principled architectural lines by the chaplain to the East India Company, the Rev. George Pigott (see pp. 129–30). However, after J. M. Derick's initial proposal was rejected in 1845, Bartle Frere, an administrator for the East India Company in the Bombay presidency, obtained an alternative design by G. G. Scott in 1847 through the Oxford Architectural Society.[102] But this too was rejected on economic grounds. The task eventually fell to the town engineer at Bombay, Henry Conybeare (1823–1884), who based his design in part on Scott's.[103] The Ecclesiological Society received a lithograph of the scheme in 1849, describing aspects of it as 'lamentable' but otherwise approving 'the general *animus* of the undertaking'. The bulk of the criticism related to Conybeare's poor attempt at adapting the building to the prevailing climatic conditions, especially as the project had been at the centre of early discussions concerning the development of Tropical Pointed architecture.[104]

In the event, Conybeare only got as far as producing a set of design drawings before standing down as town engineer in 1850 (fig. 295). In his place came Captain C. W.

296 St John's church (the Afghan Memorial church), Colaba (1850–7), by Henry Conybeare.

Tremenheere of the Royal (late Bombay) Engineers as superintending architect. While overseeing construction of the building, Tremenheere altered Conybeare's design in a number of ways. He not only reduced the pitch of the roof but also lowered the height of the tower. No doubt these alterations had much to do with concerns over cost, but Tremenheere insisted that the church still satisfied the 'requirements of the style'. Not so, according to Conybeare, who must have felt more than a little aggrieved at the unsympathetic alteration of his plans during his absence in England.[105] Although an engineer by training, Conybeare would have considered himself far more knowledgeable than Tremenheere in matters of ecclesiology. He not only grew up in close proximity to Gothic architecture (his father was dean of Llandaff cathedral) but later wrote a book on the subject, rather ironically entitled *The Ten Canons of Proportion and Composition in Gothic Architecture* (1868).

Another reason why Tremenheere would have been compelled to alter the design was that Conybeare's drawings were somewhat vague. The assistant garrison engineer, H. G. Wilcox, complained that the 'plans and estimates afford little information and only give general ideas of what was proposed to be done. There are no detailed plans or specifications sufficiently explicit to shew [*sic*] what was

297 The chancel wall of St John's church (the Afghan Memorial church), Colaba, 1879, showing decorative tiles designed by William Butterfield, in conjunction with students from the Sir Jamsetjee Jeejeebhoy School of Art.

intended.'[106] Nevertheless, work progressed steadily throughout the 1850s, and the building was all but complete (minus the tower) in 1857, allowing consecration to take place in November that year (fig. 296).

Much of the impetus behind continuing the work in a proper and dignified manner was maintained by Pigott's successor, the Rev. Philip Anderson (1816–1857), graduate of Corpus Christi College, Cambridge (BA 1838). By all accounts, Anderson had clear Tractarian leanings, having been among the list of subscribers to the *Library of the Fathers*. He was, according to his obituary, someone who attributed 'great value to the ritual and ceremony of Prayer and Praise', and was particularly concerned 'that the delights of Sound, of Colour, and of Form' were turned to their proper use in the glorification of God.[107] To be sure, the result, as *The Ecclesiologist* was quick to note, may not have been perfect, but there is little doubt that if it had not been for the efforts of Pigott, Conybeare, Tremenheere, Anderson and others, St John's would probably have been just another nondescript garrison church in the 'Commissioners' Gothic' or 'Government Grecian' mould. Despite its apparent failure to take account of the climate, the building (especially its interior) remains among India's most accomplished and attractive specimens of Anglican ecclesiology. The original set of forty-two stained glass windows were by William Wailes of Newcastle, while designs for some of the benches, seats, choir stalls and Minton tile patterns for the walls and floor were supplied by William Butterfield (fig. 297).[108]

Canada and the Cape

As discussed in Chapter 2, British North America was, for a time at least, at the forefront of colonial ecclesiology. Owing mainly to the zeal of its early bishops, colonies such as New Brunswick, Ontario and Newfoundland not only erected church buildings far superior to anything that had come before but also involved some of the leading lights of ecclesiastical architecture in Britain. The 1850s and 1860s was a period of consolidation and experiment in this region, especially with respect to parish church design in urban and suburban centres. As the settler population increased, and cities and towns grew, so too did the need for additional church accommodation.

As Tractarian-style churchmanship was reasonably widespread in Canada, even during the 1840s, one can find there the seeds of ecclesiological correctness in the design of small churches from earliest times. Perhaps the best-known example of this is St Anne's chapel, Fredericton (1845–7) (see fig. 240), orchestrated by Bishop Medley and designed by Frank Wills. Loosely based on that well-known exemplar of Longstanton, Cambridgeshire, this building was a knowing and relatively sophisticated interpretation of Early English Gothic. In a sense, it would prove something of a model for small-church design in the Canadian provinces, with its low walls and steeply pitched roof setting the tone for years to come. Moreover, its perfectly arranged and neatly decorated interior, with free and open seating, soon established the high-water mark of what was possible in that part of the world. As Phoebe Stanton observed, when complete, St Anne's was the finest small church on the North American continent, while Wills himself described it as 'the first ecclesiastical building

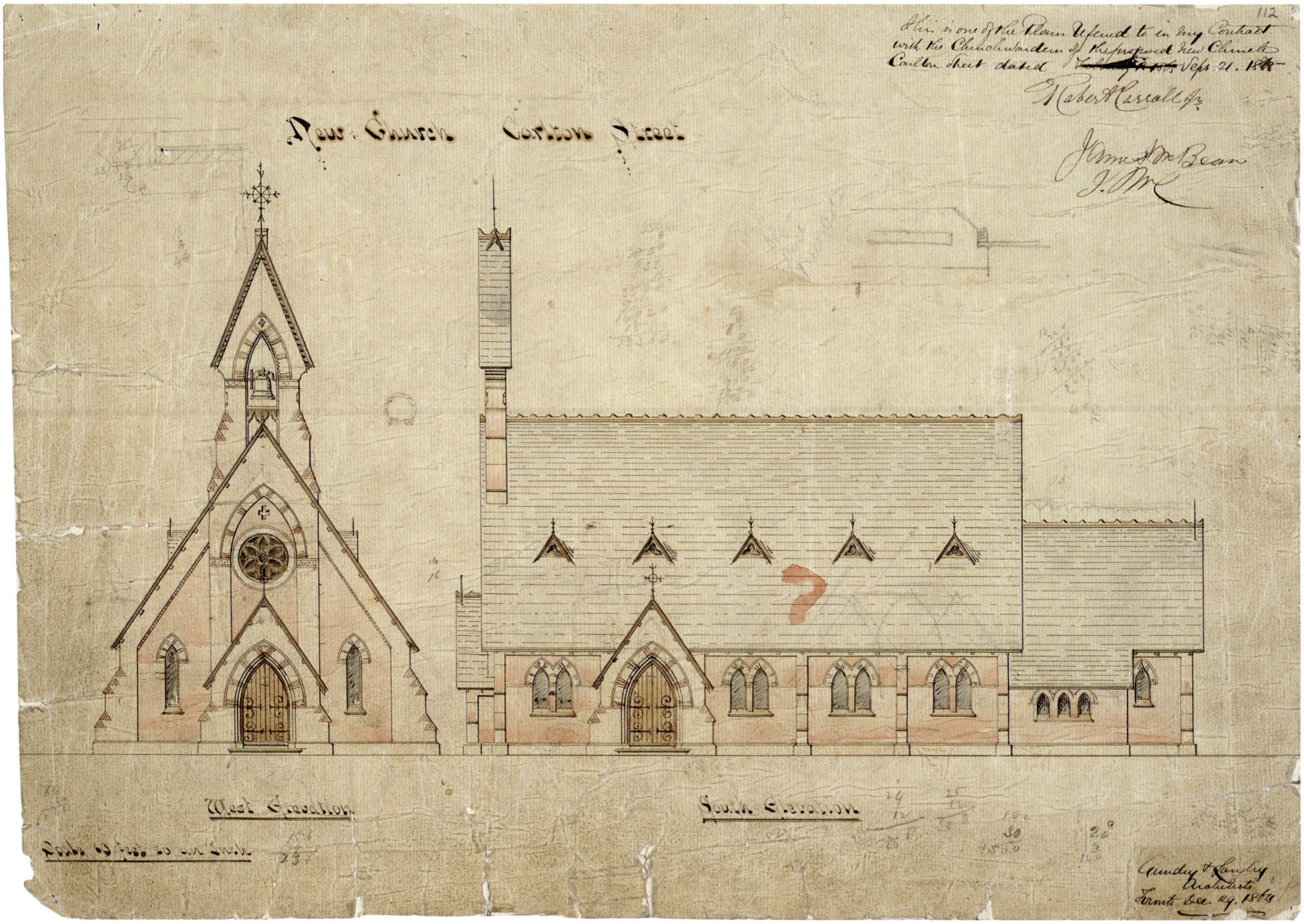

298 Elevation drawings of Henry Langley's design for St Peter's church, Carleton Street, Toronto (1864) (Toronto Public Library).

erected in the British provinces on which Ancient Architecture has been attempted to be honestly carried out'.[109]

Small churches in this vein began appearing elsewhere in Canada over the next two decades. In Toronto there came not only the distinctive brick and stone edifice of St Stephen-in-the-Fields (1858) by Thomas Fuller, but also the impressive polychrome structure of St Peter's, Carleton Street (1864), by Henry Langley, former pupil of William Hay (figs 298 and 299). In the vicinity of Ottawa rose the equally striking St John the Baptist, Lyn (1860–9), and St Paul's, Almonte (1863–4); while in the city proper there appeared St Bartholomew's (1866–8) and St Alban the Martyr (1867–77) (fig. 300).[110] All of these buildings perpetuate that characteristic appearance of very low walls and high-pitched roofs, imparting an exceptionally strong if somewhat idiomatic sense of geometric (that is, triangular) compactness. In this respect they echo buildings elsewhere in the Anglican world, such as Benjamin Mountfort's timber church at Kaiapoi, New Zealand (see p. 56).

Architecturally, these small churches had moved far beyond the rather orthodox style of St Anne's, occupying territory that was more properly High Victorian. Their distinctive massing undoubtedly originated in a need to adapt to the climate, especially the requirement to shed copious amounts of snow. This led to a very identifiable 'type', through a playful emphasis on particular forms and features. The recurrence of narrow, finely pointed lancets in the later Ottawa examples, for instance, or the use of polychrome

299 The church of St Stephen-in-the-Fields, Toronto (1858), by Thomas Fuller.

300 The church of St Alban the Martyr, Ottawa (1867–77), by Thomas Fuller and partners.

brickwork at Toronto, also confirms the progressive nature of this architecture. It was as if Beresford Hope's call for a Streetian-style ecclesiology in Canada had been heeded.

But church architects in Canada were developing (or rather rehearsing) theories of their own by this time. William Hay is one example. In an article for the *Anglo-American Magazine* entitled 'Architecture for the Meridian of Canada', Hay observed that, although 'we can scarcely hope to see a distinct style of pure architecture formed on the primitive log hut, something may be done to lead the taste of the Province into a direction which may tend to give a local character to our Canadian edifices'. In suggesting this he was combining Laugier's concept of origins with Pugin's notion of integrity, and applying these directly to the Canadian context. Here he pointed to the frontier log hut – a building that had been shaped in a distinctive way by the peculiar demands of climate and purpose – noting that 'utility and reality' were its fundamental principles.[111] Of special note in these huts were their high-pitched roofs, necessary for 'throwing off the snow and to deflect the rays of the summer sun'. Thus, rather than blindly follow the 'pagan schools of Greece and Rome', it appeared rather more sensible to concede that 'the Old English style of building is admirably adapted to the climate of Canada. Its high pitched roof, and weathered projections are just what are needed for protection against the snow and rain'.[112] The union of these two 'original types' (the frontier log hut and the old English house) would result in that elusive 'local character' so desired in modern Canadian architecture, especially in ecclesiastical buildings.[113]

301 St James the Less funeral chapel, St James's Cemetery, Parliament Street, Toronto (1857–61), by Frederic Cumberland and W. G. Storm.

Some of the architects involved in the design of churches in Canada also had English experience. Thomas Fuller (1823–1898), for example, who (along with his partners Chilion Jones and King Arnoldi) had designed St Stephen-in-the-Fields, the churches at Lyn and Almonte, and St Alban's, Ottawa, emigrated from Bath to Toronto in 1857. He would therefore have been familiar with the seismic shift that occurred in Victorian church design in England during the 1850s, bringing this knowledge with him to Canada.

Another immigrant architect was Fred Cumberland, who was responsible for St James's cathedral, Toronto (see p. 80). If this building was a less than successful attempt at extending the principles of English ecclesiology to the North American continent, then Cumberland seems to have learnt the lesson. His later effort, St James the Less funeral chapel (1857–61) at St James's Cemetery, Parliament Street, Toronto, designed in conjunction with W. G. Storm, was much more in keeping with what the Ecclesiological Society would have appreciated (fig. 301). Cumberland was no doubt assisted in this remarkable turn-around by his visit to England in the mid-1850s, from where, like Fuller, he returned with much new-found wisdom. As Shirley Morriss has observed, the rural nature of the site called for a picturesque response in terms of formal arrangement and massing.[114] The result is an exquisitely composed, asymmetrical configuration, with all the compact virility of true High Victorian architecture. To be sure, the base arrangement is orthodox, with articulated nave and chancel to the exterior, but this is offset by a strongly buttressed, protruding south-west tower and elongated western porch in timber. The walls are thick, and the forms stout and heavy, relieved only by the small, interspersed windows (lancet,

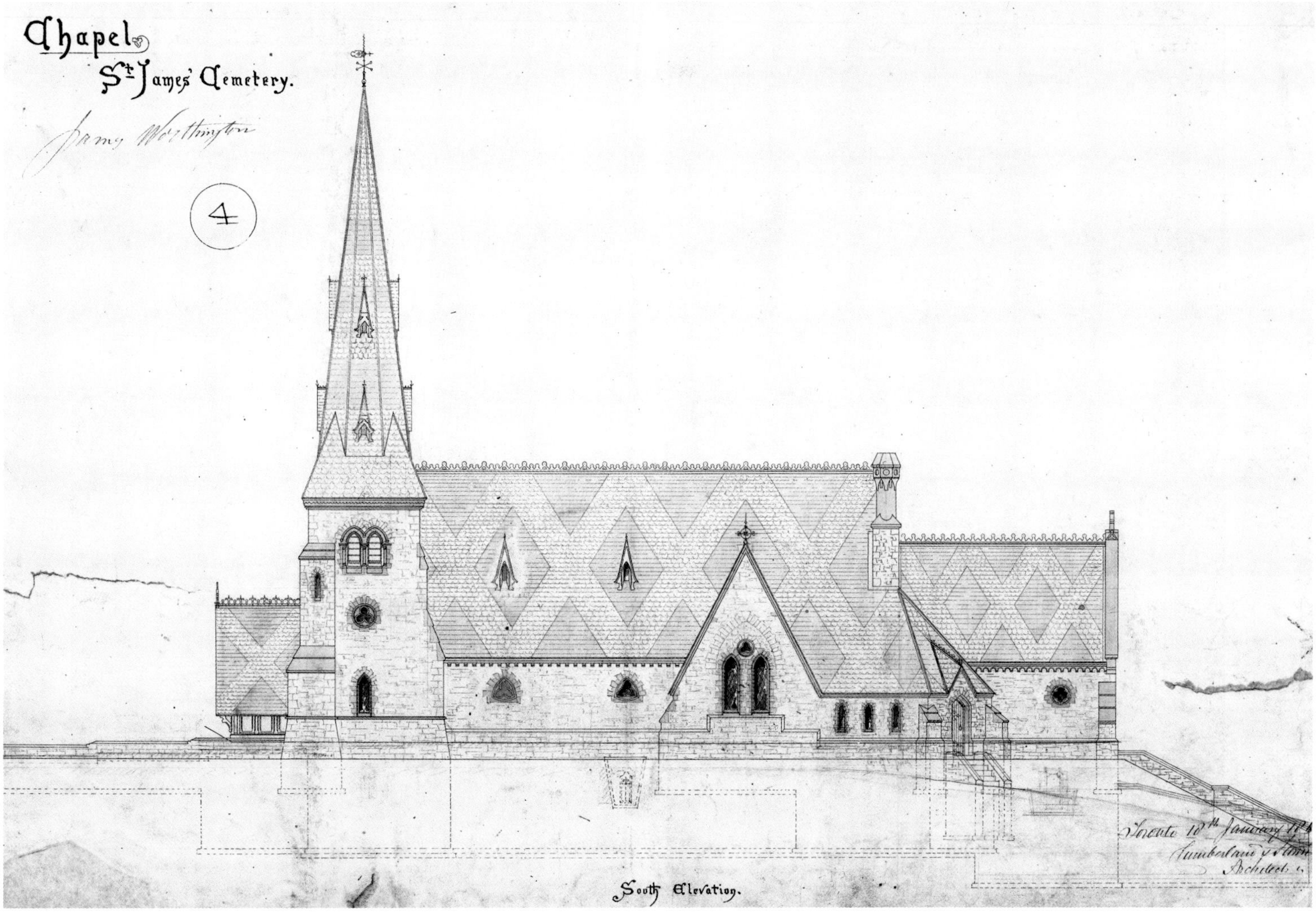

trefoil and quatrefoil) and the odd flourish of sculptural detail, including a diapered roof pattern (fig. 302). This severity continues inside, with large, uninterrupted surfaces of cream-coloured Toronto brick, over which hangs an impressive trussed roof. The most striking aspect of the interior, however, are the splayed window reveals, cut deep into the north and south walls, giving the space a sense of sculptural dynamism (fig. 303). It is details such as this that make St James the Less a gem of colonial ecclesiology.

Top 302 South elevation drawing for St James the Less funeral chapel, Toronto, by Frederic Cumberland and W. G. Storm, 1857 (Archives of Ontario, Toronto).

Bottom 303 South aisle window, interior view, St James the Less funeral chapel, Toronto (1857–61).

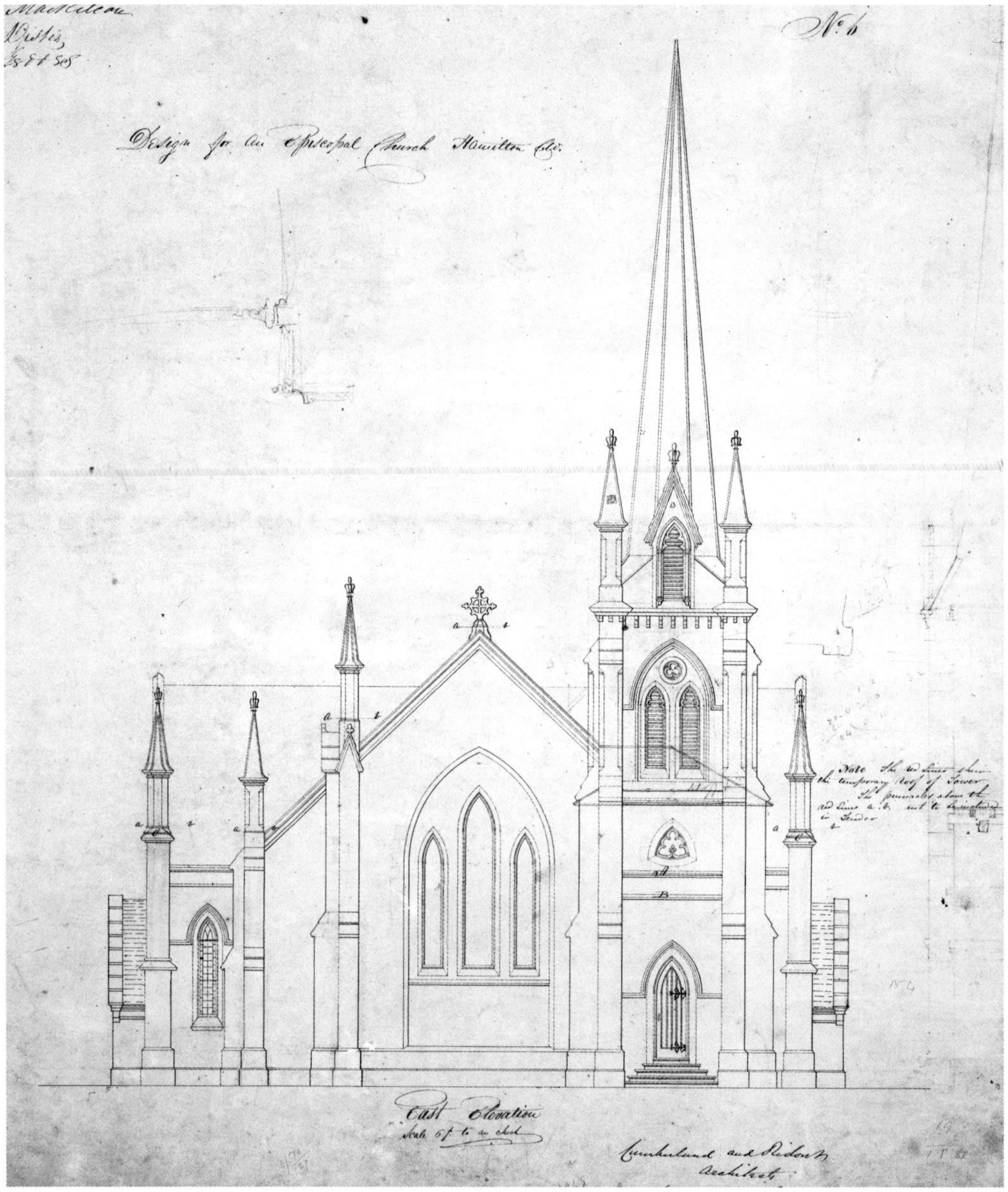

304 East elevation drawing for Frederic Cumberland's design for the Church of the Ascension, Hamilton, Ontario, 1850 (Archives of Ontario, Toronto).

Cumberland designed only one other Anglican church in his lifetime, the Church of the Ascension in Hamilton, Ontario (fig. 304). Built in 1850–1, this building was conceived before his return visit to England and is therefore of the same species as his design for St James's cathedral. It presents a mixture of periods and styles, and would definitely have been on the suspect list for *The Ecclesiologist*. However, here Cumberland introduces the same element of asymmetry as in the funeral chapel by positioning the tower off centre, this time at the north-east corner of the building. Although the chancel was extended after a fire in 1887, so changing the position of this feature in relation to the body of the building, its placement demonstrated Cumberland's growing awareness of certain developments in formal massing and arrangement in ecclesiastical design emanating from England; perhaps Cumberland was thinking of R. C. Carpenter's vision for St Paul's, Brighton (1846), a view of which had appeared in *The Ecclesiologist*.[115]

As with Mountfort in New Zealand, it is possible that Cumberland and other Canadian architects were influenced by models such as those illustrated in Truefitt's *Designs for Country Churches* (1850), or perhaps the ancient specimens contained in Raphael and J. Arthur Brandon's *Parish Churches* (1851).[116] The same weighty, voluminous and 'roofy' character of Truefitt's designs is certainly evident at St James the Less, as in many of the other churches mentioned above – examples, perhaps, of Truefitt's call '*to think* in "Gothic", exclusive of actual authority'.[117] Cumberland would also have been aware of Hay's utterances on the subject by the mid-1850s (fig. 305). Such buildings seemed to answer the needs and anxieties of Anglican clergy in expressing the determination and resolve of the English Church in British North America.

Other designs for Canada began appearing in professional journals at around the same time. For example, in 1858 *The Builder* published an interior view, looking east, of a solid Middle-Pointed design for St Paul's, Yorkville (Bloor Street), while the *Architect and Contract Reporter* carried a similar illustration of a proposal by C. Hodgson Fowler for St George's, Lennoxville (1869) (fig. 306).[118] St Paul's demonstrates that it was in fact liberal Evangelicals in the diocese of Toronto who were leading the way in progressing the cause of Anglican ecclesiology. Both internally and externally, this building was the most correct and advanced Anglican church in the city at the time of its completion (fig. 307). Though composed in a predominantly Decorated idiom, its understated muscular character, with powerfully articulated north transept, octagonal bell turret and banded roof tiling, gave it a definite, if restrained, High Victorian sensibility.

305 William Hay's design for Christ Church, Brampton, Ontario, from the *Anglo-American Magazine* (1854).

NEW CHURCH AT BRAMPTON.

There is no evidence that Fowler's proposal was ever carried out, but it is nevertheless interesting for its rich, polychrome effect. The architect's intent certainly suggested something spectacular: 'The church will be built of local brick, red and black being used for the exterior, and white and red for the interior. The black on the outside and the red inside have been sparingly used, and in purely architectural lines. Stone is difficult to obtain, but a white marble is much used, and the simple forms of the capitals and window tracery have been designed for its use. The nave and chancel piers are of polished red Aberdeen granite.' Precautions were also introduced for the climate: 'All the windows are to be double glazed, the exterior glazing being of plateglass, in wrought-iron frames, the interior, cathedral or painted glass. All the entrances have double doors.'[119] The plans also show a narthex for this purpose. If built, St George's would certainly have been one of the largest and most progressive specimens of Anglican ecclesiology in Canada.

William Hay was also active on this front. After his experience with Scott's cathedral in Newfoundland, he moved back to Scotland briefly, before returning around 1853 to Toronto, where he established a successful architectural practice. Amongst the many secular works he executed during his seven-year sojourn was the very neat brick church of St George, Newcastle (*c.*1856), as well as an unexecuted design for Brampton (1853) (fig. 305). The Brampton design was described in the *Anglo-American Magazine* as 'unmistakably English'. 'We have here no gingerbread work,' it was further observed, 'no gimcrackery, no useless pinnacles to give a trumpery effect to a commonplace erection; but a substantial looking edifice with low walls and high pitched roof, giving a bold and fearless outline, expressive at once of dignity and humility' – precisely what one would have expected from Hay at this time.[120]

Elsewhere there was St George's, Montreal (1869–70), by William Tutin Thomas, one-time apprentice carpenter to Charles Barry and A. W. N. Pugin. This church was erected

306 Interior perspective drawing and plan of C. Hodgson Fowler's design for St George's, Lennoxville, Quebec, from the *Architect and Contract Reporter* (1869).

307 Interior perspective drawing of St Paul's church, Yorkville (Bloor Street), Toronto (1858–60), by G. K. Radford and E. Radford, from *The Builder* (1858).

as a chapel of ease to cater for the overspill from Christ Church cathedral. Externally it is rather conservative, displaying only a modicum of formal and decorative flair, save the porch. Internally, however, Thomas gave his knowledge of, and evident love for, carpentry free range, with the introduction of an extraordinary double hammer-beam ceiling, creating an impressively large, column-free interior.

As we have seen already, further east, in New Brunswick, the discipline of timber ecclesiology had progressed admirably under the aegis of Edward Medley (see pp. 150–2). To the north, in Newfoundland, things had developed more or less along the lines laid down by the Rev. William Grey. We see this, for instance, in the timber churches of St John the Evangelist, Topsail (1861), and St James, Carbonear (1860–4). A little later there is evidence of something slightly more ambitious. St Andrew's, Brooklyn (begun 1867), for example, is more sophisticated than the Grey prototype, both formally and decoratively, with its articulated elements, including asymmetrically positioned tower, cusped lancets and trefoiled gable bordering (fig. 308).[121]

Out west, however, the situation was different. In British Columbia (formerly the district of New Caledonia), only designated an official British colony in 1858, development had been relatively slow until the discovery of gold in the late 1850s and early 1860s. With timber in abundance, missionary clergymen, following the diggers, were able to build a number of modest if ecclesiologically correct churches in wood. We have already discussed the example of Holy Trinity, New Westminster (see pp. 153–6), but other notable examples from this period include Christ Church, Hope (1861) (fig. 309), and St. John the Divine, Yale (1863). Further east, in the prairie lands of Saskatchewan and Man-

Top 308 St Andrew's church, Brooklyn, Newfoundland (begun 1867), by Caleb Marshall.

Bottom 309 Christ Church, Hope, British Columbia (1861).

310 St Clement's church, Mapleton, Manitoba (1862–3).

itoba – so called 'Red River country' – the situation was similar. Progress there had also been slow, owing mainly to the lingering presence of the Hudson's Bay Company and therefore the retarded pace of colonisation and economic development. The Rev. David Anderson (1814–1885), alumnus of Exeter College, Oxford (BA 1836), was consecrated first bishop of this territory, known as Rupert's Land, in May 1849. At this time the diocese was vast and Anderson took to moving around it, when he could, by canoe and dogsled. The earliest churches were, for the most part, extremely plain, giving little more than the impression of Gothic architecture, let alone making any pretension to ecclesiology. This was the case even up until the mid-1860s, as seen, for example, in buildings such as St Andrew's, St Andrews (1845–9), and St Clement's, Mapleton (1862–3) (fig. 310). It would not be until much later – in the 1880s and 1890s – that Anglican architecture in this part of the world was put on a proper ecclesiological footing.[122]

But there were some attempts at realising a more comely form of edifice before this time. The earliest was the timber church of St James, Winnipeg (1852–3), with its simple but churchlike proportions (fig. 311). Here the intention of the designer, the Rev. William Henry Taylor (1820–1873), was to create something based closely on medieval prototypes, although he readily admitted how difficult it was 'getting anything done correctly or properly' with the resources to hand.[123] A similar, if more impressive, structure was erected a few years later at Stanley Mission, Saskatchewan. Known as Holy Trinity (1854–60), this building was more along the lines of what William Grey had produced in Newfoundland (fig. 312). Here we have a church in wood, comprising distinct chancel, nave with aisles, and an articulated west-end bell tower, all raised on a foundation of rubblework.[124] Perhaps the most noteworthy church in the region during this period was the tiny stone cathedral

311 Engraving of St James's church, Winnipeg (1852–3), designed by the Rev. William Henry Taylor (Archives of Manitoba, Winnipeg).

312 Holy Trinity church, Stanley Mission, Saskatchewan (1854–60).

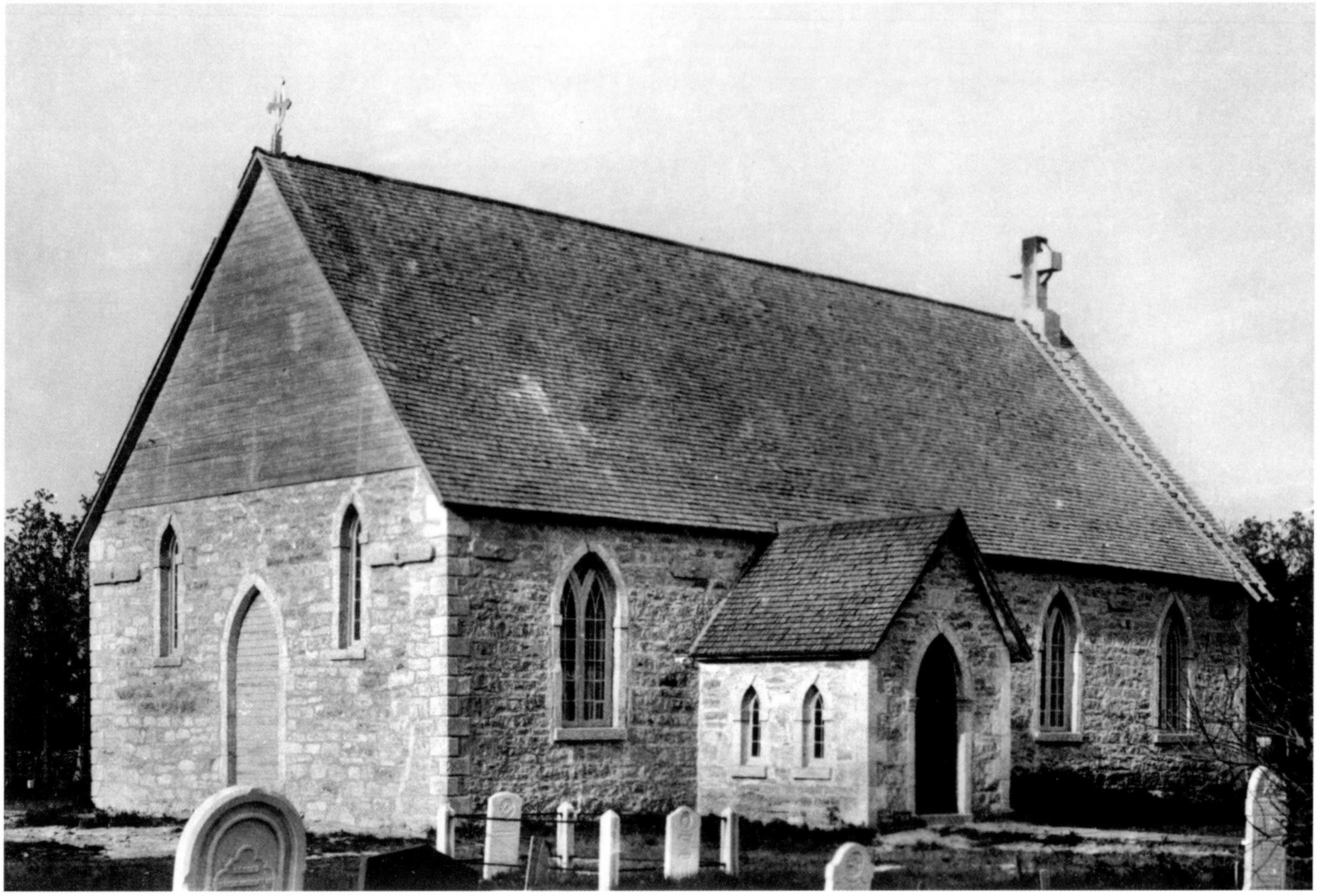

313 St John's cathedral, Winnipeg (*c.*1865).

of St John, Winnipeg (*c.*1865) (fig. 313). Although no more than a mere chapel in scale, this building was at least churchlike. Its irregular masonry construction gave it a definite air of antiquity, while its high-pitched roof with gable crosses imparted a palpable sense of ecclesiastical dignity. Under the circumstances, one cannot help but think the Ecclesiological Society would have approved. Still, it was a far cry from what had been achieved in the Atlantic Provinces by this time.

But re-creating the 'church as it should be' in the colonies was rather more difficult than some had anticipated. Among the most persistent problems in Canada, as in parts of Australia, was the lingering system of pew rents. As *The Ecclesiologist* had noted, men in England could only theorise about implementing correct church practices abroad: the real work had to be carried out by those *in situ*.[125] But not even the Ecclesiological Society would have found reason to sanction pew rents, no matter how badly in need of funds a parish or diocese claimed to be. Galleries also clung on in the colonies. We saw this earlier in the case of St Peter's, Eastern Hill, Melbourne, but St James's cathedral, Toronto, also had them. This was not in order that the 'word' might be heard more clearly, but so that more bodies might be crammed in and therefore more income generated.

To be sure, colonial bishops often had their hands tied financially, leaving them with little option but to maintain such a system if they were ever to fund major building campaigns. This was one of those predicaments, Broughton had complained, of which an endowed churchman in England 'could not easily conceive'. Church politics also intervened. It should be remembered that the abolition of box pews in certain colonial contexts was considered tantamount to Puseyism. The attempt on the part of some clergymen to sweep them away even led to charges of popery. At the heart of this anxiety, of course, as Medley, Feild, Binney and others discovered, was the perceived stripping away of lay rights and the dismantling of the parish system as a proprietary enterprise. No exchange of money meant no stake-holdings, which meant a loss of influence among the laity and the transfer of power from vestry to bishop's palace. Many colonial bishops pushed for this transfer of power for disciplinary reasons alone. But try as they might, Canadian bishops had very mixed fortunes in this regard. Despite their best efforts, neither Bishop Strachan nor Bishop Fulford, for example, was able to abolish pew rents in his cathedral.[126] In some cases, the system persisted well into the twentieth century.

In South Africa the situation – architecturally, at least – was less advanced than in the major population centres of Canada. Since the arrival of the Grays in 1848, church building in the Anglican faith had been all but monopolised by Sophy Gray, the bishop's wife. Although she was an amateur, her name has been associated with the design of nearly forty churches.[127] We have already discussed some of her more notable achievements, but it is worth making a point here about style. Because the plans that she and her husband brought with them from England dated from around the middle of the 1840s, the 'Anglo-parochial' phase in Anglican ecclesiology was perpetuated in South Africa far beyond what would have been considered its use-by date in England. To be sure, Sophy was no professional, nor could a fledgling diocese like Cape Town be expected to keep pace with the latest architectural fashions in the homeland. But mid-century Anglican architecture in South Africa does have a distinctly conservative flavour. Much like Blacket in Australia, Sophy was operating in an environment many thousands of miles removed from the source. In such a context, getting any church built was a challenge, and the Grays were obviously content to make do with what they could reasonably achieve. Nevertheless, the designs adapted by Sophy were, on the whole, correct and 'churchlike' in every respect. St Saviour's, Claremont, for example, was described in 1854 by the Rev. R. J. Mullins (then a catechist) as 'a perfect little jewel'.[128] Thus, it was clear to all that a new age of ecclesiology had dawned on the African continent, even if it was outdated by English standards.

A classic example of this persistence of style is the Armstrong Memorial chapel, Grahamstown (1856–62) (fig. 314). Built in memory of the short-lived but energetic episcopate of the Rev. John Armstrong, this building appears to have been erected to one of the original plans given to Robert and Sophy Gray by Henry Woodyer (see p. 61).[129] Although a very small and modest structure, it is nevertheless a neat and worthy specimen of its kind – again, largely typical of what passed for Anglican church architecture in the colony at the time. Indeed, it is a church that would not have looked out of place in a small rural village in England. Further examples of this kind include Holy Trinity Church, King William's Town (1850, reputedly by Charles Barry),[130] St Matthew's, Riversdale (1854), St Peter's, Cradock (1857), St Mary's, Pietermaritzburg (1858, by Bishop Colenso), All Saints', Springbok (1864), and St John's, Clanwilliam (1864).

Holy Trinity, Kalk Bay (1873) (fig. 315), is also reputed to be a Woodyer design, although the exact nature of his involvement is unclear. It may have been built to one of his original plans, or, as R. R. Langham-Carter has argued, designed afresh for Cape conditions.[131] Evidence in favour of the latter scenario can be found in the incredibly thick walls, the small, deeply recessed windows and the simple (to the point of abstract) architraves. The building also sports some rather unusual features for an 1840s design, including pronounced buttressing, ultra-minimal, chamfered mouldings around the internal doors and arches, and a huge trefoil opening in the porch. The whole has a vernacular, near rustic appearance in its use of rubblework and thatch. These features were either purposefully specified by Woodyer to meet the particular circumstances at Kalk Bay, or are the result of simplification and adaptation on the spot. Either way, some of these features have a rather High, as opposed to early, Victorian feel about them.

As discussed in Chapter 4, there were other, less architectural reasons why the earlier 'English' phase of Anglican ecclesiology was considered applicable in South Africa. In a land where making connections between religion and identity was understood to be important, the small but characteristically English churches erected throughout the province were seen as playing a particular role in transforming the landscape – not just spiritually, but culturally and politically too. The more 'identifiable' a church, the more effective it was considered to be. In such a context, the subtleties of stylistic development would have been largely lost on the colonial inhabitants. But this is not to say that something more 'modern' was not attempted. St Bartholomew's, Grahamstown (1857–60), is one such effort (fig. 316).

314 Armstrong Memorial chapel, Grahamstown, South Africa (1856–62), by Henry Woodyer and Sophy Gray.

315 Holy Trinity church, Kalk Bay, South Africa (1873), attributed to Henry Woodyer.

316 St Bartholomew's church, Grahamstown, South Africa (1857–60), by William White.

Orchestrated by Archdeacon Nathaniel Merriman, and designed by William White, this building took church architecture in South Africa to another level.[132] At first glance it hardly appears different from the churches produced by Sophy Gray. However, on closer inspection, certain details emerge that reveal its contemporary nature. For a start, we find structural polychromy in the window arches, around the opening of the porch and in the brick fence running down the north side of the building. As this was an aesthetic effect developed in England during the early 1850s, it would have been unknown to Sophy. In addition to this, there is a striking sense of muscular power and energy in the massing of forms that is quite different from that found in the churches designed by the bishop's wife. The large planar surfaces of roof and walls, combined with the strong, abstract effect of the buttressing, give a palpable impression of solidity and vigour. This is High Victorian architecture, albeit in its most stringent guise. Thus, as a building, St Bartholomew's embodies perfectly what Bishop Gray described as Merriman's 'energy, zeal, [and] self-denial' as an Anglican clergyman.[133] *The Ecclesiologist* described it as 'thoroughly good', while the *Colonial Church Chronicle* suggested that it 'seemed to embody the model of what a church might be, and could be in this country'.[134] The church was consecrated in 1860 and was an unqualified triumph for ecclesiology in the Eastern Cape. It was among the neatest and most progressive church buildings of its type anywhere in Africa, and would remain unsurpassed until the erection of St Philip's seven years later (see pp. 217–25).

While South Africa would have to wait until the 1880s for a more modern and sophisticated brand of Anglican ecclesiology brought about by the continued interventions of William White and the arrival of Herbert Baker,[135] there is a small example at Cape Town that provided something of a bridge between these two ages of church building in the colony. This is the west front of St Saviour's church, Claremont, by William Butterfield (1872–80) (fig. 317).[136] Initially intended as a memorial to Sophy Gray, who had died in 1871, it became one to the bishop as well after his death the following year. It is an example of mature Butterfield, unlike the rest of the building, which was essentially an adaptation by Sophy of Butterfield's earlier, more mimetic style (see fig. 209). The west front is a genuinely synthetic and monumental work of architecture. It surges up from the ground through the face of the building over three storeys, fully articulated, climaxing in an elegantly composed but powerful two-stage (three-arch) bellcote. The centrepiece is a beautiful three-light, reticulated window, with small ventilator slots above and below. This window was possibly one that Butterfield had designed during the earlier phases of the church's construction.[137] The erection of the west front by J. H. Sanderson was superintended *in situ* by Cape Town architects A. W. Ackerman and Thwaites. The end result is a slightly odd if intriguing juxtaposition of the younger and older Butterfield in a single building.

Through the raising of these buildings the Church of England in South Africa can at least claim to have aspired to, and in many cases reached, a certain point of ecclesiological attainment, even if the higher and more sophisticated brand of mid-century ecclesiology remained elusive.

Some Other Designs by English Architects

Throughout the period covered in this book, English architects continued to design churches for different parts of the British empire. This was mainly through the auspices of the university architectural societies, which continued to encourage and report on church building activity abroad. Indeed, between 1841 and 1868 more than 250 leading articles, reports, and notices on colonial church architecture appeared in the pages of *The Ecclesiologist*. So extensive was the coverage, and so considerable its influence, the journal claimed in its final number of 1868, that the society had 'the satisfaction of retiring from the field victors'.[138] Although there was a certain truth in this, advancements in church design could never be taken for granted, particularly in the colonies. As the ecclesiological movement was both conceived of and practised on a global scale, it is not surprising that we find some of Britain's leading ecclesiastical architects involved.

We have already examined the contribution made by some of these men to the design of colonial cathedrals. We have also touched upon the input of key figures such as William Butterfield, R. C. Carpenter and William Slater in producing designs for *Instrumenta Ecclesiastica*. But there were many other designs for churches and chapels in the empire that involved these great architects. To them, as to the numerous other members of the university societies, the cause of correct church design was something to be promoted wherever Anglicans were to be found. Apart from the three mentioned above, other notable figures who were

317 St Saviour's church, Claremont, Cape Town (1849–80) by William Butterfield and Sophy Gray. The west front was wholly designed by William Butterfield in 1872 as a memorial to Sophy Gray.

involved in colonial church design include William Burges, G. E. Street, G. F. Bodley, William White, Henry Woodyer, J. L. Pearson and the ubiquitous G. G. Scott.

Some of the more modest designs produced by these architects have already been discussed, such as White's work in South Africa (Bishop's College, Rondebosch, and St Bartholomew's and St Philip's, Grahamstown), Carpenter's in Tasmania (St John's, Prosser Plains) and Butterfield's and Woodyer's for the bishop of Cape Town. Mention has also been made of unexecuted designs, including Bodley's for Delhi and Grahamstown, and Scott's for Bombay, Calcutta and Canterbury.

Butterfield, Carpenter and Slater perhaps best represent how English architects were involved in church design at a number of levels and across wide geographical areas. They not only produced designs for churches and church furnishings in England, attracting the enthusiastic approbation of the Ecclesiological Society, but were among the most active in providing support for the colonies. Their contribution to cathedral architecture is one example of this. It has to be remembered that the opportunities presented to British architects for designing cathedrals in their own country was extremely limited, and, with reference to England, non-existent. Truro Cathedral (1881–1910) by J. L. Pearson was the first Anglican cathedral erected on English soil for some 200 years (St Paul's in London being the last, and only then because it burned down), and the first as a new establishment since Salisbury (1220). Thus, the colonial scene offered exciting prospects and scope for design initiative. These three architects also devised a number of one-off designs and models for parish churches, church furniture and other liturgical accoutrements for colonial bishops and clergymen: Butterfield designed church plate for Tasmania and Fredericton, and Slater an altar cross and candlesticks for Honolulu.[139]

318 South and west elevations of William Butterfield's unexecuted design for St Matthew's church, Auckland, 1858 (Diocese of Auckland Archives).

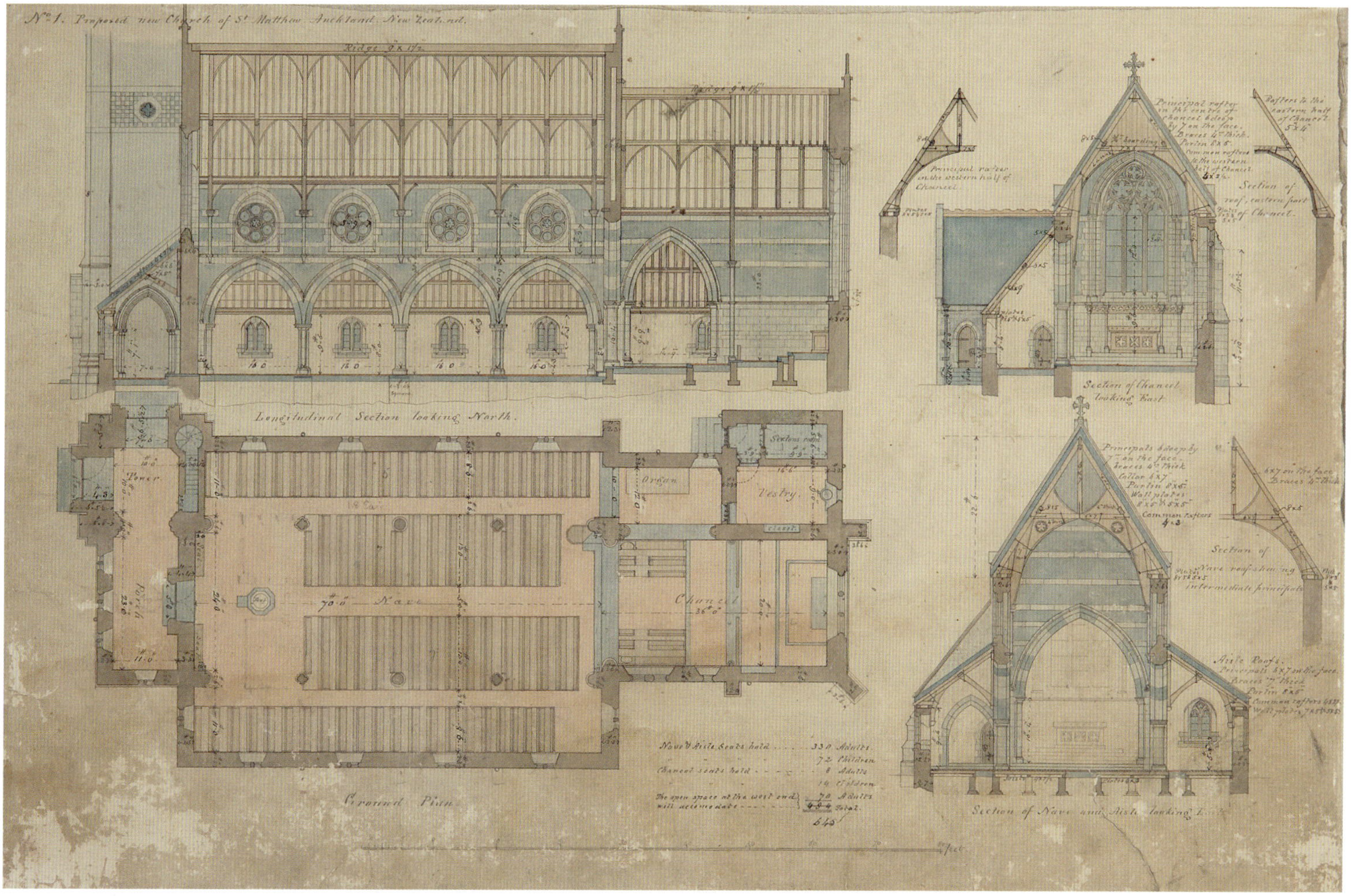

319 Plan and sections of William Butterfield's unexecuted design for St Matthew's church, Auckland, 1858 (Diocese of Auckland Archives).

Butterfield's name was associated with a number of colonial projects during the 1850s and 1860s, including proposals for simple wooden churches for Canada, the 'rearrangement' of St George's cathedral, Cape Town, the Bishop Gray Memorial Column, also in Cape Town, and St John's church, Victoria West (Cape Province).[140] But his most substantial efforts, not counting the cathedral projects (notably Melbourne), were for New Zealand. Like Scott, he was also involved with the Canterbury Settlement, producing designs in 1849 for a chapel-school to be erected upon the settlers' arrival in 1850. However, the building was never realised.[141]

Butterfield's other New Zealand design was for the parish church of St Matthew, Auckland (1858) (figs 318 and 319). This design was classic Butterfield. Praising its vigour, *The Ecclesiologist* observed approvingly that it exhibited 'that stamp of grave dignity' characteristic of the architect's style.[142] Indeed, the journal went further in suggesting that, standing as it did unobstructed in its churchyard, 'with light admitted on every side', St Matthew's was perhaps a more perfect, if reduced, version of All Saints', Margaret Street.[143] But St Matthew's was no recycled project. It was designed specifically to combat the fierce wind that regularly lashed the Auckland area. This 'enemy', as *The Ecclesiologist* called it, was accounted for and overcome in the compactness, solidity and spatial arrangement of the building. Designed to be built in local stone, its forms were rendered in a rather severe and heavy Middle-Pointed idiom, as if to cut the wind, with a narthex for additional shelter. Unusually, the tower had two separate entrances to cater for the wind blowing from different directions. It opened into the northern end of the narthex, which in turn opened into the nave though a single arch.

The exterior is impressive in its use of structural polychomy and chequered patterning along the clerestory and in the gable ends, much like what would later appear at All Saints', Babbacombe (1865–74), or Keble College, Oxford (1867–83). However, the composition is dominated by the clerestory windows, each comprising a sexfoil surrounded by six unfoliated circles set under an arch. Like the spire, the interior is composed of grey and blue banding, the effect of which is equally striking, and much like that achieved by Butterfield at Melbourne (St Paul's cathedral) twenty years later. Although an English design by an English architect, the result is one specifically tailored to local means and conditions. To be sure, this is nothing more than what would have been expected for a provincial church in Britain at the time. But here the outcome seems rather special, placing Butterfield's vision for Auckland among the most extraordinary examples of High Victorian design in colonial church architecture of the mid-nineteenth century.

Unfortunately, it was not to be. A misunderstanding between Butterfield and Frederick Thatcher, who was to superintend the construction and who met with Butterfield while in England, caused the project to fall through. It was, anyway, unlikely to have succeeded in its proposed form, especially as the estimated cost was some £7,500, far beyond the means of a small colonial parish.[144] Thus, it went the way of so many similar schemes in being considered 'too expensive' or 'inappropriate'.

Carpenter had more success, but did not escape unscathed. His design for Cookham Dean was recreated almost *in toto* at Prosser Plains (Buckland), which was uncontroversial as the church was small and the Tasmanian climate was understood to be somewhat similar to that in Britain. But his designs for Ceylon (Colombo cathedral and All Saints', Galle) fared less well, being distorted and discarded to varying degrees, although his hand is still evident in the final product. He also produced the well-known 'Design for a Wooden Church', which appeared in the second series of *Instrumenta Ecclesiastica* (1856), but was never erected anywhere in that particular form.[145]

As mentioned in Chapter 1, Carpenter also sent 'three models' of different sized churches to Tasmania via the Cambridge Camden Society in 1844. Cookham Dean was the smallest of these, while the cathedral model, proudly showcased by Bishop Nixon, was the largest (see fig 56). In the archive of the Tasmanian Museum and Art Gallery there are two further drawings by Carpenter.[146] Although very similar in style and form to the cathedral model, they are plans for a slightly smaller church. Of the three designs, these drawings would appear to represent the middle-sized church, consisting of only a four-bay nave and three-storey tower, as opposed to the five bays and four storeys of the 'cathedral'. It is this design that was probably adapted for St Mary's church, Hagley, near Hobart (1861–2) (figs 320 and 321). In the guide to the church it is suggested that the parish benefactor, Sir Richard Dry, especially commissioned Carpenter to supply designs for the church while visiting England in 1858.[147] However, Carpenter was dead by this time. The more likely scenario is that the abovementioned drawings by Carpenter, already in the possession of the diocese, were unearthed and used by the superintending architect, Henry Hunter.

When we consider the church as built, it is clear that, although he did not copy Carpenter's original design, Hunter adopted many of the same forms and features. This is evident not only in the general massing of the building but also in the window tracery. It is probable that Hunter culled elements from the larger cathedral model as well, such as the vesica-style oculus in the tower. The end result is a very neat,

320 St Mary's church, Hagley, near Hobart (1861–2), by R. C. Carpenter and Henry Hunter.

321 North elevation of R. C. Carpenter's original design of a church for Tasmania, *c.*1844 (Archives, Tasmanian Museum and Art Gallery, Hobart).

double-gabled, English parish church in a distinguished Middle-Pointed style with articulated chancel and south-west tower. The main differences between the plans and the completed building are the two- rather than three-bay chancel, and the oddly proportioned spire. Indeed, as one approaches the site from the main road, the whole scene appears like some rural idyll transported directly from the English countryside, with its surrounding oasis of European deciduous and evergreen trees. There is almost no more complete attempt at recreating the ideal of the English parish church and its environs anywhere in the British empire.

William Slater had been an assistant and then partner to Carpenter in the 1840s and early 1850s. After Carpenter's death in 1855, Slater took control of the practice. As discussed in Chapter 3, it was shortly after this that he put in an entry for the Crimean War Memorial church competition, in which he gained the unofficial fourth prize. This design demonstrated his flexibility in adapting European architectural forms to foreign contexts – a topic that one can imagine he discussed frequently with Carpenter. It therefore seems especially odd that one of the earliest designs that Slater produced for the colonies took no heed of

322 William Slater's design for a cathedral at Adelaide, South Australia, 1847 (Art Gallery of South Australia, Adelaide).

context at all (fig. 322). This was for a cathedral at Adelaide (1847) which Bishop Short appears to have taken with him to Australia. Far from what many would have considered to be a cathedral, it was rather more a perfectly correct Middle-Pointed design for a parish church. It was very much along the lines of what the Cambridge Camden Society had called for in terms of parish church design in the colonies, pointing to ancient models such as All Saints', Teversham (Cambridgeshire). In fact, the design is something of an amalgam, taking inspiration not only from Teversham but also from other well-known and prized thirteenth- and fourteenth-century English exemplars, such as SS Mary and Michael, Trumpington (Cambridgeshire), and St John the Baptist, Shottesbrooke (Berkshire). There are also profound similarities to the designs Carpenter sent to Tasmania a few years earlier, which Slater would have known.

In this respect, Slater's design represents an ideal. It was produced in the hope, perhaps, that if such exemplary models could not easily be realised at home, then they might form the basis of a new era of ecclesiology in that

'England beyond the seas'. After all, the colonies were considered lands of new opportunity. As Brian Andrews has observed, if erected, Slater's church would have been the most exquisite specimen of archaeologically correct, Gothic Revival church architecture in Australia.[148]

But it was never built. Despite having written to Governor Robe before leaving England about the prospect of erecting the church, Short would have realised almost immediately upon arrival in South Australia that such a building was far beyond the means of his fledgling diocese.[149] As mentioned in Chapter 1, he needed only to set eyes on the existing attempts at church architecture in the colony to know that his vision would remain but a dream. He was also in possession of a much plainer, more practical design for a cathedral church by William Butterfield (see p. 110). Short may have taken these two quite different designs in the hope that if one could not be realised then perhaps the other could. Whatever his original plan, he was in communication with Butterfield by May 1848.[150] Where this left Slater is not entirely clear, for he does not seem to have given up on Adelaide. When Short was in England on a return visit in 1854, he solicited an alternative, and perhaps more realistic (that is, conservative), set of plans for a cathedral from W. G. and E. Habershon.[151] At the same time, however, *The Ecclesiologist* reported Slater's having presented another design for Adelaide at a meeting of the Ecclesiological Society, describing it as 'a large cruciform structure, in late Middle-Pointed style, with a lofty central tower and spire'.[152] Whether Slater met with Short while he was in England to discuss the commission is not known. Maybe he felt that it was either his duty or his right to continue the project, having been involved with Short and Adelaide from the beginning. Unfortunately, none of the drawings for this later design survive.

The other commissions in which Slater was involved include designs for Labuan cathedral (Borneo), and a small church in Sarawak, both produced in 1863.[153] However, it is not known if any of these designs reached their intended destination, and, as with the final Adelaide proposal, none of the drawings survive.

As discussed in Chapter 2, Scott designed three of the most distinguished colonial cathedrals in Canada, South Africa and New Zealand. He also produced designs for a number of smaller churches in various parts of the empire. We have already considered those for Canterbury, Colaba and Calcutta, but there were others, such as proposals for the Bishop Patteson Memorial chapel (St Barnabas), Norfolk Island (*c.*1874), and St Paul's cathedral, Victoria (Mahé), Seychelles (1851).[154] Undoubtedly the most distinguished of these smaller designs, and the only one to be erected largely as intended, was that for St Alban's parish church, Muswellbrook, New South Wales (1864–9) (figs 323 and 324). Again, as with so many designs for the colonies at this time, the pedigree of this church points to the tapping of clerical networks. The plans (more than 100 separate sheets) were procured by the Rev. R. G. Boodle, who had designed and built the iron-bark chapel at Merriwa (see p. 154). It was while back in England that Boodle, who had been an Oriel man at the height of the agitation surrounding the Oxford Movement, secured the services of Scott at the behest of his old friend and protégé, the Rev. W. E. White of Edenglassie, who was by this time the incumbent at St Alban's.[155] The plans reached White some time in 1863, and were initially placed in the hands of Blacket, but were soon passed on to the young Horbury Hunt, who superintended the project. Scott's plans specified rough stone walling with dressed quoining and architraves. However, it was decided some time in 1864 to alter this to cut and dressed stone throughout, which dramatically increased the cost of the project (from an estimated £3,500 to over £12,000). The foundation stone was laid by Bishop Tyrrell on 11 November 1864, and the church was dedicated on St Alban's Day 1869. Very fond and proud of the church, Tyrrell was delighted to call it his 'Minster'.[156] Until the erection of Christ Church cathedral, Grafton, in the early 1880s, St Alban's, Muswellbrook, was the most impressive church in the diocese.

Considering the building's location, there is little doubt that Scott thought carefully about issues of climate. He had probably received reports from Boodle about the intense sunlight and mild humidity of the Hunter Valley, which made it somewhat similar in terms of atmosphere to parts of continental Europe. Knowledge of these conditions, along with an understanding of colonial society in Australia, seem to have inspired Scott to opt for a heavy version of early Gothic in a predominantly French idiom. Interestingly, this was a variation on a design he had previously supplied for the parish church at Hawkhurst in Kent (1859–61).[157] Nevertheless, Scott's decision to send a design in this particular style appears to have been deliberate, given the entirely different, Italianate style that he had adopted in the contemporaneous designs for Calcutta and Shanghai.

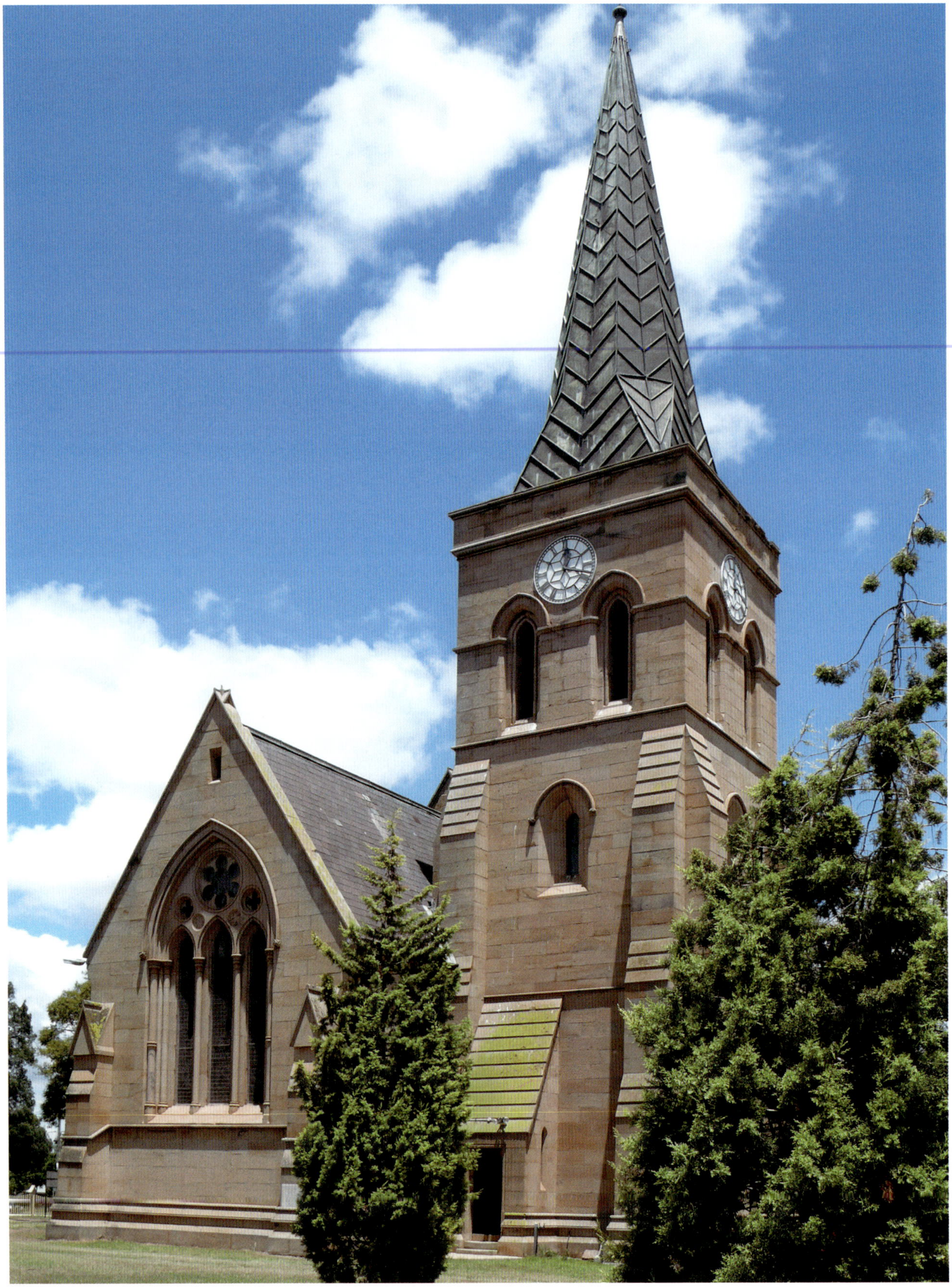

323 East end of St Alban's church, Muswellbrook, New South Wales (1864–9), by G. G. Scott and John Horbury Hunt.

324 West elevation drawing of G. G. Scott's original design for St Alban's church, Muswellbrook, 1863 (St Alban's church archive, Muswellbrook).

However, despite these apparently careful considerations on Scott's part, it appears that Hunt, while preparing a new set of construction drawings for the project, flipped the plan on its longitudinal axis, resulting in a mirror image of Scott's original layout. No reason was provided, but one may surmise that, given the intensity of the sun in northern New South Wales, a way of placing the entrance porch on the south side of the building (in the shade) had to be found, without destroying the formal balance of the scheme. The end result at Muswellbrook, notwithstanding this change, is a beautifully poised ensemble of forms, double-gabled, comprising a four-bay nave, southern aisle, chancel with choir, and north-east tower and vestry. The walls are extremely thick for a church of this size (some 3 feet 6 inches) (fig. 325), while the windows are no more than small apertures and heavily recessed, with ample use of plate tracery. Like Hunt's smaller churches in the region, St Alban's, Muswellbrook, is among the finer specimens of

325 John Horbury Hunt's revision of G. G. Scott's plan for St Alban's church, Muswellbrook, *c.*1864 (St Alban's church archive, Muswellbrook).

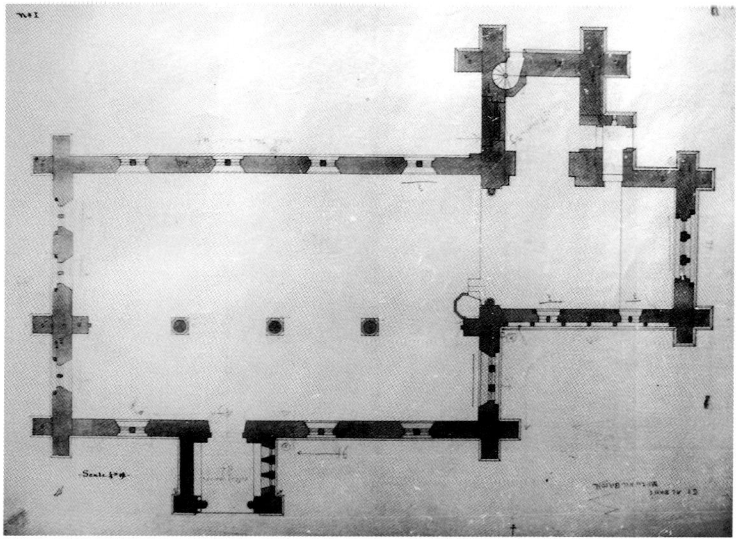

326 Pastoral staff for the bishop of Dunedin, New Zealand, 1866, designed by William Burges.

a speluncar-style church erected in Britain's colonies during the mid-nineteenth century. Even Scott would have been pleased with the outcome, especially as he was wont to complain that his colonial designs were regularly mutilated once they had left his office.[158]

Other English architects played their part, too, however small. There were designs for relatively minor items, such as Burges's pastoral staffs for the bishops of Honolulu (1862) and Dunedin (1866) (fig. 326),[159] and Scott's fountain for St Thomas's cathedral, Bombay (1866). But perhaps the most significant of these remaining contributions was George Edmund Street's proposal for the church of St John the Baptist, Hobart (1851). Orchestrated by the Rev. F. H. Cox, this was an attempt by Street to export his thinking on town churches to the colonies.[160] The site was a steeply inclined and awkwardly shaped suburban block at the intersection of two roads, making for particularly difficult terrain upon which to erect a building. However, it seems that

327 Church of St John the Evangelist, Carlton, Yorkshire (1878), by G. E. Street.

Street was determined to turn this misfortune into a virtue by making a bold and dramatic statement. The account in *The Ecclesiologist* describes an unusual, if not eccentric, design with a large and heavily buttressed oblong tower between nave and chancel (forming a choir), with an 'acutely pitched' gable roof.[161] The drawings do not survive, but the building was of the same species as his later design for Sts Philip and James, Oxford (1859), or even St Stephen's, Fylingdales (Yorkshire; 1868–70) or St John the Evangelist, Carlton (Yorkshire; 1878) (fig. 327). The tower, with its metal cresting, must have appeared somewhat like that in G. F. Bodley's design for All Saints', Selsley (Gloucestershire; 1859). Although *The Ecclesiologist* expressed concern at Street's originality, it was on the whole so impressed that it 'grudge[d] this design to Van Dieman's Land'.[162] But such an unusual type was not the most suitable for the colonies, it warned. Not surprisingly, it was never erected. Indeed, the plans, if they ever reached Hobart at all, were handed to Henry Hunter who altered them substantially to the requirements of a rather modest budget (fig. 328). To be sure, the church as built does project a certain energy, but there is little of Street's originality or flair. It is essentially a construct of Hunter's own imagination.

The buildings discussed in this chapter give a good impression of the diversity and range of colonial ecclesiology. At the same time, however, they provide clear evidence of the consistencies in both form and arrangement that linked Anglican church architecture (and its architects) across the globe. In this sense, although the formal possibilities in each case were reasonably extensive, becoming more specific and particular as the century wore on, Anglican church architecture in each location nevertheless represented not so much a distinct species as a genetic variation of the same species. The DNA, as it were, that related these buildings was the power and influence of ecclesiology as both a 'science' and an ideology – a doctrine that had been thoroughly inculcated into the minds of architects and clergymen alike by the mid-nineteenth century, including the full-scale revival of liturgical discipline (or what was otherwise termed 'correctness'). Colonial church architecture in the nineteenth century differed from that of the seventeenth and eighteenth centuries, in that the common identifying traits and their spatial equivalents were more robustly expressed.

It was the self-evident truth underpinning the idea of ecclesiology that enabled architects like G. G. Scott or William Slater to produce formally and aesthetically divergent designs for different parts of the world without violating what were perceived as the fundamental tenets of Anglican ecclesiology. Thus, what we see in the examples discussed above, by and large, is a response to Benjamin Webb's original dictum that 'the bones . . . be constructed before the flesh which covers them', after which 'any thing else may be boldly added' (see p. 127). It was this basic 'truth', once accepted, that enabled architects to break the bonds of archaeological 'copyism' and to *think* Gothic, as Truefitt had pleaded, leading to the variety of forms we see. To be sure, the pace and extent of change varied from place to place, but the key indicators remained consistent,

328 Church of St John the Baptist, Hobart (1852–6), by Henry Hunter.

even if they were not always realised to the degree anticipated. This degree of adaptation and development was affected also, as we have seen, by the personnel involved, the time at which they arrived in their various locations, and the number of times they revisited England. In some cases these factors led to dramatic step-changes in the approach towards and sophistication of church design, as in the case of Fred Cumberland.

In the wide view, then, one can see how the mantra of Anglican ecclesiology first arrived and then developed in these different parts of the world, reaching a relative high point between about 1855 and 1875 as each individual colony gained the confidence and resources to facilitate it. The final outcome was a series of forms and spaces across the globe that were, in many cases, and despite the best of intentions, almost but not quite as they should be.

7

Bringing the Empire Home

MISSION WORK AND CHURCH EXTENSION IN THE BRITISH ISLES

The Church's glorious future bursts full upon my sight:
I see the white-winged vessels, that, bound to realms afar,
Go, conquering and to conquer, upon their holy war;
. . .
Yet they breast the broad Atlantic, the Polar zone they brave,
They dash the spray-drops from their bow in that Antarctic wave;
. . .
Where earthly arms were weakness, and earthly gold were dross,
Safe go they, for they carry the unconquerable Cross;
The Cross that, planted here at first, now planted here again,
Shall bloom and flourish in the sight of angels and of men

J. M. Neale, *The Consecration of St. Augustine's, Canterbury* (1848)

If Anglicanism in the mid-nineteenth century was both perceived and directed as a global initiative, then the effects of this must necessarily have impacted on the United Kingdom. To be sure, the distinct Anglican polities of the United Church of England and Ireland and the Episcopal Church of Scotland continued to manage home affairs, largely unaffected by the extension of Anglicanism abroad. There had, of course, been upheavals, both spiritual and legal, and industrialisation exerted pressure on the ancient parochial system unlike any that had gone before, but the edifice as a whole remained largely intact, if transformed.[1] However, as discussed in Chapter 1, during this period the Church *did* awaken to its responsibilities overseas vis-à-vis Britain's empire. England remained the headquarters, as it were, of the 'global Church of England', with the Colonial Bishoprics' Fund, the newly invigorated Society for the Propagation of the Gospel and the Church Missionary Society all located in London. These organisations were, in a sense, agencies for the extraction and administration of resources from the British Isles, both human and fiscal. Their presence was felt throughout the land, whether in the circulation of publications and notices or via special collections in parish churches. Undoubtedly, this presence was felt more keenly in some places than others, such as in the diocese of Exeter, where the Coleridge family's connection with, and contribution to, the colonial Church was significant.[2]

329 The Rev. Frederick Thatcher (1814–1890).

330 Bishop Selwyn's tomb at Lichfield cathedral, with tiles depicting New Zealand scenes.

Home and Abroad:
The Expanded World of the English Church

Importantly, the effects of this process of 'globalisation' were not only visited upon the non-European world but also had perceptible, even distinct, repercussions upon the Church at home. The continual flow of information, materials and manpower from centre to periphery and back again meant that the English Church as a whole, both in Britain and throughout the empire, was part of the same expanded field of operation, in which all constituent elements were touched and transformed by the experience in some form or other. In other words, historically speaking, it is extremely difficult, if not impossible, to extricate operations entirely in any one of these constituent parts from the others, including the British Isles.

If we consider the question of manpower for a moment, then the impact of this global exchange is apparent. Large numbers of clergymen may have left for fields afar, but quite a few found their way back. As we have seen, colonial bishops made return visits to England on a regular basis, during which time they toured the country raising funds and speaking in public about their experiences. Some returned permanently (if reluctantly) to take up posts in England, such as G. A. Selwyn, who was translated to the see of Lichfield in 1867. He was followed almost immediately by his friends from Australia and New Zealand, including the Revs W. H. Walsh, Frederick Thatcher (fig. 329) and Charles Abraham. These men, who had long and distinguished colonial service records, were patronised by Selwyn, given diocesan curacies or official offices in the cathedral, or both. Thus, in this one English diocese was to be found a small but influential coterie of ex-colonial clergymen. Indeed, not only Selwyn's tomb at Lichfield (fig. 330), with its spectacular New Zealand imagery, but also Selwyn College, Cambridge (1880–2), remain as witnesses in England to his achievement as an Anglican clergyman and the global reach of the English Church. Other colonial churchmen to be commemorated in this way – as 'modern martyrs' – included the Revs C. F. Mackenzie and J. C. Patteson, both missionary bishops who were seen to have sacrificed their lives not just for the greater good of the English Church but for Christianity in general (fig. 331).[3] The consecration of colonial bishops in Westminster Abbey from 1842 can also be seen in this light.

331 Mackenzie memorial window, Haslingfield church, Cambridgeshire (1869), to designs by Frederick Preedy.

The impact of the Church's global extension at home was also evident at the level of architectural debate. In the pages of *The Ecclesiologist*, for instance, it is clear that the terms of reference for what constituted modern 'ecclesiology' were shaped and reshaped in accordance with the ever shifting limits of the Anglican Communion. As observations and requests came flooding back from clergymen stationed abroad, in climates vastly different from those they had left behind, what ecclesiology actually meant – in both theory and practice – continued to develop, informing wider debates on architectural adaptation and 'appropriateness'. Thus, the official discourse of modern ecclesiology, emanating as it did from the 'centre', was at once metropolitan *and* colonial in its constitution – that is, 'global' in its truest and most expanded sense; hence the Ecclesiological Society's understanding of itself as bestriding 'the narrow world like a Colossus'.[4] As mentioned in Chapter 2, the same can be said of Beresford Hope's *The English Cathedral of the Nineteenth Century* (1861). Here the examples identified as 'English' were almost exclusively colonial, Scottish or Irish. It is clear that Hope viewed Anglicanism precisely in these expanded terms, and that what had been achieved in these places might be learned and reapplied in England. For Beresford Hope, the British empire – that 'great England beyond the seas' – was evidently a kind of organic system in which the dynamics of cultural, economic and political transformation were assimilative and therefore liable to feedback.[5]

The most striking example of this as far as Church governance is concerned was the move by the bishop of Exeter – inspired perhaps by events in Australia – to call a diocesan synod in 1851. The general background to the issue of self-governance in the Church of England was, of course, more drawn out, dating back to calls for the revival of Convocation (suppressed since 1717) in the 1830s. But two events in particular focused minds during the early 1850s: the Gorham Judgment and the re-establishment of the Roman Catholic hierarchy in England.[6] Nevertheless, the bishop of Sydney's initiative to solve the complications of Royal Supremacy in the colonies by calling an Australasian synod set a crucial precedent. Later, during Bishop Blomfield's attempts at reinstituting Convocation, it was proposed to admit the bishop of Cape Town in order not only to assert the committee's right to determine its membership but also to imply its imperial jurisdiction.[7]

Architects, too, were part of these 'feedback loops', moving as they did between home and the colonies, as well as around the empire. For example, we have already heard about the case of William Hay. Scottish born and trained, Hay became a trusted clerk of works for G. G. Scott, having overseen the construction of Newfoundland cathedral in the late 1840s. He later established a lucrative practice in Toronto, before returning to Scotland in 1861. While in Canada he designed a number of English churches, including St George's, Newcastle, and St Paul's, Southampton. Once back in Scotland, he established a practice in 1875 with George Henderson, the son of his former employer in Edinburgh. Henderson had made his way back from Geelong in Australia, where his practice with Alexander Davidson had been an unhappy one. Hay and Henderson designed a number of churches after forming their partnership, including Old St Paul's, Edinburgh (1881). However, their greatest achievement with respect to the colonies was the Cathedral of the Most Holy Trinity, Hamilton, Bermuda (1886–1905).[8] One cannot help but wonder to what extent their collective experiences in the colonies informed their approach to ecclesiastical design in a place such as Scotland. Other examples of architects who moved between metropole and colony and around include Robert Speechley, Frank Wills and Edward Medley.

But it was in the areas of education and mission work at home that the Church of England's colonial experience was perhaps most conspicuous. We have heard how a lack of architectural expertise in the colonies precipitated calls in England for colonial clergymen to be given some training in matters architectural, but the general training of clergymen for service in Britain's overseas empire was an altogether more urgent and systemic problem. There had been calls as early as the 1830s for such a training centre in Oxford, but it did not receive sanction at the time.[9] It was not until 1848, thanks mainly to the zeal of Bishop Broughton of Australia and the Rev. Edward Coleridge of Eton, as well as the financial clout of A. J. B. Beresford Hope, that an officially sanctioned missionary training college was opened in England, at the heart of the Anglican ecclesiastical establishment in Canterbury. Known as St Augustine's College, it was architecturally impressive and occupied an important site among the old abbey buildings near the cathedral for some 130 years. Although it got off to a shaky start, St Augustine's churned out over 600 graduates up to 1905, sending them to all parts of the British empire.[10] Here was the Church of England taking ultimate responsibility on home soil for the welfare of the Anglican Communion abroad. The mandate of St Augustine's was controversial and never entirely fulfilled, and the college would in time become essentially obsolete as regional training centres were established in other parts of the empire, but its mere existence, including the people involved and the resources assembled, proved clear metropolitan intent.

Other such 'seminaries' followed in its wake, such as Cuddesdon College, Oxford, initiated by Samuel Wilberforce and opened by Bishop Selwyn while on a return visit to England in 1854.[11] In time, Cuddesdon would cultivate extensive colonial and overseas missionary links of its own.[12] Not only did Wilberforce regularly invite colonial clergymen to attend official functions at the college, thus impressing upon its students the worldwide responsibilities of the Church, but Cuddesdon was also home to the Rev. Edward Willis (vice-principal 1870–80), founder of the Oxford Mission to Calcutta (1880). If this were not enough, every time students entered the chapel a mural of St Paul by Clayton and Bell greeted them in the ante-chapel, reminding them of the missionary vocation of the Christian Church.

So-called 'home missions' also saw the tactics and language of the overseas mission field employed within the British Isles. The 'heathen' of the slums of London and the big industrial cities were targeted, but Anglican missionary activity and Church extension were also carried out across the land, in Wales, provincial England, Scotland and Ireland. Here the front line was populated by Methodists and Roman Catholics (even Mormons),[13] just as in many of Britain's colonies. Church building – or 'planting', as it was known – was central to this endeavour, as the work of the Incorporated Church Building Society demonstrates.

It is also worth considering the plight and condition of Anglicanism in Ireland in the context of this study. Essentially a colony of England in all but name, Ireland bore witness to an ecclesiastical history and series of Church reforms during the nineteenth century that liken it to many of Britain's other colonies, especially the so-called 'settler dominions'. The nature of the Church may have been different in Ireland, but the parallels are both striking and instructive. This chapter will consider issues around clerical education, home missions and the Church in Ireland.

Missionary Training and its Infrastructure: St Augustine's College, Canterbury

A training college in England for Anglican missionaries was initially suggested on the grounds that the need for such an institution was urgent, and had been for some time. Indeed, as early as 1837, Bishop Broughton of Australia had written to the Rev. Edward Coleridge stressing the necessity of establishing such a centre in England specifically dedicated to 'rearing up clergymen for the Colonies'.[14] The principal advantage of establishing such an institution at home, Wilberforce reckoned, was the ability to provide an environment where 'health, morals, and efficient teaching' could be guaranteed, which was impossible in the colonies.[15] Originally, the college was to supply missionaries for the manufacturing and mining districts of England, too, but this function was never realised.[16] Thus, with a clear plan in sight, Coleridge sought opinions from friends via a private circular issued in June 1844.[17] The response was encouraging. But it was not until the following year that the initiative was brought into the open. In May 1845 a formal 'proposal' was drafted, printed and circulated among leading clerics and laymen of the Church of England, both at home and abroad. This proposal, which went through at least two iterations, is important because it tells us a great deal about the principles that inspired the project. The supposed need was laid out in explicit terms:

> A sufficient reason for the forming of such an Institution may at once be shewn [*sic*] in the fact, that there exists at present in this country, wielding an Empire over more than a hundred millions of souls, and those chiefly Heathen, but one College or Institution of any kind, in connection with the Church of England, for the Education of Missionary Clergy. . . . The Church at home enjoys, for the supply of its pastoral ministry, an extensive and richly endowed system of Education. . . . A body of fourteen or fifteen thousand Clergy is perpetually replenished and maintained by these fruitful and beneficent Institutions. But for the Colonial Dioceses, now seventeen in number, and for the vast and populous lands of the British Colonies in the East and in the West, there exists absolutely no provision in England, and but little abroad, for the replenishment, training, or supply of a body of Missionary Pastors.[18]

There are two things that strike one in particular about this rationale. The first is the way the author connects the activity and purpose of the Church of England in Britain with that in the colonies, as though these domains were contiguous fields of operation and responsibility. The second is the mention made of the only other 'Institution' for the training of Anglican missionaries. As far as the first of these is concerned, it is evident that Coleridge put forward the idea for his college in the same spirit that animated the formation of the Colonial Bishoprics' Fund (1841); namely, that the political economy of Anglicanism as both a cultural and spiritual system was considered vital to the security and ongoing prosperity of the British Empire, including Britain itself. As we have seen throughout the course of the current study, this line of thinking, as evidenced in both theory and practice, was a relatively consistent one in Church of

332 Engraving after a portrait by Thomas Phillips of Daniel Wilson (1778–1858), bishop of Calcutta (detail) (Bodleian Library, Oxford).

England circles during the middle decades of the nineteenth century, as the Church moved to assert its moral and spiritual authority in the wake of widespread social and political reform. Concerning this point, Coleridge emphasised Britain's wider responsibility in the eyes of God. What he and his backers wanted was nothing less than a training centre equal to 'the greatness of our obligations'. Pressing the point, he exclaimed how the national Church was a 'debtor' to the far-flung peoples of the British Empire, and how every good member of it would wish to 'supply this shameful defect'. The principal 'inducement' here was not merely the supply of more men but also, and of equal importance, the bond that would be created between 'the Church at home . . . and its Colonial Dioceses'.[19] 'Moreover', he continued,

> in one high sense, the need of some such close and constraining bond will become more and more felt, in proportion as the Church in the Colonies shall become less vitally dependent on the Church at home. No greater guarantee against the estrangement, which may attend on independence, can be conceived, than the sustained intercommunication of mind and feeling between the English and the Colonial Clergy, through those, who, after Education at home, shall pass into the Church abroad: so that all future Colleges in the Colonial Dioceses will find a common source, and an assimilating centre in the Missionary College at home, as all the Colonial Churches are united together in the Church, from which they spring.[20]

Again, as with the motivation behind the CBF, this was all the more significant, politically speaking, because the Church was obliged, first, 'to her own children scattered abroad; to our emigrants and settlers; to those of the same tongue, kindred, and faith; especially to the banished and all but excommunicated population of our Penal Colonies', and then, to 'the eighty or ninety millions of heathen souls under our rule in India'.[21]

The second aspect of the project's rationale – that only one other institution for the training of missionaries existed in England – was slightly more complicated. The institution referred to here was the CMS training school at Islington. Founded in 1826, it had some influential backers, including the Rev. Daniel Wilson (future bishop of Calcutta), who was then vicar of Islington (fig. 332).[22] However, being a Low Church organisation, the CMS was an independent entity that was happy to operate outside episcopal authority. This was something that High Church Anglicans, as most of those involved in the establishment of St Augustine's were, frowned upon. Indeed, as Coleridge's proposal made clear, the very constitution of the CMS school 'limited' its field of operation. In other words, CMS men were 'missionaries' in the true sense, ministering primarily to indigenous populations and penal colonies, as demonstrated by their remits in Tasmania and New Zealand. Besides which, most CMS clergymen were considered unfit to serve as priests in colonial parish churches. This is something that A. J. B. Beresford Hope seized upon (fig. 333). Hope, whom we have met several times already in this study, was a significant figure in the founding of St Augustine's College, not only because he was a leading layman of the English Church, but also because he provided the initial funding for it, buying the site and paying for a number of the new buildings. In this respect he was its key patron.

In a letter to the dean of Canterbury, Hope firmly outlined his thoughts on the character he expected the college to take:

> I do not simply mean an institution where theology is to be taught, but one in which the predominant spirit shall be that religion is the one thing needful, & this religion not one of personal beliefs, & undirected enthusiasm, but the religion of the Christian Church, & a religion which shall take its colouring from the Prayer Book of the Church, & make itself real, by ratifying the ordinances of the Church – That as the object of the institution was to train Christian Missionary Priests, it should do so by first making its members good Christians, then good Priests, & then good Missionaries.[23]

333 Portrait of A. J. B. Beresford Hope (1820–1887), leading Church of England patron, from R. J. E. Boggis, *A History of St Augustine's College* (1907).

Although it was noted in the initial proposal that St Augustine's would be put forward 'with no party feeling', it was clear that the High Churchmen who drove and funded the enterprise would have their way. Indeed, Hope's desires were reflected in the final statutes of the college, where strict adherence to the ordinances of the English Church were insisted upon.[24] It was precisely this 'High' and disciplined objective to produce 'devoted sons of the English Church' that would distinguish St Augustine's College from the CMS school at Islington.

Apart from the real, practical want and wider geopolitical concerns that gave rise to the college, stress was also placed on the type of education the students would receive – that is, an education that would make them 'effective' missionary agents. The general syllabus offered at England's universities, from where Anglican clergymen were traditionally recruited, equipped young men with neither the specific knowledge base required to operate in the colonial mission field, nor the habits of mind that would make them fit for purpose.[25] Thus, the programme of instruction offered at the new college would 'embrace all the ordinary branches of University Education, with the addition of such as may be calculated specially to promote the usefulness of the Students in their future scenes of ministerial labour'.[26] These 'additions' included 'practical' subjects such as languages, applied mathematics, geometry, astronomy, navigation, medicine and chemistry, as well as mechanical arts such as agriculture and carpentry. However, as those from England's public schools who were inclined to undertake further education usually went to one of the universities, it was suggested that students for the college be recruited primarily from the nation's grammar schools.

But this specialist agenda went further. In both the initial proposal documents and the college's eventual charter it was stated clearly that the aim of the institution was to 'prepare' the students appropriately for their future missionary endeavours. As this preparation ended with sending them to all quarters of the globe, into conditions that were entirely alien to the average middle-class English boy, it was imperative that both the daily habits of the students, and the conditions in which they lived, be 'simple and frugal'. It was observed with regret that many of the men who found their way to the colonies, or into some or other mission field, were either naïve or unfit, or both, through 'want of appropriate Training for the duties to be discharged, the difficulties to be encountered, and the hardships . . . to be endured'.[27] Such men were rather more of a hindrance than a help in colonial contexts. With this in mind, one of the objectives of the system offered at St Augustine's was to 'discipline . . . the inmates in a proper degree of hardness', thus making them 'fit' for the 'special duties' that lay ahead and that would be entrusted to them.[28] The proposal elaborated on this 'chief point':

> In all other Institutions for Education, it is comparatively a matter of indifference, whether the future calling and profession of those under instruction be determined or no. In the case of the Missionary, it is absolutely required that his career should from the first, so far as possible, be ascertained. To mature the necessary intensity of purpose, to concentrate all the powers of the will, and to inspire the whole character with a constant and enduring force, it is necessary that the first condition on entering the College walls be – the recorded choice of a Missionary life.[29]

To this end, the statutes of the college included a clause insisting that all students sign, before admission, a 'written declaration of their deliberate intention to devote themselves with all the powers of mind and body which God in His Goodness has given them to his Service in the Ministry of the Church of England in the distant dependencies of the British Empire'.[30]

However, with this requirement came a warning:

> The true life of it [the college] is in the purpose, which it embodies. If this be compromised or weakened, the College must relax itself into a mere place of lecturing about Missions, instead of a School of Missionaries. With this view, therefore, it is needed that the whole order and discipline of the place should habitually impress the one great aim of seeking Christ's sheep, not for wages, nor for hire, but 'for the love of God'. To mature the zeal, boldness, endurance and fervent charity, without which the hardships and crosses of Missionary toil cannot be sustained, there is need of a strengthening, and a chastening system, with prayer and meditation, within walls, which bear the tokens of an apostolic life. . . .[31]

This 'chastening system' went to draconian lengths, and included everything from the clothes worn by the 'inmates' – which 'shall be grave and sober' – to the withholding of female company and the regular taking of exercise. On the point of women, Beresford Hope believed that it would be altogether 'unpleasant' to have a female residing at the college in the form of a Matron, as this would rather soften the boys. 'Young men training as Missionaries ought surely to learn to be independent as much as possible of female help,' he asserted, 'for fear that they should, as I believe is the case with Missionaries of that sect [presumably the CMS], think it necessary to set up with a wife.'[32] On the issue of exercise, the disciplinary regime was equally stern. In 1853 the *Occasional Papers* of St Augustine's College carried an article on the day in the life of a student. Here it was observed that 'after Chapel there is half an hour to spare, which twice in the week is occupied by the drill-sergeant'. In mentioning this, the author inserted a quote on missionary training from the late Rev. W. B. Hopkins, formerly of St Catharine's College, Cambridge. Reference to Hopkins was introduced, it seems, in order not only to emphasise the necessity of exercise in the training of missionaries but also to highlight its ancient and thereby authoritative pedigree. 'Doubtless it was the common practice in ancient times to associate physical with intellectual training,' mused Hopkins; 'and a gymnasium for bodily exercise was an indispensable appendage to the schools where youth were taught philosophy.' He continued: 'it is highly probable therefore that the Apostle (St Paul) enjoyed advantages of this kind, and we cannot doubt that they would afterwards prove of great service to him. . . . St Paul, in his first letter to Timothy, says that "bodily exercise" has its profitable uses. . . . To the same person he condescends to give instruction about diet. . . . It would be therefore far from wise to undervalue the importance of physical fitness, or to deny the utility of some physical training in the case of a Missionary.'[33] The fitness regime introduced at St Augustine's was no doubt influenced by the many tales of physical endurance recorded by Anglican clergy stationed in the colonies, to which Coleridge was privy. It also dovetailed precisely with the demands being made by colonial bishops with respect to the candidature of missionary clergy, and the wider ethos of manly vigour that underpinned public school education at the time (see pp. 41–3).[34] In this respect, St Augustine's College was somewhat akin to a military academy or extended boot camp, the only difference being that in this case 'soldiers of the Cross' were being trained.

This *esprit de corps*, as it were, extended to the college hierarchy. Not only were the warden and officers to come from one of the three English universities – Oxford, Cambridge and Durham – but their titles were to reflect the collegiality inherent in those establishments. On this point Beresford Hope was 'very decided' that they be called '"Fellows", & not "Professors" or "Assistants" or "Tutors"', and that they be unmarried. In this sense the students and fellows would be recognised more as a 'community [of] the Christian Church, labouring in it, for the glory of God', rather than merely teachers.[35] It was envisaged that the warden would lead by example, ordering 'all things within the College to the furtherance of Piety and Learning, . . . and lead[ing] all those who are under his charge to sober and godly Living by public and private exhortations'.[36] But Hope wanted to go even further. Writing to Coleridge in 1845, he insisted that the warden ought to be 'the head of a Catholic and not a Protestant Seminary', and that, although he could hardly expect all the Fellows to be 'of the extreme shade of High Church, (this I should like, but it is more than I can expect,) still I say that all the Fellows should be High Churchmen'.[37] These strictures, when made more widely known, immediately raised the hackles of Low Churchmen, alienating them from the cause. As expected, accusations of 'popery' and 'Puseyite' followed, with one critic describing the scheme as nothing less than 'a deep-laid Jesuitical scheme for Romanizing our Church'.[38] This no doubt caused some to withhold donations, but Coleridge was able steer the enterprise through these troubled waters, gaining both the sanction and patronage of the archbishop of Canterbury.[39]

These notions of restraint and specialist knowledge as being fundamental to the education of a missionary also came from the coal face, so to speak – that is, from those few training centres that had been established in the colonies in such places as India, New Zealand, Australia and Newfoundland. As we saw in Chapter 1, Bishop Feild extolled the virtues of austerity and plain living at Queen's College, Newfoundland, while Bishop Selwyn implemented strict religious observance and a programme of practical skills training in agriculture, weaving, printing and carpentry at St John's College, Auckland. The educational programme at St Augustine's was an attempt to absorb and learn these lessons on home soil. There were models from the ancient past, too. In 1851, at the departure of the college's first graduate, the warden, the Rev. Henry Bailey (1815–1906), sought a parallel from earliest times in justifying his training regime. 'The rule by which we are bound', he reminded those gathered, including the Rev. W. H. Walsh of Sydney, 'is designed to maintain among us a spirit of primitive piety and simplicity of living akin to that which pervaded the College at Antioch.' 'Their habit', he continued, 'was to minister to the Lord and to fast; with us too, thank God, the daily sacrifice of prayer and praise, the weekly Eucharistic service, and the observance of fast and festival according to the order of our Church, are essentials of our system.'

> But ponder for a moment the example of the primitive brotherhood at Antioch. They 'fasted and prayed'; but they had fasted and prayed before; they continued to do what they had been in the habit of doing. Their common rule of devotion was a continual preparation for critical periods; therefore excitement and over-wrought unusual display were needless, and would have been unsuitable. . . . The application of this part of the history to ourselves in our present circumstances is not difficult, and it will be encouraging to us in the degrees in which we have cultivated the spirit of those devout men at Antioch. What are our daily common prayers, our weekly and festival communions, our devotional exercises, our customary forms, but a continuous preparation.[40]

What we see here, in these appeals to asceticism, manly vigour and the Christian ideal, is a kind of invention of tradition, much like that witnessed in the colonies among colonial clergymen. As with the revival of Gothic architecture itself, this tradition was grounded in the authority of ancient precedent. With the creation of St Augustine's College, a vivid and dynamic ideology was established, based on a feedback loop between metropole and mission field as clergymen and their experiences were relayed from one place to the other and back again: hence the presence of Walsh at such a critical moment in the college's history.

These ideas of precedent and authority were given an unparalleled sense of romantic continuity in the siting of the college. Originally, the progenitors of the scheme wished to locate it near one of the ancient universities, preferably Oxford, so that Wilberforce might act as a kind of *locum* guardian.[41] But such a location was criticised by some as potentially corrupting, both socially and spiritually – socially, owing to the luxurious and profligate lifestyles led by some undergraduates, and spiritually because

334 J. M. W. Turner, *Saint Augustine's Gate, Canterbury*, *c.*1793, showing the medieval gateway leading to the ruins of St Augustine's Abbey, Canterbury (Yale Center for British Art, New Haven).

of Tractarianism.[42] All were on high alert with the recent 'going over' of Newman. Therefore, to avoid needless controversy, a site more removed was sought. Luckily, it happened that Beresford Hope had purchased the precinct and ruins of St Augustine's Abbey, Canterbury, in June 1844. After having visited the site the pervious year, he was disgusted to have found it in such a neglected state and was determined to return it to the custodianship of the English Church.[43] Upon hearing this news, Coleridge wrote to Hope asking if he meant to give the site for his missionary college. After some consideration, Hope agreed, replying 'St. Augustine's is yours, or rather of the Church.'[44] This no doubt pleased Broughton, who had been a pupil at the King's School in Canterbury.[45]

What more perfect site could there have been in England for a missionary college? Here, exclaimed Coleridge, was the 'Site of Sites',[46] the location upon which the great missionary apostle himself, St Augustine, based his operation to evangelise the Anglo-Saxon race (fig. 334). Writing to the archbishop of Canterbury on the proposed site shortly after hearing of Beresford Hope's decision, Coleridge pleaded that 'surely, as far as the genius loci c^{d} avail, no place w^{d} be more suitable, & certainly no diocese c^{d} be more proper than that of your Grace'.[47] But, once again, Hope got carried away. In a private letter to Coleridge the following year, he expressed his anxiety that the 'institution should be in some sort a restoration of the old Monastery of St Augustine, and not a mere College'. 'Don't you feel with me', he added, 'that we must have the old House of St. Augustine back again? The Monastery of St. Andrew at Rome, which sent St Augustine forth with his holy companions, was both a monastery and a mission college.'[48] We cannot know exactly what Hope's intentions were, except to say that such a notion, although appealing to the genius of the site, would have been dynamite in certain Church of England circles.

The associations inspired by the site were echoed in the public and professional press. The *Colonial Church Chronicle*, for one, observed that the College had 'a peculiar and signal advantage in the associations of its mere locality'. In the 'beauty of its buildings, whether old or restored, it may claim not only to rival, but surpass, many of the colleges at our universities, and in the memories and traditions which gather around its site, it may bear comparison with any spot, even in Oxford itself'. Although St Augustine's was comparatively poor as an institution, this mattered little, we are told, for 'there lingers around it something venerable and romantic': 'if we had had all England to choose from, we hardly *could* have selected a spot more appropriate for the training of Missionaries, to go forth from our land as the heralds of salvation, than the very spot which was assigned as a home and dwelling-place to those who first came to our land with the same blessed message of life and peace.'[49] The *Illustrated London News* also seized on the history and romance of the site, noting that 'the locality has been for ages hedged, as it were, with divinity. Twelve centuries and a half have rolled away since Augustine and his forty companions, nigh upon this very spot, met the incredulous King Ethelbert.' 'How auspicious, then', remarked the paper, 'is the site for the new foundation, seeking to become "a humble instrument in the hands of God and the Church".'[50]

The principles underpinning the institutional nature of St Augustine's College, and the historic allusions regarding its location, worked significantly to inform its architecture. Not surprisingly, William Butterfield was chosen for the job. Only someone like Butterfield, with his proven – in the eyes of ecclesiologists, at least – knowledge of, and sensitivity to, medieval architecture, would do for so important a task on such a venerated site. He was given strict instructions to work with the ruins, 'ingrafting' upon them, to use the terminology of *The Ecclesiologist*, 'what is necessary in order to fit it [the site] for its new destiny'.[51] Some of these ideas no doubt came from Beresford Hope, with whom Butterfield had spent 'many a happy hour' planning the college.[52]

Retaining what he could, in particular the fourteenth-century gateway, Butterfield produced a spacious quadrangle with ranges of buildings on three sides, including a chapel, hall, library, warden's and fellows' lodgings, and student rooms.[53] Immediately to the left of the entrance were the students' rooms, contained in a long, low-lying building raised upon a terrace. This building was marked by its impressive open cloister with reticulated tracery and asymmetrical, dual stairway turrets breaking the line of the range's south wall (figs 335 and 336). To the left, flanking the eastern side of the site, directly across the quadrangle from the entrance, was the library. This was perhaps the most striking of the new buildings. Comprising upper and lower sections, and built directly over the foundations of the former refectory, it is a high, continuous building, which dominates the scene. Pleased with this effect, *The Ecclesiologist* described it as 'a vast apartment, seventy-eight feet long by thirty-nine feet broad, with massy buttressed walls and large traceried and transomed windows, surmounted by a magnificent open roof, the ridge of which is sixty-three feet high, . . . so imposing in its dimensions as to become nearly as important an object in a view of Canterbury as the majestic hall of Trinity College, Cambridge'.[54] Beneath this was a 'crypt' or undercroft, once used by the monks as a cellar. This space was lovingly restored by Butterfield close to what would have been its original form based on the ancient remains. With its wonderfully reconstructed Early English vaulting, it made the perfect location for the college's workshop, later becoming the museum. The only deviation from the original composition, observed Beresford Hope, was one of material – the use of 'warm red brick' instead of stone for the webbing of the vaults.[55] Coming around to the open southern side of the quadrangle, we finally reach the western range, comprising the warden's house, the chapel (the east end of which protrudes into the quadrangle), fellows' lodgings, hall and main gateway (fig. 337), all of which, like the students' rooms, were constructed using local flint with Caen stone dressings. A further block, known as the 'Natives' Building', was added at the southern edge of the warden's lodge in 1861. It was here that the non-European students were housed.

As the overriding ethos of the college was one of 'economy and frugality of habits', so the architecture was to be one of humility. Indeed, as Charles Eastlake would later observe, the general appearance of the college was 'remarkable for its extreme simplicity'.[56] But this was not simplicity in terms of a niggardly approach to materials, or a lack of attention to detail, but 'simple' with respect to the character conveyed by the buildings and their spaces. It was in this idea that the architecture of the college was expected to correspond with and 'embody' its pedagogic regime, like

335 Quadrangle of St Augustine's College, Canterbury (now the King's School), designed by William Butterfield. The view is to the north-east, and shows the library (*right*) and student dormitory (*left*).

a modern-day version of Bernard of Clairvaux's 'rule' of austerity. In the instructions given to Butterfield there appears to have been a diktat to adopt plain finishes. Again, this had little to do with expense *per se*, but was based on a 'principle of avoiding bright colours', as in the case of the wallpaper.[57]

This philosophy extended to the furnishings and finishes throughout many of the college buildings, particularly in the students' quarters, as well as communal spaces such as the dining hall and library. In these spaces we find a near monastic character being cultivated. The students' rooms, for instance, were like monks' cells, or 'carrells', as *The Ecclesiologist* described them, based on the 'prophet's allowance' of 'a bed, a stool, and a candlestick'.[58] Although not quite as minimal as this in reality, they were certainly basic. The following description appeared in the *Illustrated London News*: 'They are 15 feet by 8 feet 6 inches, and being divided by a partition, form two small rooms. The furniture consists of an iron bedstead, a neatly arranged fixed washhand-stand, a fixed table, having on one side drawers for clothes and on the other a drawer for writing materials, and above this table shelves for books are fastened to the wall; an elbow chair, and two others, complete, the furniture.'[59]

This arrangement was recorded by one visitor to the college in 1850 as 'most clever and convenient'.[60] The purpose-built furniture was of the 'simplest kind'.[61] There

336 Engraving, 1848, of the cloister corridor of St Augustine's College, Canterbury, showing the main route at the lower level to the student accommodation block, from *Illustrated London News* (1848).

337 Quadrangle of St Augustine's College, Canterbury (1845–8), designed by William Butterfield. The view is to the west and shows the chapel (*left*), the hall (*centre*) and the main gateway (*right*).

338 The main upper-level corridor leading to the student accommodation block at St Augustine's College, Canterbury. The wooden panelling was designed in a restrained, minimalist fashion to reflect the missionary values of the college.

were no fireplaces either, which were standard in Oxbridge college rooms. Instead, Butterfield introduced a hot-water central heating system which was piped through each room. Of this modern convenience, *The Ecclesiologist* commented: 'We confess to some curiosity as to the working of the *sans*-fireplace system: its healthiness has been called in question – we know not with what degree of justice. The intention is obvious – viz., to simplify the routine and habits of the future missionary, by doing away with all separate meal-taking.'[62] This, of course, was part of the challenge confronting Butterfield, the need to 'combine in a group of the collegiate type the necessities of a modern, and the requirements of an ascetic, missionary college'.[63]

But modern conveniences could be taken too far. Beresford Hope believed that Butterfield at times had to be reined in. In a letter to William Hart Coleridge, first warden of the college, Hope noted that one of Butterfield's bills contained 'a charge for varnishing the Fellows rooms – Is it not surely a pity to beautify the solid simplicity of the plain oak in the Fellows rooms – which now looks so real & businesslike?'[64] He need not have worried. So Spartan were these spaces that Bishop Blomfield, while conducting an official inspection of the students' quarters, was recorded as having said (when the word 'Rome' was still pronounced 'Room') 'there is no Room-ward tendency here!'[65] What he observed was that 'chastening system' made real, its walls bearing happily those 'tokens' of apostolic life (fig. 338).

In the dining hall we see this ascetic aesthetic reach its apogee. This space had a high open timber ceiling. The genius of Butterfield was to retain the rough-hewn timbers of the extant buildings where he could. This he did in the old 'gueston hall', adjacent to the ancient gateway, which he refitted as the new dining hall (fig. 340). To match the somewhat brutal character of the timbers he designed a solid, rather masculine, wrought-timber hoarding at the southern end of the room, in much the same manner as the panelling along the corridors in the students' building (fig. 339). The furniture in this room, apart from the warden's chair, consisted mainly of 'T' tables and benches and was also entirely unpretentious. The overall effect was of a distinct vernacularism – a kind of 'Arts and Crafts' before Red House. Here meals were taken 'in common': warden, fellows and all students. But unlike at Oxbridge colleges,

339 Timber hoardings at the southern end of the dining hall, St Augustine's College, Canterbury.

340 Interior of the dining hall, St Augustine's College, Canterbury (1845–8), designed by William Butterfield.

all partook of the same fare. Again, our anonymous visitor of 1850 commented on one such occasion: 'We dined in hall at two o'clock at the high table. The dinner was very plain, and the same for the high as the low tables.'[66] Thus, in this one space, through its form and material character, as well as in the consistent spectacle of self-imposed restraint that took place within it, we find the college's disciplinary ethos writ large.

Butterfield continued this aesthetic in his interior designs for both the library and chapel. Indeed, the chapel exudes a manifest simplicity, exquisite in its balance between beauty and restraint (fig. 341). Here, again, the timberwork – from roof to floor – is fine without being fussy, in some parts appearing almost crude. 'The whole effect', contended *The Ecclesiologist*, 'is one of real, unpretending, earnest effectiveness, an austere and unworldly beauty.'[67] Such a space was perfect for the purpose to which it was put, not only for quiet prayer and divine worship, but also for the matriculation and 'swearing-in' of students, the gravitas and solemnity of which was no doubt profound.[68] Beneath was the crypt (or 'Lower Chapel'), which was a heavily vaulted space with banded marble walling (fig. 343). Two relief sculptures designed by William Burges are located in this space. Here, in 1859, on these very walls, was established the tradition of engraving the names of deceased former students, those marked in red signifying 'martyrs'. Seeing this, it is little wonder the college was not inundated with applicants, especially when the prospectus asked such pointed questions as: 'Are you without any particular family ties? and duties?'[69] It all suggested the likelihood that alumni would meet a premature end.

The library had a high open oak-beam roof much like the dining hall, only in this case on a grander scale (fig. 342). Following ancient precedent, the principal members, also rather rough-hewn, were joined using traditional carpentry techniques, without nails (fig. 344). As if by plan, these practices were literally being revived in the undercroft below, which served initially as the college's carpentry workshop. It was recorded with glee in the first number of the *Occasional Papers* how in this space had been con-

Top left 341 Interior of the chapel of St Augustine's College, Canterbury (1845–8), looking west, designed by William Butterfield.

Top right 342 Interior of the library of St Augustine's College, Canterbury (1845–8), designed by William Butterfield, showing the exposed timberwork ceiling.

Bottom 343 Crypt of St Augustine's College chapel, with the names of deceased graduates inscribed on the walls ('martyrs' were inscribed in red).

structed a 'two-roomed cottage, which . . . has met with a purchaser'. Thereafter, 'a new stock of wood being immediately laid in, another house has been begun to order. The energies of European, African, Hindoo, Esquimaux, and Australian, (representing all the five continents) being concentrated upon this building, it will probably when constructed be the most singular building of its kind in the world.'[70] It was here, too, that the western doors for Grahamstown cathedral were produced.[71]

This second cottage was, of course, seen as serving more than a mere practical purpose. As one might expect, it was understood as symbolising and embodying the global missionary enterprise. 'May it be a type of a greater building not made with hands,' the author beamed, 'a spiritual house, for which it has been the very purpose of this College to collect builders from North and South, from East and West. And may that house be built as energetically and successfully, and with as hearty union among the workmen, as our unpretending little cottage in the Crypt!'[72] The activity in the carpentry shop not only had profound biblical resonance, but also takes us back to the workshop at St John's College, Auckland, where the students laboured in a similar fashion to produce buildings for the very same cause (see pp. 157–9). In this respect, the efforts made at home and abroad in preparing missionary clergymen were linked across time and space. Indeed, as Ian Lochhead has pointed out, former students were apt to imitate aspects of the college architecture in their adopted homes. For example, at Waimate, New Zealand, the church built by the Rev. W. A. Pascoe (1872) was reported in the *Lyttelton Times* as having a west front 'reminiscent of the front of the chapel of St. Augustine's College, Canterbury'.[73] Pascoe even dedicated the church to St Augustine.

If this were not enough, the undercroft space at St Augustine's turned out to be at the very intersection of the exchange of personnel and information between the 'home' and 'colonial' branches of the English Church. It was here, for instance, that Beresford Hope entertained leading churchmen at the opening of the college in 1848, including a number of colonial churchmen; and here that Bishop Mackenzie was bidden God-speed on the eve of his departure to Central Africa. It was in this space also that bishops and clergymen on return visits from the colonies narrated their experiences from all over the world (fig. 345).[74]

As one walks around St Augustine's today, perusing contemporary descriptions and viewing old prints and photographs, one gets a distinct impression of being in a parallel universe, as if transported to the colonies. What remains of the original spaces and their fittings indicates that St Augustine's was a place similar to those that would be experienced by its students upon graduation. This was a concept akin to education by simulation. Walking into the students' quarters or the dining hall, for instance, one is reminded of conditions in places such as St John's College, Auckland; St Andrew's College, Kohimarama; or Queen's College, Newfoundland – simple, restrained and disciplined. In this sense, St

344 Detail of a timber rafter and wall shaft, St Augustine's College library, showing jointing without the use of nails.

345 Butterfield's medieval-style undercroft beneath St Augustine's College library, showing its use as a 'colonial museum' later in the nineteenth century.

Augustine's can be seen as an attempt to visit colonial conditions upon England through a carefully orchestrated set of spatial and architectural arrangements. Everywhere one turns, the words of *The Ecclesiologist* ring true, that 'same air of repose and quiet usefulness in all that the eye rests upon'.[75]

As a centre for the inculcation of Tractarian ideals, St Augustine's College, Canterbury, was a controversial enterprise. Evangelicals within the Church were highly suspicious of it, and, as a consequence, largely withheld their encouragement and support. To be sure, the education of over 600 missionaries up to 1905 was not an insignificant achievement, but there is little doubt that the roll call would have been higher had the college been broader in its theological outlook.[76] Nevertheless, located as it was at the heart of the English ecclesiastical establishment, St Augustine's was a powerful and impressive manifestation of the unified efforts of the Church and its personnel around the world, which stood as testament to Edward Coleridge's understanding of the Church of England as a truly global enterprise. Architecturally, this unity of purpose is captured in the words of that other visionary builder of global Anglicanism, Bishop John Medley: 'How happy were we to be present in a building, reared on those ancient foundations of England's primitive glory, where . . . the originator of the design, and the founder of the institution, and the builder of the fabric, had all one mind and one soul; where the building was no motley collection of ill-assorted plagiarisms, like nothing else, and yet like everything else in Christian art.'[77] In this respect, St Augustine's College was a monument to applied theology.

Home Missions: Slum Work and Church Extension in England

Concern for the missionary vocation of the English Church was echoed elsewhere at home. Recall that St Augustine's, in addition to its wider imperial mandate, was originally intended as a training centre for missionaries to the disaffected poor, irreligious and intemperate of Britain's major industrial cities, including mining districts. This proposed dual function for the college suggests two distinct yet connected ideas. First, that the people who inhabited the slums of Britain's industrial centres represented a different kind, even race, of human beings. They were people that civilisation had forgotten, and terms such as 'heathen', 'savagery' and 'barbarism' were used often to describe their circumstances. They were 'in melancholy truth', the Rev. Edward L. Cutts (1824–1901) lamented, 'little more than savages and heathen, in the midst of a civilized and Christian land'.[78] And, secondly, that this condition necessitated a special kind of training in order to prepare clergymen to enter into and cope with what were continually identified as 'unknown worlds', as if venturing into some unexplored African or Asian jungle.[79] Both these ideas were closely related to the perception of, and approach towards, 'uncivilised' races abroad. In fact, as we shall see, it is not surprising that colonial and missionary clergymen moved between slum work in Britain and the foreign mission field – the skills and experience gained in one were considered transferable and applicable to the other, and vice versa.

As Peter Keating, Felix Driver, Catherine Hall and Alison Twells, among others, have shown, these comparisons were commonplace, near clichés in Britain among various Christian organisations by the mid- to late nineteenth century.[80] But, as far as the missionary impulse within the Church of England was concerned, their origins can be traced back through the 'home mission' and Church extension movements to at least the 1840s. Without wishing to delve too deeply into the genealogy or historiography of such comparisons, suffice it to say that these ideas were bound up in the 'condition of England' question and the wider and more universal endeavour to lift the 'wretched' of this world out of poverty, ignorance and heathenism: whether in England or elsewhere, such people were still God's children, and 'harvesting souls' was the name of the game.

For example, in 1840 the Rev. John Livesey of St Philip's, Sheffield, observed in a pamphlet titled *Mechanics' Churches* that in Britain's industrial cities 'a mass of human depravity has been suffered to accumulate; and vices of every kind luxuriate, amidst the stagnant waters of corruption'. It was suggested that one of the most dangerous consequences of this disgraceful neglect of souls, and the 'heathenism' that resulted, was the potential destabilisation of society. Referring to allusions made by Lord John Manners in Parliament, Livesey declared: 'it is quite natural to suppose that in such a population, the demagogue and political firebrand will find abundant materials for sedition, treason, and rebellion'.[81] The solution was to plant churches and to extend the gospel among the working classes in a way that was both orderly and 'true' (that is, according to the ordinances of the established Church).

Again, this endeavour was associated with the wider cause of missions to the heathen, wherever they might be. Such a comparison prompted the Rev. Henry Moseley (1801–1872) to observe that 'in the field of our labours [at home] the working classes of the community are the wilderness. . . . And all these helps to the propagation of the Gospel at home they [mission societies] extend to our colonies and dependencies abroad, and to missions to the heathen. They cover, thus, the whole field of your labours'.[82] Others went further in uniting these causes and finding meaningful parallels with the wider mission field. For example, by 1861 Cutts was able to summarise the problem in its entirety, accounting for precedent, the contemporary condition and its global ramifications. Taking the long view, he began by tracing the cause back to Saxon times, comparing these to the present day:

> The missionaries who converted our Saxon forefathers addressed themselves first to their Kings, as the Missionaries in South Africa address themselves first to the Chiefs. Each King of the Heptarchy, as he was converted, encouraged the Missionary Bishop and his staff of Clergy to settle at his chief town. . . . These itinerating Clergy revisited, at stated times, the villages and hamlets thinly scattered amidst the Saxon forests; ministering to the little companies of believers whom they had gathered into the fold, and extending their operations as opportunity served, much as the Clergy are now doing in the Bush of our Australian Colonies.[83]

Out of this process was born the parish system, which had remained essentially unchanged since medieval times. But the extraordinary growth in population, combined with the pressures of modern urbanisation, caused particular evils to proliferate, which the founders of the parish system could hardly have foreseen. Like Henry Mayhew in his early exposés in the *Morning Chronicle*, or Friedrich Engels in his dramatic account in *Die Lage der arbeitenden Klassen in England* (1845), Cutts explained this evil in the following way, again making a comparison with the wider world:

> Go with a Clergyman, or medical man, or district visitor, or town missionary, on one of his visits. You turn out of the main thoroughfare into a labyrinth of narrow dirty lanes, where a respectably-dressed person, other than those we have mentioned, is seldom seen; next you turn out of one of these lanes, through a narrow passage, into a small court. . . . It is surrounded on every side by tall houses of blackened brick, with dirty windows, whose broken panes here and there are pasted over with paper, or stuffed with rags. The houses are so high, and the court so narrow, that the sun never penetrates half way down its depth; the water stands in slimy puddles on the broken pavement; and the air, full of foetid odours, stagnates as in a vault. You look around, and count twelve houses. . . . But you must banish from your mind all idea of twelve houses. . . . Fancy 120 Irish cabins, or Hottentot huts, or whatever human habitations are most miserable and foul.[84]

Moreover, as the population was increasing at the rate of around 200,000 per annum (by Cutts's estimation), this was the equivalent of allowing 100,000 heathens to migrate to Britain every year.[85]

These miserable souls described by Cutts were the kind of people whom Gustave Doré would later capture with grim immediacy in his pictorial book *London: A Pilgrimage*, published in 1872 (fig. 346). For Cutts, the solution to and wider implications of this problem were clear:

> The first and most pressing object of the Society[86] is to send missionary Clergy to labour among the degraded and heathen masses of our large towns. . . . We must not omit to suggest, however briefly, the effect which the thorough evangelization of England would have upon the evangelization of the world. How often we are told that God has marked out and fitted England to be a great missionary nation, by giving her a pure faith, and great advantages for propagating it over the world. . . . Alas! how little does she do for the conversion of the world. She scatters a few clerical missionaries here and there over the earth; but those advantages of empire, colonies, and commerce, for evangelizing the world on a grand scale, are lost and wasted. And why? Because her own sons and daughters, who control her administration, and form her colonies, and conduct her commerce, are not themselves evangelized. . . . Our colonies, instead of being centres of Christianity to the surrounding nations, themselves form a mission field which absorbs a large portion of the means and energy of one of the greatest of our Church Societies [SPG]. . . . But when England has even approximated to the condition to which it is our holy aim and our prayer to God to bring her; then what influence will her example have upon the nations of Christendom! . . . how her colonies then will be centres of civilization and religion to the heathen around! how then her commerce will carry all over the world the powerful preaching of the lives of manly, self-restraining, God-fearing, Christian men![87]

346 'Dudley Street, Seven Dials' from Gustave Doré's *London: A Pilgrimage* (1872) (private collection).

By this time Cutts's plea was a familiar one. It resonated with many of the reasons given for the founding of the CBF and the creation of the colonial episcopate at large. It also emphasised the point, as Beresford Hope had done, that Britain and its empire – socially speaking – formed an integrated system in which the 'moral health' of each 'limb' was essential to the good order and functioning of the whole. The interchangeable use of language in describing the European and non-European worlds had also become commonplace in the discourse on the plight of Britain's working classes. Moreover, and perhaps most importantly, it meshed with, and further bolstered, theories of nationalist providentialism: that this was God's will, and that Britain would be judged for its efforts both at home and abroad.

Among the earliest and most controversial home missions to the urban poor in Britain during this period was that associated with the parish of St George-in-the-East, London. A distinctly Tractarian enterprise, St George's Mission, as it became known, was initiated by the Rev. Bryan King (1811–1895) and headed by the Rev. Charles Fuge Lowder (1820–1880), probably the greatest 'slum priest' of the nineteenth century (fig. 347). King, former curate at St John's, Bethnal Green, came to St George's in 1842 where he introduced certain 'innovative' High Church practices, including lit candles on a vested altar, the intoning of psalms and preaching in a surplice. This caused much vexation in the parish at the time, leading to the so-called 'ritualism riots' of the late 1850s and early 1860s.[88] While King was fighting off (literally) his parishioners at St George's, Lowder was busy ministering to the destitute in and around the London docks and the notorious Ratcliff Highway.

According to Lowder, St George's Mission had a strong claim to being the first in the 'catholic tradition'.[89] There were others in London, such as those associated with St Barnabas's, Pimlico, and St Mary's, Soho. However, among the earliest was that established by Samuel Wilberforce at Banbury (1850), in the diocese of Oxford.[90] But St George's was unique in other, less admirable ways. For Lowder, the parish in which it operated was another world, teaming with goods and people from all over Britain's empire. Like some far-flung colony, this was a land unknown to most Englishmen, who believed, wrote Lowder, they had 'arrived at the Far East when they have reached the Bank of England'.[91] This was only the beginning – the border – of a territory much more extensive, however. Again, using language that would seem more at home in the mouths of David Livingstone or John Speke, Lowder observed that St George-in-the-East, 'notorious in the annals of newspaper history, was to them, as well as to the world in general, a *terra incognita*'. It was owing to this anonymity that he and the Rev. J. Newton Smith found themselves on a 'voyage of discovery', in what was effectively a 'new country'.[92]

347 Portrait of the Rev. Charles Fuge Lowder (1820–1880), from Maria Trench, *Charles Lowder: A Biography* (1881).

This 'new country' had parallels with the wider world in other ways, too. In his account of the mission published in 1877, *Twenty-One Years in S. George's Mission*, Lowder associated its work with missionary endeavours in India.[93] But it was in the use and appropriation of space that we see the most striking continuities. Apart from the existing eighteenth-century church of St George by Hawksmoor, the mission's first real 'plant' was the chapel of the Good Shepherd (1856), located in the garden of the Mission House on Calvert Street (now Watts Street). This was a temporary iron structure capable of holding 200 people, much like those shipped to places such as Canada and Australia in the 1850s (see pp. 163–6). Very little evidence remains regarding this structure, but it would have been something like those produced by Peter Thompson of Limehouse or Samuel Hemming in Bristol.[94] The mission would later find a more worthy home in St Peter's, London

Docks (1866), by F. H. Pownall, with its spectacular polychrome brick interior.[95] Where no building existed, the missionaries resorted to open-air preaching. There was, of course, a precedent for this in the Nonconformist tradition, but it was also something that Bishop Perry had done at the gold diggings in Victoria; that Selwyn had adopted among the Māori in New Zealand; that Robertson had introduced in Natal; and that William Turpin was forced to do at Grahamstown. At the opening of the chapel, King preached, reiterating, as many had done before him, that it was the Church's 'first and paramount responsibility' to care for her '*own children*'. Mindful of the context, he added that, in these people, 'she [the national Church] had not yet discovered the vast, the *inexhaustible* treasures of wealth, better far than the revenues of empires'.[96] As if referring to the most ignorant of heathens in a distant land, religion, he claimed, was dead to the 'poor straying souls' of the Ratcliff Highway, likening the task of their conversion to that of proselytising 'the dull and hardened hearts of aliens'.[97]

It was while ministering to these 'aliens' that Lowder realised, just as Bishop Gray and his colleagues had in South Africa, the power of ritual and ornament. Their method – again, extremely controversial – was known as the 'Way of the Cross'.[98] Comprised of 'stations', this method was one in which Lowder and his colleagues processed through the slums and rookeries of the East End, stopping to preach in any open space that would allow a crowd to gather. The missiology involved here was similar to that later employed by the Universities' Mission to Central Africa. For example, at station six, referred to as 'the Ruins', Lowder was recorded in *The Guardian* as having said: '"Jesus stripped off His garments", conveying lessons which it need scarcely be said were peculiarly applicable in such a district, where many a half-dressed woman and child was listening intently. There will be no clothes in the kingdom of heaven, said Mr Lowder, who, like a second Wesley, appealed to his hearers to dress the soul rather than the body, and never to be absent from Church because of shabby clothes.'[99] Thus, just as Bishop Tozer of the UMCA cared little for Westernising the indigenous peoples of Central Africa by 'clothing' them, focusing instead on their souls, so too Lowder was concerned less with outward appearance than with inward substance (when it came to his 'converts', at least). This was considered the only sure way to Christianise and therefore 'civilise' such people, whether in the Morambala Highlands or the back streets of Wapping.

It is therefore hardly surprising to learn that the Rev. Henry Rowley of the UMCA began his career as the schoolmaster at St George's Mission. Men came back the other way, too, such as the Rev. Edward Williams, who had been ordained by Bishop Tyrrell of Newcastle (NSW) and became missionary priest at St Saviour's and St Stephen's, Spitalfields, in 1869. Other foreign links with St George's included the Rev. Edward Gifford Shapcote, who went to South Africa as a missionary in 1864, and the Rev. C. N. Gray, son of Bishop Robert Gray of Cape Town, who assisted in extending the mission throughout the East End.

The St George's Mission even organised what it referred to as 'special' or 'preaching' missions to other towns and cities in Britain. For example, in 1862 they decamped to Bedminster, Bristol, for ten days. There they catechised children, sang hymns, preached sermons on the seven deadly sins, and gave lectures to the colliers who lived in the area, concluding the mission with a midnight visit to a neighbouring coal mine. Lowder later noted how 'a deep impression was made on many'.[100] The lives of Lowder and his colleagues, who formed a kind of brotherhood in 1855 known as Societas Sanctae Crucis (Society of the Holy Cross), were dedicated to discipline and frugality. They were followed shortly afterwards (1857) by what was essentially an order of Anglican nuns, established by Elizabeth, the sister of John Mason Neale, who called themselves the Community of the Holy Cross. This sisterhood worked alongside the St George's Mission, among the fallen women and homeless children of the area.

Numerous other so-called mission churches were erected in London during these years, among the more noteworthy of which were St Saviour's, Hoxton (1865–6), by James Brooks, and St James the Less, Pimlico (1859–61), by G. E. Street (fig. 348).[101] It was out of experiments such as these that came the famous Oxbridge and public school 'settlements' in the East End and south of London during the 1880s – enterprises that were also Tractarian in inspiration, describing themselves likewise as 'colonies' and 'missions'.[102]

❁

The changing face of religion in nineteenth-century Britain also forced the established Church to reform, consolidate, and extend its presence in other parts of the country to meet not only the demands of the Ecclesiastical Commissioners but also, and perhaps more urgently, the challenge

348 External and internal perspective drawings of St Saviour's church, Hoxton, London (1865–6), designed by James Brooks, from the *Church Builder* (1866).

of Nonconformism.[103] This was especially the case in rural or 'rusticated' regions where the parochial system was structurally weak, inefficient, and/or overstretched. One such place was the diocese of Exeter, covering all of Devon and Cornwall. In time, a new diocese would be carved out of this territory – that of Truro (1876) – but in the 1830s its ecclesiastical structures were essentially medieval, creaking under the strains of population growth, distance, non-residency and poor communication.[104] It was in this part of the country that the full force of Methodism was felt, which took advantage of the inadequacies of the diocesan and parochial systems of the established Church, and which began encroaching upon and disrupting the old world order. Official census statistics show that by 1851 adherents of the Church of England were in the minority in the south-west, especially in Cornwall.[105] Action was required.

These dual problems of negligence and Nonconformism combined to put the diocese in a condition somewhat akin to a missionary one by the 1830s.[106] The established Church had to fight back in order to prevent itself from being overrun and made all but irrelevant. Enter the Rev. Henry Phillpotts (1778–1869), bishop of Exeter from 1830. Phillpotts was at least cognisant of the real threat presented by Methodism as early as 1812.[107] Spurred on by the growing popularity of Methodism in the south-west, and by the wider agenda of ecclesiastical reform, he oversaw an extended period of Anglican renewal in the diocese, tightening discipline and invigorating the Church. He was particularly active in parochial restructuring, creating seventy-seven new parishes during his reign as bishop (forty-four in Devon and thirty-three in Cornwall), mainly through subdivision, which was allowed under the various Church acts passed during the 1830s and early 1840s. Being a patron of the Cambridge Camden Society, Phillpotts also facilitated Church extension projects throughout the diocese, including the erection of several mission chapels at Pinhoe, Exton, Travellers' Rest, Glampton, Cowley and Sidford.[108]

Heavily involved in this process was the Exeter Diocesan Architectural Society, founded in 1841 by John Medley (its first secretary, and later bishop of Fredericton) and John Armstrong (later bishop of Grahamstown), with Phillpotts as patron. Many of the foremost families of the diocese were also members, leading to a considerable degree of patronage with respect to church building and restoration.[109] Lord

349 The church of St Michael and All Angels, Baldhu, Cornwall (1847–8), by William White.

Rolle, for instance, was particularly active against Nonconformism, commissioning John Hayward, the society's architect, to design St Mary's, Bicton (1849–50).[110] The Incorporated Church Building Society was also crucial to Church extension in the diocese, providing grants for the erection and rebuilding of over 300 churches in Devon and Cornwall during Phillpotts's episcopacy (1830–69). The ICBS aimed at increasing the number of free sittings in each parish, thus encouraging poorer parishioners to abandon dissenting sects in favour of returning to the Church of England.[111] It was under the impetus of this aim that the likes of William White and G. E. Street began their solo careers. Shortly after arriving at Scott's office in London as an 'improver', White left to establish his own practice in Truro, Cornwall (1847), first designing St Michael and All Angels, Baldhu (1847–8), and then rebuilding St Gerrent's, Gerrans (1849–50) – both under the patronage of the Earl of Falmouth with grants from the ICBS (fig. 349).[112] As suggested in Chapter 4, this experience no doubt assisted him in preparing economic designs for South Africa (see pp. 212–13).[113] Although remaining in London, Street was also active in the south-west during the late 1840s, having prepared designs for churches benefiting from ICBS grants, such as St Mary the Virgin, Par (1847–51); St Peter's, Treverbyn (1848–51); and St Cuthbert's, Cubert (1849–53).

Apart from Medley and Armstrong, the other connections the diocese of Exeter had with the English Church abroad included the Rev. Francis Fulford (bishop of Montreal), Edward Coleridge (housemaster at Eton and colonial agent), Frank Wills (architect and leading figure in the New York Ecclesiological Society), the Rev. William Hart Coleridge (bishop of Barbados and first warden of St Augustine's College), and the Rev. J. C. Patteson (bishop of Melanesia). Exeter cathedral was also the site where Selwyn gave his farewell sermon in December 1841 (see p. 29).

The Incorporated Church Building Society was, in fact, fundamental to the wider cause of Anglican renewal in England and Wales during the nineteenth century. It began life in 1818 as the Church Building Society in response to the first Church-Building Act (1818), which required addi-

350 Wythop church, Cumberland (*c.*1864), before and after restoration, from the *Church Builder* (1864).

tional church accommodation for the country's rapidly expanding population.[114] Its record was impressive. By the time its first regular publication (*The Church Builder*) appeared in 1862, it had given funds for the erection, enlargement and restoration of 4,365 parish churches.[115] Although, in its early years, as Beresford Hope was quick to point out, the society was the 'sponsor of some of the most horrid monstrosities in the shape of churches which ever disfigured art',[116] by the 1850s it had been thoroughly infused with the spirit of ecclesiology, appointing a 'committee of architects' whose job it was to scrutinise and amend (even reject) plans submitted for funding. This committee included some of the most accomplished names working in the field of Anglican church architecture during the mid- to late nineteenth century, giving the projects funded by the society a consistent degree of no-fuss integrity and correctness.[117] Typical examples of the kind of church enlargement and replacement work the society was undertaking by this time can be found in Cilrheyden church, Pembrokeshire (1859–62), and Wythop church, Cumberland (*c.*1864) (fig. 350).

In addition to providing financial aid for its main purpose, the ICBS also established a 'Mission House Scheme' in 1857. Its aim was to plant the first seeds of religious teaching and observance in remote or isolated parts of the country where the presence of the established Church was either inadequate or non-existent. As with the diocese of Exeter, part of the initiative behind the scheme was to counteract the influence of dissenting and Nonconformist sects. A characteristic element of the scheme was to combine a vicarage, school and chapel in one, economical building.[118] In the first edition of the *Church Builder* it was reported that two such buildings had recently been erected in the parish of Tydd St Mary in rural Lincolnshire. The one in the Fen was described as a 'model of its kind', containing

> three living rooms for the schoolmistresses, and a room with a separate entrance for the use of the clergyman. At the west end of the building is a good staircase, which leads up to the 'large upper room furnished and prepared' for Divine Service. It has a high pitched roof, and three windows on each side, with a large east and west window in addition. . . . The cost of this Mission House has been about 700*l.* A portion of the lower end of the room is fitted up with fixed school desks and seats; but the desks are all made with flaps, so that when let down the seats are available for the school children during Divine Service. . . . A bell turret at the west end gives it a very ecclesiastical appearance.[119]

It was later observed that care should be taken in such buildings to mark the difference, architecturally, between that portion used for the school and that solely used for

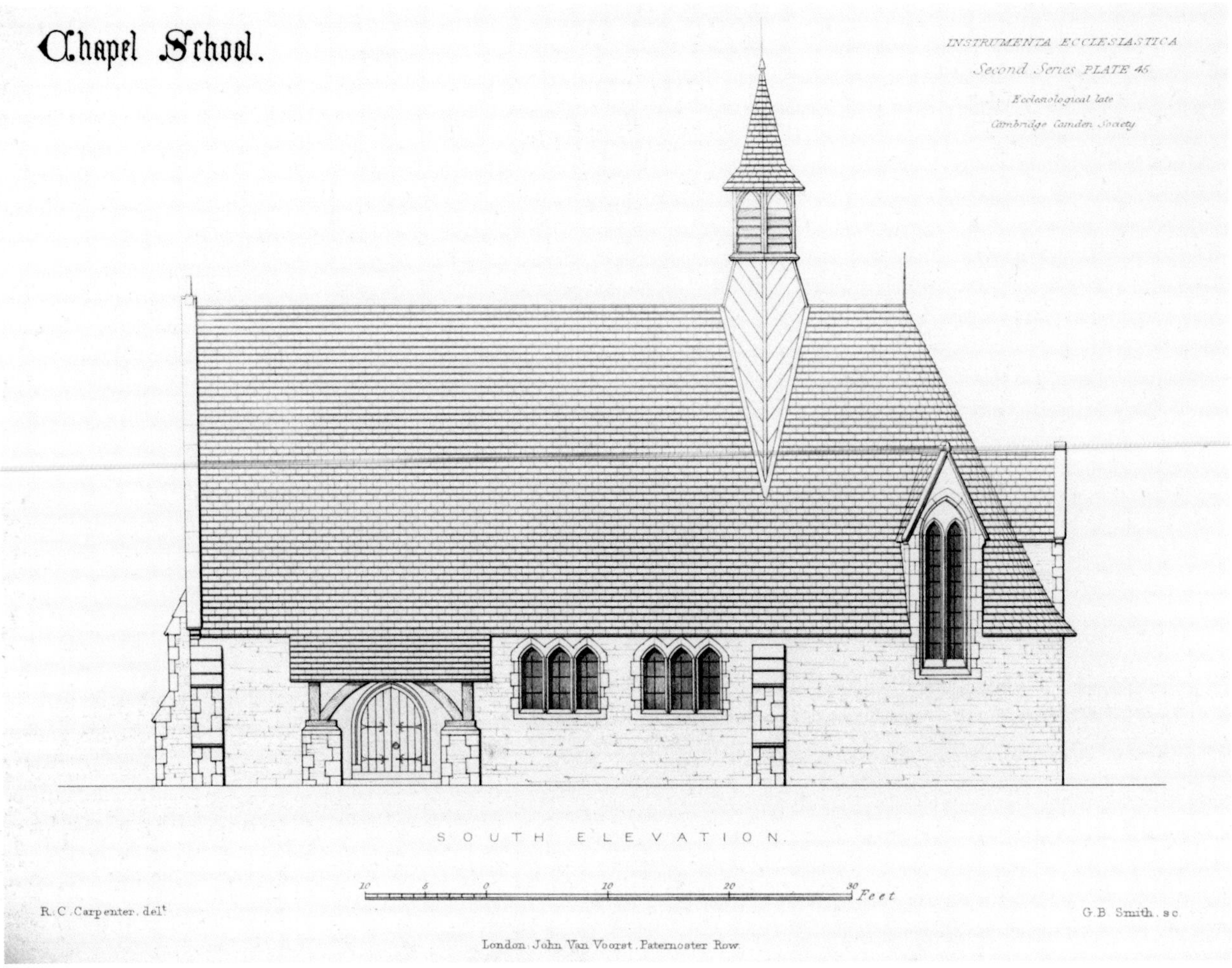

351 R. C. Carpenter's design for a 'chapel-school' from *Instrumenta Ecclesiastica*, 2nd ser. (1856).

worship. Here it was advised to provide a small chancel that might be closed off entirely with folding doors during school hours.[120] This kind of building is reminiscent of those already discussed, such as St Matthew's Mission, Poonindie, South Australia (1855), and Butterfield's design for the Canterbury Settlement, New Zealand (1849) (see pp. 36–7, 313). This building type also relates to Carpenter's design for a 'chapel-school' which appeared in the second series of *Instrumenta Ecclesiastica* (1856), which became the model for B.W. Mountfort's St John the Evangelist, Heathcote (1857–9) (figs 351 and 352).[121]

The purpose of such houses was to gather in and encourage people who had never attended any place of worship before, especially those drawn to 'dissenting congregations'. In one case, at Armley, near Leeds, the mission house was built for a population 'looked upon as the Van Diemen's land of the parish'.[122] However, being schools and churches in one, the ultimate aim of the mission house scheme was to bring such people into the polity of the established Church by educating them and thus inculcating a particular set of values and ideals:

> In the Fen dissent was popular, – and deservedly so, for it was the only channel of religious teaching, – but since the erection of the Mission House the two meetings of Dissenters have been abandoned, and with the exception of two families the whole of the neighbourhood for miles around now regularly attend the services of the Church. . . . It is not too much to say that the whole character of that district of the Fen has been altered and elevated since the Church has been fairly planted there; the manners of the people are improved, their intelli-

352 The church of St John the Evangelist, Heathcote, New Zealand (1857–9), by Benjamin Mountfort.

gence cultivated, their morals advanced. . . . About forty children are under regular instruction. . . . Truly the wilderness is blossoming and bringing forth fruit to the glory of Almighty God.[123]

As with missionary efforts in Britain's industrial cities, this enterprise was bound up with fears of social instability caused by the perceived relationship between irreligion and civil disobedience, and, in the minds of some, Nonconformism and republicanism.[124] As discussed in Chapter 5, these were also fears shared by Anglican clergymen in the colonies.

The ICBS missionary fund was augmented in the late 1850s to include aid for temporary and portable structures made of wood and iron, providing places of worship for what the society described as migratory populations – that is, 'those large bodies of artizans and labourers whose services are required by the agriculturalist, the manufacturer, and the trader, only at *certain seasons of the year*'.[125] This likened some parts of Britain to the farming districts of rural New South Wales, or the gold diggings of central Victoria, where temporary structures of wood and iron were also required for itinerant populations. Once again, it was Beresford Hope (a member of the ICBS committee) who had foreseen this continuity, architecturally speaking, between Britain and its empire. 'We should be quick at discerning the distinctive types of the town and of the country church, of the college or domestic chapel,' he exhorted listeners during a paper read before the Oxford Architectural Society in 1846.

We should make ourselves familiar with the social condition of great and crowded towns, and with their religious destitution. We should forecast the probable wants of the age, . . . and we should mediate what peculiar method the Church of the nineteenth century should assume to embody them. We should think upon the workhouse chapels, hospital chapels, and barrack chapels, and missionary churches in the midst of Leeds and Manchester. We should remember that Great Britain . . . will soon have to rear temples of the true faith in Benares and Labrador, Newfoundland and Cathay.[126]

Beresford Hope was not the only member of the ICBS who understood this connection between the endeavours of the home and colonial branches of the English Church. We find it also among two of the society's leading committee men, Joshua Watson (1771–1855), a London-based wine merchant and member of the Hackney Phalanx, and William Cotton (1786–1866), director of the Bank of England. Being close friends with a number of colonial bishops, including Broughton and Selwyn, Watson was very much concerned with Church extension in the colonies,[127] while Cotton was the father of the Rev. W. C. Cotton, Selwyn's assistant curate. It was Cotton senior who had gifted Selwyn the now famous church tent before he set sail for New Zealand in 1841.

Celtic Fringe?
Ireland and Global Anglicanism

What about Ireland? It is certainly not straightforward to argue a case for Ireland in the context of this study. Strictly speaking, it was not 'home'; nor was it a 'colony' as commonly understood in the mid-nineteenth-century sense of the term. It was formally integrated into the British political state in 1801, but its status remained ambiguous, hovering somewhere between what it actually was (legally) and what it was perceived to be (historically).[128] Complicating matters further was the fact that the Church in Ireland was different in so many ways from the Church in the distant colonies. Unlike the new world order represented in Britain's other, more recent imperial acquisitions (that is, those colonies beyond the British Isles), Anglicanism was firmly established in Ireland. There it was known as the Church of Ireland, where it had existed as an independent ecclesiastical polity since 1536. With the Act of Union – creating the United Kingdom of Great Britain and Ireland – the Church of Ireland was likewise fused with the Church of England to form the United Church of England and Ireland. This union remained in place until the Irish Church Act (1869) formally disentangled the two provinces, leading to disestablishment in Ireland in 1871.

However, despite this major historical difference, there are a number of parallels that relate the Anglican experience in Ireland to the rest of Britain's colonial empire. As Hilary Carey has recently observed, it is worth remembering that from 1801 the historic realms of England, Scotland, Ireland and Wales, as well as Britain's overseas territories, were all effectively united into a single state, ruled by a Protestant monarch, endowed with not one, but two established Churches (the United Church of England and Ireland and the Church of Scotland), and ultimately governed by a single parliament in Westminster.[129] This created a set of circumstances that both enabled and encouraged a certain degree of political, economic and religious continuity within and across the wider British state. It is therefore appropriate to make a few points here, however brief and incomplete, on what these continuities were with regard to Ireland and how they affected the perception and use of ecclesiastical architecture in what was essentially England's first overseas colony.[130]

This is important, for the long process of Irish colonisation had a distinct spatial dimension, which can be detected in the literature on Irish conquest, 'reconquest' and union from earliest times to the nineteenth century. As Mark Dorrian had shown, by considering these spatial and/or formal attributes, it is possible to gain certain insights into the Anglo-Irish experience.[131] With this spatial aspect in mind, Nicholas Canny has also observed (in relation to the Elizabethan period) how it is both desirable and instructive to view Irish history in the wider geographical context of European expansion.[132] This is equally true of the Victorian era. By situating the trials of the Irish Church in the broader context of global Anglicanism, certain connections and associations become apparent that help give greater depth and breadth to our understanding of the ecclesiastical reforms (and their architectural consequences) that took place in both Ireland and the wider British empire during the mid-nineteenth century. This also includes the architects involved, in this case namely Street, Slater and Burges.

To begin with, great swathes of early modern Ireland had been subject to a 'plantation' culture imported from Britain (both England and Scotland) during the sixteenth and seventeenth centuries. This culture was effectively a colonial one, in that its mechanisms of conquest, patronage and administration broadly corresponded to those that would later be extended elsewhere.[133] As David Fitzpatrick has convincingly argued, practically speaking, post-Union Ireland was a 'colony' in all but name.[134] More specifically, Anglicanism was understood and used as an instrument of 'civilisation' in Ireland, both during the Tudor reconquest of the sixteenth century and after. In this sense, as Wilberforce would have appreciated, the imposition and extension of the Church in Ireland was as much a political and cultural enterprise as it was a spiritual one, bound up with ideas of systematic education and religious reform, despite its ultimate failure to achieve religious hegemony.[135] In fact, for better or worse, comparison was made at the time between the way the English Church had been instituted in Ireland and how it was being rolled out in places such as India, Africa and China.[136]

The acrimony between Roman Catholics and Protestants that characterised the Irish scene was also echoed in the colonies, although not with anything like the same violence.[137] This was most evident in places such as Sydney and St John's (Newfoundland), where sizable Irish emigrant populations existed. The Irish were among the most prolific migrants to Britain's colonies during the nineteenth century. Indeed, many of the Roman Catholic clergy that ended up in the colonies were from Ireland, as were a number of the Anglican clergy.[138] As mentioned in Chapter 5, the initial shortage of willing English clergy meant that Irish churchmen, trained at Trinity College, Dublin, were relied upon more than was anticipated.[139] These clerics also brought with them their own brand of conservative Protestantism, such as that seen in Tasmania and British North America, setting them at loggerheads with Roman Catholics and High Church Anglicans alike. We have already met some of these men during the course of this study, including the Revs H. P. Fry (Tasmania), David Fitzgerald (Prince Edward Island) and Peter Beamish (NSW).

But the connections and cross-currents between Ireland and the wider British empire ran deeper still. Indeed, it was the Grey administration's reform of the Irish bishoprics in the early 1830s which inspired the now famous charge of 'national apostasy' from John Keble, subsequently sparking the Oxford Movement – a movement, as we have seen, that had profound consequences for the development of the colonial Church of England. This was mainly because Church reforms in Ireland had effectively put an end to hopes of establishment in the colonies, which might have led to a more independent outlook. Likewise, after disestablishment, the Church in Ireland found itself in an analogous situation to that in the colonies.[140] Even before this moment, parallels could be found with the controversy surrounding the increase in the Maynooth grant (1845) for Catholic education in Ireland, which effectively established a quasi-pluralist condition not entirely unlike that experienced in many of Britain's colonies, particularly in Australia.

Physically, too, conditions were similar, including widespread poverty and under-development, especially beyond 'the Pale'. To be sure, the reasons for this deficiency differed from place to place. It must be remembered that Irish sees were far wealthier than their colonial counterparts. However, the largely moribund state of the Church in Ireland – riddled with sinecures, pluralities and non-residencies – meant that the funds were not used effectively, oftentimes being misappropriated.[141] The ultimate effect of this upon the ecclesiastical landscape was clear: impoverished clergy, dilapidated or inadequate church accommodation, and small and dispersed communities of adherents in conflict with other denominations. When Archbishop William King (1650–1729) of Dublin was asked if he might contribute missionaries to Britain's overseas territories, he replied: 'we are in little better circumstances . . . than the foreign plantations themselves'.[142] Things had changed little a century later. In 1831, for example, the then bishop of Dublin, Richard Whately (1787–1863), observed sardonically that 'in large districts of Ireland the Established Church is such as, by the help of a map, you might establish in Turkey or in China – viz. no place of worship, no congregation, no payment'.[143] Thus, as Owen Chadwick has noted, lapses in the Irish Church were not only blatant but also conspicuous.[144]

Like the colonies, Ireland was a mission field. It had always been the focus of missionary attention in one form or other since the first English invasions, particularly during the late sixteenth and early seventeenth centuries. But the early part of the nineteenth century witnessed something altogether different, the so-called 'new' or 'second' Reformation.[145] As the first Protestant Reformation had failed to convert and control the Roman Catholic population of Ireland, this follow-up movement – led by organisations such as the Irish Society (1818), the Scripture Readers' Society (1822) and the Reformation Society (1827) – saw itself as finishing the job. Spurred on in part by the perceived inertia and dereliction of the Irish Church, and in part as a response to the resurgence in Roman Catholic sentiment, it was an especially zealous attempt to bring the entire Irish population into conformity with the Church as by law established.[146] No small amount of Anglo-Irish prejudice towards Celtic culture motivated this enterprise, to the point where Irish peasants were routinely compared to 'savage', 'barbaric' and 'childlike' natives in other parts of the world such as Africa and Asia.[147] The missionary impulse in nineteenth-century Ireland was therefore bound up (as in other parts of the empire) with notions of cultural trusteeship and the need to 'educate' and 'civilise'. But Roman Catholic and Celt were not the only ones that required reform: the 'errors' of Protestant Nonconformism in the guise of Presbyterianism were also targeted.

This made the Irish scene somewhat akin to that experienced by Bishop Broughton in New South Wales. Just as Broughton had complained of 'Romanists on the one side and the Dissenters on the other', so, too, the Rev. William Magee, bishop of Dublin, felt 'hemmed in by two opposite descriptions of professing Christians: the one, possessing a Church, without what *we* can properly call a religion; and the other possessing a religion, without what *we* can properly call a Church'.[148] Although, as Chadwick has suggested, the High Church party in Ireland remained aloof from such 'enthusiasms', believing that the Irish would be converted through the diffuse effects of 'reason and education',[149] leading High Churchmen such as John Jebb and Richard Mant were keen to reinstate discipline and order in the Irish Church, which included proselytising both Roman Catholics and Dissenters.[150] However, the second Reformation was effectively derailed as a missionary project following Catholic emancipation in 1829.

The CMS was also active in Ireland. There it operated in the guise of the Hibernian Society (founded 1814). However, unlike the established hierarchy of the Church of Ireland, which, in its modern form, was essentially an imported, Anglophone constitution from England (although Irish bishops did not necessarily see it that way), the strategy of the CMS was to indigenise the Anglican faith by reaching out and proselytising in the Irish tongue. In so doing it took the fight directly into the Gaelic-speaking peasant communities of rural Ireland. This strategy operated in direct contradistinction to the official policy of the established Church, which for so long had been happy to work within its traditional power bases. The *modus operandi* of the CMS therefore linked efforts in Ireland to its wider, global missionary policy under the Rev. Henry Venn.[151] In this sense, Ireland and the colonies (and beyond) were perceived by the CMS as both a unified and extended field of operation.

Importantly for this study, Tractarianism established a foothold in this evolving domain. As Peter Nockles has demonstrated, it was in the context of the fall-out from the Whig reforms during the 1830s and 1840s that a number of leading Irish High Churchmen began to sympathise with the Oxford Movement, enabling them to strengthen their argument that they belonged to a proper 'Church' as opposed to a mere sect.[152] This cause, however, had the odds stacked against it in the climate of ultra-Protestantism that prevailed in Ireland during the early decades of the nineteenth century. To many, Tractarianism appeared as an intrusive deviation – an 'unreformed' species of 'quasi-popery' – that militated against the revived Evangelicalism which had swept through and now dominated the Irish Church.[153]

But the one thing working in favour of the High Churchmen in this regard was that they could trace the genealogy of their arguments concerning catholicity and apostolic succession (or so they believed) back to a time long before the Oxford Movement. This was a claim similar to that which had been made by Bishop Strachan in Toronto (see p. 79), and one that had also characterised High Church Episcopalianism in the United States during the early nineteenth century.[154] Indeed, it was argued that clergymen in Ireland had asserted Anglican apostolical continuity and repudiated the schismatical nature of Romanism within Britain as early as the seventeenth century. Here texts such as James Ussher's *Discourse of the Religion Anciently Professed by the Irish and British* (1623) and Richard Cox's *Hibernia Anglicana* (1689) were cited in defence of the idea that the Protestant Church in Ireland was a lineal descendent of the early church of St Patrick, which was largely independent of Rome. The logical consequence of this reasoning was that Irish Romanism was seen as a later corruption.[155] This argument was essentially one that promoted the notion of the established Protestant Church as being the 'true' or 'real' Church in Ireland. In the period under discussion, this tradition of scholarly apologetic found its apogee in Richard Mant's *History of the Church of Ireland* (1840), W. G. Todd's *The Church of St. Patrick* (1844) and Henry Cotton's six-volume *Fasti Ecclesiae Hibernicae* (1848–78).[156]

Despite the apparent irony of Keble's appeal to the plight of the Irish Church as the *casus belli* for the Oxford Movement, links between High Churchmen in Ireland and the Oxford Tractarians were extensive, especially early on. Facing broad secular intrusion, and the possibility of disestablishment, Irish High Churchmen found solace in the message promulgated in the early numbers of the *Tracts for the Times* calling for bishops to 'magnify' their office.[157] These arguments also proved useful in confronting the radical and potentially destructive forces of Evangelicalism. Thus, like the CMS and other Low Church missionary organisations in Ireland, the High Churchmen, inspired by the zeal of their English brethren, also looked to inculcate their theology through education and home missions. Initially, their instrument was St Columba's College, Rathfarnham (instigated 1840). Among the scheme's chief founders was the Rev. William Sewell of Exeter College, Oxford.[158] Sewell, who, as we have seen, had connections with the Anglican Church in South Africa and was sometime president of the Oxford Architectural Society, believed that Ireland lacked not only a clergy with the necessary linguistic skills to extend the Church's influence but also a rigorous, disciplined and well-ordered system of education like that of the English public schools.[159] Established in the hope of fulfilling these needs, in particular the production of an Irish-speaking ministry that would conduct missionary work with due regard to ecclesiastical order and in accordance with the English Prayer Book, St Columba's opened its doors in April 1843. Although it would never realise its role as a missionary training centre, it did evolve to become a modern, English-style public school.

Interestingly, the tactic behind producing a Gaelic-speaking clergy for work in the remoter parts of Ireland was very similar to that later adopted by the UMCA and the Melanesian Mission, whereby attempts were made to find and exploit points of intersection between distinct religious and cultural traditions – in the case of Ireland, between Anglicanism and Roman Catholicism. The Rev. J. H. Todd, who was a leading Irish Tractarian and heavily involved in the initiative, explained this strategy in a letter to Pusey, noting that its basic aim was to provide converts 'with a resting place, which will exhibit to them our church in a catholic position and aspect, so that they may see in her that purity of which they are in search, and at the same time not to be compelled to cast off all that is primitive and catholic.'[160] This prefigures the Rev. Henry Rowley's notion several years later that by 'seeking a groundwork in [indigenous peoples'] common customs', the UMCA would find 'a surer way of making them Christians than by totally ignoring all they [knew] as useless' (see p. 172).

Much like such institutions in the colonies, St Columba's was a very modest affair, initially at least. Its first stone buildings, produced from designs by P. C. Hardwick, were chaste and correct – a 'simple example of the revived spirit of ecclesiastical art', observed *The Ecclesiologist*.[161] Its chapel, on the other hand, was a temporary wooden structure in the 'First Pointed' style, reminding one of Selwyn's effort at St John's College, Auckland. Not surprisingly, perhaps, this wooden structure was eventually superseded by a much more comely building in stone designed by none other than William Butterfield (1880), architect of St Augustine's.

As the surrounds of St Columba's demonstrated, architecture was clearly important to the aims of Sewell and Todd. They were not alone. In Ireland, as elsewhere in the British colonial world at this time, a renewed focus on architecture and liturgy was coming to be seen by High Churchmen as fundamental to the revival of order, discipline and solemnity in the Irish Church. In the context of this renewal, the historic if principled disinterest in externals of worship in Ireland suddenly became conspicuous. For instance, while on a visit to Ireland in 1846, Lord John Manners commented on the lack of ritual in church services. Almost as if reliving the nightmare of Bishop Broughton in Sydney, he complained of the cathedral in Kilkenny that 'everything . . . externally and internally, wore a cold Calvinistic hue, and gave a fair promise of success to the magnificent Roman Catholic cathedral hard by, which Mr Pugin is erecting'.[162] Lord John George Beresford, archbishop of Armagh, also knew that an unimpressive liturgy and a paucity of ritual (including music) was to blame for his cathedral's failure to attract Roman Catholics; while *The Ecclesiologist* reported that external religion in Ireland had 'fallen very low'.[163]

Painfully aware of these deficiencies, High Church clerics began restoring their churches and introducing liturgical order and solemnity into public worship. In the hope of promoting greater awareness of such things, both among Irish architects and within the wider clerical profession, the Church of Ireland formed its very own architectural societies. The first of these was the Church Architecture Society founded in 1842 in the diocese of Down by the then bishop, the Rev. Richard Mant (1776–1848). According to Mant, who was a leading Irish High Churchman, the society's aim was 'to give a more appropriate appearance to the houses of God'. This it did, particularly in and around the city of Belfast.[164] Shortly afterwards, in October 1850, came the St Patrick's Ecclesiological Society. This organisation was proposed by two of Ireland's leading Tractarians, Todd and the Rev. William Maturin.[165] Others on the founding committee included the dean of St Patrick's and Christ Church cathedrals, the Very Rev. Henry Pakenham (1787–1863); the warden of St Columba's College, the Rev. George Williams (1814–1878), member of the Ecclesiological Society; and the eminent Irish antiquary and author of *Ecclesiastical Architecture of Ireland* (1845), George Petrie (1790–1866). Its principal patron was the Eton and Christ Church educated Lord John George de la Poer Beresford (1773–1862), bishop of Armagh, primate of all Ireland and leading Irish High Churchman.

As its name suggests, the St Patrick's Ecclesiological Society was modelled closely on its namesake in England. However, it had more in common with the Ecclesiological Society than its name. Its list of vice-presidents included one 'A. J. B. Hope, Esq.', and it operated on the same principle as its counterpart in London by nominating bishops as patrons.[166] Like Mant's society, the stated aims of the St Patrick's Society also connected it to the wider ambitions of the ecclesiological cause. These included, among others, 'the study of Ecclesiastical Architecture and Antiquities, and to aid in the preservation or restoration of the ancient Architectural Monuments of the country'.[167] Indeed, its formation occurred against the backdrop of the full-scale restoration of St Patrick's cathedral, Dublin (1845–52), then taking place under the direction of the English architect and ecclesiologist R. C. Carpenter.[168]

Orchestrated by Pakenham, the restoration of St Patrick's aroused enthusiastic interest in England, especially in the pages of *The Ecclesiologist*.[169] In Ireland, however, it proved rather controversial, as the ancient accretions of the cathedral were systematically 'destroyed' in favour of a wholesale Early English makeover (fig. 354). To be sure, Carpenter's 'restoration' was both radical and comprehensive, and was interpreted as something of an English imposition. The process was initially slow owing to the famine, and then Carpenter's death (1855), but when the brewing magnate Benjamin Lee Guinness stepped in to fund the project's completion in 1860 – to the tune of a reported £130,000 – he took complete control, insisting that all subsequent work merely 'replace whatever is decayed, adhering exactly to the ancient [that is, Irish] patterns, and making no other alteration than the substitution of a better material'. His offer was contingent upon this demand.[170] Naturally the dean and chapter acquiesced, with only Todd expressing a concern that the incomplete sections of Carpenter's original plan be carried out.

But perhaps the most distinguished and thoroughgoing church restoration in Ireland during this period was the neighbouring cathedral of Christ Church (1871–8). This initiative was instigated in 1868 by the Rev. Richard Chenevix Trench (1807–1886), archbishop of Dublin (who, incidentally, had been an official guest at the opening of St Augustine's College), in conjunction with the Duke of Leinster (Augustus FitzGerald) and Edward Roe Seymour, the cathedral's precentor (fig. 353). These 'cultivated Churchmen' were aided in their endeavours by yet another leading English ecclesiastical architect, George Edmund Street, and the munificent patronage of local whisky distiller Henry Roe.[171] Trench, who had long-standing connections to Hugh James Rose and Samuel Wilberforce, was born in Ireland but educated in England, first at Harrow School

353 Portrait of Richard Chenevix Trench (1807–1886), archbishop of Dublin, from the *Illustrated London News* (1863).

354 St Patrick's cathedral, Dublin, after restoration (1845–52) to the designs of R. C. Carpenter.

and then Trinity College, Cambridge.[172] He became acquainted with Street while he was dean of Westminster (1856–63), having been involved with the erection of St James the Less, Pimlico (1859–61). Trench's sympathy for the Tractarian cause naturally inclined him towards dignified architectural settings. However, as Street and others had been quick to point out, Christ Church cathedral, although a noble medieval edifice, was anything but dignified by the nineteenth century.[173] 'So contemptible and shabby were all its surroundings', lamented Street, 'that it is not a matter for surprise if Christ Church seemed almost to have dropped out of the Cathedral category.'[174]

As with Carpenter, it was considered impolitic in some quarters of the Dublin architectural profession to have appointed an Englishman to carry out the work.[175] Worse still was the fact that, during the course of his archaeological investigations, which formed the basis of the first and second reports (1868 and 1871) submitted to the dean and chapter, Street was wont to emphasise the English foundation and patronage of the building (fig. 355).[176] He was also the first to observe, as Roger Stalley has noted, that the cathedral had been built by masons brought from the Severn Valley. If this were not insulting enough, all the new furnishings and stained glass specified for the restoration were commissioned from firms in England. As far as Street was concerned, Christ Church cathedral would remain an essentially English affair.

The idea of architecture, and what it represented, institutionally speaking, was also invoked by Irish clergy in defence of the catholic and apostolic pedigree of their Church. A leading protagonist in this respect was the Rev. John Jebb junior (1805–1886). Jebb, who studied at Trinity College, Dublin, before moving to East Farleigh, Kent, as curate in the early 1840s, was the nephew of the noted Irish High Churchman and bishop of Limerick John Jebb (1775–1833). During his time in both Ireland and England, the younger Jebb had built extensive links with leading Tractarian figures such as Newman, Pusey and the Mozley brothers.[177] Thus his theological leanings were clear. Beginning in 1866, he penned a series of articles for *The Ecclesi-*

355 Christ Church cathedral, Dublin, restored (1871–8) to designs by G. E. Street.

ologist entitled 'The Cathedrals of Ireland'. These articles are particularly interesting in the context of Church reform in Ireland during the middle decades of the nineteenth century. Alarmed by the bishop of Dublin's primary charge of 1865, in which he spoke of 'so-called cathedrals', Jebb's aim in preparing this series was not to discuss architecture exclusively but to use the notion of architecture in its widest sense as a means by which to clarify the ancient constitutional (that is, 'ecclesiastical') nature and pedigree of the Irish Church through the history of its cathedral institutions. In elaborating this agenda, Jebb appealed to the idea of architecture as the physical condensation of ecclesiastical polity, both embodying and signifying the true and proper extents of episcopal authority in Ireland, and how this authority ought to be understood and interpreted. In so doing he was further validating and defending the constitutional rights of the Protestant Church in Ireland. For example, one of the points he makes early on, and one that had a direct parallel in other British colonies at the time, was the 'double function' played by some cathedrals in Ireland – such as those at Cashel, Limerick and Kilmore – in being both parochial and diocesan churches.[178] He could see nothing contradictory or unessential in this dual roll, and affirmed that these institutions were therefore no less entitled to be recognised as 'real' than the 'so-called' cathedrals.

In this respect, Jebb may have been following Beresford Hope's conclusions that cathedral institutions need not be large or elaborate, and that serving a parochial function did not disqualify them from being the seat of a bishop. This was especially so in the case of 'modern' cathedrals, where adaptation to circumstance was more important than aping ancient precedent for its own sake.[179] Indeed, in light of such 'modernisation', the extensive reform and pending disestablishment of the Church of Ireland between 1833 and 1869 led to a reassertion of the apostolic constitution of the Irish Church, not just in an abstract sense but also in a spiritual and corporeal sense through architecture. We have seen evidence of this in the extensive restorations of St Patrick's and Christ Church, Dublin, discussed above. These initiatives were followed in short order by restorations at St Mary's cathedral, Tuam (1864–78), which was essentially a new build by T. N. Deane, and St Brigid's cathedral, Kildare (1875–81), also by G. E. Street. However, this regenerative zeal was not restricted to restorations; it extended to the erection of entirely new cathedrals. These architectural exertions, as David Lawrence and Ann Wilson have observed, directed by the High Church élite within the Irish Church, were defiant assertions of pride and identity in the face of inexorable change and debilitation.[180]

One new cathedral – mentioned by both Jebb and Beresford Hope – was that at Kilmore, Co. Cavan. Although the parishioners of Kilmore had been desirous of additional church accommodation for some time, the new cathedral only came about as a result of the amalgamation of two extant bishoprics under the Irish Temporalities Act (1833), leading to the formation in 1841 of the united bishopric of Kilmore, Elphin and Ardagh. It was not until 1857, however, that William Slater was approached to design a fitting structure, the then bishop, the Rev. Marcus Beresford (1801–1885), cousin of Lord John George Beresford, having decided to seek the 'best professional talent' available.[181] The Ecclesiastical Commissioners had put up £6,000 for the project, leaving Beresford in a situation akin to that which faced many a colonial bishop when contemplating such a building. Moreover, as Jebb noted, like most colonial cathedrals the new building was to perform the supplementary function of a parish church. What to do? *The Ecclesiologist* advised that such a 'moderate' sum called for an equally moderate solution. This was achieved by producing a design of small dimensions upon a cruciform plan, in a simple Middle-Pointed style, with the requisite liturgical features, including an 'eastern limb' (that is, choir and sanctuary) at the same height as the nave, with transepts (fig. 356). This, it was suggested, would

356 Plan of William Slater's design for the cathedral of St Feidhlimidh, Kilmore, Co. Cavan, Ireland, 1857, from A. J. B. Beresford Hope's *The English Cathedral of the Nineteenth Century* (1861).

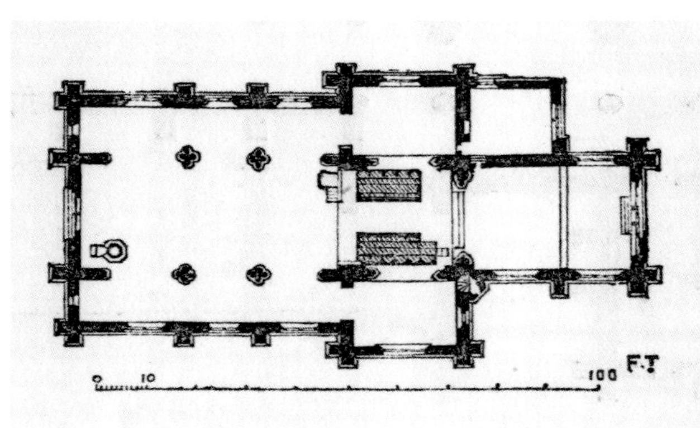

357 Interior perspective drawing of William Slater's design for Kilmore cathedral, 1857, from A. J. B. Beresford Hope's *The English Cathedral of the Nineteenth Century* (1861).

enable the building to preserve that all important 'cathedral character'.[182] 'We consider that this design', the journal added, 'very successfully fulfils its double object of being ordinarily a small parish church, and yet, in the primitive sense of the word, a more true cathedral than many of the grandest in England.'[183]

The design is certainly one that would have fulfilled all the requirements of a colonial cathedral – cheap, compact and unfussy, without losing any of its dignified, cathedral-like features (fig. 357). In this respect, Kilmore can be related to Slater's other proposals – both built and unbuilt – for colonial cathedrals. Indeed, was Kilmore a more 'moderate' version of his unrealised 1854 design for Adelaide (see p. 317)? We will never know, but Kilmore would not have looked out of place as the 'mother church' in any of the more temperate zones of the British empire during the mid-nineteenth century. Moreover, it is one of the most complete and elegantly composed Anglican cathedrals built anywhere in the world during this period – a fine specimen of muscular High Victorian Gothic in its more restrained guise (fig. 358).

One of its chief competitors for this crown was the cathedral of St Fin Barre, Cork, built between 1865 and 1878. In this case it was William Burges who got the job. Here was yet another English architect designing an Irish cathedral, although this time appointed via open competition. From the start Burges and his supporters affirmed High Church principles in the liturgical planning, arrangement and decoration of the building. Prominent here were the Rev. William Connor Magee (1821–1891), dean of the cathedral and later bishop of Peterborough (and archbishop of York for little over a month), and William Bence-Jones (1812–1882), influential landlord, essayist and prominent member of the building committee. Both Magee and Bence-Jones agitated for a building 'worthy of its high and holy use'.[184]

Magee, who was of Irish Church stock – son of William Magee, bishop of Dublin and prominent Irish High Churchman, mentioned above – worked in conjunction with the bishop of Cork, the Rev. John Gregg (1798–1878), to ensure a desirable outcome. Although of rather more Evangelical persuasion, they were both sage enough to see how such a building would work as an instrument in extending the prominence and influence of the Irish Church in the south of Ireland. As the first Irish-speaking clergyman to be made a bishop in the Church of Ireland since the early seventeenth century, Gregg was deeply interested in and concerned with extending the gospel through home mission work among the Gaelic-speaking rural poor. In this sense, as Gregg's son would later observe: 'The Bishop threw himself with characteristic energy into its [the cathedral's] construction, as a lover of art, because he believed that the building of this beautiful church would tend to improve the taste of all who looked upon it, but above all, because he believed that the building of this Cathedral in troublous times would be to the glory of God,

358 The cathedral of St Feidhlimidh, Kilmore (1858–69), by William Slater.

and would bind more firmly together the members of the Church of Ireland in the Southern Province.'[185]

Bence-Jones, on the other hand, was a committed High Churchman with extensive connections in England, having been educated at Harrow School, then Balliol College, Oxford, during the 1830s. He was already a friend of Burges and, together, they ensured (not without some resistance) that the end result would embody a distinct High Church character. At one point Burges was even able to solicit the support of G. G. Scott and Beresford Hope in arguing for his selection of materials – unsuccessfully as it turned out.[186]

The building was to replace the existing eighteenth-century church which was variously condemned as 'unsightly', 'dull', 'plain', 'unworthy' and 'shabby' (fig. 359).[187] Burges himself certainly thought little of it, believing that the whole thing ought to be swept away (except possibly the western doorway), and so it was.[188] The building that came in its place was small in one sense, with a plan little bigger than a large parish church, but colossal in another. Thus, like Scott at Newfoundland before him, Burges, faced with considerable financial constraints (initially at least), sought to identify and distil those features he believed typified a cathedral – transepts (that is, cruciform plan), triple division of the arcade, and more than one tower.[189] These features the building could not do without. However, the sense of massiveness that resulted is essentially perceived, not real, owing to the architect's clever and characteristic articulation of architectural forms (figs 360 and 361). The cathedral's most distinguished attribute in this regard is its potent yet controlled rendition of Early French Gothic.

359 The old cathedral of St Fin Barre, Cork, Ireland.

360 Plan of William Burges's design for the new cathedral of St Fin Barre, Cork (1865–78), from *The Builder* (1863).

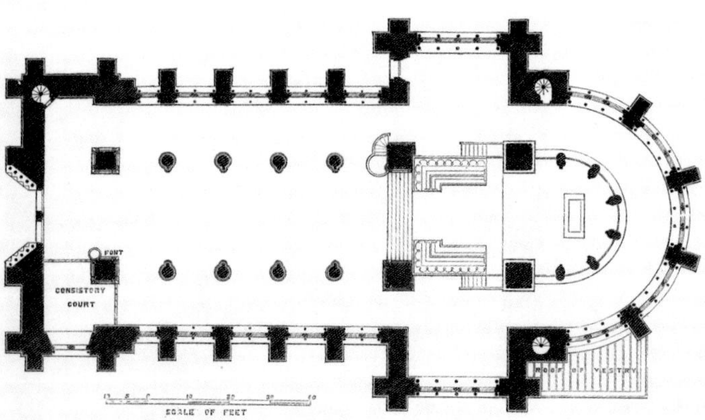

Like much of Burges's work in this manner, the principal features at Cork are over-wrought and compressed, with the details – which are equally bold and expressive – crowded in. Again, as with Brisbane, the overall effect is Michelangelesque in its *terribilità*-like dynamism, ready to erupt. 'It crouches', writes J. Mordaunt Crook, 'heavily-muscled, like some tumescent beast waiting to spring. . . . Despite its miniature scale, its design exudes weight, power, [and] majesty.'[190]

It was therefore entirely apt that bishop Gregg, with the image of Burges's design firmly before his mind's eye, and with no small amount of Ruskinian rhetoric, evoked the idea of revelation at the laying of the foundation stone in January 1865:

> My Christian brethren, we may reverentially say that God, our Maker, delights – it is no irreverence or irreligion to say it – that God our Creator, Preserver, and Redeemer, delights in beauty and grandeur. This we learn from His works in nature and from His Word of revelation. Whether we look above us or around us – in the heavens above or in the earth beneath – we see both teaming with multitudinous specimens of beauty and of grandeur. . . . Or if we look at these cathedrals of nature, not the hills which resemble churches, but at the lofty mountains do they not speak the love of their Eternal Maker – the love of grandeur and magnificence as well as greatness? . . . I would expect [in such a building] something that would strike the human mind with its sublimity. . . . Is it not exceedingly desirable that we should have something worthy of us – some church which in magnitude and altitude and finish would be worthy of the character of our beloved Church? . . . Jesus, Rock of Ages.[191]

The Ecclesiologist joined with this enthusiasm, observing that Cork would 'be among those monuments of the Gothic revival of our generation'.[192] Of its extensive sculptural programme, which steadily increased throughout the course of construction, Charles Eastlake noted that 'no finer examples of decorative sculpture have been produced during the Revival'. Like so many 'multitudinous specimens' teeming over a steep and rugged landscape, as Gregg would have it, Burges's sculpture (executed by Thomas Nicholls) represented, according to Eastlake, 'exactly . . . that intermediate condition between natural form and abstract idealism which is the essence of Medieval and

361 The new cathedral of St Fin Barre, Cork (1865–78), by William Burges.

362 Detail of figurative sculpture on the south façade of St Fin Barre's cathedral, Cork (1865–78), designed by William Burges and carved by Thomas Nicholls.

indeed of all noble art' (fig. 362).[193] Nothing like it, claimed Burges, 'had been attempted since the West front of Wells'. The *British Architect* was less enthusiastic, however, expressing concern over what it saw as the design's 'exaggerations' and 'elephantine' touch; while certain of the cathedral authorities found fault with the iconography of Burges's decorative imagery (stained glass and sculpture), attempting to have it censored.[194]

All of this mass and vigour was calculated to project a rejuvenated image of the Irish Church in the eyes of its critics. During the laying of the foundation stone the building was solemnly dedicated to 'the glorious principles of the blessed Reformation', and hailed as 'the dawn of a new era . . . which will contradict the miserable calumny that the Church of Ireland is dead'.[195] The missionary ambitions of Bishop Gregg, combined with the newly independent status of the Irish Church by 1869, thus conspired to create a set of circumstances very much akin to those faced by colonial bishops in the wider British empire. To be sure, colonial bishops could never have raised the £100,000 it took to complete St Fin Barre's cathedral, certainly not in the mid-nineteenth century, but the disestablished and increasingly competitive domain in which they largely operated meant that, in a wholly modern sense, the Irish Church and the colonial Church of England now had much in common – in other words, they both had to own and assert their independence: historically, theologically, spiritually, and not least architecturally.

As with Slater at Kilmore, there was also at Cork a direct architectural connection with the colonies. As Crook has suggested, Burges's design for St Fin Barre's is the culmination, or the 'complete embodiment', as *The Ecclesiologist* would have it, of his unbuilt schemes for the Memorial Church at Istanbul and Brisbane cathedral – all in that same Early French idiom and exhibiting many shared features, as though working towards a final resolution.[196] All Saints' cathedral, Allahabad, by William Emerson also has similarities (see pp. 139–40). It is therefore rather fitting that Cork, like these other three buildings, would become a beacon of a larger missionary endeavour connecting Ireland, if only unwittingly, to strategies (material and spatial) developed in the extended context of global Anglicanism.

This chapter has shown that the theory, practice and language of missionary work and training was current within the established Church in England in the form of training colleges, 'home missions' to the rural and urban poor, and through systematic Church extension initiatives. What this demonstrates, to a greater or lesser extent, and by a certain awareness and admission on the part of leading Church of England clerics and laymen, is a perceived degree of continuity between Britain and its colonial empire with respect to the wider cause of Anglican renewal, both in its sacramental and political aspects. Many of the key figures involved were not only associated, more or less, with Church extension at home and abroad, but also viewed these two spheres of action as being intimately entwined, if not coextensive. The connections and associations between the men involved and their ideas are clear and convincing in this regard. This is important in the sense that if one is to understand fully the phenomenon of Anglican renewal, the rise of ecclesiology and the motives behind Church extension in nineteenth-century Britain, then one must recognise and take account of its global dimensions. Although this study is concerned with the High end of the Anglican spectrum, the Low end shared in many of these same concerns and their global ramifications. In Ireland, too, we saw how many of the same personnel and ideas were engaged and tested in the context of reform and disestablishment, indicating close connections between the Church of Ireland and its counterpart in England.

Architecturally, similar ideas and patterns are observable. Whether with regard to the aesthetics of discipline, as in the case of St Augustine's College; the employment of temporary and portable buildings, as with the home mission movement; the erection of small but complete cathedrals in Ireland; or the proliferation of simple but correct churches in neglected and parochially weak areas of England, practices overlapped and analogies were drawn. Setting these developments in a wider context helps to put them into perspective by revealing their extended and, in some cases, obscured significance.

363 Christ Church Cathedral, Christchurch, New Zealand (photograph *c.*1880), by G. G. Scott and B. W. Mountfort. Among the most perfect symbols of the reach and ambition of the Anglican confession worldwide.

CONCLUSION

The Imperial Dimension

ANGLICAN ARCHITECTURE AND ITS INFLUENCE

Victorian England was religious. Its churches thrived and multiplied, its best minds brooded over divine metaphysic and argued about moral principle, its authors and painters and architects and poets seldom forgot that art and literature shadowed eternal truth or beauty, its legislators professed outward and often inward allegiance to divine law, its men of empire ascribed national greatness to the providence of God and the Protestant faith. . . . Part of their confidence was money, a people of increasing wealth and prosperity, an ocean of retreating horizons. And part was of the soul. God is; and we are his servants, and under his care, and will do our duty.

Owen Chadwick, *The Victorian Church* (1966)

[T]he practical duty [of building] divides itself into two branches, – acting and talking: – acting, as to defend us from weather or violence; talking, as the duty of monuments or tombs, to record facts and express feelings; or churches, temples, public edifices, treated as books of history, to tell us such things clearly and forcibly.

John Ruskin, *The Stones of Venice* (1851–3)

The period between *c.*1840 and *c.*1870 was a momentous one for the Church of England. These thirty years witnessed not only tremendous reforms generated from within the Church but also an awakening (as a politically established institution) to its wider responsibilities through systematic global expansion. At this moment ecclesiastical architecture in Britain was undergoing a significant reformation of its own. Combined, these factors conspired to shape the Anglican world in very particular and identifiable ways. Compared to preceding epochs in the history of colonial Church expansion, activity during this period was intense and its consequences profound.

Throughout this study we have explored the origins, development and regional variations of what may properly be termed (in its nineteenth-century, British, Anglican sense) colonial ecclesiology. The rise of this phenomenon went hand in hand with the expansion of the British State, and the cultural pressures exerted by that expansion, especially following the inauguration of the Colonial Bishoprics' Fund. It is clear that both the opportunity for, and process of, Church extension overseas had distinct spiritual and socio-political dimensions. The forms and spaces that resulted from this project were loaded with notions concerning religious tradition and identity that worked (indeed, competed) actively to influence the shape of colonial society. Thus, although Anglican clergymen often clashed with government officials over matters concerning education, religious provision and the treatment of indigenes, Church extension overseas was an 'imperial' undertaking, in as much as it was part and parcel of British State expansion and its implied 'mission' to penetrate, transform and 'improve' the wider world. This is not to say, however, that the Church of England was an extra-gubernatorial agent of State, for it was not. Rather, in the field, it was a largely autonomous cultural agency that had overlapping, but not necessarily coterminous, interests with the ambitions and policies of the State.

In the telling of this story, we have considered how advancements in both ecclesiastical organisation and architecture in the wider British world affected perceptions and practices within the Church at home. What this demonstrates most clearly is the unified and largely coherent endeavour represented by Church extension and mission work undertaken by the Church through the aegis of the Colonial Bishoprics' Fund, the Society for the Propagation of the Gospel in Foreign Parts, the Society for Promoting Christian Knowledge, and related organisations such as the Church Missionary Society and the Incorporated Church Building Society. To be sure, there were tension and debate between High and Low factions within the Church as to how best to extend and consolidate the influence of Anglicanism worldwide, but the ultimate aim of transplanting the 'true' faith was shared by all.

This study has focused on 'High' and Tractarian influences within the Church and their architectural effect as a means of assessing the ways in which the Church of England went about realising its aim. Church building, as a spatial strategy, was considered a 'chief weapon' by colonial clergymen in their struggle against heathenism and irreligion in the wider world. In this sense, architecture was used extensively and very deliberately by Anglican clergymen to promote the influence, authority and integrity of their confession and its distinctive values and ideals. Again, this strategy was as much political as it was spiritual, as leading clerics and politicians began to see the role that national religion could (indeed should) play in the shaping of the wider geo-political landscape. Bound up in this were notions of national providence and manifest destiny. In this scenario, architecture was understood as both a symbol and a mechanism of societal identity and change.

Crucially important to the realisation of the Church's global project was the steadfast cooperation of the various architectural societies in Britain, in particular the Cambridge Camden and Oxford Architectural societies. As mentioned in Chapter 6, over two hundred and fifty leading articles, reports, and notices on colonial church architecture appeared in the pages of *The Ecclesiologist* alone between 1841 and 1868. Indeed, the enthusiasm of these societies for colonial ecclesiology may be seen to have driven and directed both the pace and nature of Church extension throughout the empire, including Britain. Without the considerable impact that their influence concerning matters of style and correctness had on the development of colonial ecclesiology, it is certain that the architectural expression of the Anglican Church abroad would have been not only different but also much less coherent.

The influence wielded by these societies was largely attributable to the nature of their membership. As discussed, their roll-call included not only a number of Britain's leading architects but also many who would go on to become colonial bishops and clergymen. One of the key findings of this study is the extent to which Oxbridge-educated clergymen patronised and controlled architectural development within the colonial Church of England. In many cases, especially early on (or in remote locations), they acted as the sole arbiters of church design and construction. Thanks mainly to their knowledge of ancient church architecture, along with their continued involvement in the university architectural societies, these clerics were able to advance ecclesiastical design in ways that would not otherwise have been possible – at least until the latter part of the nineteenth century, when professional architectural advice was more reliable.

A major feature of this influence was the 'pulling' of clerical networks and old school ties. As we have seen time and again, English clergymen stationed in the colonies were part of much larger professional, familial, social and educational networks that went to the very core of the English Church.[1] This suggests that bishops appointed under the CBF were anything but 'glorified vicars'. Indeed, they were among the most hard working and inspired Anglican clerics anywhere in the world. Their connections included those with leading and influential laymen such as W. E. Gladstone and A. J. B. Beresford Hope. With the assistance of agents in England, colonial bishops and clergymen were able to tap into an array of intellectual and material resources to which they would not otherwise have had access. This not only included reliance on official agencies, such as the SPG, the SPCK or the CMS, but also personal contacts in England such as the Revs Edward Coleridge, William Scott and George Gilbert.

Bishop G. A. Selwyn of New Zealand presents a classic case of how this network operated, drawing extensively as he did on his close connections in politics (Gladstone), the Church (the Coleridge family), education (Eton and Cambridge) and architecture (the Cambridge Camden Society). Most other bishops appointed under the CBF enjoyed similar connections. Moreover, these relationships worked to maintain and strengthen ties between the Church of England in different parts of the world. This, it will be remembered, was one of the principal aims behind the establishment of the CBF and the setting up of educational institutions such as St Augustine's College in Canterbury. As the articles and reports in both *The Ecclesiologist* and the *Rules and Proceedings* demonstrate, colonial clergymen clearly believed they were emissaries of a greater cause, taking the gospel of ecclesiology, as it were, to the farthest corners of the known world.

One of the revealing, if logical, aspects of this cause was the way in which both clergymen in the colonies and the publicity machine of the Church at home constructed, in part at least, an image of the colonial Church as one of primitive origins, simplicity and authority. Constant comparison was made with the beginnings of Christianity and the early Church fathers, thus investing the idea of Church extension and missionary work abroad with an aura of romance. This included making a virtue out of the extreme hardship and privation faced by colonial clergymen. For some, this became an all-encompassing mantra of self-denial and discipline, as they cast themselves and their endeavours in a redemptive and sacrificial light. As we have seen, this idea led to certain anxieties that directly affected architectural output, as clergymen sought to embody notions of vigour and endurance through building. Even where perishable materials were used, such as timber, these anxieties were reflected in attempts to build 'solidly'. In this sense, architecture was perceived by the Anglican mind as representing the apparent stability (or not) of the Church itself, as expressed so earnestly in the efforts of Broughton and Selwyn. Here architecture also occupied the front line in the duel with competing denominations, standing as witness to the authority and righteousness of the English Church and its concerns over the social and political constitution of 'Greater Britain'.

With this in mind, we are led to the conclusion that Anglican ecclesiology during the mid-nineteenth century (its critical phase) was in every sense a global phenomenon. It is a mistake to think that it was a purely 'English' invention, exported to other parts of the world by lesser mortals, thereby losing integrity through interference along the way. After all, this is not how the Ecclesiological Society saw it. At the same time, however, there were evidently more or less successful attempts at applying ecclesiological principles to church design in the colonies, as the pressures of circumstance led on occasion to inconsistent and/or anomalous outcomes. Nevertheless, and on the whole, the level of engagement with, and consistency of, the application of these principles to Anglican church building in the colonies was remarkable. This alone testifies to the influence and currency of the 'science' of ecclesiology throughout the empire during this period.

It is also a mistake to compare church architecture in different parts of the empire at different times (especially between England and the colonies) on grounds of artistic merit alone; this is to draw a false distinction between 'good' and 'bad' architecture in a connoisseurial sense. To be sure, the Ecclesiological Society was quick to pass judgment on designs it found wanting, but it always took circumstances into account. Moreover, some of Britain's leading architects designed buildings in Britain and the colonies simultaneously. In each case they thought carefully about context, producing designs that may have been 'simple' but were nonetheless 'correct'. We must recall here the advice of *The Ecclesiologist*: 'if the church be of mud, it may still be a church'.[2] As discussed in Chapter 3, this sentiment was taken to heart in the colonies.

The principle of appropriateness, as it was known, was applied as much in Britain as it was abroad, as materials, expertise and resources varied from place to place. Ecclesiologists were realistic enough to concede that churches in the All Saints', Margaret Street, mould would not start appearing in every town and city of the empire (not even in Britain). Theories and practices of adaptation were very much at the heart of this agenda. Thus, the science of ecclesiology was not a race to the top; rather, it was a matter of horses for courses. Again, it must be remembered that men such as William Grey and John Medley were at the centre of the ecclesiological movement in Britain before leaving for the colonies. Their efforts abroad may have been modest, but this did not necessarily condemn them as a lesser or inferior brand of ecclesiology. Relative to the circumstances, they were achievements in their own right. Was there anything less correct or proper about the grass church at Morambala, or William White's design for a wooden church in Cape Town, than about St Mary's, Littlemore (the so-called model small church of its day)? Two of the three may have been considered 'inferior' on grounds of permanence, but in terms of function and arrangement they were equal. The same applied to cathedrals. Though tiny, Slater's cathedral at Kilmore, Co. Cavan, was described by *The Ecclesiologist* as 'more true' than many of the grandest in England (see pp. 357–8).

The phenomenon of Anglican ecclesiology and its cultural intent must therefore be understood as a whole and relative to circumstance if we are to gauge fully its influence and impact worldwide. This is precisely what the current study has attempted to do. What it reveals, among other things, is that ecclesiological principles with regard to church design and construction were both far-reaching and effective in transforming the Anglican world during the period discussed. There is almost no comparison with the type of Anglican church erected in Britain's colonies in 1835 with that in 1875 – a full-scale reformation in taste and attitude had been effected. In the past, this reform has been better understood with respect to Britain than the colonies. The picture as far as the wider empire is concerned has been fragmentary. But, like piecing together a great jigsaw puzzle, we now have a more complete image. We are not only better able to see how this phenomenon was played out on a global scale, but the emergent connections, parallels and patterns uniting it (once largely hidden from view) are now much clearer.

This naturally has implications for how we understand the nature and character of British imperialism as a cultural enterprise. Organised religion most certainly played its part in helping to shape the colonial world both socially and physically. Until now, too little attention has been paid to global Anglicanism and its manifestations during the great age of empire, especially with regard to the so-called 'suffragen Church' in what would later become known as the 'white-settler dominions' (Canada, Australia, South Africa and New Zealand). The Church of England can no longer be dismissed as having had little or no impact in the British world in comparison to its Nonconformist rivals. The significance and legacy of religion in Britain's empire rests upon more than conversion alone, for Anglicanism's monuments tell a very different and conspicuous story.

Finally, this study has offered a model of analysis that moves beyond the somewhat disabling dichotomies established (and perpetuated) by post-colonial theory. For too long architectural historians of empire have paid almost exclusive and uncritical deference to post-structuralist modes of analysis, all but ignoring intellectually useful and equally valid methods of historical examination that have been developed in cognate disciplines such as history, economics and social science, in particular Atlantic and Global history. To be sure, post-colonial theory and its attendant forms of discourse analysis have opened up new and exciting ways of understanding historical phenomena, including art and architecture, and continue to be useful, but their application in this context has proven limited.

As historians of imperial architecture, it is essential that we problematise forms of colonial agency and their internal conflicts to a far greater extent. Global Anglicanism was one such agency. In order to make sense of it and its architectural manifestations, this study has looked to the insights of New British history and, in particular, the pioneering work of J. G. A. Pocock as a means first to recognise and then to analyse Anglicanism as a 'planetary' phenomenon (see the Bibliographic Essay, pp. 436–41). This approach has been concerned more with enriching than debunking the conclusions reached by post-colonial theorists, focusing less on discourses surrounding the Manichean binary of coloniser/colonised and more on the complexities of agency and the networks that were crucial in assisting European expansion and dominance abroad. As cultural artefacts, buildings have proven to be an effective means of exploring the limits of this agency.

NOTES

Preface

1 John Betjeman, Foreword, in Basil F. L. Clarke, *Anglican Cathedrals Outside the British Isles* (London: SPCK, 1958), p. xxi.

2 *Journal of the Society of Architectural Historians*, vol. 18:3 (1959), pp. 119–20. George Hersey delved a little further into the subject in 1972, but even this was only based on what he could glen from *The Ecclesiologist*. See George L. Hersey, *High Victorian Gothic: A Study in Associationism* (Baltimore: Johns Hopkins UP, 1972).

3 Susan Thorne, *Congregational Missions and the Making of an Imperial Culture in Nineteenth-Century England* (Paolo Alto: Stanford University Press, 1999); Catherine Hall, *Civilising Subjects: Metropole and Colony in the English Imagination, 1830–1867* (Cambridge: Polity, 2002); Andrew Porter, *Religion versus Empire?: British Protestant Missionaries and Overseas Expansion, 1700–1914* (Manchester: Manchester UP, 2004); David Hempton, *Methodism: Empire of the Spirit* (New Haven and London: Yale UP, 2005); and, more lately, Jeffrey Cox, *The British Missionary Enterprise since 1700* (London: Routledge, 2008); Carla Gardina Pestana, *Protestant Empire: Religion and the Making of the British Atlantic World* (Philadelphia: University of Pennsylvania Press, 2008); and Hilary Carey, *God's Empire: Religion and Colonialism in the British World, c.1801–1908* (Cambridge: Cambridge UP, 2010). See also Elizabeth Elbourne, *Blood Ground: Colonialism, Missions, and the Contest for Christianity in the Cape Colony and Britain, 1799–1853* (Montreal and Kingston: McGill–Queen's UP, 2002). This global perspective on the expansion of Christianity has also begun to shape the study of Roman Catholicism. For example, see Luke Clossey, *Salvation and Globalization in the Early Jesuit Missions* (Cambridge: Cambridge UP, 2008).

4 Two outstanding exceptions to this are Sara H. Sohmer, 'Christianity without Civilization: Anglican Sources for an Alternative Nineteenth-Century Mission Methodology', *Journal of Religious History*, vol. 18:2 (1994), pp. 174–97; Howard Le Couteur, 'Anglican High Churchmen and the Expansion of Empire', *Journal of Religious History*, vol. 32:2 (2008), pp. 193–215.

5 Pamela Welch, 'Constructing Colonial Christianities: With Particular Reference to Anglicanism in Australia, ca 1850–1940', *Journal of Religious History*, vol. 32:2 (2008), pp. 237–9.

6 See also W. M. Jacob, *The Making of the Anglican Church Worldwide* (London: SPCK, 1997); and D. O'Connor *et al.* (eds), *Three Centuries of Mission: The United Society for the Propagation of the Gospel, 1701–2000* (London: Continuum, 2000).

7 Andrew Saint, 'The Late Victorian Church', in T. Sladen and A. Saint (eds.), *Churches 1870–1914*, themed issue of *Studies in Victorian Architecture and Design*, vol. 3 (2011), p. 7.

8 The same could be said of the Roman Catholic Church as it began branching out into all parts of Britain's empire, following the passing of the Roman Catholic Relief Act in 1829, and consolidating its prior missionary holdings in those places that were now under the sway of the British crown. For example, for A. W. N. Pugin and the Roman Catholic Church in Tasmania, see Brian Andrews, *Creating a Gothic Paradise: Pugin in the Antipodes* (Hobart: Tasmanian Museum and Art Gallery, 2002).

9 Estimates vary, but the general consensus is that between about 1840 and 1885 Britain's empire went from approximately 2–3 million square miles to around 9–10 million. In the 1860s it was reckoned by some to be around 4.5 million square miles, whereas others put it at more like 8.5 million, with a total population of some 225 million. See C. Bray, *The British Empire* (London: Longman & Co., 1863), p. 33. Charles A. Coke, using the official government census of 1861, devised the following figures: area, 8,778,965 square miles; population, 225,802,250 people; see C. A. Coke, *The British Empire: Area, Population, Government, etc., etc.* (London: Harrison, 1865), pp. 336–43.

10 Geoffrey Blainey, *The Tyranny of Distance: How Distance Shaped Australia's History* (Melbourne: Sun Books, 1966).

11 Rowan Strong, *Anglicanism and the British Empire, c.1700–1850* (Oxford: Oxford UP, 2007), pp. 198–221; Le Couteur, 'Anglican High Churchmen'.

12 This question might also apply to buildings designed by 'English' or 'British' architects in sovereign territories beyond British political control, such as embassy buildings. For example, see Mark Crinson's description of W. J. Smith's British Embassy building in Istanbul (1842–54) in *Empire Building: Orientalism and Victorian Architecture* (London: Routledge, 1996), pp. 126–30.

13 Recent attempts at a similar, historiographically integrated approach have emerged in cognate disciplines such as art history. One such is Tim Barringer's interlacing (at a discursive level) of the means of artistic production in colonial contexts with notions of craft-based labour in Britain. See 'Colonial Gothic' in T. Barringer, *Men at Work: Art and Labour in Victorian Britain* (New Haven and London: Yale UP, 2005), pp. 243–311. As far as architecture is concerned, at least within the 'British Atlantic world', a more integrated approach will no doubt emerge from B. L. Herman and Daniel Maudlin's edited volume entitled *Building the British Atlantic World 1600–1850* (forthcoming, University of North Carolina Press). See also Louis P. Nelson, *The Beauty of Holiness: Anglicanism and Architecture in Colonial South Carolina* (Chapel Hill: University of North Carolina Press, 2008).

14 Asa Briggs, *Victorian Cities* (1963) (Harmondsworth: Penguin Books, 1968), pp. 277–310. Some mention of this wider context is also made in Chris Brooks, *The Gothic Revival* (London: Phaidon, 1999), pp. 281–8.

15 This tendency in itself suggests a great deal about the emergent geopolitical climate that shaped global power structures in the second half of the twentieth century: the Cold War, the rise of NATO, the advent of the EU and EEC, and Britain's retreat from empire after the Second World War. David Armitage has also observed that leftist historians during the post-war period down to the 1970s were embarrassed and suspicious of empire: David Armitage, 'Greater Britain: A Useful Category of Historical Analysis?', *American Historical Review*, vol. 104:2 (1999), p. 429.

16 This point has also been made by Thomas Metcalf: see T. R. Metcalf, 'Architecture in the British Empire', in R. W. Winks (ed.), *The Oxford History of the British Empire*, vol. 5: *Historiography* (Oxford: Oxford UP, 1999), p. 594. As Julie Willis and Philip Goad have pointed out, in the case of Australia this historicising tendency has at times been accompanied by a specific agenda concerning the need for cultural self-definition and the validation of emergent Modernist forms. See Julie Willis and Philip Goad, 'A Bigger Picture: Reframing Australian Architectural History', *Fabrications*, vol. 18:1 (2008), p. 12.

17 For a recent attempt at adopting a pan-imperial approach in the Australian context, see Miles Lewis, 'The Imperial Technology Cringe' (1996), in A. Leach, A. Moulis and N. Sully (eds.), *Shifting Views: Selected Essays on the Architectural History of Australia and New Zealand* (St Lucia: Queensland UP, 2008), pp. 81–94. It is also the intention of Julie Willis and Philip Goad's new concise history of Australian architecture (forthcoming, Cambridge UP) to move beyond these insular and nationalist interpretations of colonial architecture.

18 Joan Kerr has discussed some of the problems surrounding the idea of an authentic 'Australian' Gothic Revival architecture. See Joan Kerr, 'Authentically Australian Gothic', *Transition* (Spring 1988), pp. 5–13. For the broader context, see K. L. Eggener (ed.), *American Architectural History: A Contemporary Reader* (London: Routledge, 2004), p. 15.

19 This is something that Robert Kerr observed in his preface to the third (revised) edition of James Fergusson's *History of the Modern Styles of Architecture* (1891): 'we now have to class with England on this interesting ground [architectural development since the 'epoch of 1851'], on more equal terms than formerly, not only the sister kingdoms of Scot-

land and Ireland, but the whole of the Anglo-Saxon Empire. Canada, Australia, New Zealand, the Cape, India, have all felt the same glad influence in different degrees and forms; and . . . have preferred to follow the course of English progress with a fidelity of kindred and indeed filial feeling that is most interesting and flattering to contemplate.' See J. Fergusson, *History of the Modern Styles of Architecture*, 3rd edn, rev. R. Kerr, 2 vols (London, 1891), vol. 1, p. vii.

20 For criticism of post-colonial theory in the field of history, see R. O'Hanlon and D. Washbrook, 'Orientalism: Culture, Criticism, and Politics in the Third World', *Comparative Studies in Society and History*, vol. 34:1 (1992), pp. 141–67. In art history, see J. M. MacKenzie, *Orientalism: History, Theory and the Arts* (Manchester: Manchester UP, 1995). In the fields of literary and cultural studies, see Erin O'Connor, 'Preface for a Post-Postcolonial Criticism', *Victorian Studies*, vol. 45:2 (2003), pp. 217–46, and Aijaz Ahmad, *In Theory: Classes, Nations, Literatures* (London: Verso, 1994). For discussions about the contested terrain between 'history' and 'theory', see Dane Kennedy, 'Imperial History and Post-Colonial Theory', *Journal of Imperial and Commonwealth History*, vol. 24:3 (1996), pp. 345–63, and B. Moore-Gilbert, 'Postcolonial Cultural Studies and Imperial Historiography', *Interventions*, vol. 1:3 (1999), pp. 397–411.

21 Mark Crinson, *Modern Architecture and the End of Empire* (Aldershot: Ashgate, 2003), p. 4.

Introduction

1 For an assessment of the SPG in its early years, see Andrew Porter, *Religion versus Empire? British Protestant Missionaries and Overseas Expansion, 1700–1914* (Manchester: Manchester University Press, 2004), pp. 17–28.

2 Ernest Hawkins, 'Historical Preface' in *Documents Relative to the Erection and Endowment of Additional Bishoprics in the Colonies, 1841–1855* (London: SPCK, 1855), pp. 1–11.

3 H. P. Thompson, *Into All Lands: The History of the Society for the Propagation of the Gospel in Foreign Parts, 1701–1950* (London: SPCK, 1951), p. 17. In fact, this was seen as one of the principal objectives of the SPG. See W. M. Jacob, *The Making of the Anglican Church Worldwide* (London: SPCK, 1997), pp. 43–4; C. F. Pascoe, *Two Hundred Years of the SPG: An Historical Account of the Society for the Propagation of the Gospel in Foreign Parts, 1701–1900* (London: SPG, 1901), pp. 7–8.

4 T. E. Yates, *Venn and Victorian Bishops Abroad: The Missionary Policies of Henry Venn . . . 1841–1872* (London: SPCK, 1978), pp. 22–43.

5 Elizabeth Elbourne, 'The Foundation of the Church Missionary Society: The Anglican Missionary Impulse' in John Walsh, Colin Haydon and Stephen Taylor (eds.), *The Church of England, c.1689–1833: From Toleration to Tractarianism* (Cambridge: Cambridge UP, 1993), pp. 247–64. For a succinct review of the successes and failures of the CMS in its first fifty years, see Eugene Stock, *The History of the Church Missionary Society*, 3 vols. (London: CMS, 1899), vol. 1, pp. 489–91.

6 Charles Blomfield, *A Letter to His Grace the Lord Archbishop of Canterbury, upon the Formation of a Fund for Endowing Additional Bishoprics in the Colonies* (London: B. Fellows, 1840), p. 4.

7 Geoffrey Yeo, 'A Case without Parallel: The Bishops of London and the Anglican Church Overseas, 1660–1748', *Journal of Ecclesiastical History*, vol. 44:3 (1993), pp. 469–75.

8 For instance, see Carl Bridenbaugh, *Mitre and Sceptre: Transatlantic Faiths, Ideas, Personalities, and Politics* (New York: Oxford UP, 1962), pp. 178–9. In the case of Jamaica, R. A. Minter has observed: 'whatever authority the Bishop of London may, at any time, have had *de jure* over the clergy in Jamaica, there is no doubt that throughout the period *de facto* authority was exercised by the Governor, by the local legislature, and by the vestries'. See R. A. Minter, *Episcopacy without Episcopate: The Church of England in Jamaica before 1824* (Upton-upon-Severn: Self Publishing Association, 1990), pp. 11–20 (p. 15). See also Daniel O'Connor *et al.* (eds), *Three Centuries of Mission: The United Society for the Propagation of the Gospel, 1701–2000* (London: Continuum, 2000), pp. 12–13; and Thompson, *Into All Lands*, pp. 156–7.

9 Boyd Stanley Schlenther, 'Religious Faith and Commercial Empire', in P. J. Marshall (ed.), *The Oxford History of the British Empire*, vol. 2: *The Eighteenth Century* (Oxford: Oxford UP, 1998), p. 146.

10 For the case of Virginia in the early 1770s, see Rhys Isaac, *The Transformation of Virginia, 1740–1790* (Chapel Hill: University of North Carolina Press, 1982), pp. 181–205.

11 Schlenther, 'Religious Faith and Commercial Empire', p. 146. This suspicion of, and resistance to, Anglican bishops in the American colonies was orchestrated not only by Dissenters but also by Anglican clergy who, by this time, were used to operating without *in situ* bishops. See Bridenbaugh, *Mitre and Sceptre*, especially Part II (pp. 171–340).

12 Hilary M. Carey, *God's Empire: Religion and Colonialism in the British World, c.1801–1908* (Cambridge: Cambridge UP, 2010), pp. 45–54; Porter, *Religion versus Empire?*, pp. 16–24.

13 Rowan Strong, *Anglicanism and the British Empire, c.1700–1850* (Oxford: Oxford UP, 2007), pp. 118–20.

14 Howley quoted in Yeo, 'A Case without Parallel', p. 475.

15 See the invitation by Howley to the clergy and laity of the Church of England in 1841 in *Documents Relative to the Erection and Endowment of Additional Bishoprics*, pp. 17–18.

16 For instance, see the comments of Howley and Archdeacon Henry Manning in *Proceedings at a Meeting of the Clergy and Laity Specially Called by His Grace the Lord Archbishop of Canterbury . . . Towards the Endowment of Additional Colonial Bishoprics* (London: Rivingtons, 1841), pp. 4, 25. For the bishop of Montreal, see George J. Mountain, *A Journal of Visitation to a Part of the Diocese of Quebec, by the Lord Bishop of Montreal in the Spring of 1843* (SPCK: London, 1846), p. 78.

17 Jacob, *The Making of the Anglican Church*, pp. 72–3. For the origins of this idea dating back to the seventeenth century, see Carla Gardina Pestana, *Protestant Empire: Religion and the Making of the British Atlantic World* (Philadelphia: University of Pennsylvania Press, 2008), pp. 68–9, 259–61.

18 Vincent T. Harlow, *The Founding of the Second British Empire, 1763–1793: New Continents and Changing Values*, 2 vols (London: Longmans, 1964), vol. 2, pp. 735–9; Porter, *Religion versus Empire?*, p. 20.

19 Lowth quoted in Hawkins, 'Historical Preface', p. 8.

20 Secker quoted in Frank J. Klingberg, *Anglican Humanitarianism in Colonial New York* (Philadelphia: Church Historical Society, 1940), p. 93.

21 Harlow, *The Founding of the Second British Empire*, p. 738.

22 Joseph Hardwick, 'Anglican Church Expansion and the Recruitment of Colonial Clery for New South Wales and the Cape Colony, *c.*1790–1850', *Journal of Imperial and Commonwealth History*, vol. 37:3 (2009), pp. 365–8.

23 Unpublished letter, W. G. Broughton to A. C. Campbell (9 Dec. 1834), Bodl. CAS, USPG Archive, CLR/200 (Australia).

24 Unpublished letter, W. G. Broughton to E. Coleridge (19 Oct. 1837), University of Sydney, Moore Theological College Archive, 1/3.

25 For a brief history of the CBF, see W. F. France, *The Oversea Episcopate: Centenary History of the Colonial Bishoprics Fund, 1841–1941* (London: CBF, 1941). France notes that in the first 100 years of the CBF the SPG and SPCK between them accounted for nearly one quarter of the fund's total income (pp. 22–3).

26 Broughton quoted in Hardwick, 'Anglican Church Expansion', p. 374.

27 *Proceedings at a Meeting of the Clergy and Laity*, p. 11.

28 Ibid., p. 13.

29 Ibid., p. 21.

30 Gladstone quoted in Hardwick, 'Anglican Church Expansion', p. 374.

31 Such views also came from the colonies. In his visitation diary of 1843, the bishop of Montreal, G. J. Mountain, observed that 'the Bishops and Clergy of [the English Church] will never fail to inculcate a deep and dutiful attachment to the monarchy of England, and a conscientious reverence of deportment towards the powers that be'. See Mountain, *Journal of Visitation*, p. 78. For further discussion of this inaugural CBF meeting, see Strong, *Anglicanism*, pp. 198–221. For an excellent account of the wider relationship between High Churchmanship and empire, including the SPG and CBF, see Howard Le Couteur, 'Anglican High Churchmen and the Expansion of Empire', *Journal of Religious History*, vol. 32:2 (2008), pp. 193–215.

32 *The Colonial Church Atlas, Arranged in Dioceses: With Geographical and Statistical Tables* (London: SPCK, 1843).

33 *Quarterly Review*, vol. 75 (Dec. 1844–March 1845), p. 201.

34 Andrew Porter, 'An Overview, 1700–1914' in Norman Etherington (ed.), *Missions and Empire*, The Oxford History of the British Empire Companion Series (Oxford: Oxford UP, 2005), pp. 46–53.

35 I say 'general banner' here because the Church of Scotland split during the 1840s as a result of the so-called Disruption.

36 John Wolffe, 'Whose Jerusalem? Evangelicalism and Nationalism in Nineteenth-Century England' in J. Wolffe (ed.), *Christianity and National Consciousness* (Leicester: Universities and Colleges Christian Fellowship Associates for the Historians' Study Group, 1987), pp. 39–49; Stewart J. Brown, *Providence and Empire: Religion, Politics and Society in the United Kingdom, 1815–1914* (Harlow: Pearson Longman, 2008); Brian Stanley, '"Commerce and Christianity": Providence Theory, the Missionary Movement, and the Imperialism of Free Trade, 1842–1860', *Historical Journal*, vol. 26:1 (1983), pp. 71–94.

37 An example of this idea can be found in 'A Few Thoughts on the Duty of National Religion', *Melbourne Church of England Messenger*, vol. 2 (1851), pp. 359–63.

38 Strong, *Anglicanism and the British Empire*, pp. 125–44.

39 E. B. Pusey, *The Church the Converter of the Heathen: Two Sermons Preached in Conformity with the Queen's Letter in Behalf of the Society for the Propagation of the Gospel* (Oxford: J. H. Parker, 1839), pp. 27–8. See also Pascoe, *Two Hundred Years*, p. xvi.

40 Literature relating to this cause was widely disseminated during the 1850s and 1860s. The Ramsden Sermons on the colonial Church, delivered at the universities of Oxford and Cambridge from 1852, were also instrumental in promoting this cause, as was the publication of the *Colonial Church Chronicle* from 1847. Other examples include Anthony Grant's *The Past and Prospective Extension of the Gospel by Missions to the Heathen* (London, 1843); Samuel Wilberforce's

many sermons between 1840 and 1870 relating to the missionary activities and responsibilities of the Church of England compiled in Henry Rowley (ed.), *Speeches on Missions by the Right Reverend Samuel Wilberforce, D.D.* (London: William Wells Gardner, 1874); C. Wordsworth, *National Christianity, an Article of the Christian Faith* (London: Francis and John Rivington, 1851); George W. Lyttelton, *The Colonial Empire of Great Britain, Especially in Its Religious Aspect* (London: Simpkin, Marshall & Co., 1849); and the Prince Consort's address before the SPG on the occasion of its 150th anniversary in 1851, republished in the *Mission Field*, vol. 7:74 (1862), pp. 25–7. See also J. Manners, *The Church of England in the Colonies* (London: Simpkin, Marshall & Co., 1851); C. K. Robinson, *Missions Urged upon the State on Grounds both of Duty and Policy* (Cambridge, 1853). H. Merivale, *Lectures on Colonization and Colonies*, new edn (London, 1861; repr. London: Oxford UP, 1928).

41 Bishop George J. Mountain quoted in *Documents Relative to the Erection and Endowment of Additional Bishoprics*, p. 33.

42 *Colonial Church Chronicle*, vol. 1 (July 1847), p. 39.

43 *Proceedings at a Meeting of the Clergy and Laity, Specially Called by His Grace the Lord Archbishop of Canterbury . . . for the Further Extension of the Episcopate in the Colonies and Dependencies of the British Crown* (London: Rivingtons, 1853), p. 8.

44 Ibid., p. 12.

45 Ibid., p. 14.

46 For instance, see Merivale, *Lectures*, pp. 524–3.

47 There is a large body of literature relating to missionary activity in southern Africa in this respect, especially that of Evangelical and Nonconformist societies. See: J. Comaroff and J. Comaroff, 'Christianity and Colonialism in South Africa', *American Ethnologist*, vol. 13:1 (1986), pp. 1–22; D. Stuart, '"For England and for Christ": The Gospel of Liberation and Subordination in Early Nineteenth-Century South Africa', *Journal of Historical Sociology*, vol. 6:4 (1993), pp. 377–95; J. Comaroff and J. Comaroff, *Of Revelation and Revolution: Christianity, Colonialism, and Consciousness in South Africa* (Chicago: Chicago UP, 1991), pp. 253–308. Although different in many ways from Evangelical and Nonconformist missionary societies, the activities and ideologies of Anglican missions were broadly similar, especially in their objectives respecting 'conversion'.

48 For commentary on this, see L. Bell, 'Artists and Empire: Victorian Representations of Subject People', *Art History*, vol. 5:1 (1982), p. 74.

49 G. A. Bremner, 'Between Civilisation and Barbarity: Conflicting Perceptions of the Non-European World in William Theed's *Africa*, 1864–69', *Sculpture Journal*, vol. 15 (2007), pp. 94–102.

50 For the use of these terms, see *Colonial Church Chronicle*, vol. 2 (Aug. 1848), p. 43.

51 On this point Boyd Stanley Schlenther has noted that the Church of England in the American colonies focused far more on targeting non-Anglican Protestants than on making indigenous conversions. See Schlenther, 'Religious Faith', pp. 131–5. For the way in which the SPG was beholden to the interests of the white planter society in Barbados, see Noel Titus, 'Concurrence without Compliance: SPG and the Barbadian Plantations, 1710–1834' in O'Connor, *et al.* (eds), *Three Centuries of Mission*, pp. 249–61.

52 Samuel Wilberforce, 'Upon Our Duty to the Aboriginal Inhabitants of Our Colonies' in Rowley (ed.), *Speeches on Missions*, p. 88; A. R. Ashwell and R. G. Wilberforce, *Life of the Right Reverend Samuel Wilberforce D.D.*, 3 vols (London: John Murray, 1880–2), vol. 1, pp. 158–60.

53 Rowley (ed.), *Speeches on Missions*, p. 151. For more on the 'official mind' of British imperial politics and its relationship to religion, see Le Couteur, 'Anglican High Churchmen', pp. 193–215.

54 Daniel Wilson, *A Charge Delivered to the Clergy of the Four Dioceses of Calcutta, Madras, Bombay, and Colombo, at the Second Metropolitical Visitation* (London: J. Hatchard & Son, 1849), p. 10.

55 Pusey, *The Church the Converter of the Heathen*, pp. 56–62.

56 R. W. Church, *The Oxford Movement: Twelve Years, 1833–1845* (1891) (Chicago: University of Chicago Press, 1970), p. 10. For the turmoil within the Church more generally at this time, see Owen Chadwick, *The Victorian Church*, vol. 1 (London: Adam and Charles Black, 1966), pp. 7–166; and Brown, *Providence and Empire*, pp. 70–138.

57 John Keble's Assize Sermon delivered on 14 July 1833 in St Mary's Church, Oxford, later published as *National Apostasy Considered in a Sermon Preached in St. Mary's, Oxford* (Oxford, 1833). William Palmer of Worcester College, Oxford, observed of the Church Temporalities Bill and its potential consequences that, 'at the beginning of the summer of 1833, the Church of England and Ireland seemed destined to immediate desolation and ruin'. See Michael Chandler, *An Introduction to the Oxford Movement* (London, SPCK, 2003), p. 6.

58 Alan D. Gilbert, *Religion and Society in Industrial England: Church, Chapel and Social Change, 1740–1914* (London: Longman, 1976), pp. 132–3.

59 Hans Cnattingius, *Bishops and Society: A Study of Anglican Colonial and Missionary Expansion, 1698–1950* (London: SPCK, 1952), pp. 204–5. The point was also made by Ashwell and Wilberforce, *Life . . . of Samuel Wilberforce*, p. 111. See also Strong, *Anglicanism and the British Empire*, p. 216–21.

60 G. A. Bremner, '"Imperial Monumental Halls and Tower": Westminster Abbey and the Commemoration of Empire, 1854–1904', *Architectural History*, vol. 47 (2004), p. 267; Cnattingius, *Bishops and Society*, p. 204.

61 R. E. Prothero, *The Life and Correspondence of Arthur Penrhyn Stanley, D.D.* (London: John Murray, 1893), p. 278.

62 *Illustrated London News* (27 Aug. 1842), p. 249. The five bishops consecrated were for Barbados, Guiana, Antigua, Malta and Gibraltar, and Tasmania.

63 *Colonial Church Chronicle*, vol. 1 (Aug. 1847), p. 44. For further commentary on this consecration ceremony, see *Christian Remembrancer*, vol. 14 (July–Dec. 1847), pp. 419–35.

64 Arthur P. Stanley, *Historical Memorials of Westminster Abbey*, 5th edn (London, 1882), pp. 35ff.

65 Thompson, *Into All Lands*, pp. 114–15. For more on Hawkins and the SPG, see Carey, *God's Empire*, pp. 91–7.

66 This suspicion was exacerbated by the formation of the Archbishops' Board of Examiners in 1846, the purpose of which was to examine all candidates applying for missionary service. However, it imposed no doctrinal tests on candidates, thus causing agitation in the CMS. See Thompson, *Into All Lands*, pp. 115–16; Stock, *The History of the Church Missionary Society*, pp. 398–9.

67 For example, see Christopher Webster, '"Absolutely wretched": Camdenian Attitudes to the Late Georgian Church' in C. Webster and J. Elliott (eds), *'A Church as it should be': The Cambridge Camden Society and Its Influence* (Stamford: Shaun Tyas, 2000), pp. 1–21.

68 *The Ecclesiologist* complained about the profanation of church building frequently. See James F. White, *The Cambridge Movement: The Ecclesiologists and the Gothic Revival* (Cambridge: Cambridge UP, 1962), pp. 1–16. See also Christopher Webster, *'Temples worthy of His presence': The Early Publications of the Cambridge Camden Society* (Reading: Spire Books, 2003), pp. 20–1. An impression of the different types of Anglican service one might have encountered in the late nineteenth century is given in John Shelton Reed, *Glorious Battle: The Cultural Politics of Victorian Anglo-Catholicism* (Nashville: Vanderbilt UP, 1996), pp. 4–7. E. A. Freeman recorded, upon visiting a church in an unnamed midlands village in 1846: 'I cannot conceive anything more distressing, than the circumstances of the Communion here: a damp squalid chancel, everything as bare and meagre as possible, thanks to the shameless selfishness of the non-resident pluralist who consumes the revenues of the Church on his dogs and guns, a solitary priest to officiate with no vestment but a surplice, while the worshipper is fastened up in a large pew utterly cut off from Priest, Altar, or Congregation.' See W. R. W. Stephens, *The Life and Letters of Edward A. Freeman*, 2 vols (London: Macmillan, 1895), vol. 1, p. 70.

69 'The Oxford Counter-Reformation' (1881), in J. A. Froude, *Short Studies on Great Subjects*, 4 vols (London: Longmans, Green & Co., 1891), vol. 4, pp. 231–360. 'Letter I' in this section gives a very good account of the nature of the Church of England at around the time of the advent of the Oxford Movement, including distinctions between different types of clergymen.

70 J. H. Newman, *Apologia pro vita sua: Being a Reply to a Pamphlet Entitled 'What, then, does Dr. Newman Mean?'* (London: Longman, Roberts and Green, 1864), p. 31. Some of the concerns that these men had over Ritualism are discussed in White, *The Cambridge Movement*, pp. 20–1.

71 James Patrick, 'Newman, Pugin, and Gothic', *Victorian Studies*, vol. 24:2 (1981), p. 190.

72 For further discussion of Newman's attitude towards Gothic architecture, see ibid.; David Brownlee, 'The First High Victorians: British Architectural Theory in the 1840s', *Architectura*, vol. 15:1 (1985), p. 35; and R. D. Middleton, *Newman & Bloxam: An Oxford Friendship* (London: Oxford UP, 1947), pp. 31–60. See also Peter Howell, 'Newman's Church at Littlemore', *Oxford Art Journal*, vol. 6:1 (1983), p. 52. Later, in his *Discourses* on university education, Newman observed that: 'For myself, certainly I think that that style which, whatever be its origin, is called Gothic, is endowed with a profound and a commanding beauty, such as no other style possesses, with which we are acquainted, and which probably the Church will not see surpassed till it attain to the Celestial City'. See J. H. Newman, *Discourses on the Scope and Nature of University Education: Addressed to the Catholics of Dublin* (Dublin: James Duffy, 1852), p. 116.

73 Pusey, *The Church the Converter of the Heathen*, p. 15.

74 Pusey went further in his criticisms, far beyond what either Blomfield or Wilberforce would have dared to say. In a thinly veiled attack on the CMS and its methods, he warned of the dangers of privileging 'the word' above all other forms of sanctity. Promulgating and emphasising the written word through printed bibles was at best superficial and at worst a corruption that would allow Satan into the hearts of the heathen through the back door. 'There was not a syllable of Scripture, whether of the Old or New Testament, which was not written for persons already orally instructed, and, actually provided with living teachers,' he asserted. Ibid., p. 12.

75 For Pusey's views on the English Church abroad, see Ruth Teale, 'Dr Pusey and the Church Overseas', in Perry Butler (ed.), *Pusey Rediscovered* (London: SPCK, 1983), pp. 185–209.

76 Le Couteur, 'Anglican High Churchmen', pp. 202–4.

77 C. Brad Faught, *The Oxford Movement: A Thematic History of the Tractarians and Their Times* (University Park: Pennsylvania State UP, 2003), p. 130.

78 Michael Brooks, *John Ruskin and Victorian Architecture* (London: Thames and Hudson, 1987).

79 For the wider national and imperial dimensions of this debate, see G. A. Bremner, 'Nation and Empire in the Government Architecture of Mid-Victorian London: The Foreign and India Office Reconsidered', *Historical Journal*, vol. 48:3 (2005), pp. 703–42.

80 H. M. White in the *South African Church Magazine and Ecclesiastical Review*, new ser., vol. 1 (1853), p. 131.

81 For Neale, see Michael Chandler, *The Life and Work of John Mason Neale, 1818–1866* (Leominster: Gracewing, 1995). For Webb, see J. Mordaunt Crook, 'Benjamin Webb (1819–85) and Victorian Ecclesiology' in R. N. Swanson (ed.), *The Church Retrospective* (Woodbridge: Boydell Press, 1997), pp. 423–57.

82 Letter, Neale to Benjamin Webb (1844), in Mary S. N. Lawson (ed.), *Letters of John Mason Neale D.D.* (London: Longmans, Green & Co., 1910), p. 70.

83 White, *The Cambridge Movement*. See also Webster, *'Temples worthy of His presence'*; Kenneth Clark, *The Gothic Revival: An Essay in the History of Taste* (London: John Murray, 1962), pp. 150–74.

84 S. L. Ollard, 'The Oxford Architectural and Historical Society and the Oxford Movement', *Oxoniensia*, vol. 5 (1940), pp. 146–60. For example, by 1845 the society was stating: 'The number of Churches now fast rising in every part of the country, renders it of the highest importance to provide for the cultivation of correct Architectural Taste.' See *The Rules and Proceedings of the Oxford Society for Promoting the Study of Gothic Architecture* [hereafter *Rules and Proceedings*] (1845), p. 2.

85 *The Ecclesiologist*, [1st ser.], vol. 1 (Nov. 1841), pp. 4–5. *Rules and Proceedings* (7 June 1843), p. 11; (27 June 1843), p. 13; (15 Nov. 1843), pp. 7–16; (3 June 1845), p. 81; (23 June 1846), p. 18.

86 *Eccl.*, vol. 5 (Oct. 1847), p. 86

87 *Eccl.*, vol. 5 (June 1848), p. 378.

88 This publication was originally referred to as *Instrumenta Ecclesiastica, or, A Series of Working Designs for the Furniture, Fittings, and Decorations of Churches and Their Precincts* (London: John Van Voorst, 1847).

89 For example, John M. Derick, *Views and Details of Stanton Harcourt Church, Oxfordshire* (Oxford: J. H. Parker, 1841); James P. Harrison, *Views and Details of Saint Giles' Church, Oxford* (Oxford: J. H. Parker, 1842); H. J. Underwood, *Elevations, Sections and Details of the Church of St Mary the Virgin at Littlemore, Oxfordshire* (Oxford: John Henry Parker for the Architectural Society, 1845).

90 G. W. O. Addleshaw and Frederick Etchells, *The Architectural Setting of Anglican Worship* (London: Faber and Faber, 1948), pp. 203–4; Clark, *Gothic Revival*, p. 174; and J. Mordaunt Crook, *The Dilemma of Style: Architectural Ideals from the Picturesque to the Post-Modern* (London: John Murray, 1989), p. 63.

91 Sten Nilsson, *European Architecture in India 1750–1850* (London: Faber and Faber, 1968), pp. 126–30. See also John Summerson, *Architecture in Britain, 1530–1830* (1953), 8th edn (Harmondsworth: Penguin Books, 1991), p. 516.

92 Philip Davies, *Splendours of the Raj: British Architecture in India, 1660–1947* (London: John Murray, 1985), pp. 42–3, 58–9, 78–80; Nilsson, *European Architecture in India*, pp. 127–9. See also Terry Friedman, *The Eighteenth-Century Church in Britain* (New Haven and London: Yale University Press, 2011), pp. 605–6.

93 In the foreword to M. H. Ellis's book on Greenway, Morton Herman observed that, although quick to adapt to the Australian scene, Greenway was a rather undistinguished architect while in Bristol. See foreword to M. H. Ellis, *Francis Greenway: His Life and Times* (Sydney: Angus and Robertson, 1953), p. xii.

94 Their plain interiors, Freeland adds, 'formed a fitting background to the black gown and white bands of the preacher. Elaborate ritual and ornate colourful vestments had no place in a vehemently evangelical society which saw all hope and cause for pride and pleasure in the unchallengeable rightness of the Protestant ascendancy.' See J. M. Freeland, *Architecture in Australia: A History* (Harmondsworth: Penguin Books, 1972), pp. 38–9.

95 Albert McPherson, 'Architecture, Music, Art, and Liturgy in the Diocese of Melbourne', in B. Porter (ed.), *Melbourne Anglicans: The Diocese of Melbourne, 1847–1997* (Melbourne: Mitre Books, 1997), p. 52.

96 R. R. Langham-Carter, 'The Story of the Original St. George's Cathedral', *Architect and Builder* (Oct. 1970), p. 16.

97 Stephen P. Dorsey, *Early English Churches in America, 1607–1807* (New York: Oxford UP, 1952), p. 39.

98 The evolution of Anglican church architecture in Virginia, and it relationship to colonial society, is covered extensively in Dell Upton's excellent study *Holy Things and Profane: Anglican Parish Churches in Colonial Virginia* (New York and Cambridge, Mass.: Architectural History Foundation and MIT Press, 1986). See also Isaac, *The Transformation of Virginia*, pp. 58–65; Gavin Stamp, 'Church Architecture' in Robert Fermor-Hesketh (ed.), *Architecture of the British Empire* (London: Weidenfeld and Nicolson, 1986), pp. 154–62; and Friedman, *The Eighteenth-Century Church in Britain*

(New Haven and London: Yale University Press, 2011), pp. 605–6.

99 Louis P. Nelson, 'Anglican Church Building and Local Context in Early Jamaica', *Perspectives in Vernacular Architecture*, vol. 10 (2005), p. 74. Another likely source for this would have been Gibbs's *A Book of Architecture* (1728), which was known in the Americas. See Robert Tavernor, *Palladio and Palladianism* (London: Thames and Hudson, 1991), pp. 181–2. With regard to Jamaica, Nelson has shown that, although concerned with English fashion and precedent, the planning of Anglican churches in the colony was also influenced by pre-existing Spanish church architecture and considerations of climate, such as earthquakes and hurricanes.

100 Harold Kalman, *A History of Canadian Architecture*, 2 vols (Toronto: Oxford UP, 1994), vol. 1, p. 106.

101 Ibid., pp. 144, 182–3, 189–91.

102 The second St James's church, Toronto, was designed to have a 'candle snuffer' spire, modelled on that of All Souls', Regent Street (London), by John Nash. See Shirley Morriss and Carl Benn, 'Architecture', in Carl Benn, William Cooke *et al.* (eds), *The Parish and Cathedral of St. James', Toronto, 1797–1997: A Collaborative History* (Toronto: University of Toronto Press, 1998), pp. 184–90.

103 *Eccl.*, vol. 1 (Jan. 1845), p. 31.

104 'On the Education of Missionaries', *Colonial Church Chronicle*, vol. 3 (Oct. 1849), pp. 121–33. It was also noted in *The Ecclesiologist* that 'knowledge of Ecclesiology ought to be a *sinè quâ non* in the education of the Colonial clergy'. See *Eccl.*, vol. 4 (Jan. 1847), p. 16. This view was reiterated by the Rev. William Grey of Newfoundland in *Eccl.*, vol. 11 (June 1853), p. 159. See also Bishop John Medley of Fredericton's comments in *A Charge Delivered at His Primary Visitation Held in Christ Church Cathedral, Fredericton* (Fredericton: John Simpson, 1847), pp. 30–2, and *Elementary Remarks on Church Architecture* (Exeter: P. A. Hannaford, 1841), pp. 5–6. Benjamin Webb and J. M. Neale even went so far as to say that the design of churches ought to be taken out of the hands of most 'professional' architects altogether. See Webster, '"Absolutely Wretched"', p. 15. For 'priest-architects' in the English context, see James Bettley, 'In the Footsteps of William of Wykeham: Anglican Priest-Architects of the Nineteenth Century'. *Transactions of the Ancient Monuments Society*, vol. 55 (2011), pp. 9–38.

1 In Principio

1 R. H. Forster and W. Harris, *The History of the Lady Margaret Boat Club, St. John's College, Cambridge, 1825–1890* (Cambridge: Deighton, Bell & Co., 1890), p. 14.

2 Unpublished letter, R. Gray to E. Hawkins (9 Nov. 1860), Bodl. CAS, USPG Archive, D24/A, letter 13466.

3 First 'Address' to readers in *Eccl.*, [1st ser.], vol. 1 (Nov. 1841), p. 2.

4 G. H. Curteis, *Bishop Selwyn of New Zealand, and of Lichfield* (London: Kegan Paul, Trench, 1889), p. 6. For Selwyn's attitude towards the Oxford Movement and Tractarianism see John H. Evans, *Churchman Militant: George Augustus Selwyn, Bishop of New Zealand and Lichfield* (London: George Allen and Unwin, 1964), pp. 204–25.

5 *Eccl.*, [1st ser.], vol. 1 (Nov. 1841), pp. 4–5.

6 The Rev. J. L. Patterson of the OAS would observe of the Romanesque that: 'if it were fitting when first introduced, it would be fitting in the colonies, where the Church was in an analogous position'. See *Rules and Proceedings* (29 Jan. 1845), p. 5.

7 'Letter (petition of gratitude) to Selwyn from laymen of the Anglican Communion in Melbourne, 1861', SA. In this letter Selwyn is described as 'our Augustine of the South'. The idea that New Zealand would become a Britain of the southern hemisphere was suggested by the English historian Edward Gibbon (1737–1794). See Edward Gibbon, *The History of the Decline and Fall of the Roman Empire* (1776–88), ed. J. B. Bury, 7 vols (London, 1897), vol. 3, p. 44. It was reiterated by T. B. Macaulay sixty years later in 'Von Ranke' (1840) in *Literary and Historical Essays Contributed to the Edinburgh Review* (London: Oxford UP, 1932), p. 477. Selwyn himself describes it thus in *An Idea of a Colonial College: A Sermon Preached in the Chapel of St. John the Divine, Bishops' Auckland* (Eton, 1848), p. 15.

8 *Eccl.*, [1st ser.], vol. 1 (Nov. 1841), p. 5.

9 Although Selwyn could be quite disparaging of Māori customs, he was impressed with what he considered to be the general alertness, curiosity and intelligence of the Māori, often describing them as better than 'our own People' (that is, English settlers in New Zealand). For example, see Selwyn's visitation journal, SA, 8.39.j. See also *Colonial Church Chronicle*, vol. 1 (Sept. 1847), pp. 96–108. For Marsden, see J. Hutchison, *Picture of New Zealand: Containing an Account of Its Harbours, Bays, Natural Productions . . .* (Edinburgh, 1840), pp. 15–16.

10 For the connection between ideas concerning progress, civilisation and 'sociological evolutionism' in British thought, see Duncan Forbes, '"Scientific" Whiggism: Adam Smith and John Millar', *Cambridge Journal*, vol. 7 (1953–4), pp. 643 70.

11 Johannes Fabian, *Time and the Other: How Anthropology Makes Its Object* (New York: Columbia UP, 1983), pp. 1–35.

12 For the development and pervasiveness of these concepts

in mid-Victorian thought, see Peter Bowler, *The Invention of Progress: The Victorians and the Past* (Oxford: Blackwell, 1989), pp. 75–105; and John W. Burrow, *Evolution and Society: A Study in Victorian Social Theory* (Cambridge: Cambridge UP, 1970), pp. 10–16. For the 'civilisational' perspective, see Peter Mandler, '"Race" and "Nation" in Mid-Victorian Thought', in Stefan Collini, Richard Whatmore and Brian Young (eds), *History, Religion, and Culture: British Intellectual History, 1750–1950* (Cambridge: Cambridge UP, 2000), pp. 224–44.

13 Theories would be developed later in the Victorian period that attempted to connect race with social and intellectual inferiority, but these do not apply here. For these theories, see Christine Bolt, *Victorian Attitudes to Race* (London: Routledge, 1971).

14 In a letter home to his mother in 1842 Selwyn wrote how he hoped to 'improve' the Māori and to 'advance them in the scale of society'. See unpublished letter, G. A. Selwyn to his mother (13 Sept. 1842), SA, 6.19.c.

15 The CMS had had missionaries stationed in New Zealand since 1809. For example, see William Yate, *An Account of New Zealand; and of the Formation and Progress of the Church Missionary Society's Mission in the North Island* (London: R. B. Seeley and W. Burnside, 1835). See also Allan K. Davidson, 'Culture and Ecclesiology: The Church Missionary Society and New Zealand', in Kevin Ward and Brian Stanley (eds), *The Church Mission Society and World Christianity, 1799–1999* (Richmond, Surrey: Curzon Press, 2000), pp. 198–227.

16 For example, G. L. Craik, *The New Zealanders* (London: Charles Knight, 1830). Art objects and other artefacts from New Zealand and Polynesia were also deposited in the British Museum, the offices of the CMS, and the London Missionary Society Museum, all located in London.

17 George F. Angas, *The New Zealanders Illustrated* (London: Thomas McLean, 1847).

18 This church was known to English ecclesiologists. For example, Benjamin Webb and J. M. Neale mention it in the introduction to their translation of William Durandus's *Rationale Divinorum Officiorum*. See J. M. Neale and Benjamin Webb, *The Symbolism of Churches and Church Ornaments: A Translation of the First Book of the Rationale Divinorum Officiorum, Written by William Durandus, Sometime Bishop of Mende* (Leeds: T. W. Green, 1843), pp. xxvii–xxxii.

19 *Eccl.*, [1st ser.], vol. 1 (Dec. 1841), p. 31.

20 John S. Cotman, *Architectural Antiquities of Normandy* (London: J. and A. Arch, 1822), Preface and p. 15.

21 Geoffrey Tyack, 'The Restoration of Iffley Parish Church', *Oxoniensia*, vol. 68 (2003), pp. 113–30.

22 No evidence of these drawings has come to light; nor does it appear that any buildings erected in New Zealand during Selwyn's episcopate match its description. See *Eccl.*, [1st ser.], vol. 1 (Feb. 1842), p. 51; *Rules and Proceedings* (June 1842), p. 12.

23 Ibid. (*Rules and Proceedings*).

24 The cast catalogue of the OAS lists the following items:

1 Part of the Arch of the South Doorway of Iffley Church, Oxon; of three orders, the inner continuous and richly ornamented with vegetable and animal figures, the two outer enriched with the chevron moulding and springing from shafts with rich capitals. *c.*1160.

2 Part of the outer order of the West Doorway of the same Church, with continuous mouldings, enriched with the chevron and medallion ornaments. In these two though still pure Romanesque the section is considerably affected.

3 Part of the outer order of the North Doorway of the same Ch. with the pellet & chevron Mouldings.

See 'List of Casts in the Society's Rooms', Bodl., MS. Dep.c.593. These casts survive and are now kept in the storage facility of the Oxfordshire Country Museum at Standlake.

25 The *Tomatin* was the ship upon which Selwyn and his party departed England (boarding the *Bristolian* at Sydney). See unpublished letter, Sarah Selwyn to her aunt (aboard the *Tomatin*, 18 Jan. 1842), Selwyn Papers, 1839–65, ATL, qMS – 1780–1, vol. 2, p. 7.

26 Unpublished letter, G. A. Selwyn to his mother (at sea, 18 Jan. 1842), SA, 6.10. c.

27 'Journal Kept by One of the Passengers on Board the "Tomatin"', ATL, qMS – 1082, p. 4.

28 He was also a distinguished apiarist, publishing numerous books on the subject. See Arthur R. Smith, *William Charles Cotton MA, 1813–1879: Priest, Missionary and Bee Master* (Birkenhead: Countryvise, 2006).

29 While Selwyn had been communicating with the CCS, Cotton had written to the OAS asking for a 'supply of architectural drawings and models, chiefly in the Norman and Early English styles'. See unpublished letter, W. Cotton to OAS (14 Oct. 1841), Bodl., OAS Archive, MS. Dep.c.589, letter 72.

30 For his contribution to the ICBS, see *Church Builder*, no. 21 (1867), pp. 25–46.

31 *Eccl.*, [1st ser.], vol. 1 (Nov. 1841), p. 5.

32 Ibid., p. 4, and *Eccl.*, [1st ser.], vol. 2 (April 1843), p. 136.

33 *Quarterly Papers of the SPG*, no. 32 (Jan. 1845), p. 12. See also unpublished letter, G. A. Selwyn to his mother (13 March 1843), Selwyn Letter Book, 1841–5, ATL, qMS – 1774.

34 Caroline Palmer, 'Account of the Last Days at Eton of

George Augustus and Sarah Selwyn, 1841, Before Sailing to New Zealand', Margaret Alington Note Book, ATL, MS 265, Rev. F. Thatcher – 10.

35 For example, Selwyn noted that the tent 'will be of great use to me at Nelson and Wellington, where there are at present no places appropriated to Public Worship'. See unpublished letter, G. A. Selwyn to E. Hawkins (29 July 1842), Bodl. CAS, USPG Archive, CLS/212 (New Zealand).

36 For example, Exodus, chaps 26–7.

37 In his visitation diaries Selwyn describes his tent as a 'tabernacle'. See 'Visitation Journal', SA, 8.39. j., p. 37. Caroline Palmer, a friend of the Selwyns, noted something similar, observing: 'It was a real pleasure to me to stand with them, for once, beneath this Tabernacle, wh. is to be pitched as the Lord's house in the wilderness. The first cathedral of the Island Church.' See Palmer, 'Account of the Last Days at Eton' (Monday 4 Oct.).

38 *Letters from the Bishop of New Zealand . . . with Other Information Concerning His Diocese* (London: Rivingtons, 1843), p. 3.

39 William Cotton, 'Journal of a Residence at Waimate, New Zealand, from Aug. 21 1842 to Sat. Feb. 25 1843', p. 26, Mitchell Library, State Library of New South Wales, Sydney.

40 *Eccl.*, vol. 1 (March 1845), p. 86; Cotton Journals, vol. 5, p. 156, Mitchell Library, State Library of New South Wales, Sydney. The sketch showing Selwyn and Cotton conducting divine service at Orona has been described in some detail by Robin Skinner. See Robin Skinner, 'Celebrating the Lord's Supper at Orona', in Andrew Leach and Gill Matthewson (eds), *Celebration: Proceedings of the 22nd Annual Conference of the Society of Architectural Historians, Australia and New Zealand* (Napier, NZ: Society of Architectural Historians of Australia and New Zealand, 2005), pp. 329–34.

41 G. A. Selwyn, *'How shall we sing the Lord's song in a strange land?' A Sermon, Preached in the Cathedral Church of St. Peter, Exeter . . . by the Right Reverend the Lord Bishop of New Zealand* (Exeter: P. A. Hannaford, 1842), p. 15.

42 Selwyn Journal, 1843–4, SA, E.5.j.

43 Unpublished letter, E. C. Hawtrey to G. A. Selwyn at Eton College (6 Oct. 1841), Selwyn Letter Book, 1841–5, ATL, qMS – 1774. The list of books up to 1851 that were held in what was referred to as the 'cathedral library', initially kept in the old CMS storehouse at Keri Keri, can be found in the archive of St John's College, John Kinder Theological Library, St John's College, Auckland. Those books that formed part of the original library gifted by Selwyn's Eton friends are marked with a printed inscription.

44 Sarah Selwyn, 'Reminiscences', 1809–67, ATL, qMS – 1782, p. 30. For a fuller account of the use of printed sources in early New Zealand architecture, see Ian Lochhead, 'British Architectural Books in Colonial New Zealand', *Turnbull Library Record*, vol. 34 (2001), pp. 29–44.

45 F. T. Whitington, *William Grant Broughton: Bishop of Australia* (Sydney: Angus and Robertson, 1936), pp. 180–90.

46 For the problems around Royal Supremacy in Australia, see Bruce N. Kaye, 'Broughton and the Demise of the Royal Supremacy', *Journal of the Royal Australian Historical Society*, vol. 81 (1995), pp. 39–51. For the consequences of the Church Act, see Patricia Curthoys, 'State Support for Churches, 1836–1860', in Bruce Kaye *et al.* (eds), *Anglicanism in Australia: A History* (Melbourne: Melbourne UP, 2002), pp. 31–51; Rowan Strong, *Anglicanism and the British Empire, c.1700–1850* (Oxford: Oxford UP, 2007), pp. 228–9.

47 For example, see W. G. Broughton, 'Earthly Store Prepared for God's Sanctuary', in Benjamin Harrison (ed.), *Sermons on the Church of England: Its Constitution, Mission, and Trials* (London: Bell and Daldy, 1857), pp. 222–34.

48 Austin Cooper, 'Bishop Broughton and the Diocese of Australia', in Brian Porter (ed.), *Colonial Tractarians: The Oxford Movement in Australia* (Melbourne: Joint Board of Christian Education, 1989), p. 31.

49 Unpublished letter, W. G. Broughton to A. M. Campbell (9 Dec. 1834), Bodl. CAS, USPG Archive, CLR/200 (Australia).

50 Scott quoted in Joseph Hardwick, 'Anglican Church Expansion and the Recruitment of Colonial Clergy for New South Wales and the Cape Colony, *c.*1790–1850', *Journal of Imperial and Commonwealth History*, vol. 37:3 (2009), p. 371.

51 George P. Shaw, 'The Promotion of Civilization', *Journal of the Royal Australian Historical Society*, vol. 74:2 (Oct. 1988), pp. 99–111.

52 For an example of this, see unpublished letter, W. G. Broughton to W. Boydell (29 May 1843), BPML, MS 913. Here Broughton is referring to St Mary the Virgin, Allynbrook, New South Wales (1843–5).

53 In a letter to the SPG of 1837, Broughton observes: 'the chief difficulty I encounter is in making progress with the Churches and other buildings, now projected, from the want of mechanics, or the very exorbitant wages demanded by those who apply for work'. Unpublished letter, W. G. Broughton to A. M. Campbell (1 Aug. 1837), Bodl. CAS, USPG Archive, CLR/200 (Australia). See also Joan Kerr and James Broadbent, *Gothick Taste in the Colony of New South Wales* (Sydney: David Ell, 1980), pp. 67–78.

54 Joan Kerr, *Our Great Victorian Architect: Edmund Thomas Blacket (1817–1883)* (Sydney: National Trust of Australia, 1983), pp. 8–11.

55 Ibid., p. 15.

56 Work Diary of Edmund Blacket, University of Sydney, Fisher Library (Rare Books and Special Collections),

P.3/2/5–27 July 1843. The sketchbooks that Blacket brought with him to Australia are also filled with details of Norman churches in England. See Blacket Sketch Books, University of Sydney, Fisher Library (Rare Books and Special Collections), RB 508.5 17.

57 Unpublished letter, J. Fry to Vyge Kraal (Rondebosch, 3 April 1845), Bodl. CAS, USPG Archive, C/AFS/2, p. 248. For St Helena, see Edward Cannan, *Churches of the South Atlantic Islands, 1502–1991* (Oswestry: Anthony Nelson, 1992), p. 106.

58 There was also the example of St Thomas's, North Shore (1843–5) by Conrad Martens and James Hume. See Kerr and Broadbent, *Gothick Taste*, p. 127.

59 T. T. Reed, *Historic Churches of Australia* (South Melbourne: Macmillan, 1978), pp. 80–3; unpublished letter, A. Short to E. Hawkins (6 Aug. 1852), State Library of South Australia, Adelaide, PRG 160/53.

60 The Norman style was also considered 'suitable' by the ICBS, offering 'peculiar advantages under certain circumstances, especially when the material is brick'. See 'Suggestions and Instructions', Bodl., MS. Dep.c.589.

61 *Eccl.*, [1st ser.], vol. 1 (March 1842), p. 107.

62 Ferrey was one of the 'approved' architects of the CCS, and would go on to supply designs for the diocese of Cape Town. See *Eccl.*, vol. 9 (April 1851), pp. 158–9

63 According to Judith Brown, Short studied the Tracts with 'great care and thought'. See Judith M. Brown, *Augustus Short D.D., Bishop of Adelaide* (Walkerville: Hodge Publishing, 1973), p. 14. For Short's Tractarian sympathies, see Fred T. Whitington, *Augustus Short: First Bishop of Adelaide* (Adelaide: E. S. Wigg & Son, 1887), pp. 19–41.

64 Despite the fact that the South Australia Act 1834 contained no provision for state financial support for religion, it did contain what was known as a 'chaplaincy clause', which necessitated the appointment of 'Chaplains and Clergymen of the Established Church of *England* or *Scotland*'. See David Hilliard, *Godliness and Good Order: A History of the Anglican Church in South Australia* (Netley: Wakefield Press, 1986), p. 5.

65 Douglas Pike, *Paradise of Dissent: South Australia, 1829–1857*, 2nd edn (Melbourne: Melbourne UP, 1967); N. K. Meaney, 'The Church of England in the Paradise of Dissent: A Problem of Assimilation', *Journal of Religious History*, vol. 3:2 (1964), pp. 137–57.

66 The £35,000 endowment was used to found the bishoprics of Adelaide and Cape Town. See Diana Orton, *Made of Gold: A Biography of Angela Burdett Coutts* (London: Hamish Hamilton, 1980), pp. 104–5. For three years after his arrival Short was able to rely for pecuniary assistance on the so-called 'grant-in-aid' scheme (1846–51) which offered a £1 for £1 government subsidy. See N. K. Meaney, 'The Church of England in South Australia (1836–1869)', BA Thesis (University of Adelaide, 1954), pp. 20–30.

67 Janet Scarfe, 'The Diocese of Adelaide (and the West)', in Porter (ed.), *Colonial Tractarians*, pp. 78–9.

68 Hilliard, *Godliness and Good Order*, p. 9. In the first Church Society report of 1841 it was noted how Church of England clergy were preaching in Wesleyan and Congregationalist chapels. See Arthur L. Bulbeck, *This Stone Which I Have Set Up: Christ Church, North Adelaide, 1849–1949* (Adelaide: Vardon, 1949), p. 5.

69 Before arriving in Adelaide Short had written to the governor of South Australia, Major Frederick Robe, noting that it was both his duty and obligation to assert the 'distinctive principles' of the English Church, and to build it up according to 'sound doctrine and venerable discipline'. In addition he asked that a parcel of land be purchased in South Adelaide so that church-building activity might be initiated immediately upon his arrival. See unpublished letter, A. Short to F. H. Robe (17 March 1847), State Library of South Australia, Adelaide, PRG 160/38.

70 Short quoted in Janet Scarfe, '"Bridge of Polished Steel as Fine as a Hair": The Oxford Movement in South Australia', Master's Thesis (University of Adelaide, 1974), p. 202.

71 Unpublished letter, W. J. Woodcock to E. Hawkins (6 Aug. 1847), Bodl. CAS, USPG Archive, CLR/205 (Adelaide).

72 Unpublished letter, A. Short to E. Hawkins (19 Jan. 1848), Bodl. CAS, USPG Archive, CLR/205 (Adelaide).

73 Diary of Bishop Augustus Short, 1848, State Library of South Australia, Adelaide, PRG 160/52.

74 Maurice E. Fenton, *Triad: The Anglican Churches* (unpublished manuscript, *c.*1970), State Library of South Australia, Adelaide, D5772(T). It is stated elsewhere that plans for the church and rectory were brought from England by Short, and that Stuckey acted merely as superintending architect. See Geoffrey Manning, 'The Foundation History', in Fiona White (ed.), *Christ Church North Adelaide* (Adelaide, 1998), p. 4.

75 In his diary Short also mentions regular discussions he had with the architect William Weir over the design of Christ Church. See Diary of Bishop Augustus Short, 1848, State Library of South Australia, Adelaide, PRG 160/52.

76 Meaney, 'The Church of England in the Paradise of Dissent', p. 141.

77 *Adelaide Times* (3 July 1857), n. p.

78 Unpublished letter, A. Short to T. B. Murray (10 Oct. 1848), Correspondence of Bishop Augustus Short, 1847–9, State Library of South Australia, Adelaide, PRG 160/38.

79 The design was described in *The Ecclesiologist* as consisting

of a 'Chancel, Nave, two Aisles to each, Transepts, and central Tower'. See *Eccl.*, [1st ser.], vol. 1 (Dec. 1841), p. 31.

80 Unpublished letter, A. Short to E. Hawkins (21 Dec. 1849), Bodl. CAS, USPG Archive, CLR/205 (Adelaide).

81 On this point even the Rev. William J. Woodcock, a former CMS missionary and man of marked Evangelical disposition, observed of Christ Church that it was 'in its general style, somewhat more worthy of English churchmen than any hitherto erected in the Province, and indicates a disposition, at least, amongst us, to emulate our ancestors in their laudable endeavours to give their ecclesiastical structures a distinctive architectural character'. Woodcock quoted in Bulbeck, *This Stone Which I Have Set Up*, p. 12.

82 Whitington, *Augustus Short*, p. 101.

83 *Eccl.*, [1st ser.], vol. 1 (June 1842), pp. 133–5.

84 In *A Few Words to Church Builders*, issued by the CCS in 1841, it was observed that 'where the funds are small, or of uncertain amount, an excellent plan is to finish the Chancel and Nave first, leaving it to the piety of future years to raise Aisles . . . This way of building was often adopted by our ancestors, . . . and with the happiest results; as it ought to be now in the Cathedral churches of Sydney, Montreal, and Calcutta' (pp. 8–9).

85 The Rev. Fitzherbert Adams Marriott, who travelled out with Nixon as his archdeacon, was also a member of the CCS.

86 Herbert Condon, *Francis Russell Nixon: A New Appraisal* (University of Tasmania Occasional Paper 32, Hobart, 1981), p. 5.

87 Unpublished letter, F. Nixon to E. Hawkins (21 July 1843), Bodl. CAS, USPG Archive, CLR/216 (Tasmania).

88 Ibid.

89 Nixon quoted in Condon, *Francis Russell Nixon*, p. 9.

90 Anna Maria Nixon quoted in Norah Nixon, *The Pioneer Bishop in Van Diemen's Land, 1843–1863: Letters and Memories of F. R. Nixon* (Hobart: J. Walch & Sons, 1953), p. 37.

91 *Eccl.*, vol. 5 (Oct. 1847), p. 87.

92 *Eccl.*, [1st ser.], vol. 3 (Aug. 1844), p. 133.

93 *Eccl.*, vol. 5 (Oct. 1847), p. 88; *Instrumenta Ecclesiastica* (London: John Van Voorst, 1847), Plate 49. See also Eleanor Joan Kerr, 'Designing a Colonial Church: Church Building in New South Wales, 1788–1888', DPhil thesis (University of York, 1978), p. 196.

94 *Eccl.*, vol. 5 (Oct. 1847), p. 87; *Hobart Town Courier* (23 Jan. 1850).

95 For example, see Broughton's comments in unpublished letter, W. G. Broughton to A. M. Campbell (3 Jan. 1842), Bodl. CAS, USPG Archive, CLR/201 (Australia).

96 A. P. Elkin, *The Diocese of Newcastle: A History* (Glebe, NSW: Australian Medical Publishing Co., 1955), p. 197.

97 James Grant, *Episcopally Led and Synodically Governed: Anglicans in Victoria 1803–1997* (Melbourne: Australian Scholarly Publishing, 2010), p. 42.

98 Francis Nixon, *Lectures, Historical, Doctrinal, and Practical on the Catechism of the Church of England* (London: Henry Wix, 1843), pp. 339–40. See also Geoffrey Stephens, 'The Diocese of Tasmania', in Porter (ed.), *Colonial Tractarians*, p. 55.

99 Strachan quoted in Alan L. Hayes, *Anglicanism in Canada: Controversies and Identity in Historical Perspective* (Urbana: University of Illinois Press, 2004), p. 240.

100 In this respect Selwyn's efforts were likened to those of St Paul in Crete. See *Saturday Review* (20 April 1878), p. 492. This type of heroic endeavour and its romantic associations were set against the backcloth of Tractarian ethics and spiritualism, Carlylean heroism, and Scott's medievalism. For notions of masculine self-fashioning that emerged from this combination of forces in Victorian society, see James Eli Adams, *Dandies and Desert Saints: Styles of Victorian Masculinity* (Ithaca: Connell UP, 1995), pp. 36–41, 63–5, 75–83.

101 For High Church Anglicans and asceticism, see Peter B. Nockles, *The Oxford Movement in Context: Anglican High Churchmanship, 1760–1857* (Cambridge: Cambridge UP, 1994), pp. 184–90. Peter Williams has also noted how High Anglicans were drawn to overseas missions, especially as bishops, because episcopal freedom in such places was seen as an antidote to the excesses of Erastianism in England. Quoting Gavin White, he observes that 'the undefiled wilderness could allow the undefiled bishop to exist'. See Peter Williams, '"Not transplanting": Henry Venn's Strategic Vision', in Ward and Stanley (eds), *The Church Mission Society*, p. 154.

102 Richard Chenevix Trench, *A Sermon Preached at the Church of S. Edward, Cambridge, at the First Anniversary Meeting of the Oxford, Cambridge, Dublin, and Durham Mission to Central Africa* (London: Parker & Son, 1861), p. 11. On this point Bishop Samuel Wilberforce had observed, 'The [colonial] Bishop is the one who should be the friend, the helper, the guide of his brethren. In toil the foremost to undergo it; in danger the boldest to face it; in self-denial setting the example of endurance. And I thank God that we need not refer back to the earliest times for examples of such men and such lives.' Wilberforce quoted in R. G. Boodle, *The Life and Labours of the Right Rev. William Tyrrell, D.D.* (London: Wells Gardner, Darton & Co., 1881), p. 54.

103 Unpublished letter, W. Tyrrell to E. Hawkins (28 May 1851), Bodl. CAS, USPG Archive, CLR/208 (Newcastle). See also 'Mission Work in the South Australian Bush', in Whitington, *Augustus Short*, pp. 118–42.

104 Strachan quoted in *Quarterly Review*, vol. 75 (Dec. 1844–March 1845), p. 216.

105 Armstrong, suffering from a severe bout of influenza during the early months of 1856, died after returning from a visitation of his diocese. The official cause of death was *purpura haemorrhagica* owing to a depressed immune system resulting from general exhaustion. See unpublished letter, J. Hardie to E. Hawkins (24 May 1856), Bodl. CAS, USPG Archive, D/7b – 1077. Thomas Whytehead, Selwyn's chaplain, being of weak constitution, was worn down and died soon after arriving in New Zealand.

106 G. A. Selwyn to Rev. E. Coleridge (12 Aug. 1849) in *Letters Addressed to Rev. Edward Coleridge from the Bishop of New Zealand* (1850), San Marino, Calif., Huntington Library, Rare Books, 264821.

107 C. P. Williams, '"Not quite gentlemen": An Examination of "Middling Class" Protestant Missionaries from Britain, *c.*1850–1900', *Journal of Ecclesiastical History*, vol. 31:3 (1980), pp. 301–15. See also Susan Walton, *Imagining Soldiers and Fathers in the Mid-Victorian Era: Charlotte Yonge's Models of Manliness* (Farnham: Ashgate, 2010), p. 158. See also Hardwick, 'Anglican Church Expansion', pp. 365–71.

108 For example, this was something that worried bishop Perry of Melbourne who set up his own board of examiners in England to screen candidates. See Geoffrey R. Quaife, 'Money and Men: Aspects of the Anglican Crisis in Victoria, 1850–1865', *Journal of Religious History*, vol. 5:1 (1968), pp. 58–61.

109 From the time of the Rev. Ernest Hawkins's appointment as secretary of the SPG in 1843, the approach to missionary recruitment in the Anglican Church changed. Increasingly aligned with the Church and its organisational structures at home, SPG missionaries began to reflect the broad theological shifts taking place in the Church of England at this time (namely, Tractarianism). The eventual establishment in 1846 of the Archbishops' Board of Examiners to exert control over the selection of missionaries put the SPG in marked contrast to the CMS, which chose its own candidates, independently of the Church. See H. P. Thompson, *Into All Lands: The History of the Society for the Propagation of the Gospel in Foreign Parts, 1701–1950* (London: SPCK, 1951), pp. 110–16.

110 Unpublished letter, W. G. Broughton to E. Coleridge (19 Oct. 1837), University of Sydney, Moore Theological College Archive, Broughton Papers, 1/3.

111 Unpublished letter, C. Perry to E. Hawkins (5 Oct. 1852), Bodl. CAS, USPG Archive, CLR/207 (Melbourne). See also unpublished letter, Mrs W. Martin to E. Coleridge (11 Aug. 1845), SA, 5.31.a. Tyrrell made a similar observation in 1849. See Elkin, *The Diocese of Newcastle*, p. 172; *Colonial Church Chronicle*, vol. 2 (Nov. 1848), p. 191.

112 Unpublished letter, W. G. Broughton to A. M. Campbell (17 June 1836), Bodl. CAS, USPG Archive, CLR/200 (Australia). Here Broughton also notes that colonial clergymen must be 'of an obliging, self-denying disposition, and may I mention one requisite more; which is [an] ability to undergo much bodily fatigue in travelling, exposure to weather, and frequent preaching'. See also George P. Shaw, *Patriarch and Patriot: William Grant Broughton, 1788–1853* (Melbourne: Melbourne UP, 1978), p. 115. A good portrait of one such colonial clergyman, William Dove, can be found in R. G. Boodle, 'Recollections of Ministerial Work in New South Wales', in J. J. Halcombe (ed.), *The Emigrant and the Heathen, or, Sketches of Missionary Life* (London: SPCK, n.d), pp. 125–50.

113 Merriman was renowned for his ability to walk great distances, preferring to be on foot than ride a horse. See Pauline M. Whibley, *Merriman of Grahamstown* (Cape Town: Howard Timmins, 1982), p. 3. The *Monthly Record* of the SPG would later observe of Merriman that: 'so, also, has Archdeacon Merriman manfully done his part, toiling in the noblest spirit, showing an example of self-denial and devout courage, that carries back the thoughts to the early ages of the church, when the Christian character was manifested in its primitive zeal and purity. . . . enduring hardness as a good soldier of Jesus Christ, wearing his cross for Christ's sake, holding his life cheap, enduring hunger and want, perils and privations, in an age proverbial for its softness and self-indulgent ways'. See *Monthly Record* (Dec. 1853), pp. 273–4. As Hilary Carey has observed, such stories, although true, were part of the 'self-fashioning' of colonial clergymen. See Hilary M. Carey, *God's Empire: Religion and Colonialism in the British World, c.1801–1908* (Cambridge: Cambridge UP, 2010), p. 281.

114 Samuel Wilberforce, 'Upon the Supply of Men for Mission Work in India' (1859), in Henry Rowley (ed.), *Speeches on Missions by the Right Reverend Samuel Wilberforce, D.D.* (London: William Wells Gardner, 1874), p. 124.

115 Patricia J. Leader, 'The Hon. Reverend William Grey, M.A.', MTh thesis (Queen's College, St John's, 1998), p. 17.

116 For the making of the missionary 'hero' myth, see Walton, *Imagining Soldiers and Fathers*, pp. 141–59, 173–80.

117 For the development of this phenomenon see N. Vance, 'The Ideal of Manliness', in B. Simon and I. Bradley (eds), *The Victorian Public School: Studies in the Development of an Educational Institution* (Dublin: Gill and Macmillan, 1975), pp. 115–28; J. A. Mangan and J. Walvin (eds), *Manliness and Morality: Middle-class Masculinity in Britain and America, 1800–1940* (New York: St Martin's Press, 1987).

118 Boodle, *The Life and Labours of the Right Rev. William Tyrrell*, p. 6. It was also observed of Short that 'he learned to endure hardness through a rough school life; he was a practised boxer and good horseman; he rowed in his college boat, and thus understood how to keep himself fit'. See G. H. Jose, *The Church of England in South Australia, 1836–1856* (Adelaide, 1937), p. 40.

119 In his initial visitations, Selwyn recorded that he travelled a total of 2,277 miles: 1,180 miles by sea, 762 on foot, 86 on horseback, and 249 by boat. See Carey, *God's Empire*, p. 95.

120 Cotton, for instance, was not only a finalist in the double sculls at Eton but could also ride, sail, and use a lathe. See Smith, *William Charles Cotton*, pp. 12, 25.

121 *Saturday Review* (20 Feb. 1864).

122 Walton, *Imagining Soldiers and Fathers*, pp. 173–80.

123 Gilbert was a schoolfriend of Broughton's and would go on to be associated with the establishment and funding of St Augustine's College, Canterbury. See R. J. E. Boggis, *A History of St. Augustine's College, Canterbury* (Canterbury: Cross and Jackman, 1907), p. 131.

124 Austin Cooper, 'Forgotten Australian Anglican: Edward Coleridge', *Pacifica*, vol. 3 (1990), pp. 257–67. See also Walton, *Imagining Soldiers and Fathers*, pp. 147–53, and G. F. Maclear, *S. Augustine's, Canterbury: Its Rise, Ruin, and Restoration* (London: Wells Gardner, Darton & Co., 1888), pp. 42–52. Broughton described Coleridge's efforts as 'substantial' and 'unassisted', noting that the eighteen churches for which he laid the foundation stones, and the twelve churches that he consecrated in 1845 would not have been possible without Coleridge. See *A Journal of Visitation of the Lord Bishop of Australia in 1845* (London: SPG, 1846), pp. 3–4, 53.

125 Coleridge's relationship with Selwyn is described in his autobiography. See 'Autobiography of the Rev. Edward Coleridge, Fellow of Eton', 1876, British Library, Add. MS 47555, pp. 13–14. Coleridge also had a close relationship with Broughton, describing him as his 'dear and reverend friend'. See Boggis, *A History of St. Augustine's College*, p. 32.

126 Orton, *Made of Gold*, pp. 104–5.

127 Unpublished letter, F. Nixon to E. Hawkins (23 Oct. 1852), Bodl. CAS, USPG Archive, CLR/216 (Tasmania). H. H. Montgomery, fourth bishop of Tasmania also observed: 'It is impossible to estimate the aid a man like Coleridge has been to the Church in Australia.' See Whitington, *William Grant Broughton*, p. 72. Coleridge also got his pupils at Eton to copy letters sent from colonial bishops. See Charlotte Yonge, *Life of John Coleridge Patteson: Missionary Bishop of the Melanesian Islands* 2 vols (London: Macmillan, 1874), vol. 1, p. 29.

128 Writing to Coleridge some time in the late 1830s, Broughton implored: 'Indeed I do request you and all my friends, from regard to the interests of divine truth and the cause of pure Christianity, to watch every opportunity of procuring for us such assistance.' See Boggis, *A History of St. Augustine's College*, p. 35.

129 J. Ruskin, *The Seven Lamps of Architecture* (London: Smith, Elder & Co., 1849; repr. New York: John Wiley & Son, 1865), p. 35.

130 *A Journal of Visitation*, pp. 17–18.

131 Ibid., pp. 21–22; James Grant, *Christ Church, Geelong, 1843–1983: A Brief History with Special Emphasis on the Foundation Years* (Melbourne, 1983), p. 10.

132 *A Journal of Visitation*, p. 47. Broughton also notes that he superintended construction of the church himself (p. 44). He wrote to the incumbent emphasising: 'pray take care to have the foundation made secure: that [it] is deep enough, wide enough, and strong enough'. See unpublished letter, W. G. Broughton to W. Boydell (29 May 1843), BPML, MS 913.

133 *A Journal of Visitation*, pp. 18–19.

134 Unpublished letter, W. G. Broughton to E. Hawkins (3 June 1850), Bodl. CAS, USPG Archive, CLR/201 (Australia).

135 *Eccl.*, vol. 9 (Aug. 1851)

136 *A Journal of Visitation*, p. 18. See also Broughton, 'Earthly Store Prepared'.

137 *Eccl.*, [1st ser.], vol. 1 (Nov. 1841), p. 4.

138 Kathryn Morrison, *The Workhouse: A Study of Poor-Law Buildings in England* (Swindon: English Heritage, 1999), pp. 46–8.

139 As included in the 'Suggestions and Instructions of the Incorporated Society for Promoting the Enlargement, Building, and Repairing of Churches and Chapels', *Eccl.*, [1st ser.], vol. 1 (July 1842), p. 152.

140 Unpublished letter, G. A. Selwyn to E. Coleridge (7 Aug. 1844), SA, 7.9.e. See also unpublished letter, Bishop Selwyn to a 'Friend' (probably Coleridge) (16 April 1844), Selwyn Letter Book, ATL, qMS – 1775.

141 Unpublished letter, Mary A. Martin to her father (7 Dec. 1844), SA, 5.28.a.

142 Unpublished letter, Sarah Selwyn to S. T. M. (5 March 1844), Selwyn Papers, 1839–65, ATL, qMS – 1780–1, vol. 1.

143 Unpublished letter, G. A. Selwyn to his father (22 March 1844), Selwyn Letter Book, 1841–5, ATL, qMS – 1744. Selwyn had also noted of St Stephen's that, 'being of solid stone', it 'was a most refreshing sight in the midst of the wilderness of weather board'. The chapel fell down during a storm: it has been suggested that its construction was defective.

144 The failure of Selwyn's early stone churches near Auckland has been variously attributed to weak mortar, gale-force winds and earthquakes. However, Cyril Knight has suggested that they most likely failed owing to the red clay soil of the district, which tended to undermine foundations unless they were put down on the bedrock beneath. See C. R. Knight, *The Selwyn Churches of Auckland* (Wellington: A. H. and A. W. Reed, 1972), p. 21.

145 This was a practice generally endorsed by ecclesiologists. For example, later, in the diocese of Melbourne, one can find 'instructions and suggestions' for church building stipulating that 'temporary walls and filling up of arches should be so built as clearly to show that they are temporary and that the building is incomplete'. See *Building of Churches & Parsonages* (1869), Anglican Diocese of Melbourne Archive.

146 Margaret H. Alington, *An Excellent Recruit: Frederick Thatcher – Architect, Priest and Private Secretary in Early New Zealand* (Auckland: Polygraphia, 2007), p. 54.

147 He also states how 'Mr Thatcher may act as my surveyor to estimate the work'. See unpublished letter, G. A. Selwyn to W. Bolland (20 March 1844), ATL, St Mary's Church Archive, New Plymouth, Micro-MS-0233.

148 Unpublished letter, G. A. Selwyn to W. Bolland (25 May 1844), ATL, St Mary's Church Archive, New Plymouth. (I wish to thank Margaret Alington for a copy of this letter.) See also Margaret H. Alington, *Goodly Stones & Timbers: A History of St Mary's Church New Plymouth* (New Plymouth: St Mary's Church, 1988), p. 4.

149 As Selwyn had copies of *The Ecclesiologist* for 1843 in his library, he was no doubt reassured in this approach by an article which appeared that year titled 'On Simplicity of Composition, Especially in Churches of the Early-English Style'. See *Eccl.*, [1st ser.], vol. 2 (April 1843), pp. 118–22.

150 'A building may be plain, and yet perfectly graceful and pleasing'. *Eccl.*, [1st ser.], vol. 2 (April 1843), p. 121.

151 H. R. Walden, 'New Zealand Anglican Church Architecture 1814–1963', Master's thesis (University of Auckland, 1964), pp. 39–40.

152 Selwyn Diary, 1843, SA. See also unpublished letter, G. A. Selwyn to E. Hawkins (23 Dec. 1847), Bodl. CAS, USPG Archive, CLS/212 (New Zealand).

153 Cotton, 'Journal of a Residence at Waimate' (initial pages).

154 William Cotton, 'Diary of a Journey from Whanganui to Wellington, Nelson, Taranahi, Auckland, and the Waimate: from Nov. 27th, 1843 to March 1st 1844', p. 4, Mitchell Library, State Library of New South Wales, Sydney.

155 Charles Lyell, *Principles of Geology: Being an Inquiry How Far the Former Changes of the Earth's Surface Are Referable to Causes Now in Operation*, 4 vols (London: John Murray, 1835), vol. 4, p. 401.

156 Michael Hall, 'What do Victorian Churches Mean? Symbolism and Sacramentalism in Anglican Church Architecture, 1850–1870', *JSAH*, vol. 59:1 (2000), pp. 81–5. For Ruskin, geology revealed the 'intelligent reverence of the great Builder'. See Michael W. Brooks, *John Ruskin and Victorian Architecture* (London: Thames and Hudson, 1987), p. 89; Alastair Grieve, 'Ruskin and Millais at Glenfinals', *Burlington Magazine*, vol. 138 (1996), pp. 228–34; Nicholas Penny, 'Ruskin's Ideas on Growth in Architecture and Ornament', *British Journal of Aesthetics*, vol. 13:3 (1973), pp. 276–86. For wider associations between architecture, science and nature during this time, see Carla Yanni, *Nature's Museums: Victorian Science and the Architecture of Display* (Baltimore: Johns Hopkins UP, 1999).

157 For instance, as J. W. Burrow has pointed out, William Paley's *Natural Theology, or, Evidences of the Existence and Attributes of the Deity* (1802) was part of the prescribed course of study for the Cambridge Tripos. See J. W. Burrow, 'Introduction', in Charles Darwin, *The Origin of Species* (Harmondsworth: Penguin, 1968), p. 23.

158 For instance, see discussion on timber ecclesiology in *Rules and Proceedings* (Nov. 1843), where it was hoped that knowledge on timber church design in both England and Norway would be transferred to Newfoundland and New Zealand (pp. 15–16); *Eccl.*, vol. 1 (July 1845), pp. 148–50; vol. 6 (Aug. 1848), pp. 14–27. Selwyn's library held a copy of the *Rules and Proceedings* for 1843.

159 See also Davidson, 'Culture and Ecclesiology', pp. 199–203; Deidre Brown, 'The Maori Response to Gothic Architecture', *Architectural History*, vol. 43 (2000), pp. 253–8; and Richard A. Sundt, *Whare Karakia: Māori Church Building, Decoration & Ritual in Aotearoa New Zealand, 1834–1836* (Auckland: Auckland UP, 2010).

160 The types and qualities of native New Zealand timbers were laid out in *The New Zealand Church Almanac* (1847).

161 For the history of the CMS station at Te Waimate, see M. W. Standish, *The Waimate Mission Station* (Wellington: National Historic Places Trust, 1962).

162 G. A. Selwyn, unpublished letter (11 Jan. 1843), ATL, Micro-MS-202. Sarah, his wife, was less generous. She described it as an 'apology' for a church, and noted how it was 'melancholy to see wood so perverted'. See 'Mrs Selwyn's Letters (1842–62)', ATL, qMS – 1766 (Aug 1842).

163 A full account of St John's College is given in Allan K. Davidson, *Selwyn's Legacy: The College of St. John the Evangelist Te Waimate and Auckland 1843–1992* (Auckland: St John's College, 1993).

164 Unpublished letter, G. A. Selwyn to E. Coleridge (11 May 1846), Selwyn Letters, ATL, MS-Papers-7188-02.

165 Cotton quoted in Alington, *An Excellent Recruit*, p. 98.

166 This level of control was typical of Selwyn. For instance, in *The New Zealand Church Almanac* (1847), it is stated: 'The plans of the Buildings must be approved by the Bishop, or by some person appointed by him.' In a letter to his brother of 1845, Selwyn also states how 'a plan which is now being drawn by one of our own Architects under my direction will effectively, I think, secure them against earthquake or *wind*; the latter of which is I think much more to be feared than the former'. See unpublished letter, G. A. Selwyn to W. Selwyn (24 April 1845), SA, 8.22.h.

167 Sarah Selwyn, 'Reminiscences', pp. 74, 79.

168 Cotton Journals, vol. 8, pp. 31, 34–5, Mitchell Library, State Library of New South Wales, Sydney; Sarah Selwyn, 'Reminiscences'.

169 He goes on to say: 'and before he gave over had not only the ground plan of the whole establishment [St John's College], but also a beautiful general sketch of his ideas of the whole'. See unpublished letter, W. Cotton to his sisters (9 Sept. 1844), SA, 3.34.a.

170 Alington, *An Excellent Recruit*, p. 93. At the time, the Rev. Robert Maunsell (CMS missionary) described this church as a 'little Gothic building [which] I hope will serve as a neat model for a New Zealand church'. Maunsell quoted in Ian Lochhead, 'Remembering the Middle Ages: Responses to the Gothic Revival in Colonial New Zealand', in J. Anderson (ed.), *Crossing Cultures: Conflict, Migration and Convergence. The Proceedings of the 32nd International Congress in the History of Art* (Carlton, Victoria: Miegunyah Press, 2009), p. 536. It is possible that Thatcher may have picked up this technique from Pugin's *True Principles* (1841), where he suggests adopting various modes of 'ornamented construction' in timber buildings, providing an illustration of external 'curvilineal bracing' (pp. 43–4). We know that Selwyn had a copy of this book. See Lochhead, 'British Architectural Books', p. 32. A copy of P. R. Robinson's *Village Architecture* (1837) was also in the college library. See Jonathan Mane-Wheoki, 'Selwyn Gothic: The Formative Years', *Art New Zealand*, no. 54 (Autumn 1990), p. 78.

171 Unpublished letter, T. B. Hutton to his father (20 May 1847), SA, 5.26.a. According to Hutton, the bracing elements were first painted in boiled oil and then painted with a 'tinge of umber'.

172 Cotton Journals, vol. 11, p. iv, Mitchell Library, State Library of New South Wales, Sydney. In commenting on the same technique used on other of the college buildings, Cotton observed how it made for a 'very substantial manner'. See unpublished letter, W. Cotton to E. Coleridge (27 June 1845), Cotton Letters, ATL, MS-Papers-7188-13.

173 Patteson quoted in Lochhead, 'Remembering the Middle Ages', p. 537.

174 For a short but good account of the mode of building, see Mane-Wheoki, 'Selwyn Gothic', pp. 76–81.

175 Unpublished letter, G. A. Selwyn to W. Selwyn (24 April 1845), Selwyn Letter Book, 1841–5, ATL, qMS – 1744.

176 See entry for 15 October 1841 in Palmer, 'Account of the Last Days at Eton'.

177 Alington, *An Excellent Recruit*, p. 183. Selwyn was involved in the design of the CMS chapel at Maraetai. See Sundt, *Whare Karakia*, p. 11.

178 Ian Lochhead, 'St. Bartholomew's Church Kaiapoi: A Mountfort-Selwyn Connection', *Bulletin of New Zealand Art History*, vol. 9:1 (1985), pp. 14–18.

179 Mountfort's A-frame technique might also have been influenced by the 'V-hut' that was used very early on in Christchurch as a makeshift church. See Marie Peters, *Christchurch-St Michael's: A Study in Anglicanism in New Zealand, 1851–1972* (Christchurch: Canterbury UP, 1986), pp. 3–4. Robert Bateman Paul also alluded to the V-hut in his description of the church, and how it was adapted for a 'windy climate'. See Robert Bateman Paul, *Letters from Canterbury, New Zealand* (London: Rivingtons, 1857), p. 57.

180 Brian Andrews, *Australian Gothic: The Gothic Revival in Australian Architecture from the 1840s to the 1950s* (Melbourne: Melbourne UP, 2001), pp. 27–9.

181 *Eccl.*, [1st ser.], vol. 1 (June 1842), pp. 133–4.

182 Nigel Yates, *Buildings, Faith, and Worship: The Liturgical Arrangement of Anglican Churches 1600–1900* (Oxford: Clarendon Press, 1991), p. 133. See also Roderick O'Donnell, '". . . blink [him] by silence"? The Cambridge Camden Society and A.W.N. Pugin', in C. Webster and J. Elliott (eds), *'A church as it should be': The Cambridge Camden Society and Its Influence* (Stamford: Shaun Tyas, 2000), pp. 98–120.

183 *British Critic*, vol. 25 (1839), pp. 495–504.

184 In *Reminiscences*, Mozley claims to have 'designed' Littlemore, having produced sketches, then handing these to Underwood upon Newman's approval, who then produced working drawings. See Thomas Mozley, *Reminiscences, Chiefly of Oriel College and the Oxford Movement*, 2 vols (London: Longmans, Green & Co., 1882), vol. 1, pp. 245–6.

185 *Eccl.*, vol. 1 (Jan. 1845), p. 33.

186 Peter Howell, 'Newman's Church at Littlemore', *Oxford Art Journal*, vol. 6:1 (1983), p. 52. See also John Rothenstein, 'Christian Gothic: Newman and Littlemore', *Architectural Review*, vol. 98 (1945), p. 176.

187 Bishop Edward Feild of Newfoundland, for instance, fancied

Littlemore as a 'useful model', and had requested the OAS to send plans. See unpublished letter, E. Feild to W. Scott (24 Oct. 1844), ADAENL, 100.43-Box 2.

188 *Eccl.*, [1st ser.], vol. 2 (April 1843), p. 122.

189 *Eccl.*, [1st ser.], vol. 1 (June 1842), pp. 133–4.

190 *Eccl.*, [1st ser.], vol. 1 (May 1842), p. 132. National achievement associated with England's medieval architecture pervades both *Contrasts* (1836) and *True Principles* (1841) by Pugin.

191 See 'Ancient Models', *Eccl.*, [1st ser.], vol. 3 (Aug. 1844), p. 134.

192 These plans were published by the Society as folio-sized working drawings. The purpose of these drawings was 'to furnish Clergymen and others residing beyond the reach of competent professional assistance with cheap working plans of Churches, which, in point of style or design, either in part or altogether, furnish good models for imitation'. See *Rules and Proceedings* (June 1842), p. 14.

193 *Eccl.*, vol. 1 (Jan. 1845), p. 23. See also in the same volume 'Sixth Annual Report of the Committee of the Cambridge Camden Society' (p. 3.).

194 I am aware that I am using the term 'Canada', and to a lesser extent 'Australia', in an anachronistic sense here, given that these regions consisted of a number of autonomous crown colonies prior to federation. However, for the modern reader, these terms are used occasionally to facilitate ease of geographical comprehension in instances concerning the making of general points.

195 Marion MacRae (with Anthony Adamson), *Hallowed Walls: Church Architecture of Upper Canada* (Toronto: Clarke, Irwin & Co., 1975), pp. 158–9, 174; Harold Kalman, *A History of Canadian Architecture* (Toronto: Oxford University Press, 1994), vol. 1, pp. 280–2, 290.

196 John Elliott, 'A Trusted Disciple: Richard Cromwell Carpenter', in C. Webster and J. Elliott (eds), *'A church as it should be': The Cambridge Camden Society and Its Influence* (Stamford: Shaun Tyas, 2000), p. 160.

197 Kerr, *Our Great Victorian Architect*, p. 41.

198 *Eccl.*, vol. 3 (May 1848), p. 117.

199 It was later observed by Edward J. Boyce, one of the founding members of the CCS, that 'it may be said without exaggeration that not only from every part of the British Isles, but from almost every colony of the British Empire, applications for designs and for advice were received almost every month without intermission'. M. S. N. Lawson (ed.), *Letters of John Mason Neale D.D.* (London: Longmans, Green & Co., 1910), p. 17.

200 *Eccl.*, vol. 2 (Jan. 1846), p. 20. Edward Feild noted how he had received *Instrumenta* by October 1844. See unpublished letter, E. Feild to W. Scott (24 Oct. 1844), ADAENL.

201 Unpublished letter, H. M. White to W. White (3 Dec. 1849), Bishop's College Archive, Cape Town.

202 Kerr, 'Designing a Colonial Church', p. 190.

203 Ian Lochhead, *A Dream of Spires: Benjamin Mountfort and the Gothic Revival* (Christchurch: Canterbury UP, 1999), pp. 79–82.

204 *Eccl.*, vol. 11 (Feb. 1853), pp. 50–1. This building was identified as Christ Church, now known as Christ Episcopal Church.

205 Unpublished letter, J. Strachan to E. Hawkins (10 Oct. 1845), Bishop Strachan Papers, Ontario Archives, MS 35/R 11, p. 68. These sentiments were echoed by Strachan's colleague, the Rev. Jasper Hume Nicolls (1818–1877), principal of Bishop's College, Lennoxville, Quebec. See *Eccl.*, vol. 8 (Oct. 1850), pp. 211–12.

206 W. A. Pantin, 'The Oxford Architectural and Historical Society, 1839–1939', *Oxoniensia*, vol. 4 (1939), p. 179.

207 John Medley, *A Charge Delivered at His Primary Visitation Held in Christ Church Cathedral, Fredericton* (Fredericton: John Simpson, 1847), p. 32. See also 'The Cathedral', newspaper clipping, University of New Brunswick, Provincial Archives, Diocese of Fredericton Records, DB-1-1C.

208 Selwyn's books appear in the original 1850 catalogue of St John's College library. See John Kinder Theological Library, St John's College, Auckland.

209 Cotton Journals, vol. 8, p. 31 (4 Sept. 1844), Mitchell Library, State Library of New South Wales, Sydney.

210 Kerr, 'Designing a Colonial Church', pp. 210–21.

211 Unpublished letter, H. M. White to W. White (3 Dec. 1849), Bishop's College Archive, Cape Town.

212 Charles Gray (ed.), *The Life of Robert Gray, Bishop of Capetown and Metropolitan of Africa*, 2 vols (London: Rivingtons, 1876), vol. 1, p. 338. It is reckoned that Sophy played a hand in the design of over a hundred buildings in South Africa. See A. J. R. Beddy, 'The List of Churches, Chapels and Schools associated with Bishop Gray and Mrs Gray, 1847–1872', University of the Witwatersrand, William Cullen Library, CPSA Archive, AB1946f.

213 For instance, Gray mentions Butterfield in one of his visitation diaries. See *Church in the Colonies: Diocese of Cape Town (Part 1)* (London: SPCK, 1849), p. 20. On another occasion, just before leaving for South Africa, Gray noted in his diary that he had been promised plans of a church by Scott in Cirencester (Gray (ed.), *The Life of Robert Gray*, vol. 1, p. 131). See also Desmond Martin, 'The Churches of Bishop Robert Gray & Mrs Sophia Gray: An Historical and Architectural Overview', PhD thesis (University of Cape Town, 2002); R. R. Langham-Carter, 'South Africa's First Woman Architect', *Architect and Builder* (March 1967), pp. 14–18.

214 The Underwood plans were most likely supplied courtesy of the OAS. These plans were, after all, published by the society. See H. J. Underwood, *Elevations, Sections, and Details, of the Church of St. Mary the Virgin, at Littlemore* (Oxford: John Henry Parker for the Architectural Society, 1845). Holy Trinity, on the other hand, was adapted from Underwood's, *Oxford Parish Burial Ground Chapels* (Oxford, 1849).

215 Unpublished letter, R. Gray to E. Hawkins (23 Sept. 1848), Bodl. CAS, USPG Archive, CLR/113 (Cape and Mauritius).

216 In a letter of 1849, Bishop Gray noted as he passed through George that he 'found things in a very satisfactory condition; the church (Littlemore) is rising rapidly, and will be very respectably built'. See Gray, *The Life of Robert Gray*, vol. 1, p. 255. A copy of Underwood's plan for Littlemore remains in the Diocesan Archives at George.

217 Diary entries for March 1842 and March 1843. See Robert Gray Diary, 1837–44, University of the Witwatersrand, William Cullen Library, CPSA Archive, AB1161/A7. See also Martin, 'The Churches of Bishop Robert Gray', pp. 27, 31, 40.

218 Kerr, 'Designing a Colonial Church', p. 209.

219 Blacket Sketch Books, University of Sydney, Fisher Library (Rare Books and Special Collections), RB 508.5 17.

220 University of the Witwatersrand, William Cullen Library, CPSA Archive, AB2070.

221 Unpublished letter, G. A. Selwyn to a 'Friend' (probably Coleridge) (16 April 1844), Selwyn Letter Book, ATL, qMS – 1775.

222 Unpublished letter, G. A. Selwyn to E. Coleridge (22 July 1843), SA, 7.5.e.

223 Unpublished letter, G. A. Selwyn to E. Coleridge (20 Oct. 1845), Selwyn Letters, ATL, MS-Papers-7188-02.

224 *Instrumenta Ecclesiastica* (London: John Van Voorst, 1847), Plate 6.

225 John Medley, *A Charge Delivered in the Cathedral Church of Christ Church, Fredericton . . . at the Second Triennial Visitation* (Saint John, New Brunswick: W. L. Avery, 1850), p. 49. He had also asked the Ecclesiological Society to send out 'small plain wooden models of wooden churches in the country'. See *Eccl.*, vol. 5 (June 1848), pp. 362, 381.

226 *Eccl.*, vol. 3 (July 1846), p. 36.

227 Medley presiding at the Annual General Meeting of the Exeter Diocesan Architectural Society (21 May 1852). See *Eccl.*, vol. 10 (Aug. 1852), p. 293.

228 I am grateful to Michael Hall for this suggestion.

229 Harriet Partridge, '"Boyish Effort" or Manly Masterpiece? An Early Work by G. F. Bodley in Guernsey – St. Stephen's Church, 1862–1865', MA thesis (University of Edinburgh, 2008), p. 29.

230 For the use of architectural casts, see Isabelle Flour, '"On the Formation of a National Museum of Architecture": The Architectural Museum versus the South Kensington Museum', *Architectural History*, vol. 51 (2008), pp. 211–38.

231 I am grateful to Geoffrey Tyack for bringing this model to my attention. The model, which measures 7¾ × 13¼ inches, was uncovered in 2008.

232 Kerr, *Our Great Victorian Architect*, p. 46. See also newspaper clipping 'St. Andrew's Cathedral – Public Meeting', Bodl. CAS, USPG Archive, D/17 (Sydney).

233 This interpretation of architectural models comes from Albert C. Smith, *Architectural Models as Machine: A New View of Models from Antiquity to the Present Day* (Oxford: Architectural Press, 2004), pp. 1–32.

234 'Report of the Annual Meeting of Subscribers to the Cathedral Building Fund (1850)', Anglican Diocesan Archive, Sydney, 1992/16/15. Here it was stated that the cathedral should be 'worthy of the divinity whom we worship', as this 'was so at Jerusalem'.

235 W. G. Broughton, 'Cathedral Churches, Useful and Necessary', in Benjamin Harrison (ed.), *Sermons on the Church of England: Its Constitution, Mission, and Trials* (London: Bell and Daldy, 1857), pp. 206–21.

236 *Eccl.*, vol. 1 (Jan. 1845), p. 24.

237 For example, John Armstrong of Grahamstown had appealed to this model or 'pattern', as he called it. See John Armstrong, *The Pattern for Church Building: A Sermon Preached in Aid of the Erection of a Chapel of Ease* (London: J. H. Parker, 1852).

238 Broughton, 'Earthly Store Prepared', p. 226.

239 *Eccl.*, vol. 9 (Aug. 1851), p. 265.

2 *The Colonial Cathedral*

1 For instance, see Philip Aspin, '"Our Ancient Architecture": Contesting Cathedrals in Late Georgian England', *Architectural History*, vol. 54 (2011), pp. 213–32.

2 A. J. B. Beresford Hope, *The English Cathedral of the Nineteenth Century* (London: John Murray, 1861), pp. 21, 27.

3 *The Times* (17 Dec. 1857).

4 Beresford Hope, *The English Cathedral*, p. 1.

5 The two influential pamphlets at the time in favour of cathedral reform were: Robert Henley, *Plan of Church Reform* (1832) and Thomas Arnold, *Principles of Church Reform* (1833).

6 Owen Chadwick, *The Victorian Church*, 2 vols (London: Adam and Charles Black, 1966), vol. 1, pp. 137–41. Many of the changes that were forced upon English cathedrals came in the form of the Dean and Chapter Act of 1840.

7 Ibid., p. 138.

8 Roger Jupp, '"Nurseries of a Learned Clergy": Pusey and the Defence of Cathedrals', in P. Butler (ed.), *Pusey Rediscovered* (London: SPCK, 1983), pp. 139–61.

9 *Eccl.*, [1st ser.], vol. 2 (April 1843), pp. 135–6. See also unpublished letters: G. A. Selwyn to E. Coleridge (27 July 1842), SA, 7.1.e; G. A. Selwyn to A. M. Campbell (29 July 1842), Bodl. CAS, USPG Archive, CLS/212 (New Zealand); G. A. Selwyn to William Selwyn (25 Feb. 1845), Selwyn Letters, ATL, MS-Papers-0700-3.

10 Beresford Hope, *The English Cathedral*, pp. 19–20.

11 For Broughton's views in this respect, see F. T. Whitington, *William Grant Broughton, Bishop of Australia* (Sydney: Angus and Robertson, 1936), pp. 48–54.

12 W. G. Broughton, 'Cathedral Churches, Useful and Necessary', in Benjamin Harrison (ed.), *Sermons on the Church of England: Its Constitution, Mission, and Trials* (London: Bell and Daldy, 1857), p. 209.

13 Ibid., pp. 213–14.

14 W. G. Broughton, 'Earthly Store Prepared for God's Sanctuary', in Harrison (ed.), *Sermons on the Church of England*, p. 231.

15 G. A. Selwyn, *'How shall we sing the Lord's song in a strange land?' A Sermon, Preached in the Cathedral Church of St. Peter, Exeter . . . by the Right Reverend the Lord Bishop of New Zealand* (Exeter: P. A. Hannaford, 1842), pp. 12–16.

16 Peter B. Nockles, *The Oxford Movement in Context: Anglican High Churchmanship, 1760–1857* (Cambridge: Cambridge UP, 1994), pp. 146–56.

17 John Medley, *The Episcopal Form of Church Government: Its Antiquity, Its Expediency, and Its Conformity to the Work of God* (London: John W. Parker, 1835); Wilson's comments in *Final Report of St. Paul's Cathedral, Calcutta, to which is Prefixed the Sermon Delivered on the Occasion of the Consecration* (Calcutta: Bishop's College, 1847).

18 Tract No. 15, 'On the Apostolical Succession of the English Church', in *Tracts for the Times by Members of the University of Oxford*, vol. 1 (London: Rivingtons, 1834), p. 4.

19 Tract No. 1, 'Thoughts on the Ministerial Commission, respectfully addressed to the Clergy', in *Tracts for the Times*, vol. 1, p. 2.

20 For example: 'The Catholic Church', 'On Arguing Concerning the Apostolical Succession', 'The Episcopal Church Apostolical', 'The Scripture View of the Apostolic Commission', and 'Adherence to the Apostolical Succession the Safest Course'.

21 Selwyn, *'How shall we sing the Lord's song in a strange land?'*, p. 8.

22 Curtis Fahey, *In His Name: The Anglican Experience in Upper Canada, 1791–1854* (Ottawa: Carleton UP, 1991), pp. 99–103.

23 Beresford Hope, *The English Cathedral*, pp. 26–7. He later made the same point by observing that critics of the cathedral system could not see past magnificence as a prerequisite. Hence, a 'Missionary Cathedral would . . . be not merely impossible but inconceivable. It would be like a town hall in the tangles of an African jungle, or a sword of state in the hand of a village constable. . . . The Cathedral of those theorists is nothing more than a gorgeous building.' See A. J. B. Beresford Hope, 'Cathedrals in Their Missionary Aspect', in J. S. Howson (ed.), *Essays on Cathedrals* (London: John Murray, 1872), p. 77.

24 Ibid., pp. 79, 85.

25 Ibid., p. 78.

26 Wilson was praised by Beresford Hope for this. See Beresford Hope, *The English Cathedral*, pp. 97–102.

27 Eyre Chatterton, *A History of the Church of England in India* (London: SPCK, 1924), p. 175. See also Hans Cnattingius, *Bishops and Society: A Study of Anglican Colonial and Missionary Expansion, 1698–1950* (London: SPCK, 1952), p. 159.

28 T. E. Yates, *Venn and Victorian Bishops Abroad: The Missionary Policies of Henry Venn . . . 1841–1872* (London: SPCK, 1978), pp. 24–8.

29 For instance, Lord William Bentinck, governor-general of India (1828–35), perceived Wilson's sermon on the 'apostolic commission' as evidence of High Church leanings. See ibid., p. 27.

30 Daniel Wilson, *The Apostolical Commission Considered, with Reference to the Authority of the Clergy of the Church of England* (1833) (London: SPCK, 1841), pp. 3–4, 5.

31 E. M. Gibbs, *The Anglican Church in India, 1600–1970* (Delhi: Indian SPCK, 1972), p. 118.

32 The clearest expression of this is Wilson's sermon at the consecration of St Paul's cathedral (1847). See 'A Sermon', in *Final Report*, pp. 1–29.

33 D. Wilson (14 June 1839) in Josiah Bateman, *The Life of the Right Rev. Daniel Wilson, D.D., Late Lord Bishop of Calcutta and Metropolitan of India*, 2 vols (London: John Murray, 1860), vol. 2, pp. 171–2.

34 Wilson quoted in *Eccl.*, vol. 5 (April 1848), p. 267. It was also noted in a special meeting held at the University of Oxford in 1840 that Wilson conceived of the cathedral in the same manner as that 'founded by Augustine at Canterbury'. See *Final Report*, p. xxxviii.

35 Unpublished letter, D. Wilson to A. M. Campbell (15 Feb. 1840), Bodl. CAS, USPG Archive, CLR/2 (East Indies).

36 Gibbs, *The Anglican Church in India*, p. 117.

37 The original spire of the cathedral collapsed in the earthquake of 1897, and then again, after having been rebuilt, in the subsequent earthquake of 1934. The whole tower had

to be pulled down, and this time it was rebuilt in the image of Bell Harry Tower at Canterbury. See Arabindo N. Mukherjee (ed.), *A Short History of St. Paul's Cathedral Calcutta* (Calcutta, 1956), p. 27. West's window was originally painted for St George's chapel, Windsor, many years earlier (1796–1808). Never fully completed, however, it was given to Wilson by Queen Victoria in 1845. It was destroyed by a hurricane in 1864. See Jerry D. Meyer, 'Benjamin West's Window Designs for St. George's Chapel, Windsor', *American Art Journal*, vol. 11:3 (1979), pp. 53–65.

38 *Eccl.*, vol. 5 (April 1848), pp. 265, 270–1. Beresford Hope would later observe that, given Wilson's 'just appreciation of the cathedral institution', it was 'with reluctance that I am bound to note that the architecture of Calcutta Cathedral, the work of a colonel of engineers, can only be described as a sort of corrupt Perpendicular, apparently founded on some rude print of the Duomo of Milan'. See Beresford Hope, *The English Cathedral*, p. 100.

39 *Eccl.*, vol. 3 (July 1846), p. 36.

40 The foundation stone for St Andrew's was in fact *re*laid owing to the abandonment of the original cathedral project in 1820. It was first laid 'according to ancient custom' on 31 August 1819 by governor Lachlan Macquarie (1761–1824) for what would have been a Gothick-inspired edifice by the convict architect Francis Greenway (1777–1837). But the work was halted and no further action was taken until Broughton became primate twenty years later. See S. M. Johnstone, *The Book of St. Andrew's Cathedral Sydney* (1937) (Sydney: Angus and Robertson, 1968), pp. 1–2.

41 'St. Andrew's Cathedral', in *The Sydney Diocesan Directory for the Year of Our Lord 1881* (Sydney: Joseph Cook & Co., 1881), p. 25.

42 These measured drawings still exist in the State Library of New South Wales, Sydney, Mitchell Library, D204^{-1}/77.

43 Joan Kerr and James Broadbent, *Gothick Taste in the Colony of New South Wales* (Sydney: David Ell, 1980), p. 68.

44 Broughton quoted in Whitington, *William Grant Broughton*, pp. 148–9.

45 Eleanor Joan Kerr, 'Designing a Colonial Church: Church Building in New South Wales, 1788–1888', DPhil Thesis (University of York, 1978), pp. 140–1.

46 It is important to note that Broughton did not give up hope on his cathedral project, even in the most despairing of times. In 1844, during the suspension of works, he wrote to Ernest Hawkins stating that: 'Though disappointed, I am not disheartened, and rely on the favour of God to raise up some resources for the completion of a work which would stand a monument of our veneration for His Holy name; and would tend, I feel assured, more than perhaps any other external means or material agency could, to fix in the minds of this community a sense of the importance of religion, and of the respect which is due even to its visible Ordinances.' See unpublished letter, W. G. Broughton to E. Hawkins (3 April 1844), Bodl. CAS, USPG Archive, CLR/201 (Australia).

47 Blacket's appointment was a close run thing, as several key members of the committee wished James Hume to remain as superintending architect. It was not until May that Blacket was finally elected. See Building Committee Minutes, 4 May 1846, Anglican Diocesan Archive, Sydney, [1992/16/15].

48 Cotton Journals, vol. 7, p. 17, Mitchell Library, State Library of New South Wales, Sydney. Blacket was forced to resign as architect in 1850 owing to his appointment as architect to the colonial government; T. W. Sheppard was appointed clerk of works to carry out the design. Blacket was reinstated as architect of St Andrew's in October 1854 after retiring from his position as government architect.

49 Building Committee Minutes, 24 Aug. 1846, Anglican Diocesan Archive, Sydney, [1992/16/15]. See also report from the *Sydney Morning Herald* in *Eccl.*, vol. 5 (April 1848), p. 272.

50 Kerr, 'Designing a Colonial Church', pp. 181–2.

51 'St. Andrew's Cathedral', p. 29.

52 *Eccl.*, vol. 5 (April 1848), p. 274; *Eccl.*, vol. 12 (Feb. 1854), p. 19.

53 A concise summation of this sentiment can be found in the Rev. W. H. Walsh's letter to Rev. G. Gilbert of Grantham (19 April 1852). See 'Memorial to the Late Bishop of Sydney', BPML, FM4/225. See also speeches made at a public gathering in 1862 in support of the cathedral's completion: *Sydney Morning Herald* (18 March 1862). *The Ecclesiologist* noted that this meeting was deserving of especial attention as it indicated 'alike a growing appreciation of the meaning and value of the cathedral system, and in connection with it of the real character of the Church of England itself'. See *Eccl.*, vol. 20 (June 1862), p. 160.

54 *Sydney Morning Herald* (14 Aug. 1868).

55 Unpublished letter, W. G. Broughton to E. Coleridge (19 Oct. 1837), University of Sydney, Moore Theological College Archive, Broughton Papers, 1/3.

56 Broughton, 'Cathedral Churches', p. 218.

57 For Strachan's biography, see J. L. H. Henderson, *John Strachan, 1778–1867* (Toronto: University of Toronto Press, 1969).

58 Fahey, *In His Name*, pp. 127–30.

59 Ibid., pp. 239–53. Henderson has noted that Strachan's strong line on apostolicity was initially influenced by bishop J. H. Hobart of New York. See Henderson, *John Strachan*, pp. 58–9. The Anglican Church in Canada began with similar privileges to that in Australia, with one seventh of all public

land turned over to the 'Protestant Clergy'. This system was known as the 'Clergy Reserves'. However, as in Australia, the act that granted these privileges was eventually repealed by the colonial government (1854). See Alan L. Hayes, *Anglicans in Canada: Controversies and Identity in Historical Perspective* (Urbana: University of Illinois Press, 2004), pp. 59–61.

60 Perhaps Strachan's most articulate and committed exposition of this principle came in *A Sermon, Preached at York, Upper Canada, Third of July, 1825, On the Death of the Late Lord Bishop of Quebec* (Kingston, Ontario, 1826).

61 J. Strachan to J. H. Newman (15 Aug. 1839), Archives of Ontario, Toronto, Bishop Strachan Papers, MS 35/R3. As Curtis Fahey has observed, if Strachan eventually repudiated Newman for his defection to Rome, he was never in any doubt as to the basic tenets of Tractarian theology and its affinity with his own High Church principles. See Fahey, *In His Name*, p. 243. For the extended correspondence between Strachan and Newman, see John S. Moir, 'The Correspondence of Bishop Strachan and John Henry Newman', *Canadian Journal of Theology*, vol. 3:4 (1957), pp. 219–25.

62 The most complete history of St James's cathedral in its various phases is Shirley Morriss and Carl Benn, 'Architecture', in Carl Benn, William Cook *et al.* (eds), *The Parish and Cathedral of St. James', Toronto, 1797–1997: A Collaborative History* (Toronto: University of Toronto Press, 1998), pp. 179–215.

63 This choice of style proved mistaken, however. Not long after the building's completion a visitor from England commented that 'instead of the decorative style which they of the dark ages knew so well, . . . and which has been of late years so happily copied in England, . . . the building as it stands is one of the commonest possible . . . and but for the ill-proportioned stumpy attempt at a spire, might answer as well . . . for a corn exchange'. See Morriss and Benn, 'Architecture', p. 194.

64 William G. Cooke, 'The Diocese of Toronto and Its Two Cathedrals', *JCCHS*, vol. 27:2 (1985), p. 99.

65 For example, see unpublished letter from J. Strachan to E. Hawkins (13 April 1849), Public Archives of Ontario, Toronto, Bishop Strachan Papers, MS 35/R11, p. 109. He also wrote to the Rev. T. Murray of the SPCK observing that 'we are unable to attempt the building of a large Cathedral – but the New Church might be erected in the Cathedral style'. See J. Strachan to T. Murray (14 April 1849), ibid., p. 28.

66 Curtis Fahey notes how Strachan's sympathy for the 'externals' of worship grew significantly after he was exposed to Tractarian theology. See Fahey, *In His Name*, p. 244.

67 John Strachan, *Thoughts on the Rebuilding of the Cathedral Church of St. James* (Toronto, 1850), p. 10.

68 St James, Toronto, Cathedral Archive, Vestry Minute Book, 1842–1907, 1-C-22.

69 St James, Toronto, Cathedral Archive, Building Committee Minutes, 1849–50, 4-F-5.

70 *Eccl.*, vol. 15 (Dec. 1857), p. 359. There had been mention earlier in *The Ecclesiologist* of the rebuilding of St James, of which the Society approved, in particular comments made by Strachan. See *Eccl.*, vol. 9 (Feb. 1851), p. 79.

71 The most comprehensive biographical history of Medley and his achievements is Barry L. Craig, *Apostle to the Wilderness: Bishop John Medley and the Evolution of the Anglican Church* (Madison: Fairleigh Dickinson UP, 2005). Other sources include W. Q. Ketchum, *The Life and Work of the Most Reverend John Medley, D.D.* (Saint John, New Brunswick: J. and A. McMillan, 1893); Eugene R. Fairweather, 'A Tractarian Patriarch: John Medley of Fredericton', *Canadian Journal of Theology*, vol. 6:1 (1960), pp. 15–24; Lyman N. Harding, '"John, by divine permission": John Medley and the Church in New Brunswick', *JCCHS*, vol. 8:4 (1966), pp. 76–87; and Christopher F. Headon, 'Developments in Canadian Anglican Worship in Eastern and Central Canada, 1840–1868', *JCCHS*, vol. 17:2 (1975), pp. 26–36. For Medley and architecture, see Craig, *Apostle to the Wilderness*, pp. 95–113; Phoebe B. Stanton, *The Gothic Revival & American Church Architecture: An Episode in Taste, 1840–1856* (Baltimore: Johns Hopkins UP, 1968); Alan Gregg Finley, '"Habits of reverence and awe": Bishop John Medley and the Promise of Ecclesiology', *JCCHS*, vol. 35 (1993), pp. 3–22; Robert L. Watson, *Christ Church Cathedral, Fredericton: A History* (Fredericton: Bishop and Chapter of Fredericton Cathedral, 1984); and Douglas Richardson, 'Christ Church Cathedral, Fredericton, New Brunswick', MA thesis (Yale University, 1966).

72 For instance, in 1841 Medley wrote a pamphlet titled *Elementary Remarks on Church Architecture*, which was recommended 'most safely' by *The Ecclesiologist*. See *Eccl.*, [1st ser.], vol. 1 (Nov. 1841), p. 15. See also his comments on architecture in 'The Advantages of Open Seats', *Exeter Architectural Review*, no. 1 (1843), pp. 1–2, 4–5.

73 Gladstone said of Medley that 'his was the wisest head that wore a mitre'. See Fairweather, 'A Tractarian Patriarch', p. 18.

74 The extent of the relationship between Armstrong and Medley is unknown, as no correspondence between the two has yet been discovered. Presumably it was close, as they were not only both heavily involved in the Exeter Diocesan Architectural Society, but Armstrong was also priest-vicar at Exeter cathedral while Medley was a prebend. An article in the *Western Luminary* (13 May 1845) reported that Arm-

strong, along with the Rev. C. C. Bartholomew, were responsible for raising £1571.2s.6*d*. for Medley's cathedral project before he left for New Brunswick. Medley later observed that this money was raised by 'two old and zealous friends'. See 'Account of Architecture', in John Medley, *A Charge to the Clergy of the Diocese . . . at His Third Triennial Visitation* (Fredericton: Royal Gazette Office, 1853), p. 31.

75 For example, see Christopher Headon, 'An Unpublished Correspondence between John Medley and E. B. Pusey', *JCCHS*, vol. 16:4 (1974), pp. 72–4.

76 Thomas Mozley, *Reminiscences, Chiefly of Oriel College and the Oxford Movement*, 2 vols (London: Longmans, Green & Co., 1882), vol. 2, p. 9.

77 John Medley, *'The Harvest Field of the World': A Sermon Preached in the Cathedral Church of St. Peter, Exeter . . .* (Exeter: P. A. Hannaford, 1843), p. 30. See also his comments in *A Charge Delivered in the Cathedral Church of Christ-Church, Fredericton . . . at the Second Triennial Visitation* (Saint John, New Brunswick: W. L. Avery, 1850), p. 13.

78 W. O. Raymond, 'John Medley', in W. B. Heeney (ed.), *Leaders of the Canadian Church* (London: SPCK, 1920), p. 108. Medley later described Selwyn as that 'truly apostolic prelate' who, 'with the highest prospects before him, left all to follow Christ'.

79 'Annual Report' (21 May 1852) in *Transactions of Exeter Diocesan Architectural Society*, vol. 4 (1853), p. 251. On this point Medley had observed: 'Wherever there is a bishop, there is not only a centre of unity, but a rallying point for action, . . . a Cathedral Church, the mother-Church of the diocese, Jerusalem and her daughters.' Medley quoted in Fairweather, 'A Tractarian Patriarch', p. 23.

80 Ibid., p. 21.

81 *Western Luminary* (13 May 1845). Coleridge was also chairman of the Exeter Diocesan Architectural Society. For Coleridge's architectural activity in Barbados, see Barbara Hill and Henry Fraser, *Historic Churches of Barbados* (Bridgetown: Art Heritage Publications, 1984).

82 'An Interview with His Lordship Seven Years Ago, on the Occasion of the Eightieth Anniversary of His Birthday', University of New Brunswick, Provincial Archives, Diocese of Fredericton Records, DB-1-20F.

83 Medley, 'Account of Architecture', p. 31.

84 *Eccl.*, vol. 2 (Feb. 1846), p. 81.

85 *Quarterly Papers of the SPG*, no. 35 (Oct. 1845), p. 5.

86 *Eccl.*, vol. 5 (June 1848), p. 362. As Jane Russell-Corbett has shown, Medley's deference to the opinion of the Ecclesiological Society demonstrated its influence in British North America. See Jane Russell-Corbett, '"The Ecclesiologist" and Anglican Church Architecture in the Canadian Colonies', *Bulletin of the Society for the Study of Architecture in Canada*, vol. 21:4 (1997), pp. 91–2.

87 *Eccl.*, vol. 5 (June 1848), p. 362.

88 Bishop Medley's Journal, University of New Brunswick, Provincial Archives, Diocese of Fredericton Records, DB-1-1B.

89 Watson, *Christ Church Cathedral*, p. 5.

90 Headon, 'Developments in Canadian Anglican Worship', p. 28; Finley, '"Habits of reverence and awe"', p. 18. Medley's cause was not helped by Newman's 'perversion' to Rome shortly after his arrival in Fredericton.

91 John Medley, *The Staff of Beauty and the Staff of Bands: A Sermon Preached in St. Anne's Chapel, Fredericton* (Saint John, New Brunswick: W. L. Avery, 1847), pp. 14–15. This sermon was preached at the consecration of St Anne's chapel, Fredericton – another of Wills's creations.

92 Medley, *A Charge Delivered in the Cathedral of Christ-Church*, pp. 46–7. Here Medley refers to a passage in Ruskin's *Seven Lamps of Architecture* (1849). This was the general notion of 'Levitical sacrifice' postulated by Ruskin in the 'Lamp of Sacrifice'.

93 Medley, *A Charge Delivered in the Cathedral of Christ-Church*, p. 48.

94 Medley, *The Staff of Beauty*, pp. 19–20.

95 Stanton, *The Gothic Revival*, p. 143.

96 Kalman, *A History of Canadian Architecture*, vol. 1, p. 191.

97 Bishop Fulford, Journal, vol. 4, entry for 4 Feb. 1857, Christ Church, Montreal, Cathedral Archive. Wills was appointed at a meeting of the Cathedral Building Committee in March 1857. See unpublished letters, F. Fulford to F. Wills (17 Jan. 1857) and J. Drake to W. Hay (28 March 1857), Finance & Building Committee Ledger, No. 4, Christ Church, Montreal, Cathedral Archive.

98 Bishop Fulford, Journal, vol. 4, entry for 11 Jan. 1857, Christ Church, Montreal, Cathedral Archive. See also unpublished letter, F. Fulford to E. Hawkins (14 Feb. 1857), Bodl. CAS, USPG Archive, CLR/155 (Montreal). Shortly after his appointment, Wills's credentials were disclosed in the *Montreal Weekly Herald* (11 April 1857). For Wills elsewhere in Canada, see Malcolm Thurlby, 'Two Churches by Frank Wills: St. Peter's, Barton, and St. Paul's, Glanford, and the Ecclesiological Gothic Revival in Ontario', *JSSAC*, vol. 32:1 (2007), pp. 49–60.

99 Frank Wills, *Ancient English Ecclesiastical Architecture and Its Principles Applied to the Wants of the Church at the Present Day* (New York: Stanford and Swords, 1850).

100 Fulford was associated with the Tractarian cause through a defence of the Anglican position in his book *The Progress of the Reformation in England* (1841).

101 Fennings Taylor, *The Last Three Bishops Appointed by The Crown, for the Anglican Church of Canada* (Montreal: John Lovell, 1869), pp. 67–87.

102 For instance, see Fulford's sermon on the occasion of the cathedral's opening in the *Montreal Gazette* (29 Nov. 1859).

103 *Eccl.*, vol. 15 (Dec. 1857), p. 359. Others were not quite so generous in their praise. For instance, see the *Church Journal* (New York) (26 Aug. 1857).

104 Here Stanton notes Wills's closeness to Pugin. Stanton, *The Gothic Revival*, pp. 286–96.

105 For the construction history of Christ Church cathedral, see Philip J. Turner, *Christ Church Cathedral Montreal*, Series XIII (Art and Architecture), no. 17 (Montreal: McGill University Publications, 1927).

106 A total of 24,994 cubic feet of Caen stone arrived in Montreal for the cathedral's construction. See Finance & Building Committee Ledger, No. 4, Christ Church, Montreal, Cathedral Archive.

107 G. G. Scott, *Personal and Professional Recollections* (1879), ed. G. Stamp (Stamford: Paul Watkins, 1995), p. 373.

108 Scott's major works in this respect are: *A Plea for the Faithful Restoration of Our Ancient Churches* (Oxford: J. H. Parker, 1850); *Remarks on Secular & Domestic Architecture, Present and Future* (London: John Murray, 1857); and *Lectures on the Rise and Development of Mediæval Architecture*, 2 vols (London: John Murray, 1878–9).

109 J. N. Mané, 'Gilbert Scott's Colonial Churches', in M. Belcher and H. Debenham (eds), *Australasian Victorian Studies Association: Conference Papers 1987* (Christchurch: University of Canterbury for the AVSA, 1987), pp. 31–42.

110 See Robin Skinner, 'Drawing from an Indigenous Tradition? George Gilbert Scott's First Design for Christchurch Cathedral, 1861–62', *Architectural History*, vol. 53 (2010), p. 256. See also Chris Miele, 'Scenes from Clerical Life: The Young Scott' (forthcoming).

111 Supplying plans to cash-strapped dioceses on this basis was not particularly unusual. For example, we see it in the case of William Slater's design for St George's cathedral, Basse Terre, and with Charles Tiffin in Queensland. See *Eccl.*, vol. 18 (June 1860), p. 142, and Stuart King, 'Colony and Climate: Positioning Public Architecture in Queensland, 1859–1909, unpublished PhD thesis (University of Melbourne, 2010), p. 92. Scott also gave his services to the ICBS for nothing. See *Church Builder*, no. 34 (1870), p. 39.

112 Scott later described Newfoundland cathedral as one of his most important works up to 1862. See Scott, *Personal and Professional Recollections*, pp. 147–8. For the cathedral's architecture, see Peter Coffman, *Newfoundland Gothic* (Quebec: Éditions MultiMondes, 2008), pp. 77–112, 157–68. Scott was never really a fan of imitation as initially encouraged by the ecclesiologists. In a letter to E. A. Freeman on restoring churches he complained: 'every [window] which does not conform to the canons of the ecclesiologist or which is not *the* pet window of the "restorer" is to be removed to make way for a fancy specimen from Bloxham [*sic*] or the [J. H. Parker's] Glossary [that is, the *Glossary of Terms*]'. See unpublished letter, G. G. Scott to E. A. Freeman (9 Oct. 1849), University of Manchester, John Rylands Library, Freeman Papers, FA1/1/94a. I wish to thank Jonathan Conlin for this reference.

113 *The Times* (Newfoundland) (27 Jan. 1841). See also unpublished letter, A. Spencer to Lord Stanley (26 Aug. 1842), Bodl. CAS, USPG Archive, C/CAM/NFL6–71.

114 Unpublished letter, A. Spencer to A. M. Campbell (23 Sept. 1842), Bodl. CAS, USPG Archive, CRL/159 (Newfoundland). The OAS design is most likely that prepared by John Derick at the request of the Rev. Thomas Bridge in 1841. Derick's plans were sent by the society some time around the middle of 1842, but do not seem to have been followed particularly carefully by Purcell. See *Rules and Proceedings* (6 June 1842).

115 The correspondence of Edward Feild seems to corroborate this. In a letter to William Scott, he observes: 'I must relieve Derrick [*sic*] from implication of having designed the wretched imitation of a Ch: intended and accepted for our Cathedral. The drawings which he sent were very handsome and I should think correct.' See unpublished letter, E. Feild to W. Scott (24 Oct. 1844), ADAENL.

116 Unpublished letter, E. Feild to E. Hawkins (19 June 1845), Bodl. CAS, USPG Archive, CLR/159 (Newfoundland).

117 Unpublished letter, E. Feild to E. Hawkins (19 July 1844), Bodl. CAS, USPG Archive, CLR/159 (Newfoundland). The stone had been arranged by Purcell and shipped from Cork.

118 *Report of the Cathedral Building Committee . . . St. John's, Newfoundland* (St John's: Ryan and Withers, 1844), pp. 8–9.

119 For Feild, see Frederick Jones, 'Bishop Feild: A Study in Politics and Religion in Nineteenth-Century Newfoundland', PhD thesis (University of Cambridge, 1972).

120 For instance, see Edward Feild, *Order and Uniformity in the Public Services of the Church . . . : A Charge Delivered to the Clergy of the Diocese of Newfoundland* (St John's: John W. McCoubrey, 1844). Jones notes that within one month of arriving in St John's, Feild had moved the fittings of the parish church to show his clergy the 'proper arrangement'. See Jones, 'Bishop Feild', p. 96.

121 Unpublished letter, E. Hawkins to E. Feild (18 July 1846), Bodl. CAS, USPG Archive, CLS/113 (Newfoundland).

122 Unpublished letter, E. Hawkins to E. Feild (3 Aug. 1846), Bodl. CAS, USPG Archive, CLS/113 (Newfoundland). See also, unpublished letter, G. G. Scott to E. Hawkins (17 Aug. 1846), Bodl. CAS, USPG Archive, C/CAN/NFL6–76.

123 Although sketches of the parish-style scheme were still being produced by 1847, Scott had all but given up on this and opted for the cruciform version. See unpublished letter, G. G. Scott to E. Hawkins (1 Jan. 1847), Bodl. CAS, USPG Archive, C/CAN/NFL6–80a.

124 Indeed, when Ernest Hawkins was making inquiries into suitable architects in England, he recorded how Scott had noted: 'the Church to be built should be of solid & *severe* character with small windows, as best suited to the climate and the condition of the Colony'. See unpublished letter, E. Hawkins to E. Feild (18 July 1846), Bodl. CAS, USPG Archive, CLS/113 (Newfoundland).

125 Unpublished letter, E. Hawkins to E. Feild (3 March 1847), Bodl. CAS, USPG Archive, CLS/113 (Newfoundland). It was probably on the recommendation of the Rev. William Scott, who was a committee member of the CCS at the time, that Scott was offered the commission.

126 G. G. Scott, 'Argument in Favour of a Cross Church', *c.* Jan. 1847, Bodl. CAS, USPG Archive, C/CAM/NFL6–80b, pp. 1–2.

127 Ibid., pp. 3–4.

128 Ibid., pp. 4–5.

129 Beresford Hope, *The English Cathedral*, pp. 26–7.

130 F. M. Buffett, *The Story of the Church in Newfoundland* (Toronto: Board of Religious Education, 1939). See also 'In Memoriam – Edward Feild, D.D., Bishop of Newfoundland 1844–1876', newspaper obituary, University of New Brunswick, Provincial Archives, Diocese of Fredericton Archives, DB-1-1C.

131 Letter (or speech) by Edward Feild on the building of the cathedral at St John's, Newfoundland (*c.*1848), Bodl. CAS, USPG Archive, C/CAM/NFL6–81. He later described the expenditure of upwards of £25,000 on such a project at this stage as 'midsummer madness'. See H. W. Tucker, *Memoir of the Life and Episcopate of Edward Feild, D.D., Bishop of Newfoundland, 1844–76* (London: W. Wells Gardner, 1877), p. 68.

132 For example, see unpublished letter, G. G. Scott to E. Feild (3 Aug. 1847), Memorial University of Newfoundland, Centre for Newfoundland and Labrador Studies, Coll. 45, File 3.

133 Mané, 'Gilbert Scott's Colonial Churches', p. 37.

134 Scott, *A Plea for the Faithful Restoration of Our Ancient Churches*, p. 95.

135 Webb says: 'Under these conditions, a most impracticable climate, no available native materials, an unpliant ritual, and the need of retaining a parochial character, – we think that such a combination, as in the parallel case of a tropical climate, would have justified an attempt at developement [*sic*]. Mr. Scott, has, however, chosen to build by precedent: and the result, though scrupulously correct, appears to us deficient in the indescribable character, the moral feeling, if we may so say – of originality.' *Eccl.*, 5 (April 1848), p. 277.

136 John Ruskin, *On the Nature of Gothic Architecture: And Herein of the True Functions of the Workman on Art* (London: Smith Elder, & Co., 1854), pp. 4–5. As Peter Coffman has observed, Scott even seems to have opted for a peculiarly northern-English style of moulded capital with a fillet running through its neck. This may have been further reference to a style of architecture suitable to colder climates. See Coffman, *Newfoundland Gothic*, p. 104.

137 Unpublished letter, G. G. Scott to E. Feild (27 Nov. 1846), St John's, Newfoundland, Cathedral Archive, Arch 600, p. 55. Hay had operated in this capacity for other architects in the past, having superintended the erection of St Columba's, Edinburgh (1846), and Trinity College, Glenalmond (1843). He also seemed eminently qualified for the task, having dedicated much of his professional career to the study of ecclesiastical architecture. See unpublished letters: W. Hay to E. Feild (30 Oct. 1846), ADAENL, 100.43, Box 1, File 6; W. Hay to E. Feild (7 Nov. 1846), Memorial University of Newfoundland, Centre for Newfoundland and Labrador Studies, Coll. 45, File 1.

138 Coffman, *Newfoundland Gothic*, pp. 109–11.

139 *The Builder* (22 Jan. 1881), p. 99; *Building News* (18 Sept. 1885), p. 446.

140 *Eccl.*, 5 (April 1848), pp. 275, 278.

141 Rhodes University, Grahamstown, Cory Library, St George's Vestry Minute Book, 1829–62, MS 16 604/1.

142 Unpublished letter, F. H. Williams (dean of the cathedral) probably to J. H. Scott, 18 July 1878), Rhodes University, Grahamstown, Cory Library, MS 16 758/10. The Vestry Minute Book indicates that Cotterill (who was bishop, 1856–71) had Scott's plans by August 1862. Cotterill also noted in a letter to J. H. Scott, the executor of Scott's will, that he had received design drawings from Scott for the cathedral. See unpublished letter, J. H. Scott to F. H. Williams (2 Dec. 1878), Cory Library, MS 16 758/10.

143 See '"Notes from South Africa" by the Bishop of Grahamstown', Bodl. CAS, USPG Archive, D7b (Letters received: Cape Town and Grahamstown).

144 T. T. Carter, *A Memoir of John Armstrong, D.D., Late Bishop of Grahamstown* (J. H. Parker: Oxford, 1857), p. 278.

145 Despite being headed 'Vision for a Cathedral', it is possible that this drawing by Armstrong was an alternative version

for the college chapel at St Andrew's College, Grahamstown, as it is next to another sketch of the college. See J. Armstrong, manuscript '"Notes from South Africa" by the Bishop of Grahamstown', Bodl. CAS, USPG Archive, D7b (Letters received: Cape Town and Grahamstown).

146 This approach was also recommended by the CCS, where funds were meagre or piecemeal. See *A Few Words to Church Builders* (Cambridge: Cambridge Camden Society, 1841), pp. 8–9.

147 'Declaration (under the north-west corner of the Cathedral Tower)', Rhodes University, Grahamstown, Cory Library, MS-16-649.

148 Carter, *A Memoir*, p. 278.

149 Scott, *A Plea for the Faithful Restoration of Our Ancient Churches*, p. 115. Scott described the Early English as 'our' (that is, 'English' and 'Christian') architecture.

150 Scott's correspondence, Rhodes University, Grahamstown, Cory Library, MS 16 758/10; Rhodes University, Grahamstown, Cory Library, St George's Vestry Minute Book, 1829–62, MS 16 604/1, entries for 20 Aug. 1874 and 30 May 1878.

151 Rhodes University, Grahamstown, Cory Library, St George's Vestry Minute Book, MS 16 758/10, entry for 20 Sept. 1910. See also M. Berning, *The Tower, Clock and Bells of Grahamstown Cathedral: An Outline History* (Grahamstown, 1987); Basil F. L. Clarke, *Anglican Cathedrals Outside the British Isles* (London: SPCK, 1958), p. 27.

152 Unpublished letters: J. E. FitzGerald to Lord Lyttelton (20 Aug. 1858), Canterbury Museum Library, Lyttelton Papers, 79/50-Folder 23, item 487; G. G. Scott to H. J. C. Harper (24 Feb. 1862), Christchurch Anglican Diocesan Archive, PAR0015 (Christchurch Cathedral).

153 *Canterbury Papers: Information Concerning the Principles, Objects, Plans, & Proceedings of the Founders of the Settlement of Canterbury in New Zealand* (London: John W. Parker, 1850), nos. 1 and 2, p. 6.

154 Ibid., p. 5.

155 Gladstone quoted in a letter from FitzGerald to Bishop Harper. See Mané, 'Gilbert Scott's Colonial Churches', p. 31.

156 W. P. Morrell, *The Anglican Church in New Zealand: A History* (Dunedin: Anglican Church of the Province of New Zealand, 1973), p. 52.

157 Marie Peters, 'Homeland and Colony', in C. Brown, M. Peters, and J. Teal (eds), *Shaping a Colonial Church: Bishop Harper and the Anglican Diocese of Christchurch, 1856–1890* (Christchurch: Canterbury UP, 2006), p. 19; L. C. Webb, 'Aspiration and Achievement', in J. Hight and C. R. Straubel (eds), *A History of Canterbury*, vol. 1 (Christchurch: Whitcome and Tombs, 1957), pp. 224–33.

158 *The Press* (25 Oct. 1862).

159 *The Press* (20 Dec. 1862).

160 Ian Lochhead, *A Dream of Spires: Benjamin Mountfort and the Gothic Revival* (Christchurch: Canterbury UP, 1999), pp. 134–41. Lochhead's chapter on Christchurch cathedral is the most complete and comprehensive architectural history of the building. A wider history of the cathedral and its associations can be found in Colin Brown, *Vision & Reality: Christchurch's Cathedral in the Square* (Christchurch: Christchurch Cathedral Chapter, 2000).

161 FitzGerald quoted in Brown, *Vision & Reality*, p. 129.

162 *Eccl.*, vol. 8 (Dec. 1850), pp. 262–3. This association is identified by Lochhead in *A Dream of Spires*, p. 137.

163 Lochhead, *A Dream of Spires*, p. 138. See also Skinner, 'Drawing from an Indigenous Tradition?', pp. 250–2.

164 The use of timber in this way to construct the house of God is also reminiscent of Selwyn's continual references to 'trees' and 'growth' in his parting sermon at Exeter in December 1841. See Selwyn, *'How shall we sing the Lord's song in a strange land?'*.

165 Unpublished letter, H. J. C. Harper to G. G. Scott (10 April 1863), Christchurch Diocesan Archives: PAR0015 (Christchurch Cathedral).

166 For example, on Scott's recommendation of Mountfort, see unpublished letters: G. G. Scott to H. J. C. Harper (18 May and 20 Oct. 1863), Christchurch Diocesan Archives: PAR0015 (Christchurch Cathedral). Mountfort had written to Scott pleading his case, including photos of his work which seemed to impress him.

167 *The Press* (3 Aug. 1864).

168 The Cathedral Commission threatended Speechley with legal action unless he returned the drawings. See unpublished letter, Hon. Treasurer of the Cath. Comm. to R. Speechley (24 Feb. 1869), Christchurch Diocesan Archives: PAR0015 (Christchurch Cathedral). He eventually returned them.

169 Ian Lochhead, 'Experiments in Ecclesiology: Anglican Church Building in Colonial New Zealand', in G. A. Bremner (ed.), *Ecclesiology Abroad: The British Empire and Beyond*, themed issue of *Studies in Victorian Architecture and Design*, vol. 4 (2012), pp. 71–2.

170 Unpublished letter, G. G. Scott to H. J. C. Harper (18 May 1863), Christchurch Anglican Diocesan Archive, PAR0015 (Christchurch Cathedral). Working in Mountfort's favour here was the fact that the Ecclesiological Society had earlier recommended that 'where a part only of a church is to be built, it is ordinarily better to begin with the nave'. See *Eccl.*, vol. 13 (Feb. 1855), p. 50.

171 For a detailed account of the construction of the cathedral, see Lochhead, *A Dream of Spires*, pp. 141–65.

172 Interestingly, an understanding of Scott's oeuvre in this sense had become such that by the early twentieth century *The Builder* magazine could say of his chapel at St John's College, Cambridge (1863–9), that it had 'the air of an interloper on the scene, with the look of a colonial cathedral rather than a college chapel'. See *The Builder*, vol. 86 (1904), p. 241. I am grateful to Simon Bradley for this reference.

173 For instance, see Clarke, *Anglican Cathedrals Outside the British Isles*.

174 *Eccl.*, vol. 5 (Dec. 1847), p. 141.

175 Beresford Hope, *The English Cathedral*, p. 104.

176 Southwell had lost its west-end spires by the time Butterfield came to design Adelaide (they were not replaced until the 1880s), but there were many images in circulation of what it had originally looked like, some of which were no doubt known to Butterfield. The replacement spires were based on the originals. I wish to thank Peter Coffman for pointing this out.

177 Interestingly, Short had earlier noted that the north Adelaide site would have made the perfect spot for 'one of our "*Minster*" Churches'. See unpublished letter, A. Short to E. Hawkins (31 Dec. 1847), Bodl. CAS, USPG Archive, CLR/205 (Adelaide).

178 J. Mordaunt Crook, 'The Reality of Brick: William Butterfield and Benjamin Webb', in Crook, *The Architect's Secret: Victorian Critics and the Image of Gravity* (London: John Murray, 2003), p. 57. See also Paul Thompson, 'Form: The Mass', in Thompson, *William Butterfield* (Cambridge, Mass.: MIT Press, 1971), pp. 275–303.

179 Three publications that went some way to enlivening interest in the use of brick were Benjamin Webb's *Sketches of Continental Ecclesiology* (1848), John Ruskin's *The Stones of Venice* (1851–3), and G. E. Street's *Brick and Marble in the Middle Ages* (1855). For the influence of constructional polychromy, see Neil Jackson, 'Christ Church, Streatham, and the Rise of Constructional Polychromy', *Architectural History*, vol. 43 (2000), pp. 241–6. For Street's views on 'developement', see H.-R. Hitchcock, 'G. E. Street in the 1850s', *JSAH*, vol. 19:4 (1960), pp. 148–50.

180 G. E. Street, 'The True Principles of Architecture, and the Possibility of Development', *Eccl.*, vol. 10 (Aug. 1852), p. 261.

181 Owen Chadwick, *From Bossuet to Newman: The Idea of Doctrinal Development* (Cambridge: Cambridge UP, 1957), pp. 116, 119; David Brownlee, 'The First High Victorians: British Architectural Theory in the 1840s', *Architectura*, vol. 15:1 (1985), pp. 35–7.

182 For a detailed account of Freeman's thinking on this, see G. A. Bremner and Jonathan Conlin, 'History as Form: Architecture and Liberal Anglican Thought in the Writings of E. A. Freeman', *Modern Intellectual History*, vol. 8: 2 (2011), pp. 299–326.

183 Beresford Hope, *The English Cathedral*, p. 31. For the concept of architectural development in general, see Michael Hall, '"Our Own": Thomas Hope, A. J. B. Beresford Hope and the Creation of the High Victorian Style', in Rosemary Hill and Michael Hall (eds), *The 1840s, Studies in Victorian Architecture and Design*, vol. 1 (London: Victorian Society, 2008), pp. 61–75. For Beresford Hope and 'progressive eclecticism', see J. Mordaunt Crook, 'Progressive Eclecticism: The Case of Beresford Hope', *Architectural Design*, vol. 53:7–8 (1983), pp. 56–62.

184 The critical arguments concerning this shift are to be found in 'The Artistic Merit of Mr Pugin', *Eccl.*, vol. 2 (Jan. 1846), pp. 10–16, and 'Past and Future Developements [*sic*] of Architecture', *Eccl.*, vol. 2 (Feb. 1846), pp. 48–53.

185 Michael Hall, 'What do Victorian Churches Mean?: Symbolism and Sacramentalism in Anglican Church Architecture, 1850–1870', *JSAH*, vol. 59:1 (2000), pp. 78–95. See also Michael W. Brooks, *John Ruskin and Victorian Architecture* (London: Thames and Hudson, 1987), pp. 88–9. For the influence of the idea of 'development' in Victorian architecture, see Brownlee, 'The First High Victorians', pp. 33–46.

186 John Ruskin, *The Stones of Venice: The Foundations*, vol. 1 (London: Smith, Elder & Co., 1851), p. 286.

187 Crook, 'The Reality of Brick', pp. 35–83.

188 Augustus Short, *The Primary Charge, Delivered by the Right Reverend Augustus, Lord Bishop of Adelaide* (Adelaide: H. Hussey, 1851), pp. 3–5. See also Short's comments on the cathedral in *South Australian Register* (17 Jan. 1855).

189 Interestingly, at the time he recommissioned Butterfield to design the cathedral, Short had had in his possession since 1854 a far more conventional plan by W. G. and E. Habershon. See Brian Andrews, *Gothic in South Australian Churches* (Adelaide: Flinders University, 1984), p. 32. See also Donald Leslie Johnson, 'French and English Influences on the Architecture of St. Peter's Cathedral, Adelaide', *Architecture Australia* (June 1988), pp. 70–6.

190 Paul Thompson, 'Exporting the Gothic Revival: Butterfield's Australian Cathedrals, 1', *Country Life* (9 Sept. 1971), p. 622.

191 Unpublished letter, A. Short to E. Hawkins (6 July 1870), Bodl. CAS, USPG Archive, CLR/206 (Adelaide).

192 It seemed that neither did Burges have a full understanding of where he was designing his cathedral, believing Brisbane to be in South Australia, nor did the bishop of Brisbane know of the proposal. See the *Moreton Bay Courier*, 14 August 1860, p. 3.

193 *Eccl.*, vol. 19 (Feb. 1861), p. 21.

194 J. Mordaunt Crook, 'Early French Gothic', in S. Macready and F. H. Thompson (eds), *Influences in Victorian Art and Architecture* (London: Society of Antiquaries of London, 1985), pp. 49–58; Gavin Stamp, 'High Victorian Gothic and the Architecture of Normandy', *JSAH*, vol. 62:2 (2003), pp. 194–211. For 'muscularity' in Victorian church architecture, see C. M. Smart, *Muscular Churches: Ecclesiastical Architecture of the High Victorian Period* (Fayetteville: University of Arkansas Press, 1989).

195 J. Mordaunt Crook, *William Burges and the High Victorian Dream* (London: John Murray, 1981), p. 199. In his predilection for foreign forms, Burges was somewhere between what Charles Eastlake described as the 'adaptational or artistic school' and the 'independent or eclectic school' in British architecture. See Charles L. Eastlake, *A History of the Gothic Revival* (London: Longmans, 1872), p. 359.

196 Ruskin, *The Stones of Venice*, vol. 1, p. 86.

197 In issuing his first address to his see from England, Bromby noted that one of two things he would do upon arrival was 'the commencement of a cathedral'. See *The Standard* (12 Aug. 1864).

198 *Church News* (20 Jan. 1864).

199 Ibid.

200 Bromby's Easter Day service at St Paul's church, Cheltenham, quoted in *Church Times* (20 June 1864).

201 Herbert H. Condon, 'Henry Bromby, Second Bishop of Tasmania', MA thesis (University of Tasmania, 1964), p. 283. I wish to thank Michael Hall for supplying me with this reference.

202 I wish to thank Michael Hall for bringing this to my attention.

203 J. H. B. Mace, *Henry Bodley Bromby* (London: Longmans, Green & Co., 1913), p. 9.

204 Michael Hall, 'The Rise of Refinement: G. F. Bodley's All Saints', Cambridge, and the Return to English Models in Gothic Architecture of the 1860s', *Architectural History*, vol. 36 (1993), pp. 106–10.

205 Tasmanian State Library and Archives, Hobart, Minutes of the Meetings of the New Cathedral Committee, NS282/4/1.

206 Hall, 'The Rise of Refinement', pp. 103–26.

207 *Eccl.*, vol. 25 (Feb. 1867), p. 57.

208 The first reference to Bodley's design appeared in *Eccl.*, vol. 23 (Aug. 1865), p. 231. I wish to thank Michael Hall for sharing his thoughts and research findings on Hobart cathedral.

209 *Church News* (19 Jan. 1866).

210 *Church News* (20 April 1866).

211 I wish to thank Michael Hall for bringing this to my attention. Bodley experimented with the same motif later at Holy Angels, Hoar Cross (1872–3), and St Mary the Virgin, Clumber Park, Nottinghamshire (1886).

212 It should be noted that Bodley's first scheme for Hobart was not all continental muscularity. It did have geometric traceried windows and therefore contained something of his broader move towards refinement. See Michael Hall, *George Frederick Bodley* (forthcoming).

213 *Church News* (18 March and 2 April 1867). Concerns about these initial plans were evident almost immediately after they were received. For example, the initial plan contained a side altar 'against which we should decidedly protest', declared *Church News* (19 Jan. 1866).

214 *Church News* (20 June 1864).

215 See Bromby's pastoral letter reprinted in *Church News* (1 Sept. 1866).

216 Beresford Hope, *The English Cathedral*, p. 282.

217 Ibid., pp. 182–4.

218 For example, Bishop Chapman of Colombo had envisioned his cathedral also acting as the chapel of a much larger, enclosed collegiate complex, much like Christ Church, Oxford. See J. Chapman, *Address on Laying the Corner-Stone of the Cathedral Church at St. Thomas' College, Colombo* (Colombo: College Press, 1852).

219 Especially St John's cathedral, Brisbane (1889–2008), which Pearson designed only a few years after Truro. See Anthony Quiney, *John Loughborough Pearson* (New Haven and London: Yale UP, 1979), pp. 133–48, 199–201.

220 Beresford Hope, *The English Cathedral*, p. 143.

221 Ibid., p. 264.

3 Adaptation and Invention

1 *Eccl.*, vol. 4 (Jan. 1847), pp. 15–16.

2 Benjamin Webb, 'On the Adaptation of Pointed Architecture to Tropical Climates', *Transactions of the Cambridge Camden Society, 1843–45* (1845), p. 218.

3 A. J. B. Beresford Hope, *The English Cathedral of the Nineteenth Century* (London: John Murray, 1861), p. 31. For Beresford Hope, see J. Mordaunt Crook, 'Progressive Eclecticism: The Case of Beresford Hope', *Architectural Design*, vol. 53:7–8 (1983), pp. 56–62. See also G. A. Bremner, '"Some Imperial Institute": Architecture, Symbolism, and the Ideal of Empire in Late Victorian Britain, 1887–93', *JSAH*, vol. 62:1 (2003), pp. 67–9.

4 *Eccl.*, vol. 4 (March 1847), pp. 89–90.

5 David Brownlee, 'That "regular mongrel affair": G. G. Scott's Design for the Government Offices', *Architectural History*, vol. 28 (1985), pp. 159–82. For the Battle of the

Styles debate and its bearing on issues of empire, see G. A. Bremner, 'Nation and Empire in the Government Architecture of Mid-Victorian London: The Foreign and India Office Reconsidered', *Historical Journal*, vol. 48:3 (2005), pp. 703–42.

6 Webb, 'On the Adaptation', p. 216. The OAS was also in concordance with this view. See *Rules and Proceedings* (23 June 1846), p. 18.

7 Ibid., p. 201.

8 E. A. Freeman, *A History of Architecture* (London: Joseph Master, 1849), p. 47. See also G. A. Bremner and Jonathan Conlin, 'History as Form: Architecture and Liberal Anglican thought in the Writings of E. A. Freeman', *Modern Intellectual History*, vol. 8: 2 (2011), p. 316.

9 Webb, 'On the Adaptation of Pointed Architecture', p. 215.

10 John Mason Neale, 'On the Ecclesiology of Madeira', *Transactions of the Cambridge Camden Society, 1843–45* (1845), pp. 219–35.

11 *Eccl.*, vol. 6 (Dec. 1848), p. 186.

12 William Scott, 'Some Thoughts on the Cathedral of Las Palmas, with a Few Thoughts on Tropical Architecture', *Eccl.*, vol. 9 (Feb. 1851), pp. 29–45.

13 Ibid., p. 39.

14 I would like to thank Michael Hall for encouraging me to consider Scott's views in relation to Ruskin's 'Lamp of Power'.

15 Scott, 'Some Thoughts on the Cathedral of Las Palmas', p. 40.

16 E.g. *Eccl.*, 12 (April 1854), p. 150; *Eccl.*, vol. 17 (Feb. 1859), pp. 54–5.

17 E.g. *Eccl.*, vol. 3 (Nov. 1846), pp. 165–6. Crusader churches were suggested because they were 'built by Christian architects, in days when Christian architecture was a living thing, for the use of a climate far more sultry than that to which they had been themselves accustomed' (p. 166).

18 This suggestion was made by the Rev. John Frederick Bourne of Guiana. In a letter to *The Ecclesiologist* he observed: 'Now, if in a brick or stone church we were to construct large semi-circular or polygonal buttresses, hollow, and pierced externally to windward, and internally on higher planes than the external piercings, these would form admirable ventilators.' He thought such an adaptation necessary in locations where strong breezes were a problem, thus not allowing large, open windows. See *Eccl.*, vol. 6 (Dec. 1848), p. 186.

19 J. E. Millard, 'On the Style of Architecture to be Adopted in Colonial Churches', *Rules and Proceedings* (26 Feb. 1845), pp. 10–12. Millard's basic point was that 'perfection may be gained by the gradual exaltation of a national style, rather than by plunging an untried borrowed one into a region not in character with it'. In this respect he was not so far from Webb; only the degree of stylistic influence was debatable.

20 *Eccl.*, vol. 3 (Nov. 1846), pp. 166–8.

21 Beresford Hope, *The English Cathedral*, p. 87.

22 This was a concern expressed by the Rev. J. F. Bourne in a paper titled 'On Tropical Architecture'. See *Eccl.*, vol. 9 (June 1851), p. 169.

23 *Eccl.*, vol. 9 (Feb. 1851), p. 21.

24 *Eccl.*, vol. 5 (April 1848), p. 79. See also Beresford Hope, *The English Cathedral*, p. 96; J. N. Mané, 'Gilbert Scott's Colonial Churches', in M. Belcher and H. Debenham (eds), *Australasian Victorian Studies Association: Conference Papers 1987* (Christchurch: University of Canterbury for the AVSA, 1987), p. 37.

25 Indeed, on the matter of ecclesiology in general, Beresford Hope had urged as early as 1846: 'do not the achievements of modern science, do not our increased acquaintance with the products of all lands, their marbles, their woods, their ornamental work; do not our increased means of commerce all point to fresh stores of artistical wealth, which may hereafter be devoted to the service of the sanctuary'. See *Eccl.*, vol. 2 (Feb. 1846), p. 52.

26 *Eccl.*, vol. 5 (Dec. 1847), p. 147. For the interest in and influence of Albi cathedral among ecclesiologists and architects in Britain, see John Thomas, *Albi Cathedral and British Church Architecture* (London: Ecclesiological Society/Society of Antiquaries of London, 2002).

27 *Eccl.*, [1st ser.], vol. 1 (July 1842), p. 180; *Eccl.*, [1st ser.], vol. 2 (Jan. 1843), pp. 74–5. The idea of 'approval' here, with respect to Salvin, refers to those architects 'approved' of and 'condemned' by the CCS. See index to [1st ser.], vol. 3 (1844) of *The Ecclesiologist*.

28 A description of the design can be found in *Eccl.*, [1st ser.], vol. 1 (Jan. 1843), pp. 74–5.

29 Unpublished letter, G. Pigott to OAS (26 Feb. 1843), Bodl., OAS Archive, MS. Dep.c.589.

30 *Rules and Proceedings* (15 Nov. 1843), pp. 8–9.

31 *Rules and Proceedings* (27 June 1843), p. 13. For the dispute between the two societies over who received the initial request, see correspondence between E. Venables and J. H. Parker (29 June 1843), and T. Thorp and W. K. Fletcher (3 Sept. 1843), Bodl., OAS Archive, MS. Dep.c.589, letters 166 and 169.

32 *Rules and Proceedings* (15 Nov. 1843), p. 9.

33 See illustrations in *Rules and Proceedings* (17 June 1844).

34 Webb, 'On the Adaptation of Pointed Architecture', p. 216.

35 Ibid., p. 215.

36 See unpublished letter, J. Tucker to OAS (Madras, 16 Oct. 1839), Bodl., OAS Archive, MS. Dep.c.589, letter 20.

37 *Rules and Proceedings* (3 June 1845), p. 81.

38 *The Ecclesiologist* noted that: 'architecturally speaking, there is . . . much to lament, particularly in the want of any special adaptation to the climate'. See *Eccl.*, vol. 6 (June 1849), p. 399.

39 F. Lorenz Beven (ed.), *A History of the Diocese of Colombo: A Centenary Volume* (Colombo: Times of Ceylon, 1946), pp. 68–9.

40 *Eccl.*, vol. 2 (May 1846), p. 191.

41 He might also have had in mind earlier CMS churches such as Christ Church, Baddegama (1821–4), which was surrounded by a substantial veranda.

42 *Eccl.*, vol. 2 (May 1846), p. 192; *Eccl.*, vol. 5 (Oct. 1847), pp. 88–92.

43 This basic format is similar to that adopted by Carpenter in his unexecuted design for Inverness cathedral (1855). See Beresford Hope, *The English Cathedral*, p. 80.

44 This is how it was described by Beresford Hope. Ibid., p. 84.

45 *Eccl.*, vol. 5 (Oct. 1847), p. 89.

46 Beresford Hope, *The English Cathedral*, pp. 81–4.

47 John Elliott, 'A Trusted Disciple: Richard Cromwell Carpenter', in C. Webster and J. Elliott (eds), *'A church as it should be': The Cambridge Camden Society and Its Influence* (Stamford: Shaun Tyas, 2000), pp. 149–72.

48 See Webb's criticism of Derick's attempt to make the outer cloister in his design for the Afghan Memorial church appear like a traditional aisle in 'On the Adaptation of Pointed Architecture', p. 216.

49 *Eccl.*, vol. 9 (Feb. 1851), p. 20.

50 'Houses of Prayer in Heathen Countries', *Colonial Church Chronicle*, vol. 4 (March 1851), p. 351.

51 *Eccl.*, vol. 9 (Feb. 1851), pp. 29–45.

52 Ibid., p. 23.

53 To be fair to Scott, he did point this out himself. Ibid., p. 44.

54 *Eccl.*, vol. 9 (June 1851), p. 170.

55 E.g. *Eccl.*, vol. 12 (April 1854), p. 150.

56 The two men responsible for supplying the plans for the cathedral (as built) and superintending its construction were a 'Captain Pickering' of the Royal Artillery, and a 'Corporal Moore' of the 15th Regiment. It has been supposed that Pickering was in contact with Carpenter at the time the plans were revised. This is certainly plausible as the cathedral, although reduced, remained a neat and ecclesiologically 'correct' design. See Beven (ed.), *A History of the Diocese of Colombo*, pp. 82, 237–40. See also Basil F. L. Clarke, *Anglican Cathedrals Outside the British Isles* (London: SPCK, 1958), pp. 15–16.

57 *Eccl.*, vol. 12 (Dec. 1854), p. 387. Despite the lack of innovation, the bishop was able to note: 'All that we have done is I hope well done; solid granite, rudely perhaps squared, but still with good effect, the colour being grey and Church like; and the interior fittings, all of really good, and rather elaborate native workmanship, being satin wood in the nave, stalls, pulpit and throne, and of ebony in the Chancel, rails, sedilia, credence, altar table and chairs; and all of good pattern and style.' See Bodl. CAS, USPG Archive, C/IND/COL 1–1247.

58 It seems that Clarke's designs were further 'adapted' by men on the ground, in particular the architect to the Public Works Department, J. G. Smither. See Beven, *A History of the Diocese of Colombo*, p. 274.

59 *Eccl.*, vol. 19 (June 1861), p. 199. See also, *Eccl.*, vol. 20 (Feb. 1862), pp. 32–3.

60 Beresford Hope also made note of the extra-thick walls. Beresford Hope, *The English Cathedral*, p. 85.

61 *The Builder* (12 July 1856), p. 386.

62 For an in-depth account of the design of this building, see Mark Crinson, *Empire Building: Orientalism and Victorian Architecture* (London: Routledge, 1996), pp. 136–66.

63 *Eccl.*, vol. 19 (Feb. 1861), p. 21.

64 For an account of Pearson's involvement at Brisbane, see Anthony Quiney, *John Loughborough Pearson* (New Haven and London: Yale UP, 1979), pp. 199–203.

65 *Illustrated London News* (6 Feb. 1847), p. 84. See also *Eccl.*, vol. 4 (April 1847), p. 153.

66 *Eccl.*, vol. 6 (June 1849), p. 397. The plans for this church were originally furnished by the OAS (drawn by James Cranstoun). See unpublished letters, E. Feild to W. Scott (10 March 1846), ADAENL; and E. Feild to E. Hawkins (19 March 1846), Bodl. CAS, USPG Archive, CLR/113 (Newfoundland). For further discussion of this building, see Barry Magrill, '"Development" and Ecclesiology in the Outpost of the British Empire: William Hay's Gothic Solutions for Church Building in Tropical Climates (1840–1890)', *JSSAC*, vol. 29:1–2 (2004), pp. 15–26.

67 *Eccl.*, vol. 14 (June 1856), p. 214.

68 Beresford Hope noted of this building that, although sturdy, it was comparatively light. 'He [Slater] had not only to provide for the admission of air, but to provide against the risk of a sudden overthrow [cyclone or earthquake] by making his church flexible, and as it were elastic. . . . Mr Slater gave a church broad but not lofty, the dangerous bulk of triforium and clerestory being dispensed with. The pillars

are slender, but not too slender for the weight they have to bear. The aisles, instead of being thrown into the relief of deep shade, are brought forward, as in the large town churches of later Gothic, to contribute to the general effect of air spaciousness.' Beresford Hope, *The English Cathedral*, p. 88.

69 See Louis P. Nelson, 'Anglican Church Building and Local Context in Early Jamaica', *Perspectives in Vernacular Architecture*, vol. 10 (2005), p. 68.

70 *Eccl.*, vol. 7 (April 1850), p. 421.

71 'Journal of the Bishop of Antigua' quoted in *Colonial Church Chronicle*, vol. 13 (May 1859), p. 185.

72 *Eccl.*, vol. 14 (April 1856), p. 109.

73 *Eccl.*, vol. 6 (Dec. 1848), p. 186.

74 This is an observation made by Philip Davies. See Philip Davies, *Splendours of the Raj: British Architecture in India, 1660–1947* (Harmondsworth: Penguin, 1987), p. 191.

75 John Taylor, *All Saints' Cathedral, Allahabad* (n.d.).

76 *The Builder* (18 Feb. 1865), pp. 118–19.

77 The first church was opened for service on Christmas Day 1718. However, the building was not consecrated until June 1816, and not made a cathedral until February 1838. See *The Gazetteer of Bombay City and Island*, vol. 3 (1910), pp. 240–7.

78 Beresford Hope, *The English Cathedral*, p. 96. See also *Eccl.*, 5 (April 1848), pp. 274–9. This is something that Feild's predecessor, Bishop Spencer, also noted: 'The material must be stone, which will offer at once some security from fire, and some resistance to the deleterious qualities of these hyperborean climates.' *Rules and Proceedings* (12 May 1841), p. 12.

79 Beresford Hope, *The English Cathedral*, p. 94. Ernest Hawkins noted in a letter to Francis Fulford that Beresford Hope had mentioned Montreal as a likely place to erect Street's design. See unpublished letter, E. Hawkins to F. Fulford (22 May 1857), Bodl. CAS, USPG Archive: CLS/110 (Montreal).

80 For example, see 'Church on the Banks of Lake Huron, Canada', *The Builder* (17 Dec. 1859), p. 825.

81 Unpublished letter, T. B. Fuller to E. Hawkins (14 July 1845), Bodl. CAS, USPG Archive, C/CAN/TOR/4/523/56.

82 Unpublished letter, T. Bridge to OAS (24 May 1841), Bodl., OAS Archive, MS. Dep.c.589, letter 47.

83 *Eccl.*, 5 (April 1848), p. 275.

84 It was observed by the Rev. William Grey that 'I hear a good many complaints of the expensiveness of stone buildings; it seems that they want constant and costly repairs, owing to the ravages made on the cement by the intense frost, and the sudden changes to rapid thaw, which we have more or less every winter.' See *Eccl.*, 11 (June 1853), pp. 157–8.

85 On this point Feild observed that 'rough walls are sometimes built of this country's stone, but these generally fall in 3 or 4 years unless built very thick and carefully looked after'. See unpublished letter, E. Feild to W. Scott (7 Aug. 1844 and 10 March 1846), ADAENL, letters between Bishop Feild and the Rev. William Scott transcribed by Tim Power (under the direction of S. O'Dea). For St Saviour's, see ADAENL, 302. f03, Box 2.

86 *Eccl.*, vol. 11 (June 1853), p. 160.

87 We see this, for instance, in the letters of bishops Medley and Feild, as well as the Rev. Frederick Coster and his son, George. For the Costers, see *Rules and Proceedings* (23 Nov. 1842), p. 15; (24 May 1843), p. 8; and (28 Feb. 1844), pp. 10–11. See also, David Prout, '"The Oxford Society for Promoting the Study of Gothic Architecture" and the "Oxford Architectural Society," 1839–1860', *Oxoniensia*, vol. 54 (1989), p. 384.

88 *Rules and Proceedings* (26 Feb. 1845), p. 15. Millard invoked well-known examples of ancient timber churches in defence of his argument, such as St Andrew's, Greensted, Essex, and St Oswald's, Lower Peover, Cheshire.

89 For example, see Harold Kalman and John de Visser, *Pioneer Churches* (Toronto: McClelland and Stewart, 1976).

90 *Rules and Proceedings* (15 Nov. 1843), p. 15. Bishop Feild of Newfoundland had hoped to receive copies of these lithographs. See unpublished letter, E. Feild to W. Scott (1 July 1844), ADAENL, letters between Bishop Feild and the Rev. William Scott transcribed by Tim Power (under the direction of S. O'Dea).

91 *Eccl.*, vol. 6 (Aug. 1848), p. 14.

92 Ibid., p. 16.

93 Ibid., p. 18.

94 *Instrumenta Ecclesiastica*, 2nd ser. (London: John Van Voorst, 1856), plates 19–26. Although the full design was published in 1856, Carpenter had been working on this church as early as 1850. See *Eccl.*, vol. 8 (Dec. 1850), p. 248.

95 *Eccl.*, vol. 6 (Aug. 1848), p. 22.

96 Ibid., p. 18. These were mentioned by Scott in his paper. In particular he mentioned two churches 'known to Mr. George Scott, both of the timber and plaister [*sic*] construction'.

97 See unpublished letter, E. Feild to W. Scott (15 May 1845), ADAENL, letters between Bishop Feild and the Rev. William Scott transcribed by Tim Power (under the direction of S. O'Dea).

98 See unpublished letter, E. Feild to W. Scott (7 Aug. 1844), ADAENL, letters between Bishop Feild and the Rev. William Scott transcribed by Tim Power (under the direction of S. O'Dea).

99 See obituary in *The Times* (9 Oct. 1872), and Stephen Matthews, '"Your dutiful son": The Newfoundland Letters of the Revd William Grey', *Report and Transactions of the Dev-*

onshire Association for the Advancement of Science, Literature and the Arts, vol. 136 (2004), pp. 149–50.

100 For instance, see Grey's contributions in Bodl., MS. Top. Oxon. D. 168.

101 Thomas Mozley, *Reminiscences, Chiefly of Oriel College and the Oxford Movement*, 2 vols (London: Longmans, Green & Co., 1882), vol. 1, pp. 334–5.

102 *Eccl.*, vol. 11 (June 1853), p. 159.

103 In his letters back to England, Feild describes Grey as 'a very valuable acquisition' and describes his 'qualifications as an architect . . . so good and useful'. See unpublished letters, E. Feild to E. Hawkins (21 and 30 May 1849), Bodl. CAS, USPG Archive: CLR/159 (Newfoundland).

104 *Eccl.*, vol. 11 (June 1853), p. 159.

105 *The Times* (9 Oct. 1872).

106 *Colonial Church Chronicle*, vol. 8 (Jan. 1855), p. 247.

107 *The Times* (9 Oct. 1872).

108 For Grey's ecclesiological interests in a wider context, see P. J. Leader, 'The Hon. Reverend William Grey, M.A.', MTh thesis (Queen's College, St John's, 1998), pp. 48–52, 91–107. For a specific discussion of the churches mentioned above, see Shane O'Dea and Peter Coffman, 'William Grey: "Missionary" of Gothic in Newfoundland', *JSSAC*, vol. 32:1 (2007), pp. 39–48. See also Grey's diaries, which confirm his involvement in church building activity in Newfoundland, kept at the John Rylands Library, University of Manchester: EGR4/8/1/5–6. I wish to thank James Bettley for bringing this reference to my attention.

109 For example, see Grey's letter of 12 Oct. 1849 printed in Matthews, '"Your dutiful son"', pp. 156–8. See also William Grey, *Sketches of Newfoundland and Labrador* (Ipswich: S. H. Cowell, 1857).

110 On this point Grey noted that 'the sudden changes from frost to thaw, the high winds with furious snow-drifts, together with the poor materials, render a very simple outline quite necessary'. *Eccl.*, vol. 11 (June 1853), p. 159.

111 Grey also mentions the so-called 'black and white' technique from Cheshire in his letter on Newfoundland ecclesiology. Ibid., p. 160.

112 'If the clap board be nailed on, some horizontally, some obliquely, with the frame-work painted with red and the clap board with yellow ochre, the building will have a much more pleasing appearance.' Ibid.

113 For Placentia Bay, see Bodl. CAS, USPG Archive, D/9a, pp. 923–9; for St Francis' Harbour, see *Quarterly Papers of the SPG* (Oct. 1850). The design for St Francis' Harbour was praised in *The Ecclesiologist*. See *Eccl.*, 8 (Oct. 1850), pp. 200–1.

114 Peter Coffman, *Newfoundland Gothic* (Quebec: Éditions MultiMondes, 2008), p. 138. The Grey diaries suggest that the design for this building may have dated back to 1851. See William Grey diaries, John Rylands Library, University of Manchester: EGR4/8/1/5–6, 10–11; EGR4/8/6/7, 10. I wish to thank James Bettley for these references. According to O'Dea and Coffman, St Saviour's, Hermitage, might also have been designed by Grey. See O'Dea and Coffman, 'William Grey', p. 41.

115 *Eccl.*, vol. 5 (June 1848), p. 381; vol. 6 (Aug. 1848), p. 49.

116 For a full account of Edward Medley and his churches, see Douglas S. Richardson, 'Hyperborean Gothic, or Wilderness Ecclesiology and the Wood Churches of Edward Medley', *Architectura*, vol. 1 (1972), pp. 48–74.

117 Ibid., pp. 56–7, 64.

118 Ibid., p. 70.

119 *Eccl.*, vol. 6 (Feb. 1849), p. 216.

120 The full appeal runs: 'In this country [England] we have the greatest difficulty in ascertaining any particulars whatever, of the climate, the local materials, the native way of building, the colonial adaptations of domestic architecture, and the like: we start with some knowledge of Ecclesiological principles, but of course cannot be successful in trying to develope [*sic*] them under new conditions, which we can only guess at by trying to frame a whole out of the conflicting, incomplete, and erroneous information we pick up at hearsay.' *Eccl.*, vol. 4 (Jan. 1847), p. 15.

121 Butterfield was one of the 'apostles', the other was R. C. Carpenter. See G. G. Scott, *Personal and Professional Recollections* (1879), ed. G. Stamp (Stamford: Paul Watkins, 1995), p. 112.

122 'The Nature of Gothic' was originally published as part of Ruskin's *The Stones of Venice* (1851–3).

123 Although *The Ecclesiologist* insisted that stone was a preferable material wherever it could be found, 'cheap' or ready-to-hand material was acceptable so long as ecclesiological dictates were adhered to. This point was made in relation to White's designs for the diocesan school in Cape Town that would eventually become Bishops College. See *Eccl.*, vol. 10 (Aug. 1852), pp. 283, 301. For William White's work in South Africa, see Gill Hunter, 'William White: The Early Years', in Rosemary Hill and Michael Hall (eds), *The 1840s, Studies in Victorian Architecture and Design*, vol. 1 (London: Victorian Society, 2008), pp. 106–16.

124 M. H. Alington, *An Excellent Recruit: Frederick Thatcher – Architect, Priest and Private Secretary in Early New Zealand* (Auckland: Polygraphia, 2007), pp. 50–1.

125 *Mission Life* (1 Feb. 1867), p. 93.

126 See unpublished manuscript, 'History of the Parish of Merriwa' (*c.*1930), University of Newcastle Archive, Auchmuty Library, A5453(v), pp. 7–12. It is noted here that 'To save expense Mr Boodle prepared the plans as much like

early English architecture as could be erected in the wood available – the timber being iron bark slabs.' Boodle also mentions this himself in R. G. Boodle, 'Recollections of Ministerial Work in New South Wales', in J. J. Halcombe (ed.), *The Emigrant and the Heathen, or, Sketches of Missionary Life* (London: SPCK, n.d), pp. 75–6. The 'foundation sleeper' of the church was laid on 17 October 1850. The church was consecrated by Bishop Tyrrell on 19 March 1855.

127 Joan Kerr, 'Authentically Australian Gothic', *Transition* (Spring 1988), p. 6.

128 Extract from the *New Westminster Times* (1860) in Barry Downs, *Sacred Places: British Columbia's Early Churches* (Vancouver: Douglas and McIntyre, 1980), p. 87.

129 The details of this building are contained in a letter from the Rev. Edward Steere. See unpublished letter, E. Steere (22 Oct. 1863), Bodl. CAS, UMCA Archive, A1(III) B-1-245.

130 G. A. Bremner, 'The Architecture of the Universities' Mission to Central Africa: Developing a Vernacular Tradition in the Anglican Mission Field, 1861–1910', *JSAH*, vol. 68:4 (2009), pp. 518–20. The UMCA had erected a similar church, St Paul's, at one of its other mission stations – Magomero (Malawi). See *Colonial Church Chronicle*, vol. 16 (Aug. 1862), pp. 285–6.

131 George Kubler, *The Religious Architecture of New Mexico in the Colonial Period and since the American Occupation* (Colorado Springs: Taylor Museum, 1940).

132 Downs, *Sacred Places*, p. 87.

133 For more on these buildings, see Gregg Finley and Lynn Wigginton, *On Earth as it is in Heaven: Gothic Revival Churches of Victorian New Brunswick* (Fredericton: Goose Lane Editions, 1995), pp. 109–49. See also Phoebe B. Stanton, *The Gothic Revival & American Church Architecture: An Episode in Taste, 1840–1856* (Baltimore: Johns Hopkins UP, 1968), pp. 154–7.

134 For instance, see criticism of Frank Wills's use of timber buttresses at Grace Church, Albany, in *Eccl.*, vol. 8 (Oct. 1850), p. 201. Wills claimed that the buttresses were not sham but 'of the greatest utility' owing to their encasing of structural members. But he seems to have missed the point of the criticism. See Frank Wills, *Ancient English Ecclesiastical Architecture and Its Principles, Applied to the Wants of the Church at the Present Day* (New York: Stanford and Swords, 1850), p. 113.

135 *Eccl.*, vol. 6 (Aug. 1848), p. 19.

136 This is a point also made about New Zealand architecture by Michael Austen in 'Kiwi Architecture: Modernism Recycled', *Fabrications*, vol. 14:1–2 (Dec. 2004), p. vi.

137 G. A. Selwyn, *New Zealand. St. John's College, Bishops' Auckland: Industrial System* (Eton, 1846). In the preface to this document is contained a number of quotes from Thessalonians and Acts concerning 'St Paul's Rule'; for example, 'That ye study to be quiet, and to do your own business, and to work with your own hands, as we commanded you.' Thessalonians, iv. 11. In the details of the system it is noted that, apart from other trades such as printing and tailoring, carpentry be pursued for the 'embellishment of Churches' (p. 3.). See also Allan K. Davidson, *Selwyn's Legacy: The College of St. John the Evangelist Te Waimate and Auckland 1843–1992* (Auckland: St John's College, 1993), pp. 57–64. Selwyn also considered Abraham a suitable role model for colonists. See *Church Chronicle for the Diocese of Montreal*, vol. 1:1 (May 1860), p. 15.

138 Selwyn, *Industrial System*, p. 3.

139 Unpublished letter, G. A. Selwyn to his family in England (1 Dec. 1847), SA, 6.24.c.

140 C. R. Knight, *The Selwyn Churches of Auckland* (Wellington: A. H. and A. W. Reed, 1972), p. 25; Alington, *An Excellent Recruit*, pp. 130–2.

141 H. R. Walden, 'New Zealand Anglican Church Architecture 1814–1963', Master's thesis (University of Auckland, 1964), pp. 44–5.

142 G. A. Selwyn, *An Idea of a Colonial College: A Sermon Preached in the Chapel of St. John the Divine, Bishops' Auckland* (Eton, 1848), p. 11.

143 *Instrumenta Ecclesiastica* (1856), plates 19–26. Although the full design was published in 1856, Carpenter had been working on this church as early as 1850. See *Eccl.*, vol. 8 (Dec. 1850), p. 248.

144 He would later design Christ Church cathedral, Nelson (1886–7), which is a magnificent specimen of this type. For a detailed account of Mountfort's early timber churches, see Ian Lochhead, *A Dream of Spires: Benjamin Mountfort and the Gothic Revival* (Christchurch: Canterbury UP, 1999), pp. 62–90. Another excellent example of this tradition in New Zealand is the second incarnation of St Michael and All Angels, Christchurch (1872), by William FitzJohn Crisp.

145 Unpublished letter, F. T. McDougall to T. F. Stooks (6 Jan. 1849), Bodl. CAS, USPG Archive, C/ASI/SIN – 2 (Borneo).

146 Unpublished letter, F. T. McDougall to T. F. Stooks (26 Oct. 1848), Bodl. CAS, USPG Archive, C/ASI/SIN – 2 (Borneo).

147 On this point McDougall noted how Rajah James Brooke's house was falling apart after only four years because it was not built of the right materials. See unpublished letter, F. T. McDougall to T. F. Stooks (6 Jan. 1849), Bodl. CAS, USPG Archive, C/ASI/SIN – 2 (Borneo). In the case of St Thomas's, balean shingles were also used for the roof. See Harriette McDougall, *Sketches of Our Life in Sarawak*, with intro. by R. H. W. Reece and A. J. M. Saint (Singapore: Oxford UP, 1992), p. 46. Although the material was not entirely

indestructible, it did take a lot longer than most timbers to deteriorate.

148 Only the main structural members of the church were constructed using balean. The exterior was clad in a cedar-type wood that was sawn and shipped from Singapore. This cladding, however, tended to split apart in the burning heat of the midday sun, forcing McDougall to paint it. See F. T. McDougall to T. F. Stooks (9 June 1849 and 12 Sept. 1850), Bodl. CAS, USPG Archive, C/ASI/SIN – 2 (Borneo).

149 Donald Watson, 'Outside Studding: Some Claims to Architectural Taste', *Historic Environment*, vol. 6:2–3 (1988), pp. 22–31. Watson quotes from one of Suter's letters that 'he had been all his life connected with church matters' (p. 29).

150 Ibid., p. 30. See also Miles Lewis, 'Architecture from Colonial Origins' in *The Heritage of Australia: The Illustrated Register of the National Estate* (South Melbourne: Macmillan, 1981), p. 82. Suter's instructions were to paint these elements as near to their natural colours as possible.

151 Selwyn and Cotton often complained about the maintenance associated with timber buildings. John Medley, for example, lamented that 'wooden Churches are really more expensive than stone buildings. In twenty years they cost as much in painting and continual repairs: sixty or seventy years they grow old, and hasten to decay.' See John Medley, *A Charge Delivered at His Primary Visitation Held in Christ Church Cathedral, Fredericton* (Fredericton: John Simpson, 1847), p. 35.

152 These iron, flat-pack, portable buildings for overseas included everything from military barracks, verandahs, train stations, hotels and elaborate kiosks. See Robert Thorne, 'Inventing a New Design Technology: Building and Engineering', in John M. MacKenzie (ed.), *The Victorian Vision: Inventing New Britain* (London: V&A Publications, 2001), pp. 180–1; Jonathan Clarke, '"Like a huge birdcage from the earth": Watson's Esplanade Hotel, Mumbai (1867–71), and Its Place in Structural History', *Construction History*, vol. 18 (2002), pp. 37–77.

153 *Instrumenta Ecclesiastica* (1856), plates 67–72. The problem stated in the accompanying text to the illustrations was: 'how to employ iron for an ecclesiastical building in accordance with the qualities and conditions of the material'.

154 Even though it was declared in *The Ecclesiologist* that several of Slater's designs were shipped to the colonies, no trace of them has been found. See *Eccl.*, vol. 14 (Aug. 1856), p. 280.

155 Michael W. Brooks, *John Ruskin and Victorian Architecture* (London: Thames and Hudson, 1987), pp. 131–4. See also, Charles L. Eastlake, *A History of the Gothic Revival* (London: Longmans, 1872; repr. 1975), p. 268. Ruskin was doubtful about cast iron because he believed that the builder had no command over its chemical composition or modes of decay. Nor did cast iron show any evidence of 'art' – that is, the combination of hand and mind. In this sense Ruskin did not view it as an 'architectural' material. His prejudice against iron came from his reading of the ancient Greek word ἀρχη meaning 'authority over materials'. See John Ruskin, *The Seven Lamps of Architecture* (London: Smith, Elder & Co., 1849; repr. New York: John Wiley & Son, 1865), p. 34. See also his lecture 'The Work of Iron, in Nature, Art, and Policy', in *The Two Paths: Being Lectures on Art and Its Application to Decoration and Manufacture* (London: Smith, Elder & Co., 1859).

156 Buildings of this kind were shown at the Great Exhibition (1851), with production peaking around the 1880s. See Ian Smith, *Tin Tabernacles: Corrugated Iron Mission Halls, Churches & Chapels of Britain* (Salisbury: Camrose Organisation, 2004).

157 Three further iron churches were imported from England to Victoria in the 1850s. These were located at Sandridge (Port Melbourne), Gisbourne, and Bacchus Marsh. For initial correspondence regarding these buildings, see the *Melbourne Church of England Messenger*, vol. 4 (1853), pp. 189–90, 251–2. For reference to Gisbourne see the *Church of England Record for Victoria*, no. 4 (Oct. 1855), p. 30. For Bacchus Marsh, see Betty Osborn, *A History of Holy Trinity Church of England Bacchus Marsh* (Bacchus Marsh: Bacchus Marsh and District Historical Society, 1971), pp. 9–10.

158 For a brief account of this building, see J. B. Moroney, *Anchorage of Faith: A Short History of Holy Trinity Parish Church, Williamstown* (Williamstown: Holy Trinity Church of England, 1971), pp. 11–13. See also James Grant, 'The Great Church Societies' (an address given to the Anglican Historical Society, 16 Oct. 2002), Anglican Diocesan Archive, Melbourne, Australia, St Paul's cathedral; *Diamond Jubilee, Holy Trinity Church, Port Melbourne* (n.p., c.1954), pp. 1–3.

159 James Grant, *Episcopally Led and Synodically Governed: Anglicans in Victoria 1803–1997* (Melbourne: Australian Scholarly Publishing, 2010), p. 44.

160 Stuart Underhill, *The Iron Church* (Victoria, BC: Braemar Books, 1984). The bishop mentions the 'coming' of this church in January 1860. See *Colonial Church Chronicle*, vol. 14 (April 1860), p. 145.

161 The plan was to fill the cavity between the internal and external lining of the buildings with wool, straw, sawdust, or mud bricks. See *Colonial Church Chronicle*, vol. 6 (May 1853), p. 432.

162 Osborn, *A History of Holy Trinity*, p. 9. Iron buildings were also prone to leak: see Underhill, *The Iron Church*, p. 14. There had been an idea to transport an iron church to Barbados as early as 1843, but I cannot discover if this was ever sent. One can only imagine how uncomfortable an iron church would have been in such a climate. The bishop

of Barbados, however, thought otherwise: 'My object is, of course, to ascertain whether there is any good foundation for this statement respecting *Cast Iron Churches* or Chapels; and, if so, where we are likely to get them faithfully prepared with something of correct architectural design, in a simple way. We have already *Cast Iron* hospitals here; and I do not see why we should not have Cast Iron Chapels also. They would be better adapted to this climate, with reference to Hurricanes and Earthquakes, than Stone, and be more durable than wood. It would be a new era in our Ecclesiastical Architecture; and perhaps, as we cannot in these countries attempt elaborate buildings, and all we aim at is correctness and simplicity, with sufficient amplitude, iron might answer our purpose better than the common materials.' Unpublished letter, Bishop of Barbados to A. M. Campbell (23 Dec. 1843), Bodl. CAS, USPG Archive, CLR/187 (Barbados)

163 *Eccl.*, vol. 14 (Aug. 1856), pp. 280–1. For a broader account of the discontent surrounding the use of cast iron as an architectural material more generally during the mid-nineteenth century, see Stephan Muthesius, 'The "Iron Problem" in the 1850s', *Architectural History*, vol. 13 (1970), pp. 58–63. See also Andrew Saint, *Architect and Engineer: A Study in Sibling Rivalry* (New Haven and London: Yale UP, 2007), pp. 99–118, 131–42.

164 *Instrumenta Ecclesiastica* (1856), plate 67.

165 A complaint was made by a correspondent to *The Ecclesiologist* that Slater's design in *Instrumenta Ecclesiastica* went against all worthy principles of design and notions of truth to materials. It was asserted that Slater's design was merely a stone or brick design for a parish church rendered in iron, thus ignoring the unique potential and qualities of the material. See *Eccl.*, vol. 14 (Aug. 1856), p. 280.

166 *Instrumenta Ecclesiastica* (1856), plate 67.

167 After the applied render had dried, the walls and pillars were rubbed with rock crystal and brought to a high polish. See J. F. A. McNair, *Prisoners Their Own Warders* . . . (Singapore: A. Constable, 1899), p. 100. This finish was based on indigenous techniques and used widely by the British in India. See the Rev. J. Tucker's comments on its use in an unpublished letter, J. Tucker to OAS (16 Oct. 1839), Bodl., OAS Archive, MS. Dep.c.591, letter 20.

168 Charles B. Buckley, *An Anecdotal History of Old Times in Singapore* (1902) (Singapore: Oxford UP, 1984), p. 294.

169 Bremner, 'The Architecture of the Universities' Mission', p. 522.

170 Two examples are St Saviour's, Hermitage, Newfoundland (1850–4), and St Paul's cathedral, St Helena (1850–2), by Benjamin Ferrey. It was noted of St Saviour's that: 'It represents a typical English village church, and is built of brick and stone. Its Gothic style of architecture is chaste, and in most of its features it is purely English. It is the gift of the late Thomas Newman Hunt, of the firm of Messrs. Newman Hunt & Co., of Broad Street, London, who formerly had branches of their business in Hermitage Bay, as well as in Forteau Bay, N.F. A gift intended for the glory and worship of God, and for the use of the employees of their business, as well as for the settlers in and around Hermitage. Every stone used in its construction was cut and carved in England. Every brick and every slate and every piece of timber was brought from "the old country". Even the lime to mix the mortar was burnt of imported English limestone. English masons were engaged for the building about the year 1850. Their want of experience, as to Newfoundland climate, was not a help towards solid work; but the work went on, sometimes checked by frost, sometimes from want of the proper English material.' See ADAENL, 302. f03, Box 2. For St Paul's, see Edward Cannan, *Churches of the South Atlantic Islands, 1502–1991* (Oswestry: Anthony Nelson, 1992), pp. 103–13.

171 *Rules and Proceedings* (15 Nov. 1843), p. 9.

172 *Eccl.*, vol. 2 (May 1846), p. 191, and vol. 4 (May 1847), p. 169. It was noted of Slater's design for Honolulu that: 'there is stone which can be used for carving, mouldings, tracery, or ashlar walling. Accordingly a severe early type has been chosen . . . a design at once original and successful in the high qualities of breadth, simplicity, and dignity'. See *Eccl.*, vol. 20 (June 1862), p. 159.

173 *Eccl.*, vol. 9 (Feb. 1851), pp. 41–2. As Scott is not known to have been to the tropics, he would no doubt have gleaned this information from the letters of friends or first hand from those who had travelled and lived there.

174 There is a large body of literature relating to missionary activity in southern Africa in this respect, especially that of Evangelical and Nonconformist societies. See Jean and John Comaroff, 'Christianity and Colonialism in South Africa', *American Ethnologist*, vol. 13:1 (1986), pp. 1–22; Doug Stuart, '"For England and for Christ": The Gospel of Liberation and Subordination in Early Nineteenth-Century South Africa', *Journal of Historical Sociology*, vol. 6:4 (1993), pp. 377–95; J. and J. Comaroff, *Of Revelation and Revolution: Christianity, Colonialism, and Consciousness in South Africa* (Chicago: Chicago UP, 1991), pp. 253–308; and Elizabeth Elbourne, *Blood Ground: Colonialism, Missions, and the Contest for Christianity in the Cape Colony and Britain, 1799–1853* (Montreal and Kingston: McGill–Queen's UP, 2002).

175 For a time the CMS, under the stewardship of Henry Venn, had a policy of cultural assimilation in the mission field. See Peter Williams, '"Not transplanting": Henry Venn's Strategic Vision', in Kevin Ward and Brian Stanley (eds), *The Church*

Mission Society and World Christianity, 1799–1999 (Richmond, Surrey: Curzon Press, 2000), pp. 147–72.

176 Sara H. Sohmer, 'Christianity without Civilization: Anglican Sources for an Alternative Nineteenth-Century Mission Methodology', *Journal of Religious History*, vol. 18:2 (1994), pp. 174–97.

177 Allan K. Davidson, 'Culture and Ecclesiology: The Church Missionary Society in New Zealand', in Kevin Ward and Brian Stanley (eds), *The Church Mission Society and World Christianity, 1799–1999* (Richmond, Surrey: Curzon Press, 2000), p. 199.

178 *Rangiātea: Ko Ahau te Huarahi te Pono me te Ora* (Wellington: National Library of New Zealand, 2003), pp. 14–21, 32–3. This Milky Way pattern, otherwise known as the *purapura whetū* (stardust) motif, was supposed to illustrate the hope of the incumbent chief, in this case Te Rauparaha, that there would be as many Christian converts as there were stars in the sky. See Deidre Brown, *Māori Architecture: From Fale to Wharenui and Beyond* (Rosedale: Raupo [Penguin Group], 2009), p. 47. A similar approach to incorporating indigenous symbols and motifs into ecclesiastical architecture was adopted by evangelical missionaries in the Pacific Islands. See Sujit Sivasundaram, *Nature and the Godly Empire: Science and Evangelical Mission in the Pacific, 1795–1850* (Cambridge: Cambridge UP, 2005), p. 170.

179 The most complete study of these unique churches is Richard A. Sundt, *Whare Karakia: Māori Church Building, Decoration & Ritual in Aotearoa New Zealand, 1834–1863* (Auckland: Auckland UP, 2010).

180 Quote from the proceedings of the CMS Conference on Missions, held in Liverpool in 1860, in Williams, '"Not transplanting"', p. 148. For more on Venn and CMS policy, see T. E. Yates, *Venn and Victorian Bishops Abroad: The Missionary Policies of Henry Venn 1841–1872* (SPCK: London, 1978).

181 *Eccl.*, vol. 9 (June 1851), p. 233.

182 Both Selwyn and Cotton describe in their journals earlier examples of such buildings. In his visitation journal of 1843, Selwyn describes one such chapel at Waikanae, to hold 500 people, which had a ridge pole formed from a single tree trunk 76 feet long. See 'Selwyn's Visitation Journal', SA, 8.38.j, p. 37. Cotton described a similar building at Matamata in 1843: 'It is the largest native building in the island 82 × 45, entirely of native work and very lofty. The ridge pole is supported by two upright magnificent round trees. I should think between 30 to 40 feet high. . . . It must have been a tremendous work to get the ridge pole into its place. It was done I believe by means of scaffolding, and ropes of Kauri. There are 14 principal . . . slabs, all adzed out of single trees. . . . These divide the walls into so many compartments, which are filled up with the stalk of the fern placed horizontally. The ends are hidden behind the slabs, and a lacing of Kauri runs down the middle of each panel, giving a very neat appearance to very rude materials.' See Cotton Journals, vol. 5, pp. 98–9, Mitchell Library, State Library of New South Wales, Sydney. See also Sundt, *Whare Karakia*, pp. 102–3.

183 Crinson, *Empire Building*, pp. 107–20. In granting the land for the church to the British, Muhammad Ali (khedive of Egypt), in the *hodget* (title deed), stipulated that whatever was built should 'harmonize with the neighbouring buildings' (p. 112).

184 *Eccl.*, vol. 3 (Nov. 1846), pp. 165–9. On the point concerning a 'developed' solution, it was noted of Wild's design that: 'the English Church will, we fear, be made contemptible to all the various tribes of a mixed nation, catholic, infidel, and heretic, through a mistaken spirit of eclecticism' (p. 168).

185 Competition regulations reprinted in *The Builder* (12 July 1856), 386, and *Eccl.*, vol. 14 (Aug. 1856), pp. 79, 295.

186 'The Memorial Church at Constantinople', Bodl. CAS, USPG Archive, D29b/1591-9. Here Beresford Hope observed specifically that the Church ought to take into consideration both the 'climate and locality'.

187 Crinson, *Empire Building*, pp. 141–53. In the competition brief it was stated that 'The numerous and beautiful instances existing in Southern Europe of this modification of Pointed Architecture amply justify the preference thus given to it.' *Eccl.*, vol. 14 (Aug. 1856), p. 295. Beresford Hope, who was on the judging committee for the church, had suggested that the architects look to examples in Italy, Spain and Portugal, as well as the Crusader churches of Palestine. See Beresford Hope, 'The Memorial Church at Constantinople'.

188 G. E. Street's *Brick and Marble in the Middle Ages: Notes on a Tour in the North of Italy* (London: John Murray, 1855) would also have been influential.

189 Beresford Hope, *The English Cathedral*, p. 90.

190 'Memorial Church at Constantinople: To Architects', Bodl. CAS, USPG Archive, D2/53–4.

191 Bremner, 'The Architecture of the Universities' Mission', pp. 514–16.

192 Unpublished letter, W. G. Tozer to Bishop of Lincoln (17 June 1865), Bodl. CAS, UMCA Archive, A1(I)A.

193 Henry Rowley, *The Story of the Universities' Mission to Central Africa* (London: Saunders, Otley & Co., 1866), pp. 267–70. In this sense, Rowley's approach not only had features in common with that of other High Anglican missionaries working at the margins of the British empire, but also prefigured in some sense the missionary application of F. D. Maurice's concept of Christian solidarity, developed by Westcott. Westcott argued for a broadly conciliatory

approach to missionary theology, viewing other religions – such as Hinduism and Islam – not as idolatrous and false but as yet 'incomplete' or partial revelations of the true faith. For the initial articulation of this idea, see B. F. Westcott, *On Some Points in the Religious Office of the Universities* (London: Macmillan, 1873), pp. 25–44. For its effect on the Cambridge Mission to Delhi (established 1876) see Jeffrey Cox, *Imperial Fault Lines: Christianity and Colonial Power in India, 1818–1940* (Stanford: Stanford UP, 2002), pp. 46–8, 140. This idea also had much in common with Butler's concept of 'mediation' which centred on analogy or the process of applying the understanding of the familiar to the unfamiliar. See Sohmer, 'Christianity without Civilization', pp. 187–7.

194 Unpublished letter, W. G. Tozer to Bishop of Cape Town (8 Jan. 1864), Bodl. CAS, UMCA Archive, A1(I)1, 'Letters of Bishop Tozer and Steere', pp. 47–8. On this point Tozer further noted: 'I dare say some would think it was hopeless to teach such children Christianity, before you had clad them in some more decent (because more English looking) costume, coat and trousers at the least and perhaps shoes and stockings as well. But the effect would be at once to bring out an irritation of the skin, especially in the region of the abdomen and anus, which is exactly like the Itch in its effects. The African skin must have plenty of air and a constant application of water to keep it in health. The former is secured by the native form of dress, and thus [to] make Africans look like Europeans at the expense of health and cleanliness, would surely be a great mistake.' See unpublished letter from W. G. Tozer to Bishop of Lincoln (17 June 1865), UMCA Archive: A1(I)A. See also commentary on Tozer's views in *Colonial Church Chronicle* 23 (Dec. 1869), pp. 482–5.

195 Bremner, 'The Architecture of the Universities' Mission', pp. 520–7.

196 The mission's church services had already caused trouble in Stone Town, and there were elements within the Muslim community intent on undermining the mission's activity. See unpublished letter, E. Steere (2 June 1875), Bodl. CAS, UMCA Archive, A1(III)A – 1-489. See also the letter by Steere published in *The Builder* (4 Sept. 1875), p. 795.

197 *Cathedral Church of Christ Zanzibar* (Zanzibar: UMCA, 1927), pp. 2–3. It was also reported in *The Builder* (4 Sept. 1875) that a set of C. F. Hayward's plans were received by the sultan. This probably took place during the sultan's visit to Britain in 1875. In reality there was very little the sultan could have done if Steere had ignored his request for a height limit. He was effectively in the pocket of the British agent in Zanzibar, John Kirk (1832–1922), who had installed him as sultan after the death of his brother in 1870. Nevertheless, Steere erred on the side of caution, seeking a hybrid solution for the cathedral's design. His discretion was, in effect, an act of architectural diplomacy.

198 For a detailed account of the use of the narthex in Anglican missionary architecture, see G. A. Bremner 'Narthex Redux: Reinventing Disciplinary Space in the Anglican Mission Field, 1847–1903' (forthcoming).

199 The ante-chapel was described by Steere as a 'narthex'. See unpublished letter, E. Steere (22 Oct. 1863), Bodl. CAS, UMCA Archive, A1(III)B – 1-245.

200 John Mason Neale, *A History of the Holy Eastern Church* (London: John Masters, 1850), pp. 207–10. For more contemporary scholarship on nartheces and their various uses, see N. Spatz, 'Church Porches and the Liturgy in Twelfth-Century Rome', in Thomas J. Heffernan and E. Ann Matter (eds), *The Liturgy of the Medieval Church* (Kalamazoo: Michigan Medieval Institute Publications, 2001), pp. 327–67. See also Richard Krautheimer, *Early Christian and Byzantine Architecture* (Baltimore: Johns Hopkins UP, 1965), pp. 19, 69, 361.

201 *Church Times* (12 March 1864).

202 The *pronaos* section of the church was described by Tozer as the 'ante-chapel', where the indigenous boys would 'stand and kneel and squat' during church services. See Gertrude Ward (ed.), *Letters of Bishop Tozer and His Sister* (London: UMCA, 1902), p. 42. Although the introduction of such a spatial device had clear disciplinary and historical associations, it may also have been influenced by a desire on the part of the UMCA missionaries to dispel an idea that had grown up in the minds of their indigenous followers that when they went into their church for prayer they were conducting magic. To be sure, the missionaries wished to encourage a certain notion of 'mystery' around the Eucharist, but did not want their activities to be misinterpreted (or so it seems, at least) as some kind of witchcraft. An impression of this is given by Rowley in *The Story of the Universities' Mission*, p. 208.

203 These practices of spatial division and conversion hierarchies continued to be used by the UMCA into the twentieth century. See Justin Willis, 'The Nature of a Mission Community: The Universities' Mission to Central Africa in Bonde', *Past and Present*, no. 140 (1993), pp. 144–6. See also, Bremner, 'The Architecture of the Universities' Mission'.

204 See 'Extracts from Journal Continued (1857)', Bodl. CAS, USPG Archive, E/4–345.

205 Henrietta Robertson described a similar building to the Mackenzies in a letter from 1861. See Anne Mackenzie (ed.), *Mission Life among the Zulu-Kafirs: Memorials of Henrietta Robertson Wife of the Rev. R. Robertson* (London: Deighton, Bell & Co., 1866), pp. 162–4.

206 Although Mackenzie did not mention such a division in his

description of the church, a nave 60 feet long does seem rather large for such a building. See Bremner, 'The Architecture of the Universities' Mission', p. 517.

207 A brief description of the content of Neale's lecture, entitled '*Narthex* of Ancient – especially the Eastern – Church with Reference to its Adoption in England's Missionary Colonial Dioceses', can be found in: *Eccl.*, 5 (June 1848), p. 380.

208 Beresford Hope, *The English Cathedral*, p. 84.

209 The standard work on this is John McAndrew, *The Open-Air Churches of Sixteenth-Century Mexico: Atrios, Posas, Open Chapels, and Other Studies* (Cambridge, Mass.: Harvard UP, 1965). I wish to thank Barry Bergdoll for bring this book to my attention.

210 'Extracts from Journal Continued (1857)', Bodl. CAS, USPG Archive, E/4–345. It is not absolutely certain that the figure depicted in this sketch is Robertson, even though it was found in the archive accompanying a report written by him. The scene is recorded as having taken place on or near the river Bashee, British Kaffraria.

211 The Ecclesiological Society advised that it was indeed necessary for a Christian church in such a location to have a narthex for 'purposes of discipline'. See *Eccl.*, 4 (May 1847), p. 170. The narthex in Carpenter's design was reported as follows: 'In Mr Carpenter's design the narthex was situated locally within the nave; that is to say, the western part of the nave was screened off for a narthex.'

212 Chapman was here referring to the precepts of Buddhism and the influence of Roman Catholicism, both of which were prevalent on the island at the time. See unpublished letter, Bishop of Colombo to E. Hawkins, 4 June 1852, Bodl. CAS, USPG Archive, CLR/28 (Colombo).

213 This building was considered a good model to follow as it was erected in a warm climate, using English resources and craftsmen (it was believed). See *Eccl.*, 15 (April 1857), p. 99. The church had a connection to St Andrew's abbey in Chesterton, Cambridgeshire.

214 *The Builder* (14 March 1857), pp. 150–1.

215 The *proaulion* is mentioned by Neale in his *History of the Holy Eastern Church* (pp. 208–9) as a kind of 'second narthex'.

216 *Eccl.*, vol. 19 (Aug. 1861), pp. 109, 235. The porch of St Germain had been described (and illustrated) by Viollet-le-Duc only a few years earlier in his *Dictionnaire raisonné* (vol. 7, 1854). Like Neale before him, Viollet identified porches and narthexes as spaces that were used in early medieval times for the accommodation of catechumens and penitents. See the section on porches in Eugène Viollet-le-Duc, *Dictionnaire raisonné de l'architecture française du XIe au XVIe Siècle*, vol. 6 (Paris: B. Banche, 1853), pp. 411–12; and vol. 7 (1854), pp. 259–312. For example, Viollet notes of porches that: 'les plus anciennes églises chrétiennes possédaient, devant la nef reservée aux fidèles, un porche ouvert ou fermé, destiné à contenir les catéchumènes et les pénitents' (p. 259).

217 *Eccl.*, vol. 20 (June 1862), pp. 114, 158–60.

218 *Final Report of St. Paul's Cathedral, Calcutta to which is Prefixed the Sermon Delivered on the Occasion of the Consecration* (Calcutta: Bishop's College, 1847), p. 11. It is stated that: 'The designs of the Sacred Building remain the same as were stated in the Proposals of 1839, embracing a Native Mission, as well as a Distinct and Cathedral Church.'

219 Wilson had always wanted to see the ancient Syrian churches of India. He noted of them that they all 'presented a certain degree of similarity' and were 'constructed on a thoroughly primitive model'. See Josiah Bateman, *The Life of the Right Rev. Daniel Wilson, D.D., Late Lord Bishop of Calcutta and Metropolitan of India*, 2 vols (London: John Murray, 1860), vol. 2, pp. 50, 67–8.

220 According to a letter sent from the head of Bishop's College in Calcutta, Professor Alfred Wallis Street, the laying of the foundation stone at St Peter's, Barripûr, took place on 13 January 1843. See unpublished letter, A. Street to E. Hawkins (17 Feb. 1843), Bodl. CAS, USPG Archive, CLR/12 (Calcutta). The plans for these churches were supposedly drawn up by Driberg, but a local architect by the name of Townsend is mentioned in relation to their completion.

221 During the consecration service for St Peter's, Barripûr, two wealthy Hindus from the area entered the church and stood by the altar. Upon seeing these men, one among the native congregation 'quietly removed [them] . . . to that part of the sacred building which is appropriated to the unbaptized catechumens'. See C. E. Driberg, *A Narrative of the Progress and Condition of the Barripûr Mission . . . with an Account of the Consecration of the Churches of Barripûr and Mogra Hât* (London: SPG, 1847), p. 31. Porches in medieval English parish churches were used for this purpose. See Dave Postles, 'Micro-Spaces: Church Porches in Pre-Modern England', *Journal of Historical Geography*, vol. 33:4 (2007), pp. 756–7. See also 'The Porch', *Church Builder*, no. 6 (1863), p. 69.

222 Humphrey quoted in Yates, *Venn and Victorian Bishops Abroad*, pp. 79–80. In the event Humphrey's plans were never realised, his ideas being considered too 'High' for both his employer (the CMS) and the bishop of Madras.

223 *Eccl.*, vol. 19 (Aug. 1861), pp. 108, 282; F. J. Western, *The Early History of the Cambridge Mission to Delhi* (Delhi, 1950), p. 50.

224 Western, *The Early History of the Cambridge Mission.*

225 *The Story of the Delhi Mission* (Westminster, 1908), p. 22. The bishop's report, published in the *Colonial Church Chronicle*, noted of the church that: 'At the main entrance a small portion is divided off by pillars, forming a Narthex or unconsecrated outer court for the heathen, which, at the consecration, was crowded with a quiet and respectful con-

gregation of spectators.' See *Colonial Church Chronicle*, vol. 22 (March 1868), p. 103. It was also reported in the *Mission Field* that: 'The daily services are attended not only by the Christian congregation, but by many Hindus and Mohometans, especially in the evening, when there are often as many as twenty or thirty in the porch built for them.' See *Mission Field*, vol. 13 (May 1868), p. 129.

226 The immersion font at St Stephen's was in the shape of a coffin because it was accompanied by the inscription: 'Ye are buried with Him by baptism into death, wherein also ye are risen with Him.' It was also felt by the mission that owing to the climate in India there was no reason why the normal rule of the Christian Church in regard to baptism should not be observed. *The Story of the Delhi Mission*, p. 22. The full-immersion font was not actually used a great deal until the early twentieth century, when it was decided that most adult baptisms would be conducted using it. See *Delhi Mission News*, vol. 2 (April 1899), pp. 6, 64.

227 For the meanings and various uses of the term *baraza* in Swahili culture, see Angelique Haugerud, *The Culture of Politics in Modern Kenya* (Cambridge: Cambridge UP, 1995), pp. 61–2.

228 R. M. Heanley, *A Memoir of Edward Steere: Third Missionary Bishop in Central Africa* (London, 1890), p. 120.

229 Bodl. CAS, UMCA Archive, A1(III)B, 416--25. It was also noted in Anderson-Morshead's account that: 'At the west end is a gallery for such Arab ladies as could not, according to Eastern etiquette, mingle with men on the church floor.' See Anna E. M. Anderson-Morshead, *The History of the Universities' Mission to Central Africa*, 3 vols (London, 1909), vol. 1, p. 87. For a contemporary account on the historical usage of narthexes and 'women's galleries', see Neale, *A History of the Holy Eastern Church*, pp. 207–10.

230 The women's gallery was added in the early 1880s. Steere observed that: 'There are known to be some [women] who would be glad to come if a fitting place were provided for them.' See Bodl. CAS, UMCA Archive, A1(III)B, 416–25.

4 *Symbolism and Identity*

1 James White has observed that it is hard to overestimate the importance of the Camden Society's publications at the time. *A Few Words to Church Wardens* had sold 5,000 copies within the first six weeks, and 13,000 copies were in circulation by 1843. A copy probably reached almost every parish church in England. See James F. White, *The Cambridge Movement: The Ecclesiologists and the Gothic Revival* (Cambridge: Cambridge UP, 1962), pp. 113–16.

2 *Eccl.*, vol. 1 (Jan. 1845), p. 1.

3 John Mason Neale and Benjamin Webb, *The Symbolism of Churches and Church Ornaments: A Translation of the First Book of the Rationale Divinorum Officiorum, Written by William Durandus, Sometime Bishop of Mende* (Leeds: T. W. Green, 1843).

4 Ibid., p. xxvi. For Neale and Webb 'sacramentalism' was the *sine qua non* of true 'Catholick Architecture'. See also 'A Catena Symbolica, from Writers of the Western Church, A.D. 540–1736', *Eccl.*, vol. 8 (Dec. 1850), pp. 217–26. For a discussion of the general significance of meaning in Victorian religious architecture, see William Whyte, 'Sacred Space as Sacred Text: Church and Chapel Architecture in Victorian Britain' in J. Sterrett and P. Thomas (eds.), *Sacred Text – Sacred Space: Architectural, Spiritual, and Literary Convergences in England and Wales* (Leiden: Brill, 2011), pp. 247–67.

5 A. J. B. Beresford Hope, 'The Present State of Ecclesiological Science', *Rules and Proceedings* (23 June 1846), p. 26. This essay begins with a very good account of the recent history of ecclesiology and its concern for national 'English' forms.

6 John Mason Neale, *Hierologus, or, The Church Tourists* (London: James Burns, 1843), p. 2.

7 That modern British architecture ought to be based on peculiarly indigenous forms of medieval architecture was a sentiment shared by G. G. Scott. See G. G. Scott, *Remarks on Secular & Domestic Architecture, Present and Future* (London: John Murray, 1857).

8 A. J. B. Beresford Hope, *The English Cathedral of the Nineteenth Century* (London: John Murray, 1861), pp. 32–3.

9 *Eccl.*, vol. 9 (Feb. 1851), p. 1.

10 *Eccl.*, vol. 6 (Aug. 1848), p. 14. It was also observed of ornamental symbolism in *A Few Words to Church Builders* that 'Our Lord in a ship . . . was generally taken by the Fathers as a type of the Holy Church' (p. 18).

11 *A Journal of a Visitation in the 'Hawk' Church Ship, on the Coast of Labrador, and Round the Whole Island of Newfoundland, in the Year 1849* (London: SPG, 1850). According to Bishop Feild, William Scott had asked William Butterfield to design a 'suitable Communion table and Lecturn' for this ship. See unpublished letter, E. Feild to E. Hawkins (18 July 1844), Bodl. CAS, USPG Archive, CLS/113 (Newfoundland).

12 G. A. Selwyn, *'How shall we sing the Lord's song in a strange land'? A Sermon, Preached in the Cathedral Church of St. Peter, Exeter . . . by the Right Reverend the Lord Bishop of New Zealand* (Exeter: P. A. Hannaford, 1842), p. 10.

13 Nicholas Penny, 'Ruskin's Ideas on Growth in Architecture and Ornament', *British Journal of Aesthetics*, vol. 13:3 (1973), p. 280.

14 Dave Postles, 'Micro-Spaces: Church Porches in Pre-Modern England', *Journal of Historical Geography*, vol. 33:4 (2007), pp. 749–69.

15 *A Few Words to Church Builders* (Cambridge: Cambridge Camden Society, 1841), p. 16. Neale and Webb also note in their 'Introductory Essay' to the *Rationale Divinorum Officiorum* that 'Porches are usually on the south side. For as the east was considered in an especial manner connected with the Kingdom of Heaven, so was the north imagined to be under the Prince of the Power of the Air.' See Neale and Webb, *The Symbolism of Churches and Church Ornaments*, p. xcv.

16 *Eccl.*, vol. 5 (Oct. 1847), p. 87.

17 *The Orientator: A Simple Contrivance for Ascertaining the Orientation of Churches* (Cambridge: Thomas Stevenson on behalf of the Cambridge Camden Society, 1844). The first paragraph of this publication states: 'The design of this instrument is, in general, to determine the point of the compass to which a church is directed; and more particularly to ascertain whether that point be the sun's place of rising on the festival of the Saint in whose honour the church is dedicated' (p. 1.).

18 *Eccl.*, vol. 6 (Dec. 1848), pp. 183–4.

19 *Eccl.*, vol. 8 (Oct. 1850), p. 201.

20 For example, see Peter Donovan and June Donovan, *150 Years of Stained and Painted Glass* (Adelaide: Wakefield Press, 1986).

21 Lynn Pearson, 'Decorative Tile and Terracotta Exports by British Manufacturers, 1840–1940', *Journal of the Tiles and Architectural Ceramics Society*, vol. 11 (2005), pp. 27–32. See also Gary B. Magee and Andrew S. Thompson, *Empire and Globalisation: Networks of People, Goods and Capital in the British World, c.1850–1914* (Cambridge: Cambridge UP, 2010), p. 158.

22 Extracts of unpublished letter, Sarah Selwyn to Ms C.H.P. (25 March 1843), Mrs Selwyn's Letters, 1842–62, ATL, qMS – 1776. Sujit Sivasundaram has described how indigenous islanders in the Pacific reacted in a similar way to seeing missionary churches for the first time. See Sujit Sivasundaram, *Nature and the Godly Empire: Science and Evangelical Mission in the Pacific, 1795–1850* (Cambridge: Cambridge UP, 2005), pp. 169–70.

23 Unpublished letter, Sarah Selwyn to W. Selwyn (6 Sept. 1842), Selwyn Papers, 1839–1865, ATL, MS-1780-81.

24 Cotton Journals, vol. 4, pp. 11–12, 151, Mitchell Library, State Library of New South Wales, Sydney.

25 Unpublished letter, Sarah Selwyn (Aug. 1842), Mrs Selwyn's Letters, 1842–62, ATL, qMS – 1776. For Māori tattoos, or *moko*, see Ngahuia Te Awekotuku (with Linda Waimarie Nikora, Mohi Rua and Rolinda Karapu), *Mau Moko: The World of the Māori Tattoo* (Rosedale, NZ: Penguin, 2007).

26 Bishop Tozer's Journals, Stone Town, Zanzibar National Archives, CB1/1B, 35.

27 *Eccl.*, vol. vol. 9 (Aug. 1851), pp. 264–5.

28 For an analysis of the philosophical underpinnings of Ruskin's writings on art and architecture, see Cornelis J. Baljon, 'Interpreting Ruskin: The Argument of *The Seven Lamps of Architecture* and *The Stones of Venice*', *Journal of Aesthetics and Art Criticism*, vol. 55:4 (1997), pp. 401–14.

29 John Ruskin, *The Stones of Venice* (London: Smith, Elder & Co., 1851), p. 213.

30 John Ruskin, *The Seven Lamps of Architecture* (1849) (New York: Dover, 1989), p. 103. Ruskin makes the point in *The Stones of Venice* that 'all I mean to allege is, that beautiful ornament, wherever found, or however invented, is always either an intentional or unintentional copy of some constant natural form; and that in this particular instance, the pleasure we have in these geometrical figures of our own invention is dependant for all its acuteness on the natural tendency impressed on us by our Creator to love the forms into which the earth He gave us to tread, and out of which He formed our bodies, knit itself as it was separated from the deep'. Ruskin, *The Stones of Venice*, pp. 219–20.

31 Charles L. Eastlake, *A History of the Gothic Revival* (American Life Foundation, 1975 [first published 1872]), pp. 264–80.

32 G. G. Scott, *A Plea for the Faithful Restoration of Our Ancient Churches* (Oxford: J. H. Parker, 1850), p. 8.

33 On this point Scott noted that 'All works of pure decoration, whether in sculpture or painting, must be remodelled by reference to Nature, – an implicit and unconditional falling back upon which, not as our copy, but as our guide and starting point, must be the great, all-pervading characteristic of the future style'. Scott, *Remarks on Secular & Domestic Architecture*, p. 268.

34 Neale and Webb quoted in Dale Dishon, 'Three Men in a Gondola: Ruskin, Webb and Street', in Christopher Webster and John Elliott (eds), *'A church as it should be': The Cambridge Camden Society and Its Influence* (Stamford: Shaun Tyas, 2000), p. 194.

35 *Eccl.*, vol. 9 (Feb. 1851), p. 44.

36 *Eccl.*, vol. 9 (June 1851), p. 172.

37 *Eccl.*, vol. 15 (Feb. 1857), pp. 32–4. See also, Angus Trumble, 'Gilbert Scott's "Bold and Beautiful Experiment", Part I: The Tomb of Sir Charles Hotham in Melbourne', *Burlington Magazine*, vol. 141 (1999), p. 742. Here Trumble notes that the sculptor Bernie Philip was supplied by Lady Hotham with the address of a London nursery where he could see and copy Australian flora.

38 For the ecclesiastical side of this cross-fertilisation of ideas, see Michael Hall, 'What do Victorian Churches Mean?: Symbolism and Sacramentalism in Anglican Church Architecture, 1850–1870', *JSAH*, vol. 59:1 (2000), pp. 78–95.

39 For Montreal, see *Eccl.*, vol. 17 (Dec. 1859), p. 426. At Adelaide some of the decorative bosses are of native plants, such as Banksia.

40 *The Builder* (14 Jan. 1865), p. 31.

41 G. A. Bremner, 'Nation and Empire in the Government

Architecture of Mid-Victorian London: The Foreign and India Office Reconsidered', *Historical Journal*, vol. 48:3 (2005), pp. 703–42.

42 For these changes in architecture in Australia, see Brian Andrews, *Australian Gothic: The Gothic Revival in Australia Architecture from the 1840s to the 1950s* (Melbourne: Melbourne UP, 2001), pp. 133–42.

43 For instance, in 1847 it was stated in *The Ecclesiologist* that: 'We are not now insisting on the propriety of building costly churches, nor even on their being exclusively of perfect Christian architecture; but on their correct arrangement – which is the very soul of a church.' *Eccl.*, vol. 4 (Jan. 1847), p. 16.

44 G. G. Scott, 'A Paper Read before the Buckinghamshire Architectural and Archæological Society (1848)', in Scott, *A Plea for the Faithful Restoration of Our Ancient Churches*, p. 18.

45 Chris Brooks, *The Gothic Revival* (London: Phaidon, 1999); Michael J. Lewis, *The Gothic Revival* (London: Thames and Hudson, 2002).

46 Simon Bradley, 'The Englishness of Gothic: Theories and Interpretations from William Gilpin to J. H. Parker', *Architectural History*, vol. 45 (2002), pp. 325–46. See also J. M. Frew, 'Gothic is English: John Carter and the Revival of the Gothic as England's National Style', *Art Bulletin*, vol. 64:2 (1982), pp. 315–19.

47 Ruskin, *The Seven Lamps*, pp. 199–214.

48 Bremner, 'Nation and Empire'; David Brownlee, 'That "regular mongrel affair": G. G. Scott's Design for the Government Offices', *Architectural History*, vol. 28 (1985), pp. 159–97. For more general accounts of the history of the Foreign Office, see Ian Toplis, *The Foreign Office: An Architectural History* (London: Mansell, 1987); Michael H. Port, *Imperial London: Civil Government Building in London, 1851–1915* (New Haven and London: Yale UP, 1995).

49 For instance, see W. J. Rorabaugh, 'Politics and the Architectural Competition for the Houses of Parliament, 1834–1837', *Victorian Studies*, vol. 18 (1973), p. 166; Michael H. Port, 'The Houses of Parliament Competition', in Michael H. Port (ed.), *The Houses of Parliament* (New Haven and London: Yale UP, 1976), pp. 20–52; Andrea Fredericksen, 'Parliament's *Genius Loci*: The Politics of Place after the 1834 Fire', in Christin Riding and Jacqueline Riding (eds), *The Houses of Parliament: History, Art, Architecture* (London: Merrell, 2000), pp. 99–111; Roland Quinault, 'Westminster and the Victorian Constitution', *Transactions of the Royal Historical Society*, vol. 2 (1992), pp. 79–104.

50 Scott, 'A Paper Read before the Buckinghamshire Architectural and Archæological Society', p. 12.

51 Scott, *A Plea for the Faithful Restoration of Our Ancient Churches*, p. 115.

52 Scott, *Remarks on Secular & Domestic Architecture*, p. 9.

53 Ibid., p. 278.

54 G. A. Bremner and Jonathan Conlin, 'History as Form: Architecture and Liberal Anglican Thought in the Writings of E. A. Freeman', *Modern Intellectual History*, vol. 8:2 (2011), pp. 322–3.

55 G. G. Scott, 'Lecture 1: The Claims of Mediæval Architecture upon Our Study', in *Lectures on the Rise and Development of Mediæval Architecture*, 2 vols (London: John Murray, 1878), vol. 1, p. 17.

56 Ibid., p. 16.

57 Scott, *Remarks on Secular & Domestic Architecture*, pp. 10–11, 262.

58 *Eccl.*, [1st ser.], vol. 1 (July 1842), p. 161.

59 *Eccl.*, [1st ser.], vol. 1 (June 1842), pp. 133–4; [1st ser.], vol. 1 (May 1842), p. 132.

60 Howard Le Couteur, 'Anglican High Churchmen and the Expansion of Empire', *Journal of Religious History*, vol. 32:2 (2008), pp. 196–7.

61 In this respect he also perceived it as the Church's 'right arm'. Samuel Wilberforce, 'Upon Our Duty to the Aboriginal Inhabitants of Our Colonies' (1840), in Henry Rowley (ed.), *Speeches on Missions by the Right Reverend Samuel Wilberforce, D.D.* (London: William Wells Gardner, 1874), p. 89.

62 Samuel Wilberforce, 'Upon South Africa, India, etc.', in Rowley (ed.), *Speeches on Missions*, p. 143.

63 Ibid., pp. 144, 148–50. The Great Sepoy Revolt was interpreted in the same way by many in Britain at the time. See Stewart J. Brown, *Providence and Empire: Religion, Politics and Society in the United Kingdom, 1815–1914* (London: Longman, 2008), pp. 199–201.

64 Samuel Wilberforce, 'Upon Our Indian Empire' (1867), in Rowley (ed.), *Speeches on Missions*, p. 133. Wilberforce's sermons are littered with such warnings and pronouncements. For example, in 1864 he observed of the Great Sepoy Revolt: '[C]ould anything be more marked, than that the shaking of that great dominion was a judgement from on high on the people to whom He had given that power, in order to warn them, that if they would not there do His will, the Empire should be taken from them . . . ?'. Wilberforce, 'Upon the Work of Missions in India' (1864), in Rowley (ed.), *Speeches on Missions*, p. 119.

65 See the 'Royal Proclamation' reprinted in Jane Samson (ed.), *The British Empire* (Oxford: Oxford UP, 2001), p. 173.

66 An example of this is the continued struggle Wilberforce had over the Missionary Bishops Bill. See A. R. Ashwell and R. G. Wilberforce, *Life of the Right Reverend Samuel Wilberforce, D.D.*, 3 vols (London: John Murray, 1880–2), vol. 2, pp. 378–80, 443–5; vol. 3, pp. 37–42, 52–3.

67 Gregg Finley and Lynn Wigginton, *On Earth as it is in Heaven: Gothic Revival Churches of Victorian New Brunswick* (Fredericton: Goose Lane Editions, 1995), p. 95.

68 Medley quoted in Finley and Wigginton, *On Earth as it is in Heaven*, p. 95.

69 Jacobs and FitzGerald quoted in Ian Lochhead, 'Remembering the Middle Ages: Responses to the Gothic Revival in Colonial New Zealand', in Jaynie Anderson (ed.), *Crossing Cultures: Conflict, Migration and Convergence. The Proceedings of the 32nd International Congress in the History of Art* (Carlton, Victoria: Miegunyah Press, 2009), p. 539.

70 W. G. Broughton, 'The English Reformation, and the Empire of England', in Benjamin Harrison (ed.), *Sermons on The Church of England: Its Constitution, Mission, and Trials* (London: Bell and Daldy, 1857), pp. 53–4.

71 Ibid., p. 57.

72 Ibid., p. 55. See also unpublished letter, W. G. Broughton to E. Coleridge (3 April 1840), University of Sydney, Moore Theological College Archive, Broughton Papers, 1/9.

73 Bruce N. Kaye, 'Broughton and the Demise of the Royal Supremacy', *Journal of the Royal Australian Historical Society*, vol. 81 (1995), pp. 44–5.

74 Ibid., p. 65.

75 For example, when Tahiti was taken by France in 1844, protest meetings were held in both Victoria and New South Wales over the apparently ever-increasing 'creep' of Roman Catholicism in its religious, cultural, and political forms. If religious, and thereby national, sympathies were to be altered substantially in Australia, some feared political take-over through the back door. See Michael Roe, *Quest for Authority in Eastern Australia, 1835–1851* (Parkville: Melbourne UP, 1965), p. 139.

76 For the perceived relationship between trade, civilisation and religion, see Brian Stanley, '"Commerce and Christianity": Providence Theory, the Missionary Movement, and the Imperialism of Free Trade, 1842–1860', *Historical Journal*, vol. 26:1 (1983), pp. 71–94; Andrew Porter, '"Commerce and Christianity": The Rise and Fall of a Nineteenth-Century Missionary Slogan', *Historical Journal*, vol. 28:3 (1985), pp. 597–621.

77 Samuel Wilberforce, 'Upon the Universities' Mission to Central Africa' (1860), in Rowley (ed.), *Speeches on Missions*, p. 189.

78 'Cape of Good Hope', *Colonial Church Chronicle*, vol. 2 (Jan. 1849), p. 244.

79 A. T. Wirgman, *The History of the English Church and People in South Africa* (London: Longmans, Green & Co., 1895); Peter Hinchliff, *The Anglican Church in South Africa* (London: Darton, Longman and Todd, 1963), pp. 1–26.

80 This was made possible in part owing to the fact that the Dutch Reformed Church remained the 'established' Church of the Cape even after the British had taken control of the territory. Its status was legally enshrined in the eighth article of the Deed of Capitulation. See John M'Carter, *The Dutch Reformed Church in South Africa* (Edinburgh, 1869), pp. 34–5; D. H. Varley and H. M. Matthew (eds), *The Cape Journals of Archdeacon N. J. Merriman, 1848–1855* (Cape Town: Van Riebeeck Society, 1957), p. x.

81 Bengt Sundkler and Christopher Steed, *A History of the Church in Africa* (Cambridge: Cambridge University Press, 2000), p. 357.

82 'From the Bishop of Cape Town', *Colonial Church Chronicle*, vol. 1 (Jan. 1848), p. 267.

83 Unpublished letter, R. Gray (2 Oct. 1848), University of the Witwatersrand, William Cullen Library, CPSA Archive, AB1161/Ba. Further evidence of Gray's zeal in erecting new churches throughout his diocese can be found in: *Church in the Colonies: Diocese of Cape Town (Part 1)* (London: SPCK, 1849) [transcript of the diary of Robert Gray, bishop of Cape Town].

84 *Church in the Colonies: Diocese of Cape Town (Part 2)* (London: SPCK, 1852), pp. 9, 15, 21, 61, 197.

85 Unpublished letters, R. Gray to E. Hawkins (6 Aug. 1861 and 9 Nov. 1860), Bodl. CAS, USPG, D24/A, letters 9541, 13466.

86 In a diary entry for 1839 Gray noted that he was 'much pleased' with the *Tracts of the Times*, and hoped that the attention of the wider clergy would be drawn to the 'blessed sacraments'. See Robert Gray Diary, 1837–44, University of the Witwatersrand, William Cullen Library, CPSA Archive, AB1161/A7. Further indications of Gray's Tractarian sympathies can be seen in a letter he wrote to the Rev. W. T. Bullock in 1865, complaining about the wayward clergy in the diocese of Natal after the Colenso affair: 'I have done all that I can to guide the Diocese at this juncture, in accordance with the views of ArchBp. S. Oxon, Parker, Pusey, Keble . . . and a host of others; – i.e., I have urged them to elect their Bp, organize themselves as a Ch. in Com. with the Ch. of E., and apply to the ArchBp to return them to communion.' Unpublished letter, R. Gray to W. T. Bullock (27 May 1865), Bodl. CAS, USPG Archive, D24/B, letter 8638. See also Charles Gray (ed.), *The Life of Robert Gray, Bishop of Cape Town and Metropolitan of Africa*, 2 vols (London: Rivingtons, 1876), vol. 1, pp. 68–9; Frank England, 'Tracing South African Anglicanism', in Frank England and Torguil Paterson (eds), *Bounty in Bondage: The Anglican Church in Southern Africa. Essays in Honour of Edward King, Dean of Cape Town* (Johannesburg: Ravan Press, 1989), pp. 20–5.

87 It is known from Gray's account of his visit to Cambridge in 1867 that he dined with Benjamin Webb and discussed with him the issue of ritualism, noting how he admired the

'beautiful chapel in St. John's which [George Gilbert] Scott is building' (Gray (ed.), *The Life of Robert Gray*, vol. 2, pp. 372–3). Gray's diary during his visit to England in 1858 also contains many references to architecture. For instance, see 'England, 1858', University of the Witwatersrand, William Cullen Library, CPSA Archive, AB1161/A11.

88 Unpublished letter, R. Gray to W. T. Bullock (14 May 1866), Bodl. CAS, USPG Archive, D24/B, letter 9458.

89 'Pastoral Letter' (Jan. 1850), University of the Witwatersrand, William Cullen Library, CPSA Archive, Chronicles of the Diocese of Capetown, AB1159 Fol.

90 For Gray's use of the term 'appliance' in this context, see unpublished letter, R. Gray to E. Hawkins (9 Nov. 1860), Bodl. CAS, USPG Archive, D24/A, letter 13466.

91 Gray quoted in Thelma Gutsche, *The Bishop's Lady* (Cape Town: H. Timmins, 1970), p. 119. Writing to the church building committee in Bloemfontein in 1850, Gray also observed how the Rev. W. A. Steabler, who was located there, would point out details that were wrong in church building. See Desmond Martin, 'Bishop Robert Gray and Mrs Sophia Gray: Building Anglican Churches in South Africa, 1848–72', in G. A. Bremner (ed.), *Ecclesiology Abroad: The British Empire and Beyond*, themed issue of *Studies in Victorian Architecture and Design*, vol. 4 (2012), pp. 111–25.

92 *Three Months' Visitation, by the Bishop of Capetown, in the Autumn of 1855* (London: Bell and Daldy, 1856), p. 79.

93 For instance, Green is described by the Rev. A. Theodore Wirgman in the preface to his *Life of James Green* (1909) as someone who, 'had he remained in England, . . . would have been numbered [among the] veterans of the Tractarian epoch'. See A. T. Wirgman, *Life of James Green* (London: Longmans, Green, & Co., 1909), p. vii.

94 Pauline M. Whibley, *Merriman of Grahamstown* (Cape Town: Howard Timmins, 1982), p. 24.

95 I wish to thank Gill Hunter for supplying me with information about this connection.

96 While at Balliol, White would no doubt have encountered W. G. Ward (1812–1882) and Frederick Oakeley (1802–1880), both of whom were among the most trenchant and influential of Tractarians in Oxford at the time. See Owen Chadwick, *The Victorian Church*, 2 vols (London: Adam and Charles Black, 1966–70), vol. 1, pp. 199–201.

97 For example, when William White was working out his designs for the bishop's diocesan college in Cape Town, he was told by Henry to go to see William Sewell for advice on designing correct school buildings. Sewell was one of the founders and the third warden (1853–61) of St Peter's College (now Radley College), which was held up as a new and improved model of Anglican education. See unpublished letter, H. M. White to W. White (27 April 1849), Bishop's College Archive, Cape Town. H. M. White's association with Sewell (and with W. B. Heathcote, second warden of Radley) is affirmed in Gray's biography. Gray (ed.), *The Life of Robert Gray*, vol. 1, p. 211.

98 Whibley, *Merriman of Grahamstown*, p. 6. While at Oxford, Merriman also became close friends with W. E. Gladstone, who himself had begun turning towards Tractarianism by the late 1830s. Gladstone finally entered the public domain of politics; the two remained good friends for life.

99 Newman was also an Oxford man. He gained his MA from Trinity College, Dublin, but he was admitted to Trinity College, Oxford, 'ad eundem' in 1847.

100 For instance, see *South African Church Magazine and Ecclesiastical Review*, vol. 1:2 (1850), pp. 33–40, 167–75.

101 Ibid., pp. 34–5.

102 For instance, *The Ecclesiologist* had itself praised Walter Scott for his 'truthful and attractive pictures' of medieval life in Britain. See White, *The Cambridge Movement*, p. 8.

103 H. M. White in the *South African Church Magazine and Ecclesiastical Review*, new ser., vol. 1 (1853), p. 131.

104 Ibid., p. 200.

105 *Eccl.*, 7 (Oct. 1849), p. 102. See also Vestry Minute Book, St Paul's church Rondebosch, 1848–1910, University of the Witwatersrand, William Cullen Library, CPAS Archive, entries for 7 and 19 Aug. 1848. See also Martin, 'The Churches of Bishop Robert Gray', pp. 53–8.

106 On this point Gray noted in a letter home that: 'Contributions of Theological books, works on architecture, plans, drawings, &c. of churches, schools, or houses, will be of great use'. University of the Witwatersrand, William Cullen Library, Chronicles of the Diocese of Capetown, CPSA Archive, AB1159 Fol., p. 3.

107 Bodl. CAS, USPG Archive, C/AFS/3, pp. 335–6.

108 Unpublished letter, H. M. White to W. White (27 April 1849), Bishop's College Archive, Cape Town. Radley was chosen as the model not only because it had a more liberal and modern system of accommodation than most public schools in England at the time, having been created in 1847, but also because it was established on strict High Church principles.

109 *Eccl.*, 10 (Aug. 1852), p. 283.

110 See unpublished letter, H. M. White to W. White (28 Nov. 1849), Bishop's College Archive, Cape Town.

111 For a full account of these buildings, see Gill Hunter, *William White: Pioneer Victorian Architect* (Reading: Spire Books, 2010), pp. 49–58. See also Gill Hunter, 'William White: The Early Years', in Rosemary Hill and Michael Hall (eds), *The 1840s, Studies in Victorian Architecture and Design*, vol. 1 (London: Victorian Society, 2008), pp. 106–16.

112 See A. J. R. Beddy, 'The List of Churches, Chapels and

Schools Associated with Bishop Gray and Mrs Gray, 1847–1872', University of the Witwatersrand, William Cullen Library, CPSA Archive, AB1946f. The most complete study of Sophia Gray's churches to date is Desmond Martin, 'The Churches of Bishop Robert Gray & Mrs Sophia Gray: An Historical and Architectural Overview', PhD thesis (University of Cape Town, 2002). See also R. R. Langham-Carter, 'South Africa's First Woman Architect', *Architect and Builder* (March 1967), pp. 14–18.

113 *Church in the Colonies (Part 2)*, p. 338.

114 Sophy Gray quoted in Gutsche, *The Bishop's Lady*, p. 112.

115 It is known that the Grays were in possession of plans by Butterfield. As a basic plan, the Coalpit Heath church is the most likely source of influence for Sophy's churches. As noted in Chapter 1, St Mark's was based on Underwood's design for Littlemore church, Oxfordshire.

116 Desmond Martin attributes the design of Belvidere to the Norman-style chapel that appeared in Underwood's, *Oxford Parish Burial Ground Chapels* (Oxford, 1849). See Desmond Martin, *The Bishop's Churches: The Churches of Anglican Bishop Robert Gray* (Cape Town: Struik, 2005), p. 33.

117 Paul Thompson, *William Butterfield: Victorian Architect* (Cambridge, Mass.: MIT Press, 1971), p. 60. The fact that Bishop Gray noted in his diary that he used a plan supplied by Butterfield for Belvidere suggests the Eginton source. See *Church in the Colonies (Part 1)*, p. 20.

118 See John Armstrong, 'Notes from South Africa', Bodl. CAS, USPG Archive, D7b, p. 94.

119 *Mission Field*, vol. 5 (Dec. 1861), p. 274.

120 G. A. Selwyn, *A Charge Delivered to the Clergy of the Diocese of New Zealand at the Diocesan Synod*, 1847 (London: Francis and John Rivington, 1849), p. 17.

121 G. Cuthbertson, 'The English-Speaking Churches and Colonialism', in C. Villa-Vicencio (ed.), *Theology & Violence: the South African Debate* (Grand Rapids: Eerdmans, 1998), pp. 15–30.

122 *Mission Field*, vol. 11 (June 1866), p. 125.

123 For Evangelical missionaries and their approach to mission station architecture in the Pacific, see Sivasundaram, *Nature and the Godly Empire*, pp. 148–9, 169–72.

124 Unpublished letter, W. Greenstock to SPG (11 May 1857), Bodl. CAS, USPG Archive, D7b, letter 7435/1857.

125 *Colonial Church Chronicle*, vol. 5 (June 1852), p. 461.

126 *South African Church Magazine and Ecclesiastical Review*, vol. 1 (1853), p. 68.

127 Richard A. Sundt, *Whare Karakia: Māori Church Building, Decoration & Ritual in Aotearoa New Zealand, 1834–1863* (Auckland: Auckland UP, 2010), p. 16.

128 Gray, *Church in the Colonies (Part 2)*, pp. 336–7.

129 Mary M. Goedhals, 'Nathaniel James Merriman, Archdeacon and Bishop, 1849–1882: A Study in Church Life and Government', PhD Thesis (Rhodes University, 1982), pp. 88–92.

130 Armstrong quoted in Gill Hunter, 'William White in the Colonies', in G. A. Bremner (ed.), *Ecclesiology Abroad: The British Empire and Beyond*, themed issue of *Studies in Victorian Architecture and Design*, vol. 4 (2012), p. 100. Robert Gray made a similar remark in 1869. See Martin, 'Bishop Robert Gray and Mrs Sophia Gray', p. 122.

131 His reputation suffered in England, too. For his apparent meddling he was characterised in the House of Commons as that 'turbulent priest'. See *Colonial Church Chronicle*, vol. 10 (Aug. 1856), p. 69.

132 For a full account of this episode, see K. R. Howe, '"The Bishop Alien": Selwyn and the New Zealand Wars of the 1860s', in Warren E. Limbrick (ed.), *Bishop Selwyn in New Zealand, 1841–68* (Palmerston North, NZ: Dunmore Press, 1983), pp. 94–119.

133 W. A. Newman quoted in *Colonial Church Chronicle*, vol. 8 (May 1855), pp. 430–1.

134 T. T. Carter, *A Memoir of John Armstrong, D. D., Late Bishop of Grahamstown* (Oxford: J. H. Parker, 1857), p. 91. Armstrong also designed and superintended the construction of buildings while in South Africa, including the main school building of St Andrew's College, and Bishopsbourne House, both in Grahamstown (pp. 381, 390).

135 Armstrong was one of the founders of the House of Mercy at Bussage, Gloucestershire, at which White had designed permanent buildings, including a chapel, in 1853. I wish to thank Michael Hall for this information. See also Hunter, *William White*, p. 70.

136 *Colonial Church Chronicle*, vol. 15 (Oct. 1861), pp. 391–2.

137 The 'Fingoes' – a term derived from a Bantu word (*amaMfengu*) meaning 'destitute people in search of work' – were a coalescence of various indigenous refugees driven south from Natal by tribal warfare. See 'Grahamstown Missions', *Mission Field*, vol. 12 (May 1867), p. 189; Hinchliff, *The Anglican Church in South Africa*, pp. 45–8.

138 See Grey's speech on his policy printed in *The Cape Monitor* (17 March 1855). For more on Grey and his governorship, see J. Rutherford, *Sir George Grey, KCB 1812–1898: A Study in Colonial Government* (London, 1961), pp. 291–439.

139 For Gray and Armstrong's response to Grey's plans, see Bodl. CAS, USPG Archive, CLR/114 (South Africa), letters received, 23 Dec. 1854; 28 Dec. 1854; 10 Feb. 1855; 20 March 1855; 6 June 1855; 14 July 1855; 5 Feb. 1865.

140 See Cory Library, PR 3514 (d); Cory Library, annual report, St Bartholomew's church, 1862, PR 3514 (f). The Rev. William Turpin, the mission's incumbent, had also expressed the pressing need for such a building in 1862. Merriman also sent a message back to England the same year seeking

assistance to this end. See Bodl. CAS, USPG Archive, D/24c (Grahamstown), and E/9a (Kaffir Mission, Grahamstown, Report), p. 446.

141 Cory Library, annual report, St Bartholomew's church, PR 3514 (f).

142 *Eccl.*, vol. 18 (1860), p. 113.

143 Ibid.

144 For the history of the commission, see G. A. Bremner, 'Out of Africa: G. F. Bodley, William White, and the Anglican Mission Church of St. Philip, Grahamstown, 1857–67', *Architectural History*, vol. 51 (2008), pp. 192–200.

145 Hunter, *William White*, p. 18. See also Basil F. L. Clarke, *Church Builders of the Nineteenth Century: A Study of the Gothic Revival in England* (London, 1938), p. 157.

146 *RIBA Journal* (10 Feb. 1900), p. 146; Eastlake, *A History*, p. 292.

147 For example, C. M. Smart, *Muscular Churches: Ecclesiastical Architecture of the High Victorian Period* (Fayetteville: University of Arkansas Press, 1989).

148 Edward N. Kaufman, '"The weight and vigour of their masses": Mid-Victorian Country Churches and "The Lamp of Power"', in John Dixon Hunt and Faith M. Holland (eds), *The Ruskin Polygon: Essays on the Imagination of John Ruskin* (Manchester: Manchester UP, 1982), pp. 94–121.

149 Beresford Hope, *The English Cathedral*, pp. 58–9.

150 For example, *Mission Field*, vol. 12 (June, 1867), p. 224. Such qualities seemed to be endemic to Merriman's character. For example, while a student at Winchester he won the school's gold medal for an essay titled 'Simplicity is the Essential of True Greatness'. See Whibley, *Merriman*, p. 2.

151 White quoted in Kaufman, '"The weight and vigour of their masses"', p. 100. In fact, it almost appears as though White had taken the advice offered by the Ecclesiological Society on this matter over ten years earlier. In 1847 Benjamin Webb had noted that the use of brick in colonial church architecture ought to be treated in 'bold and broad masses' and 'thrown into different planes', as much for effect as for integrity. See *Eccl.*, vol. 5 (Dec. 1847), pp. 146–7.

152 'St. Philip's Mission, Grahamstown', *Mission Field*, vol. 10 (September 1865), pp. 176–8. Turpin noted that there was likely to be only enough money to complete the nave at first and that the chancel would have to be added later. The church was opened for divine service on 4 November 1866 but not consecrated until the following year (23 June 1867). See quarterly mission report by W. H. Turpin in Bodl. CAS, USPG Archive, E/21 (Grahamstown), pp. 215–19. See also 'A Chief Account of St. Philips Mission from its Commencement in 1860', Bodl. CAS, USPG Archive, D24/c – 2529; *Illustrated London News* (6 April 1867), pp. 336–7. Building progressed slowly because of the limited funds. For example, after the foundations had been laid in 1864, it was decided that only enough money remained to build about two-thirds of the church as planned. See Bodl. CAS, USPG Archive, E/15 (Mission Report, St Philip's), p. 205.

153 *St. Philip's Church, Grahamstown* ([Grahamstown], 1960), Rhodes University, Cory Library, MS 16 811–12.

154 Indeed, Turpin did complain that the SPG had not given 'one farthing towards this Church', which made him all the more determined to 'make this a strictly African Mission, supplied from African funds alone'. Turpin quoted in Hunter, 'William White in the Colonies', p. 102.

155 Hinchliff, *The Anglican Church in South Africa*, pp. 45–8. The benefits of this approach appealed to Gray and were adopted as the basis for Anglican missions. See Gray's comments in Gray (ed.), *The Life of Robert Gray*, pp. 198, 269. See also 'An Appeal to the Church of England in Behalf of the Heathen of South Africa', Bodl. CAS, USPG Archive, D/7a; 'Kafir Industrial Institution', *Colonial Church Chronicle*, vol. 14 (March 1860), p. 120; and *Mission Field*, vol. 12 (Feb. 1867), pp. 59–63.

156 John Armstrong, *The Pattern for Church Building: A Sermon Preached in Aid of the Erection of a Chapel of Ease* (London: J. H. Parker, 1852). Gray had a similar view. See Martin, 'The Churches of Bishop Robert Gray', p. 46.

157 This is something that was also recognised by W. A. Newman. For example, see *South African Church Magazine and Ecclesiastical Review*, new ser., vol. 5 (1857), p. 335.

158 *Mission Field*, vol. 10 (Sept. 1865), p. 177. This sense of 'excitement' was also observed by Henry Cotterill, then bishop of Grahamstown, in relation to the opening of the Grahamstown mission school chapel in 1861, where he noted that the converts felt that it was 'specially for themselves'. See Bodl. CAS, USPG Archive, D/24c – 4148.

159 'A Chief Account of St. Philip's Mission from Its Commencement in 1860', Bodl. CAS, USPG Archive, D24/c – 2529; *Illustrated London News* (6 April 1867), pp. 336–7.

160 For instance, the close friendship that Bishop Short had with Governor Robe of South Australia brought certain exclusive concessions. He was able to frank his letters at government expense and to travel free of charge on the government schooner, *Yatala*, when visiting distant outposts of his diocese. N. K. Meaney, 'The Church of England in the Paradise of Dissent: A Problem of Assimilation', *Journal of Religious History*, vol. 3:2 (1964), p. 141.

5 *Conflict and Confrontation*

1 E. D. Daw, 'Church and State in the Empire: The Conference of Australian Bishops, 1850', *Journal of Imperial and Commonwealth History*, vol. 5:3 (1977), pp. 251–69.

2 Unpublished letter, J. Chapman to E. Hawkins (4 June 1852), Bodl. CAS, USPG Archive, CLR/28 (Colombo).

3 Unpublished letter, J. Chapman to E. Hawkins (13 Aug. 1850), Bodl. CAS, USPG Archive, C/IND/COL 1.

4 Unpublished letter, J. Chapman to E. Hawkins (13 Feb. 1852), Bodl. CAS, USPG Archive, C/IND/COL 1.

5 Ibid.

6 See John S. Moir, *The Church in the British Era: From the British Conquest to Confederation* (Toronto: McGraw-Hill, 1972).

7 'Petition of the Committee to Promote Subscriptions for the Newfoundland Fire to the Queen, 27 July 1846', Memorial University Libraries, CNLS, Coll. 45, File 2.

8 See unpublished letter, Earl Grey to Sir J. G. LeMarchant (governor) (18 May 1847), Memorial University Libraries, CNLS, Coll. 45, File 3.

9 Unpublished letter, E. Feild to Earl Grey (Nov. 1846), Memorial University Libraries, CNLS, Coll. 45, File 2. He added: 'As we shall be compelled to build of stone [government granted land on the condition that a stone edifice be built], a very large sum of money will be required to build the plainest Church, substantial, and sufficient for our requirements.'

10 Unpublished letter, E. Feild to Earl Grey (25 June 1847), Memorial University Libraries, CNLS, Coll. 45, File 3.

11 Unpublished letter, E. Feild to the Administrator of Newfoundland (17 April 1847), Memorial University Libraries, CNLS, Coll. 45, File 3.

12 For more on this, see Peter Coffman, *Newfoundland Gothic* (Quebec: Éditions MultiMondes, 2008), pp. 90–5.

13 Rowan Strong, *Anglicanism and the British Empire, c.1700–1850* (Oxford: Oxford UP, 2007), pp. 232–9. Broughton's successor, the Rev. Frederic Barker, described Sydney not only as 'godless' but also as a 'barren, melancholy wilderness'. See K. J. Cable, 'Protestant Problems in New South Wales in the Mid-Nineteenth Century', *Journal of Religious History*, vol. 3:2 (1964), p. 119.

14 Austin Cooper, 'Bishop Broughton and the Diocese of Australia', in Brian Porter (ed.), *Colonial Tractarians: The Oxford Movement in Australia* (Melbourne: Joint Board of Christian Education, 1989), pp. 23–34.

15 See also Strong, *Anglicanism and the British Empire*, p. 231.

16 Unpublished letter, W. G. Broughton to E. Coleridge (3 April 1840), University of Sydney, Moore Theological College Archive, Broughton Papers, 1/9.

17 Unpublished letter, G. King to E. Hawkins (8 April 1846), Bodl. CAS, USPG Archive, CLR/202 (Australia).

18 Unpublished letter, W. G. Broughton to E. Hawkins (17 May 1843), Bodl. CAS, USPG Archive, CLR/201 (Australia). For Broughton's firm position on the legal status of the English Church in Australia, see K. J. Cable, 'Religious Controversies in New South Wales in the Mid-Nineteenth Century, I: Aspects of Anglicanism, 1848–1850', *Royal Australian Historical Society Journal*, vol. 49:1 (1963), p. 60.

19 P. A. Micklem, *Australia's First Bishop: A Brief Memoir of William Grant Broughton* (Sydney: Angus and Robertson, 1936), p. 34. See also George P. Shaw, *Patriarch and Patriot: William Grant Broughton, 1788–1853* (Melbourne: Melbourne UP, 1978), p. 164.

20 Unpublished letter, W. G. Broughton to E. Coleridge (27 March 1843), University of Sydney, Moore Theological College Archive, Broughton Papers, 1/22.

21 On this point Broughton observed: 'It was the first instance since the Reformation, of the Pope's having established a Metropolitan See within the realm of England with a title derived from a city within that realm.' See F. T. Whitington, *William Grant Broughton: Bishop of Australia* (Sydney: Angus and Robertson, 1936), p. 193. Although Broughton's observation was technically correct, Roman Catholicism was tolerated by the British in Quebec after they had seized control of the territory following the Seven Years' War (1756–63).

22 Unpublished letter, W. G. Broughton to E. Hawkins (17 May 1843), Bodl. CAS, USPG Archive, CLR/201 (Australia). Broughton again wrote to Coleridge in 1846, observing that: 'here, upon the very spot whence I now write to you, will take place the most tremendous struggle, perhaps of all, between the opposing powers; and here the Reformation will have to be defended eminently and expressly according to our system'. Broughton quoted in Whitington, *William Grant Broughton*, p. 189.

23 Broughton quoted in Whitington, *William Grant Broughton*, p. 197.

24 For example, Owen Chadwick, *The Victorian Church*, 2 vols (London: Adam and Charles Black, 1966–70), vol. 1, pp. 291–309.

25 For Nixon and Short, see Patricia Curthoys, 'State Support for Churches, 1836–1860', in Bruce Kaye *et al.* (eds), *Anglicanism in Australia: A History* (Melbourne: Melbourne UP, 2002), pp. 32–9.

26 Royal Supremacy (enacted 1534 and 1559), refers to the legally established status of the Church of England – that is, the legal consolidation of Church and State. Although the 'established' nature of the English Church in the colonies had always been tenuous, and later was repealed entirely, many Anglican bishops nevertheless felt morally obliged to uphold the idea of 'supremacy' in lands governed by the British crown. Anglican bishops also believed themselves to be in a legally superior position to their counterparts from other Christian Churches because they carried letters patent

from the queen, recognising them as official appointees of the crown; however, local governors did not always view them as having privileged status.

27 For example, Broughton wrote to Coleridge in 1839: 'I feel that I have no second, no advisor to rely on for counsel, and I may say . . . a hundred times a day, "I am not able to bear all this people alone, because it is too heavy for me". Let me have your constant prayers that I may be more than equal to what is required of me.' Broughton quoted in Cooper, 'Bishop Broughton', p. 31.

28 This was a general and growing opinion among Anglican bishops in the colonies. For instance, fearing the consequences of too cosy a connection with the State, the Evangelical bishop of Melbourne, the Rev. Charles Perry, observed that: 'an endowed church was bound to be a lazy church'. See H. W. Nunn, *A Short History of the Church of England in Victoria* (Melbourne: Anglican Diocese of Melbourne, 1947), p. 23. Despite this conviction, Perry did bow to necessity and accepted state aid. James Grant, *Episcopally Led and Synodically Governed: Anglicans in Victoria, 1803–1997* (Melbourne: Australian Scholarly Publishing, 2010), p. 43.

29 See Strong, *Anglicanism and the British Empire*, pp. 250–5; Shaw, *Patriarch and Patriot*, pp. 250–70. The matter of education proved a continual sticking point for Broughton in his battle with the State. The creation of the Board of Education by the colonial government in 1839 essentially secularised elementary education in the state of New South Wales. This deeply concerned Broughton, as he believed that the classroom was the best place to inculcate Protestant and, in particular, Anglican ideals. See Curthoys, 'State Support', p. 36; Cooper, 'Bishop Broughton', p. 29.

30 Bruce N. Kaye, 'The Strange Birth of Anglican Synods in Australia and the 1850s Bishops' Conference', *Journal of Religious History*, vol. 27:2 (2003), pp. 177–97. Daw, 'Church and State in the Empire', pp. 251–69.

31 For example, unpublished letters, W. G. Broughton to E. Hawkins (17 May 1843 and 3 July 1843), Bodl. CAS, USPG Archive, CLR/201 (Australia). See also *Letters and Extracts from Letters, from the Lord Bishop of Australia, to the Rev. the Secretary of the Society for the Propagation of the Gospel* (1843), p. 1.

32 For the repeal of the Church and Schools Corporation, see Kelvin Grose, 'What Happened to the Clergy Reserves of New South Wales?', *Journal of the Royal Australian Historical Society*, vol. 72:2 (1987), pp. 93–5.

33 Curthoys, 'State Support', pp. 32–9.

34 Unpublished letter, W. G. Broughton to E. Coleridge (26 July 1836), University of Sydney, Moore Theological College Archive, Broughton Papers, 1/1.

35 Unpublished letter, W. G. Broughton to E. Coleridge (14 April 1842), University of Sydney, Moore Theological College Archive, Broughton Papers, 1/16. Three months later Broughton further observed that he 'regretted to perceive that the walls of the vast Roman C. Church opposite to it had risen visibly within the week. They now overtop ours: and I suppose they will open the building for public worship before the close of this year'. Unpublished letter, W. G. Broughton to E. Coleridge (11 July 1842), Broughton Papers, 1/17.

36 Brian Andrews, *Australian Gothic: The Gothic Revival in Australian Architecture from the 1840s to the 1950s* (Melbourne: Melbourne UP, 2001), pp. 70–1.

37 Unpublished letter, W. G. Broughton to E. Coleridge (16 Feb. 1843), University of Sydney, Moore Theological College Archive, Broughton Papers, 1/21.

38 For Pugin in Tasmania, see Brian Andrews, *Creating A Gothic Paradise: Pugin in the Antipodes* (Hobart: Tasmanian Museum and Art Gallery, 2002).

39 Unpublished letter, W. G. Broughton to A. M. Campbell (2 June 1837), Bodl. CAS, USPG Archive, CLR/200 (Australia).

40 W. G. Broughton, 'Cathedral Churches, Useful and Necessary', in Benjamin Harrison (ed.), *Sermons on the Church of England; its Constitution, Mission, and Trials* (London: Bell and Daldy, 1857), pp. 206–21.

41 Unpublished letter, W. G. Broughton to E. Coleridge (19 Oct. 1837), University of Sydney, Moore Theological College Archive, Broughton Papers, 1/3.

42 For example, in a letter dated April 1842, the Rev. Thomas Whytehead, who was laid over in Sydney for some months before continuing on to New Zealand, noted how Nonconformism there was 'extremely feeble'. See unpublished letter, T. Whytehead to Marriot (27 April 1842), Letters of C. J. Abraham, ATL, qMS – 1778.

43 Broughton quoted in Micklem, *Australia's First Bishop*, p. 32.

44 Unpublished letter, W. G. Broughton to E. Coleridge (6 Feb. 1838), University of Sydney, Moore Theological College Archive, Broughton Papers, 1/4.

45 Unpublished letter, G. King to E. Hawkins (15 Feb. 1845), Bodl. CAS, USPG Archive, CLR/201 (Australia).

46 For example, see unpublished letter, G. A. Selwyn to his father (22 March 1844), Selwyn Letter Book (1841–45), ATL, qMS – 1774; and Cotton Journals, vol. 10, pp. 16–17, Mitchell Library, State Library of New South Wales, Sydney.

47 For example, see I. Breward, 'Selwyn in Ecumenical Perspective: His Theology of Unity and Mission', in Warren E. Limbrick (ed.), *Bishop Selwyn in New Zealand, 1841–68* (Palmerston North, NZ: Dunmore Press, 1983), p. 138. Although Selwyn could not see eye to eye with Wesleyans, he did assist them in other ways. In a letter to Edward

Coleridge he notes that: 'You are probably aware of the rule which I make in visiting Missions connected with other bodies of Christians. I abstain from taking part in their services, but I endeavour to give them every encouragement and advice, which my acquaintance with the Mission work enables me to suggest. With the Wesleyan Missions I can go no further; as the popery of their system, in spreading the name of Wesley, and the authority of the Conference, over their whole Mission field, precludes all hope of communion, till the main body in England shall have changed its present opinion, on the advantage of separation from the Church, which their founder loved and venerated to the day of his death.' See letter from G. A. Selwyn to E. Coleridge (17 Aug. 1849) in letters printed by E. Coleridge and presented to H. Merivale (Secretary of State for the Colonies), Rare Books Collection, Huntington Library (San Marino, California). See also T. E. Yates, *Venn and Victorian Bishops Abroad: The Missionary Policies of Henry Venn . . . 1841–1872* (London: SPCK, 1978), pp. 52–3.

48 Cotton Journals, vol. 9, pp. 197–9, Mitchell Library, State Library of New South Wales, Sydney.

49 Cotton Journals, vol. 11, p. 162, Mitchell Library, State Library of New South Wales, Sydney.

50 On this point Christopher Wakeling notes how the CCS believed Nonconformism to be beyond the pale. See Christopher Wakeling, 'Nonconformity and Victorian Architecture', in Bridget Cherry (ed.), *Dissent and the Gothic Revival* (London: Chapels Society, 2007), p. 50.

51 See unpublished letter, G. A. Selwyn to E. Coleridge (1843), SA, 8.31.h. See also Yates, *Venn and Victorian Bishops Abroad*, pp. 51–2.

52 See 'Church Fund: Regulations for the Management of Church Property in New Zealand', in *New Zealand Church Almanac* (1847).

53 Unpublished letter, G. A. Selwyn to E. Coleridge (14 Dec. 1843), SA, 7.6.e.

54 Unpublished letter, R. Gray to E. Hawkins (20 March 1855), Bodl. CAS, USPG Archive, CLR/114 (South Africa).

55 Gray's impression of Grey was that he instinctively favoured his own Church over those of others. He felt that the goodwill and trust Grey had towards the Church of England might be squandered if they refused his generous offer. Writing to Ernest Hawkins in 1854, he noted that Grey had mentioned to him that 'the Church has now an opportunity of retrieving her character – of recovering lost ground. She will greatly embarrass my Government, if she does not rise up [to] her duty.' See unpublished letter, R. Gray to E. Hawkins (23 Dec. 1854), Bodl. CAS, USPG Archive, CLR/114 (South Africa).

56 'Speech by Sir George Grey on the matter of the "crisis" regarding the state of relations between the European population of the Cape and the native population of Kaffraria – what to do?', *Cape Monitor* (17 March 1855).

57 Writing to Hawkins in 1855, Armstrong reported that: 'The Governor on his part will immediately pay into the Bank for the erection of buildings on these several missions the total sum of £4,000 this present year intending also to make some further addition next year that the buildings may be complete.' See unpublished letter, J. Armstrong to E. Hawkins (10 Feb. 1855), Bodl. CAS, USPG Archive, CLR/114 (South Africa).

58 William Westfall, *Two Worlds: The Protestant Culture of Nineteenth-Century Ontario* (Kingston and Montreal: McGill–Queen's UP, 1989), p. 138.

59 Jobson quoted in Wakeling, 'Nonconformity and Victorian Architecture', p. 49. Serious consideration of Gothic architecture for Nonconformist churches can be traced back even further, to the Wesleyan's Model Plan Committee (established 1846) and an article on Nonconformist chapels that appeared in the *Congregational Year Book* for 1847.

60 Leslie A. Hewson, *They Seek a City: Methodism in Grahamstown* (Grahamstown: Institute of Social and Economic Research, Rhodes University, 1981), pp. 63–77.

61 See Miles Lewis (ed.), *Victorian Churches: Their Origins, Their Story & Their Architecture* (Melbourne: National Trust of Australia, 1991).

62 Westfall, *Two Worlds*, p. 142.

63 Indeed, in parts of British India, for example, Presbyterian clergy were allowed to appropriate Anglican churches from time to time to minister to Scottish soldiers in the Indian army. See *Colonial Church Chronicle*, vol. 15 (Feb. 1861), pp. 41–53. An argument of this kind had also been made by Francis Makemie in the eighteenth century. See Boyd Stanley Schlenther, 'Religious Faith and Commercial Empire', in P. J. Marshall (ed.), *The Oxford History of the British Empire*, vol. 2: *The Eighteenth Century* (Oxford: Oxford UP, 1998), p. 138.

64 Michael Roe, *Quest for Authority in Eastern Australia, 1835–1851* (Parkville: Melbourne UP, 1965), p. 134.

65 For the Gothic Revival in Australia, see Andrews, *Australian Gothic*.

66 Unpublished letter, T. B. Hutton (St John's College, Waimate, 9 July 1844), SA, 5.21.a.

67 Hans Cnattingius, *Bishops and Society: A Study of Anglican Colonial and Missionary Expansion, 1698–1950* (London: SPCK, 1952), pp. 225–9; Yates, *Venn and Victorian Bishops Abroad*, p. 53; and W. P. Morrell, 'Selwyn's Relations with the Church Missionary Society', in Warren E. Limbrick (ed.), *Bishop Selwyn in New Zealand, 1841–68* (Palmerston North, NZ: Dunmore Press, 1983), pp. 75–93.

68 The clearest rendition of Selwyn's position on the unity of governance and purpose of mission in the New Zealand Church can be found in the episcopal charge he delivered at St John's College in 1847. See G. A. Selwyn, *A Charge Delivered to the Clergy of the Diocese of New Zealand at the Diocesan Synod* (London: Francis and John Rivington, 1849).

69 One example of this can be found in a reference by the CMS missionary the Rev. William Williams to the practices of Selwyn as 'Tractarian'. See Williams quoted in Richard A. Sundt, *Whare Karakia: Māori Church Building, Decoration & Ritual in Aotearoa New Zealand, 1834–1836* (Auckland: Auckland UP, 2010), p. 33. See also Yates, *Venn and Victorian Bishops Abroad*, p. 53.

70 Unpublished letter, T. B. Hutton (St John's College, Waimate, 9 July 1844), SA, 5.21.a.

71 For an account of the Low Church movement in Australia, see Stuart Piggin, *Evangelical Christianity in Australia: Spirit, Word, and World* (Melbourne: Oxford UP, 1996).

72 For concepts of religious freedom, radicalism, and egalitarianism in Australia, see Roe, *Quest for Authority*, pp. 133–7.

73 Cable, 'Religious Controversies', pp. 62–9.

74 Shaw, *Patriarch and Patriot*, pp. 193–4; Cooper, 'Bishop Broughton', p. 32.

75 See extracts from the Rev. Peter Beamish's letter to Broughton in Shaw, *Patriarch and Patriot*, pp. 222–3. See also Cable, 'Religious Controversies', p. 66; Roe, *Quest for Authority*, p. 133.

76 Cable, 'Religious Controversies', p. 67.

77 Broughton, 'Cathedral Churches', pp. 210, 216–18.

78 Unpublished letter, W. H. Walsh to E. Hawkins (6 Oct. 1840), Bodl. CAS, USPG Archive, CLR/200 (Australia).

79 *Eccl.*, vol. 9 (Aug. 1851), p. 261.

80 Ibid. See also Joan Kerr, *Our Great Victorian Architect: Edmund Thomas Blacket (1817–1883)* (Sydney: National Trust of Australia, 1983), pp. 43–4.

81 For example, Broughton noted in his journal for 1845 that: 'The Church is provided with an organ of great compass and sweetness of tone, and an excellent choir. I have heard objections stated to some of the arrangements in the celebration of Divine Worship as savouring of novelty and innovation; but I am bound to say that there is no contrariety in any part of the practice to the most approved usages of the Church of England, and with which I have been from my earlier years . . .' Broughton quoted in Laura Mary Allen, *A History of Christ Church S. Laurence Sydney* (Sydney, 1939), p. 16. For suspicions of Walsh's theology and that of his successor, the Rev. George Vidal, see Allen, pp. 32, 42ff. See also Eleanor Joan Kerr, 'Designing a Colonial Church: Church Building in New South Wales, 1788–1888', DPhil thesis (University of York, 1978), pp. 191–3.

82 *Eccl.*, vol. 2 (April 1846), pp. 158–9.

83 Piggin, *Evangelical Christianity*, pp. 35–6. New crosses donated by Bishop Barker met a similar fate in January the following year.

84 Colin Holden, *From Tories at Prayer to Socialists at Mass: St. Peter's, Eastern Hill, Melbourne, 1846–1990* (Melbourne: Melbourne UP, 1996), pp. 12–13.

85 N. K. Meaney, 'The Church of England in the Paradise of Dissent: A Problem of Assimilation', *Journal of Religious History*, vol. 3:2 (1964), pp. 137–57.

86 For this episode in the Anglican history of Tasmania, see Neil Batt and Michael Roe, 'Conflict within the Church of England in Tasmania, 1850–1858', *Journal of Religious History*, vol. 4:1 (1966), pp. 39–62. The Gorham Judgment was the outcome of a legal dispute between the Rev. George Cornelius Gorham and the bishop of Exeter, the Rev. Henry Phillpotts, over the nature of baptismal regeneration, which was itself a point of contention between Evangelicals and High Churchmen. It caused much consternation at the time because many Anglican clergymen believed that a secular court should not have been able to pass judgment on an ecclesiastical, and therefore strictly spiritual, matter. Ironically, the Gorham Judgment, while further repelling conservative Laudians, such as Nixon, from the Church–State connection, prompted Evangelicals to cherish it.

87 Nixon quoted in Batt and Roe, 'Conflict within the Church', p. 43.

88 F. R. Nixon, *A Charge Delivered to the Clergy of the Diocese of Tasmania, at the Visitation, Held in the Cathedral Church of St. David, Hobart Town . . . 22 May 1851* (Hobart: H. and C. Best, 1851), pp. 42–8.

89 Nixon quoted in Batt and Roe, 'Conflict within the Church', p. 49.

90 *Eccl.*, vol. 5 (June 1848), p. 361.

91 For example, see Christopher Webster, 'Patterns of Church Seating from Waterloo to 1850, and the Role of the Cambridge Camden Society', in Trevor Cooper and Sarah Brown (eds), *Pews, Benches and Chairs: Church Seating in English Parish Churches from the Fourteenth Century to the Present* (London: Ecclesiological Society / Society of Antiquaries, 2011), pp. 197–210.

92 John Medley, *A Charge Delivered at His Primary Visitation Held in Christ Church Cathedral, Fredericton* (Fredericton: John Simpson, 1847), p. 34.

93 Ibid., p. 30.

94 *Eccl.*, vol. 11 (June 1853), p. 156.

95 Writing to William Scott in March 1846, Feild noted his disappointment at the then Presbyterian governor, Sir John Harvey, commenting on his marked dislike of the Church of England. In this respect, the problems Feild faced with

Harvey, and later Hamilton, were similar to those Broughton faced with Governor Bourke in New South Wales. See unpublished letter, E. Feild to W. Scott (10 March 1846), ADAENL, letters between Bishop Feild and the Rev. William Scott, transcribed by Tim Power (under the direction of S. O'Dea).

96 Feild quoted in Frederick Jones, *Edward Feild: Bishop of Newfoundland, 1844–1876* (St John's: Newfoundland Historical Society, 1976), p. 11.

97 Feild quoted in Frederick Jones, 'Bishop Feild: A Study in Politics and Religion in Nineteenth-Century Newfoundland', PhD thesis (University of Cambridge, 1972), p. 31.

98 See unpublished letter, B. Webb to W. Scott (15 May 1845), Memorial University of Newfoundland, Queen's College Archive, Feild Correspondence, 303.3.31 – c.2. Webb described the political tensions surrounding the society at this time in his letter to Scott. Strangely, Feild was happy to act as a patron of the OAS. His name appears in the patron list of the society for 1850–3. See membership list in *Oxford Architectural Society: Reports of Meetings (1850–53).*

99 J. F. White, *The Cambridge Movement: The Ecclesiologists and the Gothic Revival* (Cambridge: Cambridge UP, 1962), pp. 131–55. Writing to Scott in May 1845, Feild observed of his nomination that, despite sympathising with the CCS: 'You can easily understand what suspicion and jealousies would be excited in this country if I were reported as a vicepatron or Member (newly elected) of the Cambridge Camden Society. You know how shamefully and perseveringly that Society is attacked in the Newspapers which are the authorities here, and do all the mischief.' See unpublished letter, E. Feild to W. Scott (20 May 1845), ADAENL, letters between Bishop Feild and the Rev. William Scott, transcribed by Tim Power (under the direction of S. O'Dea).

100 Edward Feild, *Order and Uniformity in the Public Services of the Church . . .: A Charge Delivered to the Clergy of the Diocese of Newfoundland* (St John's: John W. McCoubrey, 1844).

101 Edward Feild, *The Means and Methods of a Christian Life, as Told and Taught by the Form and Arrangement of a Christian Church* (London: W. Clinkskel, 1870), pp. 11, 15.

102 Vernon G. Kent, 'The Right Reverend Hibbert Binney, Colonial Tractarian, Bishop of Nova Scotia, 1851–1887', MA thesis (King's College, Dalhousie University, 1966), pp. 1–34. As Binney's numerous early charges and sermons illustrate, he was determined to change this Low tendency in the Nova Scotian Church. Perhaps his most notable dispute was with the Rev. James Cuppaidge Cochran, who insisted upon preaching in a Geneva gown, despite Binney's express orders 'ex cathedra' not to (pp. 153–8). See also Peter Coffman, 'The Introduction of Ecclesiology to Nova Scotia', in G. A. Bremner (ed.), *Ecclesiology Abroad: The British Empire and Beyond*, themed issue of *Studies in Victorian Architecture and Design*, vol. 4 (2012), pp. 80–91.

103 This was particularly the case in Halifax. Ibid., pp. 35–82, 158.

104 Excerpt from the *Church Times* (9 June 1855), quoted in Kent, 'The Right Reverend Hibbert Binney', p. 131.

105 For the history of St Peter's and its congregation, see H. M. Peter Westin, *An Act of Faith: The First Fifty Years of St. Peter's Cathedral* (Charlottetown, Prince Edward Island: St Peter Publications, 1994). See also Malcolm Thurlby, 'Nineteenth-Century Churches in Prince Edward Island and Their Place in the Gothic Revival', *JSSAC*, vol. 31:2 (2006), pp. 78–9.

106 'A Journal Kept at the Cape', *Colonial Church Chronicle*, vol. 3 (Jan. 1850), p. 252. Others had made similar observations. A correspondent to *The Ecclesiologist*, for instance, damned the church as a 'most miserable specimen of colonial taste', while an officer in the Royal Navy, writing to the *Colonial Church Chronicle*, regretted that 'it is but a heathenish looking place'. See *Eccl.*, vol. 7 (Oct. 1849), p. 101; 'Extract of a Letter from the Cape of Good Hope', *Colonial Church Chronicle*, vol. 1 (April 1848), p. 383.

107 Peter Hinchliff, *The Anglican Church in South Africa: An Account of the History and Development of the Church of the Province of South Africa* (London: Darton, Longman and Todd, 1963), pp. 22–4.

108 'Letter from Gray to Louisa' (11 March 1848), University of the Witwatersrand, William Cullen Library, CPSA Archive, AB1161/Ba.

109 'Letter from Gray to Williamson' (8 April 1848) and 'Letter from Gray to Annie' (29 June 1848), University of the Witwatersrand, William Cullen Library, CPSA Archive, AB1161/Ba – b.

110 Meaney, 'The Church of England in the Paradise of Dissent', p. 137

111 For Australia, see Roe, *Quest for Authority*, pp. 133–7. For the condition of Anglicanism in South Africa and the Colenso affair, see Hinchliff, *The Anglican Church in South Africa*, pp. 48–9, 82–100. The 'Colenso affair' refers to the dispute between the Rev. John William Colenso (1814–1883) and the bishop of Cape Town and metropolitan of South Africa, the Rev. Robert Gray; it aroused great controversy and led to Colenso's eventual excommunication from the Church of England in South Africa. The dispute concerned Colenso's extremely controversial interpretation of and commentary on the book of Romans in the Bible, denying eternal punishment and rejecting much traditional sacramental theology. In 1863 he was formally deposed by Gray as bishop of Natal. However, Colenso appealed to the judicial committee of the Privy Council in England, which overruled Gray's decision (1865). This created a schism in the English

Church in South Africa, with Colenso remaining as an independent Anglican bishop in Natal beyond the legal authority of Gray as metropolitan.

112 Kaye, 'The Strange Birth of Anglican Synods in Australia', pp. 177–97. See also Daw, 'Church and State in the Empire', p. 264.

113 Fred D. Schneider, 'The Anglican Quest for Authority: Convocation and the Imperial Factor, 1850–60', *Journal of Religious History*, vol. 9:2 (1976), p. 142.

114 Ibid., pp. 143–54.

115 Daw, 'Church and State in the Empire', pp. 252–3, 265.

116 For New Zealand, see W. P. Morrell, *The Anglican Church in New Zealand: A History* (Dunedin: Anglican Church of the Province of New Zealand, 1973), pp. 48–71; for Canada, see Alan L. Hayes, *Anglicans in Canada: Controversies and Identity in Historical Perspective* (Urbana: University of Illinois Press, 2004), pp. 82–113; for South Africa, see Hinchliff, *The Anglican Church in South Africa*, pp. 48–53, 111–17.

117 Daw, 'Church and State in the Empire', p. 265.

6 *'A church [almost] as it should be'*

1 The quotation in this chapter heading, originally uttered by the CCS, refers to the title of Christopher Webster and John Elliott's edited volume *'A church as it should be': The Cambridge Camden Society and Its Influence* (Stamford: Shaun Tyas, 2000).

2 Brian Andrews, *Australian Gothic: The Gothic Revival in Australian Architecture from the 1840s to the 1950s* (Melbourne: Melbourne UP, 2001), pp. 27–62.

3 Joan Kerr, *Our Great Victorian Architect: Edmund Thomas Blacket (1817–1883)* (Sydney: National Trust of Australia, 1983), p. 8.

4 Blacket quoted in ibid., p. 9.

5 Report of the Cathedral Committee, 22 April 1850, Building Committee Minutes, 1846–66, vol. 1, Anglican Diocesan Archive, Sydney, 1992/16/15.

6 *Eccl.*, vol. 4 (June 1847), pp. 234–6. A few years later Walsh would also note in his report to the society entitled 'The Ecclesiology of New South Wales': 'To one individual, . . . Mr Edmund Blacket, is mainly owing the great improvement in taste and construction which is so visible in the later churches of the colony'. *Eccl.*, vol. 9 (Aug. 1851), p. 262.

7 Blacket found an illustration of Holy Trinity, Horncastle, in the *Illustrated London News* of April 1847. See Kerr, *Our Great Victorian Architect*, p. 22.

8 Eleanor Joan Kerr, 'Designing a Colonial Church: Church Building in New South Wales, 1788–1888', DPhil thesis (University of York, 1978), p. 219.

9 Morton Herman, *The Blackets: An Era of Australian Architecture* (Sydney: Angus and Robertson, 1977), p. 12. Walsh also observed that the church on the site that preceded Blacket's bore 'the palm for ugliness'. *Eccl.*, vol. 9 (Aug. 1851), p. 254.

10 Andrews, *Australian Gothic*, pp. 102–3. Here Andrews quotes Kerr: 'In Sydney, Bishop Broughton had been waiting for someone like Blacket for years; a gentleman, a churchman, a medieval architectural enthusiast, a draftsman who could draw details that an illiterate builder in the country could get right without supervision, . . . and a reliable estimator of time of building programmes.'

11 Work Diary of Edmund Blacket, University of Sydney, Fisher Library (Rare Books and Special Collections), P.3/2/5.

12 For reference to this, see the *Church of England Record for Victoria*, no. 4 (Oct. 1855), p. 28.

13 It was originally planned to have a spire, but this was never added. See *Geelong Advertiser* (14 Nov. 1844).

14 A competition for the design was initially held in 1860 and was won by a local architect by the name of William Gould, but when Bishop Thomas arrived he was determined to get a design from England. He at first approached J. L. Pearson (1869) to prepare plans for the new cathedral, but the commission eventually ended up in the hands of Blacket. See William C. Stegemann, *An Ornament to the City: A History of the Cathedral Church of St. Saviour, Goulburn, 1874–1988* (Canberra: Anglican Diocese of Canberra and Goulburn, 1988), pp. 21, 31–2.

15 Unlike Blacket, Scott did design a number of polychrome churches, but he is most noted for his rather conventional but impressive Middle-Pointed churches such as St Giles's, Camberwell (1844), and All Souls', Halifax (1859).

16 J. M. Freeland, *Architect Extraordinary: The Life and Work of John Horbury Hunt, 1838–1904* (Melbourne: Cassell, 1970), pp. 10–11.

17 Ibid., p. 22.

18 After some experience as a deacon at Kidderminster, White returned to Australia in 1860. See A. P. Elkin, *The Diocese of Newcastle: A History* (Glebe, NSW: Australian Medical Publishing Co., 1955), pp. 739–40.

19 See list of members in *Oxford Architectural Society: Reports of Meetings* (1853–6), p. 25.

20 Freeland, *Architect Extraordinary*, p. 38.

21 Charles Eastlake, *A History of the Gothic Revival* (London: Longmans, 1872), p. 359. For what is otherwise an excellent biographical monograph, failure to make this connection is an inexplicable oversight on the part of Freeland (*Architect Extraordinary*).

22 Michael Hall, 'The Rise of Refinement: G. F. Bodley's All Saints', Cambridge, and the Return to English Models in

Gothic Architecture of the 1860s', *Architectural History*, vol. 36 (1993), pp. 103–26.

23 The plans for this church bear Hunt's signature. See the Blacket and sons collection of architectural plans and drawings *c.*1840–1915), State Library of New South Wales, $D201^{-1}/15$–20.

24 A. J. B. Beresford Hope, *The English Cathedral of the Nineteenth Century* (London: John Murray, 1861). Beresford Hope's book was known to Hunt. See Andrews, *Australian Gothic*, p. 52.

25 Bishop Turner quoted in Andrews, *Australian Gothic*, p. 103.

26 Freeland, *Architect Extraordinary*, pp. 60–2.

27 Beresford Hope, *The English Cathedral*, pp. 58–9.

28 Andrews, *Australian Gothic*, pp. 117–18. See also Brian Andrews, *Creating a Gothic Paradise: Pugin at the Antipodes* (Hobart: Tasmanian Museum and Art Gallery, 2002), pp. 142–4.

29 See 'Melbourne Statistics', 31 Aug. 1853, and unpublished letter, C. Perry to W. T. Bullock (27 June 1866), Bodl. CAS, USPG Archive, CLR/207 (Melbourne). See also Albert McPherson, 'Architecture, Music, Art, and Liturgy in the Diocese of Melbourne', in Brian Porter (ed.), *Melbourne Anglicans: The Diocese of Melbourne, 1847–1997* (Melbourne: Mitre Books, 1997), p. 54.

30 See 'The Ballarat Gold Fields', *Melbourne Church of England Messenger*, vol. 2 (1851), pp. 321–31.

31 Perry quoted in N. K. Meaney, 'The Church of England in the Paradise of Dissent: A Problem of Assimilation', *Journal of Religious History*, vol. 3:2 (1964), p. 146.

32 Perry quoted in Geoffrey Serle, *The Golden Age: A History of the Colony of Victoria, 1851–1861* (Melbourne: Melbourne UP, 1963), p. 338. For the funding scene in general, see Geoffrey R. Quaife, 'Money and Men: Aspects of the Anglican Crisis in Victoria, 1850–1865', *Journal of Religious History*, vol. 5:1 (1968), pp. 45–61.

33 Writing to Ernest Hawkins in 1852, Perry noted with alarm: 'I am afraid that our brethren in England wholly misappropriated the effect of the discovery of gold upon the Church in this colony. They seem to think that it relieves them from the obligation of taking any more thought about us; whereas it ought to make us more than ever the object of their sympathy, their prayers, and their effectual help. I do not hesitate to say, that we are in a *much worse position* in a pecuniary point of view now than we were before. Then there was a good prospect, with God's blessing, of the Church, notwithstanding all its difficulties, becoming almost wholly self-supporting: but now the increased amount of money which we are able to raise *bears no proportion* whatever to the increased cost of building Churches and maintaining Clergymen for the multitude which is flocking to our shores.' See unpublished letter, C. Perry to E. Hawkins (5 Oct. 1852), Bodl. CAS, USPG Archive, CLR/207 (Melbourne).

34 *Eccl.*, vol. 11 (Feb. 1853), pp. 49–50.

35 A brief history of this church can be found in James Grant, *Old St. Paul's: The Story of St. Paul's Church Melbourne and Its Congregation, 1850–1891* (Melbourne: St. Paul's Cathedral, 2000).

36 Colin Holden, *From Tories at Prayer to Socialists at Mass: St. Peter's, Eastern Hill, Melbourne, 1846–1990* (Melbourne: Melbourne UP, 1996), p. 30.

37 Ibid., p. 29; Serle, *The Golden Age*, p. 337. See also Farnham E. Maynard, *A Talk About St. Peter's, Eastern Hill, Melbourne* (n.d.), p. 15. Perry was not as dim as this might suggest, however. By all accounts he was a brilliant scholar while at university, taking a first in classics at Trinity College, Cambridge, in 1828.

38 David Hilliard, 'Anglo-Catholicism in the Religious Ecology of Melbourne', in Colin Holden (ed.), *Anglo-Catholicism in Melbourne: Papers to Mark the 150th Anniversary of St Peter's Eastern Hill, 1846–1996* (Melbourne: Melbourne UP, 1997), pp. 169–70.

39 Billing is mentioned in *The Ecclesiologist* as having at one time been 'Mr Scott's clerk of works'. See *Eccl.*, vol. 9 (June 1851), p. 170. See also Miles Lewis, 'Architectural Drawings as Historical Sources', *Latrobe Library Journal*, vol. 5:20 (1977), p. 73.

40 Vestry Minutes quoted in Stuart Soley, *'The Highest of the High' in 'Marvellous Melbourne': All Saints' East St Kilda as Melbourne's Original High Church* (East St Kilda: All Saints' Parish, 1998), p. 21.

41 Ibid., p. 7. Initially, Gregory had been a 'bush missionary'. He was employed by Perry as an itinerant on the Bendigo goldfields, moving from place to place in his 'mobile vicarage' (covered wagon) and, like Selwyn in New Zealand, conducting services from his church tent. H. W. Nunn, *A Short History of the Church of England in Victoria, 1847–1947* (Melbourne: Anglican Diocese of Melbourne, 1947), p. 64.

42 Soley, *'The Highest of the High'*, p. 6.

43 Gregory quoted in ibid., p. 21.

44 Ibid., p. 22. See also, Stuart Soley, '"The Highest of the High": All Saints, St Kilda as Melbourne's Original High Church', in Colin Holden, *Anglo-Catholicism in Melbourne: Papers to Mark the 150th Anniversary of St Peter's Eastern Hill, 1846–1996* (Melbourne: Melbourne UP, 1997), pp. 23–4.

45 This denominational competition was especially prevalent in the goldfields. For example, see the *Melbourne Church of England Messenger*, new ser., vol. 1 (1854), p. 78.

46 Quaife, 'Money and Men', pp. 54–5.

47 For a comprehensive study of Mountfort, see Ian Lochhead,

A Dream of Spires: Benjamin Mountfort and the Gothic Revival (Christchurch: Canterbury UP, 1999). See also *B. W. Mountfort and the Gothic Revival in Canterbury: A Centennial Exhibition* (Christchurch: Robert McDougall Art Gallery, 1998) [exhibition catalogue].

48 Lochhead, *A Dream of Spires*, pp. 33–8.

49 *Lyttelton Times* (1 May 1852).

50 Lochhead, *A Dream of Spires*, pp. 36, 69.

51 Ibid., p. 76.

52 Ibid., p. 87.

53 Here Lochhead makes the point that there was a widespread belief at the time that even masonry towers of Anglo-Saxon churches incorporated stone strips in imitation of timber-work. Ibid., p. 88.

54 For example, see 'Letter I', in Robert Bateman Paul, *Letters from Canterbury, New Zealand* (London: Rivingtons, 1857), pp. 8–22. For further background on the Settlement and its difficulties, see Marie Peters, 'Homeland and Colony', in C. Brown, M. Peters, and J. Teal (eds.), *Shaping a Colonial Church: Bishop Harper and the Anglican Diocese of Christchurch* (Christchurch: Canterbury UP, 2006), pp. 19–33; W. P. Morrell, *The Anglican Church in New Zealand: A History* (Dunedin: Anglican Church of the Province of New Zealand, 1973), pp. 51–7.

55 Marie Peters, *Christchurch-St Michael's: A Study in Anglicanism in New Zealand 1851–1972* (Christchurch: Canterbury UP, 1986), pp. 1–2.

56 *The Press* (25 Oct. 1862).

57 Prior to this, the only reputedly 'substantial' Anglican church in the settlement was that at Avonside, just outside Christchurch. This was made of cob with brick quoins. It was supposedly a copy of 'one of our village churches at home'. See Paul, *Letters from Canterbury*, p. 61.

58 David Hilliard, *God's Gentlemen: A History of the Melanesian Mission, 1849–1942* (Brisbane: University of Queensland Press, 1978), p. 3.

59 Selwyn quoted in ibid., p. 7. See also R. M. Ross, *Melanesians at Mission Bay: A History of the Melanesian Mission in Auckland* (Wellington: New Zealand Historic Places Trust, 1983), p. 9.

60 Hilliard, *God's Gentlemen*, pp. 8–9. See also Allan K. Davidson, 'An "Interesting Experiment": The Founding of the Melanesian Mission', in A. K. Davidson (ed.), *The Church of Melanesia, 1849–1999* (Remuera, NZ: College of St John the Evangelist, 2000), p. 21.

61 Indeed, a comparison was often drawn between these two missions as the first 'missionary bishoprics'. Such was their affinity that Mackenzie's sister wrote to Patteson after her brother's untimely death offering his copy of Thomas à Kempis and a sextant. See Charlotte M. Yonge, *Life of John Coleridge Patteson, Missionary Bishop of the Melanesian Islands*, 2 vols. (London: Macmillan, 1874), vol. 2, p. 159.

62 Selwyn quoted in Ross, *Melanesians at Mission Bay*, p. 28.

63 For the relationship between Patteson, Yonge and *The Daisy Chain*, see Susan Walton, *Imagining Soldiers and Fathers in the Mid-Victorian Era: Charlotte Yonge's Models of Manliness* (Farnham: Ashgate, 2010), pp. 161–80.

64 Yonge, *Life of John Coleridge Patteson*, vol. 1, pp. 426–7.

65 *Eccl.*, vol. 24 (April 1866), p. 126. Buckeridge did have some experience in designing mission churches, and was probably engaged by a member of Merton College, Oxford, which operated a special fund for the Melanesian Mission. For Buckeridge, see Andrew Saint, 'Charles Buckeridge and His Family', *Oxoniensia*, vol. 38 (1973), pp. 357–71.

66 Patteson wrote to his sisters asking for lengths of crimson cloth to hang in the chapel so that it would 'look better'. See unpublished letter, J. C. Patteson to his sisters (20 May 1862), Bodl. CAS, USPG Archive, C/NZ/MELI, 2393.

67 The chapel was only ever intended as a temporary solution. See unpublished letter, J. C. Patteson to his father (29 June 1859), Bodl. CAS, USPG Archive, C/NZ/MELI, 1905.

68 Yonge, *Life of John Coleridge Patteson*, vol. 2, p. 79. Patteson had planned to build a stone chapel at Kohimarama using Charlotte's money, but did not manage to do so. See unpublished letter, J. C. Patteson to his father (18 Jan. 1860), Bodl. CAS, USPG Archive, C/NZ/MELI, 1985.

69 H. N. Drummond, *Bishop Patteson, Pioneer and Martyr, with an Account of the Memorial Chapel* (Parkstone (UK): Ralph and Brown, 1930), pp. 21–45.

70 There appears to have been some discussion between Codrington and Jackson over the type of building required. The Rev. Robert H. Codrington noted in a letter to Bullock of the SPG that he was anxious to begin the chapel as soon as he had received a plan which 'appeared practicable'. See unpublished letter, R. H. Codrington to W. T. Bullock (5 Aug. 1875), Bodl. CAS, USPG Archive, D42. Jackson also noted in his recollections that he was cautioned to design a building for earthquake conditions, and appeared concerned about hurricanes as well. See Basil H. Jackson (ed.), *Recollections of Thomas Graham Jackson, 1835–1924* (Oxford: Oxford UP, 1950), p. 132.

71 These windows were designed specifically for the chapel. See A. C. Sewter, *The Stained Glass of William Morris and His Circle: A Catalogue* (New Haven and London: Yale UP, 1975), p. 213.

72 Sara H. Sohmer, 'Christianity without Civilization: Anglican Sources for an Alternative Nineteenth-Century Mission Methodology', *Journal of Religious History*, vol. 18:2 (1994), pp. 180ff.

73 Allan K. Davidson, 'The Legacy of Robert Henry Codrington', *International Bulletin of Missionary Research*, vol. 27:4

(2003), pp. 171–6. Before arriving in New Zealand, Codrington had also been an associate of the Rev. Edmund Hobhouse, future bishop of Nelson.

74 Drummond, *Bishop Patteson*, p. 28.

75 Sohmer, 'Christianity without Civilization', pp. 186–7. For instance, Codrington would later explain his approach in 'Various Forms of Paganism', in G. A. Spottiswoode (ed.), *The Official Report of the Missionary Conference of the Anglican Communion* (London: SPCK, 1894), pp. 112–16.

76 Codrington quoted in Sohmer, 'Christianity without Civilization', p. 187.

77 Davidson, 'The Legacy of Robert Henry Codrington', p. 175.

78 For this type of church architecture, see Edward N. Kaufman, '"The weight and vigour of their masses": Mid-Victorian Country Churches and "The Lamp of Power"', in John Dixon Hunt and Faith M. Holland (eds.), *The Ruskin Polygon: Essays on the Imagination of John Ruskin* (Manchester: Manchester UP, 1982), pp. 94–121.

79 Jackson (ed.), *Recollections of Thomas Graham Jackson*, p. 133.

80 Unpublished letter, J. C. Patteson to his sister Frances Patteson (27 Aug. 1859), Bodl. CAS, USPG Archive, C/NZ/MELI, 1961.

81 Drummond, *Bishop Patteson*, pp. 43–4.

82 Riánna M. Williams, *From Royal Garden to Gothic Splendor: The History of St. Andrew's Cathedral* (Honolulu: St Andrew's Cathedral, 1996), p. 9. I would like to thank Peter Hoffenberg for providing this reference.

83 Robert Louis Semes, 'Hawai'i's Holy War: English Bishop Staley, American Congregationalists, and the Hawaiian Monarchs, 1860–1870', *Hawaiian Journal of History*, vol. 34 (2000), p. 115.

84 *Eccl.*, vol. 20 (June 1862), pp. 158–60. See also *Eccl.*, vol. 24 (Aug. 1866), p. 217.

85 *Eccl.*, vol. 24 (Aug. 1866), p. 217.

86 Benjamin Ingelow has been cited as the actual author of this project. See Rhoda E. A. Hackler, *The Cathedral Church of Saint Andrew, Honolulu, Hawaii* (Honolulu, 1991), p. 6. However, although Ingelow was working in the office of Slater and Carpenter, it is likely that he was only the project architect responsible for design development and the drafting of plans. Indeed, he is listed in *The Directory of British Architects, 1834–1914*, rev. Antonia Brodie *et al.* (London: Continuum, 2001) as an 'improver and assistant' in Slater's office at this time.

87 *Building News* (11 Jan. 1867), p. 24. Indeed, all the columns, arch-mouldings, strings, cornices, windows and doors were to be sent from England.

88 W. M. Jacob, *The Making of the Anglican Church Worldwide* (London: SPCK, 1997), pp. 98–9.

89 Robert E. Frykenberg, 'Christian Missions and the Raj', in Norman Etherington (ed.), *Missions and Empire* (Oxford: Oxford UP, 2005), pp. 107–31.

90 *Colonial Church Chronicle*, vol. 4 (Feb. 1851), p. 286.

91 One of the most vociferous proponents of this idea in High Church circles was Samuel Wilberforce, bishop of Oxford. For example, see his pronouncements on the matter in Henry Rowley (ed.), *Speeches on Missions by the Right Reverend Samuel Wilberforce, D.D.* (London: William Wells Gardner, 1874), pp. 103–36.

92 Vincent Kumaradoss, 'The SPG and the Impact of Conversion in Nineteenth-Century Tirunelveli', in D. O'Connor *et al.* (eds), *Three Centuries of Mission: The United Society for the Propagation of the Gospel, 1701–2000* (London: Continuum, 2000), p. 274–89.

93 Churches of this kind are mentioned in Gavin Stamp, 'Church Architecture', in Robert Fermor-Hesketh (ed.), *Architecture of the British Empire* (London: Weidenfeld and Nicolson, 1986), pp. 148–85. See also, Omar Khan, *From Kashmir to Kabul: Photography, 1860–1900* (Ahmedabad: Maplin Publishing, 2002), pp. 22–3, 43–4.

94 It was reported in the *Colonial Church Chronicle* that the foundation stone of this church was laid in July 1862. The designer was probably Walter Granville, but a 'Colonel Yule' is mentioned. Construction was overseen by the district commissioner, B. Thornhill. See *Colonial Church Chronicle*, vol. 16 (July 1862), pp. 461–3; vol. 17 (April 1863), p. 155. See also Philip Davies, *Splendours of the Raj: British Architecture in India, 1660–1947* (London: John Murray, 1985), p. 138.

95 For the Emerson churches see Christopher W. London, *Bombay Gothic* (Mumbai: India Book House, 2002), pp. 67–71.

96 'Consecration of a Church', Bodl. CAS, USPG Archive, CLR/28 (Ceylon).

97 *Eccl.*, vol. 19 (June 1861), p. 192; vol. 20 (Aug. 1862), p. 224.

98 Victoria and Albert Museum, London, South and South-East Asian Collection, IS.1–2000. See also *Eccl.*, vol. 22 (June 1864), p. 149.

99 *North-China Herald and Market Report* (11 Feb. 1865). I wish to thank Hal Kalman for this reference.

100 Wray is identified as the 'architect' in *The Ecclesiologist*. See *Eccl.*, vol. 22 (June 1864), p. 149. See also, *The Parish Church of St. James the Great, Calcutta* (Calcutta, 1962), p. 2.

101 Philip Davies has linked Granville, architect to the East Bengal Railway Company, with St James's. However, no sources are given. See Davies, *Splendours of the Raj*, p. 191.

102 *Rules and Proceedings* (3 June 1845), p. 81. See also London, *Bombay Gothic*, p. 16. For further reference to Scott in Bombay, see Richard Butler, 'George Gilbert Scott and the

University of Bombay', *The Victorian*, no. 37 (July 2011), pp. 10–13; and Dana Arnold, 'George Gilbert Scott and Bombay: India's Gothic Architecture', *Apollo* (Feb. 1991), pp. 87–90.

103 Conybeare's official title was Superintendent of Repairs to the Board of Conservancy. For more on Conybeare's involvement in the urban development of Bombay, see Mariam Dossal, *Imperial Designs and Indian Realities: The Planning of Bombay City, 1845–1875* (Delhi: Oxford UP, 1991), pp. 46–50, 109–13.

104 *Eccl.*, vol. 6 (June 1849), p. 398. It was characterised as a 'large and inferior First-Pointed church, with some *purpurei panni* [superficial effects], borrowed from ancient examples'. Conybeare seems to have learnt little in this respect over the next seven years, for his entry in the competition for the Crimean War Memorial church was rejected for similar reasons.

105 See unpublished letter, C. Weddington to Lord Elphinstone (Public Works Department, India, 7 June 1856), Elphinstone College Archive, Mumbai. In the margin of this letter, after the account of Tremenheere's excuse, is written in brackets 'Mr Conybeare says *no*.'

106 See unpublished 'Explanation' as appendix to 'Estimates for Completion of "Monumental Church at Colaba"', 28 March 1856, Elphinstone College Archive, Mumbai, Ecclesiastical 3/56 (1856), p. 58. See also unpublished letter, C. Weddington to Lord Elphinstone (see note 105). Here it is stated that, despite his apparent shortcomings, Tremenheere superintended the work with 'assiduous attendance, and . . . minutely supervised the execution, and prepared working plans and estimates very carefully. The funds were also well husbanded and their economical application looked to.'

107 *Bombay Quarterly Review*, vol. 6 (1857), pp. 391–4.

108 Paul Thompson, *William Butterfield: Victorian Architect* (Cambridge, Mass.: MIT Press, 1971), p. 513; London, *Bombay Gothic*, p. 18. However, Christopher London notes that some of Butterfield's designs were altered by students at the Sir Jamsetjee Jeejeebhoy School of Art.

109 Phoebe B. Stanton, *The Gothic Revival & American Church Architecture: An Episode in Taste, 1840–1856* (Baltimore: Johns Hopkins UP, 1968), p. 130; Frank Wills, *Ancient English Ecclesiastical Architecture and Its Principles, Applied to the Wants of the Church at the Present Day* (New York: Stanford and Swords, 1850), p. 109.

110 For further description and analysis of these buildings, see Marion MacRae (with Anthony Adamson), *Hallowed Walls: Church Architecture of Upper Canada* (Toronto: Clarke, Irwin & Co., 1975), pp. 158–61; Harold Kalman, *A History of Canadian Architecture*, 2 vols (Toronto: Oxford UP, 1994), vol. 1, pp. 290–2.

111 *Anglo-American Magazine*, vol. 2 (Jan.–July, 1853), p. 253.

112 Ibid., p. 254.

113 Two of Hay's designs that are almost literal realisations of this 'fusion' are the mission churches at St Francis' Harbour, Labrador (1850) and Lammuline, Newfoundland (1855). I wish to thank Candace Iron for bringing the Lammuline design to my attention.

114 Shirley G. Morriss, 'The Nine-Year Odyssey of a High Victorian Goth: Three Churches by Fred Cumberland', *Journal of Canadian Art History*, vol. 2:1 (1975), p. 50.

115 Ibid., p. 44. See also Geoffrey Simmins, *Fred Cumberland: Building the Victorian Dream* (Toronto: University of Toronto Press, 1997), pp. 118–22.

116 Shirley Morriss has suggested this. See Morriss, 'The Nine-Year Odyssey', p. 51. For St James the Less see, in particular, Truefitt's 'Design No. IX'. Geoffrey Simmins has also observed that Cumberland had a copy of Brandon's *Parish Churches* in his library. See Simmins, *Fred Cumberland*, p. 146.

117 George Truefitt, *Designs for Country Churches* (London, 1850), p. 7.

118 These designs are mentioned in Jane Russell-Corbett, '"The Ecclesiologist" and Anglican Church Architecture in the Canadian Colonies', *Bulletin of the Society for the Study of Architecture in Canada*, vol. 21:4 (1997), p. 94; MacRae (with Adamson), *Hallowed Walls*, p. 158.

119 *Architect and Contract Reporter* (20 Feb. 1869), p. 104.

120 *Anglo-American Magazine*, vol. 4 (Jan.–June, 1854), p. 21.

121 For these churches, see Peter Coffman, *Newfoundland Gothic* (Quebec: Éditions MultiMondes, 2008), pp. 142–8.

122 For these churches, see Kelly Crossman, *A Study of Anglican Church Buildings in Manitoba* (Winnipeg, 1989). I would like to thank Neil Bingham for bringing this publication to my attention.

123 Taylor quoted in ibid., p. 13. Indeed, the construction method used, so-called 'Red River frame', originated with French (Roman Catholic) traders. See Harold Kalman and John de Visser, *Pioneer Churches* (Toronto: McClelland and Stewart, 1976), p. 165.

124 Kalman, *A History of Canadian Architecture*, vol. 1, p. 340.

125 *Eccl.*, vol. 4 (Jan. 1847), pp. 15–16.

126 It is worth noting here that Medley was a leading opponent of pew rents and had in fact written a tract on their abolition. See John Medley, 'The Advantages of Open Seats', *Exeter Architectural Review*, no. 1 (1843), pp. 1–10.

127 See R. R. Langham-Carter, 'Buildings Wholly or Partly Designed by Mrs Gray', University of the Witwatersrand, William Cullen Library, CPSA Archive, AB1733.

128 W. M. Levick, 'The Diary of Robert John Mullins, 1854–61', University of the Witwatersrand, William Cullen Library, CPSA Archive, AB482, p. 5.

129 A letter in the Cory Library, Grahamstown, does identify one 'Mr Woodyer' as architect of the chapel. See unpublished letter (Cape Town, 6 Sept. 1864), Rhodes University, Cory Library, MS 16 698/1. See also R. R. Langham-Carter, 'A "Reconstruction" of the Armstrong Chapel, Grahamstown', *Architect and Builder* (Dec. 1981), pp. 22–3.

130 Desmond Martin, *The Bishop's Churches: The Churches of Anglican Bishop Robert Gray* (Cape Town: Struik, 2005), p. 13.

131 R. R. Langham-Carter, 'The Church of Holy Trinity at Kalk Bay in the Cape', *Architect and Builder* (May 1981), pp. 2–7.

132 The Vestry Minute Book from St Bartholomew's church shows that William White was paid £60 for supplying drawings. See Rhodes University, Cory Library, PR 3514 (d). During a return trip to England in 1855, Merriman was able to raise some £1,700 for the project, including the donation of church plate and furnishings.

133 Gray quoted in Gill Hunter, *William White: Pioneer Victorian Architect* (Reading: Spire Books, 2010), p. 58.

134 *Eccl.*, vol. 15 (1857), p. 65; *Colonial Church Chronicle*, vol. 14 (Oct. 1860), p. 392. The *Colonial Church Chronicle* also observed how its 'church-like aspect is a great relief to the eye after seeing the cathedral'.

135 For example, William White's chancel at St Paul's, Rondebosch (1880–4). See Hunter, *William White*, pp. 223–4. Herbert Baker was responsible for St Alban's cathedral, Pretoria (1905–9), and (with Francis Masey) the reconstruction of St George's cathedral, Cape Town (1901–39). John Oldrid Scott was largely responsible for reworking his father's design for the choir and nave of Grahamstown cathedral in a more elaborate form between 1890 and 1912. See Basil F. L. Clarke, *Anglican Cathedrals Outside the British Isles* (London: SPCK, 1958), pp. 25–31.

136 See unpublished letter, R. Gray (15 July 1872), University of the Witwatersrand, William Cullen Library, CPSA Archive, AB1161/Bb; T. G. Le Mesurier, 'Historical Sketch of St. Saviour's Church, Claremont', University of the Witwatersrand, William Cullen Library (University of Witwatersrand), CPSA Archive, AB2038f; R. R. Langham-Carter, 'St. Saviour's Church, Claremont, Cape', *Architect and Builder* (Sept. 1972), pp. 8–10. See also Thompson, *William Butterfield*, p. 448.

137 Butterfield was apparently responsible for designing and superintending the work on several stone arches and windows for St Saviour's, which were then sent out from England. See *South African Church Magazine and Ecclesiastical Review*, new ser., vol. 5 (1857), p. 335.

138 *Eccl.*, vol. 26 (Dec. 1868), p. 315.

139 *Eccl.*, vol. 8 (Aug. 1850), pp. 89–91; vol. 21 (Feb. 1863), p. 72.

140 *Eccl.*, vol. 6 (Aug. 1848), p. 49; vol. 20 (Aug. 1862), p. 225. *Cape Times* (14 Dec. 1964); R. R. Langham-Carter, 'The Bishop Gray Memorial', *The Gateway* (May 1983), pp. 11–12; Thompson, *William Butterfield*, p. 432.

141 For the Butterfield chapel-school, see Lochhead, *Dream of Spires*, pp. 48–9.

142 *Eccl.*, vol. 16 (April 1858), p. 92.

143 Ibid., p. 91.

144 The interaction between Butterfield and Thatcher is covered in Margaret H. Alington, *An Excellent Recruit: Frederick Thatcher – Architect, Priest and Private Secretary in Early New Zealand* (Auckland: Polygraphia, 2007), p. 173.

145 Perhaps the closest anyone came to erecting this design was the Rev. J. H. Thompson of Bishop's College, Lennoxville (Quebec). See *Eccl.*, vol. 13 (Feb. 1855), p. 49.

146 See the archive of the Tasmanian Museum and Art Gallery, Hobart, R1993.3.1847–8. I would like to thank Brian Andrews for bring these plans to my attention.

147 E. G. Scott, *St. Mary's Church, Hagley: History of the Church* ([Hobart], n.d.), p. 2.

148 Andrews, *Australian Gothic*, p. 28.

149 See unpublished letter, A. Short to F. Robe (1847), State Library of South Australia, PRG 160/54. Here Short observes: 'I propose dedicating £100 towards purchasing an eligible site in South Adelaide, and building a Church of substantive dimensions for the large Church population there assembled; if I can obtain subscriptions commensurate for this project, it might be an ornament to the town and perhaps not unsuitable here after for the Cathedral Church of the Bishopric.'

150 See Diary of Bishop Augustus Short, 1848, entry for 14 May, State Library of South Australia, PRG 160/52.

151 Brian Andrews, *Gothic in South Australian Churches* (Adelaide: Flinders University, 1984), p. 32. See also Donald Leslie Johnson, 'French and English Influences on the Architecture of St. Peter's Cathedral, Adelaide', *Architecture Australia* (June 1988), pp. 70–6.

152 *Eccl.*, vol. 13 (Feb. 1855), p. 50.

153 *Eccl.*, vol. 21 (Aug. 1863), p. 233.

154 For Norfolk Island, see 'Bishop Patteson's Memorial Chapel, Norfolk Island', n.d., RIBA Drawings Collection, PA 1723/SCGGS [100] 1. For the Seychelles, see J. N. Mané, 'Gilbert Scott's Colonial Churches', in M. Belcher and H. Debenham (eds), *Australasian Victorian Studies Association: Conference Papers 1987* (Christchurch: University of Canterbury for the AVSA, 1987), p. 37.

155 'Sketch of the History of Muswellbrook Parish', n.d., University of Newcastle Archive, Auchmuty Library, A5453(i), p. 9.

156 Ibid., p. 16.

157 All Saints', Hawkhurst, was built in 1861. I would like to thank Brian Andrews for pointing out the Hawkhurst con-

nection. Although formally quite similar, the Muswellbrook plans were, however, a separate design, taking into account the contextual limitations of its Australian setting. All Scott's drawings carried a different date from the Hawkhurst design and were headed 'St Alban's Church, Muswell Brook [*sic*]'. The Hawkhurst association is also mentioned in David Cole, *The Work of Sir Gilbert Scott* (London: Architectural Press, 1980), p. 114.

158 From *Church Chronicle of the Diocese of Sydney, Newcastle and Goulburn* (Feb. 1866) quoted in Mané, 'Gilbert Scott's Colonial Churches', p. 39.

159 *Colonial Church Chronicle*, vol. 16 (July 1862), p. 274; *Eccl.*, vol. 24 (Feb. 1866), p. 63.

160 See 'On the Proper Characteristics of a Town Church', *Eccl.*, vol. 8 (Dec. 1850), pp. 227–33.

161 *Eccl.*, vol. 9 (April 1851), p. 152.

162 Ibid.

7 *Bringing the Empire Home*

1 For a concise account of these changes, see Alan D. Gilbert, *Religion and Society in Industrial England: Church, Chapel and Social Change, 1740–1914* (London: Longman, 1976), pp. 125–43.

2 For the Coleridge family and their connection to the diocese of Exeter, see Bernard Coleridge, *The Story of a Devonshire House* (London: T. Fisher Unwin, 1906).

3 I wish to thank Simon Bradley for bringing the Mackenzie memorial window in Haslingfield church, Cambridgeshire, to my attention.

4 *Eccl.*, vol. 1 (Jan. 1845), p. 24.

5 Beresford Hope had used organic metaphors in relation to architecture before. For example, see his reference to the new government offices building, quoted in G. A. Bremner, 'Nation and Empire in the Government Architecture of Mid-Victorian London: The Foreign and India Office Reconsidered', *Historical Journal*, vol. 48:3 (2005), p. 721.

6 This episode is covered in G. C. B. Davies, *Henry Phillpotts, Bishop of Exeter, 1778–1869* (London: SPCK, 1954), pp. 264–86.

7 Fred D. Schneider, 'The Anglican Quest for Authority: Convocation and the Imperial Factor, 1850–60', *Journal of Religious History*, vol. 9:2 (1976), pp. 143–54. Further background as to why a colonial bishop was considered desirable on the committee is given in A. R. Ashwell and R. G. Wilberforce, *Life of the Right Reverend Samuel Wilberforce, D.D.*, 3 vols (London: John Murray, 1880–2), vol. 2, pp. 443–5.

8 Barry Magrill, '"Development" and Ecclesiology in the Outpost of the British Empire: William Hay's Gothic Solutions for Church Building in Tropical Climates (1840–1890)', *JSSAC*, vol. 29:1–2 (2004), pp. 15–26. Between returning to Scotland and making his partnership with Henderson, Hay designed St Peter's Anglican church in the town of St George, Bermuda (1871). However, this church was never completed (Magrill, pp. 16–17).

9 R. J. E. Boggis, *A History of St. Augustine's College, Canterbury* (Canterbury: Cross and Jackman, 1907), pp. 30–1.

10 Frederick Bullock has observed that the numbers of students were at first disappointing, with only six enrolled at the time of the college's opening in 1848. See F. W. B. Bullock, *A History of Training for the Ministry of the Church of England in England and Wales, 1800–1874* (St Leonards-on-Sea: Budd and Gillatt, 1955), p. 88.

11 G. A. Selwyn, *'A little one shall become a thousand': A Sermon Preached at the Opening of the Cuddesdon Theological Institution* (London: Rivingtons, 1854). The bishop of Natal was also present at the opening.

12 S. C. Gayford, *Cuddesdon College, 1854–1904: A Record and Memorial* (Longmans, Green & Co., 1904), pp. 73–95. Although Cuddesdon was established for the purposes of the Church at home, by 1904 approximately ten per cent of its graduates were to be found in the colonial and foreign mission field. For a general account of the college's establishment, see Owen Chadwick, *The Founding of Cuddesdon* (Oxford: Oxford UP, 1954).

13 Henry Moseley described Mormons as 'pagans' and considered them a threat to ordered and dignified religion in Britain. See Henry Moseley, *The Home Missions of the Church: A Sermon, Preached on the Seventeenth Anniversary of the Bath & Wells Diocesan Societies* (London: J. W. Parker, 1856), p. 9.

14 Unpublished letter, W. G. Broughton to E. Coleridge (19 Oct. 1837), University of Sydney, Moore Theological College Archive, Broughton Papers, 1/3.

15 Bishop Samuel Wilberforce quoted in Boggis, *A History of St. Augustine's College*, p. 40.

16 See entry for 16 June 1844 in 'Statement Drawn up for Provisional Committee Meeting at King's College – Read at the Meeting, King's College, July 1847', Canterbury Cathedral Archives (UK), U88 A1/1/2.

17 For example, a copy of this circular exists in the National Library of New Zealand, where it came as part of G. A. Selwyn's letters. See ATL, MS – 1841.

18 *A Proposal for the Establishment of a Missionary College to Educate Clergy for the Colonies and Dependencies of Great Britain* (privately printed, *c.*1845) [circular], Canterbury Cathedral Archives (UK), U88/A1/1/3, p. 1.

19 Ibid., p. 2.

20 Ibid.

21 Ibid. It was also observed on this point in an earlier draft of the proposal that: 'our fellow-subjects in the Colonies

will not be deemed less our Brethren – less dear objects of Christian Charity, because they have been induced by the spirit of honest enterprise, or compelled by severe necessity, to settle in a distant part of our Empire'. See 'Proposal for the Foundation of a Missionary College' (*c.*1846), Canterbury Cathedral Archives (UK), U88/A1/1/4, p. 2.

22 Bullock, *A History of Training for the Ministry*, p. 31.

23 He went on to say: 'All along I have been desirous that the course which they should follow towards attaining this perfection should be that of our own Prayer Book, that they should be made Christian by being Churchmen, and Churchmen by being devoted sons of the English Church.' See unpublished draft of letter, A. J. B. Beresford Hope to the dean of Canterbury (*c.*1845), Canterbury Cathedral Archives (UK), U88 A1/1/1.

24 See *The Charter and Statues of the Missionary College of Saint Augustine, Canterbury* (1848).

25 *Colonial Church Chronicle*, vol. 1 (Sept. 1847), pp. 81–2.

26 See *Proposal for the Foundation of a Missionary College*, p. 1. For the academic subjects studied, see H. M. Carey, *God's Empire: Religion and Colonialism in the British World, c.1801–1908* (Cambridge: Cambridge UP, 2010), p. 279.

27 'Proposal for the Foundation of a Missionary College' (*c.*1846), Canterbury Cathedral Archives (UK), U88/A1/1/4, p. 1. In a later document this aim was phrased in the following way: 'It is therefore the object of the College now in progress, to provide an education to qualify young men for the services of the Church in Foreign Settlements, with such strict regard to economy and frugality of habits, as may fit them for the special duties to be discharged, the difficulties to be encountered, and the hardships to be endured.' See 'Missionary College for the Church of England Now in Course of Erection at Canterbury', Sept. 1846, Canterbury Cathedral Archives (UK), U88 A1/1/7.

28 Ibid.

29 *A Proposal for the Establishment of a Missionary College*, p. 3.

30 'Statutes of the Missionary College of Saint Augustine, Canterbury', Canterbury Cathedral Archives (UK), U88 A1/2/18, p. 20.

31 *A Proposal for the Establishment of a Missionary College*, p. 3. See also *Colonial Church Chronicle*, vol. 2 (Aug. 1848), p. 45.

32 Unpublished letter, A. J. B. Beresford Hope to W. H. Coleridge (14 Nov. 1847), Canterbury Cathedral Archives (UK), U88 A2/9 – C32.

33 *Occasional Papers from St. Augustine's College*, no. 1 (May 1853), p. 5. It was also observed in the *Colonial Church Chronicle* that: 'for all students, abundance of out-door exercise is of primary importance: a robust frame, a hardy temperament, which makes light of, and rather enjoys "roughing it," . . . is an immense advantage . . . to him who aspires to be a successful Missionary. . . . The body is not only the tabernacle, but the tool, the *ὄργανον*, of the spirit. . . . We trust that at St. Augustine's, both by labour and open-air exercises, and by a nutritious and well-chosen dietary, all care will be taken to preserve in unimpaired health and vigour the bodily frames of those whom a generous emulation may excite to serve and long-continued mental exertion.' See *Colonial Church Chronicle*, vol. 12 (March 1858), p. 110.

34 On this point the *Colonial Church Chronicle* noted that: 'We do not know whether such things as cricket, single-stick, swimming, and other athletic sports, are considered by the authorities too undignified and boyish for those destined hereafter for such grave and responsible posts; but we must confess to a high esteem for such games . . . : a great deal is learned from them, courage, endurance, self-possession, command of temper, patience'. Ibid.

35 Unpublished draft of letter, A. J. B. Beresford Hope to the dean of Canterbury (*c.*1845), Canterbury Cathedral Archives (UK), U88 A1/1/1.

36 'Statutes of the Missionary College of Saint Augustine, Canterbury', Canterbury Cathedral Archives (UK), U88 A1/2/18, p. 4.

37 Boggis, *A History of St. Augustine's College*, pp. 55–6.

38 Ibid., p. 57.

39 For instance, writing to the archbishop about the college in 1844, Coleridge included the following excerpt from a letter from Broughton: 'Pangs of the heart *cannot* escape, when I look round, and behold the barren wilderness given to me to cultivate; the extent of which and of its wants, and the comparative nothingness of the means at my disposal, have been revealed to me more distressingly than ever during my late visitation of the Port Phillip District. You must not, and I am sure, for the love of God, you will not let go your design for the Colonial Institution for Clergymen. It will be the one and only measure by which we can stand.' See entry for 30 May 1844 in 'Statement Drawn up for Provisional Committee Meeting at King's College – Read at the Meeting, King's College, July 1847', Canterbury Cathedral Archives (UK), U88 A1/1/2.

40 Henry Bailey, *A Sermon Preached in the Chapel of Saint Augustine's College, by the Rev. Henry Bailey, B.D., Warden, with an Address Delivered in the College Hall, by the Rev. William H. Walsh, M.A., Christ Church, Sydney, . . . August 1851, before the Departure of Charles Joseph Gillett, Student, to the Diocese of Sydney* (Canterbury: St Augustine's College, 1851), pp. 6–8.

41 See excerpt from unpublished letter, E. Coleridge to the bishop of Oxford (Feb. 1843), in 'Statement Drawn up for Provisional Committee Meeting at King's College – Read at the Meeting, King's College, July 1847', Canterbury Cathedral Archives (UK), U88 A1/1/2.

42 Boggis, *A History of St. Augustine's College*, p. 55.

43 He had apparently been inspired to rescue the site upon reading a letter by Robert Brett published in the *English Churchman* in September 1843. See G. F. Maclear, *S. Augustine's, Canterbury: Its Rise, Ruin, and Restoration* (London: Wells Gardner, Darton, & Co., 1888), p. 40.

44 Boggis, *A History of St. Augustine's College*, pp. 60–1.

45 Broughton was one of the college's consistent and vociferous supporters. Ibid., pp. 62, 80–1.

46 Unpublished letter, E. Coleridge to G. Gilbert (20 March 1845), Canterbury Cathedral Archives (UK), U88 A2/13 – C215. Maclear also observed that he was 'fired by the associations of place'. See Maclear, *S. Augustine's*, p. 46.

47 See excerpt from unpublished letter, E. Coleridge to the archbishop of Canterbury (14 June 1844), in 'Statement Drawn up for Provisional Committee Meeting at King's College – Read at the Meeting, King's College, July 1847', Canterbury Cathedral Archives (UK), U88 A1/1/2.

48 Boggis, *A History of St. Augustine's College*, p. 55.

49 *Colonial Church Chronicle*, vol. 12 (March 1858), p. 107.

50 *Illustrated London News* (8 July 1848), p. 5.

51 *Eccl.*, vol. 6 (Aug. 1848), p. 2.

52 Boggis, *A History of St. Augustine's College*, p. 65. Indeed, Coleridge agreed to leave the architectural side of the college to Beresford Hope and Butterfield (p. 63).

53 From the very beginning it was intended that the new buildings would be raised, in part at least, 'on the foundations of the old Abbey'. See unpublished letter, E. Coleridge to G. Gilbert (20 March 1845), Canterbury Cathedral Archives (UK), U88 A2/13 – C215.

54 *Eccl.*, vol. 6 (Aug. 1848), p. 7.

55 A. J. B. Beresford Hope, 'Architectural Notes on St. Augustine's College, Canterbury', in *St. Augustine's Abbey and St. Augustine's College* (Canterbury: St Augustine's College, n.d.), p. 21. However, as Paul Thompson has pointed out, the remains of this undercroft were only fragmentary, and Butterfield probably modelled the vaulting technique on the undercroft at Lambeth Palace. See Paul Thompson, *William Butterfield: Victorian Architect* (Cambridge, Mass.: MIT Press, 1971), p. 172.

56 Charles L. Eastlake, *A History of the Gothic Revival* (London: Longmans, 1872), p. 226.

57 Unpublished letter, W. Butterfield to W. H. Coleridge (n.d.), Canterbury Cathedral Archives (UK), U88 A2/8 – C10/6.

58 *Eccl.*, vol. 6 (Aug. 1848), p. 4; Boggis, *A History of St. Augustine's College*, p. 162.

59 *Illustrated London News* (8 July 1848), p. 6.

60 Anon., travel diary, 1850, Canterbury Cathedral Archives (UK), U88 A3/4/35, p. 3.

61 *Descriptive Account of the Cathedral of Canterbury, . . . with a Short Description of St. Augustine's Monastery, Now Converted into a Missionary College, for the Church of England* (Canterbury: Henry Ward, 1850), p. 47. Butterfield also talked about how he experimented in designing chairs for these rooms in a manner that was 'quite simple'. See unpublished letter, W. Butterfield to W. H. Coleridge (14 Nov. 1847), Canterbury Cathedral Archives (UK), U88 A2/9 – C32.

62 *Eccl.*, vol. 6 (Aug. 1848), p. 4.

63 Ibid., p. 5.

64 Upublished letter, Beresford Hope to W. H. Coleridge (21 July 1847), Canterbury Cathedral Archives (UK), U88 A2/9 – C29.

65 Blomfield quoted in Boggis, *A History of St. Augustine's College*, p. 163.

66 Anon., travel diary, 1850, Canterbury Cathedral Archives (UK), U88 A3/4/35, p. 4.

67 *Eccl.*, vol. 6 (Aug. 1848), p. 7. Originally the chapel interior contained encaustic tiles, mosaics, and stained glass, most of which has since been removed or covered up.

68 At this swearing-in service, the students had to respond aloud to the following vow: 'Is it your deliberate intention to devote yourself, with all the powers of mind and body which God in His goodness has given you, to His service in the ministry of the Church of England in the distant dependencies of the British Empire or in the Foreign Mission Field?' See Boggis, *A History of St. Augustine's College*, p. 138.

69 'A Voice of Affectionate Inquiry from the Missionary College, Canterbury', *St. Augustine's College Tracts*, no. 2 (n.d.), p. 1.

70 *Occasional Papers of St. Augustine's College*, no. 1 (May 1853), p. 10.

71 The destination of these doors was unknown to the students at the time, until two who had worked on them were sent to Grahamstown, where, upon arrival, they recognised their handiwork. See Boggis, *A History of St. Augustine's College*, pp. 149–50.

72 *Occasional Papers of St. Augustine's College*, no. 1 (May 1853), p. 10.

73 *Lyttelton Times* quoted in Ian Lochhead, 'Remembering the Middle Ages: Responses to the Gothic Revival in Colonial New Zealand', in Jaynie Anderson (ed.), *Crossing Cultures: Conflict, Migration and Convergence. The Proceedings of the 32nd International Congress in the History of Art* (Carlton, Victoria: The Miegunyah Press, 2009), p. 538.

74 Boggis, *A History of St. Augustine's College*, pp. 150–1. Later, in the early 1880s, the undercroft was turned into the college museum. Although the function of the space was changed specifically for this purpose, it was infused with the same sense of global reach. Here were displayed an incredible array of maps, specimens and objects from around the world, sent for the most part by colonial clergymen.

75 *Eccl.*, vol. 6 (Aug. 1848), p. 3.

76 Carey, *God's Empire*, pp. 284–6.

77 *Colonial Church Chronicle*, vol. 2 (Sept. 1848), p. 104.

78 Edward L. Cutts, *Home Missions and Church Extension* (London: Rivingtons, *c.*1861), p. 7.

79 The comparison with Africa had been used as early as 1842 by James Grant: 'The great masses of the metropolitan community are as ignorant of the destitution and distress which prevail in large districts of London . . . as if the wretched creatures were living in the very centre of Africa.' Grant quoted in H. J. Dyos, 'The Slums of Victorian London', in David Cannadine and David Reeder (eds), *Exploring the Urban Past: Essays in Urban History by H. J. Dyos* (Cambridge: Cambridge UP, 1982), p. 135.

80 Peter Keating (ed.), *Into Unknown England, 1866–1913: Selections from the Social Explorers* (Manchester: Manchester UP, 1976); Felix Driver, *Geography Militant: Cultures of Exploration and Empire* (Oxford: Blackwell, 2001), pp. 170–98; Alison Twells, *The Civilising Mission and the English Middle Class, 1792–1850* (Basingstoke: Palgrave Macmillan, 2009); Catherine Hall, *Civilising Subjects: Metropole and Colony in the English Imagination, 1830–1867* (Cambridge: Polity, 2002), p. 372. For a particularly informative account of the 1840s and 1850s, see Dyos, 'The Slums of Victorian London', pp. 129–53.

81 John Livesey, *Mechanics' Churches: A Letter to the Right Honourable Sir Robert Peel, Bart. M.P., on Church Extension in Populous Towns and Manufacturing Districts* (London: Hatchard, 1840), p. 7.

82 Moseley, *The Home Missions of the Church*, pp. 9–10.

83 Cutts, *Home Missions*, p. 3.

84 Ibid., p. 7.

85 Ibid., p. 5.

86 The Society for Promoting the Employment of Additional Curates in Populous Places.

87 Cutts, *Home Missions*, pp. 13–15.

88 For an account of the controversy around King, see David Kent, 'High Church Rituals and Rituals of Protest; The "Riots" at St George-in-the-East, 1859–60', *London Journal*, vol. 32:2 (2007), pp. 145–65. See also Owen Chadwick, *The Victorian Church*, 2 vols (London: Adam and Charles Black, 1966–70), vol. 1, pp. 495–501.

89 C. F. Lowder, *Twenty-One Years in S. George's Mission: An Account of its Origin, Progress, and Works of Charity* (London: Rivingtons, 1877), p. 7.

90 Ashwell and Wilberforce, *Life of . . . Samuel Wilberforce*, vol. 2, pp. 30–4.

91 Lowder, *Twenty-One Years in S. George's Mission*, p. 30.

92 Ibid., p. 18.

93 Ibid., p. 7.

94 It is mentioned by Basil Clarke in his book on nineteenth-century church builders, but no clue is given as to who produced it. See Basil F. L. Clarke, *Church Builders of the Nineteenth Century: A Study of the Gothic Revival in England* (London: SPCK, 1938), p. 219. See also Michael Reynolds, *Martyr of Ritualism: Father Mackonochie of St. Alban's, Holborn* (London: Faber and Faber, 1965), pp. 43–4.

95 *Illustrated London News* (30 Jan. 1869), p. 113.

96 Bryan King, *The Recovery of the Lost Sheep of the Church of England by Home Missions in Her Large and Destitute Parishes: A Sermon Preached at the Opening of the Mission Chapel, Calvert Street, S. George's, East* (London: Joseph Masters, 1856), p. 12.

97 Ibid., p. 16.

98 Initially there was violent reaction to the mission on the part of some in the area, which included the throwing of bricks and other 'dangerous missiles' at Lowder and his colleagues. This was perpetrated mainly by Irish Catholic migrants, now working at the docks – no doubt the same 'rude' and 'savage' folk that were the focus of Anglican mission work in Ireland (see below). See 'St. George's Mission, St. George's-in-the-East, London', *The English Church Union Kalendar: An Ecclesiastical Almanac, Part V* (1863), p. 19. Of the approximately 6,000 people living in the immediate vicinity of the mission, 2,000 were Irish Catholics. See Reynolds, *Martyr of Ritualism*, p. 43.

99 Lowder, *Twenty-One Years*, p. 69.

100 Ibid., p. 72.

101 Like St Peter's London Docks, the mission associated with St Saviour's started off in a temporary iron church. See *Church Builder*, no. 19 (1866), p. 103.

102 Nigel Scotland, *Squires in the Slums: Settlements and Missions in Late-Victorian London* (London: I. B. Tauris, 2007). See also N. B. Kent (ed.), *Cambridge in South London: The Work of the College Missions, 1883–1914* (Cambridge: W. Heffer & Sons, 1914).

103 Gilbert, *Religion and Society in Industrial England*, pp. 125–43, 162–72. For the conflict and rivalry between the established Church and Methodism dating back to the late eighteenth and early nineteenth centuries, see David Hempton, *Methodism and Politics in British Society, 1750–1850* (London: Hutchinson, 1987), pp. 77–80.

104 Bruce Coleman, 'The Nineteenth Century: Nonconformity', in Nicholas Orme (ed.), *Unity and Variety: A History of the Church in Devon and Cornwall* (Exeter: University of Exeter Press, 1991), p. 132. See also Gilbert, *Religion and Society in Industrial England*, pp. 98–103.

105 Of the total Christian population who worshipped in Cornwall, only 27.2 per cent were Anglican. See John Turner, 'The Nineteenth Century: The Church of England',

in Nicholas Orme (ed.), *Unity and Variety: A History of the Church in Devon and Cornwall* (Exeter: University of Exeter Press, 1991), p. 112.

106 It was later reported in the *Church Builder* that the work of the Church in such places was 'essentially a *Missionary* one'. See *Church Builder*, no. 7 (1863), p. 141.

107 Davies, *Henry Phillpotts*, p. 19.

108 R. J. E. Boggis, *A History of the Diocese of Exeter* (Exeter: William Pollard, 1922), pp. 493–5.

109 Chris Brooks, 'Building the Rural Church: Money, Power and the Country Parish', in Chris Brooks and Andrew Saint (eds), *The Victorian Church: Architecture and Society* (Manchester: Manchester UP, 1995), p. 63.

110 Ibid.; see also Coleman, 'The Nineteenth-Century', p. 132.

111 Chris Miele, '"Their interest and habit": Professionalism and the Restoration of Medieval Churches, 1837–77', in Chris Brooks and Andrew Saint (eds), *The Victorian Church: Architecture and Society* (Manchester: Manchester UP, 1995), p. 166. It was reported in the first edition of the *Church Builder* that, in its forty-three-year history, the ICBS had aided in supplying 1,000,000 additional sittings, 895,526 of which were free. See *Church Builder*, no. 1 (1862), pp. 4, 7. It was required of new churches receiving a grant from the society that at least half the sittings be free (p. 7).

112 Gill Hunter, *William White: Pioneer Victorian Architect* (Reading: Spire Books, 2010), pp. 18–24. See also Gill Hunter, 'William White: The Early Years', in Rosemary Hill and Michael Hall (eds), *The 1840s, Studies in Victorian Architecture and Design*, vol. 1 (London: Victorian Society, 2008), p. 108.

113 Gill Hunter has noted that White may also have been involved in the design of a temporary wooden church for Truro in 1849. See Hunter, *William White*, p. 318. He would later go on to design other churches for the diocese, with the aid of the ICBS, such as St Peter's, Mithian (consecrated 1862). *Church Builder*, no. 1 (1862), p. 21.

114 It became incorporated in 1828. See M. H. Port, *600 New Churches: The Church Building Commission, 1818–1856* (Reading: Spire Books, 2006), pp. 28–9.

115 *Church Builder*, no. 1 (1862), p. 7.

116 Ibid., p. 124.

117 In 1870 this committee comprised G. F. Bodley, David and Raphael Brandon, Ewan Christian, Joseph Clarke, Benjamin Ferrey, J. H. Hakewill, J. L. Pearson, J. P. St Aubyn, G. G. Scott, G. E. Street and T. H. Wyatt.

118 As Alison Twells has shown, Nonconformist groups had been establishing chapel schools since the late 1830s and early 1840s among the working classes in and around Britain's industrial centres. See Twells, *The Civilising Mission*, pp. 102–3.

119 *Church Builder*, no. 1 (1862), p. 15.

120 *Church Builder*, no. 7 (1863), p. 142.

121 It was noted in the accompanying text to Carpenter's chapel-school: 'The want has been generally felt in many colonial dioceses of some building which might serve, not only for a Place of Worship, but also for a School. And in our country there are many hamlets of comparatively small population, where both a Chapel and a School are wanted, and yet where it is impossible, from want of means, to provide more than one of these two buildings. . . . The building is divided internally by a screen. On one side is an oblong apartment . . . which may serve both for a Schoolroom and for the Nave, or congregational part, of a small Chapel: the other portion is treated as a chancel. . . .' *Instrumenta Ecclesiastica*, 2nd ser. (London: John Van Voorst, 1856), plate 18.

122 *Church Builder*, no. 10 (1864), p. 74.

123 *Church Builder*, no. 1 (1862), pp. 15–16. See also report on the mission houses at Great Yarmouth and Reach in the *Church Builder*, no. 8 (1863), pp. 173–5.

124 This idea, bound up with the need for extra church accommodation, extended back to the early nineteenth century. See Port, *600 New Churches*, pp. 15–18.

125 *Church Builder*, no. 7 (1863), p. 140.

126 A. J. B. Beresford Hope, 'The Present State of Ecclesiological Science', *Rules and Proceedings* (23 June 1846), p. 29.

127 Edward Churton (ed.), *Memoir of Joshua Watson*, 2 vols (Oxford: J. H. and Jas. Parker, 1861), vol. 1, pp. 49, 163–89; vol. 2, pp. 17–18, 84–138, 224–5, 307.

128 The ambiguity of Ireland's status as 'colony' or 'kingdom', and the historical debates that attend it, has recently been highlighted by Nicholas Canny in the foreword to Kevin Kenny (ed.), *Ireland and the British Empire* (Oxford: Oxford UP, 2004), p. viii. See also 'Introduction', in Brendan Smith, *Colonisation and Conquest in Medieval Ireland: The English in Louth, 1170–1330* (Cambridge: Cambridge UP, 1999), pp. 1–9; R. R. Davies, *Domination and Conquest: The Experience of Ireland, Scotland and Wales, 1100–1300* (Cambridge: Cambridge UP, 1990), pp. 11–15.

129 Carey, *God's Empire*, p. 41.

130 For a justification of the use of the term 'colony' in relation to parts of medieval Ireland, see Robin Frame, *Colonial Ireland, 1169–1369* (Dublin: Helicon, 1981), pp. vi–x.

131 Mark Dorrian, 'On Some Spatial Aspects of the Colonial Discourse on Ireland', *Journal of Architecture*, vol. 6:1 (2001), pp. 27–51.

132 Nicholas Canny, 'The Ideology of English Colonization: From Ireland to America', *William and Mary Quarterly*, 3rd ser., vol. 30:4 (1973), pp. 575–98.

133 For a critical overview of Ireland as a British colonial/imperial territory, see Alvin Jackson, 'Ireland, the Union, and the Empire, 1800–1960' in Kevin Kenny (ed.), *Ireland and the British Empire* (Oxford: Oxford UP, 2004), pp. 123–35. For the 'conquest', 'colonization' and 'civilization' element of this history during the sixteenth and seventeenth centuries, see also Nicholas Canny, *Making Ireland British, 1580–1650* (Oxford: Oxford UP, 2001).

134 David Fitzpatrick, 'Ireland and Empire', in A. Porter (ed.), *The Oxford History of the British Empire*, vol. 3: The *Nineteenth Century* (Oxford: Oxford UP, 1999), pp. 494–521.

135 For the earlier period, see Canny, *Making Ireland British*. For the nineteenth century, see Stewart J. Brown, 'The New Reformation Movement in the Church of Ireland, 1801–29', in Stewart J. Brown and David W. Miller (eds), *Piety and Power in Ireland, 1760–1960: Essays in Honour of Emmet Larkin* (Belfast: Queen's University, 2000), pp. 182–92.

136 For example, see C. Peter Williams, '"Too peculiarly Anglican": The Role of the Established Church in Ireland as a Negative Model in the Development of the Church Missionary Society's Commitment to Independent Native Churches, 1856–1872', in W. J. Sheils and Diana Wood (eds), *The Churches, Ireland and the Irish* (Oxford: Basil Blackwell, 1989), pp. 299–310.

137 For a concise account of the Church in Ireland at this time, see Chadwick, *The Victorian Church*, vol. 1, pp. 47–60.

138 For Church of Ireland clergy in British North America, see Alan L. Hayes, *Anglicans in Canada: Controversies and Identity in Historical Perspective* (Urbana: University of Illinois Press, 2004), pp. 6–7; Curtis Fahey, *In His Name: The Anglican Experience in Upper Canada, 1791–1854* (Ottawa: Carleton UP, 1991), p. 255; John S. Moir, *The Church in the British Era: From the British Conquest to Confederation* (Toronto: McGraw-Hill, 1972), p. 111. For Australia, see James Grant, *Episcopally Led and Synodically Governed: Anglicans in Victoria, 1803–1997* (Melbourne: Australian Scholarly Publishing, 2010), p. 47. For Irish Catholics in the empire, see Carey, *God's Empire*, pp. 114–45.

139 Joseph Hardwick, 'Anglican Church Expansion and the Recruitment of Colonial Clergy for New South Wales and the Cape Colony, *c.*1790–1850', *Journal of Imperial and Commonwealth History*, vol. 37:3 (2009), p. 374.

140 At this moment the Church of Ireland looked to the churches of the Anglican Communion in places such as Australia and New Zealand as models of self-government. See Charles A. Webster, 'The Restoration of the Church', in Walter Alison Phillips (ed.), *History of the Church of Ireland from the Earliest Times to the Present Day*, 3 vols (Oxford: Oxford UP, 1933), vol. 3, pp. 362–3.

141 S. J. Connolly, *Religion, Law, and Power: The Making of Protestant Ireland 1660–1760* (Oxford: Oxford UP, 1992), pp. 178–9.

142 King quoted in ibid., p. 179.

143 Whately quoted in E. Jane Whately, *The Life and Correspondence of Richard Whately D.D.* (London: Longmans, Green & Co., 1868), p. 63.

144 Chadwick, *The Victorian Church*, vol. 1, p. 48.

145 Desmond Bowen, *The Protestant Crusade in Ireland, 1800–70* (Dublin: Gill and Macmillan, 1978); John Wolffe, *The Protestant Crusade in Great Britain, 1829–1860* (Oxford: Oxford UP, 1991), pp. 32–41.

146 Brown, 'The New Reformation Movement in the Church of Ireland', p. 181.

147 This prejudice stretched back centuries. For the sixteenth and seventeenth centuries, see Canny, 'The Ideology of English Colonization'. For the nineteenth century, see L. P. Curtis, *Anglo-Saxons and Celts: A Study of Anti-Irish Prejudice in Victorian England* (Bridgeport, Conn.: Conference on British Studies at the University of Bridgeport, 1968); Patrick O'Farrell, *England and Ireland since 1800* (Oxford: Oxford UP, 1975); Dorrian, 'On Some Spatial Aspects of the Colonial Discourse on Ireland', pp. 43–6.

148 Magee (1822) quoted in Brown, 'The New Reformation Movement in the Church of Ireland', p. 181.

149 Chadwick, *The Victorian Church*, vol. 1, p. 48.

150 Brown, 'The New Reformation Movement in the Church of Ireland', p. 188.

151 Williams, '"Too peculiarly Anglican"'.

152 Peter Nockles, 'Church or Protestant Sect? The Church of Ireland, High Churchmanship, and the Oxford Movement, 1822–1869', *Historical Journal*, vol. 41:2 (1998), pp. 457–93. See also Austin Cooper, 'Ireland and the Oxford Movement', *Journal of Religious History*, vol. 19:1 (1995), pp. 62–74.

153 Nockles, 'Church of Protestant Sect?', p. 460.

154 This was especially the case with clerics such as bishops John Henry Hobart (1775–1830) and George W. Doane (1799–1859). See Raymond W. Albright, *A History of the Protestant Episcopal Church* (New York: Macmillan, 1964), pp. 180–5. See also Henry Caswall, *America, and the American Church* (London: John and Charles Mozley, 1851).

155 Nockles, 'Church or Protestant Sect?', p. 462.

156 Ibid.

157 Ibid., p. 467.

158 For Sewell's pivotal role in the foundation of St. Columba's, see G. K. White, *A History of St. Columba's College, 1843–1974* (Dublin: Old Columban Society, 1980), pp. 1–21.

159 Sewell also had brothers in Australia and New Zealand. His elder brother (Richard) established a legal practice in Mel-

bourne, later becoming reader in law at the University of Melbourne; while his younger brother (Henry) became the first premier of New Zealand. See M. C. Owen, *The Sewells of the Isle of Wight* (Manchester: privately printed, 1908), pp. 11, 40–4.

160 Todd quoted in Nockles, 'Church or Protestant Sect?', pp. 479–80.

161 *Eccl.*, vol. 10 (June 1852), p. 175.

162 Manners quoted in Nockles, 'Church or Protestant Sect?', p. 476.

163 Ibid.; see also *Eccl.*, vol. 8 (Dec. 1850), p. 248.

164 See N. D. Emerson, 'Church Life in the 19th Century', Walter Alison Phillips (ed.), *History of the Church of Ireland from the Earliest Times to the Present Day*, 3 vols (Oxford: Oxford UP, 1933), vol. 3, p. 356.

165 Nockles, 'Church or Protestant Sect?', pp. 473–7.

166 *Eccl.*, vol. 9 (April 1851), pp. 144–6

167 Ibid., p. 144.

168 A full account of the restoration of St Patrick's cathedral is given in Michael O'Neill, 'Nineteenth-Century Architectural Restorations', in John Crawford and Raymond Gillespie (eds), *St. Patrick's Cathedral, Dublin: A History* (Dublin: Four Courts Press, 2009), pp. 328–49.

169 For example, see *Eccl.*, vol. 2 (May 1846), p. 204.

170 O'Neill, 'Nineteenth-Century Architectural Restorations', pp. 340–1. Here O'Neill observes that Guinness and his builder, Timothy Murphy, identified in Carpenter's plans a fixation with the Early English and a corresponding lack of awareness of the nuances of Irish Gothic architecture (p. 342).

171 A full account of this restoration is given by Roger Stalley in the introduction to Roger Stalley (ed.), *George Edmund Street and the Restoration of Christ Church Cathedral, Dublin* (Dublin: Four Courts Press, 2000), pp. 11–34. For Street's specific philosophy to ecclesiastical restoration as it applied to Christ Church, see Seán O'Reilly, 'A Philosophy of Restoration: George Edmund Street at Dublin's Christ Church', *Irish Architectural and Decorative Studies*, vol. 1 (1998), pp. 200–20.

172 For Trench's Tractarian connections, see John Bromley, *The Man of Ten Talents: A Portrait of Richard Chenevix Trench, 1807–86* (London: SPCK, 1959), pp. 50–1; Kenneth Milne, *Richard Chenevix Trench, 1807–1886* (Dublin: Church of Ireland Historical Society, 2010), pp. 6–7.

173 *Eccl.*, vol. 10 (June 1852), pp. 169–70. See also G. E. Street and E. Seymour, *The Cathedral of the Holy Trinity Commonly Called Christ Church Cathedral, Dublin* (1882), reprinted in Stalley (ed.), *George Edmund Street*, pp. 79–80.

174 Ibid., p. 80.

175 Stalley, 'Introduction', p. 32.

176 For example, in his first report (1868), Street says: 'whatever Church existed on the site before the time of the English Invasion, was entirely removed in order to provide the necessary foundations for one on a large scale'. See G. E. Street, *Report to the Dean and Chapter of Christ Church Cathedral, Dublin, on the Restoration of the Cathedral Church* (1868), reprinted in Stalley (ed.), George Edmund Street, p. 45.

177 Nockles, 'Church or Protestant Sect?', p. 469.

178 *Eccl.*, vol. 24 (Oct. 1866), p. 267.

179 A. J. B. Beresford Hope, *The English Cathedral of the Nineteenth Century* (London: John Murray, 1861).

180 David Lawrence and Ann Wilson, *The Cathedral of St. Fin Barre at Cork: William Burges in Ireland* (Dublin: Four Courts Press, 2006), pp. 37–41. See also Maurice Craig, *The Architecture of Ireland from the Earliest Times to 1880* (London: B. T. Batsford, 1982), p. 315.

181 *Eccl.*, vol. 18 (Feb. 1860), p. 20; Beresford Hope, *The English Cathedral*, p. 79.

182 *Eccl.*, vol. 15 (Aug. 1857), p. 254.

183 Ibid., p. 255.

184 Charles A. Webster quoted in Lawrence and Wilson, *The Cathedral of St. Fin Barre*, p. 29. For a concise account of this building, see J. Mordaunt Crook, *William Burges and the High Victorian Dream* (London: John Murray, 1981), pp. 195–208.

185 R. S. Gregg, *'Faithful unto death': Memorials of the Life of John Gregg D.D., Bishop of Cork, Cloyne, and Ross* (Dublin: George Herbert, 1879), p. 249.

186 Lawrence and Wilson, *The Cathedral of St. Fin Barre*, pp. 31, 38.

187 Ibid., p. 28.

188 Crook, *William Burges*, p. 196.

189 *Building News* (17 July 1863), p. 550.

190 Crook, *William Burges*, p. 199.

191 *Belfast News Letter* (16 Jan. 1865).

192 *Eccl.*, vol. 21 (Aug. 1863), p. 214.

193 Eastlake, *A History of the Gothic Revival*, p. 354.

194 This attempt was ultimately unsuccessful. See Lawrence and Wilson, *The Cathedral of St. Fin Barre*, pp. 77–90.

195 Crook, *William Burges*, pp. 196–7.

196 Ibid., p. 199; *Eccl.*, vol. 21 (Aug. 1863), p. 214.

Conclusion

1 For further analysis of this, see Howard Le Couteur, 'Using the "Old Boys" Network: Bishop Tufnell's Search for Men and Money', paper delivered at the Australian Historical Association conference, Hobart (1998).

2 *Eccl.*, vol. 4 (Jan. 1847), p. 16.

BIBLIOGRAPHIC ESSAY

Rethinking British Architecture

TOWARDS AN EXPANDED METHODOLOGY

One of the aims of this book, as mentioned in the Preface, is to reconsider some of the terminology and scholarly assumptions surrounding the study of architecture in Britain's former territorial empire. An abiding factor in this undertaking has been the problem of geography, which is nothing less than global in scope. To achieve this aim, methods new to the study of architecture were necessarily required in order to bring together factors pertaining to the rise of global Anglicanism and its architectural manifestations worldwide that might otherwise have been considered disparate or even unrelated historical phenomena. In this respect, much has been drawn from recent approaches to the study of empire in the cognate disciplines of New British history, as well as regional, World and Global historiographies.

In conjunction with the Preface, this bibliographic essay is intended to sketch out something of the rationale underpinning this study, discussing at length the sources drawn upon and the relevance of these to a new and extended understanding of 'British' architecture in the mid-nineteenth century.

Scholarly Precedent: Taking a Lesson from History

Perhaps a good place to begin such a discussion is with past scholarship in the history of architecture. One of the earliest works of scholarship to attempt an expansive history of the kind pursued here was on the art and architecture of early modern Spain and Portugal. First published as part of the Pelican History of Art series in 1959, *Art and Architecture in Spain and Portugal and their American Dominions, 1500 to 1800* by George Kubler and Martin Soria was a colossal and visionary work that charted the development of architecture, painting and sculpture in Spain, Portugal and their colonial empires in the Caribbean and Central and South America. As impressive in its scope as this history was (no less than ten years in the making), it fell short of what the authors had originally envisioned. They had hoped the study would go so far as to 'treat the art and architecture of the Iberian Empires from the Renaissance to the Napoleonic Wars', including 'Asia, Oceania, Africa and the rest of Europe'.[1] Although overly ambitious, the fundamental premise of Kubler and Soria's study is worth pondering, for it was a work of scholarship that saw (as a matter of course) the development of Spanish and Portuguese art and architecture as not merely an Iberian phenomenon but one that encompassed the entire known world. In other words, they considered buildings such as Jaén Cathedral in Spain and the Catedral Metropolitana in Mexico City, São Pedro dos Clérigos in Oporto and N. S. da Glória do Outeiro in Rio de Janeiro as part of the same genealogy of forms – of Spanish and Portuguese architecture, and of 'Iberian' architecture more generally.

Kubler and Soria's study should not be mistaken for 'grand narrative', however. Rather, it is concerned with their interest in the geography of art and its inherent complexities.[2] They appreciated not only the variations in style and materials that accompanied the spread of European forms into the New World, but also, and more importantly, the social, administrative and spiritual continuities that tied these forms to a wider network of culturally specific influences and ideas. It is clear from looking at their study that they conceived of this network as constituting a complete body – a kind of web of artistic production that stretched across land and sea – connecting the empire as a whole.[3] In this respect, it may be suggested that Kubler and Soria's book achieved for the study of Iberian architecture precisely what Basil Clarke's *Anglican Cathedrals Outside the British Isles* had failed to do for British architecture (see Preface, p. xi).

In looking back at Kubler and Soria's study in this way we must also accept it for what it is. It was published in 1959 and therefore has certain limitations as far as problems in contemporary scholarship are concerned. Nevertheless, this should not detract from its fundamental premise – that is, its scope and what it was essentially trying to achieve methodologically. These are still entirely valid.

Needless to say, there is no equivalent of Kubler and Soria's book in the study of British architecture. Although a product of its time, Sir John Summerson's 1953 classic *Architecture in Britain, 1530–1830* could only manage a sixteen-page appendix on 'English Architecture in America.'[4] Along with Scottish architecture, such a subject was clearly at the margins, both literally and figuratively.[5] To find anything like the geographical breadth of Kubler and Soria's book one must turn to studies dealing with the pre-modern world, a time that witnessed the first *imperium* on British soil since antiquity, that of the Normans.

The nineteenth-century French architect and antiquary Victor Ruprich-Robert (1820–1887), for example, sought to show that the architecture of a militaristic, colonising people such as the Normans, who conquered lands in Britain, northern France and Italy, could (and perhaps should) be viewed as a single artistic tradition.[6] Although there is no room here to discuss the Norman empire and its architecture in detail, the analogy between the development of ecclesiastical architecture throughout the Norman kingdoms during the eleventh and twelfth centuries and that of the Anglican church in the British empire during the mid-nineteenth century is striking. Although modern scholars did not follow Ruprich-Robert's lead, a number of monographs on nineteenth-century British architects have since appeared in which some discussion of their buildings abroad has been included.[7] Even in these rare examples, however, colonial works are treated as largely incidental and are mentioned only in passing.

More promising has been the work undertaken on Britain's most celebrated architects of empire, Edwin Lutyens and Herbert Baker. The scholarship of Robert Irving, in particular, has presented the work of these architects in its proper imperial context, highlighting the very real and significant political agenda embodied in buildings such as Lutyens's Viceroy's House in New Delhi.[8] Equally encouraging has been the research into certain British architects who migrated to the colonies during the nineteenth century. This work has done much to call attention to the strong architectural and ideological ties between Britain and its colonial empire with respect to 'ecclesiology' and the Gothic Revival.[9] Included here is Phoebe Stanton's *The Gothic Revival & American Church Architecture* (1968), which is somewhat similar to Kubler and Soria's enterprise. Although her book is primarily a study of church building in the United States, Stanton couches her subject within the wider geographical context of Anglican ecclesiology during the mid-nineteenth century, and includes a chapter on the British colony of New Brunswick.[10]

But perhaps the most significant contribution to a wider and more inclusive understanding of British architecture in recent years has come from the study of 'colonial cultures' and their engagement with architecture and urbanism as instruments of change. This type of scholarship is different in scope and intent from more orthodox studies of the history of architecture, and has emerged in response to the rise of post-colonial theory and especially the work of the Marxist historian Anthony D. King and the literary critic Edward Said.[11] Although studies of this kind have been better at conceptualising the colonial encounter and therefore presenting architecture as a form of cultural practice – imbued with all the prejudices and preconceptions of the societies that produced it – they too have been reluctant to assert the interconnectedness of British domestic and colonial architecture as a methodological imperative.

Anthony King's *The Bungalow: The Production of a Global Culture* (1984) is perhaps the only study that has taken seriously the global nature and implications of an essentially British architectural form.[12] His book is singular in its outlook and methodology, effectively tracing the origins and proliferation of this unique form from seventeenth-century British India to other parts of the modern world, including Britain. In so doing, it highlights the largely inseparable trajectories of empire, architecture and what King has called 'cultural globalisation.'[13]

Among the numerous outcomes of adopting this enlarged perspective (and the deep-seated relationships between architecture and imperial culture it reveals) has been a shift of focus back to the metropolis (that is, Britain). For a long while the metropolis, especially its capital city, London, was conspicuous for its absence in the study of British imperial and colonial architecture. In recent years, however, architectural historians, urban geographers and landscape historians have begun re-examining the buildings and landscapes of Britain in new and diverse ways, uncovering the various political, cultural and economic agendas that lay behind building campaigns in London and the country estates of the British aristocracy.[14]

Others have moved in the opposite direction, away from the metropolis to the emerging communities of the colonial and post-colonial world. With the increasing emphasis placed on the study of material culture (and the 'deep readings' of site-specific objects), this move has seen a desire among some scholars to eschew wider connections and to argue for 'exceptionalism' with respect to colonial architecture. This is particularly evident in scholarship on the history of architecture in colonial North America, and is exemplified by the work of historians and archaeologists such as Dell Upton and James Deetz.[15]

However, as good as these studies have been at identifying particular ethnic and regional traits, and at probing the boundaries between national and international forms, their approach tends towards what Michael Warner and Jack P. Greene have described as a preoccupation with 'localism' at the expense of wider, transatlantic contexts of empire, identity and trade.[16] Despite their insistence on difference, these studies are necessarily based on the implicit acknowledgement that even vernacular forms have developed from, and are derivative of, customs and practices brought from elsewhere, however remote their echoes may appear to us today. Contemporary trends in imperial scholarship now demand that we keep these broader connections constantly in view.

Reframing the Subject: Influences and Historiography

The particular approach developed in this book concerning the nature and extents of Anglican ecclesiology has been informed by three major considerations: the contemporary context; the relationship between Britain and its empire during the mid-nineteenth century; and recent advancements in British imperial and domestic historiography. Although it is worth commenting on these considerations individually, it is not my intention here to sketch out a complete intellectual genealogy. Instead, I wish simply to discuss each briefly, highlighting those aspects that have been important in shaping the evolution of the present study.

The first of these considerations, evident throughout the course of this book, concerns the observation that many of the architects and clergymen (and their sponsors) associated with the Anglican cause worldwide were closely related, either through family ties, social and political connections, educational background or professional networks.[17] Moreover, nearly all were interested to some degree or other in architecture and the role it played in the growth and consolidation of Anglican discipline and spirituality. Periodicals such as *The Ecclesiologist* and the *Colonial Church Chronicle*, both of which enjoyed a worldwide reputation and distribution, sustained these ties, keeping colonial clergymen not only in touch with 'home' but also informed of the activities of their colleagues abroad.[18] These considerations alone were enough to make me rethink the historiographic divide between colony and metropole with respect to architecture, and are loosely based on a prosopographic conception of 'Anglican lives' within Britain's empire. As my research progressed, it became clear that the organization and maintenance of these connections revealed Britain and its empire to be a continuous field of Anglican activity and agency.[19] Indeed, agency and networking have become major themes in the study of empire in recent years. Clergymen were of course as reliant as anyone else on these factors in extending their influence.[20]

The second consideration, which follows naturally from the first, concerns the way in which the bond between Britain and its colonies was perceived during the mid-nineteenth century. Although there was considerable debate at the time as to the fiscal and administrative relationship that Britain ought to maintain with its colonial empire, there was little doubt that the colonies were perceived to be, as William Huskisson observed, 'kindred in blood, in habits, and in feeling', especially the so-called 'settler' dominions.[21] It is hardly surprising, therefore, to find a high church grandee like A. J. B. Beresford Hope (1820–1887) drawing extensively on examples from Britain's colonies in his book *The English Cathedral of the Nineteenth Century* (1861). After all, Hope believed, the colonies were 'that great England beyond the seas'.[22]

This perception, although somewhat naïve, was an increasingly common (if unevenly distributed) one during the nineteenth century, representing the social and cultural ties that were seen to connect the 'mother country' to its colonial 'offspring'. The British and other European emigrants who ventured out to all parts of Britain's empire, forging new societies in their wake, were often described, according to this familial metaphor, as 'sons', 'daughters', 'children' or, as the clergy preferred, 'brethren'. For the most part the sentiment was reciprocal. As the travel accounts of Englishmen such as Charles Dilke and Anthony Trollope reveal, most colonists were happy to identify themselves as 'Britons' in some form or other, and to view the British Isles as 'home'.[23] In this sense, the object of colonisation was, as J. A. Robuck succinctly put it, 'the creation of so many happy Englands'.[24] In fact, some settlements, such as Canterbury in New Zealand and, to a lesser extent, Adelaide in South Australia, were precisely this: concerted experiments in the creation of more congenial forms of English society abroad, architecture included.[25]

Not everyone of course was an enthusiast of empire or an 'imperialist'. Empire had its critics. Moreover, the majority of people living in Britain at the time had neither the knowledge nor the experience to make sense of their nation's involvement in empire, or to understand how it affected their lives.[26] But the establishment and maintenance of the British empire was never a populist enterprise. It was something presided over by the élite and educated classes whose confidence in Britain's social, legal and political institutions, and their self-evident reproducibility, compelled them to adopt these whenever and wherever they could. It was this trust in the apparent universal validity of English culture that is often referred to as Britain's imperial 'mission', and it applied to all parts of the empire, including India. Even after the horrors of the great Sepoy Revolt (Indian Mutiny) of 1857, the British government knew that it could not simply walk out on India and its people. It felt morally obliged to continue its self-appointed course of 'civilisation'.[27] This sense of unabashed obligation accorded precisely with the Church of England's renewed concern for the propagation of the Anglican faith abroad, as both a national and institutional responsibility.

But the connections between Britain and its empire ran deeper still. The economic ties that linked the two were seen to engender a 'special relationship' of their own. We get some sense of what this relationship might have meant to the mid-Victorian generation in the view expressed by John Stuart Mill in his *Principles of Political Economy* (1848). In Book III Mill writes:

> [Britain's colonies] are hardly to be looked upon as countries, carrying on an exchange of commodities with other countries, but more properly as outlying agricultural or manufacturing establishments belonging to a larger community. Our West Indian colonies, for example, cannot be regarded as countries, with a productive capital of their own. If Manchester, instead of being where it is, were on a rock in the North Sea (its present industry nevertheless continuing), it would still be but a town of England, not a country trading with England; it would be merely, as now, a place where England finds it convenient to carry on her cotton manufacture. The West Indies, in like manner, are the place where England finds it convenient to carry on the production of sugar, coffee, and a few other tropical commodities.[28]

In this view Britain's colonies were not, as Mill explains, considered to be independent countries but, again, part of a 'larger community', however variegated it may have been.[29] Although referring specifically to the economy of production, Mill's concept has implications for the way we might perceive the corporate nature of missionary Anglicanism and its architectural achievement worldwide.

As discussed throughout this book, by 1840 a great deal of anxiety had built up around the Church of England's responsibility vis-à-vis the spiritual needs of empire. Accordingly, it launched itself headlong into missionary activity abroad, not only for the sake of 'harvesting' souls (as important and essential as this was) but also for reasons of imperial security.[30] Indeed, with the assistance of a newly invigorated Society for the Propagation of the Gospel in Foreign Parts, and the establishment of the Colonial Bishoprics' Fund (1841), the Anglican Church went global. With these mechanisms in place, and its moral conscience somewhat mollified, the Church of England was able to proclaim with no small satisfaction that 'the sun now never sets upon the Kingdom of the Saviour'.[31]

This sense of duty that the mid-Victorians maintained towards empire necessarily transformed my perception of Anglican ecclesiology and its extension abroad. The need to plant 'correct' and worthy church buildings wherever the English Church went was no mere afterthought; rather, it was a faithful attempt at proffering a particular set of architectural forms and practices within a 'Greater Britain'. This is precisely what John Mason Neale and Benjamin Webb meant when they declared that the Ecclesiological Society bestrode 'the narrow world like a Colossus'.[32] To them, architecture, culture, religion and empire went hand in hand.

This leads me onto the third consideration that has influenced the thesis developed in this book, which is New British history.[33] This approach first emerged in a series of ground-breaking articles published between 1974 and 1982 by the New Zealand historian J. G. A. Pocock, in which he sought to redefine what was meant by the term 'British history'. His initial observations had led to the conclusion that there was nothing that could properly be described as 'British history', and that what generally passed for the history of Britain, or the British Isles, was in fact the history of England.[34] In his opening salvo, 'British History: A Plea for a New Subject', published in the *New Zealand Journal of History* in 1974, Pocock noted of this problem that 'when one considers what "Britain" means – that it is the name of a realm inhabited by two, and more than two, nations, whose history has been expansive to the extent of planting settlements and founding derivative cultures beyond the Four Seas – it is evident that the history of this complex expression has never been seriously attempted.'[35] In short, Pocock's principal contention was that British history, in its most plural and comprehensive sense, was an 'unknown' subject.

Clearly, from where Pocock was standing, British history was not only something different from the history of England but also something far more expansive, both geographically and historiographically. This included not only English political and cultural expansion and domination within the British Isles – what Pocock refers to as 'the Anglo-Norman transformation of the Atlantic Archipelago' – but also expansion beyond this into North America, India and Australasia. This was essentially Pocock's challenge to the modern historian: that one can 'conceive of "British history" no longer as being an archipelagic or even an Atlantic-American phenomenon, but as having occurred on a planetary scale'.[36]

At first Pocock's thesis proved controversial.[37] He was asking historians who had hitherto taken a very insular and Eurocentric view of English history to re-evaluate their position fundamentally, and to consider both the intra- *and* extra-archipelagic events that shaped the modern nation state as being part of the same historical record.[38] Although it might be argued that Pocock's historiographical agenda was accompanied by no small amount of post-imperial anxiety, his conclusions were such that they could only have been reached (indeed, appreciated) by a scholar looking from the outside in, especially from the margins of Britain's former colonial empire. Nevertheless, his 'plea', as it were, certainly reminds one of J. R. Seeley's observation of a hundred years earlier – that empire was 'the great fact of modern English history' – and was the first trenchant articulation since Seeley's time of the now largely accepted thesis that neither the domestic nor the imperial histories of Britain can be fully appreciated in isolation.[39]

Pocock's ideas have since found resonance in much scholarship on British domestic and imperial history, and the 'enlarged' perspective that his work represents has flourished more generally.[40] Scholars such as David Armitage, C. A. Bayly, Duncan Bell, Linda Colley, Richard Drayton, Catherine Hall, David Hancock and Andrew Thompson, to name but a few, have sought to highlight the intimately entwined and therefore largely inseparable conditions of British domestic and imperial history.[41] As architecture is one of the most immediate and conspicuous forms of cultural production, it would seem that this approach and the insights it offers have much to recommend them to the study of architecture broadly conceived, and might just as easily apply to 'British architecture' as they do to 'British history'.[42]

Unfortunately, the discipline of architectural history has been much slower in taking up this challenge. Very few scholars of architecture, apart from those already mentioned, have been either willing or able to place regional and national histories in a genuine dialogue with the spread and development of architectural forms worldwide, particularly with respect to European imperialism. Although much work has been done on the various ways in which British architecture has been influenced by ideas from abroad, this is not the same as proposing or insisting upon a historiographically integrated approach. Extensive bodies of literature have been built up around the study of British domestic and colonial architectures respectively, but, as mentioned, there has been no serious attempt as yet to make a methodological connection between the two. However, as I have tried to argue here, there is no reason why the histories of British domestic and colonial architecture should be treated separately; or why the subject cannot be seen as a 'unitary field of analysis', to borrow a phrase from Bernard Cohn, especially when it comes to the extension of an institution such as the Church of England.[43] To return finally to the insight of Pocock: if colonial history is British history in the sense that nearly all its determinants are the product of British expansion, then cannot the same be said for colonial architecture? This has been the underlying concern of the present book.

1 George Kubler and Martin Soria, *Art and Architecture in Spain and Portugal and Their American Dominions, 1500 to 1800*, Pelican History of Art (Harmonsdworth: Penguin Books, 1959), p. xxv.

2 For an analysis of Kubler's approach to the geography of art, see: Thomas DaCosta Kaufmann, *Toward a Geography of Art* (Chicago: University of Chicago Press, 2004), pp. 219–38.

3 A recent study that takes a similarly inclusive approach is Maria Georgopoulou's, *Venice's Mediterranean Colonies: Architecture and Urbanism* (Cambridge: Cambridge UP, 2001). Although the subject matter of this book is largely 'peripheral' as opposed to metropolitan, it does make an argument for formal and ideological continuity between the architecture of Venice and its colonies.

4 See: 'Appendix II: English Architecture in America', in John Summerson, *Architecture in Britain, 1530–1830* (1953), 8th edn (Harmondsworth: Penguin Books, 1991), pp. 512–27.

5 As Marlene Heck has recently observed, Summerson's treatment of the subject tended towards the conclusion that British colonial architecture in America was really nothing more than an inferior copy or sub-species of respectable architecture in Britain, with little or no vitality of its own. See: M. E. Heck, 'Mind the Gap: Rewriting Sir John Summerson's American Architectural History', in Frank Salmon (ed.), *Summerson and Hitchcock: Centenary Essays on Architectural Historiography* (New Haven and London: Yale UP, 2006), pp. 117–32.

6 Victor Ruprich-Robert, *L'architecture normande aux XIe et XIIe siècles en Normandie et en Angleterre* (Paris: Librairie des Imprimeries Réunies, 1884–9). For a long while now historians have viewed the Norman empire as a culturally and geographically continuous phenomenon. See: John le Patourel, *The Norman Empire* (Oxford: Clarendon Press, 1976). More recent scholarship, however, has sought to complicate this view but still acknowledges the large degree of continuity. See: David Bates, 'Normandy and England after 1066', *English Historical Review*, vol. 104 (1989), pp. 851–80; Brian Golding, *Conquest and Colonisation: The Normans in Britain, 1066–1100* (Basingstoke: Palgrave Macmillan, 2001). Although modern scholars of Norman architecture have been reluctant to cast as wide a net as Ruprich-Robert, the stylistic associations between Norman architecture in Britain and northern France are still part of modern historiography. See: Eric Fernie, *The Architecture of Norman England* (Oxford: Oxford UP, 2000).

7 For example: Paul Thompson, *William Butterfield: Victorian Architect* (Cambridge, Mass.: MIT Press, 1971); Anthony Quiney, *John Loughborough Pearson* (New Haven and London: Yale UP, 1979); and Gill Hunter, *William White: Pioneer Victorian Architect* (Reading: Spire Books, 2010).

8 R. G. Irving, *Indian Summer: Lutyens, Baker and Imperial Delhi* (New Haven and London: Yale UP, 1981); R. G. Irving, 'Architecture for Empire's Sake: Lutyens's Palace for Delhi', *Perspecta*, vol. 18 (1982), pp. 7–23; R. G. Irving, 'Bombay and Imperial Delhi: Cities as Symbols', in Andrew Hopkins and Gavin Stamp (eds), *Lutyens Abroad: The Work of Sir Edwin Lutyens Outside the British Isles* (London: British School at Rome, 2002), pp. 169–80. See also Jane Ridley, 'Edwin Lutyens, New Delhi, and the Architecture of Imperialism', *Journal of Imperial and Commonwealth History*, vol. 26:2 (1998), pp. 67–83.

9 Margaret H. Alington, *Frederick Thatcher and St. Paul's: An Ecclesiological Study* (Wellington: New Zealand Historic Places Trust, 1965); Joan Kerr, *Our Great Victorian Architect: Edmund Thomas Blacket (1817–1883)* (Sydney: National Trust of Australia, 1983); Ian Lochhead, *A Dream of Spires: Benja-*

min Mountfort and the Gothic Revival (Christchurch: Canterbury UP, 1999). For recent scholarship on British architects who were involved in designing buildings for the colonies but did not emigrate, see: Brian Andrews, *Creating a Gothic Paradise: Pugin at the Antipodes* (Hobart: Tasmanian Museum and Art Gallery, 2002); and J. N. Mané, 'Gilbert Scott's Colonial Churches', in Margaret Belcher and Helen Debenham (eds), *Australasian Victorian Studies Association: Conference Papers 1987* (Christchurch: University of Canterbury for the AVSA), pp. 31–42.

10 Phoebe B. Stanton, *The Gothic Revival & American Church Architecture: An Episode in Taste, 1840–1856* (Baltimore: Johns Hopkins UP, 1968). Here too may be mentioned George L. Hersey, *High Victorian Gothic: A Study in Associationism* (Baltimore: Johns Hopkins UP, 1972). In addition to these may be counted a handful of books that have appeared over the past two decades on certain architectural styles and movements from Palladianism to the Gothic Revival. Although much more general in their treatment, these books have made some attempt to consider the wider geographical and cultural reverberations of these styles and movements within the British colonial world. For instance, see: Chris Brooks, *The Gothic Revival* (London: Phaidon, 1999); M. J. Lewis, *The Gothic Revival* (London: Thames and Hudson, 2002); Robert Tavernor, *Palladio and Palladianism* (London: Thames and Hudson, 1991); and Dell Upton, *Architecture in the United States* (Oxford: Oxford UP, 1998).

11 There are too many such studies to mention them all, but some of the initial and most noteworthy include: A. D. King, *Colonial Urban Development: Culture, Social Power and Environment* (London: Routledge, 1976); T. R. Metcalf, *An Imperial Vision: Indian Architecture and Britain's Raj* (London: Faber and Faber, 1989); the essays in Nezar AlSayyad (ed.), *Forms of Dominance: On the Architecture and Urbanism of the Colonial Enterprise* (Aldershot: Avebury, 1992); and Mark Crinson, *Empire Building: Orientalism and Victorian Architecture* (London: Routledge, 1996). For Said, see E. W. Said, *Orientalism: Western Conceptions of the Orient* (London: Routledge and Kegan Paul, 1978), and E. W. Said, *Culture and Imperialism* (London: Chatto and Windus, 1993).

12 An excellent recent addition to this approach, although on a reduced geographic scale (taking an 'Atlantic' rather than a global perspective) is Louis P. Nelson's *The Beauty of Holiness: Anglicanism and Architecture in Colonial South Carolina* (Chapel Hill: University of North Carolina Press, 2008). In many respects Nelson's book presents a precursor to this study regarding the spread of Anglican culture and its architecture throughout Britain's colonial empire. B. L. Herman and Daniel Maudlin's edited volume entitled *Building the British Atlantic World 1600–1850* (forthcoming, University of North Carolina Press) will also add to this broader perspective.

13 See also King's recent comments on this form in: A. D. King, 'Imperialism, Colonialism and Architects of the Arts and Crafts in Britain', Chapter 10 in A. D. King, *Spaces of Global Cultures: Architecture, Urbanism, Identity* (London: Routledge, 2004), pp. 161–86.

14 For London, see Felix Driver and David Gilbert, 'Heart of Empire? Landscape, Space and Performance in Imperial London', *Environment and Planning D: Society and Space*, vol. 16 (1998), pp. 1–17; Federico Freschi, 'The Fine Art of Fusion: Race, Gender and the Politics of South Africanism as Reflected in the Decorative Programme of South Africa House, London (1933)', *De Arte*, no. 71 (April 2005), pp. 14–34; G. A. Bremner, 'Nation and Empire in the Government Architecture of Victorian London: The Foreign and India Office Reconsidered', *Historical Journal*, vol. 48:3 (2005), pp. 703–42; G. A. Bremner, '"Some Imperial Institute": Architecture, Symbolism, and the Ideal of Empire in Late Victorian Britain, 1887–93', *JSAH*, vol. 62:1 (2003), pp. 50–73. For country estates, see James Walvin, 'The Colonial Origins of English Wealth', *Journal of Caribbean History*, vol. 39:1 (2005), pp. 38–53; Patrick Eyres, 'Neoclassicism on Active Service: Commemoration of the Seven Years' War in the English Landscape Garden', *New Arcadian Journal*, no. 35–36 (1993), pp. 62–122. For other accounts on the various relationships between architecture and imperialism in capital cities, see M. H. Port, *Imperial London: Civil Government Building in London, 1851–1915* (New Haven and London: Yale UP, 1995); Jonathan Schneer, *London 1900: The Imperial Metropolis* (New Haven and London: Yale UP, 1999); and the essays in Felix Driver and David Gilbert (eds), *Imperial Cities: Landscape, Display and Identity* (Manchester: Manchester UP, 1999).

15 For example, see the introduction to Dell Upton (ed.), *America's Architectural Roots: Ethnic Groups that Built America* (New York: Preservation Press, 1998), pp. 7–15.

16 M. Warner, 'What is Colonial about Colonial America?', in R. Blair St. George (ed.), *Possible Pasts: Becoming Colonial in Early America* (Ithaca: Cornell UP, 2000), p. 50; J. P. Greene, 'Colonial History and National History: Reflections on a Continuing Problem', *The William and Mary Quarterly*, vol. 64:2 (2007), pp. 235–50. For a broader critique of the exceptionalist thesis in North American historiography, see Joyce E. Chaplin, 'Expansion and Exceptionalism in Early American History', *Journal of American History*, vol. 89:4 (2003), pp. 1431–55.

17 For example: Howard Le Couteur, 'Using the "Old Boys" Network: Bishop Tufnell's Search for Men and Money',

paper delivered at the Australian Historical Association conference, Hobart (1998); Austin Cooper, 'Forgotten Australian Anglican: Edward Coleridge', *Pacifica*, vol. 3 (1990), pp. 257–67; Susan Walton, 'Edward Coleridge and the Eton Connection', in Susan Walton, *Imagining Soldiers and Fathers in the Mid-Victorian Era: Charlotte Yonge's Models of Manliness* (Farnham: Ashgate, 2010), pp. 147–53. The connections between Selwyn and many of his colleagues at Eton and Cambridge are also mentioned in Warren E. Limbrick, '"A most indefatigable man"', in Warren E. Limbrick (ed.), *Bishop Selwyn in New Zealand, 1841–68* (Palmerston North, NZ: Dunmore Press, 1983), pp. 13–15.

18 Pamela Welch, 'Constructing Colonial Christianities: With Particular Reference to Anglicanism in Australia, ca 1850–1940', *Journal of Religious History*, vol. 32:2 (2008), p. 249.

19 Under the general compulsion of Anglican renewal, the Church of England was not only reaching out to the farthest parts of the British empire but was also organising 'home missions' and 'church extension' in Britain, especially in Cornwall and Devon, Wales and certain parts of London. Like the colonies, parts of east London were at times described in contemporary accounts as 'terra incognita' and 'this new country'. See C. F. Lowder, *Ten Years in St George's Mission* (London, 1867), p. 5. See also *Church Builder* (1862–1916). For a detailed account of this phenomenon in the last quarter of the nineteenth century, see Felix Driver, *Geography Militant: Cultures of Exploration and Empire* (Oxford: Blackwell, 2001), pp. 170–98.

20 For example, on networking and empire see David Hancock, *Citizens of the World: London Merchants and the Integration of the British Atlantic Community, 1735–1785* (Cambridge: Cambridge UP, 1995); Alison Games, *The Web of Empire: English Cosmopolitans in an Age of Expansion* (Oxford: Oxford UP, 2008); John Darwin, *The Empire Project: The Rise and Fall of the British World-System, 1830–1970* (Cambridge: Cambridge UP, 2009); Gary B. Magee and Andrew S. Thompson, *Empire and Globalisation: Networks of People, Goods and Capital in the British World, c.1850–1914* (Cambridge: Cambridge UP, 2010); and Emma Rothschild, *The Inner Life of Empires: An Eighteenth-Century History* (Princeton: Princeton UP, 2010). This point has also been made by J. H. Elliott in 'How They Made the Empire', *New York Review of Books*, vol. 58:13 (2011), p. 22.

21 Huskisson quoted in A. G. L. Shaw, 'British Attitudes to the Colonies, *ca.* 1820–1850', *Journal of British Studies*, vol. 9:1 (1969), p. 83. This was observed by Huskisson as early as 1828. For accounts of these debates, attitudes to imperial expansion, and the significance of imperial sentiment in mid-Victorian Britain, see: Ged Martin, '"Anti-Imperialism" in the Mid-Nineteenth Century and the Nature of the British Empire, 1820–70', in Ronald Hyam and Ged Martin, *Reappraisals in British Imperial History* (London: Macmillan, 1975), pp. 88–120; A. P. Thornton, *The Imperial Idea and Its Enemies* (London: Macmillan, 1959); C. C. Eldridge, *England's Mission: The Imperial Idea in the Age of Gladstone & Disraeli, 1868–1880* (Chapel Hill: University of North Carolina Press, 1973); J. S. Galbraith, 'Myths of the "Little England" Era' (1961), in A. G. L. Shaw (ed.), *Great Britain and the Colonies, 1815–1865* (London: Methuen, 1970), pp. 27–45; John Gallagher and Ronald E. Robinson, 'The Imperialism of Free Trade', *Economic History Review*, vol. 6:1 (1953), pp. 1–15; and more recently, John Darwin, 'Imperialism and the Victorians: The Dynamics of Territorial Expansion', *English Historical Review*, vol. 112 (1997), pp. 614–42.

22 A. J. B. Beresford Hope, *The English Cathedral of the Nineteenth Century* (London: John Murray, 1861), p. 19.

23 For instance, see what Trollope had to say about colonists in New Zealand (and elsewhere) regarding their sense of 'Englishness' in *Australia and New Zealand* (Melbourne: George Robertson, 1874), pp. 631–2. See also: C. W. Dilke, *Greater Britain: A Record of Travel in English-Speaking Countries during 1866 and 1867* (London: Macmillan, 1868).

24 Robuck quoted by W. E. Gladstone in 'An Address delivered to the Members of the Mechanics' Institute, at Chester, November 12, 1855', repr. in Paul Knaplund, *Gladstone and Britain's Imperial Policy* (London: Routledge, 1966), p. 202.

25 Edward Gibbon Wakefield, the father of 'systematic colonisation', was quick to point out that the Canterbury Settlement was made up of 'not merely a nice, but a choice society of English people'. Wakefield quoted in Keith Sinclair, *A History of New Zealand* (Harmondsworth: Penguin Books, 1976), p. 92. Both Canterbury and Adelaide were based on Wakefield's principles of systematic colonisation. The Canterbury Settlement, in particular, was envisioned as a Church of England colony. See L. C. Webb, 'The Canterbury Association and Its Settlement', in James Hight and C. R. Straubel (eds) *A History of Canterbury*, vol. 1 (Christchurch: Whitcome and Tombs, 1957), pp. 135–233. See also Marie Peters, 'Homeland and Colony', in Colin Brown, Marie Peters, and Jane Teal (eds), *Shaping a Colonial Church: Bishop Harper and the Anglican Diocese of Christchurch, 1856–1890* (Christchurch: Canterbury UP, 2006), pp. 19–34.

26 Although somewhat overstated, Bernard Porter's point that a large proportion of Britain's population was essentially ignorant of empire and its implications is valid. See Bernard Porter, '"Empire, what empire?" Or, Why 80% of Early- and Mid-Victorians Were Deliberately Kept in Ignorance of It', *Victorian Studies*, vol. 46:2 (2004), pp. 256–63; Bernard Porter,

The Absent-Minded Imperialists: Empire, Society, and Culture in Britain (Oxford: Oxford UP, 2004).

27 On this point C. C. Eldridge has noted: 'To the mid-Victorian generation the empire entailed a duty, and for many the imperial idea was beginning to assume a sense of mission.' See Eldridge, *England's Mission*, p. 40.

28 J. S. Mill, *Principles of Political Economy*, new edn, ed. W. J. Ashley (London: Longmans, Green & Co., 1909), pp. 685–6.

29 The summation of this idea in the 'official mind' is captured eloquently in a passage from Herman Merivale's lectures on colonisation delivered at Oxford between 1839 and 1841: 'May we not conceive England as retaining the seat of the chief executive authority, the prescriptive reverence of her station, the superiority belonging to her vast accumulated wealth, and as the commercial metropolis of the world; and united, by these ties only, with a hundred nations, – not unconnected, like those which yielded to the spear of the Roman, but her own children, owing one faith and one language? May we not figure to ourselves, scattered thick as stars over the surface of this earth, communities of citizens owing the name of Britons, bound by allegiance to a British sovereign, and uniting heart and hand in maintaining the supremacy of Britain on every shore which her unconquered flag can reach?' See Herman Merivale, *Lectures on Colonization and Colonies*, new edn (London, 1861; repr. London: Oxford UP, 1928), p. 634. Dilke's concept of 'Greater Britain' is also applicable here. For an excellent recent account of this idea, see Duncan Bell, *The Idea of Greater Britain: Empire and the Future of World Order, 1860–1900* (Princeton: Princeton UP, 2007).

30 For instance, see Samuel Wilberforce's many sermons between 1840 and 1870 relating to the missionary activities and responsibilities of the Church of England in Henry Rowley (ed.), *Speeches on Missions by the Right Reverend Samuel Wilberforce, D.D.* (London: William Wells Gardner, 1874). See also *Documents Relative to the Erection and Endowment of Additional Bishoprics in the Colonies, 1841–1855* (London: SPCK, 1855); and J. C. Wynter, *Hints on Church Colonization* (London: J. W. Parker, 1850). For an excellent account of the politics surrounding Church of England expansion into the empire, see Rowan Strong, *Anglicanism and the British Empire, c.1700–1850* (Oxford: Oxford UP, 2007), pp. 198–221.

31 C. T. Longley (1794–1868), bishop of Ripon, quoted in Daniel O'Connor *et al.*, *Three Centuries of Mission: The United Society for the Propagation of the Gospel, 1701–2000* (London: Continuum, 2000), p. 47.

32 *Eccl.*, vol. 1 (Jan. 1845), p. 24. In 1851 they further observed: 'We are a "large party," and the world fear us.' See *Eccl.*, vol. 9:46 (Feb. 1851), p. 1.

33 I have also been influenced significantly in this approach by the expansive methodological perspectives developed over the past few years in so-called Atlantic history. For some definitions of this method of historical analysis and its resonances with this study, see David Armitage, 'Three Concepts of Atlantic History', in David Armitage and Michael J. Braddick (eds), *The British Atlantic World, 1500–1800* (Basingstoke: Palgrave Macmillan, 2002), pp. 11–27; and Alison Games, 'Atlantic History: Definitions, Challenges, and Opportunities', *American Historical Review*, vol. 111:3 (2006), pp. 741–57.

34 J. G. A. Pocock, *The Limits and Divisions of British History* (Studies in Public Policy, no. 31, University of Strathclyde, 1979), p. 7.

35 J. G. A. Pocock, 'British History: A Plea for a New Subject', *New Zealand Journal of History*, vol. 8:1 (1974), p. 5.

36 J. G. A. Pocock, 'The Limits and Divisions of British History: In Search of the Unknown Subject', *American Historical Review*, vol. 87:2 (1982), p. 319. Here Pocock also observes that: '"British history," both cultural and political, is discovered to have exceeded even the archipelagic and Atlantic dimension and to have established itself in a number of areas in the southern hemisphere. The history of these settler nations . . . makes a claim to be considered part of "British history" and to enlarge the meaning of that term.' For the same argument in a related context, see J. G. A. Pocock, 'The New British History in Atlantic Perspective: An Antipodean Commentary', *American Historical Review*, vol. 104:2 (1999), pp. 490–500.

37 See the criticisms of Pocock's initial thesis by A. J. P. Taylor, Gordon Donaldson and Michael Hechter, as well as his own reply to those criticisms, in the *Journal of Modern History*, vol. 47:4 (1975), pp. 601–21.

38 On this point Pocock notes that: 'Some fifteen years ago, there appeared among English scholars and publicists a strong tendency to assert that England – or Britain if they happened to use the word – had always formed part of Europe and the history of Europe; and this was plainly a myth – like all myths containing much incidental truth – designed to accompany the entry of the United Kingdom into the European Economic Community. The decision to seek this entry was as we know founded upon the proposition that Britain's independent role as an imperial power was now irretrievably lost. The accompanying myth – the insistence on the inherently European character of British history – conveyed the message that the history of that imperial role either had never happened, or had never counted and could now be forgotten.' See Pocock, 'The Limits and Divisions of British History', p. 2.

39 J. R. Seeley, *The Expansion of England* (London: Macmillan, 1883), p. 12. For further reflections on Pocock's thesis, see J. G. A. Pocock, *The Discovery of Islands: Essays in British History* (Cambridge: Cambridge UP, 2005). Although, as David Armitage has recently suggested, Seeley and Pocock were approaching the same problem from different perspectives, and at radically different moments in history, the conclusions they reached were essentially the same: that it is vital to integrate the history of the state and the empire if the history of Britain is to be properly understood. David Armitage, *The Ideological Origins of the British Empire* (Cambridge: Cambridge UP, 2000), pp. 20–1.

40 See note 3 in J. G. A. Pocock, 'The Field Enlarged: An Introduction', in Pocock, *The Discovery of Islands*, p. 48. This especially applies to histories of Britain such as 'Three Kingdoms' and 'Four Nations'. For example, see Hugh Kearney, *The British Isles: A History of Four Nations* (1989), 2nd edn (Cambridge: Cambridge UP, 2006).

41 On this point Hall has recently confessed that 'in order to understand the specificity of the [British] national formation, we have to look outside it', while Bayly has argued that 'all local, national, or regional histories must, in important ways, . . . be global histories. It is no longer really possible to write "European" or "American" history in a narrow sense.' See Catherine Hall, *Civilising Subjects: Metropole and Colony in the English Imagination 1830–1867* (Cambridge: Polity, 2002), p. 9; and C. A. Bayly, *The Birth of the Modern World, 1780–1914* (Oxford: Blackwell, 2004), p. 2. See also Richard Drayton, *Nature's Government: Science, Imperial Britain, and the 'Improvement' of the World* (New Haven and London, Yale UP, 2000), pp. xiii–xv.

42 In fact, as Bayly has noted, a global perspective on modern history must also include the numerous forms of cultural practice and production, including architecture. See: Bayly, *The Birth of the Modern World*, pp. 1, 384–5.

43 Bernard S. Cohn, *Colonialism and Its Forms of Knowledge: The British in India* (Princeton: Princeton UP, 1996), p. 4.

BIBLIOGRAPHY

Newspapers, Periodicals, Magazines and Occasional Papers

Adelaide Times
Anglo-American Magazine
Architect and Contract Reporter
Bombay Quarterly Review
British Critic
Builder
Building News
Cape Monitor
Christian Remembrancer
Church Builder
Church Chronicle for the Diocese of Montreal
Church Journal (New York)
Church News (Tasmania)
Church of England Record for Victoria
Church Times
Colonial Church Chronicle (London)
Delhi Mission News
English Churchman
Exeter Architectural Review
Gazetteer of Bombay City and Island
Geelong Advertiser (Victoria, Australia)
Hobart Town Courier
Illustrated London News
Lyttelton Times (New Zealand)
Melbourne Church of England Messenger
Mission Life (London)
Monthly Record (SPG)
Montreal Gazette
Montreal Weekly Herald
New Westminster Times (British Columbia, Canada)
New Zealand Church Almanac
North-China Herald and Market Report
Occasional Papers from St. Augustine's College
Quarterly Paper of the SPG
RIBA Journal
The Rules and Proceedings of the Oxford Society for Promoting the Study of Gothic Architecture
St. Augustine's College Tracts
Saturday Review (London)
South African Church Magazine and Ecclesiastical Review
South Australian Register
Sydney Morning Herald
The Ecclesiologist
The Times
The Press (Christchurch, New Zealand)
The Standard (London)
Transactions of Exeter Diocesan Architectural Society
Western Luminary (Exeter)

Archival Sources

Archival material for this study, including original correspondence, vestry minute books, clergymen's diaries, unpublished diocesan records, architects' sketch books, rare ephemera, architectural plans and drawings, historic photographs and other manuscript material, was sourced from the following repositories. Specific references to each can be found in the notes to the main text.

Alexander Turnbull Library, National Library of New Zealand, Wellington, New Zealand
Anglican Diocesan Archive, Adelaide, Australia
Anglican Diocesan Archive, Kolkata, India
Anglican Diocesan Archive, Melbourne, Australia
Anglican Diocesan Archive, Montreal, Canada
Anglican Diocesan Archive, Newcastle, Australia
Anglican Diocesan Archive, Sydney, Australia
Anglican Diocesan Archive, Victoria, British Columbia, Canada
Anglican Diocesan Archives of Eastern Newfoundland and Labrador, St John's, Newfoundland, Canada
Archive of the United Society for the Propagation of the Gospel (formerly the Society for the Propagation of the Gospel in Foreign Parts), Bodleian Library of Commonwealth and African Studies, Oxford
Archives of Ontario, Toronto, Canada
Auckland War Memorial Museum Library, Auckland, New Zealand
Bishop's College Archive, Cape Town, South Africa
Bishop's College Library and Archive, Kolkata, India
Brotherhood of the Ascended Christ Library, Delhi, India
Canterbury Museum, Christchurch, New Zealand
Centre for Newfoundland Studies, Memorial University Libraries, St John's, Newfoundland, Canada
Christchurch Anglican Diocesan Archive, New Zealand
Cory Library, Rhodes University, Grahamstown, South Africa
Drawings and Archives Collections, Royal Institute of British Architects Library, Victoria and Albert Museum, London
Elphinstone College Library and Archive, Mumbai, India
Huntington Library, San Marino, California, USA
John Kinder Theological Library, St John's College, Auckland, New Zealand
Mitchell Library, State Library of New South Wales, Sydney, Australia
National Archives of Singapore, Singapore
Provincial Archives, University of New Brunswick, Fredericton, Canada
Queen's College Archive, Memorial University of Newfoundland, Canada
Rare Books and Manuscripts, Cambridge University Library
Rare Books and Special Collections, McGill University Library, Montreal, Canada
Rare Books and Special Collections, University of Cape Town Libraries, South Africa
Rare Books and Special Collections, University of Sydney Library, Australia
Royal Asiatic Society Library, Kolkata, India
Selwyn College Library Archive, Selwyn College, University of Cambridge
Special Collections, Hong Kong University Library, Hong Kong
State Library of South Australia, Adelaide, Australia
State Library of Victoria, Melbourne, Australia
Tasmanian Museum and Art Gallery, Hobart, Australia
Tasmanian State Library and Archives, Hobart, Australia
The Rooms Provincial Archives, St John's, Newfoundland, Canada
Trinity College Library, University of Melbourne, Australia
University of Newcastle Archive, Auchmuty Library, Newcastle, Australia
Western Manuscripts and Rare Books, Bodleian Library, Oxford
William Cullen Library, University of the Witwatersrand, Johannesburg, South Africa
Zanzibar National Archives, Stone Town, Zanzibar (Tanzania)

Unpublished Sources

Condon, H. H., 'Henry Bromby, Second Bishop of Tasmania', MA thesis (University of Tasmania, 1964)
Fenton, M. E., *Triad: The Anglican Churches* (unpublished manuscript, *c.*1970), State Library of South Australia, D5772(T)
Goedhals, M. M., 'Nathaniel James Merriman, Archdeacon and Bishop, 1849–1882: A Study in Church Life and Government', PhD thesis (Rhodes University, 1982)
Jones, F., 'Bishop Feild: A Study in Politics and Religion in Nineteenth-Century Newfoundland', PhD thesis (University of Cambridge, 1972)
Kent, V. G., 'The Right Reverend Hibbert Binney, Colonial Tractarian, Bishop of Nova Scotia, 1851–1887', MA thesis (King's College, Dalhousie University, 1966)
Kerr, E. J., 'Designing a Colonial Church: Church Building in New South Wales, 1788–1888', DPhil thesis (University of York, 1978)

King, S., 'Colony and Climate: Positioning Public Architecture in Queensland, 1859–1909', PhD thesis (University of Melbourne, 2010)

Leader, P. J., 'The Hon. Reverend William Grey, M.A.', MTh thesis (Queen's College, St John's, 1998)

Martin, D., 'The Churches of Bishop Robert Gray & Mrs Sophia Gray: An Historical and Architectural Overview', PhD thesis (University of Cape Town, 2002)

Meaney, N. K., 'The Church of England in South Australia (1836–1869)', BA thesis (University of Adelaide, 1954)

Moore, G. M., 'Antipodean Gothic', MA thesis (University of Melbourne, 1984)

Partridge, H., '"Boyish Effort" or Manly Masterpiece? An Early Work by G. F. Bodley in Guernsey – St. Stephen's Church, 1862–1865', MA thesis (University of Edinburgh, 2008)

Richardson, D., 'Christ Church Cathedral, Fredericton, New Brunswick', MA thesis (Yale University, 1966)

Scarfe, J., '"Bridge of Polished Steel as Fine as a Hair": The Oxford Movement in South Australia', Master's thesis (University of Adelaide, 1974)

Walden, H. R., 'New Zealand Anglican Church Architecture 1814–1963', Master's thesis (University of Auckland, 1964)

Printed Sources

Adams, J. E., *Dandies and Desert Saints: Styles of Victorian Masculinity* (Ithaca: Connell UP, 1995)

Addleshaw, G. W. O., and Etchells, F., *The Architectural Setting of Anglican Worship* (London: Faber and Faber, 1948)

A Few Words to Church Builders (Cambridge: Cambridge Camden Society, 1841)

Ahmad, A., *In Theory: Classes, Nations, Literatures* (London: Verso, 1994)

A Journal of a Visitation in the 'Hawk' Church Ship, on the Coast of Labrador, and Round the Whole Island of Newfoundland, in the Year 1849 (London: SPG, 1850)

A Journal of Visitation of the Lord Bishop of Australia in 1845 (London: SPG, 1846)

Albright, R. W., *A History of the Protestant Episcopal Church* (New York: Macmillan, 1964)

Alington, M. H., *Frederick Thatcher and St. Paul's: An Ecclesiological Study* (Wellington: New Zealand Historic Places Trust, 1965)

——, *Goodly Stones & Timbers: A History of St Mary's Church New Plymouth* (New Plymouth, NZ: St Mary's Church, 1988)

——, *An Excellent Recruit: Frederick Thatcher – Architect, Priest and Private Secretary in Early New Zealand* (Auckland: Polygraphia, 2007)

Allen, L. M., *A History of Christ Church S. Laurence Sydney* (Sydney, 1939)

All Saints', East St. Kilda, 1858–1958 (Melbourne, 1958)

AlSayyad, N. (ed.), *Forms of Dominance: On the Architecture and Urbanism of the Colonial Enterprise* (Aldershot: Avebury, 1992)

Anderson-Morshead, A. E. M., *The History of the Universities' Mission to Central Africa* (London: UMCA, 1909); rev. edn (1955), with vol. 2 [1907–32] and vol. 3 [1933–57] by A. G. Blood

Andrews, B., *Gothic in South Australian Churches* (Adelaide: Flinders University, 1984)

——, *Australian Gothic: The Gothic Revival in Australian Architecture from the 1840s to the 1950s* (Melbourne: Melbourne UP, 2001)

——, *Creating a Gothic Paradise: Pugin at the Antipodes* (Hobart: Tasmanian Museum and Art Gallery, 2002)

Angas, G. F., *The New Zealanders Illustrated* (London: Thomas McLean, 1847)

A Proposal for the Establishment of a Missionary College to Educate Clergy for the Colonies and Dependencies of Great Britain (privately printed, *c.*1846) [circular]

Armitage, D., 'Greater Britain: A Useful Category of Historical Analysis?', *American Historical Review*, vol. 104:2 (1999), pp. 427–45

——, *The Ideological Origins of the British Empire* (Cambridge: Cambridge UP, 2000)

——, 'Three Concepts of Atlantic History', in D. Armitage and M. J. Braddick (eds), *The British Atlantic World, 1500–1800* (Basingstoke: Palgrave Macmillan, 2002), pp. 11–27

Armstrong, J., *The Pattern for Church Building: A Sermon Preached in Aid of the Erection of a Chapel of Ease* (London: J. H. Parker, 1852)

Arnold, D., 'George Gilbert Scott and Bombay: India's Gothic Architecture', *Apollo* (Feb. 1991), pp. 87–90

Ashwell, A. R., and Wilberforce, R. G., *Life of the Right Reverend Samuel Wilberforce D.D.*, 3 vols (London: John Murray, 1880–2)

Aspin, P., ' "Our Ancient Architecture": Contesting Cathedrals in Late Georgian England', *Architectural History*, vol. 54 (2011), pp. 213–32

Austen, M., 'Kiwi Architecture: Modernism Recycled', *Fabrications*, vol. 14:1–2 (Dec. 2004), pp. iii–xi

Bagot, W. H., *Architecture and Growth of St. Peter's Cathedral, Adelaide* (Adelaide, 1934)

Bailey, H., *A Sermon Preached in the Chapel of Saint Augustine's College, by the Rev. Henry Bailey, B.D., Warden, with an Address Delivered in the College Hall, by the Rev. William H. Walsh, M.A., Christ Church, Sydney, . . . August 1851, before the Departure of Charles Joseph Gillett, Student, to the Diocese of Sydney* (Canterbury: St Augustine's College, 1851)

Baljon, C. J., 'Interpreting Ruskin: The Argument of the Seven Lamps of Architecture and the Stones of Venice', *Journal of Aesthetics and Art Criticism*, vol. 55:4 (1997), pp. 401–14

Barringer, T., *Men at Work: Art and Labour in Victorian Britain* (New Haven and London: Yale UP, 2005)

Bateman, J., *The Life of the Right Rev. Daniel Wilson, D.D., Late Lord Bishop of Calcutta and Metropolitan of India*, 2 vols (London: John Murray, 1860)

Bates, D., 'Normandy and England after 1066', *English Historical Review*, vol. 104 (1989), pp. 851–80

Batt, N., and Roe, M., 'Conflict within the Church of England in Tasmania, 1850–1858', *Journal of Religious History*, vol. 4:1 (1966), pp. 39–62

Bayly, C. A., *The Birth of the Modern World, 1780–1914* (Oxford: Blackwell, 2004)

Bell, D., *The Idea of Greater Britain: Empire and the Future of World Order, 1860–1900* (Princeton: Princeton UP, 2007)

——, 'John Stuart Mill on Colonies', *Political Theory*, vol. 38:1 (2010), pp. 34–64

Bell, L., 'Artists and Empire: Victorian Representations of Subject People', *Art History*, vol. 5:1 (1982), pp. 73–86

Beresford Hope, A. J. B., 'Architectural Notes on St. Augustine's College, Canterbury', in *St. Augustine's Abbey and St. Augustine's College* (Canterbury: St Augustine's College, n.d.)

——, *The English Cathedral of the Nineteenth Century* (London: John Murray, 1861)

——, 'Cathedrals in Their Missionary Aspect', in J. S. Howson (ed.), *Essays on Cathedrals* (London: John Murray, 1872), pp. 77–105

Berning, M., *The Tower, Clock and Bells of Grahamstown Cathedral: An Outline History* (Grahamstown, 1987)

Bettley, J., 'In the Footsteps of William of Wykeham: Anglican Priest-Architects of the Nineteenth Century'. *Transactions of the Ancient Monuments Society*, vol. 55 (2011), pp. 9–38

Beven, F. L. (ed.), *A History of the Diocese of Colombo: A Centenary Volume* (Colombo: Times of Ceylon, 1946)

Blainey, G., *The Tyranny of Distance: How Distance Shaped Australia's History* (Melbourne: Sun Books, 1966)

Blomfield, C., *A Letter to His Grace the Lord Archbishop of Canterbury, upon the Formation of a Fund for Endowing Additional Bishoprics in the Colonies* (London: B. Fellows, 1840)

Body, G., *The Life and Letters of Arthur Fraser Sim, Priest of the Universities' Mission to Central Africa* (Westminster: UMCA, 1896)

Boggis, R. J. E., *A History of St. Augustine's College, Canterbury* (Canterbury: Cross and Jackman, 1907)

——, *A History of the Diocese of Exeter* (Exeter: William Pollard, 1922)

Bolt, C., *Victorian Attitudes to Race* (London: Routledge, 1971)

Boodle, R. G., 'Recollections of Ministerial Work in New South Wales', in J. J. Halcombe (ed.), *The Emigrant and the Heathen, or, Sketches of Missionary Life* (London: SPCK, n.d.)

——, *The Life and Labours of the Right Rev. William Tyrrell, D.D.* (London: Wells Gardner, Darton & Co., 1881)

Bowen, D., *The Protestant Crusade in Ireland, 1800–70* (Dublin: Gill and Macmillan, 1978)

Bowler, P., *The Invention of Progress: The Victorians and the Past* (Oxford: Blackwell, 1989)

Bradley, S., 'The Englishness of Gothic: Theories and Interpretations from William Gilpin to J. H. Parker', *Architectural History*, vol. 45 (2002), pp. 325–46

Bray, C., *The British Empire* (London: Longman & Co., 1863)

Bremner, G. A., '"Some Imperial Institute": Architecture, Symbolism, and the Ideal of Empire in Late Victorian Britain, 1887–93', *JSAH*, vol. 62:1 (2003), pp. 50–73

——, '"Imperial Monumental Halls and Tower": Westminster Abbey and the Commemoration of Empire, 1854–1904', *Architectural History*, vol. 47 (2004), pp. 251–82

——, 'Nation and Empire in the Government Architecture of Mid-Victorian London: The Foreign and India Office Reconsidered', *Historical Journal*, vol. 48:3 (2005), pp. 703–42

——, 'Between Civilisation and Barbarity: Conflicting Perceptions of the Non-European World in William Theed's *Africa*, 1864–69', *Sculpture Journal*, vol. 15 (2007), pp. 94–102

——, 'Out of Africa: G. F. Bodley, William White, and the Anglican Mission Church of St. Philip, Grahamstown, 1857–67', *Architectural History*, vol. 51 (2008), pp. 185–210

——, 'The Architecture of the Universities' Mission to Central Africa: Developing a Vernacular Tradition in the Anglican Mission Field, 1861–1910', *JSAH*, vol. 68:4 (2009), pp. 514–39

——, 'Narthex Redux: Reinventing Disciplinary Space in the Anglican Mission Field, 1847–1903' (forthcoming)

——, and Conlin, J., 'History as Form: Architecture and Liberal Anglican Thought in the Writings of E. A. Freeman', *Modern Intellectual History*, vol. 8:2 (2011), pp. 299–326

Breward, I., 'Selwyn in Ecumenical Perspective: His Theology of Unity and Mission', in W. E. Limbrick (ed.), *Bishop Selwyn in New Zealand, 1841–68* (Palmerston North, NZ: Dunmore Press, 1983), pp. 136–54

Bridenbaugh, C., *Mitre and Sceptre: Transatlantic Faiths, Ideas, Personalities, and Politics* (New York: Oxford UP, 1962)

Briggs, A., *Victorian Cities* (1963) (Harmondsworth: Penguin Books, 1968)

Bromley, J., *The Man of Ten Talents: A Portrait of Richard Chenevix Trench, 1807–86* (London: SPCK, 1959)

Brooks, C., 'Building the Rural Church: Money, Power and the Country Parish', in C. Brooks and A. Saint (eds), *The Victorian Church: Architecture and Society* (Manchester: Manchester UP, 1995), pp. 51–81

——, *The Gothic Revival* (London: Phaidon, 1999)

Brooks, M. W., *John Ruskin and Victorian Architecture* (London: Thames and Hudson, 1987)

Broughton, W. G., 'Cathedral Churches, Useful and Necessary', in B. Harrison (ed.), *Sermons on the Church of England: Its Constitution, Mission, and Trials* (London: Bell and Daldy, 1857), pp. 206–21

——, 'Earthly Store Prepared for God's Sanctuary', in B. Harrison (ed.), *Sermons on the Church of England: Its Constitution, Mission, and Trials* (London: Bell and Daldy, 1857), pp. 222–34

——, 'The English Reformation, and the Empire of England', in B. Harrison (ed.), *Sermons on the Church of England: Its Constitution, Mission, and Trials* (London: Bell and Daldy, 1857), pp. 51–67

Brown, C., *Vision & Reality: Christchurch's Cathedral in the Square* (Christchurch: Christchurch Cathedral Chapter, 2000)

Brown, D., 'The Maori Response to Gothic Architecture', *Architectural History*, vol. 43 (2000), pp. 253–70

——, *Māori Architecture: From Fale to Wharenui and Beyond* (Rosedale: Raupo [Penguin Group], 2009)

Brown, J. M., *Augustus Short D.D., Bishop of Adelaide* (Walkerville: Hodge Publishing, 1973)

Brown, S. J., 'The New Reformation Movement in the Church of Ireland, 1801–29', in S. J. Brown and D. W. Miller (eds), *Piety and Power in Ireland, 1760–1960: Essays in Honour of Emmet Larkin* (Belfast: Queen's University, 2000), pp. 180–208

——, *Providence and Empire: Religion, Politics and Society in the United Kingdom, 1815–1914* (Harlow: Pearson Longman, 2008)

Brownlee, D., 'That "regular mongrel affair": G. G. Scott's Design for the Government Offices', *Architectural History*, vol. 28 (1985), pp. 159–97

——, 'The First High Victorians: British Architectural Theory in the 1840s', *Architectura*, vol. 15:1 (1985), pp. 33–46

Buckley, C. B., *An Anecdotal History of Old Times in Singapore* (1902) (Singapore: Oxford UP, 1984)

Buffett, F. M., *The Story of the Church in Newfoundland* (Toronto: Board of Religious Education, 1939)

Bulbeck, A. L., *This Stone Which I Have Set Up: Christ Church, North Adelaide, 1849–1949* (Adelaide: Vardon, 1949)

Bullock, F. W. B., *A History of Training for the Ministry of the Church of England in England and Wales, 1800–1874* (St Leonards-on-Sea: Budd and Gillatt, 1955)

Burrow, J. W., 'Introduction', in Charles Darwin, *The Origin of Species* (Harmondsworth: Penguin Books, 1968), pp. 11–48

——, *Evolution and Society: A Study in Victorian Social Theory* (Cambridge: Cambridge UP, 1970)

Butler, R., 'George Gilbert Scott and the University of Bombay', *The Victorian*, no. 37 (July 2011), pp. 10–13

Cable, K. J., 'Religious Controversies in New South Wales in the Mid-Nineteenth Century, I: Aspects of Anglicanism, 1848–1850', *Royal Australian Historical Society Journal*, vol. 49:1 (1963), pp. 58–74

——, 'Protestant Problems in New South Wales in the Mid-Nineteenth Century', *Journal of Religious History*, vol. 3:2 (1964), pp. 119–36

Cannan, E., *Churches of the South Atlantic Islands, 1502–1991* (Oswestry: Anthony Nelson, 1992)

Canny, N., 'The Ideology of English Colonization: From Ireland to America', *William and Mary Quarterly*, 3rd ser., vol. 30:4 (1973), pp. 575–98

——, *Making Ireland British, 1580–1650* (Oxford: Oxford UP, 2001)

Canterbury Papers: Information Concerning the Principles, Objects, Plans, & Proceedings of the Founders of the Settlement of Canterbury in New Zealand (London: John W. Parker, 1850)

Carey, H. M., *God's Empire: Religion and Colonialism in the British World, c.1801–1908* (Cambridge: Cambridge UP, 2010)

Carter, T. T., *A Memoir of John Armstrong, D.D., Late Bishop of Grahamstown* (Oxford: J. H. Parker, 1857)

Caswall, H., *America, and the American Church* (London: John and Charles Mozley, 1851)

Cathedral Church of Christ Zanzibar (Zanzibar: UMCA, 1927)

Chadwick, O., *The Founding of Cuddesdon* (Oxford: Oxford UP, 1954)

——, *From Bossuet to Newman: The Idea of Doctrinal Development* (Cambridge: Cambridge UP, 1957)

——, *Mackenzie's Grave* (London: Hodder and Stoughton, n.d. [1959])

——, *The Victorian Church*, 2 vols (London: Adam and Charles Black, 1966–70)

Chandler, M., *The Life and Work of John Mason Neale, 1818–1866* (Leominster: Gracewing, 1995)

——, *An Introduction to the Oxford Movement* (London: SPCK, 2003)

Chaplin, J. E., 'Expansion and Exceptionalism in Early American History', *Journal of American History*, vol. 89:4 (2003), pp. 1431–55

Chapman, J., *Address on Laying the Corner-Stone of the Cathedral Church at St. Thomas' College, Colombo* (Colombo: College Press, 1852)

Chatterton, E., *A History of the Church of England in India* (London: SPCK, 1924)

Church, R. W., *The Oxford Movement: Twelve Years, 1833–1845* (1891) (Chicago: University of Chicago Press, 1970)

Church in the Colonies: Diocese of Cape Town (London: SPCK, 1849) [transcript of the diary of Robert Gray, bishop of Cape Town]

Churton E. (ed.), *Memoir of Joshua Watson*, 2 vols (Oxford: J. H. and Jas. Parker, 1861)

Clark, K., *The Gothic Revival: An Essay in the History of Taste* (London: John Murray, 1962)

Clarke, B. F. L., *Church Builders of the Nineteenth Century: A Study of the Gothic Revival in England* (London: SPCK, 1938)

——, *Anglican Cathedrals Outside the British Isles* (London: SPCK, 1958)

Clarke, J., ' "Like a huge birdcage from the earth": Watson's Esplanade Hotel, Mumbai (1867–71), and Its Place in Structural History', *Construction History*, vol. 18 (2002), pp. 37–77

Clossey, L., *Salvation and Globalization in the Early Jesuit Missions* (Cambridge: Cambridge UP, 2008)

Cnattingius, H., *Bishops and Society: A Study of Anglican Colonial and Missionary Expansion, 1698–1950* (London: SPCK, 1952)

Coffman, P., *Newfoundland Gothic* (Quebec: Éditions Multi-Mondes, 2008)

——, 'The Introduction of Ecclesiology to Nova Scotia', in G. A. Bremner (ed.), *Ecclesiology Abroad: The British Empire and Beyond*, themed issue of *Studies in Victorian Architecture and Design*, vol. 4 (2012), pp. 79–93

Cohn, B. S., *Colonialism and Its Forms of Knowledge: The British in India* (Princeton: Princeton UP, 1996)

Coke, C. A., *The British Empire: Area, Population, Government, etc., etc.* (London: Harrison, 1865)

Cole, D., *The Work of Sir Gilbert Scott* (London: Architectural Press, 1980)

Cole, K., *A History of All Saints' Church Bendigo: The Rise and Demise of a Cathedral* (Bendigo: Keith Cole, 1990)

Coleman, B., 'The Nineteenth Century: Nonconformity', in N. Orme (ed.), *Unity and Variety: A History of the Church in Devon and Cornwall* (Exeter: University of Exeter Press, 1991), pp. 129–56

Coleridge, B., *The Story of a Devonshire House* (London: T. Fisher Unwin, 1906)

Comaroff, J., and Comaroff, J., 'Christianity and Colonialism in South Africa', *American Ethnologist*, vol. 13:1 (1986), pp. 1–22

——, and ——, *Of Revelation and Revolution: Christianity, Colonialism, and Consciousness in South Africa* (Chicago: Chicago UP, 1991)

Condon, H., *Francis Russell Nixon: A New Appraisal* (University of Tasmania Occasional Paper 32, Hobart, 1981)

Connolly, S. J., *Religion, Law, and Power: The Making of Protestant Ireland, 1660–1760* (Oxford: Oxford UP, 1992)

Cooke, W. G., 'The Diocese of Toronto and Its Two Cathedrals', *JCCHS*, vol. 27:2 (1985), pp. 98–115

Cooper, A., 'Bishop Broughton and the Diocese of Australia', in B. Porter (ed.), *Colonial Tractarians: The Oxford Movement in Australia* (Melbourne: Joint Board of Christian Education, 1989), pp. 23–34

——, 'Forgotten Australian Anglican: Edward Coleridge', *Pacifica*, vol. 3 (1990), pp. 257–67

——, 'Ireland and the Oxford Movement', *Journal of Religious History*, vol. 19:1 (1995), pp. 62–74

Cotman, J. S., *Architectural Antiquities of Normandy* (London: J. and A. Arch, 1822)

Cox, J., *Imperial Fault Lines: Christianity and Colonial Power in India, 1818–1940* (Stanford: Stanford UP, 2002)

——, *The British Missionary Enterprise since 1700* (London: Routledge, 2008)

Craig, B. L., *Apostle to the Wilderness: Bishop John Medley and the Evolution of the Anglican Church* (Madison: Fairleigh Dickinson UP, 2005)

Craig, M., *The Architecture of Ireland from the Earliest Times to 1880* (London: B. T. Batsford, 1982)

Craik, G. L., *The New Zealanders* (London: Charles Knight, 1830)

Crinson, M., *Empire Building: Orientalism and Victorian Architecture* (London: Routledge, 1996)

——, *Modern Architecture and the End of Empire* (Aldershot: Ashgate, 2003)

Crook, J. M., *William Burges and the High Victorian Dream* (London: John Murray, 1981)

——, 'Progressive Eclecticism: The Case of Beresford Hope', *Architectural Design*, vol. 53:7–8 (1983), pp. 56–62

——, 'Early French Gothic', in S. Macready and F. H. Thompson (eds), *Influences in Victorian Art and Architecture* (London: Society of Antiquaries of London, 1985), pp. 49–58

——, *The Dilemma of Style: Architectural Ideals from the Picturesque to the Post-Modern* (London: John Murray, 1989)

——, 'Benjamin Webb (1819–85) and Victorian Ecclesiology', in R. N. Swanson (ed.), *The Church Retrospective* (Woodbridge: Boydell Press, 1997), pp. 423–57

——, *The Architect's Secret: Victorian Critics and the Image of Gravity* (London: John Murray, 2003)

Crossman, K., *A Study of Anglican Church Buildings in Manitoba* (Winnipeg, 1989)

Curl, J. S., *Piety Proclaimed: An Introduction to Places of Worship in Victorian England* (London: Historical Publications, 2002)

——, *Victorian Architecture: Diversity and Invention* (Reading: Spire Books, 2007)

Curteis, G. H., *Bishop Selwyn of New Zealand, and of Lichfield* (London: Kegan Paul, Trench, 1889)

Curthoys, P., 'State Support for Churches, 1836–1860', in B. Kaye *et al.* (eds), *Anglicanism in Australia: A History* (Melbourne: Melbourne UP, 2002), pp. 31–51

Curtis, L. P., *Anglo-Saxons and Celts: A Study of Anti-Irish Prejudice in Victorian England* (Bridgeport, Conn.: Conference on British Studies at the University of Bridgeport, 1968)

Cuthbert, D., *Christ Church in South Yarra: A Social History, 1850–1990* (Melbourne: Christ Church South Yarra, 1996)

——, 'Christ Church South Yarra: An Archetypical Parish?', in C. Holden (ed.), *People of the Past? The Culture of Melbourne Anglicanism and Anglicanism in Melbourne's Culture* (Melbourne: University of Melbourne, 2000), pp. 165–68

Cuthbertson, G., 'The English-Speaking Churches and Colonialism', in C. Villa-Vicencio (ed.), *Theology & Violence: The South African Debate* (Grand Rapids: Eerdmans, 1998), pp. 15–30

Cutts, E. L., *Home Missions and Church Extension* (London: Rivingtons, *c.*1861)

DaCosta Kaufmann, T., *Toward a Geography of Art* (Chicago: University of Chicago Press, 2004)

Darwin, J., 'Imperialism and the Victorians: The Dynamics of Territorial Expansion', *English Historical Review*, vol. 112 (1997), pp. 614–42

——, *The Empire Project: The Rise and Fall of the British World-System, 1830–1970* (Cambridge: Cambridge UP, 2009)

Davidson, A. K., *Selwyn's Legacy: The College of St. John the Evangelist Te Waimate and Auckland, 1843–1992* (Auckland: St John's College, 1993)

——, 'An "Interesting Experiment": The Founding of the Melanesian Mission', in A. K. Davidson (ed.), *The Church of Melanesia, 1849–1999* (Remuera, NZ: College of St John the Evangelist, 2000), pp. 13–48

——, 'Culture and Ecclesiology: The Church Missionary Society and New Zealand', in K. Ward and B. Stanley (eds), *The Church Mission Society and World Christianity, 1799–1999* (Richmond, Surrey: Curzon Press, 2000), pp. 198–227

——. 'The Legacy of Robert Henry Codrington', *International Bulletin of Missionary Research*, vol. 27:4 (2003), pp. 171–6

Davies, G. C. B., *Henry Phillpotts, Bishop of Exeter, 1778–1869* (London: SPCK, 1954)

Davies, P., *Splendours of the Raj: British Architecture in India, 1660–1947* (London: John Murray, 1985; paperback edn Harmondsworth: Penguin Books, 1987)

Davies, R. R., *Domination and Conquest: The Experience of Ireland, Scotland and Wales, 1100–1300* (Cambridge: Cambridge UP, 1990)

Daw, E. D., 'Church and State in the Empire: The Conference of Australian Bishops, 1850', *Journal of Imperial and Commonwealth History*, vol. 5:3 (1977), pp. 251–69

Derick, J. M., *Views and Details of Stanton Harcourt Church, Oxfordshire* (Oxford: J. H. Parker, 1841)

Descriptive Account of the Cathedral of Canterbury, . . . with a Short Description of St. Augustine's Monastery, now Converted into a Missionary College, for the Church of England (Canterbury: Henry Ward, 1850)

Diamond Jubilee, Holy Trinity Church, Port Melbourne (n.p., *c.*1954)

Dilke, C. W., *Greater Britain: A Record of Travel in English-Speaking Countries during 1866 and 1867*, 2 vols (London: Macmillan, 1868)

Dishon, D., 'Three Men in a Gondola: Ruskin, Webb and Street', in C. Webster and J. Elliott (eds), *'A church as it should be': The Cambridge Camden Society and Its Influence* (Stamford: Shaun Tyas, 2000), pp. 190–210

Documents Relative to the Erection and Endowment of Additional Bishoprics in the Colonies, 1841–1855 (London: SPCK, 1855)

Donovan, P., and Donovan, J., *150 Years of Stained and Painted Glass* (Adelaide: Wakefield Press, 1986)

Dorrian, M., 'On Some Spatial Aspects of the Colonial Discourse on Ireland', *Journal of Architecture*, vol. 6:1 (2001), pp. 27–51

Dorsey, S. P., *Early English Churches in America, 1607–1807* (New York: Oxford UP, 1952)

Dossal, M., *Imperial Designs and Indian Realities: The Planning of Bombay City, 1845–1875* (Delhi: Oxford UP, 1991)

Downs, B., *Sacred Places: British Columbia's Early Churches* (Vancouver: Douglas and McIntyre, 1980)

Drayton, R., *Nature's Government: Science, Imperial Britain, and the 'Improvement' of the World* (New Haven and London: Yale UP, 2000)

Driberg, C. E., *A Narrative of the Progress and Condition of the Barripûr Mission . . . with an Account of the Consecration of the Churches of Barripûr and Mogra Hât* (London: SPG, 1847)

Driver, F., *Geography Militant: Cultures of Exploration and Empire* (Oxford: Blackwell, 2001)

——, and Gilbert, D., 'Heart of Empire? Landscape, Space and Performance in Imperial London', *Environment and Planning D: Society and Space*, vol. 16 (1998), pp. 1–17

——, and —— (eds), *Imperial Cities: Landscape, Display and Identity* (Manchester: Manchester UP, 1999)

Drummond, H. N., *Bishop Patteson, Pioneer and Martyr, with an Account of the Memorial Chapel* (Parkstone (UK): Ralph and Brown, 1930)

Dyos, H. J., 'The Slums of Victorian London', in D. Cannadine and D. Reeder (eds), *Exploring the Urban Past: Essays in Urban History by H. J. Dyos* (Cambridge: Cambridge UP, 1982), pp. 129–53

Eastlake, C. L., *A History of the Gothic Revival* (London: Longmans, 1872; repr. 1975)

Eggener K. L. (ed.), *American Architectural History: A Contemporary Reader* (London: Routledge, 2004)

Elbourne, E., 'The Foundation of the Church Missionary Society: The Anglican Missionary Impulse', in J. Walsh, C. Haydon, and S. Taylor (eds), *The Church of England, c.1689–1833: From Toleration to Tractarianism* (Cambridge: Cambridge UP, 1993), pp. 247–64

——, *Blood Ground: Colonialism, Missions, and the Contest for Christianity in the Cape Colony and Britain, 1799–1853* (Montreal and Kingston: McGill–Queen's UP, 2002)

Eldridge, C. C., *England's Mission: The Imperial Idea in the Age of Gladstone & Disraeli, 1868–1880* (Chapel Hill: University of North Carolina Press, 1973)

Elkin, A. P., *The Diocese of Newcastle: A History* (Glebe, NSW: Australian Medical Publishing Co., 1955)

Elliott, J., 'A Trusted Disciple: Richard Cromwell Carpenter', in C. Webster and J. Elliott (eds), *'A church as it should be': The Cambridge Camden Society and Its Influence* (Stamford: Shaun Tyas, 2000), pp. 149–72

Elliott J. H., 'How They Made the Empire', *New York Review of Books*, vol. 58:13 (2011), pp. 20–2

Ellis, M. H., *Francis Greenway: His Life and Times* (Sydney: Angus and Robertson, 1953)

Emerson, N. D., 'Church Life in the 19th Century', in W. A. Phillips (ed.), *History of the Church of Ireland from the Earliest Times to the Present Day*, 3 vols (Oxford: Oxford UP, 1933), vol. 3, pp. 325–59

England, F., 'Tracing South African Anglicanism', in F. England and T. Paterson (eds), *Bounty in Bondage: The Anglican Church in Southern Africa. Essays in Honour of Edward King, Dean of Cape Town* (Johannesburg: Ravan Press, 1989), pp. 20–5

Evans J. H., *Churchman Militant: George Augustus Selwyn, Bishop of New Zealand and Lichfield* (London: George Allen and Unwin, 1964)

Eyres, P., 'Neoclassicism on Active Service: Commemoration of the Seven Years' War in the English Landscape Garden', *New Arcadian Journal*, no. 35–6 (1993), pp. 62–122

Fabian, J., *Time and the Other: How Anthropology Makes Its Object* (New York: Columbia UP, 1983)

Fahey, C., *In His Name: The Anglican Experience in Upper Canada, 1791–1854* (Ottawa: Carleton UP, 1991)

Fairweather, E. R., 'A Tractarian Patriarch: John Medley of Fredericton', *Canadian Journal of Theology*, vol. 6:1 (1960), pp. 15–24

Faught, C. B., *The Oxford Movement: A Thematic History of the Tractarians and Their Times* (University Park: Pennsylvania State UP, 2003)

Feild, E., *Order and Uniformity in the Public Services of the Church . . . : A Charge Delivered to the Clergy of the Diocese of Newfoundland* (St John's: John W. McCoubrey, 1844)

——, *The Means and Methods of a Christian Life, as Told and Taught by the Form and Arrangement of a Christian Church* (London: W. Clinkskel, 1870)

Fergusson, J., *History of the Modern Styles of Architecture*, 3rd edn, rev. R. Kerr, 2 vols (London, 1891)

Fernie, E., *The Architecture of Norman England* (Oxford: Oxford UP, 2000)

Final Report of St. Paul's Cathedral, Calcutta, to which is Prefixed the Sermon Delivered on the Occasion of the Consecration (Calcutta: Bishop's College, 1847)

Finley, A. G., '"Habits of reverence and awe": Bishop John Medley and the Promise of Ecclesiology', *JCCHS*, vol. 35 (1993), pp. 3–22

Finley, G., and Wigginton, L., *On Earth as it is in Heaven: Gothic Revival Churches of Victorian New Brunswick* (Fredericton: Goose Lane Editions, 1995)

Fitzpatrick, D., 'Ireland and Empire', in A. Porter (ed.), *The Oxford History of the British Empire*, vol. 3: *The Nineteenth Century* (Oxford: Oxford UP, 1999), pp. 494–521

Flour, I., '"On the Formation of a National Museum of Architecture": The Architectural Museum versus the South Kensington Museum', *Architectural History*, vol. 51 (2008), pp. 211–38

Forbes, D., '"Scientific" Whiggism: Adam Smith and John Millar', *Cambridge Journal*, vol. 7 (1953–4), pp. 643–70

Forster, R. H., and Harris, W., *The History of the Lady Margaret Boat Club, St. John's College, Cambridge, 1825–1890* (Cambridge: Deighton, Bell & Co., 1890)

Fox, R. N., *Parish of Buckland, Tasmania, Church of St. John the Baptist: History of the Church and Window* (Hobart, n.d.)

Frame, R., *Colonial Ireland, 1169–1369* (Dublin: Helicon, 1981)

France, W. F., *The Oversea Episcopate: Centenary History of the Colonial Bishoprics Fund 1841–1941* (London: CBF, 1941)

Fredericksen, A., 'Parliament's *Genius Loci*: The Politics of Place after the 1834 Fire', in C. Riding and J. Riding (eds), *The Houses of Parliament: History, Art, Architecture* (London: Merrell, 2000), pp. 99–111

Freeland, J. M., *Architect Extraordinary: The Life and Work of John Horbury Hunt, 1838–1904* (Melbourne: Cassell, 1970)

——, *Architecture in Australia: A History* (Harmondsworth: Penguin Books, 1972)

Freeman, E. A., *A History of Architecture* (London: Joseph Master, 1849)

Freschi, F., 'The Fine Art of Fusion: Race, Gender and the Politics of South Africanism as Reflected in the Decorative Programme of South Africa House, London (1933)', *De Arte*, no. 71 (April 2005), pp. 14–34

Frew, J. M., 'Gothic is English: John Carter and the Revival of the Gothic as England's National Style', *Art Bulletin*, vol. 64:2 (1982), pp. 315–19

Friedman, T., *The Eighteenth-Century Church in Britain* (New Haven and London: Yale University Press, 2011)

Froude, J. A., *Short Studies on Great Subjects*, 4 vols (London: Longmans, Green & Co., 1891)

Frykenberg, R. E., 'Christian Missions and the Raj', in N. Etherington (ed.), *Missions and Empire* (Oxford: Oxford UP, 2005), pp. 107–31

Galbraith, J. S., 'Myths of the "Little England" Era' (1961), in A. G. L. Shaw (ed.), *Great Britain and the Colonies, 1815–1865* (London: Methuen, 1970), pp. 27–45

Gallagher J., and Robinson, R. E., 'The Imperialism of Free Trade', *Economic History Review*, vol. 6:1 (1953), pp. 1–15

Games, A., 'Atlantic History: Definitions, Challenges, and Opportunities', *American Historical Review*, vol. 111:3 (2006), pp. 741–57

——, *The Web of Empire: English Cosmopolitans in an Age of Expansion* (Oxford: Oxford UP, 2008)

Gayford, S. C., *Cuddesdon College, 1854–1904: A Record and Memorial* (London: Longmans, Green & Co., 1904)

Georgopoulou, M., *Venice's Mediterranean Colonies: Architecture and Urbanism* (Cambridge: Cambridge UP, 2001)

Gibbon, E., *The History of the Decline and Fall of the Roman Empire* (1776–88), ed. J. B. Bury, 7 vols (London: Methuen, 1897)

Gibbs, E. M., *The Anglican Church in India, 1600–1970* (Delhi: Indian SPCK, 1972)

Gilbert, A. D., *Religion and Society in Industrial England: Church, Chapel and Social Change, 1740–1914* (London: Longman, 1976)

Golding, B., *Conquest and Colonisation: The Normans in Britain, 1066–1100* (Basingstoke: Palgrave Macmillan, 2001)

Grant, A., *The Past and Prospective Extension of the Gospel by Missions to the Heathen* (London, 1843)

Grant, J., *Christ Church, Geelong, 1843–1983: A Brief History with Special Emphasis on the Foundation Years* (Melbourne, 1983)

——, *Old St. Paul's: The Story of St. Paul's Church Melbourne and Its Congregation, 1850–1891* (Melbourne: St Paul's Cathedral, 2000)

——, *Episcopally Led and Synodically Governed: Anglicans in Victoria, 1803–1997* (Melbourne: Australian Scholarly Publishing, 2010)

Gray, C. (ed.), *The Life of Robert Gray, Bishop of Cape Town and Metropolitan of Africa*, 2 vols (London: Rivingtons, 1876)

Gray, R., *Church in the Colonies: Diocese of Cape Town (Part 1)* (London: SPCK, 1849)

——, *Church in the Colonies: Diocese of Cape Town (Part 2)* (London: SPCK, 1852)

Greene, J. P., 'Colonial History and National History: Reflections on a Continuing Problem', *William and Mary Quarterly*, vol. 64:2 (2007), pp. 235–50

Gregg, R. S., *'Faithful unto death': Memorials of the Life of John Gregg D.D., Bishop of Cork, Cloyne, and Ross* (Dublin: George Herbert, 1879)

Grey, W., *Sketches of Newfoundland and Labrador* (Ipswich: S. H. Cowell, 1857)

Grieve, A., 'Ruskin and Millais at Glenfinals', *Burlington Magazine*, vol. 138 (1996), pp. 228–34

Grose, K., 'What Happened to the Clergy Reserves of New South Wales?', *Journal of the Royal Australian Historical Society*, vol. 72:2 (1987), pp. 92–103

Gutsche, T., *The Bishop's Lady* (Cape Town: H. Timmins, 1970)

Hackler, R. E. A., *The Cathedral Church of Saint Andrew, Honolulu, Hawaii* (Honolulu, 1991)

Halcombe, J. J. (ed.), *The Emigrant and the Heathen, or, Sketches of Missionary Life* (London: SPCK, n.d.)

Hall, C., *Civilising Subjects: Metropole and Colony in the English Imagination, 1830–1867* (Cambridge: Polity, 2002)

Hall, M., 'The Rise of Refinement: G. F. Bodley's All Saints, Cambridge, and the Return to English Models in Gothic Architecture of the 1860s', *Architectural History*, vol. 36 (1993), pp. 103–26

——, 'What do Victorian Churches Mean? Symbolism and Sacramentalism in Anglican Church Architecture, 1850–1870', *JSAH*, vol. 59:1 (2000), pp. 78–95

——, ' "Our own": Thomas Hope, A. J. B. Beresford Hope and the Creation of the High Victorian Style', in R. Hill and

M. Hall (eds), *The 1840s, Studies in Victorian Architecture and Design*, vol. 1 (London: Victorian Society, 2008), pp. 61–75

Hancock, D., *Citizens of the World: London Merchants and the Integration of the British Atlantic Community, 1735–1785* (Cambridge: Cambridge UP, 1995)

Harding, L. N., '"John, by divine permission": John Medley and the Church in New Brunswick', *JCCHS*, vol. 8:4 (1966), pp. 76–87

Hardwick, J., 'Anglican Church Expansion and the Recruitment of Colonial Clergy for New South Wales and the Cape Colony, *c.*1790–1850', *Journal of Imperial and Commonwealth History*, vol. 37:3 (2009), pp. 361–81

Harlow, V. T., *The Founding of the Second British Empire, 1763–1793: New Continents and Changing Values*, 2 vols (London: Longmans, 1964)

Harrison, B. (ed.), *Sermons on the Church of England: Its Constitution, Mission, and Trials* (London: Bell and Daldy, 1857)

Harrison, J. P., *Views and Details of Saint Giles' Church, Oxford* (Oxford: J. H. Parker, 1842)

Haugerud, A., *The Culture of Politics in Modern Kenya* (Cambridge: Cambridge UP, 1995)

Haw, S. (with P. Newman and T. Heywood), *St. John the Evangelist, Toorak: The History for 140 years, 1859–1999* (Melbourne: St John's Anglican Church, 1999)

Hayes, A. L., *Anglicans in Canada: Controversies and Identity in Historical Perspective* (Urbana: University of Illinois Press, 2004)

Headon, C. F., 'An Unpublished Correspondence between John Medley and E. B. Pusey', *JCCHS*, vol. 16:4 (1974), pp. 72–4

——, 'Developments in Canadian Anglican Worship in Eastern and Central Canada, 1840–1868', *JCCHS*, vol. 17:2 (1975), pp. 26–36

Heanley, R. M., *A Memoir of Edward Steere: Third Missionary Bishop in Central Africa* (London, 1890)

Heck, M. E., 'Mind the Gap: Rewriting Sir John Summerson's American Architectural History', in F. Salmon (ed.), *Summerson and Hitchcock: Centenary Essays on Architectural Historiography* (New Haven and London: Yale UP, 2006), pp. 117–32

Hempton, D., *Methodism and Politics in British Society, 1750–1850* (London: Hutchinson, 1987)

——, *Methodism: Empire of the Spirit* (New Haven and London: Yale UP, 2005)

Henderson, J. L. H., *John Strachan, 1778–1867* (Toronto: University of Toronto Press, 1969)

Herman, M., *The Blackets: An Era of Australian Architecture* (Sydney: Angus and Robertson, 1977)

Hersey, G. L., *High Victorian Gothic: A Study in Associationism* (Baltimore: Johns Hopkins UP, 1972)

Hewson, L. A., *They Seek a City: Methodism in Grahamstown* (Grahamstown: Institute of Social and Economic Research, Rhodes University, 1981)

Hill, B., and Fraser, H., *Historic Churches of Barbados* (Bridgetown: Art Heritage Publications, 1984)

Hilliard, D., *God's Gentlemen: A History of the Melanesian Mission, 1849–1942* (Brisbane: University of Queensland Press, 1978)

——, *Godliness and Good Order: A History of the Anglican Church in South Australia* (Netley: Wakefield Press, 1986)

——, 'Anglo-Catholicism in the Religious Ecology of Melbourne', in C. Holden (ed.), *Anglo-Catholicism in Melbourne: Papers to Mark the 150th Anniversary of St Peter's Eastern Hill, 1846–1996* (Melbourne: Melbourne UP, 1997), pp. 169–87

Hinchliff, P., *The Anglican Church in South Africa: An Account of the History and Development of the Church of the Province of South Africa* (London: Darton, Longman and Todd, 1963)

Hitchcock, H.-R., 'G. E. Street in the 1850s', *JSAH*, vol. 19:4 (1960), pp. 145–71

Holden, C., *'Awful Happenings on the Hill: E. S. Hughes and Melbourne Anglo-Catholicism before the War* (Melbourne: St Peter's Church, 1992)

——, *From Tories at Prayer to Socialists at Mass: St. Peter's, Eastern Hill, Melbourne, 1846–1990* (Melbourne: Melbourne UP, 1996)

Howe, K. R., '"The Bishop Alien": Selwyn and the New Zealand Wars of the 1860s', in W. E. Limbrick (ed.), *Bishop Selwyn in New Zealand, 1841–68* (Palmerston North, NZ: Dunmore Press, 1983), pp. 94–119

Howell, P., *Victorian Churches* (London: RIBA, 1968)

——, 'Newman's Church at Littlemore', *Oxford Art Journal*, vol. 6:1 (1983), pp. 51–6

——, *The Faber Guide to Victorian Churches* (London: Faber and Faber, 1989)

Hunter, G., 'William White: The Early Years', in R. Hill and M. Hall (eds), *The 1840s*, Studies in Victorian Architecture and Design, vol. 1 (London: Victorian Society, 2008), pp. 106–16

——, *William White: Pioneer Victorian Architect* (Reading: Spire Books, 2010)

——, 'William White in the Colonies', in G. A. Bremner (ed.), *Ecclesiology Abroad: The British Empire and Beyond*, themed issue of *Studies in Victorian Architecture and Design*, vol. 4 (2012), pp. 95–109

Hutchison, J., *Picture of New Zealand: Containing an Account of Its Harbours, Bays, Natural Productions . . .* (Edinburgh, 1840)

Instrumenta Ecclesiastica, or, A Series of Working Designs for the Furniture, Fittings, and Decorations of Churches and Their Precincts (London: John Van Voorst, 1847)

Instrumenta Ecclesiastica, 2nd ser. (London: John Van Voorst, 1856)

Irving, R. G., *Indian Summer: Lutyens, Baker and Imperial Delhi* (New Haven and London: Yale UP, 1981)

——, 'Architecture for Empire's Sake: Lutyens's Palace for Delhi', *Perspecta*, vol. 18 (1982), pp. 7–23

——, 'Bombay and Imperial Delhi: Cities as Symbols', in A. Hopkins and G. Stamp (eds), *Lutyens Abroad: The Work of Sir Edwin Lutyens Outside the British Isles* (London: British School at Rome, 2002), pp. 169–80

Isaac, R., *The Transformation of Virginia, 1740–1790* (Chapel Hill: University of North Carolina Press, 1982)

Jackson, A., 'Ireland, the Union, and the Empire, 1800–1960', in K. Kenny (ed.), *Ireland and the British Empire* (Oxford: Oxford UP, 2004), pp. 123–35

Jackson, B. H. (ed.), *Recollections of Thomas Graham Jackson, 1835–1924* (Oxford: Oxford UP, 1950)

Jackson, E. T., *Meadowbank – St. John's [Auckland]* (Auckland: MBE Mount Eden, 1976)

Jackson, N., 'Christ Church, Streatham, and the Rise of Constructional Polychromy', *Architectural History*, vol. 43 (2000), pp. 241–6

Jacob, W. M., *The Making of the Anglican Church Worldwide* (London: SPCK, 1997)

Johnson, D. L., 'French and English Influences on the Architecture of St. Peter's Cathedral, Adelaide', *Architecture Australia* (June 1988), pp. 70–6

Johnstone, S. M., *The Book of St. Andrew's Cathedral Sydney* (1937) (Sydney: Angus and Robertson, 1968)

Jones, F., *Edward Feild: Bishop of Newfoundland, 1844–1876* (St John's: Newfoundland Historical Society, 1976)

Jose, G. H., *The Church of England in South Australia, 1836–1856* (Adelaide, 1937)

Jupp, R., '"Nurseries of a Learned Clergy": Pusey and the Defence of Cathedrals', in P. Butler (ed.), *Pusey Rediscovered* (London: SPCK, 1983), pp. 139–61

Kalman, H., *A History of Canadian Architecture*, 2 vols (Toronto: Oxford UP, 1994)

——, and de Visser, J., *Pioneer Churches* (Toronto: McClelland and Stewart, 1976)

Kaufman, E. N., ' "The weight and vigour of their masses": Mid-Victorian Country Churches and "The Lamp of Power" ', in J. D. Hunt and F. M. Holland (eds), *The Ruskin Polygon: Essays on the Imagination of John Ruskin* (Manchester: Manchester UP, 1982), pp. 94–121

Kaye, B. N. 'Broughton and the Demise of the Royal Supremacy', *Journal of the Royal Australian Historical Society*, vol. 81:1 (1995), pp. 39–51

——, 'The Strange Birth of Anglican Synods in Australia and the 1850s Bishops' Conference', *Journal of Religious History*, vol. 27:2 (2003), pp. 177–97

Kearney, H., *The British Isles: A History of Four Nations* (1989), 2nd edn (Cambridge: Cambridge UP, 2006)

Keating, P. (ed.), *Into Unknown England, 1866–1913: Selections from the Social Explorers* (Manchester: Manchester UP, 1976)

Kennedy, D., 'Imperial History and Post-Colonial Theory', *Journal of Imperial and Commonwealth History*, vol. 24:3 (1996), pp. 345–63

Kenny, K., (ed.), *Ireland and the British Empire* (Oxford: Oxford UP, 2004)

Kent, D., 'High Church Rituals and Rituals of Protest: The "Riots" at St George-in-the-East, 1859–60', *London Journal*, vol. 32:2 (2007), pp. 145–65

Kent, N. B. (ed.), *Cambridge in South London: The Work of the College Missions, 1883–1914* (Cambridge: W. Heffer & Sons, 1914)

Kerr, J., *Our Great Victorian Architect: Edmund Thomas Blacket (1817–1883)* (Sydney: National Trust of Australia, 1983)

——, 'Authentically Australian Gothic', *Transition* (Spring 1988), pp. 5–13

——, and Broadbent, J., *Gothick Taste in the Colony of New South Wales* (Sydney: David Ell, 1980)

Ketchum, W. Q., *The Life and Work of the Most Reverend John Medley, D.D.* (Saint John, New Brunswick: J. and A. McMillan, 1893)

Khan, O., *From Kashmir to Kabul: Photography, 1860–1900* (Ahmedabad: Maplin Publishing, 2002)

King, A. D., *Colonial Urban Development: Culture, Social Power and Environment* (London: Routledge, 1976)

——, *Spaces of Global Cultures: Architecture, Urbanism, Identity* (London: Routledge, 2004)

King, B., *The Recovery of the Lost Sheep of the Church of England by Home Missions in Her Large and Destitute Parishes: A Sermon Preached at the Opening of the Mission Chapel, Calvert Street, S. George's, East* (London: Joseph Masters, 1856)

Klingberg, F. J., *Anglican Humanitarianism in Colonial New York* (Philadelphia: Church Historical Society, 1940)

Knaplund, P., *Gladstone and Britain's Imperial Policy* (London: Routledge, 1966)

Knight, C. R., *The Selwyn Churches of Auckland* (Wellington: A. H. and A. W. Reed, 1972)

Krautheimer, R., *Early Christian and Byzantine Architecture* (Baltimore: Johns Hopkins UP, 1965)

Kubler, G., *The Religious Architecture of New Mexico in the Colonial Period and since the American Occupation* (Colorado Springs: Taylor Museum, 1940)

——, and Soria, M., *Art and Architecture in Spain and Portugal and Their American Dominions, 1500 to 1800*, Pelican History of Art (Harmondsworth: Penguin Books, 1959)

Kumaradoss, V., 'The SPG and the Impact of Conversion in Nineteenth-Century Tirunelveli', in D. O'Connor *et al.*, *Three Centuries of Mission: The United Society for the Propagation of the Gospel, 1701–2000* (London: Continuum, 2000), pp. 274–89

Langham-Carter, R. R., 'South Africa's First Woman Architect', *Architect and Builder* (March 1967), pp. 14–18

——, 'The Story of the Original St. George's Cathedral', *Architect and Builder* (Oct. 1970), pp. 16–18

——, 'St. Saviour's Church, Claremont, Cape', *Architect and Builder* (Sept. 1972), pp. 8–10

——, 'The Church of Holy Trinity at Kalk Bay in the Cape', *Architect and Builder* (May 1981), pp. 2–7

——, 'A "Reconstruction" of the Armstrong Chapel, Grahamstown', *Architect and Builder* (Dec. 1981), pp. 22–3

——, 'The Bishop Gray Memorial', *The Gateway* (May 1983), pp. 11–12

Lawrence, D., and Wilson, A., *The Cathedral of St. Fin Barre at Cork: William Burges in Ireland* (Dublin: Four Courts Press, 2006)

Lawson, M. S. N. (ed.), *Letters of John Mason Neale D.D.* (London: Longmans, Green & Co., 1910)

Le Couteur, H., 'Anglican High Churchmen and the Expansion of Empire', *Journal of Religious History*, vol. 32:2 (2008), pp. 193–215

Le Patourel, J., *The Norman Empire* (Oxford: Clarendon Press, 1976)

Letters and Extracts from Letters, from the Lord Bishop of Australia, to the Rev. the Secretary of the Society for the Propagation of the Gospel (1843)

Letters from the Bishop of New Zealand . . . with Other Information Concerning His Diocese (London: Rivingtons, 1843)

Lewis, M., 'Architectural Drawings as Historical Sources', *Latrobe Library Journal*, vol. 5:20 (1977), pp. 69–89

——, 'Architecture from Colonial Origins', in *The Heritage of Australia: The Illustrated Register of the National Estate* (South Melbourne: Macmillan, 1981), pp. 68–72

—— (ed.), *Victorian Churches: Their Origins, Their Story & Their Architecture* (Melbourne: National Trust of Australia, 1991)

——, 'The Imperial Technology Cringe' (1996), in A. Leach, A. Moulis and N. Sully (eds), *Shifting Views: Selected Essays on the Architectural History of Australia and New Zealand* (St Lucia: Queensland UP, 2008), pp. 81–94

Lewis, M. J., *The Gothic Revival* (London: Thames and Hudson, 2002)

Limbrick, W. E., '"A most indefatigable man"', in W. E. Limbrick (ed.), *Bishop Selwyn in New Zealand, 1841–68* (Palmerston North, NZ: Dunmore Press, 1983), pp. 11–23

Livesey, J., *Mechanics' Churches: A Letter to the Right Honourable Sir Robert Peel, Bart. M.P., on Church Extension in Populous Towns and Manufacturing Districts* (London: Hatchard, 1840)

Lochhead, I., 'St. Bartholomew's Church Kaiapoi: A Mountfort-Selwyn Connection', *Bulletin of New Zealand Art History*, vol. 9:1 (1985), pp. 14–18

——, 'Antipodean Gothic: Gilbert Scott, Benjamin Mountfort and the Medieval Vision in New Zealand', *L'art et les révolutions: Actes [du] XXVIIe Congrès International d'Histoire de l'Art* (Strasbourg : Société Alsacienne pour le Développement de l'Histoire de l'Art, 1992), pp. 215–30

——, *A Dream of Spires: Benjamin Mountfort and the Gothic Revival* (Christchurch: Canterbury UP, 1999)

——, 'British Architectural Books in Colonial New Zealand', *Turnbull Library Record*, vol. 34 (2001), pp. 29–44

——, 'Remembering the Middle Ages: Responses to the Gothic Revival in Colonial New Zealand', in J. Anderson (ed.), *Crossing Cultures: Conflict, Migration and Convergence. The Proceedings of the 32nd International Congress in the History of Art* (Carlton, Victoria: Miegunyah Press, 2009), pp. 536–40

——, 'Experiments in Ecclesiology: Anglican Church Building in Colonial New Zealand', in G. A. Bremner (ed.), *Ecclesiology Abroad: The British Empire and Beyond*, themed issue of *Studies in Victorian Architecture and Design*, vol. 4 (2012), pp. 57–77

London, C. W., *Bombay Gothic* (Mumbai: India Book House, 2002)

Lowder, C. F., *Ten Years in St George's Mission* (London, 1867)

——, *Twenty-One Years in S. George's Mission: An Account of Its Origin, Progress, and Works of Charity* (London: Rivingtons, 1877)

Lyell, C., *Principles of Geology: Being an Inquiry How Far the Former Changes of the Earth's Surface are Referable to Causes now in Operation*, 4 vols (London: John Murray, 1835)

Lyttelton G. W., *The Colonial Empire of Great Britain, Especially in Its Religious Aspect* (London: Simpkin, Marshall & Co., 1849)

McAndrew, J., *The Open-Air Churches of Sixteenth-Century Mexico: Atrios, Posas, Open Chapels, and Other Studies* (Cambridge, Mass.: Harvard UP, 1965)

M'Carter, J., *The Dutch Reformed Church in South Africa* (Edinburgh: W. and C. Inglis, 1869)

Macaulay, T. B., *Literary and Historical Essays Contributed to the Edinburgh Review* (London: Oxford UP, 1932)

McDougall, H., *Sketches of Our Life in Sarawak*, with intro. by R. H. W. Reece and A. J. M. Saint (Singapore: Oxford UP, 1992)

Mace, J. H. B., *Henry Bodley Bromby* (London: Longmans, Green & Co., 1913)

Mackenzie, A. (ed.), *Mission Life among the Zulu-Kafirs: Memorials of Henrietta Robertson, Wife of the Rev. R. Robertson* (London: Deighton, Bell & Co., 1866)

MacKenzie, J. M., *Orientalism: History, Theory and the Arts* (Manchester: Manchester UP, 1995)

Maclear, G. F., *S. Augustine's, Canterbury: Its Rise, Ruin, and Restoration* (London: Wells Gardner, Darton & Co., 1888)

McNair, J. F. A., *Prisoners Their Own Warders . . .* (Singapore: A. Constable, 1899)

McPherson, A., 'Architecture, Music, Art, and Liturgy in the Diocese of Melbourne', in B. Porter (ed.), *Melbourne Anglicans: The Diocese of Melbourne, 1847–1997* (Melbourne: Mitre Books, 1997), pp. 49–81

MacRae, M. (with A. Adamson), *Hallowed Walls: Church Architecture of Upper Canada* (Toronto: Clarke, Irwin & Co., 1975)

Magee, G. B., and Thompson, A. S., *Empire and Globalisation: Networks of People, Goods and Capital in the British World, c.1850–1914* (Cambridge: Cambridge UP, 2010)

Magrill, B., '"Development" and Ecclesiology in the Outpost of the British Empire: William Hay's Gothic Solutions for Church Building in Tropical Climates (1840–1890)', *JSSAC*, vol. 29:1–2 (2004), pp. 15–26

Mandler, P., '"Race" and "Nation" in Mid-Victorian Thought', in S. Collini, R. Whatmore and B. Young (eds), *History, Religion, and Culture: British Intellectual History, 1750–1950* (Cambridge: Cambridge UP, 2000), pp. 224–44

Mané, J. N., 'Gilbert Scott's Colonial Churches', in M. Belcher and H. Debenham (eds), *Australasian Victorian Studies Association: Conference Papers 1987* (Christchurch: University of Canterbury for the AVSA, 1987), pp. 31–42

Mane-Wheoki, J., 'Selwyn Gothic: The Formative Years', *Art New Zealand*, no. 54 (Autumn 1990), pp. 76–81

Mangan, J. A., and Walvin, J. (eds), *Manliness and Morality: Middle-Class Masculinity in Britain and America, 1800–1940* (New York: St Martin's Press, 1987)

Manners, J., *The Church of England in the Colonies* (London: Simpkin, Marshall & Co., 1851)

Manning, G., 'The Foundation History', in F. White (ed.), *Christ Church North Adelaide* (Adelaide, 1998), pp. 3–6

Martin, D., *The Bishop's Churches: The Churches of Anglican Bishop Robert Gray* (Cape Town: Struik, 2005)

——, 'Bishop Robert Gray and Mrs Sophia Gray: Building Anglican Churches in South Africa, 1848–1872', in G. A. Bremner (ed.), *Ecclesiology Abroad: The British Empire and Beyond*, themed issue of *Studies in Victorian Architecture and Design*, vol. 4 (2012), pp. 111–25

Martin, G., '"Anti-Imperialism" in the Mid-Nineteenth Century and the Nature of the British Empire, 1820–70', in R. Hyam and G. Martin, *Reappraisals in British Imperial History* (London: Macmillan, 1975), pp. 88–120

Matthews, S., '"Your dutiful son": The Newfoundland Letters of the Revd William Grey', *Report and Transactions of the Devonshire Association for the Advancement of Science, Literature and the Arts*, vol. 136 (2004), pp. 149–50

Maynard, F. E., *A Talk About St. Peter's, Eastern Hill, Melbourne* (n.d.)

Meaney, N. K., 'The Church of England in the Paradise of Dissent: A Problem of Assimilation', *Journal of Religious History*, vol. 3:2 (1964), pp. 137–57

Medley, J., *The Episcopal Form of Church Government: Its Antiquity, Its Expediency, and Its Conformity to the Word of God* (London: John W. Parker, 1835)

Medley, J., *Elementary Remarks on Church Architecture* (Exeter: P. A. Hannaford, 1841)

——, 'The Advantages of Open Seats', *Exeter Architectural Review*, no. 1 (1843), pp. 1–10

——, *'The Harvest Field of the World': A Sermon Preached in the Cathedral Church of St. Peter, Exeter* (Exeter: P. A. Hannaford, 1843)

——, *A Charge Delivered at His Primary Visitation Held in Christ Church Cathedral, Fredericton* (Fredericton: John Simpson, 1847)

——, *The Staff of Beauty and the Staff of Bands: A Sermon Preached in St. Anne's Chapel, Fredericton* (Saint John, New Brunswick: W. L. Avery, 1847)

——, *A Charge Delivered in the Cathedral Church of Christ-Church, Fredericton . . . at the Second Triennial Visitation* (Saint John, New Brunswick: W. L. Avery, 1850)

——, *A Charge to the Clergy of the Diocese . . . at His Third Triennial Visitation* (Fredericton: Royal Gazette Office, 1853)

Merivale, H., *Lectures on Colonization and Colonies*, new edn (London, 1861; repr. London: Oxford UP, 1928)

Metcalf, T. R., *An Imperial Vision: Indian Architecture and Britain's Raj* (London: Faber and Faber, 1989)

——, 'Architecture in the British Empire', in R. W. Winks (ed.), *The Oxford History of the British Empire*, vol. 5: *Historiography* (Oxford: Oxford UP, 1999), pp. 584–95

Meyer, J. D., 'Benjamin West's Window Designs for St. George's Chapel, Windsor', *American Art Journal*, vol. 11:3 (1979), pp. 53–65

Micklem, P. A., *Australia's First Bishop: A Brief Memoir of William Grant Broughton* (Sydney: Angus and Robertson, 1936)

Middleton, R. D., *Newman & Bloxam: An Oxford Friendship* (London: Oxford UP, 1947)

Miele, C., '"Their interest and habit": Professionalism and the Restoration of Medieval Churches, 1837–77', in C. Brooks and A. Saint (eds), *The Victorian Church: Architecture and Society* (Manchester: Manchester UP, 1995), pp. 151–72

Milne, K., *Richard Chenevix Trench, 1807–1886* (Dublin: Church of Ireland Historical Society, 2010)

Mill, J. S., *Principles of Political Economy*, new edn, ed. W. J. Ashley (London: Longmans, Green & Co., 1909)

Minter, R. A., *Episcopacy without Episcopate: The Church of England in Jamaica before 1824* (Upton-upon-Severn: Self Publishing Association, 1990)

Moir, J. S., 'The Correspondence of Bishop Strachan and John Henry Newman', *Canadian Journal of Theology*, vol. 3:4 (1957), pp. 219–25

——, *The Church in the British Era: From the British Conquest to Confederation* (Toronto: McGraw-Hill, 1972)

Moore-Gilbert, B., 'Postcolonial Cultural Studies and Imperial Historiography', *Interventions*, vol. 1:3 (1999), pp. 397–411

Moroney, J. B., *Anchorage of Faith: A Short History of Holy Trinity Parish Church, Williamstown* (Williamstown, Victoria: Holy Trinity Church of England, 1971)

Morrell, W. P., *The Anglican Church in New Zealand: A History* (Dunedin: Anglican Church of the Province of New Zealand, 1973)

——, 'Selwyn's Relations with the Church Missionary Society', in W. E. Limbrick (ed.), *Bishop Selwyn in New Zealand, 1841–68* (Palmerston North, NZ: Dunmore Press, 1983), pp. 75–93

Morrison, K., *The Workhouse: A Study of Poor-Law Buildings in England* (Swindon: English Heritage, 1999)

Morriss, S. G., 'The Nine-Year Odyssey of a High Victorian Goth: Three Churches by Fred Cumberland', *Journal of Canadian Art History*, vol. 2:1 (1975), pp. 42–53

——, and Benn, C., 'Architecture', in C. Benn, W. Cooke *et al.* (eds), *The Parish and Cathedral of St. James', Toronto, 1797–1997: A Collaborative History* (Toronto: University of Toronto Press, 1998), pp. 179–215

Moseley, H., *The Home Missions of the Church: A Sermon, Preached on the Seventeenth Anniversary of the Bath & Wells Diocesan Societies* (London: J. W. Parker, 1856)

Mountain, G. J., *A Journal of Visitation to a Part of the Diocese of Quebec, by the Lord Bishop of Montreal in the Spring of 1843* (London: SPCK, 1846)

Mozley, T., *Reminiscences, Chiefly of Oriel College and the Oxford Movement*, 2 vols (London: Longmans, Green & Co., 1882)

Mukherjee, A. N. (ed.), *A Short History of St. Paul's Cathedral Calcutta* (Calcutta, 1956)

Muthesius, S., 'The "Iron Problem" in the 1850s', *Architectural History*, vol. 13 (1970), pp. 58–63

Neale, J. M., *Hierologus, or, The Church Tourists* (London: James Burns, 1843)

——, 'On the Ecclesiology of Madeira', *Transactions of the Cambridge Camden Society, 1843–45* (1845), pp. 219–35

——, *A History of the Holy Eastern Church* (London: John Masters, 1850)

——, and Webb, B., *The Symbolism of Churches and Church Ornaments: A Translation of the First Book of the Rationale Divinorum Officiorum, Written by William Durandus, Sometime Bishop of Mende* (Leeds: T. W. Green, 1843)

Nelson, L. P., 'Building "Cross-wise": Reconstructing Jamaica's Eighteenth-Century Anglican Churches', *Jamaican Historical Review*, vol. 23 (2003), pp. 11–39

——, 'Anglican Church Building and Local Context in Early Jamaica', *Perspectives in Vernacular Architecture*, vol. 10 (2005), pp. 63–79

——, *The Beauty of Holiness: Anglicanism and Architecture in Colonial South Carolina* (Chapel Hill: University of North Carolina Press, 2008)

Newman, J. H., *Discourses on the Scope and Nature of University Education, Addressed to the Catholics of Dublin* (Dublin: James Duffy, 1852)

——, *Apologia pro vita sua: Being a Reply to a Pamphlet Entitled 'What, then, does Dr. Newman Mean?'* (London: Longman, Roberts and Green, 1864)

Nilsson, S., *European Architecture in India, 1750–1850* (London: Faber and Faber, 1968)

Nixon, F. R., *Lectures, Historical, Doctrinal, and Practical on the Catechism of the Church of England* (London: Henry Wix, 1843)

——, *A Charge Delivered to the Clergy of the Diocese of Tasmania, at the Visitation, Held in the Cathedral Church of St. David, Hobart Town . . . 22 May 1851* (Hobart: H. and C. Best, 1851)

Nixon, N., *The Pioneer Bishop in Van Diemen's Land, 1843–1863: Letters and Memories of F. R. Nixon* (Hobart: J. Walch & Sons, 1953)

Nockles, P. B., *The Oxford Movement in Context: Anglican High Churchmanship, 1760–1857* (Cambridge: Cambridge UP, 1994)

——, 'Church or Protestant Sect? The Church of Ireland, High Churchmanship, and the Oxford Movement, 1822–1869', *Historical Journal*, vol. 41:2 (1998), pp. 457–93

Nunn, H.W., *A Short History of the Church of England in Victoria, 1847–1947* (Melbourne: Anglican Diocese of Melbourne, 1947)

O'Connor, D., *et al.*, *Three Centuries of Mission: The United Society for the Propagation of the Gospel, 1701–2000* (London: Continuum, 2000)

O'Connor, E., 'Preface for a Post-Postcolonial Criticism', *Victorian Studies*, vol. 45:2 (2003), pp. 217–46

O'Dea, S., and Coffman, P., 'William Grey: "Missionary" of Gothic in Newfoundland', *JSSAC*, vol. 32:1 (2007), pp. 39–48

O'Donnell, R., ' ". . . blink [him] by silence"? The Cambridge Camden Society and A.W.N. Pugin', in C. Webster and J. Elliott (eds), *'A Church as it should be': The Cambridge Camden Society and Its Influence* (Stamford: Shaun Tyas, 2000), pp. 98–120

O'Farrell, P., *England and Ireland since 1800* (Oxford: Oxford UP, 1975)

O'Hanlon, R., and Washbrook, D., 'Orientalism: Culture, Criticism, and Politics in the Third World', *Comparative Studies in Society and History*, vol. 34:1 (1992), pp. 141–67

Ollard, S. L., 'The Oxford Architectural and Historical Society and the Oxford Movement', *Oxoniensia*, vol. 5 (1940), pp. 146–60

O'Neill, M., 'Nineteenth-Century Architectural Restorations', in J. Crawford and R. Gillespie (eds), *St. Patrick's Cathedral, Dublin: A History* (Dublin: Four Courts Press, 2009), pp. 328–49

O'Reilly, S., 'A Philosophy of Restoration: George Edmund Street at Dublin's Christ Church', *Irish Architectural and Decorative Studies*, vol. 1 (1998), pp. 200–20

Orton, D., *Made of Gold: A Biography of Angela Burdett Coutts* (London: Hamish Hamilton, 1980)

Osborn, B., *A History of Holy Trinity Church of England Bacchus Marsh* (Bacchus Marsh: Bacchus Marsh and District Historical Society, 1971)

Owen, M. C., *The Sewells of the Isle of Wight* (Manchester: privately printed 1908)

Pantin, W. A., 'The Oxford Architectural and Historical Society, 1839–1939', *Oxoniensia*, vol. 4 (1939), pp. 174–94

Pascoe, C. F., *Two Hundred Years of the SPG: An Historical Account of the Society for the Propagation of the Gospel in Foreign Parts, 1701–1900* (London: SPG, 1901)

Patrick, J., 'Newman, Pugin, and Gothic', *Victorian Studies*, vol. 24:2 (1981), pp. 185–207

Paul, R. B., *Letters from Canterbury, New Zealand* (London: Rivingtons, 1857)

Pearson, L., 'Decorative Tile and Terracotta Exports by British Manufacturers, 1840–1940', *Journal of the Tiles and Architectural Ceramics Society*, vol. 11 (2005), pp. 27–32

Penny, N., 'Ruskin's Ideas on Growth in Architecture and Ornament', *British Journal of Aesthetics*, vol. 13:3 (1973), pp. 276–86

Pestana, C. G., *Protestant Empire: Religion and the Making of the British Atlantic World* (Philadelphia: University of Pennsylvania Press, 2008)

Peters, M., *Christchurch-St Michael's: A Study in Anglicanism in New Zealand, 1851–1972* (Christchurch: Canterbury UP, 1986)

——, 'Homeland and Colony', in C. Brown, M. Peters and J. Teal (eds), *Shaping a Colonial Church: Bishop Harper and the Anglican Diocese of Christchurch, 1856–1890* (Christchurch: Canterbury UP, 2006), pp. 19–34

Petit, J. L., *Remarks on Church Architecture*, 2 vols (London: James Burnes, 1841)

Piggin, S., *Evangelical Christianity in Australia: Spirit, Word, and World* (Melbourne: Oxford UP, 1996)

Pike, D., *Paradise of Dissent: South Australia, 1829–1857*, 2nd edn (Melbourne: Melbourne UP, 1967)

Pocock, J. G. A., 'British History: A Plea for a New Subject', *New Zealand Journal of History*, vol. 8:1 (1974), pp. 3–21

——, *The Limits and Divisions of British History* (Studies in Public Policy, no. 31, University of Strathclyde, 1979)

——, 'The Limits and Divisions of British History: In Search of the Unknown Subject', *American Historical Review*, vol. 87:2 (1982), pp. 311–36

——, 'The New British History in Atlantic Perspective: An Antipodean Commentary', *American Historical Review*, vol. 104:2 (1999), pp. 490–500

——, *The Discovery of Islands: Essays in British History* (Cambridge: Cambridge UP, 2005)

Port, M. H., 'The Houses of Parliament Competition', in M. H. Port (ed.), *The Houses of Parliament* (New Haven and London: Yale UP, 1976), pp. 20–52

——, *Imperial London: Civil Government Building in London, 1851–1915* (New Haven and London: Yale UP, 1995)

——, *600 New Churches: The Church Building Commission, 1818–1856* (Reading: Spire Books, 2006)

Porter, A., ' "Commerce and Christianity": The Rise and Fall of a Nineteenth-Century Missionary Slogan', *Historical Journal*, vol. 28:3 (1985), pp. 597–621

——, *Religion versus Empire? British Protestant Missionaries and Overseas Expansion, 1700–1914* (Manchester: Manchester UP, 2004)

——, 'An Overview, 1700–1914', in N. Etherington (ed.), *Missions and Empire*, The Oxford History of the British Empire Companion Series (Oxford: Oxford UP, 2005), pp. 46–53

Porter, B., ' "Empire, what empire?" Or, Why 80% of Early- and Mid-Victorians Were Deliberately Kept in Ignorance of It', *Victorian Studies*, vol. 46:2 (2004), pp. 256–63

——, *The Absent-Minded Imperialists: Empire, Society, and Culture in Britain* (Oxford: Oxford UP, 2004)

Postles, D., 'Micro-Spaces: Church Porches in Pre-Modern England', *Journal of Historical Geography*, vol. 33:4 (2007), pp. 749–69

Proceedings at a Meeting of the Clergy and Laity, Specially Called by His Grace the Lord Archbishop of Canterbury . . . for the Further Extension of the Episcopate in the Colonies and Dependencies of the British Crown (London: Rivingtons, 1853)

Proceedings at a Meeting of the Clergy and Laity Specially Called by His Grace the Lord Archbishop of Canterbury . . . Towards the Endowment of Additional Colonial Bishoprics (London: Rivingtons, 1841)

Prothero, R. E., *The Life and Correspondence of Arthur Penrhyn Stanley, D.D.* (London: John Murray, 1893)

Prout, D., ' "The Oxford Society for Promoting the Study of Gothic Architecture" and the "Oxford Architectural Society", 1839–1860', *Oxoniensia*, vol. 54 (1989), pp. 379–91

Pugin, A. W. N., *The True Principles of Pointed or Christian Architecture* (London: John Weale, 1841)

Pusey, E. B., *The Church the Converter of the Heathen: Two Sermons Preached in Conformity with the Queen's Letter in Behalf of the Society for the Propagation of the Gospel* (Oxford: J. H. Parker, 1839)

Quaife, G. R., 'Money and Men: Aspects of the Anglican Crisis in Victoria, 1850–1865', *Journal of Religious History*, vol. 5:1 (1968), pp. 45–61

Quinault, R., 'Westminster and the Victorian Constitution', *Transactions of the Royal Historical Society*, vol. 2 (1992), pp. 79–104

Quiney, A., *John Loughborough Pearson* (New Haven and London: Yale UP, 1979)

Rangiātea: Ko Ahau te Huarahi te Pono me te Ora (Wellington: National Library of New Zealand, 2003)

Raymond, W. O., 'John Medley', in W. B. Heeney (ed.), *Leaders of the Canadian Church* (London: SPCK, 1920)

Reed, J. S., *Glorious Battle: The Cultural Politics of Victorian Anglo-Catholicism* (Nashville: Vanderbilt UP, 1996)

Reed, T. T., *Historic Churches of Australia* (South Melbourne: Macmillan, 1978)

Report of the Cathedral Building Committee . . . St. John's, Newfoundland (St John's: Ryan and Withers, 1844)

Reynolds, M., *Martyr of Ritualism: Father Mackonochie of St. Alban's, Holborn* (London: Faber and Faber, 1965)

Richardson, D. S., 'Hyperborean Gothic, or Wilderness Ecclesiology and the Wood Churches of Edward Medley', *Architectura*, vol. 1 (1972), pp. 48–74

Ridley, J., 'Edwin Lutyens, New Delhi, and the Architecture of Imperialism', *Journal of Imperial and Commonwealth History*, vol. 26:2 (1998), pp. 67–83

Robin, A. de Q., *Anglicans in Geelong, 1842–1990* (Geelong: Geelong Historical Society, 1991)

Robinson, C. K., *Missions Urged upon the State on Grounds both of Duty and Policy* (Cambridge, 1853)

Roe, M., *Quest for Authority in Eastern Australia, 1835–1851* (Parkville: Melbourne UP, 1965)

Rorabaugh, W. J., 'Politics and the Architectural Competition for the Houses of Parliament, 1834–1837', *Victorian Studies*, vol. 18 (1973), pp. 155–75

Ross R. M., *Melanesians at Mission Bay: A History of the Melanesian Mission in Auckland* (Wellington: New Zealand Historic Places Trust, 1983)

Rothenstein, J., 'Christian Gothic: Newman and Littlemore', *Architectural Review*, vol. 98 (1945), pp. 176–7

Rothschild, E., *The Inner Life of Empires: An Eighteenth-Century History* (Princeton: Princeton UP, 2010)

Rowley, H., *The Story of the Universities' Mission to Central Africa* (London: Saunders, Otley & Co., 1866)

—— (ed.), *Speeches on Missions by the Right Reverend Samuel Wilberforce, D.D.* (London: William Wells Gardner, 1874)

Ruprich-Robert, V., *L'architecture normande aux XIe et XIIe siècles en Normandie et en Angleterre*, 2 vols (Paris: Librairie des Imprimeries Réunies, 1884–9)

Ruskin, J., *The Seven Lamps of Architecture* (London: Smith, Elder & Co., 1849; repr. New York: John Wiley & Son, 1865)

——, *The Stones of Venice: The Foundations*, 2 vols (London: Smith, Elder & Co., 1851–3)

——, *On the Nature of Gothic Architecture: And Herein of the True Functions of the Workman on Art* (London: Smith Elder, & Co., 1854)

——, 'The Work of Iron, in Nature, Art, and Policy', in *The Two Paths: Being Lectures on Art and Its Application to Decoration and Manufacture* (London: Smith, Elder, & Co., 1859)

Russell-Corbett, J., ' "The Ecclesiologist" and Anglican Church Architecture in the Canadian Colonies', *Bulletin of the Society for the Study of Architecture in Canada*, vol. 21:4 (1997), pp. 89–94

Rutherford, J., *Sir George Grey, KCB, 1812–1898: A Study in Colonial Government* (London: Cassell, 1961)

Said, E. W., *Orientalism: Western Conceptions of the Orient* (London: Routledge and Kegan Paul, 1978)

——, *Culture and Imperialism* (London: Chatto and Windus, 1993)

Saint, A., 'Charles Buckeridge and His Family', *Oxoniensia*, vol. 38 (1973), pp. 357–71

——, *Architect and Engineer: A Study in Sibling Rivalry* (New Haven and London: Yale UP, 2007)

——, 'The Late Victorian Church', in T. Sladen and A. Saint (eds.), *Churches 1870–1914*, themed issue of *Studies in Victorian Architecture and Design*, vol. 3 (2011), pp. 7–25

St. James' Dandenong, 1864–1989 (Dandenong: St James's Anglican Church, 1989)

St. Philip's Church, Grahamstown ([Grahamstown], 1960)

Samson J. (ed.), *The British Empire* (Oxford: Oxford UP, 2001)

Scarfe, J., 'The Diocese of Adelaide (and the West)', in B. Porter (ed.), *Colonial Tractarians: The Oxford Movement in Australia* (Melbourne: Joint Board of Christian Education, 1989), pp. 75–104

Schlenther, B. S., 'Religious Faith and Commercial Empire', in P. J. Marshall (ed.), *The Oxford History of the British Empire*, vol. 2: *The Eighteenth Century* (Oxford: Oxford UP, 1998), pp. 128–50

Schneer, J., *London 1900: The Imperial Metropolis* (New Haven and London: Yale UP, 1999)

Schneider, F. D., 'The Anglican Quest for Authority: Convocation and the Imperial Factor, 1850–60', *Journal of Religious History*, vol. 9:2 (1976), pp. 139–57

Scotland, N., *Squires in the Slums: Settlements and Missions in Late-Victorian London* (London: I. B. Tauris, 2007)

Scott, E. G., *St. Mary's Church, Hagley: History of the Church* ([Hobart], n.d.)

Scott, G. G., *A Plea for the Faithful Restoration of Our Ancient Churches* (Oxford: J. H. Parker, 1850)

——, *Remarks on Secular & Domestic Architecture, Present and Future* (London: John Murray, 1857)

——, *Lectures on the Rise and Development of Mediæval Architecture*, 2 vols (London: John Murray, 1878–9)

——, *Personal and Professional Recollections* (1879), ed. G. Stamp (Stamford: Paul Watkins, 1995)

Seeley, J. R., *The Expansion of England* (London: Macmillan, 1883)

Selwyn, G. A., *'How shall we sing the Lord's song in a strange land?' A Sermon, Preached in the Cathedral Church of St. Peter, Exeter . . . by the Right Reverend the Lord Bishop of New Zealand* (Exeter: P. A. Hannaford, 1842)

——, *New Zealand. St. John's College, Bishops' Auckland: Industrial System* (Eton, 1846)

——, *An Idea of a Colonial College: A Sermon Preached in the Chapel of St. John the Divine, Bishops' Auckland* (Eton, 1848)

——, *A Charge Delivered to the Clergy of the Diocese of New Zealand at the Diocesan Synod* (London: Francis and John Rivington, 1849)

——, *'A little one shall become a thousand': A Sermon Preached at the Opening of the Cuddesdon Theological Institution* (London: Rivingtons, 1854)

Semes, R. L., 'Hawai'i's Holy War: English Bishop Staley, American Congregationalists, and the Hawaiian Monarchs, 1860–1870', *Hawaiian Journal of History*, vol. 34 (2000), pp. 113–38

Serle, G., *The Golden Age: A History of the Colony of Victoria, 1851–1861* (Melbourne: Melbourne UP, 1963)

Sewter, A. C., *The Stained Glass of William Morris and His Circle: A Catalogue* (New Haven and London: Yale University Press, 1975)

Shaw, A. G. L., 'British Attitudes to the Colonies, *ca.* 1820–1850', *Journal of British Studies*, vol. 9:1 (1969), pp. 71–95

Shaw, G. P., *Patriarch and Patriot: William Grant Broughton, 1788–1853* (Melbourne: Melbourne UP, 1978)

——, 'The Promotion of Civilization', *Journal of the Royal Australian Historical Society*, vol. 74:2 (1988), pp. 99–111

Short, A., *The Primary Charge, Delivered by the Right Reverend Augustus, Lord Bishop of Adelaide* (Adelaide: H. Hussey, 1851)

Simmins, G., *Fred Cumberland: Building the Victorian Dream* (Toronto: University of Toronto Press, 1997)

Sinclair, K., *A History of New Zealand* (Harmondsworth: Penguin Books, 1976)

Sivasundaram, S., *Nature and the Godly Empire: Science and Evangelical Mission in the Pacific, 1795–1850* (Cambridge: Cambridge UP, 2005)

Skinner, R., 'Celebrating the Lord's Supper at Orona', in A. Leach and G. Matthewson (eds), *Celebration: Proceedings of the 22nd Annual Conference of the Society of Architectural Historians, Australia and New Zealand* (Napier, NZ: Society of Architectural Historians of Australia and New Zealand, 2005), pp. 329–34

——, 'Drawing from an Indigenous Tradition? George Gilbert Scott's First Design for Christchurch Cathedral, 1861–62', *Architectural History*, vol. 53 (2010), pp. 245–70

Smart, C. M., *Muscular Churches: Ecclesiastical Architecture of the High Victorian Period* (Fayetteville: University of Arkansas Press, 1989)

Smith, A. C., *Architectural Models as Machine: A New View of Models from Antiquity to the Present Day* (Oxford: Architectural Press, 2004)

Smith, A. R., *William Charles Cotton MA, 1813–1879: Priest, Missionary and Bee Master* (Birkenhead: Countryvise, 2006)

Smith, B., *Colonisation and Conquest in Medieval Ireland: The English in Louth, 1170–1330* (Cambridge: Cambridge UP, 1999)

Smith, I., *Tin Tabernacles: Corrugated Iron Mission Halls, Churches & Chapels of Britain* (Salisbury: Camrose Organisation, 2004)

Sohmer, S. H., 'Christianity without Civilization: Anglican Sources for an Alternative Nineteenth-Century Mission Methodology', *Journal of Religious History*, vol. 18:2 (1994), pp. 174–97

Soley, S., '"The Highest of the High": All Saints, St Kilda as Melbourne's Original High Church', in C. Holden (ed.), *Anglo-Catholicism in Melbourne: Papers to Mark the 150th Anniversary of St Peter's Eastern Hill, 1846–1996* (Melbourne: Melbourne UP, 1997), pp. 21–32

——, *'The Highest of the High', in 'Marvellous Melbourne': All Saints' East St Kilda as Melbourne's Original High Church* (East St Kilda: All Saints' Parish, 1998)

Spatz, N., 'Church Porches and the Liturgy in Twelfth-Century Rome', in T. J. Heffernan and E. A. Matter (eds), *The Liturgy of the Medieval Church* (Kalamazoo: Michigan Medieval Institute Publications, 2001), pp. 327–67

Spottiswoode, G. A. (ed.), *The Official Report of the Missionary Conference of the Anglican Communion* (London: SPCK, 1894)

Stalley, R. (ed.), *George Edmund Street and the Restoration of Christ Church Cathedral, Dublin* (Dublin: Four Courts Press, 2000)

Stamp, G., 'Church Architecture', in R. Fermor-Hesketh (ed.), *Architecture of the British Empire* (London: Weidenfeld and Nicolson, 1986), pp. 148–85

——, 'High Victorian Gothic and the Architecture of Normandy', *JSAH*, vol. 62:2 (2003), pp. 194–211

Standish, M. W., *The Waimate Mission Station* (Wellington: National Historic Places Trust, 1962)

Stanley, A. P., *Historical Memorials of Westminster Abbey*, 5th edn (London, 1882)

Stanley, B., '"Commerce and Christianity": Providence Theory, the Missionary Movement, and the Imperialism of Free Trade, 1842–1860', *Historical Journal*, vol. 26:1 (1983), pp. 71–94

Stanton, P. B., *The Gothic Revival & American Church Architecture: An Episode in Taste, 1840–1856* (Baltimore: Johns Hopkins UP, 1968)

Stegemann, W. C., *An Ornament to the City: A History of the Cathedral Church of St. Saviour, Goulburn, 1874–1988* (Canberra: Anglican Diocese of Canberra and Goulburn, 1988)

Stephens, G., 'The Diocese of Tasmania', in B. Porter (ed.), *Colonial Tractarians: The Oxford Movement in Australia* (Melbourne: Joint Board of Christian Education, 1989), pp. 49–62

Stephens, W. R. W., *The Life and Letters of Edward A. Freeman*, 2 vols (London: Macmillan, 1895)

Stock, E., *The History of the Church Missionary Society*, 3 vols (London: CMS, 1899)

Strachan, J., *A Sermon, Preached at York, Upper Canada, Third of July, 1825, On the Death of the Late Lord Bishop of Quebec* (Kingston, Ontario, 1826)

——, *Thoughts on the Rebuilding of the Cathedral Church of St. James* (Toronto, 1850)

Street, G. E., *Brick and Marble in the Middle Ages: Notes on a Tour in the North of Italy* (London: John Murray, 1855)

Strong, R., 'The Reverend John Wollaston and Colonial Christianity in Western Australia, 1840–1863', *The Journal of Religious History*, vol. 25:3 (2001), pp. 261–85

——, *Anglicanism and the British Empire, c.1700–1850* (Oxford: Oxford UP, 2007)

Stuart, D., '"For England and for Christ": The Gospel of Liberation and Subordination in Early Nineteenth-Century South Africa', *Journal of Historical Sociology*, vol. 6:4 (1993), pp. 377–95

Summerson, J., *Architecture in Britain, 1530–1830* (1953), 8th edn (Harmondsworth: Penguin Books, 1991)

Sundkler, B., and Steed, C., *A History of the Church in Africa* (Cambridge: Cambridge UP, 2000)

Sundt, R. A., *Whare Karakia: Māori Church Building, Decoration & Ritual in Aotearoa New Zealand, 1834–1836* (Auckland: Auckland UP, 2010)

Tavernor, R., *Palladio and Palladianism* (London: Thames and Hudson, 1991)

Taylor, F., *The Last Three Bishops Appointed by the Crown, for the Anglican Church of Canada* (Montreal: John Lovell, 1869)

Taylor, J., *All Saints' Cathedral, Allahabad* (n.d.)

Te Awekotuku, N. (with Linda Waimarie Nikora, Mohi Rua and Rolinda Karapu), *Mau Moko: The World of the Māori Tattoo* (Rosedale, NZ: Penguin Books, 2007)

Teale, R., 'Dr Pusey and the Church Overseas', in P. Butler (ed.), *Pusey Rediscovered* (London: SPCK, 1983), pp. 185–209

The Charter and Statues of the Missionary College of Saint Augustine, Canterbury ([Canterbury], 1848)

The Colonial Church Atlas, Arranged in Dioceses: With Geographical and Statistical Tables (London: SPCK, 1843)

The Orientator: A Simple Contrivance for Ascertaining the Orientation of Churches (Cambridge: Thomas Stevenson on behalf of the Cambridge Camden Society, 1844)

The Parish Church of St. James the Great, Calcutta (Calcutta. 1962)

The Story of the Delhi Mission (Westminster, 1908)

The Sydney Diocesan Directory for the Year of Our Lord 1881 (Sydney: Joseph Cook & Co., 1881)

Thomas, J., *Albi Cathedral and British Church Architecture*

(London: Ecclesiological Society/Society of Antiquaries of London, 2002)
Thompson, H. P., *Into All Lands: The History of the Society for the Propagation of the Gospel in Foreign Parts, 1701–1950* (London: SPCK, 1951)
Thompson, P., 'Exporting the Gothic Revival: Butterfield's Australian Cathedrals, 1', *Country Life* (9 Sept. 1971), pp. 622–4
——, *William Butterfield: Victorian Architect* (Cambridge, Mass.: MIT Press, 1971)
Thorne, R., 'Inventing a New Design Technology: Building and Engineering', in J. M. MacKenzie (ed.), *The Victorian Vision: Inventing New Britain* (London: V&A Publications, 2001), pp. 173–85
Thorne, S., *Congregational Missions and the Making of an Imperial Culture in Nineteenth-Century England* (Paolo Alto: Stanford University Press, 1999)
Thornton, A. P., *The Imperial Idea and Its Enemies* (London: Macmillan, 1959)
Three Months' Visitation, by the Bishop of Capetown, in the Autumn of 1855 (London: Bell and Daldy, 1856)
Thurlby, M., 'Nineteenth-Century Churches in Prince Edward Island and Their Place in the Gothic Revival', *JSSAC*, vol. 31:2 (2006), pp. 65–85
——, 'Two Churches by Frank Wills: St. Peter's , Barton, and St. Paul's, Glanford, and the Ecclesiological Gothic Revival in Ontario', *JSSAC*, vol. 32:1 (2007), pp. 49–60
Titus, N., 'Concurrence without Compliance: SPG and the Barbadian Plantations, 1710–1834', in D. O'Connor *et al.*, *Three Centuries of Mission: The United Society for the Propagation of the Gospel, 1701–2000* (London: Continuum, 2000), pp. 249–61
Toplis, I., *The Foreign Office: An Architectural History* (London: Mansell, 1987)
Tracts for the Times by Members of the University of Oxford, 6 vols (London: Rivingtons, 1834–41)
Trench, R. C., *A Sermon Preached at the Church of S. Edward, Cambridge, at the First Anniversary Meeting of the Oxford, Cambridge, Dublin, and Durham Mission to Central Africa* (London: Parker & Son, 1861)
Trollope, A., *Australia and New Zealand* (Melbourne: George Robertson, 1874)
Truefitt, G., *Designs for Country Churches* (London, 1850)
Trumble, A., 'Gilbert Scott's "Bold and Beautiful Experiment", Part I: The Tomb of Sir Charles Hotham in Melbourne', *Burlington Magazine*, vol. 141 (1999), pp. 739–48
Tucker, H. W., *Memoir of the Life and Episcopate of Edward Feild, D.D., Bishop of Newfoundland, 1844–76* (London: W. Wells Gardner, 1877)
Turner, J., 'The Nineteenth Century: The Church of England', in Nicholas Orme (ed.), *Unity and Variety: A History of the Church in Devon and Cornwall* (Exeter: University of Exeter Press, 1991)
Turner, P. J., *Christ Church Cathedral Montreal*, Series XIII (Art and Architecture), no. 17 (Montreal: McGill University Publications, 1927)
Twells, A., *The Civilising Mission and the English Middle Class, 1792–1850* (Basingstoke: Palgrave Macmillan, 2009)
Tyack, G., 'The Restoration of Iffley Parish Church', *Oxoniensia*, vol. 68 (2003), pp. 113–30
Underhill, S., *The Iron Church* (Victoria, BC: Braemar Books, 1984)
Underwood, H. J., *Elevations, Sections and Details, of the Church of St. Mary the Virgin, at Littlemore* (Oxford: John Henry Parker for the Architectural Society, 1845)
——, *Oxford Parish Burial Ground Chapels* (Oxford, 1849)
Upton, D., *Holy Things and Profane: Anglican Parish Churches in Colonial Virginia* (New York and Cambridge, Mass.: Architectural History Foundation and MIT Press, 1986)
—— (ed.), *America's Architectural Roots: Ethnic Groups that Built America* (New York: Preservation Press, 1998)
——, *Architecture in the United States* (Oxford: Oxford UP, 1998)
Vance, N., 'The Ideal of Manliness', in B. Simon and I. Bradley (eds), *The Victorian Public School: Studies in the Development of an Educational Institution* (Dublin: Gill and Macmillan, 1975), pp. 115–28
Varley, D. H., and Matthew, H. M. (eds), *The Cape Journals of Archdeacon N. J. Merriman, 1848–1855* (Cape Town: Van Riebeeck Society, 1957)
Viollet-le-Duc, E., *Dictionnaire raisonné de l'architecture française du XIe au XVIe siècle*, 10 vols (Paris: B. Banche, 1853–68)
Wakeling, C., 'Nonconformity and Victorian Architecture', in B. Cherry (ed.), *Dissent and the Gothic Revival* (London: Chapels Society, 2007), pp. 40–71
Wallace, D. M., *A History of Christ Church Castlemaine, Church of England, 1852–1970* (Castlemaine, 1970)
Walton, S., *Imagining Soldiers and Fathers in the Mid-Victorian Era: Charlotte Yonge's Models of Manliness* (Farnham: Ashgate, 2010)
Walvin, J., 'The Colonial Origins of English Wealth', *Journal of Caribbean History*, vol. 39:1 (2005), pp. 38–53
Ward, G. (ed.), *Letters of Bishop Tozer and His Sister* (London: UMCA, 1902)
Warner, Michael, 'What is Colonial about Colonial America?', in R. B. St. George (ed.), *Possible Pasts: Becoming Colonial in Early America* (Ithaca: Cornell UP, 2000), pp. 49–70

Watson, D., 'Outside Studding: Some Claims to Architectural Taste', *Historic Environment*, vol. 6:2–3 (1988), pp. 22–31

Watson, R. L., *Christ Church Cathedral, Fredericton: A History* (Fredericton: Bishop and Chapter of Fredericton Cathedral, 1984)

Webb, B., 'On the Adaptation of Pointed Architecture to Tropical Climates', *Transactions of the Cambridge Camden Society, 1843–45* (1845), pp. 199–218

——, *Sketches of Continental Ecclesiology, or, Church Notes in Belgium, Germany and Italy* (London: John Masters, 1848)

Webb, L. C., 'The Canterbury Association and Its Settlement', in J. Hight and C. R. Straubel (eds), *A History of Canterbury*, vol. 1 (Christchurch: Whitcome and Tombs, 1957), pp. 135–233

——, 'Aspiration and Achievement', in J. Hight and C. R. Straubel (eds), *A History of Canterbury*, vol. 1 (Christchurch: Whitcome and Tombs, 1957), pp. 224–33

Webster, C., '"Absolutely wretched": Camdenian Attitudes to the Late Georgian Church', in C. Webster and J. Elliott (eds), *'A Church as it should be': The Cambridge Camden Society and Its Influence* (Stamford: Shaun Tyas, 2000), pp. 1–21

——, *'Temples worthy of His presence': The Early Publications of the Cambridge Camden Society* (Reading: Spire Books, 2003)

——, 'Patterns of Church Seating from Waterloo to 1850, and the Role of the Cambridge Camden Society', in T. Cooper and S. Brown (eds), *Pews, Benches and Chairs: Church Seating in English Parish Churches from the Fourteenth Century to the Present* (London: Ecclesiological Society / Society of Antiquaries, 2011), pp. 197–210

Webster, C. A., 'The Restoration of the Church', in W. A. Phillips (ed.), *History of the Church of Ireland from the Earliest Times to the Present Day*, 3 vols (Oxford: Oxford UP, 1933), vol. 3, pp. 360–86

Welch, P., 'Constructing Colonial Christianities: With Particular Reference to Anglicanism in Australia, ca 1850–1940', *Journal of Religious History*, vol. 32:2 (2008), pp. 234–55

Westcott, B. F., *On Some Points in the Religious Office of the Universities* (London: Macmillan, 1873)

Western, F. J., *The Early History of the Cambridge Mission to Delhi* (Delhi, 1950)

Westfall, W., *Two Worlds: The Protestant Culture of Nineteenth-Century Ontario* (Kingston and Montreal: McGill–Queen's UP, 1989)

Westin, H. M. P., *An Act of Faith: The First Fifty Years of St. Peter's Cathedral* (Charlottetown, Prince Edward Island: St Peter Publications, 1994)

Whately, E. J., *The Life and Correspondence of Richard Whately D.D.* (London: Longmans, Green & Co., 1868)

Whibley, P. M., *Merriman of Grahamstown* (Cape Town: Howard Timmins, 1982)

White, G. K., *A History of St. Columba's College, 1843–1974* (Dublin: Old Columban Society, 1980)

White, J. F., *The Cambridge Movement: The Ecclesiologists and the Gothic Revival* (Cambridge: Cambridge UP, 1962)

Whitington, F. T., *Augustus Short: First Bishop of Adelaide* (Adelaide: E. S. Wigg & Son, 1887)

——, *William Grant Broughton: Bishop of Australia* (Sydney: Angus and Robertson, 1936)

Whyte, W., 'Sacred Space as Sacred Text: Church and Chapel Architecture in Victorian Britain' in J. Sterrett and P. Thomas (eds.), *Sacred Text – Sacred Space: Architectural, Spiritual, and Literary Convergences in England and Wales* (Leiden: Brill, 2011), pp. 247–67

Williams, C. P., '"Not quite gentlemen": An Examination of "Middling Class" Protestant Missionaries from Britain, *c.*1850–1900', *Journal of Ecclesiastical History*, vol. 31:3 (1980), pp. 301–15

——, '"Too peculiarly Anglican": The Role of the Established Church in Ireland as a Negative Model in the Development of the Church Missionary Society's Commitment to Independent Native Churches, 1856–1872', in W. J. Sheils and D. Wood (eds), *The Churches, Ireland and the Irish* (Oxford: Basil Blackwell, 1989), pp. 299–310

Williams, P., '"Not transplanting": Henry Venn's Strategic Vision', in K. Ward and B. Stanley (eds), *The Church Mission Society and World Christianity, 1799–1999* (Richmond, Surrey: Curzon Press, 2000), pp. 147–72

Williams R. M., *From Royal Garden to Gothic Splendor: The History of St. Andrew's Cathedral* (Honolulu: St Andrew's Cathedral, 1996)

Willis, J., 'The Nature of a Mission Community: The Universities' Mission to Central Africa in Bonde', *Past and Present*, no. 140 (1993), pp. 127–54

Willis, J., and Goad, P., 'A Bigger Picture: Reframing Australian Architectural History', *Fabrications*, vol. 18:1 (2008), p. 6–23

Wills, F., *Ancient English Ecclesiastical Architecture and Its Principles, Applied to the Wants of the Church at the Present Day* (New York: Stanford and Swords, 1850)

Wilson, D., *The Apostolical Commission Considered, with Reference to the Authority of the Clergy of the Church of England* (1833) (London: SPCK, 1841)

——, *A Charge Delivered to the Clergy of the Four Dioceses of Calcutta, Madras, Bombay, and Colombo, at the Second Metropolitical Visitation* (London: J. Hatchard & Son, 1849)

Wirgman, A. T., *The History of the English Church and People in South Africa* (London: Longmans, Green & Co., 1895)

——, *Life of James Green* (London: Longmans, Green & Co., 1909)

Wolffe, J., 'Whose Jerusalem? Evangelicalism and Nationalism in Nineteenth-Century England', in J. Wolffe (ed.), *Christianity and National Consciousness* (Leicester: Universities and Colleges Christian Fellowship Associates for the Historians' Study Group, 1987), pp. 39–49

——, *The Protestant Crusade in Great Britain, 1829–1860* (Oxford: Oxford UP, 1991)

Wordsworth, C., *National Christianity, an Article of the Christian Faith* (London: Francis and John Rivington, 1851)

Wynter, J. C., *Hints on Church Colonization* (London: J. W. Parker, 1850)

Yanni, C., *Nature's Museums: Victorian Science and the Architecture of Display* (Baltimore: Johns Hopkins UP, 1999)

Yate, W., *An Account of New Zealand; and of the Formation and Progress of the Church Missionary Society's Mission in the North Island* (London: R. B. Seeley and W. Burnside, 1835)

Yates, N., *Buildings, Faith, and Worship: The Liturgical Arrangement of Anglican Churches, 1600–1900* (Oxford: Clarendon Press, 1991)

Yates, T. E., *Venn and Victorian Bishops Abroad: The Missionary Policies of Henry Venn . . . 1841–1872* (London: SPCK, 1978)

Yeo, G., 'A Case without Parallel: The Bishops of London and the Anglican Church Overseas, 1660–1748', *Journal of Ecclesiastical History*, vol. 44:3 (1993), pp. 450–75

Yonge, C. M., *Life of John Coleridge Patteson: Missionary Bishop of the Melanesian Islands*, 2 vols (London: Macmillan, 1874)

PICTURE CREDITS

Albany Museum (History), Grahamstown 217, 218, 316; Alexander Turnbull Library, Wellington 20, 21, 38, 47, 94, 100, 329, 363; All Saints' Church, St Kilda (Melbourne) 269; Brian Andrews 262, 272; Anglican Diocesan Archives of Eastern Newfoundland and Labrador, St John's, Newfoundland 137, 139; Anglican Diocesan Archive, Melbourne 266; Archdiocese of Hobart Archives 227; Archives of Manitoba, Winnipeg 311, 312, 313; Archives of Ontario, Toronto 233, 302, 304; Archives of the Tasmanian Museum and Art Gallery 112, 264, 321; Art Gallery of South Australia 322; Auchmuty Library, University of Newcastle (Australia) 146; Auckland Art Gallery 45; Auckland War Memorial Museum 150; Bishops Diocesan College, Rondebosch 208; Simon Bradley 331; G. A. Bremner 3, 7, 27, 28, 31, 35, 52, 57, 58, 59, 69, 85, 86, 93, 126, 127, 148, 149, 154, 168, 178, 180, 181, 182, 186, 191, 192, 195, 196, 197, 198, 203, 210, 211, 213, 219, 220, 229, 240, 245, 248, 251, 254, 255, 256, 259, 260, 263, 265, 268, 270, 273, 274, 279, 297, 301, 303, 309, 317, 320, 323, 335, 339, 344, 355, 361, 362; Cambridge University Library 226; Canterbury Museum, Christchurch 276, 277, 280, 281, 352; Ken Charlton and the Australian Heritage Photographic Library 261; Christchurch Anglican Diocesan Archive, New Zealand 48, 95, 96, 97, 98, 99; Christ Church Cathedral, Montreal 75, 76; Peter Coffman 140, 141, 142, 241, 300, 308; Cory Library, Rhodes University 91, 206, 314; Diocese of Auckland Archives 318, 319; Diocese of Nova Scotia and Prince Edward Island Archives 243; Eton College, reproduced by permission of the Provost and Fellows 19, 200; Geelong City Library 253; Wallace Hale, Christ Church, Maugerville 55; Hocken Collections, University of Otago 46; Gill Hunter 204, 349; John Kinder Theological Library, St John's College, Auckland 36, 37, 41, 44, 235; Library and Archives Canada 74; Memorial University Libraries, St John's, Newfoundland 134; National Library of Australia 9; National Library of Ireland 354; National Portrait Gallery, London 2; Nova Scotia Museum, Halifax 11; M. O'Brien and the Australian Heritage Photographic Library 258; Provincial Archives, University of New Brunswick, Fredericton 70, 73; Puke Ariki, New Plymouth, New Zealand 144; Rare Books and Special Collections, University of Sydney 53; RIBA Library Drawings and Archives Collections, Victoria and Albert Museum, London 79, 87, 88, 121, 172, 295, 326; Royal BC Museum, Victoria, British Columbia 145, 160; St Alban's Church, Muswellbrook 324, 325; St David's Cathedral, Hobart 239; St James's Cathedral Archive, Toronto 65; St Mary's Church, New Plymouth, New Zealand 39; St Paul's Cathedral, Wellington 153; St Paul's Church, Rondebosch 207; St Peter's Cathedral, Adelaide 105; Selwyn College Archive, University of Cambridge 40, 42 (bottom); Staffordshire County Buildings Picture Collection 14; State Library of New South Wales, Sydney 18, 22, 34, 42 (top), 50, 61, 188, 223, 224, 228, 234, 237, 249, 252, 257; State Library of

Queensland 158; State Library of South Australia 25, 26, 29, 101; State Library of Tasmania 30, 56, 109, 111, 328; State Library, Victoria (Australia) 159, 230, 231, 238, 267, 271; The National Galleries of Scotland 80; The Rooms, St John's, Newfoundland 77, 222; Malcolm Thurlby 244; Tina Machado (www.machadoink.com) 340, 341, 343, 345; Toronto Public Library 298, 299; USPG (African and Commonwealth Library, Bodleian Library, University of Oxford) 78, 84, 90, 92, 110, 120, 123, 129, 135, 147, 155, 156, 166, 167, 169, 170, 171, 189, 215, 221, 242, 282, 283, 285, 286, 292, 332; Victoria and Albert Museum, London 6, 179, 193, 293, 296, 337; Wadham College, University of Oxford, by permission of the Warden and Fellows 67; Mark Watson 103; William Cullen Library, University of the Witwatersrand 54, 209, 212, 214; Woods Bagot Architects, Adelaide 102, 104; Yale Center for British Art, New Haven 334.

INDEX

NOTE: Page numbers in italics refer to illustrations; page numbers followed by *n* and a number refer to information in an endnote. Individual buildings abroad are listed under countries or for larger entries under provinces (Canada), states (Australia) and some major cities; churches in Britain appear under the names of cities, towns or villages. In larger entries the buildings are listed after the general index headings.

No. 1. Proposed new Church of St. Matthew Auckland, New Zealand.

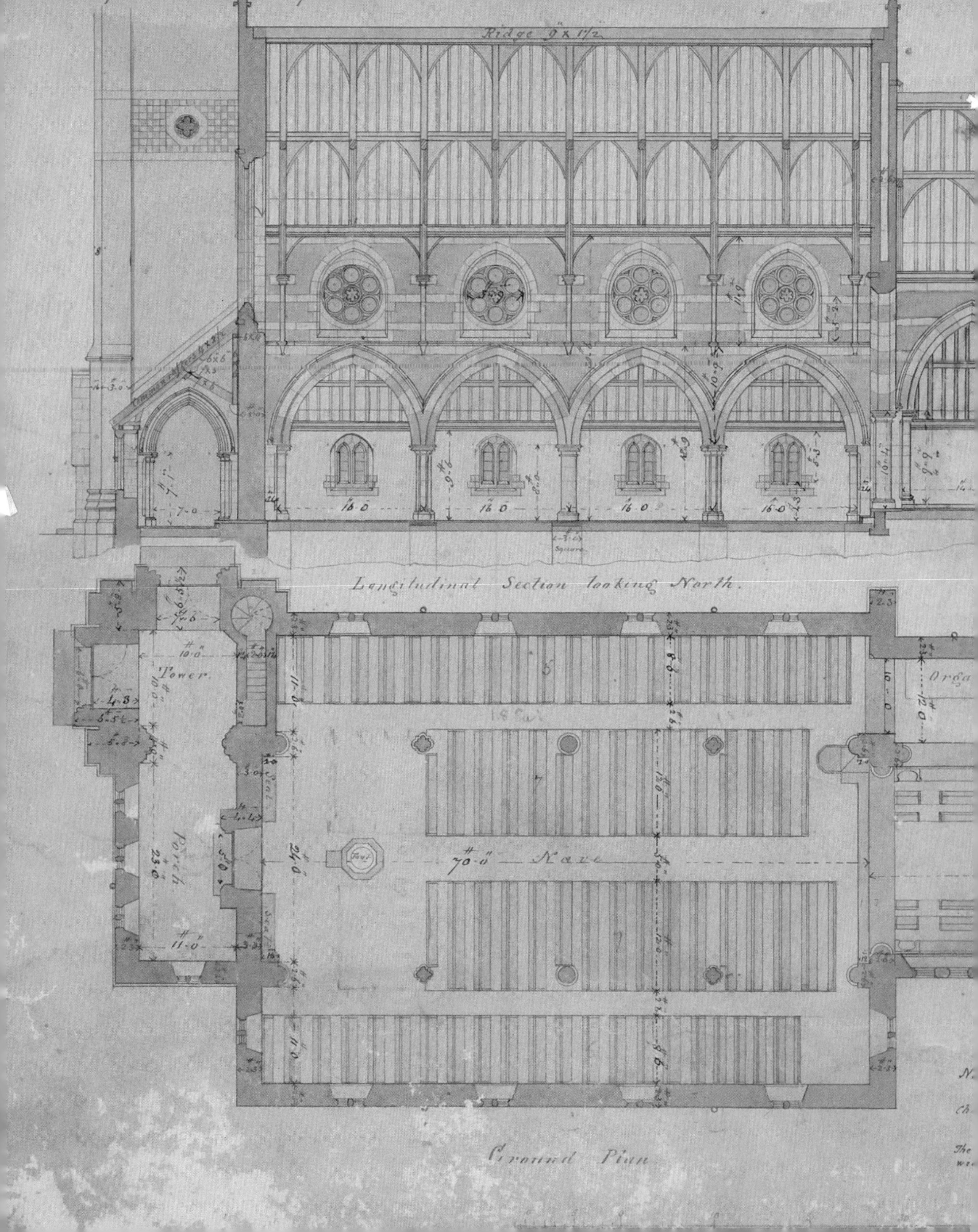

Longitudinal Section looking North.

Ground Plan